What's New in This Edition

You will find much new information in *Microsoft Internet Information Server 3 Unleashed, Second Edition*, ranging from new notes and tips to completely new chapters. For the most part, these additions explain how to take advantage of the new components of the Internet Information Server and how to use the Microsoft Proxy Server to provide additional security to your network.

The new information explains how you can do the following:

- Enhance the Internet Information Server by installing and managing the Microsoft Proxy Server to limit access to your intranet and Internet resources. Add components of the Commercial Internet Server to your current installation; configure the Microsoft Chat server and the Microsoft Network News server. (*Chapter 11*)

- Take advantage of active server pages to create dynamic content on your Web site. Start with the basic sample of an active server page based on the JScript language. (*Chapter 21*)

- Exploit the various tools currently available to create streaming multimedia. Start with the sample page that displays a streaming audio-video file using the embedded Microsoft NetShow On-Demand ActiveX control. (*Chapter 22*)

- Use the Seagate Crystal Reports for Internet Information Server to create structured reports on your Web server's activity. (*Chapter 25*)

- Set up the Index Information Server to index your Web site for easier client access. Start with the sample code to build a custom search page. (*Chapter 26*)

What's Enhanced in This Edition

In addition to new information, many chapters in this edition provide enhanced material. This updated information explains how to do the following:

- Upgrade your Internet Information Server 2.0 installation to version 3.0. Step-by-step instructions show you how to install Microsoft Active Server Pages, the NetShow On-Demand server, Index Information Server, Seagate Crystal Reports for Internet Information Server, and FrontPage 97 server extensions. (*Chapters 2 and 5*)

- Use HTML (coverage updated for Internet Explorer 3.0) to create frames, use style sheets, and insert meta information within your HTML documents. (*Chapter 12*)

- Upgrade to FrontPage 97. (*Chapter 13*)

- Use Microsoft Office 97 to directly create HTML documents for publishing on the World Wide Web. Office 95 and Word 6.0 users who have decided not to upgrade can still use the Internet Assistants. (*Chapter 14*)

- Configure the NetShow On-Demand server using the Internet Service Manager. (*Chapter 6*)

- Install, configure, and use Microsoft Internet Explorer 3.0, rather than version 2.0. (*Chapter 7*)

- Include the latest tags as defined by the HTML 3.2 draft when writing your own HTML documents. (*Appendix B*)

In addition, you can refer to Appendix C for additional information on various registry keys for some of the Commercial Internet Service services.

Microsoft® Internet Information Server 3

Second Edition

Arthur Knowles

sams
net

201 West 103rd Street
Indianapolis, IN 46290

UNLEASHED

International Standard Book Number: 1-57521-271-4

Library of Congress Catalog Card Number: 96-72166

2000   99   98   97   4   3   2   1

Interpretation of the printing code: the rightmost double-digit number is the year of the book's printing; the rightmost single-digit, the number of the book's printing. For example, a printing code of 97-1 shows that the first printing of the book occurred in 1997.

Composed in AGaramond and MCPdigital by Macmillan Computer Publishing

Printed in the United States of America

Trademarks

Publisher and President   *Richard K. Swadley*

Publishing Manager   *Dean Miller*

Director of Editorial Services   *Cindy Morrow*

Director of Marketing   *Kelli S. Spencer*

Assistant Marketing Managers   *Kristina Perry*
Rachel Wolfe

Acquisitions Editor
Kim Spilker

Development Editor
Sunthar Visuvalingam

Software Development Specialist
Patty Brooks

Resource Coordinator
Deborah Frisby

Production Editor
June Waldman

Indexer
Tom Dinse

Technical Reviewer
Jeff Perkins

Editorial Coordinator
Katie Wise

Technical Edit Coordinator
Lynette Quinn

Editorial Assistants
Carol Ackerman
Andi Richter
Rhonda Tinch-Mize

Cover Designer
Tim Amrhein

Book Designer
Gary Adair

Copy Writer
Peter Fuller

Production Team Supervisors
Brad Chinn
Charlotte Clapp

Production
Jena Brandt
Michael Dietsch
Dana Rhodes
Deirdre Smith

Overview

Introduction   **xxv**

Part I   Introduction to the Internet Information Server

1   An Internet Overview   **3**

2   An Internet Information Server Overview   **25**

Part II   Building Your Foundation for the Internet Information Server

3   A Windows NT Server Overview   **43**

4   Choosing a Platform for Windows NT Server   **69**

5   Internet Information Server Preparation and Installation   **97**

Part III   Administering Your Site

6   Using the Internet Service Manager   **137**

7   Using Internet Explorer   **169**

8   Working with Microsoft Exchange   **199**

9   Using DHCP, WINS, and DNS   **215**

10   Advanced Security Issues   **273**

11   Enhancing Internet Information Server   **319**

Part IV   Web Page Development

12   An HTML Primer   **375**

13   Designing and Managing a Web Site with FrontPage   **407**

14   Publishing on the Web with Microsoft Office   **431**

15   Using Asymetrix Web3D and Corel's Web.Designer   **465**

16   Using Sausage Software's HotDog Pro   **479**

Part V   Advanced Web Page Development

17   The Internet Information Server SDK   **509**

18   Unleashing the Power of VBScript   **527**

19   Introduction to Windows NT CGI Programming   **571**

20   Writing Java Applets   **603**

21   Creating Dynamic Content with Active Server Pages   **627**

22   Using NetShow Live   **637**

Part VI   Using Internet Information Server with Databases

23   Interfacing Internet Information Server with ODBC Databases   **649**

24   Building Dynamic Web Pages with SQL Server   **693**

25   Using Crystal Reports for Internet Information Server   **719**

26   Indexing Your Web Site with the Index Information Server   **727**

Part VII   Performance-Tuning and Optimization Techniques

27   The Performance Monitor   **749**

28   Tuning the Server   **767**

Part VIII   Appendixes

A   Glossary   **811**

B   HTML Reference   **839**

C   The Registry Editor and Registry Keys   **889**

Index   **921**

Contents

Introduction xxv

Part I Introduction to the Internet Information Server

1 An Internet Overview 3

A Little History, Please 4

The Birth of ARPAnet and TCP/IP 6

The Birth of the Internet 6

Connecting to the Internet 6

Defining Your Goals 7

Defining Your Internet Service Requirements 9

Choosing a Connection Type 10

Choosing an Internet Provider or an Internet Service

Provider 14

Using the Internet 17

Publishing Data 17

Collecting Data 21

Selling Products 22

Summary 24

2 An Internet Information Server Overview 25

What Is the Internet Information Server? 26

A Collection of Windows NT Services 26

Moving Beyond the Basic Internet Information Server

Services 29

An Extensible Platform 30

What Can the Internet Information Server Do for You? 32

Internet and Intranet Publishing 32

How Well Can the Internet Information Server Perform? 35

Publicizing Your Web Site 37

Directory Listings 37

Newsgroups 38

Summary 38

Part II Building Your Foundation for the Internet Information Server

3 A Windows NT Server Overview 43

The Windows NT Design 44

The Windows NT System Design Model 47

The Windows NT Environmental Subsystem Design Model 50

Additional Windows NT Features 52
    The New Technology File System 52
    Fault-Tolerant Capabilities 54
    Centralized Administration 56
Windows NT Server Concepts 60
    Workgroups Versus Domains 60
    Controllers Versus Servers 62
    Domain Models 63
Summary 68

4   Choosing a Platform for Windows NT Server   69
Choosing the Right Hardware 71
    Choosing a Processor Platform 71
    Choosing an I/O Bus 72
    Choosing a Disk Subsystem 76
    Easy Performance Gains 79
Hardware Upgrades 83
    System Memory Upgrades 83
    Hardware RAID Alternatives 84
    Adding Network Adapters 85
    Adding Processors 91
Choosing the Right Server Model 91
The Software Configuration 92
Summary 95

5   Internet Information Server Preparation and Installation   97
Determining Where to Install the Internet Information Server 98
    IIS on a Limited Budget 98
    IIS on an Unlimited Budget 99
    Choosing a Location for Your Data 99
IIS Preinstallation Requirements 100
    Installing the TCP/IP Protocol and Utilities 102
    Installing the Dynamic Host Configuration Protocol 106
    Installing the Windows Internet Name Service 108
    Installing the RIP for Internet Protocol Service 108
    Installing the Domain Name Server Service 109
    Installing the Simple Network Management Protocol 110
    Installing the Simple TCP/IP Service 112
    Installing the Microsoft TCP/IP Printing Service 112
The Remote Access Service 113
    Installing the Remote Access Service 114
    Configuring the Remote Access Service 119
    The Remote Access Administrator 120
    Using Remote Access as a Gateway to the Internet 121

Installing the Internet Information Server 123
    Installing IIS 2.0 Components 124
    Installing IIS 3.0 Components 126
Summary 133

Part III Administering Your Site

6 Using the Internet Service Manager   137

Basic Operations of the Internet Service Manager 138
    Controlling the Internet Services 139
    Managing Internet Information Server Sites 140
    Using a View to Manage Multiple Sites 140
Configuring the WWW Service 141
    Configuring the WWW Service 141
    Configuring the WWW Service Directories 143
    Logging WWW Activity 149
    Limiting Access to Your WWW Site 150
Configuring the FTP Service 151
    Configuring the FTP Service 152
    Configuring the FTP Service Messages 153
    Configuring the FTP Service Directories 154
Configuring the Gopher Service 156
    Configuring the Gopher Service 157
    Configuring the Gopher Service Directories 158
Configuring the NetShow On-Demand Service 160
    Configuring the NetShow On-Demand Service Directories 161
    Logging NetShow On-Demand Activity 162
Logging Site Access with SQL Server 163
    Building the Database 163
    Assigning Permissions to Access the Database 165
    Building the ODBC Data Source 165
Summary 167

7 Using Internet Explorer   169

Installing Internet Explorer 171
Configuring Internet Explorer 172
    Configuring the Appearance 173
    Configuring the Internet Connection 176
    Configuring the Start and Search Pages and History Settings... 179
    Associating Programs and File Types 181
    Configuring Internet Explorer Security 186
    Configuring Internet Explorer Advanced Settings 191
Using Internet Explorer 195
Summary 197

8 Working with Microsoft Exchange 199

Using Exchange Server on the Internet 200

Installing the Internet Mail Connector 201

Configuring the Internet Mail Connector 202

Using the Internet to Connect Multiple

Exchange Server Sites 209

Microsoft Exchange Security Issues 210

Protecting Your Server 210

Protecting Your E-Mail Messages from Tampering or Theft 212

Protecting Your Clients from Viruses 213

Summary 214

9 Using DHCP, WINS, and DNS 215

Using the Dynamic Host Configuration Protocol 216

The Design Goals for the Microsoft DHCP Protocol 217

Planning Your DHCP Installation 219

Installing the DHCP Server Service 230

Managing Your DHCP Server with the DHCP Manager 230

Managing the DHCP Databases 241

DHCP Server Registry Keys 242

Using the Windows Internet Name Service 243

Design Goals for the WINS Server Service 244

Planning Your WINS Installation 245

Installing the WINS Service 250

Configuring the WINS Service with the WINS Manager 250

Managing Your WINS Clients 257

Managing the WINS Databases 258

Using the Performance Monitor to Monitor the

WINS Server Service 259

WINS Server Registry Keys 261

Using the Domain Name System 263

The Design Goals for the Microsoft DNS Service 263

Planning Your DNS Installation 264

The DNS Configuration Files 265

Summary 270

10 Advanced Security Issues 273

Security and the Internet 274

Application and Document Security Issues 274

Firewalls, Proxy Agents, and Other Ways to Limit Access 280

Security and Windows NT Server 284

Using User Accounts to Limit Access 285

Using NTFS to Protect Your Data 288

Setting Permissions on a Directory or File 290

Security and Dial-Up Networking 296
Configuring Windows NT Server as a Mini-Firewall 300
Determining Who Is Using Your System 306
Configuring the System to Enable Auditing............................ 307
Auditing Directories and Files 308
Using the Windows NT Event Viewer 312
The Internet Information Server Logs...................................... 317
Summary.. 317

11 Enhancing Internet Information Server   319

Using the Microsoft Proxy Server 320
Installing the Microsoft Proxy Server 321
Configuring the Microsoft Proxy Server 326
Using the Microsoft Chat Server 345
Installing the Microsoft Chat Server 347
Configuring the Microsoft Chat Server 348
Using the Microsoft News Server 363
Installing the Microsoft News Server 364
Configuring the Microsoft News Server 366
Summary.. 370

Part IV Web Page Development

12 An HTML Primer   375

What Is an HTML Document?.. 376
What Is a Markup Language? 377
HTML to the Rescue 378
Basic HTML Styles 380
Changing Paragraph Attributes 382
Changing Text Attributes 383
Displaying Text Using a Fixed-Width Font 386
Creating Document Headers 387
Changing Page Attributes 388
Creating Numbered and Bulleted Lists 390
Additional List Styles 391
Miscellaneous Styles 393
Advanced HTML Styles 394
Inserting Graphics 394
Creating Tables 397
Creating Hypertext Links 399
Creating Frames 401
Using Styles 403
Inserting Meta Information 404
Summary.. 406

13 Designing and Managing a Web Site with FrontPage 407

Installing FrontPage 408

FrontPage Server 410

Changing the Default Port of FrontPage Server 411

FrontPage Server Administrator 412

    Installing Server Extensions 412

    Managing Server Extensions 414

FrontPage Explorer 416

FrontPage To Do List 419

Verifying Links.. 420

FrontPage Editor 421

    Designing Web Pages Using the FrontPage Editor 421

Summary.. 430

14 Publishing on the Web with Microsoft Office 431

Publishing on the Web with Microsoft Office 97 432

    Installing Office 97 for Web Development 433

    Publishing on the Web with Microsoft Word 97 434

    Publishing on the Web with Microsoft Excel 97 438

    Publishing on the Web with Microsoft PowerPoint 441

    Publishing on the Web with Microsoft Access 444

Publishing on the Web with Microsoft Office 95 446

    Publishing on the Web with Microsoft Word 446

    Publishing on the Web with Microsoft Excel 452

    Publishing on the Web with Microsoft PowerPoint 456

    Publishing on the Web with Microsoft Access 459

Summary.. 463

15 Using Asymetrix Web3D and Corel's Web.Designer 465

Using Asymetrix Web 3D 466

    How Does Asymetrix Web 3D Work?..................................... 467

    Creating Your Home Page with Web 3D 469

Using Corel's Web.Designer 473

    Using CorelWEB.DESIGNER 473

    Using CorelWEB.GALLERY 474

    Using CorelWEB.Transit 476

Summary.. 477

16 Using Sausage Software's HotDog Pro 479

Why Use HotDog Pro? 480

Getting Started with HotDog Pro 481

    Installing HotDog Pro 482

    The HotDog Pro Tutorial 483

    Customizing HotDog Pro 484

Working with Documents and Templates 495
    Creating an HTML Document 495
    Creating a Template from an HTML Document 505
    Publishing Your Documents 505
Working with Projects 506
Summary 506

Part V Advanced Web Page Development

17 The Internet Information Server SDK 509

What Is an ISAPI Application? 510
    A CGI Application Versus an ISAPI Application 511
    A Few ISAPI Application Considerations 511
    The Basic ISAPI Interface 512
    An Internet Server Application Skeleton 521
Summary 524

18 Unleashing the Power of VBScript 527

Introduction to VBScript 528
How VBScript Works 528
Hello World! 529
    The Hello World! Dialog Box 530
    The Time Dialog Box 531
    The Date Dialog Box 531
VBScript Operators 533
    The Addition Operator 533
    The Subtraction Operator 533
    The Multiplication Operator 533
    The Exponential Operator 533
    The Floating-Point Division Operator 533
    The Integer-Division Operator 534
    The String-Concatenation Operator 534
    The MOD Operator 534
    Boolean Operators 534
    The Equivalence Operator 536
    The Object-Reference Operator 536
    Comparison Operators 536
VBScript Control Structures 537
    Call 537
    Dim 537
    Do...While...Until...Loop 539
    Erase 539
    Exit 540
    For...Next 540

For Each…Next 540

Function 541

If…Then…Else 542

Let 542

LSet 542

Mid 542

On Error 543

Private 543

Public 543

Randomize 543

Rem 543

RSet 544

Set 544

Static 544

Sub 544

While…Wend 545

VBScript Functions 545

Abs 545

Array 545

Asc 545

Atn 546

CBool 546

CByte 546

CDate 546

CDbl 546

Chr 546

CInt 546

CLng 546

Cos 546

CSng 547

CStr 547

CVErr 547

Date 547

DateSerial 547

DateValue 547

Day 547

Exp 548

Hex 548

Hour 548

InputBox 548

InStr 548

Int, Fix 549

IsArray 549
IsDate 549
IsEmpty 549
IsError 549
IsNull 549
IsNumeric 549
IsObject 549
LBound 550
LCase 550
Left 550
Len 550
Log 550
LTrim, RTrim, Trim 550
Mid 550
Minute 550
Month 550
MsgBox 551
Now 552
Oct 552
Right 552
Rnd 552
Second 552
Sgn 552
Sin 552
Sqr 553
Str 553
StrComp 553
String 553
Tan 553
Time 553
TimeSerial 553
TimeValue 553
UBound 554
UCase 554
Val 554
VarType 554
Weekday 555
Year 555
Applications of VBScript 555
Simple Calculator 556
Labeling an Image 566
Summary 570

19 Introduction to Windows NT CGI Programming   571

Introduction to CGI 572
    Benefits of an Interactive Web Site 573
Applications of CGI 574
CGI Basics 574
    How CGI Works 575
CGI Issues 577
    Security 578
    Processing Time 579
    Multiple Instances of the Same Script 579
CGI Environment Variables 580
CGI Perl Scripts 584
    Perl Resources on the Internet 585
CGI C Scripts 586
"Content Type" Returned by CGI Applications 586
A Few Things to Note About Developing CGI Applications 587
Hello World! CGI Scripts 588
    Hello World! CGI Script in Perl 588
    Hello World! CGI Script in C 590
Accessing Environment Variables Available to CGI Scripts 592
    Accessing CGI Environment Variables from a C Program 592
    Accessing CGI Environment Variables from a Perl Script 593
Using CGI to Provide Customized Content 594
Setting Up a Feedback Form 599
Summary 602

20 Writing Java Applets   603

Java Break 604
Understanding Java 605
    Applets Work on Any Computer 605
    Object-Oriented Programming 606
    Secure and Robust 607
    What Can You Do with Java? 607
Creating a Java Applet 608
    Parameters for the Marquee Applet 609
    The Marquee Applet's Code 610
    Imported Java 613
    Head of the Class 614
    The init Method 615
    Painting Applets 619
    Threads 622
Compiling Java Applets 624

Embedding Java Applets in HTML 625
    The <APPLET> Tag 626
    The <PARAM> Tag 626
    Summary 626

21 Creating Dynamic Content with Active Server Pages 627
What Is an Active Server Page? 628
    Creating a Simple Active Server Page 629
    Including Files in an Active Server Page 633
Additional Considerations for Active Server Pages 635
Summary 636

22 Using NetShow Live 637
What Is Microsoft NetShow Live? 638
    What Is a Stream? 639
    NetShow Live Stream Types 640
Building a Streaming Audio-Video File 641
Putting It All Together 643
Summary 646

Part VI Using Internet Information Server with Databases

**23 Interfacing Internet Information
Server with ODBC Databases 649**
Installing Microsoft dbWeb 650
Using the Microsoft dbWeb Administrator 655
    Configuring dbWeb Preferences 655
    Creating the ODBC Data Source 660
    Creating the Database Schema 664
Creating a Custom Guest Book Using Microsoft dbWeb 687
Summary 691

24 Building Dynamic Web Pages with SQL Server 693
Using the Internet Database Connector 694
    Creating the Web Page Forms 695
Using the SQL Server Web Assistant 712
Summary 718

25 Using Crystal Reports for Internet Information Server 719
What Is Crystal Reports for Internet Information Server? 720
Creating a Report 721
Using Crystal Reports Live on Your Web Server 723
Summary 726

26 Indexing Your Web Site with the Index Information Server   727
  Using the Index Information Server 728
    Preparing Your Documents for the Index Information
      Server 729
    Creating the Search Page 730
    Creating the Internet Data Query File 734
    Creating the HTML Extension File 739
  Summary 745

Part VII Performance-Tuning and Optimization Techniques

27 The Performance Monitor   749
  Using the Performance Monitor 750
    The Performance Monitor Toolbar 751
    Creating Charts 752
    Creating Logs 756
    Creating Reports 758
    Creating Alerts 760
  Summary 766

28 Tuning the Server   767
  Performance Tuning with the Performance Monitor 768
    Finding Processor Bottlenecks 769
    Finding Memory Bottlenecks 774
    Finding Disk Bottlenecks 780
    Finding Network Bottlenecks 783
    Finding IIS Bottlenecks 786
  Configuring SQL Server 793
  Summary 807

Part VIII Appendixes

A Glossary   811

B HTML Reference   839
  How This Reference Is Structured 840
  HTML Element List 841
    <A> 841
    <ABBREV> 842
    <ACRONYM> 842
    <ADDRESS> 843
    <APP> 843
    <APPLET> 843
    <AREA> 844

<AU> 844

<B> 844

<BANNER> 845

<BASE> 845

<BASEFONT> 845

<BDO> 846

<BGSOUND> 846

<BIG> 846

<BLINK> 846

<BLOCKQUOTE> 847

<BODY> 847

<BQ> 848

 848

<CAPTION> 848

<CENTER> 848

<CITE> 849

<CODE> 849

<COL> 849

<COLGROUP> 850

<CREDIT> 850

<DD> 850

<DEL> 851

<DFN> 851

<DIR> 851

<DIV> 852

<DL> 852

<DT> 852

<EM> 852

<EMBED> 853

<FIG> 853

<FN> 853

<FONT> 854

<FORM> 854

<FRAME> 854

<FRAMESET> 855

<H1> 855

<H2> 855

<H3> 856

<H4> 856

<H5> 856

<H6> 857

<HEAD> 857

<HP*n*> 857

<HR> 857

<HTML> 858

<I> 858

<IMG> 858

<INPUT> 859

<INS> 859

<ISINDEX> 860

<KBD> 860

<LANG> 860

<LH> 861

<LI> 861

<LINK> 861

<LISTING> 861

<MAP> 862

<MARQUEE> 862

<MENU> 863

<META> 863

<NEXTID> 863

<NOBR> 864

<NOEMBED> 864

<NOFRAMES> 864

<NOTE> 864

<OL> 865

<OPTION> 865

<OVERLAY> 865

<P> 866

<PARAM> 866

<PERSON> 866

<PLAINTEXT> 866

<PRE> 867

<Q> 867

<S> 867

<SAMP> 868

<SELECT> 868

<SMALL> 868

<SPAN> 869

<STRIKE> 869

<STRONG> 869

<STYLE> 869

<SUB> 870

<SUP> 870

<TAB> 870
<TABLE> 870
<TBODY> 871
<TD> 871
<TEXTAREA> 872
<TFOOT> 872
<TH> 872
<THEAD> 873
<TITLE> 873
<TR> 873
<TT> 874
<U> 874
<UL> 874
<VAR> 874
<WBR> 875
<XMP> 875
Defining Special Characters on Your Web Page 875
HTML Summary for the Internet Information Server
and the Internet Assistant for Word for Windows 880

C The Registry Editor and Registry Keys   889
The Registry 890
The Registry Editor 892
Useful Registry Keys 895
System Service Configuration Registry Keys 896
NetBEUI Frame Protocol Configuration Registry Keys 912
Memory-Related Registry Keys 915
Miscellaneous Registry Keys 918

Index   921

Acknowledgments

Although an author might write the chapters himself, developing the book into a viable project is really a team effort. Therefore, I would like to thank my agent, Valda Hilley, for getting me involved in the project; Sams.net Publishing for the opportunity; and my family—my mother Antoinette Knowles and my two cats (Kit and Kat)—for their support. Special thanks go to Kim Spilker, Sunthar Visuvalingam, and Deborah Frisby of Sams.net Publishing and to June Waldman, the freelance production editor. All these people helped to make this a better book. I also would like to thank Eric Beauchamp and Alex Sampera of WinBook Computer Corporation, for without their loan of a WinBook XP5 portable computer this book could not have been completed.

About the Author

Arthur Knowles is president and founder of Knowles Consulting, a firm specializing in systems integration, training, and software development. Art is a Microsoft Certified System Engineer. His specialties include Microsoft Windows NT Server, Windows NT Workstation, SQL Server, Systems Management Server, Windows 95, and Windows for Workgroups. Art is the author of *Microsoft BackOffice 2 Administrator's Survival Guide* (Sams Publishing) and has served as a contributing author to several books, including *Designing and Implementing Microsoft Internet Information Server 2* (Sams.net), *Windows 3.1 Configuration Secrets*, *Windows NT Unleashed* (Sams Publishing), and *Mastering Windows 95*. He is the forum manager of the Portable Computers Forum on The Microsoft Network. You can reach Art on the Internet at webmaster@nt-guru.com or on his Web site at http://www.nt-guru.com.

Tell Us What You Think!

As a reader, you are the most important critic and commentator of our books. We value your opinion and want to know what we're doing right, what we could do better, what areas you'd like to see us publish in, and any other words of wisdom you're willing to pass our way. You can help us make strong books that meet your needs and give you the computer guidance you require.

Do you have access to CompuServe or the World Wide Web? Then check out our CompuServe forum by typing **GO SAMS** at any prompt. If you prefer the World Wide Web, check out our site at http://www.mcp.com.

> **NOTE**
>
> If you have a technical question about this book, call Macmillan Technical Support at 317-581-3833.

As the team leader of the group that created this book, I welcome your comments. You can fax, e-mail, or write me directly to let me know what you did or didn't like about this book—as well as what we can do to make our books stronger. Here's the information:

Fax: 317-581-4669

E-mail: opsys_mgr@sams.mcp.com

Mail: Dean Miller
         Comments Department
         Sams.net Publishing
         201 W. 103rd Street
         Indianapolis, IN 46290

Introduction

This book explains how you can use Microsoft Internet Information Server in the real world—with special emphasis on using the Internet Information Server to publish information on the World Wide Web. *Microsoft Internet Information Server 3 Unleashed* is designed for the intermediate to advanced reader (network administrators, network supervisors, upper-management personnel, and so on) and covers the basic concepts required for connecting your Microsoft Network to the Internet. The book highlights some of the more arcane aspects of the Internet and includes plenty of information on daily maintenance, troubleshooting, and problem solving.

This book uses step-by-step procedures interspersed with figures captured from the actual tools and fulfills the following needs:

- Prepares you to use the Microsoft Internet Information Server as a tool to enter the world of unlimited connectivity on the Internet.

- Prepares you to set up and administer an Internet Information Server site using the Internet Service Manager. This book includes information and sample code that enable you to use the Index Information Server to index your Web server and provide a real-time search engine interface for your users. The book explains how to use Crystal Reports to determine who is using your site—and its most popular pages—and also explains how to use HTML pages to display real-time Web site statistics.

- Prepares you to publish on the Internet using Microsoft Windows NT Server and the tools provided by the Internet Information Server, including NetShow Live—to multicast live audio streams—and Active Server Pages—to build dynamic content. The book also discusses various third-party tools you can use to build Web pages.

- Provides information and sample code that enable you to build Web pages that interact with the user, using VBScript or JavaScript, or with your ODBC databases, using the Internet Database Connector or Microsoft dbWeb. This book includes information on how to customize your Web server using the Internet Information Server SDK and CGI scripts.

- Prepares you to deal with issues relating to Internet security. The book describes how to use Windows NT Server as a mini-firewall to prevent unauthorized access to your network and also how to use and configure the Microsoft Proxy Agent for full-service protection.

Conventions Used in This Book

This book uses the following conventions:

- Menu names are separated from menu options by a vertical bar (|). For example, File | Open means "Select the File menu and choose the Open option."

- New terms appear in *italic*.

- Placeholders (words that stand for what you actually type) in regular text appear in *italic*.

- All code appears in monospace, as do filenames and directory names.

- Placeholders in code appear in *italic monospace*.

- When a line of code is too long to fit on one line of this book, the code is broken at a convenient place and continued to the next line. The continuation of the line is preceded by a code continuation character (➡). You should type a line of code that has this character as one long line without breaking it.

IN THIS PART

■ An Internet Overview 3

■ An Internet Information Server
Overview 25

Introduction to the Internet Information Server

I

PART

An Internet Overview

IN THIS CHAPTER

- A Little History, Please   4
- Connecting to the Internet   6
- Using the Internet   17

CHAPTER 1

This chapter begins with a short (really, I kept it brief) history of the creation and growth of the Internet. After your look back into history, you'll learn about various ways to connect to the Internet and examine their associated costs. This listing is not meant to be all-inclusive. Rather, my intention is to give you some idea of what is available and an estimate of how much you should expect to pay to implement each option. You can be assured that the cost of your Internet connection, particularly a high-speed connection, will be the largest portion of your Internet budget.

Getting on the Internet is easy. Paying for it is not. The most common reason to want to get on the Internet is to host a World Wide Web (WWW) site, so in this chapter you learn about alternative ways to get your Web site on the Internet. Many service providers offer a Windows NT Server–based WWW server. Your Web site might even be hosted on a server running the Internet Information Server (IIS). You will look into some of these Web site hosting options, but the premise of this book is that you want to host your own site using the IIS.

Your first job is to learn a bit about what the Internet is and where it might be going. Then, because connection speed is the factor that determines how many simultaneous clients you can support on the Internet, your next task is a look at some of the types of connections you can obtain. You also learn how to choose a provider to get you connected to the Internet. This choice is not one you want to make lightly. Although I can point out specific areas of concern, I cannot recommend any particular provider that will suit all of your needs. You will need to conduct your own research.

TIP

Two good methods for finding a suitable service provider are to look into local computer magazines for local providers and to use the Internet for additional research. For example, I found my provider—after a couple of months of research—in a local magazine called *Computer's Edge*. You can often find this type of (generally free) magazine in your local computer store. Most of the advertisements include uniform resource locators (URLs) for the provider company's Web site and information about its services and pricing structures.

The final section of this chapter describes what you can do on the Internet with the IIS. I hope this information will give you an idea of the services you can offer to your clients.

A Little History, Please

The Internet is a difficult subject to describe because you can't simply point to any single location and say, "This is the Internet." So before you can really understand what the Internet is, you must first understand how it was created. The Internet started in the late 1960s with the Advanced Research Projects Agency (ARPA) in the Department of Defense. This agency funded a study to link computer networks together so that they could reliably communicate with each other. This reliability requirement led to the development of a *packet-switched network proto-col*, which passes data from the source computer to the destination computer through interme-diary computers rather than through a direct two-way connection. For example, suppose you need to link three computer networks as shown in Figure 1.1.

FIGURE 1.1.
A sample packet-switched network.

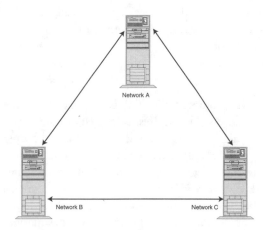

In a *circuit-switched network*, each connection from the source computer to the destination computer is a direct two-way connection called a *switch*. For example, if you wanted to send data from Network A to Network B, the path you would use would be switch AB. If you de-cided to send data from Network A to Network C, the path would be switch AC. This method works fine as long as the physical connection, or switch, is active. But what happens if the con-nection between Network A and Network B fails? How can you get the data from Network A to Network B? In a circuit-switched network, you can't. But in a packet-switched network, you can. In a packet-switched network, the data is encapsulated in a *wrapper* that contains the destination computer's address. When a computer receives a packet that is not addressed to it, it forwards, or *routes*, the packet to the next computer. Therefore, if the physical connection between Networks A and B fails, but the connections between Networks A and C and Net-works C and B are working, Network A can send the packet to Network C, which can then forward the packet to Network B. The reply from Network B to Network A can follow the same route in reverse.

NOTE

The capability to route packets is one of the Internet's greatest strengths because it practi-cally ensures that the data will arrive at its destination. However, it is also the reason you sometimes encounter a slowdown when receiving data, because the route the data takes from source to destination can change drastically. A longer route means a longer delay.

The Birth of ARPAnet and TCP/IP

In 1970 ARPA created ARPAnet, the first packet-switched network, which connected the University of California at Los Angeles, the University of California at Santa Barbara, Stanford University, and the University of Utah in Salt Lake City. By late 1972 more than 40 computers were connected using ARPAnet as a backbone. Later, ARPA was renamed Defense Advanced Research Projects Agency (DARPA), and research on network connectivity continued. In 1974 Vinton Cerf and Robert Kahn released the *Internet Protocol* (IP) and *Transmission Control Protocol* (TCP) protocols, which work together to provide a connection between computers. Consequently, the protocol is called *TCP/IP,* rather than just TCP or IP.

IP is a lower-level protocol than TCP. Each node, sometimes referred to as a *host,* is assigned a unique 32-bit address. This address is formed by combining four numbers (each number consisting of three digits between 0 and 255) separated by periods (for example, my server's IP address is 206.170.127.65). TCP is a higher-level protocol and is used to handle large amounts of data, ensure data integrity, and perform data sequencing. If a message is too large to fit in a single packet, TCP may subdivide the message into smaller messages. These messages are in turn assigned a checksum and a sequence number and are encapsulated in an IP layer before being sent to the destination computer. On the destination computer, these smaller messages are then passed to the TCP layer and returned to their original format.

The Birth of the Internet

Although ARPAnet serviced many research centers, it was not the only network in town. In 1977 the University of Wisconsin decided to create a new network for the advancement of computer science technology. This idea eventually became CSnet. By the 1980s CSnet was connected to ARPAnet using a gateway and the TCP/IP protocol. It was at this point, you could argue, that the Internet was born. After all, a method of connecting disparate networks and communicating with a common protocol is what enables you and me to connect our networks (which may or may not use TCP/IP internally) to the Internet as well.

In the late 1980s the National Science Foundation created NFSnet to support a small network of supercomputers. This network used state-of-the-art transmission capabilities to provide a high-speed backbone between central sites. At the same time other changes were also occurring. In 1983 NFSnet was slowly replacing ARPAnet. CSnet was also absorbing smaller networks, but by 1991 it was finally replaced by NFSnet as well. Now NFSnet is being slowly replaced with the very high speed Backbone Network Service (vBNS) to provide even higher transmission capabilities.

Connecting to the Internet

So you have decided that you want to connect to the Internet, but you have not decided how you will accomplish it. Will you need to connect just one computer, many computers, or possibly even your entire local area network? Will you need to support one-way or two-way network traffic? Do you need just a WWW site, or do you need full Internet services? If you need only a WWW site, will you use your own hardware or your Internet provider's hardware to host your site? How do you find an Internet provider? And what is the difference between an Internet provider and an Internet service provider (ISP)? These are some of the questions I either answer in this chapter or, at the very least, give you enough information to get you started in your search for Internet connectivity.

Defining Your Goals

Before you begin talking to external agencies or going crazy on the Web in your search for connectivity solutions, let me offer a piece of advice: *Don't!* Don't solicit advice outside your company until you have some idea of the services you want to provide. Why? Because it is a cruel world out there. The information flow is staggering, and you can waste incredible amounts of time looking on the Internet and thinking about what you want. When you finally get everything connected, all your network clients can surf the Internet as well. As your network clients go surfing on the Internet, they can be eating up valuable network bandwidth, thus slowing down your entire network. These same network clients may spend so much time on the Internet that they might not even get the work they are paid for done on time. Between dealing with your numerous users and maintaining your WWW site instance, you'll probably run out of time to sleep, much less eat, unless you have an extremely competent staff to aid you.

You can also spend too much time looking at the wrong avenues to actually get connected to the Internet. Most people will tell you to start your search for connectivity with the InterNIC. (The InterNIC is the agency that maintains IP address allocations [to ensure routability of IP addresses] and domain name registration.) However, I'll save you some time by passing on some advice from the InterNIC: When the time comes for you to connect to the Internet, look at your requirements first. Then find an Internet provider or an ISP to fulfill them. (I explain the difference in the section "Choosing an Internet Provider or an Internet Service Provider.") Your provider will furnish the interface to the InterNIC. In essence, if you are not an ISP, you do not need to worry about the InterNIC.

> **TIP**
>
> Tracking and providing the finite number of routable IP addresses are some of the InterNIC's primary concerns. Even though you can obtain a small block of IP addresses from the InterNIC, the InterNIC may be unable to guarantee their routability. A *routable* IP address is a unique IP address guaranteed to be accessible by any host on the Internet. If your IP addresses are not routable, you may have problems finding external hosts and external clients may have problems finding your hosts. Therefore, your first stop should be your ISP because the IP addresses it assigns will be fully routable.

Instead of racing willy-nilly all over the place, take the time to write out your goals. Then determine how you will achieve them. Create a schedule for each milestone and then try to meet it. But don't push the schedule. Give yourself time to find the information you need for each step. I spent several months looking for a local provider, but then again, I live in a rural area about 45 miles from the nearest large city. If you are located in a major city, you should be able to cut this time down to a few weeks.

Connecting the World to You

You can use Windows NT Server with the IIS to provide an Internet presence to the world, but not to your internal network clients (those on your LAN). In this configuration, you could create either a separate dedicated network or just a single server to provide your presence on the Internet. Neither of these configurations has a direct connection from your "Internet computers" to your local area network, which reduces the risk for potential damage to your network from the Internet. The wide open Internet often contains malicious programs, or users, that could wreak havoc on your network. Consequently, security is a big issue with Internet connectivity. Chapter 10, "Advanced Security Issues," addresses this subject in greater detail.

> **NOTE**
>
> Even though your server has no direct connection between the Internet and your LAN, you can still access the Internet (via a dial-up connection) to manage it. Most NT tools are Remote Procedure Call (RPC) enabled, which means you can manage your server remotely, that is, managing the various services; adding users; or changing WWW, FTP, or Gopher content.

Your Internet presence could consist of three additional services:

- WWW Server—The main reason you probably want to use the IIS is to create a *World Wide Web* (WWW) site. You can use this site to promote your ideas and your company products, to provide technical support for your customers, and to sell your products electronically. You will learn more about WWW capabilities in the section "Using the Internet" later in this chapter.

> **TIP**
>
> If all you want to provide is a WWW or FTP site, you may be better off putting your WWW server directly on the Internet provider's network. Your server could be a virtual server hosted on an Internet provider's computer, or it could be a server supplied and maintained by you. Each of these choices has different financial options, which you should discuss with your Internet provider.

- FTP Server—The *File Transfer Protocol* (FTP) server is used to exchange files over the Internet with FTP clients. Much as you use a communication program (such as Terminal) to transfer files using the Xmodem protocol, you can use the FTP protocol over the Internet.

- Gopher Server—This service enables you to search and display large amounts of text. For example, you could use it to provide an online catalog.

Connecting You to the World

You can also use Windows NT Server and the IIS to connect your entire network to the world. If your network is small enough, you can use a single server that is connected to the Internet as your network router. You can also purchase a dedicated router that is connected to both the Internet and your internal network. In either case, you need a router to bridge the gap between your network and the Internet. Meeting this goal involves additional implementation and security details. Chapter 5, "Internet Information Server Preparation and Installation," describes the implementation issues, and Chapter 10 covers the additional security issues and offers some configuration ideas you can use to minimize your risk.

If you are providing full Internet access for your network clients, you may want to implement services that IIS does not offer. If so, you will need additional software, for example, Microsoft Exchange to provide corporate-wide e-mail. If you are providing full Internet connectivity for all your LAN clients, you will also need an IP address for each client. Remember that you cannot just make up your IP address. In order to provide a fully routable IP address (read "successful connectivity"), you need an IP address provided by your Internet provider or the InterNIC. Even if you do obtain a block of IP addresses from the InterNIC, your Internet provider may decline to use them. This situation can leave you weeks to months behind your schedule to provide full Internet access. You should therefore assess your physical IP address requirements, but talk to your Internet provider before actually obtaining them or changing your network client configuration.

In any event, be prepared to update all your clients' network software. This process may take a great deal of time, sometimes months, so allow for that in your schedule. A full migration to provide complete Internet access may also require additional on-site technical support personnel and even classes for your network clients. You need to prepare for all contingencies.

Defining Your Internet Service Requirements

Now comes the tough part. Before you finally talk with your Internet provider, you need to determine what Internet services you want. When connecting to the Internet, you have more to consider than just providing WWW, FTP, or Gopher sites. Consider some of the following issues:

- Supported clients—Have you considered how may Internet clients you want to support? Your Internet connection will have a limited bandwidth, so it can support only a limited number of simultaneous connected users. The more users you want to support, the more you will pay for the connection. You can assume that each supported client will consume at least 57,600bps (a standard 14,400bps modem connection) of your available bandwidth. To calculate your required bandwidth, just multiply 57,600 by the number of simultaneous client connections you want to support. The result is a rough estimate of your needs.

■ IP addresses—For each host (a computer or peripheral) that you want to be visible on the Internet, you will need an Internet routable IP address. Will your provider be able to fulfill your needs? Check this one out carefully before you sign on the dotted line. Some providers are too small to service large IP address allocations. Others charge extra for each additional IP address.

■ Domain name—If you want your WWW site to have a specific name (such as my WWW site's www.nt-guru.com), you will need to obtain a *domain name*. Domain names are registered with the InterNIC and require that you have a static IP address and two *domain name service* (DNS) servers fully functional on your network at all times. Normally your Internet provider will register your domain name and provide the primary and secondary DNS servers. But it will also collect the additional fees!

■ Hardware—Before you purchase any additional hardware, like a router, check with your Internet provider. Your provider may not support a particular piece of hardware or may offer a discount on hardware purchased directly from it as part of a service agreement.

■ E-mail—Will you use an e-mail server provided by your Internet provider or use your own? If you use your own server, you may want to use one provided by the Internet provider as a backup. Otherwise, if your connection between the Internet provider and your network fails, you may lose some mail.

Choosing a Connection Type

The three established mechanisms for connecting to the Internet are dial-up, leased line, or frame relay. Each offers additional capabilities, at an additional cost. Because prices vary from state to state and from Internet provider to Internet provider, I can't offer standard pricing structures for you. Instead, you should discuss these with your Internet provider and possibly your phone company. I have provided some estimates based on information I obtained in my search for an Internet connection that may prove helpful to you.

CAUTION

If your site will be critical to the well-being of your company, you should consider obtaining two connections, possibly from two different Internet providers. Then if the connection between your network and the Internet fails, you can use your backup connection to keep your system online.

Dial-Up Connections

A *dial-up connection* is by far the easiest to work with. It consists of an analog modem connected to your computer via a serial cable. Your analog modem is in turn connected to your plain old telephone system (POTS) jack. Analog modems are currently capable of achieving carrier rates of 28,800bps, and, with 4:1 compression, they can obtain a throughput of 115,200bps. These types of connections are relatively inexpensive. Many major Internet providers offer a local phone number with unlimited access for less than $20 a month. If you do not have a local phone number, though, prices can skyrocket. For example, a call outside of my local (that is, toll free) area costs about a penny a minute. That doesn't sound like much, but it adds up to $14.40 a day, or $432 a month. If you can afford it and you need to support only one to five simultaneous clients on your WWW site, a dial-up connection with an analog modem will suit you just fine.

NOTE

Recently, U.S. Robotics and Rockwell International have introduced 56Kbps modems, which may one day rock the industry in terms of dial-up solutions. Unfortunately, this technology will not be readily available for some time, as it requires modifications to the existing dial-in modem pools or remote access servers that ISPs use. Until your ISP updates its equipment, the best you can hope for is a 28.8Kbps connection.

56KB Leased Line

If you need to support more users, you might want to consider a 56KB *leased line*. Unlike a regular phone line that routes calls dynamically to their destination and can offer many different endpoints (such as when you call your friend and then your mother from the same phone), a leased line has only one routing and connection option. In essence, your leased line can connect to only one phone number. Many leased line services are flat-rate services, but arrangements vary depending on the local phone company. In California, Pacific Bell charges about $1,000 to install a leased line and $125.00 per month for the service. A 56KB leased line provides a minimum of twice the throughput of a 28,800bps modem, so it can support additional users.

You will incur additional costs with this solution, however, because you need to purchase supplementary equipment. You will need a channel service unit/data service unit (CSU/DSU) and a router. If you are connecting an existing Ethernet-based network, you may need an additional hub as well. A CSU/DSU can run from $300 to a $1,500, and a router from $1,500 to $3,000. Some Internet providers include the price of the equipment in your service contract or sell the equipment at a discount. In some cases, though, you are expected to purchase the hardware for both your site and the Internet provider's site, so check the fine print carefully.

Frame Relay

When you need additional speed, you may want to consider *frame relay*. It comes in several flavors: from 56KB to 1.5MB, depending on your hardware, Internet provider, and phone company. With a frame relay connection, you do not own the entire line. Instead, you are purchasing a portion of its carrying capacity, or bandwidth. The feature that makes frame relay so useful as an Internet connectivity solution is its potential for growth. Depending on the hardware you choose (and, once again, you will need a CSU/DSU and router), you can start with a 56KB connection. As your needs grow, your provider and phone company can increase the bandwidth—at increased prices, of course. Frame relay is a good option for midsize companies.

1.5Mbps and Beyond

If you need higher bandwidths than those offered by frame relay and your service provider supports the newer high-speed options, such as Switched Multimegabit Data Service (SMDS) or Asynchronous Transfer Mode (ATM), you might consider using Fractional T1, T1, T2, or T3 connections. The prices for these services vary significantly from vendor to vendor, so you should discuss the pricing with them directly.

Fractional T1 is similar to frame relay in that you lease only a portion of the available bandwidth. Fractional T1 includes twenty-four 64Kbps channels. You can start with one channel; then, as with frame relay, you can add bandwidth by adding channels and paying an additional fee to your service provider. If you choose to go the full route with a T1 (1.5Mbps) line, you will also need a CSU/DSU and router. (In fact, you need similar equipment for any of the options discussed in this section.) A T2 line falls in the midrange of the SMDS options with 6.3Mbps. Both T3 and ATM can achieve rates as high as 45Mbps. From what I have seen in the market, though, SMDS is slowly replacing the options for midrange Tx connections, so Tx connectivity may be unavailable in your area.

Integrated Services Digital Network

Two types of *Integrated Services Digital Network* (ISDN) connections are available. The first is the *Basic Rate Interface* (BRI). A BRI consists of two 64Kbps bearer channels and one 16Kbps data channel. The second is the *Primary Rate Interface* (PRI), which consists of 24 bearer channels and one 16Kbps data channel. That's as big as a T1 line, offering 1.5Mbps. Although in California you may find that some ISDN bearer channels offer only a 56Kbps throughput, the missing 8Kbps per channel is combined and used for the 16Kbps data channel. In the future this situation will change so that even California residents can enjoy the full 64Kbps offered by ISDN, and the rest of this discussion assumes that a bearer channel offers 64Kbps. You can combine two bearer channels to provide an effective carrier rate of 128Kbps. Compression can quadruple this rate to 512Kbps, which is enough bandwidth to support a small (less than 15 users) network's Internet connection. With 512Kbps you also have enough bandwidth to support from 10 to 50 WWW simultaneous client connections.

You can establish an ISDN connection as described above by connecting a digital modem to your server. Then use Dial-Up Networking to connect to another digital modem at your ISP's end. Finally, by configuring your server as a software router, you can route network requests to (or from) the Internet from (or to) your network clients.

Another alternative is to purchase an ISDN router, which combines the functions of a dedicated router and an ISDN modem. ISDN routers often have four bearer channels that require a total of two ISDN BRI connections to obtain full efficiency. When connecting a small network to the Internet via ISDN, using an ISDN router is the preferred method because it provides additional network security.

I paid Pacific Bell $80 to install a single BRI ISDN connection and pay $25 a month for the service. My Motorola BitSURFER Pro cost $400, and my ISP charges $371 ($150 goes to PacBell as a data transport fee) a month for dedicated single-bearer channel ISDN access. The setup fees included $150 to convert the ISDN line to a dedicated line. In addition, I paid $100 to register my domain name and pay a $50 yearly fee. Dedicated dual-bearer channel access would have cost me $550 a month. If you decide to use ISDN, make sure you to can obtain a dedicated connection because this type of connection does not have any associated toll charges. Otherwise, you may find yourself paying more in phone company charges than you pay your Internet service provider!

BETTER THAN ISDN?

Recently, I've changed my Internet connection from a single BRI ISDN connection to a digital data service (DDS) 56Kbps connection. This solution uses an Ascend Pipeline 130 router with a built-in DDS 56 and ISDN (currently not used) connectivity solution.

The DDS 56Kbps connection provides faster throughput than a single or dual BRI ISDN connection. At least it will if you use an external ISDN modem, such as I used previously, because a router is a synchronous device. It operates at the maximum transmission rate of your connection. On the other hand, an external ISDN modem—or any other external modem—is an asynchronous device with the limiting factor being the speed of the serial port to which it is connected.

The port I used was the 16550 UART, which has a maximum transmission rate of 115,200bps. I was never able to transmit or receive a continuous data stream at 56Kbps, or at 115,200Kbps with a dual ISDN BRI connection, because the UART just couldn't keep up with the data stream. Instead, I received brief peaks of high-speed transmissions/receptions, rather than a continuous data stream, because the UART would signal the modem to pause its operations whenever the burden became too great to handle.

The monthly cost for my new connection is roughly the same as the cost of the single BRI ISDN connection. The router set me back an additional $1,400. This worthwhile investment provides several additional benefits, including Internet access for my network clients whether the server is up or not (previously I used NT Server as my router), improved utilization of the available connection bandwidth, and improved security. (Ascend recently introduced dynamic firewall capabilities for its routers.)

Choosing an Internet Provider or an Internet Service Provider

The most important factor to the success of your Internet connectivity effort is your choice of an Internet provider or an Internet service provider (ISP). You may be wondering what the difference is between an Internet provider and ISP, as did I when I first started this quest. The answer is very simple. An Internet provider, sometimes called an Internet access provider (IAP), provides only a raw connection to the Internet. You must accomplish everything else on your own. If you are a large commercial organization, the services of an IAP may be sufficient. On the other hand, most people prefer to work with an ISP because an ISP provides additional services, which can include the following:

- Domain name registration—Your ISP will, for a fee ($100 to the InterNIC and a monthly/yearly fee to the ISP), register your domain name with the InterNIC. It will also ensure that its DNS will equate your domain name with a routable IP address. Thus your clients can find you by entering http://www.*YourDomainName*.com, rather than http://www.*YourISPDomainName*.com.*YourE-MailAddress* in their Web browser.

- Server hosting—If you cannot afford the high-speed Internet connectivity options but need the bandwidth to support your clients, maybe putting your server on the ISP's network is the answer. Many ISPs allow you to place your hardware directly on their Internet backbone for a fee as low as $500 a month. You will have to watch this option carefully, however, because many ISPs also charge extra if you have more than a specific amount of traffic on your site. A very active WWW site can cause your monthly costs to soar!

- Virtual server—The step down the chain is a virtual server. A *virtual server* is a host (computer) that contains several sites. This server might have your domain, your next-door neighbor's domain, and many more as well. In essence, you are sharing resources (the computer's processor, disk storage, and Internet connection) and their associated costs. Consequently, you pay a lower fee to your ISP.

> **NOTE**
>
> The IIS can also support virtual domains. You can find out more about this capability in Chapter 6, "Using the Internet Service Manager."

- FTP drop box—An *FTP drop box* is a directory on your ISP's hardware where you can place files for clients to retrieve, or vice versa. These are generally included for free with your initial service account as long as you stay below 5MB of total storage. If you go over that you will be required to pay additional fees.

- News—The Internet contains many newsgroups, or public bulletin boards where users can meet to discuss their ideas. A newsgroup feed from your Internet provider will cost more and can run to over 90MB of data a day. Last, but not least, the IIS does not include any software to exploit the newsfeed. If you want this option, you will need to find additional software.

- E-mail services—Many ISPs will also host e-mail accounts on their servers. The charge for each additional e-mail account is generally between $10 and $20. This fee is perfectly reasonable for a small network but may be more expensive than dedicated hardware and software at your company site for midrange to large networks. Again, you should discuss your service provider's options to find the best solution.

- Turnkey solutions—With the variety of hardware available today, incompatibilities are likely to arise with the equipment you use to connect to your service provider. For this reason, many service providers offer complete solutions. These packages can include a CSU/DSU, router, server, and possibly even the software. If you purchase equipment directly from your service provider, the provider often supports it—that is, if your server hardware fails, the service provider will send someone out to repair it.

- Domain name or WWW page advertising—After you have your domain name and Web site, you have to find a way to tell the public about it. You can do this yourself, by registering your domain and Web site names at the appropriate places, or you can pay your service provider to do it for you. You will learn more about the do-it-yourself options in Chapter 2, "An Internet Information Server Overview."

- Professional WWW page development—Do you have the staff to create your own Web pages, or do you need a helping hand? If your answer is the latter, check with your service provider. It may offer Web page packages that include a virtual server, a domain name, and a WWW site designed and maintained by the service provider. Some service providers also offer Web page consulting services. If yours does, be prepared to pay between $50 and $100 per hour.

Does Your ISP Measure Up?

Before you settle on a particular ISP, you should make a few inquiries. Consider the following questions as a starting point:

How long have you been in business?

If the company has not been in business for at least a year, you should reconsider doing business with it. The Internet is big business, and many new companies are starting up to offer services. Many of these same companies fold up within a year of opening their doors. If your ISP goes out of business, what would you do?

How long have you been providing Internet connectivity solutions?

Believe it or not, almost anybody can become an ISP. Many ISPs are marketing companies looking to provide a presence on the Web—and to make money at it by offering you a connectivity solution as well. But they really do not know much about providing customer service and support. On the other hand, your ISP may be a couple of techies with a server or two in a basement. They may know quite a bit about the Internet, but may not know much about customer service or technical support. In addition, their hardware may prove to be unreliable for a long-term connection. Again, if an ISP hasn't been in business for at least a year, keep on looking.

How large is your company?

This is one way to find out if your ISP is a basement ISP or a real company. If your ISP employs fewer than 10 people, I suggest you look around some more. Smaller companies are more likely to collapse from disinterest, financial strain, or hardship, which can leave you in the lurch.

How many people in your company are dedicated to providing technical support?

This question is another test to see if your provider can really meet your needs. A reliable ISP will have several members on-site to provide technical support. If the ISP has only one or two technical support people, you may want to look for another ISP. You should also check out an ISP's technical support by placing a few calls during the week to see how they respond.

How many network professionals do you have on-site?

This question is another test of technical support capacity. The idea is to find out if the ISP has enough competent network professionals to address non–Internet-specific problems. The big question is, Will a trained technician be available to help when you need it, or will someone be given a manual and drafted to help you out? When you need help, you need it now. If your technical support personnel are unfamiliar with the hardware and software, you are not going to get much help from them. You may even know more about the system then they do.

Can you supply me with any references?

References are important because they are a means of determining whether the ISP has performed well enough to at least make some of its customers happy. Obviously, the ISP will not give you a reference from anyone who had a bad experience. If it cannot supply any references, maybe its customers had only bad experiences.

What plans do you have for future growth?

Every company will tell you it plans to grow, but you want to find out what plans the ISP has to increase the scalability of its hardware. Your ISP needs to work hard to keep up with the phenomenal growth rate of the Internet. Otherwise, as the ISP adds clients, your shared link, or bandwidth, to the Internet will deteriorate.

Assume for the moment that you have a 1.5Mbps T1 connection with your provider. Your provider has a 45Mbps T3 connection to the Internet. This T3 connection is the Internet backbone that all your ISP's clients share. If your client has only 10 T1 clients, it still has enough capacity left in the backbone to support an additional 20 T1 clients. But when your ISP's client list grows beyond the capacity of the backbone, what happens to you? Well, you'll still pay for a 1.5Mbps connection, but you'll be getting less than that from it. Your provider must plan to increase its carrying capacity as the company grows. Without proper planning by the provider, once more you will pay the price.

What type of connection to the Internet do you have?

As I've mentioned, the ISP backbone's carrying capacity affects the performance of your site. If your provider has a single T1 line or less as its backbone, it probably cannot service your needs. Look for someone else with multiple T1 lines or their equivalent carrying capacity. I recommend avoiding any ISP with less than a T3 (45Mbps) backbone.

Using the Internet

In the previous discussions you learned something about the history of the Internet and how to get connected, but you didn't learn much about what you can really do on the Internet. Using the Internet—specifically, what you can do on the Internet with Windows NT Server and the IIS—is the subject for the rest of this chapter. First, you can publish data on the Internet. Publishing uses any one, or all, of the IIS services. You can also use the WWW and FTP services to collect data. You can even use the WWW service to actually sell your company's products.

Publishing Data

Publishing data, or content, is the most frequently selected reason for getting on the Internet and is how you create a presence on the Internet. If your content is particularly appealing, clients will flock to your WWW, FTP, or Gopher sites. The big question is when and how to use each of these services. If you only want a repository for files that clients can upload or download, use the FTP service. To display large amounts of text online, use the Gopher service. To provide a GUI-driven application to play sounds or display graphics, animations, movies, and text, use the WWW service. In fact, the capabilities of a WWW server used in conjunction with a GUI Web browser far overshadow almost all other services provided with IIS. This book focuses its attention on the WWW server accordingly. You can use the WWW server to display just about anything, although you may need additional software to fully exploit your WWW server software. The following examples help explain these options.

Providing Technical Support

Let's assume for the moment that you are a computer manufacturer. You need to provide a simple, user-friendly interface to your customers for technical support. The reason you might choose to use the IIS to host a Web site is that after you create the HTML document, you can support any client computer that has a connection to the Internet and a Web browser. An HTML document is a hardware- and software-independent mechanism. (Almost every platform has a Web browser designed for it.) The goal for this example is to provide a means for your customers to download a flash BIOS replacement. A Web page, such as that displayed in Figure 1.2, may just fit the bill. It includes enough information for the user to make a choice as to what to get. The description (Motherboard #1) specifies the type of motherboard, and it includes a built-in link (Award BIOS upgrade) to your FTP server to retrieve the file.

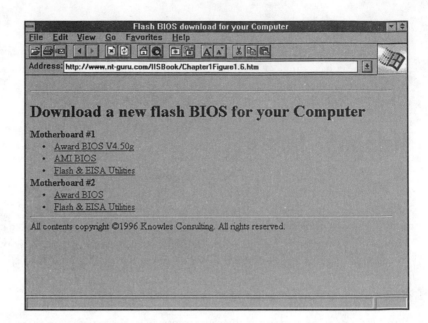

The code to create this Web page is simple as well. In fact, it's so simple you should take a look at it. You can find the source for the document Chapter1Figure1.6.HTM on the accompanying CD-ROM in the directory SOURCE\CHAP1, and you can use any ASCII text editor, such as Notepad, to create it. You'll learn much more about HTML in Chapter 12, "An HTML Primer," which describes the basic syntax and usage of the HTML tags. For now, though, I want to point out a few of the highlights.

```html
<html>

<head>
<title>Flash BIOS download for your Computer</title>
</head>

<body>

<P>
<hr>

<h2>Download a new flash BIOS for your Computer</h2><br>

<B>Motherboard #1</B><br>
<UL><LI><A href="ftp://nt-guru.com/autoexec.bat">Award BIOS V4.50g</a>
    <LI><A href="ftp://nt-guru.com/autoexec.bat">AMI BIOS</A>
    <LI><A href="ftp://nt-guru.com/autoexec.bat">Flash & EISA Utilities</A>
    </ul>
```

```
<B>Motherboard #2</B>
<UL><LI><A href="ftp://nt-guru.com/autoexec.bat">Award BIOS</A>
<LI><A href="ftp://nt-guru.com/autoexec.bat">Flash & EISA Utilities</A>
</UL>

<hr>
All contents copyright &#169 1996 Knowles Consulting. All rights reserved.

</body>
</html>
```

A *Hypertext Markup Language* (HTML) document is an ASCII document. It contains tags to format the text. Almost every tag has a corresponding end tag. The document starts with an `<html>` tag and ends with an `</html>` tag. The `<head>` and `</head>` mark the document heading; within these tags the `<title>` and `</title>` tags enclose the document title that is displayed on the caption bar of your Web browser. The `<body>` and `</body>` tags delineate the body, or major component, of the document. The `<h2>` and `</h2>` tags mark the enclosed text as a level 2 header. A `<P>` marks the end of a paragraph. The `<B>` and `</B>` mark text as bold, and `<UL>` and `</UL>` mark text as underlined. I could go on and on about this subject, but the only really important tags are the `<LI>`, `<A href=ftp:// ...>`, and `</A>` tags, which create a link to your FTP server. When a user clicks one of these items, the actual file is downloaded to his computer. In this sample all the choices will download a copy of my `autoexec.bat` file. But if this document was a real Web page, it could just as easily download the actual flash BIOS update files.

So, simply by spending a few minutes with a text editor, such as Notepad, you can be on your way to creating a Web page for your customers to use. The user needs to know only the domain name of your Web site, and then, when the page is retrieved, just one click of the mouse will download the BIOS upgrade. It can't get much easier than that.

Publishing a Product Catalog

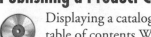

Displaying a catalog of your products is quite similar to publishing data. You create a table of contents Web page, or perhaps a search page, with links to actual document pages. The very simple sample page in Figure 1.3 displays an image of the product (in this case a WinBook XP) followed by a product review. The background is set to white to make reading the large amount of text easier. You can find the source for this sample (`Chapter1Figure1.7.HTM`) on the accompanying CD-ROM in the directory `SOURCE\CHAP1`.

> **NOTE**
>
> Don't be dismayed by the simplicity of the samples in this chapter. In the latter half of this book, you will learn more than you'll want to know about how to create HTML documents.

FIGURE 1.3.

Sample WWW page with product information.

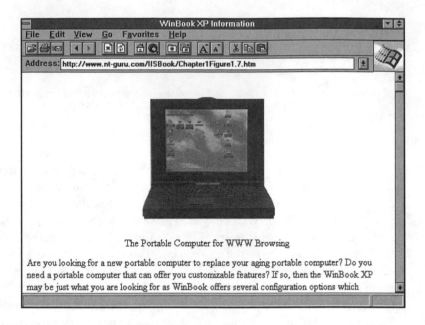

The previous example is a *static* example; that is, you must physically create the Web page, and it must physically reside on your hard disk. To make a change to this page, you must edit the page in a text editor and then save it, which can be quite time-consuming. This requirement can also cause a problem because many product catalogs change rapidly. You may spend more time editing Web pages than you actually do selling products. So what can you do about it? You can create dynamic Web pages. A *dynamic* Web page is actually a template assembled by another program (such as an ISAPI extension or Common Gateway Interface (CGI) script) from an external source, for example, a SQL Server database that contains all your product information (picture, price, and description). This information could be assembled into files on your Web server, which could then be displayed by your customers' Web browsers. Because the files are assembled every time a user requests the information (that is, dynamically), your catalog is as up-to-date as your database.

Publishing Very Large Amounts of Text

If you have an entire book or library of books, you will want to consider using the Gopher service. This particular service is designed to support text databases. You can search a Gopher site by keywords, or your menu structure could provide an index with hypertext links to the actual information, as shown in Figure 1.4. Notice in this figure that I am using the Internet Explorer (IE) Web browser. Rather than using a character-based application, I find the point-and-click capability is too nice a feature to give up, and the text is just as easy to read. You can use Internet Explorer with your FTP sites as well.

FIGURE 1.4.
*The UCSD Gopher
Server's library index.*

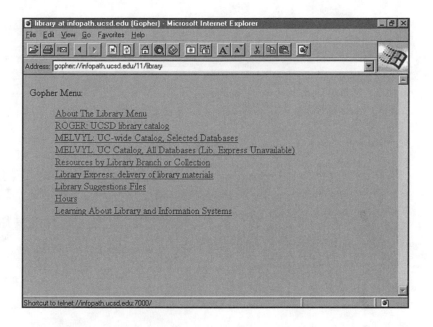

Publishing large amounts of text with the Gopher service is fairly easy, but it doesn't provide any capabilities other than text retrieval. Consequently, many Gopher sites are being converted to Web sites. For example, although an encyclopedia is useful in text form, it's much more fun to use with audio-video pictures of animals at the zoo. The audio-video encyclopedia can convey more information as well as emotional impact.

Collecting Data

You might want to collect information from network clients that access your Web server for several reasons. Perhaps you want to create an order-entry database for your roving salesperson, for example. He or she could connect to the Internet from your client's office via a simple phone call to a local provider. Then the salesperson could access your Web site and choose from the menu to place an order. As the user enters each item, your Web server can verify that the item is in stock. At the end of the order, your Web server could display an actual invoice form that your salesperson can print in the client's office. In other words, you have turned your Web server into an online database.

You could also capture customer or prospect information. The IIS includes a sample HTML page, as shown in Figure 1.5, that demonstrates this feature. The information you collect could include such items as the user's name, address, phone numbers, marital status, or anything else the user is willing to tell you that strikes your fancy. After all, you can't force people to visit your Web page and fill out all the forms if they don't want to, but you can entice them into doing so. Many sites include teasers, such as free gifts, when users supply information. As part of your form design, you can enforce a rule that specific fields must be filled out in order for the form to be submitted.

FIGURE 1.5.
Collecting customer information.

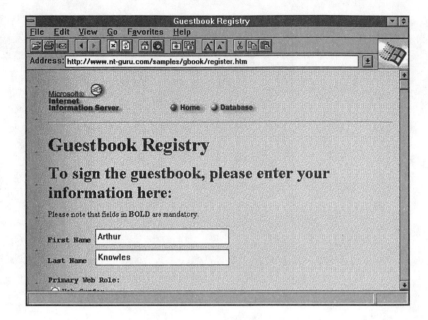

You might use this capability to collect information for a mailing list of potential customers. Your form could ask if the client is planning to purchase a house within 90 days, six months, or one year. The user could select radio buttons on the form to request further information from you about the services you could provide within that time frame. You may, for example, choose to keep the user informed, via e-mail, of special discounts for new homeowners during the time period specified on the client's form. Then, a month or so before the person's selected time frame is up, you could generate a new mailing list to check that person's status. You might hit just the right time to convert a prospect into a new customer, and you might just sell another house.

Selling Products

Selling products directly on the Internet is a little bit different. Your first concern here has to be related to security, which means that the *Secure Socket Layer* (SSL) is going to play an important part in your life. SSL is the most widely used support security mechanism for sensitive data. What's sensitive? Well, at the very least, your customers' credit card numbers should be considered sensitive information. I certainly wouldn't want my credit card numbers floating around the Internet. Therefore, your Web pages and forms may require some additional work, and you'll have to file for an SSL certificate. You'll learn more gory details of this and future security layers in Chapter 10.

> **NOTE**
>
> If selling products is your number-one priority, I recommend that you take a look at the Microsoft Merchant Server. This product is based on the IIS and also runs on Windows NT Server, but it is specifically geared toward selling products over the Internet in a secure and safe fashion.

Although I can't cover all the commercial possibilities or legal implications of selling products on the Internet, I can give you a glimpse at the process: A client (or customer) who sees a product she wants to buy on her Web browser can order that product and have it delivered to her front door just by filling out a form and clicking a button.

The two basic issues in selling merchandise on the Internet are (1) how you can do it safely and (2) how your users will interact with your company. The first issue—safety—is addressed by using SSL to secure the communication channel between your server and the client. SSL enables you to obtain the customer's credit card number without inadvertently giving that information to someone else on the Internet; the key is encryption. Keep in mind that the security of the data you collect should remain inviolate. You are responsible for keeping prying eyes away from this data. You should secure your server physically (that is, put it in a locked room) from intruders. You also need to keep the electronic thieves at bay, which I cover a bit more in Chapter 10.

The second issue—how your users will interact with your company—directly translates to how you will use the available network bandwidth. The phrase *available network bandwidth* applies to how much time your clients will spend waiting to view any data you publish. Although you might have a 1.5Mbps T1 line or higher-speed Internet connection, many of your customers will be using 14,400bps modems.

The longer a user has to wait to download a Web page, the more frustrated that user gets, making it less likely that he will bother to visit that Web page again. If the people visiting your site don't stick around long enough to download your Web page, you aren't going to get any potential customers. If you want to supply an online catalog with pictures of your products, for example, then you should be frugal with your customers' available network bandwidth. You don't want to antagonize your prospects and customers by forcing them to download a 8- by 10-inch, 24-bit picture when a 1- by 1.5-inch (or smaller), 8-bit picture will suffice. Giving the user the option to download an 8- by 10-inch, 24-bit picture, maybe by clicking the smaller image, is an acceptable use of someone's available network bandwidth. However, because the practice of creating multiple pictures can be a bit tedious, you'll probably want to use only small pictures. In that case you'll need to provide good textual descriptions to compensate for the lack of detail in the pictures.

Summary

This chapter starts with a short history of the Internet. The important lesson is that rapid expansion of the Internet will affect you in the future, and you need to prepare for it. You learn about various technologies for connecting to the Internet and how to select an ISP. The last part of the chapter introduces the IIS and various ways to publish content on the World Wide Web. Chapter 2 will examine the IIS in more depth, exploring the capabilities provided by the core services and how to extend your Web server's capabilities.

An Internet Information Server Overview

IN THIS CHAPTER

- What Is the Internet Information Server?   26

- What Can the Internet Information Server Do for You?   32

- Publicizing Your Web Site   37

CHAPTER 2

The Microsoft Internet Information Server (IIS) is not the only product that allows you to publish content on the Internet using Windows NT, but none of the others (such as those included with the Windows NT Resource Kit) offers the same range of features as Internet Information Server does. After reading this chapter, you may wonder if I work for Microsoft. I'm not a Microsoft employee, but I do like what the Internet Information Server can do. I think you will, too.

Although the idea of using the Internet to provide information is not new, the concept of publishing content on the Internet is new. People who have no experience with HTML can now create simple Web pages using a standard word processor, such as Word for Windows, and a template, such as the one provided by the Internet Assistant. For a more professional-looking Web page, you can use dedicated programs like Sausage Software's HotDog Pro, SoftQuad's HoTMetaL, or Microsoft's FrontPage. These Windows applications insert HTML tags and format documents for you.

Unlike the early years of the Internet when only a handful of users published relatively small amounts of information, today almost anyone can place huge amounts of information (including information from large internal databases) on the Internet for millions of users to view. Three changes have occurred to make this possible. First, the available bandwidth on the Internet has increased tremendously. Second, the Internet now allows commercial activity. Finally, you no longer have to use UNIX or a derivative operating system to provide your Internet services.

This chapter starts by examining the various components of the Internet Information Server. The chapter then moves on to look at what the Internet Information Server can do for you and how it compares to the competition. Finally, you take a brief look into publicizing your Web site so that potential customers can find you. After all, it does you little good to create an Internet Web site if no one knows how to find you, right?

What Is the Internet Information Server?

This question is not really as easy to answer as it seems because the Internet Information Server is more than just a port of a few Internet services to Windows NT Server. Consequently, a complete description of the Internet Information Server requires a description of the collection of services it provides. The one feature that really characterizes the Internet Information Server is that it is an extensible platform. Hence you can customize the Internet Information Server to suit your individual requirements.

A Collection of Windows NT Services

The Internet Information Server consists of three specific Windows NT services that enable you to publish content (data) using TCP/IP, the Transmission Control Protocol/Internet Protocol as the underlying transmission mechanism. These services are a World Wide Web (WWW) server, a File Transfer Protocol (FTP) server, and a Gopher server. The Internet Information Server provides the servers of a client/server product. Without a client application, such as a Web browser like Internet Explorer, the server really doesn't do much good. The underlying transport mechanism defines how a client/server application functions. (See Figure 2.1.)

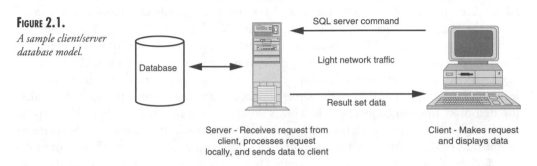

FIGURE 2.1.

A sample client/server database model.

In Figure 2.1 the computer on the right executes an application such as Microsoft Access, that is, the client application. The computer on the left executes SQL Server, that is, the server application. In essence, the client application makes a request (for example, to retrieve a row of data). This request is then passed to SQL Server over your network. SQL Server processes the request and returns only the data to the client application for display. Only the commands from the client application to the server application and the data from the server application to the client application pass over the network. Now compare this client/server model with a monolithic database model, as shown in Figure 2.2.

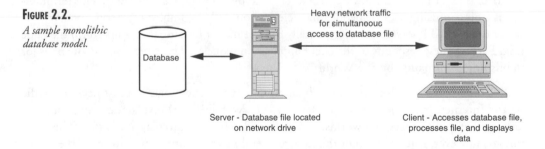

FIGURE 2.2.

A sample monolithic database model.

In this model, you can assume that the client computer is running Microsoft Access, rather than accessing a SQL Server database, although the database, or the file that contains the database, is stored on a network server. The database could just as easily be located on your local hard drive, but for comparison purposes I've placed the data on the file server. Instead of splitting the task between two separate applications, Microsoft Access performs all the processing. If you were to search a database, the entire contents of the database would have to be passed to

Microsoft Access, which in turn would process the database row by row until it found the requested information. This procedure places a heavier load on your network than the client/server model shown in Figure 2.1.

One reason that Internet services, such as FTP, WWW, Gopher, Archie, finger, telnet, rcp, rsh, and so on, also use a client/server model is to lower the bandwidth requirements. In essence, the Internet is a very large wide area network (WAN). A WAN is a collection of computers that are not physically in the same location as your network (or local area network). Most WANs use very slow connections (56Kbps) to connect them to your LAN. Some use higher-speed connections (up to 45Mbps). The connection speed determines how much information can be passed between the server application and the client application. Considering that most Internet connections by clients occur at 14.4Kbps to 28.8Kbps (57.6Kbps to 115.2Kbps with compression), there is a significant need to lower the bandwidth requirements as much as possible. After all, the speed of a 14.4Kbps connection is only 25 percent of the speed of the slowest WAN link in use today. If the bandwidth does not transmit the most important information first, your Internet client will be sitting in front of his or her Web browser waiting for the complete page to appear. One reason to use the client/server model is that it provides a mechanism for the client to obtain the text (the most important part) of a document first, followed by any graphical objects (which really just make the page look better, but usually contain no additional content).

WWW Publishing Service

The Microsoft WWW Publishing Service is a WWW server. It uses the Hypertext Transfer Protocol (HTTP) to communicate with its client application (a Web browser). This terminology is a bit confusing because people may refer to your WWW Publishing Service as a WWW server or an HTTP server; however, it really doesn't matter because they all perform the same task. Each of these responds to the client application requests. These requests are the basis for publishing information on the World Wide Web.

The World Wide Web is a content-rich environment and encompasses most network traffic on the Internet. It can be used to display (on your Web browser) text, static graphic images, animated graphic images, 3D worlds, and audio-video files, and to play audio files. This technology, however, is just the tip of the iceberg. Vendors are adding new features to their Web browsers almost constantly, which means you must add extensions to your Web server to support them.

The new generation of Web browsers does more than support Web servers. You can use Web browsers to connect to FTP and Gopher sites and to access newsgroups. Future versions may encompass other Internet services as well, such as e-mail, telnet, and remote shells. There's no telling exactly what the future will bring in the World Wide Web client/server arena.

FTP Publishing Service

Whereas the WWW Publishing Service is an HTTP server, the simpler FTP publishing service is an FTP server and is used primarily as a data repository. This repository can contain various types of files that users can upload or download to their systems using an FTP client application. FTP is similar to a communications program, such as Procomm for Windows, that you would use to access a bulletin board system (BBS). When you decide to download a file from a BBS, you have to specify a download protocol, usually ZMODEM.

Gopher Publishing Service

The Gopher publishing service is used much less frequently than either the WWW or FTP publishing services. It is primarily used to publish very large amounts of textual data, for example, an encyclopedia. The biggest benefit of the Gopher publishing service is that it can be searched with a relatively speedy response and that the data can actually span multiple servers.

Moving Beyond the Basic Internet Information Server Services

The Internet Information Server is the backbone of Microsoft's Internet product line, which also includes the Merchant Server, the Transaction Server (previously code-named "Viper"), and the Commercial Internet Server (previously code-named "Normandy"). The Merchant Server is a one-stop package to sell merchandise on the Internet. The Transaction Server can be considered a customizable version of the Merchant Server. The Commercial Internet Server is a full-blown set of Internet applications for Internet service providers (ISPs) and on-line service providers (such as CompuServe or AOL). You will learn more about some of the Commercial Internet Server components, in Chapter 11, "Enhancing Internet Information Server."

Although this series of products can be confusing, it can basically be summed up as follows:

- Internet Information Server—The core product that includes WWW, FTP, and Gopher servers. This product provides basic Internet services and is especially appropriate for small companies or individuals desiring a presence on the Internet. It also makes an outstanding intranet server.

- Merchant Server—This product builds upon the Internet Information Server to provide a means to sell products on the Internet. It includes templates to help you design your virtual store and includes basic order-entry–processing software.

- Transaction Server—This product is designed for medium to large corporations that desire a customized solution. This platform is specifically geared for developers to design, track, administer, and deploy business applications for use on the intranet and Internet. It requires a good development staff, or a really good consultant, to get the most out of it.

■ Commercial Internet Server—This product basically includes additional Internet services, such as an Internet Relay Chat server, a Newsgroup server, and content replication. It is designed for ISPs or other on-line service providers.

An Extensible Platform

The key to *any* successful project is extensibilty. Every project either grows to encompass new features and keep the customer satisfied, or it stagnates and dies. This requirement is true of the Internet Information Server, as well. The good news here is that the Internet Information Server is so extensible that you may be overwhelmed by the possibilities; it seems to have something for everyone. The software development kits available for the Internet Information Server include both legacy support, such as the Common Gateway Interface (CGI), and brand-new APIs, which bring the power of OLE (using ActiveX objects) to the World Wide Web. Although this chapter cannot cover all these possibilities in depth, it does provide a brief sampling.

The Internet Information Server Software Development Kit

The Internet Server Application Programming Interface (ISAPI) is a proprietary programming interface introduced with the Internet Information Server as a replacement for CGI development tasks. You can create ISAPI applications to extend the functionality of the Internet Information Server just as you would a CGI application. The biggest difference between a CGI application and an ISAPI application is that a CGI application executes in a separate process, whereas an ISAPI application is really a dynamic link library (DLL) that executes in the same address space as the WWW Publishing Service. An ISAPI DLL is much faster than a CGI application that performs the same task. In addition, ISAPI consumes fewer resources than CGI, which means you can service many more users.

CAUTION

ISAPI DLLs do have a downside. Because they share the same address space as the HTTP server, an errant ISAPI application could crash the WWW Publishing Service as well. Therefore, you must test your new ISAPI applications thoroughly *before* you implement them. If you are using a third-party ISAPI application, make sure it has passed the Microsoft certification tests *before* you install it on your server.

So just what can you do with an ISAPI application? Well, you could create an online calculator, for example; users could interact with the calculator screen that appears on their Web browsers. The WWW server would perform the actual calculations and return the result to the client's Web browser for display. If this task isn't challenging enough for you, here are a couple more possibilities:

■ The Internet Information Server includes the ISAPI Internet Database Connector. This DLL provides access to open database connectivity (ODBC) drivers. Consequently, your ISAPI applications can access any ODBC-compliant database, including SQL Server, Oracle, RBase, Access, Paradox, and dBASE, or any other database for which you have a 32-bit ODBC driver. The client's Web browser can display or download anything you store in the database.

■ You could create an ISAPI filter that would be called whenever the WWW Publishing Service received an HTTP request. You could use this approach to trap HTTP messages in much the same way that you would trap mouse messages to control the behavior of the mouse in Windows. You could use this process to perform data encryption, data compression, user logging, or similar tasks.

ActiveX

ActiveX is where the real heart-and-soul changes are going to be occurring in future products. ActiveX basically brings the power of OLE objects to the Internet. With ActiveX you will be able to create custom controls for Web browsers to enhance their functionality. If you are currently using a custom control, you should be able to migrate it to ActiveX without much trouble. In addition, you will be able to insert your custom controls into Visual Basic applications, which suggests the possibility of inserting them into a Visual C++ application—or into any application environment that supports the OLE custom controls.

ActiveX also introduces the OLE document-object concept, which enables you to create, or host, documents in a frame within a Web browser. (In this context a *document* can be any object for which you have developed a custom control.) You could view a Word document, for example, inside a frame of your Web browser. Or you could go so far as to turn your Web browser into a full-fledged word processor as you do today with OLE automation. This technology is going to revolutionize the Web, and you can be a part of it.

ActiveX is such a huge a topic that it requires its own book, but I do want to point out that ActiveX supports two new scripting languages. The first is JavaScript, which is based on Sun Microsystems's Java language. Java is based on C++ and provides interactive applications, commonly called *applets*, that you can integrate into your Web browser. The second new scripting language is VBScript, which performs a similar function, but is based on Microsoft's Visual Basic. Both of these languages have been trimmed down to remove potentially dangerous functions.

The Common Gateway Interface

The CGI has been around on the World Wide Web for quite some time. If you already have CGI applications, you can continue to use them. If not, you may want to consider writing some. If you are new to WWW development, you should decide whether to develop CGI or ISAPI applications. If your development skills are up to snuff and you have been writing

Windows applications using C++ for quite some time, there is really no contest. Use ISAPI—and start coding today.

On the other hand, if you are new to application development using C++ or if you prefer C, FORTRAN, Pascal, or another language, you may want to consider developing CGI applications. A *CGI application* is any application that supports the `stdin` (standard input) and `stdout` (standard output) interfaces and that can access environment variables. You can also use CGI with the Perl scripting language instead of a compiled application, such as a C++ executable, to rapidly develop applications to extend your Web server's functionality. You will learn more about these possibilities in Chapter 18, "Unleashing the Power of VBScript," and Chapter 19, "Introduction to Windows NT CGI Programming."

What Can the Internet Information Server Do for You?

The most common reason to use the Internet Information Server is to create a WWW or FTP site for your organization. The next section examines how the Internet Information Server stacks up to the competition when you use it to create an Internet or intranet Web site.

Internet and Intranet Publishing

The Internet is taking the corporate and home markets by storm. People everywhere are looking for ways to leverage the Internet. The Internet services most commonly used include the World Wide Web and FTP. For the most part, these services have always been used externally; that is, they have been provided by sources outside the local area network. Even when a corporation begins to provide these services, they have been used to supply information to external users, sell products, or possibly even to provide technical support to customers. These services, however, have been used only to provide a means for external users, or Internet clients, to access these resources. But this policy is changing as third-party manufacturers add Internet capabilities to their products. Lotus Notes is one such application. It started as a groupware product used internally on the corporate LAN to facilitate user collaboration; however, it has been enhanced to provide Internet support as well.

The Internet has become such a rich source of materials that it is becoming difficult to live without. If a tool does not provide Internet support, it is not nearly as useful as it could be. Take, for example, Lotus Notes. Your current version of Lotus Notes may have a great deal of corporate information in its proprietary database, but now that you plan to connect to the Internet, you want to share some of this information with your Internet customers. The current version of Lotus Notes enables you to use this information internally within your corporate LAN and externally as well.

Although Lotus Notes is a powerful tool, not everyone has embraced it. Notes is an expensive product, and the functionality it provides doesn't suit everyone's needs. But the tools you use today, such as a WWW browser, can now be used internally on your local area network to provide similar functionality. These tools are less developed than the current crop of groupware products, but they are also less expensive to use. More important, however, is that they are also much easier to maintain, configure, and access from various operating system platforms. Almost every operating system in existence today provides a TCP/IP stack and associated tools. With the Internet Information Server and a newer Web browser, you can do the following:

- Create corporate directories—You can easily create a static Web page with document links to specific sections within a document. One possible application is to put your entire office directory (user name, office location, phone number, and so on) on your Web server to provide access to the most up-to-date information.

- Distribute corporate documentation—Your corporation probably has ample company documentation, such as employee handbooks, accounting procedures, and EEO guidelines, that you can place on a Web server to provide instant access to the materials. Think of how many trees you could save by placing this type of material on your LAN's Web server.

- Support a help desk—Many of you may already use proprietary software in customer relations department. This software usually helps track customer problems as you work on providing a solution. Yet the expense of such software is often too high for many smaller companies. Even when a company can afford it, the software is often difficult to use and is not customizable. However, you can customize a forms-based Web page to your heart's content.

  You could use this implementation internally to provide a complete tracking mechanism—just like the proprietary implementation. You could also make this information available directly to your customers over the Internet. They can then obtain up-to-the-minute information with simple form submission using their customer tracking number. Remember, an informed customer is a happy customer. It's even possible to provide hooks to your FTP site within the customer response form so that customers can download the latest patch created specifically to solve their problem.

- Implement online inventory/order entry—Many corporations have inside and outside salespeople who use an online database. This database contains information on the current inventory as well as information on customer orders. To access this information, you use a database front end, such as Microsoft Access or a custom application. As an alternative, you could use a Web-based form to query the database or to place an order. Hence your Web browser could replace your current front end.

  When an outside salesperson arrives at a client's office, he or she could either dial your server directly or connect to the Internet via a local number and access your Web server. When the customer places an order via a form on your Web page, the salesperson could verify that the requested items are in stock. If the items are in stock, the order can be passed to the appropriate department and shipped to the client. If the item is not in stock, an order can be sent to your supplier. This entire process could take place in real time, right at the customer's office.

Many more possibilities exist for integrating your Web server and your online databases. For example, you can create forms for ad hoc queries, create dynamic Web pages where the database formats its output in a standard HTML format, or create high-performance search engines. The possibilities are limited only by your imagination and your ability to write custom applications.

Intranet publishing is not suitable for every task, nor is it for everyone. To publish data internally requires significant resources. The pros and cons of intranet publishing are summarized in Table 2.1.

Table 2.1. The pros and cons of intranet publishing.

Pro	*Con*
An intranet is an excellent platform for publishing information internally.	Collaborative applications for intranets are not nearly as powerful as those available in traditional groupware products such as Lotus Notes.
A Web browser is available for almost any operating system, unlike the proprietary clients used for traditional groupware applications.	Unlike a groupware product that has all the applications integrated into a single product, you will need to install separate clients for Web browsing, using e-mail, and so on.
Web servers, especially Internet Information Server, do not require less raw processing power and hard disk space than traditional groupware products.	Although linking an ODBC-complaint database to your Internet Information Server Web server is fairly easy, few tools are available to link other back-end components. You can use the Software Development Kits (SDKs) provided with the BackOffice components, including Internet Information Server, to integrate your Web server; however, if your third-party product does not have such a development kit, you will be unable to link the information.
You can use numerous Internet products to access your data. These products generally operate together quite well.	Intranet publishing requires TCP/IP. If your LAN uses another protocol, you may be forced to change to TCP/IP or install a gateway before these products will function properly. If you plan to access the Internet as well, you will also need to obtain routable IP addresses.

Pro	*Con*
The Internet Information Server is a scalable platform. As you need additional horsepower, you can migrate your system to another processor platform, or even add additional processors to improve performance.	There are no built-in replication services to distribute your data.
With the availability of new HTML authoring tools, such as FrontPage, Hot Dog, and HoTMetaL, creating Web pages is quite simple.	HTML, by itself, is not powerful enough to create client/server applications. Although new standards, such as ActiveX, VBScript, JavaScript, and so on are available, they are still in their infancy. To use these tools will require custom development.

To sum up this discussion, I would like to point out one major benefit of intranets. If you start with an intranet publishing site, when the time comes for you to enter the world of Internet publishing, you will be ready. Converting an intranet site to an Internet site is a straightforward process. Specifically, you will need to consider the following issues:

- Routable IP addresses—You can obtain these addresses from your ISP or from InterNIC. If you think you may migrate to the Internet someday, you should follow the InterNIC guidelines for intranets. You can find a wealth of information on this subject at http://www.internic.net.

- A domain name—If you plan to let users find your site using the form www.*yourcompanyname*.com, you will need to register your domain name with InterNIC. Your ISP may be able to perform this task for you.

- Security—The Internet is like a jungle where wild animals are roaming free. You will need to consider using hardware or software tools to prevent possible damage to your system. These tools include products such as routers, firewalls, and network isolation. Also, you will need to create policies based on common sense. For example, you should never execute an application downloaded from the Internet without checking it first for viruses.

How Well Can the Internet Information Server Perform?

The key factor in almost everyone's mind today is performance. If a product performs poorly, then your company suffers, which in turn means that you too may suffer for recommending the product. On the other hand, if the product performs well, everyone is happy, and you may even be rewarded for your product recommendation. The one key item, however, that most people seem to forget is that performance is relative. To determine a performance level, a product must be compared to another product that performs a similar function.

In an open throughput testing scenario, the Internet Information Server outperformed the Netscape Communication Server 1.12 for Windows NT on the same hardware platform (a Hewlett-Packard NetServer LS with an Intel Pentium 133MHz processor, 32MB RAM, a 1MB L2 cache, two 1GB hard drives, and a DEC 10/100MB Ethernet adapter) by four to one. It also outperformed the Netscape Communication Server 1.12 for BSD UNIX, which required 128MB RAM to complete the test, by three to one. When compared to Novell NetWare's Web Server version 2.0, the Internet Information Server surpassed it by two to one. These results are pretty impressive, considering that the Internet Information Server requires fewer resources, which translates directly into providing faster client response times and the ability to handle larger peak loads than the competition.

> **NOTE**
>
> The complete white paper on which this section is based is available on the Microsoft WWW site at `http://microsoft.com/infoserv/docs/Iisperf.htm`.
>
> You can find additional information concerning the benchmarks and testing procedures performed by Haynes & Company and Shiloh Consulting at `http://microsoft.com/infoserv/haynes1.htm`. This information was based on a prerelease version of the Internet Information Server. The actual performance benchmarks may differ from those of the released product, although I have found that the released product generally improves performance.

Similar results were obtained based on the number of connections per second. The average response time results were even more impressive, which indicates that even for small Web sites, the Internet Information Server is the best solution. But more important, the Internet Information Server provides the means to use APIs to create custom solutions, such as dynamic Web pages, that outperform the competition as well. When comparing CGI to ISAPI on the same server using the Internet Information Server, the ISAPI applications transferred almost five times as much data as a similar CGI application. When comparing ISAPI to Netscape-proprietary APIs (NSAPIs), ISAPI is almost three times faster.

What all this data really means to you is that you can create a high-performance Web site that outperforms other platforms, including RISC servers such as Sun's SPARCServer-20 or Hewlett-Packard 9000 Model HP 200 workstations. The Internet Information Server clearly provides more bang for the buck, which is important to any company. The test results also mean that you can achieve greater scalability and handle larger peak loads using the Windows NT Server and Internet Information Server combination.

Publicizing Your Web Site

Once you design your WWW site and are ready to publish data on the Internet, you still need to take care of a few additional details if you want people to find your site. Some ISPs will publicize your site (usually for a fee), and letting someone else do the work for you can simplify your life. If your budget doesn't include funds for this purpose, then you can try to get your site published in a directory listing or newsgroup.

Directory Listings

A directory listing enables Internet users to search for an item by keywords. Usually the individual directory listing, such as Yahoo!, will index your entire Web site. This technique helps users find your Web site, even when they cannot remember your site name. Although you can submit your Web site to an individual directory listing service, an easier procedure is to submit your site to Submit It at `http://submit-it.permalink.com/submit-it/`. This site uses a form-based approach to submit information about your WWW site. Submit It automatically submits your information to a number of directory listing sites, including Apollo, ElNet Galaxy, Jump Station, Harvest, Infoseek, Lycos, OpenText, Web Index, New Riders' WWW Yellow Pages, Netcenter, Nikos, Pronet, Starting Point, WebCrawler, What's New Too, Whole Internet Catalog, World Wide Web Worm, Yahoo!, and Yellow Pages.com. You can expect a two- to four-week delay between the time you submit your site and when it becomes available in these directory listings.

Submit It's list does not include Excite at `http:www.excite.com`, NCSA's What's New page at `http://www.ncsa.uiuc.edu/SDG/Software/Mosaic/Docs/whats-new.html`, and the Open Market Commercial Sites Index at `http://www.directory.net`.

The Webaholics Top 50 Links at `http://www.ohiou.edu/~rbarret/webaholics/favlinks/entries.html` is another good list to try. The lists here rotate constantly. You can also try to get on numerous cool sites of the day and week, as well as other popular pages. If you do, you'll be assured that some people will stop by to take a look at your site. And the more people who stop by, the more publicity you will receive. Word of mouth is still one of the most popular ways for people to find hot sites on the Internet.

Another way to publicize your site is to use a posting service such as PostMaster at `http://www.netcreations.com/postmaster/`. This service also uses a form to post information to 17 Web sites free of charge. For a fee of $500, you can post to a larger list of 300 print and broadcast media contacts.

Also try Digital's AltaVista engine at `http://www.altavista.digital.com`. It's a good bet that your site will already be listed, but if it's not, you can fill out a form and be on your way. Keep in mind that when you do go searching for your site, don't just stop with your home page.

Look for all the pages you want to be sure Internet users will find. When you see your listing, check out the description for the page. If you do not like what you see, change your Web page. Many of these services will use the title of your Web page plus the first few lines on the page as a teaser.

You should also check out the online malls because many of them consist of links to other sites where you can post your link free of charge. Check the Index of Commercial Databases and Malls posted by the Multimedia Marketing Group at `http://hevanet.com/online/com.html` for a list. You can also appear in the Yellow Pages of the Entire United States on the WWW at `http://www.telephonebook.com`, which is made available by American Business Information in Omaha, Nebraska. If you are not already listed, you can get a free listing by filling out a form.

Newsgroups

Publishing information about your Web site in a newsgroup (or an online BBS) is another way for people to notice that you have arrived on the Web. Before you try any postings in a newsgroup, however, keep in mind three rules:

- Never post a message about a commercial Web site in a noncommercial newsgroup.
- Keep your postings short and to the point. A paragraph or two should be sufficient.
- Always read a few messages in the newsgroups in which you plan to post information about your Web site to make sure that the format and content are applicable.

If you don't follow these rules, you may receive a lot of hate mail or flames, neither of which will do much to attract users to your Web site. The newsgroup for general announcements of a new Web site is `comp.infosystems.www.announce`. But if your Web site deals with a specific topic, try to post an announcement in associated newsgroups.

Summary

This chapter just touches on some of the basic concepts of the Internet Information Server. It describes some possible uses for the Internet Information Server within your organization and some tools you can use to extend your Web server's functionality—ISAPI, ActiveX, JavaScript, VBScript, CGI, and Perl. In future chapters you will get your hands dirty by learning how to develop some basic applications to demonstrate the functionality of these development tools. Although the amount of information can be daunting, you don't need to become proficient in all the available methodologies at the start.

This chapter briefly describes how you can use the Internet Information Server to publish information within your company before you use it for full Internet access. The chapter also highlights the basic performance characteristics of the Internet Information Server. It takes advantage of the Windows NT architecture to provide a scalable platform that is more efficient (that is, faster) than other Web servers, including many RISC platforms that cost thousands of dollars more. Finally, this chapter describes some ways to publicize your Web site. With careful planning and attention to detail, your Web site could become very popular.

In the next chapter, you will learn more about Windows NT Server so that you can build a more efficient platform to host the Internet Information Server. This information will empower you to plan and build a truly awesome Web server.

II

PART

IN THIS PART

- A Windows NT Server Overview   43

- Choosing a Platform for Windows NT Server   69

- Internet Information Server Preparation and Installation   97

Building Your Foundation for the Internet Information Server

A Windows NT Server Overview

IN THIS CHAPTER

- The Windows NT Design   44

- Additional Windows NT Features   52

- Windows NT Server Concepts   60

CHAPTER 3

Now that you've looked at some of the basics of the Internet Information Server, it's time to look at the operating system IIS runs on: Windows NT Server. The purpose of this chapter is to introduce you to some design features of Windows NT Server and to explain some of the buzzwords associated with Windows NT Server to give you a better understanding of the operating system and its capabilities. The goal for this chapter is to prepare you to build an outstanding Web server using Windows NT Server and the Internet Information Server. For those of you who have not worked with Windows NT Server before, this chapter has a lot to offer. In this chapter you will learn why Windows NT Server is often considered one of the best network file and print servers available in today's market, and why you will soon be hearing more about Windows NT Server's WWW publishing capabilities. If some of the discussion is a bit too confusing or technical for you, take a look at another book of mine called *Microsoft BackOffice Administrator's Survival Guide*, as well as *Windows NT Server 4 Unleashed*, both published by Sams Publishing, for more in-depth discussions of the material.

The Windows NT Design

The current version of Windows NT Server (version 4.0) includes some enhancements (discussed a bit later in this chapter), but the basic component model has stayed the same in each release. If you have been reading any of the literature produced by Microsoft about Windows NT Server, you've probably been confused by the scattering of buzzwords and how these buzzwords relate to your day-to-day activities as a webmaster. That's what you are going to look at here. Although I have not included all of these buzzwords, I have included those that I think will make the biggest difference in your life:

■ Robust—When you hear this word used in conjunction with Windows NT, it simply means that Windows NT is designed not to crash when an application fails. Windows NT accomplishes this by using two specific features. First, all applications execute in their own address space (with the exception of 16-bit Windows applications). Second, all the operating system components are protected-mode components. Unlike Windows 3.*x*, Windows NT does not rely on any real-mode components (a real-mode application can access any memory or Input/Output [I/O] location arbitrarily, which can lead to a system crash) to interact with your computer hardware. These features are both good and bad, but they are the price we have to pay for an operating system that will not crash easily.

> **NOTE**
>
> It is possible to execute 16-bit Windows applications in separate address spaces by manually starting them from the command line with the START *ApplicationName* /SEPARATE switch, where *ApplicationName* is the name of a 16-bit Windows executable. As an alternative, you can change the program item's properties and enable the Run in Separate Memory Space option to execute the application in a separate address space.

Because Windows NT does not use the BIOS (a real-mode component) to access the hard disk controller, not all hard disk controllers will work with NT. If you want your unsupported hard disk and controller to work with NT, you will need a Windows NT device driver to support it. And because NT prevents applications from accessing the hardware directly, not all MS-DOS and Windows 3.*x* applications will work when running under NT. In such cases, a virtual device driver, or VDD, is required to support the hardware access.

■ Fault tolerant—This particular feature is so important that I have covered it in more detail later in this chapter. For now, you can just consider it to mean that when faced with a system failure, Windows NT Server provides the means to protect your data and to keep the server running if at all possible. It does so by detecting various software and hardware failures. If a hardware failure is detected, the redundant hardware will be used, if available, to continue providing access to your network server by your network clients. If a software failure occurs, Windows NT will attempt to resolve the failure and to continue operating if possible.

■ Secure—The good news about this particular feature is that Windows NT provides reliable methods to limit access to any computer resource, including access to the server and your data as well as access from one application to another application. The first aspect to consider for this item is related to limiting access to the network file server's shared resources and the server itself. This level of security is accomplished through user identifications (a user ID) and password, or local or group identifiers. (These topics will be covered in more detail in the section "User Management.") The second aspect is related to keeping your data secure from unauthorized access and is covered in the section "The New Technology File System."

■ Scalable—When scalability is mentioned in the same breath with Windows NT Server, it generally refers to providing additional performance. Most people only consider adding resources, such as another CPU or disk channel (a disk controller and disk drives). But scalability refers to the capability of Windows NT to execute on different hardware platforms, such as the Intel 80x86 processors, the NEC MIPS processor, the DEC Alpha processor, and the IBM/Motorola PowerPC processor. Each of these platforms can provide additional levels of performance.

■ Symmetric multiprocessing—Windows NT's internal design utilizes a symmetric processing model, which means that all processors can access system resources (memory, interrupts, and so on) and that any process/thread can execute on any processor. This design is quite different from an asynchronous multiprocessing model, in which one processor is responsible for the operating system functionality and another processor is responsible for executing applications. With Windows NT, any process can execute on any processor, enabling you to make more efficient use of available processor resources.

■ Multithreading—A *thread* is the minimum executable resource in Windows NT. The difference between a *thread* and a *process* is that a process is the container for an address space, whereas a thread executes within that address space. A process by itself is not executable; it is the thread that is scheduled and executed. Threads are unique because a single process can have more than one thread of execution. For instance, a multithreaded application can have one thread for user input (keyboard and mouse), another for printing, and another for file access. When you print a file, or even save a file, these threads run in the background and the user thread runs in the foreground. Your application continues to respond to your input, and you never see the hourglass as you do in Windows 3.*x*.

NOTE

Windows NT Server's capability to support multiple processors and multiple threads of execution is one of the main reasons that the Internet Information Server performs as well as it does. Don't overlook this capability when comparing IIS to other WWW Server platforms.

■ Compatible—Compatibility refers to the ability to execute your legacy applications. These applications include your MS-DOS, 16-bit Windows, and OS/2 character-mode applications. The compatibility for a POSIX application does not include the ability to execute binary images. Instead, the compatibility is limited to executing recompiled POSIX 1003.1–compliant applications. Each of these applications executes in a different environmental subsystem. Subsystems are discussed a bit later, in the section "The Windows NT Environmental Subsystem Design Model."

Along with the ability to execute your legacy application with Windows NT is the ability to use the Windows 95 user interface. Therefore, if you have applications designed specifically for Windows 95, they should run under Windows NT as well. This is a big benefit because Windows 95 includes the same Explorer interface to the file system, the Telephone Application Programming Interface (TAPI) to your modems, a desktop interface that enables you to create shortcuts, customize your display properties (even changing video resolution on the fly without rebooting the system), and various other enhancements as well. The biggest benefit occurs because you do not need to re-train your users to use Windows NT if they are already familiar with Windows 95.

■ Integratable—Integration is one of the joys of working with Windows NT Server because it means that you do not have to tear up your existing network. Instead, Windows NT Server can happily coexist with your UNIX, Novell, Banyan, and LAN Manager networks if you desire. It also enables you to migrate your existing Novell and LAN Manager networks to Windows NT networks over a period of time, or to even emulate an existing Novell server. More importantly though, you can integrate any of these network operating systems with the Internet.

The Windows NT System Design Model

There is much more to the Windows NT design than can be explained in a few simple words. It is important for you to understand the under-the-hood features of Windows NT because, as a webmaster, you will be responsible for supporting or developing applications that will interact with these components. The Internet Information Server, for example, relies on these key items to function. As you enhance your Web server with ISAPI DLLs or CGI applications, or attempt to tune Windows NT Server and the Internet Information Server, you will be interrelating with these components directly. As you've probably heard, a picture is worth a thousand words, and I'm going to put that theory to the test. Figure 3.1 is a basic picture of the Windows NT system design model and illustrates several of the system's more important features. I like to think of Windows NT as a mainframe operating system that has been scaled down a bit to run on your desktop. As such, it includes many of the features of a mainframe operating system. Specifically, I would like you to note that, like a mainframe operating system, Windows NT incorporates a split in the process hierarchy. This split includes a user mode (ring 3 on Intel CPUs), where your applications, the environmental subsystems, and services execute, and a kernel mode (ring 0 on Intel CPUs), where the core operating system executes.

This split architecture prevents an errant application from bringing down the operating system. And just like a mainframe operating system, it cannot protect you from design flaws in the kernel, such as poorly written device drivers. Any error in the kernel is trapped, and if possible, an error handler will execute to maintain system integrity. However, if a device driver or other kernel component has an error that is unrecoverable, Windows NT will display a kernel core dump. I, and many others, often refer to this as the "blue screen of death," because what you will see on the screen is a blue background with white characters. This dump includes an error code, a device driver listing with an address location, and a stack dump of the offending driver(s). Just to ease your mind a bit, core dumps are very infrequent with Windows NT Server. If you use supported hardware and software, there is a good chance you will never even see one.

> **WARNING**
>
> Development tools, such as Visual C++, interrelate with the operating system at very low levels during the build and debug stages. It is possible during one of these actions to hang the Win32 subsystem or the complete operating system. Therefore, if you will be developing applications for Windows NT Server, never do so on a production server. Always create a standalone network (server and workstations) for your development efforts to avoid any potential server downtime.

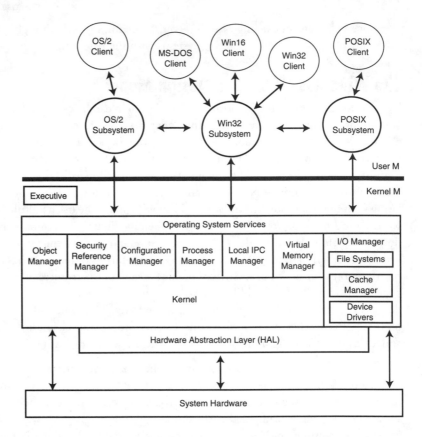

FIGURE 3.1.
The Windows NT design model.

To continue the discussion of kernel components, take a closer look at Figure 3.1 and notice that the core operating system component is called the *executive* and includes many subcomponents. From left to right and top to bottom, these are

- Object Manager—As the name implies, this component is responsible for basic object management. These objects include the object name space (used to resolve an object name to an object handle for use by an application), resource sharing, some security-related usage, and user visible events (such as windows, processes, events, and files). Although Windows NT is not an object-oriented operating system, everything in Windows NT is an object. And the object is the key to all the security features provided by Windows NT because an object (of which there are many) includes the basic data structures used by the Security Reference Manager to perform such actions as process tracking, file auditing, and user authentication.

- Security Reference Manager—This component is used with the Object Manager to determine if a user or process has sufficient privileges to access or create an object. As an object is created, it is assigned a security descriptor, which can later be used to limit access to the object. If no security descriptor is explicitly assigned, the owner's (the owner is the person who created the object) security descriptor will be applied by default.

■ Configuration Manager—This item is used to access the registry. You will learn more about the registry in Appendix C, "The Registry Editor and Registry Keys." For now you can consider the registry as the .ini file replacement for Windows 3.*x*. It is the storehouse for all configuration data for Windows NT.

■ Process Manager—This component is responsible for managing (creating, terminating, suspending, and resuming) processes and threads executing on the system.

■ Local IPC Manager—This component is the heart of the message-passing mechanism that enables Windows NT to be such a good distributed-computing operating system. It includes a fast and efficient mechanism, based on the industry standard remote procedure call (RPC) interface, to facilitate interprocess communication (IPC). This IPC mechanism passes messages between the various clients (MS-DOS, Win16, Win32, POSIX, and OS/2) and the environmental subsystem servers (Win32, POSIX, and OS/2) as well as between the environmental subsystems and the executive. Building on this interface also provides the ability to communicate between remote computers and provide full client/server functionality across the entire network.

> **NOTE**
>
> One of the interesting things produced by this mechanism is the capability to convert an RPC-enabled application to an LPC-enabled application. Whereas an RPC-enabled application is usually designed to operate on physically separate computers, or to provide a communication mechanism between applications on different environments (such as a Windows application and a POSIX application), an LPC-enabled application is designed to operate on the same computer. An LPC-enabled application is an application that has both the client and the server applications executing on the same computer instead of on two computers. Simply changing the server name in the communication linkage to a single period will enable LPC instead of RPC for the transport mechanism. Also, LPC is faster than RPC for the same action. For instance, if you are using SQL Server to create dynamic WWW pages on your WWW Server, you might want to configure your development WWW Server to use a non-local SQL Server database by creating a named pipe with the format \\ServerName\Pipe\SQL\Query and use RPC. Then, when you have finished development, you can create a pipe with the format \\.\Pipe\SQL\Query and use LPC for increased performance (assuming that your WWW Server and SQL Server are on the same computer).

■ Virtual Memory Manager—This component is responsible for all memory manipulation, including, but not limited to, the virtual-to-logical-to-physical memory address translation, shared memory between processes, and memory-mapped files. Virtual Memory Manager also includes the management of your paging files because this is where your virtual memory, memory-mapped files (by default, although memory mapped files can use a different filename if the application supports it), and stop event debugging information is read/written.

- I/O manager—This component is special because, unlike the other components that manage only one object type, the I/O manager contains several subcomponents. These subcomponents are all I/O related, but they have different tasks to accomplish. These subcomponents include the file system drivers (NTFS, FAT, HPFS, CDFS, and any third-party additions), the cache manager (which hooks in the file systems to cache all file access including network access), the device drivers (used to access system resources), and network device drivers.

- Kernel—This small component (about 60KB) is responsible for all process and thread scheduling, multiprocessor synchronization, and management of all exceptions (software generated) and interrupts (hardware generated). It is nonpageable (which means it always resides in physical memory) and nonpreemptive (no other thread of execution has a higher priority), but it is interruptable (so it can handle hardware-generated interrupts).

- Hardware Abstraction Layer (HAL)—The HAL is the major interface to the hardware on the computer system. It is designed to isolate hardware-dependent code and is written in assembly language (unlike the other components, which are written in C) for maximum performance. Most executive components access the system hardware through interfaces provided by the HAL, but the kernel and I/O manager can access some hardware resources directly.

The Windows NT Environmental Subsystem Design Model

That summary pretty much takes care of the kernel-mode components. The user-mode components encompass everything else, including services (such as the LAN Manager Server, which is used to share resources on the network; and the LAN Manager Workstation, which is used to access shared resources) and the environmental subsystems (such as the OS/2, POSIX, and Win32 subsystems). The reason these components are called *environmental subsystems* is that each of these subsystems creates a simulation of a particular operating system (the environment) that the applications (MS-DOS, Win16, Win32, and so on) execute under. What is important here is that the subsystems execute in entirely different process address spaces and are therefore protected from each other. Consequently, if a POSIX application crashes, it has no effect on the other applications you may be running.

Nearly all these subsystems are completely isolated from each other and have no communication facilities between them except through supported RPC functions such as named pipes or sockets. There are two exceptions. First, the Win32 subsystem is responsible for all I/O interaction, which includes the mouse, the keyboard, and all rendering on the screen. Every subsystem must request such support from the Win32 subsystem (by using local procedure calls), which is why the entire system becomes unusable if the Win32 subsystem hangs, unless the Win32 subsystem can be restarted (possible, but very unlikely). Second, the Win32 subsystem also contains the support for your MS-DOS and 16-bit Windows applications. Both 16-bit and 32-bit Windows applications can pass messages back and forth to each other as well as make use of the standard OLE and DDE facilities.

The 16-bit Windows subcomponent is referred to as the *Windows on Win32* (WOW) layer and can be restarted without complications (as far as I have seen to date). These subcomponents use the Virtual 8086 mode of the Intel processor's hardware support to emulate an Intel 8086 (on RISC processors this emulation is entirely in software) and provide completely independent address spaces for the MS-DOS and 16-bit applications (if desired) to execute under. Figure 3.2 illustrates the MS-DOS virtual DOS machine (VDM) architecture, and Figure 3.3 illustrates the WOW architecture.

FIGURE 3.2.

The virtual DOS machine architectural model.

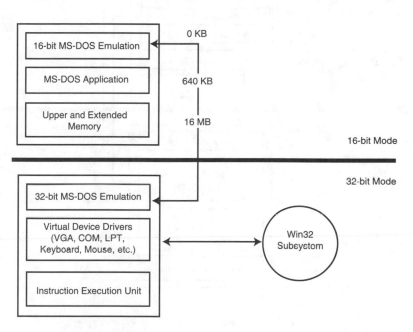

The OS/2 and POSIX subsystems are similar but less complicated because they are not built on the VDM concept. Instead, they just use the subsystem to directly support the application environment. For the MS-DOS and WOW emulation to directly support hardware access by an application, a virtual device driver must be available to support the emulation of the device and control access to it. This requirement explains why many MS-DOS disk utilities fail under Windows NT and why many Windows fax applications (which use virtual device drivers in enhanced mode) fail to execute under NT. It also explains that protected applications (which use a dongle hanging off the parallel port) fail because the standard NT parallel port driver does not support access to the required I/O ports in the fashion the protected application expects. Another interesting thing about WOW applications is that by default they all run in a shared VDM. This provides the greatest level of compatibility, but if one WOW application fails, it can crash the entire WOW layer. To provide additional protection (at the expense of compatibility), each 16-bit application can run in its own VDM. This feature gives you the ability to preemptively multitask your 16-bit Windows applications but prevents these same applications from making use of any shared memory (because they run in their own address spaces). This is one reason you cannot execute the 16-bit versions of Microsoft Mail and Schedule Plus in separate address spaces. (They make use of shared memory.)

FIGURE 3.3.

The Windows on Win32 architectural model.

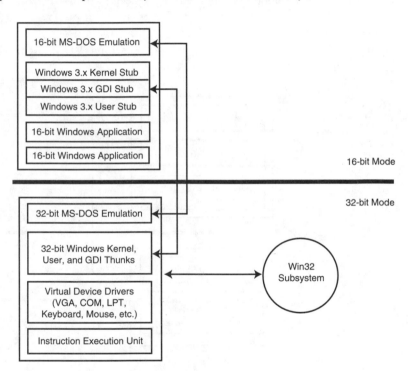

Additional Windows NT Features

There is more to the Windows NT design than its user/kernel-mode architecture. Many other network operating systems incorporate similar architectural concepts. However, not every network operating system includes the New Technology File System, the additional fault tolerant features, and the centralized administration capabilities. These are the focus of the next discussion, where you will learn why they are so important to you in your role as a webmaster.

The New Technology File System

Windows NT includes a new file system called, appropriately enough, the New Technology File System, or NTFS. This file system includes several enhancements over file systems currently in use today on most network file servers. To begin with, it is entirely transaction based.

Much like the transaction log that SQL Server uses to maintain data integrity, the NTFS file system utilizes a transaction log to maintain file system integrity. This does not mean you cannot lose data, but it does mean that you have a much greater chance of accessing your file system even if a system crash occurs. This capability stems from the use of the transaction log to roll back outstanding disk writes the next time Windows NT is booted. It also uses this log to check the disk for errors, instead of scanning each file allocation table entry as does the FAT file system. The NFTS file system has several other beneficial features:

- Security—The NTFS file system can assign access control entries (ACEs) to an access control list (ACL). The ACE contains either a group identifier or a user identifier encapsulated in a security descriptor, which can be used to limit access to a particular directory or file. This access attribute can provide the ability to grant or deny read, write, delete, execute, or ownership privileges of a directory or file. An ACL, on the other hand, is the container that encapsulates one or more ACEs. You will not be working with ACEs or ACLs directly unless you write your own application servers or IIS enhancements. For the most part, you will use File Manager or the Windows Explorer to set share-level, directory, or file-level access permissions to restrict access to your WWW Server's data.

- Long filenames—Long filenames are filenames that exceed the normal MS-DOS 8.3 limitation. These names can be up to 255 characters long, can be any mix of upper- or lowercase (although access to the file is not case sensitive except for applications executing in the POSIX subsystem), and can also include UNICODE characters if desired. One of the key features of NTFS is that it automatically generates an equivalent MS-DOS–compatible filename. It uses the first characters of the long filename as the base, adds a tilde, adds a sequence number, and uses the first three characters of the last file extension (the last word following a period). For example, if you had a long filename such as `Accounts Payable.July.1995.XLS`, the equivalent MS-DOS 8.3–compatible filename would be `ACCOUN~1.XLS`.

- Compression support—This feature was introduced with Windows NT 3.51. It enables you to compress any NTFS file, directory, or volume, unlike MS-DOS compression packages, which create a virtual disk as a hidden file on your uncompressed host drive and which require you to compress all data on the compressed drive. Windows NT uses an additional layer in the file system to compress, or decompress, files on demand without creating a virtual disk. This feature is particularly useful for compressing either a partial disk (such as the directory containing your HTML documents or your FTP site directories) or specific file types on a disk (such as graphics files). One thing you'll find with NTFS compression is that it is not designed for maximum compression as the MS-DOS compression schemes are; instead it is designed for reliability and performance.

Fault-Tolerant Capabilities

The primary purpose of a file server is to provide the ability to share resources. These can include CPU, file, and print resources. But what happens if you have a hardware failure? In many cases, this means your entire server and all the resources you share with it go down. And if you can't get everything back online quickly enough, your job may go down, too. This is where the fault-tolerant capabilities come into play to protect both your data and your job.

The previous section noted how an NTFS partition can provide data integrity at the file system level, but this may not be enough for mission-critical data. *Mission-critical data* is any data that is required to continue your business practice, for example, a SQL Server database or the source code for your WWW pages. Windows NT Server provides three options that you can use either separately or together to safeguard your data:

- Disk mirroring—This method works at the partition level to make a duplicate copy of your data. For every write to the primary partition, a second write is made to the secondary partition. If the fault-tolerant driver detects a device failure while accessing the primary partition, it can automatically switch to the secondary partition and continue providing you with access to your data.

- Disk duplexing—This method works at the partition level as well, but also includes the capability to detect disk controller errors. It does this by using two separate disk controllers with separate disk subsystems. Should you have a failure to access data on the primary partition, or a hardware failure of the primary disk controller, access to your data can be maintained by using the redundant copy on the secondary controller and disk subsystem.

- Disk striping with parity—This option works by combining equally sized disk partitions on separate physical drives (a minimum of 3 to a maximum of 32 disk drives) to create one logical partition. Data is written to the disk in discrete blocks. Each of these blocks is referred to as a *stripe*. When data is written to the disk, an error correction code stripe is written as well. In the case of a disk failure, the data stripes can be combined with the error correction code stripe to rebuild the missing data stripe.

> **TIP**
>
> The best types of disk subsystems are SCSI based because they support several important features. First, most SCSI controllers are bus masters (which means they have their own dedicated controller to transfer data to/from the disk and to/from system memory). Second, most SCSI drives support command queuing (used to issue several commands to a disk) and bus detachment (meaning that while the disk is processing the request, it detaches from the SCSI bus so another SCSI peripheral can connect to the bus and possibly transfer data). Most SCSI controllers also include a dedicated CPU so that your system CPU does not have to watch over each byte of data transferred from the SCSI controller, as most IDE disk controllers do. That means your CPU can continue processing data and enhancing

system throughput. One other important feature is that SCSI drives have spare sectors, which can be mapped to a failing sector (IDE drives have a similar feature, but do not support a specific command to replace a failing sector); the NTFS file system driver can take advantage of this.

The question is when do you use each of these techniques? Each technique provides increased data integrity, but at a cost. For instance, disk mirroring can be used to split a single disk into two partitions, using one partition to contain the primary data and the second partition to contain the copy (that is, the mirror) of the data of the primary partition. However, in order to create this copy, your disk controller must make two physical writes, one to each disk partition. And if the entire disk becomes defective, all your data is lost. To offset this problem, you might use two separate disk drives, but if the disk controller becomes defective, you again lose access to your data. Table 3.1 summarizes the capabilities of the fault-tolerant drivers.

Table 3.1. Summary of the fault-tolerant driver capabilities.

Fault-Tolerant Driver	*Pro*	*Con*
Disk mirroring	May be used on a single physical disk with at least two equally sized partitions. Can be used to mirror separate physical disks on a single disk controller as well.	Does not protect against disk failure if a single disk is used. Does not protect against controller errors. Limits disk storage to half of system capacity. Performance hit for disk writes.
Disk duplexing	Used to mirror separate physical disks on separate physical disk controllers. Protects against disk failures and disk controller errors.	Requires twice the hardware (two disk drives, two disk controllers) to provide half of the storage capacity.
Stripe set with parity	Provides fault tolerance for single drive failure. Increases disk read performance.	Does not provide protection from disk controller errors. Does not protect against multiple disk failures. Requires percentage of disk partition to contain ECC stripe. Slight CPU performance degradation for disk writes to calculate ECC stripe.

My preference is to use striping with parity because it provides fault tolerance and increased performance (particularly if you also place the paging file on the striped set). However, if you need maximum data protection, use the disk duplexing option. Continuing with this basic premise of keeping your server functional during hardware failures, you might want to consider using one of these optional techniques:

■ Uninterruptible power supply—This device is used for two purposes. First, it protects against temporary power outages by providing a battery to supply AC power to the computer. In the case of a long-term power outage, the uninterruptible power supply service will shut down the server in a graceful fashion. Second, an uninterruptible power supply is used to filter your AC power. This feature is most important because poor power (spikes, surges, low-line conditions) can cause more damage to your server's peripherals than anything else.

■ Symmetric multiprocessing—When this feature is installed on a platform with multiple CPUs, both the performance of your server and its fault tolerance increase. Should one CPU fail, it will be disabled, but processing will continue on the other CPUs. On a uniprocessor computer, if the CPU fails, the entire server goes down.

■ Multiple network adapters—Installing multiple network adapters provides several advantages. First, the adapters can be used to increase network performance by providing several channels for spreading the network load. Second, they can increase performance of a specific network transport by binding that transport to a single adapter. Conversely, by binding all the transports to all the network adapters, fault tolerance is increased. If a single adapter fails, it will be disabled and the load will spread among the additional adapters.

Centralized Administration

One of the major benefits of using Windows NT is the ability to manage your entire network from any NT Server, NT Workstation, Windows 95, or Windows 3.*x* workstation running in enhanced mode. I have divided these management tools into two sections: computer management and user management. Specifics on how to utilize these tools will be covered in later chapters. For now, I just want to mention what is available and why you will want to use it for your day-to-day system management.

Computer Management

Computer management includes all the administration tools used to configure either your local computer or a remote client computer. While I won't mention them all, I will point out the most useful tools:

■ Event Viewer—This tool is seriously underrated; indeed, many administrators never even bother to use it. This tool is your first line of defense in isolating any system- or security-related problems. It provides the ability to look at an NT computer and

determine whether any system, service, application, or security problems have occurred in the past. If you enable system auditing on a directory, for example, all the
information about who accessed the directory and when it was accessed will be
contained within the security log.

NOTE

Every administrator should review all three logs on a daily basis to determine what type of
problems may be accumulating. Not all problems are immediately flagged and sent to the
administrator in an alert. Monitoring your system log can warn you of imminent failures. My
portable computer, for example, has been reporting SCSIDISK bad partition warnings on a
SCSI drive, indicating that this drive is getting ready to fail completely. You can also
determine whether a security breach has occurred by viewing the information contained in
the security log.

- File Manager—As you might expect from its name, File Manager is responsible for
  creating network *sharepoints* (a shared directory) as well as manipulating your own files
  and directories as you may have done with the Windows 3.*x* File Manager. File
  Manager can be used to assign permissions to directories and files, to take ownership
  of existing directories or files, or to enable auditing of directories and files. (For more
  information on this refer to Chapter 10, "Advanced Security Issues.") One other
  feature, which is included in no other tool, is the capability to view who currently has
  a specific file open.

- Internet Server Manager—This tool is used to configure your WWW, FTP, and
  Gopher Servers on the network. It can also be used to control (stop, start, pause, and
  continue) the WWW, FTP, and Gopher Server services on a local or remote computer.

- Print Manager—You can use this tool to create new printers by installing a printer
  driver, to connect to existing printers on the network, and to manage your local and
  remote print queues. The Print Manager also is used to assign permissions and to take
  ownership of existing printers on the network as well as to enable auditing of your
  printers.

- Remote Access Server (RAS) Administrator—This tool is used to completely control
  the remote access service on either a local or remote NT computer. The Remote
  Access Server Administrator is capable of starting the service, authorizing users to
  make use of the RAS connectivity features, and sending messages to connected RAS
  clients on a per-port basis. The remote access service also can be used to provide a
  cost-effective, WAN solution, particularly if you use either a 28Kbps modem or an
  ISDN connection.

> **TIP**
>
> Until you authorize a user to use the RAS service, he will not be authenticated if he connects and will not be able to access any network resource.

■ Server Manager for Domains—Using this tool is the first step in controlling access to your domain. This tool is responsible for creating the computer account your NT Workstation clients will use to gain a trusted connection to your server. Without a computer account, the network client computer cannot be authenticated even if the user attempting to log on to the domain from the workstation has a valid user identification. Server Manager for Domains also can be used to control the services on a remote Windows NT client as well as determine who is connected and what resources they have in use. You can even disconnect such users if desired and, if installed, the FTP service can be monitored from the Server Manager for Domains as well. A few additional capabilities are included to provide the configuration of the replication and alert services.

■ Dynamic Host Configuration Protocol (DHCP) Manager—This tool is used to create DHCPs and configure scopes (that is, subnets) on your TCP/IP network. DHCP can automate the assignment of IP addresses to network clients and, when their lease (or time-out) expires, retrieve the IP address for allocation to a new user. IP address reservations (a reassignment mechanism) can also be created with this tool.

■ Windows Internet Naming Service (WINS) Manager—This tool manages all NetBIOS computer names to IP name resolution. It effectively performs the same task as a UNIX domain name server performs. A useful feature of WINS is the capability to replicate the database among several other WINS servers on the network automatically.

> **TIP**
>
> WINS is not designed to work with network clients that are not WINS aware, such as UNIX clients. However, there are two possible solutions. First, you can use the Microsoft domain name server service, which can be configured to interoperate with the WINS service to provide NetBIOS name resolution. Second, you can use a WINS proxy agent. A WINS proxy agent is either a Windows for Workgroups 3.11, a Windows NT Workstation, or a Windows NT Server computer that will act as an intermediary between the WINS server and the client that is not WINS aware. The WINS proxy agent forwards the IP address to the client, based on the NetBIOS name the client is attempting to find. To enable the WINS proxy agent feature, check the WINS Proxy Agent check box in the TCP/IP-32 configuration dialog box on the Windows for Workgroups 3.11 computer, or the WINS Proxy Agent check box in the Advanced Microsoft TCP/IP Configuration dialog.

User Management

User management includes adding new users to the network and manipulating current user characteristics. Most of this is accomplished with User Manager for Domains, which is covered in detail in Chapter 10. For now I just want to introduce you to some of the features provided in the basic user management area in case you will also be using your IIS server as an Internet gateway for local or remote network clients. The tools you will be using include the following:

- User Manager for Domains—This tool is the heart of all user and group management. User Manager for Domains is used to enable system auditing on a global level and to create and manipulate local and global groups (local groups are unique to the computer they are created on while global groups are domainwide). It is used to create and manipulate user accounts, to configure system user policies (such as the minimum password length, the maximum password age, and account lockout features), and to specify which computers the user can log on from and the time of day the user can be logged on to the system. You can also use User Manager to set up the user's profile, logon script, and any home directory if desired.

NOTE

Unlike Novell NetWare and other network operating systems, Windows NT Server does not provide the ability to limit the amount of file space a user can access. So be prepared to implement a system policy of notifying users who exceed your maximum disk quotas, backing up their data, and then deleting it when file space runs low. As an alternative, you can look into third-party add-ons for Windows NT Server, such as DiskQuota from New Technology Partners, to provide this functionality.

- User Profile Editor—This tool is used to create the initial user profile. A user profile is the environment in which the user works and includes all File Manager, Print Manager, and any other user-specific settings. A profile can be either user specific and non-sharable or sharable and non-user specific. It cannot be both. A sharable profile is called a mandatory profile and is used to restrict a group of users from changing their user environment, such as the .ini entries for Windows 3.x.

NOTE

One of the interesting features of profiles is the capability to use the same profile on more than one computer. As the user logs on from a different computer, her profile is used to configure the computer. She will see the same desktop and can use the same applications (as long as they are installed in the same directories on the local computer or are on a network sharepoint) that she uses on her primary computer. But this will occur only if the

continues

> *continued*
>
> user profile has been created and is available (shared) from a server that is accessible from the new location. Profiles are also server specific, unlike logon scripts, which can be replicated from server to server and can be executed from the server that authenticates the user.

■ Logon scripts—Logon scripts aren't really managed through a specific tool, although they are assigned (named) in User Manager for Domains. Basically, a *logon script* is a batch program that is executed when the user logs on to the domain and can include such capabilities as mapping sharepoints or printers, automatically checking the hard disk, running programs to keep track of a user's time on a project, or any other program that can be run from the command line.

Windows NT Server Concepts

Windows NT Server introduces several new concepts for you (the network administrator) to consider when designing your network. This section looks at the difference between workgroups and domains and introduces the trust concept. Then it looks at the difference between the various Windows NT Server modes of operation. Following this discussion is an introduction to the various domain models supported by Windows NT Server. Next you'll learn about the System Management Server implementation methodologies. And by the time you have finished this section, you will be ready for the next chapter, where you will learn about implementing your network based on the concepts in this chapter.

Workgroups Versus Domains

When you install Windows NT Server, you have to decide whether your Windows NT Server is to be a domain member or a workgroup member. If you choose to be a member of a domain, your server will also have to be either a domain controller, backup domain controller, or server. If you choose to be a server, you also have the choice to be a workgroup member. If you make the wrong choice, your only supported option to change this decision is to reinstall Windows NT Server and lose any system settings you have already implemented. Because a Windows NT Server installation can be quite time-consuming, not to mention the loss of user accounts and other system configuration options that occur when you reinstall, you want to make sure that you do it right the first time. And that's where I come in, to help you make the best decision possible and limit your downtime.

What Is a Workgroup?

A workgroup is a casual affiliation of computers that are logically grouped into a single access point. This cuts down on the clutter when your users browse for resources on the network.

Instead of seeing all the resources that are shared on the network, they will first see the shared resources of the workgroup they belong to. They will see resources in other workgroups only if they explicitly browse the other workgroup. Workgroups also cut down on the network traffic because each browse request requires that either a browse master (a computer that maintains a static list of computers that are online and belong to the workgroup) or the computer being browsed for shared resources responds with a list of the resources being shared.

All security in a workgroup is based on the local (the one sharing the resource) computer. This is a serious administrative chore because it requires that all workgroup computers have the same user accounts defined if you want to allow other computer users to access your shared resources transparently (without supplying a different user account and password) in a user-level access environment. A user-level access environment provides the ability to limit access to shared resources on an individual-user basis. Each user can have different access restrictions. In a large workgroup (more than five computers) environment, it is easier to only use share-level access to limit access to your shared resources. Share-level access uses an individual password for read-only access and another password for full access to your shared resources.

What Is a Domain?

A domain is similar to a workgroup in that it provides the same grouping ability as a workgroup. However, unlike a workgroup, a domain has a centralized user database that resides on the domain controller. All user logon authentication is based on this central user database. This makes your life as a network administrator much easier because you only have one user database to worry about, rather than one user database per computer (as the workgroup model uses).

Domains also include the ability to establish a secure, or trusted, connection. This concept of trust begins with the computer account assignment either when you install Windows NT or when you manually create the computer account with Server Manager for Domains. You cannot be a domain member without a computer account, although you can access shared resources on a domain if you are a workgroup member as long as you have a user account on the domain and no trust relationships are defined for the domain.

> **NOTE**
>
> If you have a two-way trust relationship defined on your domain, you cannot apply the user account and password mapping of the workgroup authentication model. Even if you have a user account and a password on your domain controller, you cannot use it to access a shared resource. This condition occurs because you are not a trusted member of the domain (that is, you have no computer account on the domain) and will therefore be denied access to the shared resource.

A trust relationship provides the ability to use the user accounts and global groups defined in one domain (the trusted domain) in a completely different domain (the trusting domain). If this explanation sounds a bit fuzzy, don't worry—it even confuses me on some days. You'll learn more about trust relationships and domain models in an upcoming discussion in the next chapter.

Controllers Versus Servers

When you install Windows NT Server you have three choices that basically define a specific mode of operation. Each of these operating modes provides different functional capabilities and performance options. These choices include the following:

■ Primary domain controller—The primary domain controller contains the master copy of the user database, which includes all your global groups, user accounts, and computer accounts. In addition, your primary domain controller is used to authenticate your users when they log on to the network or access a shared resource. Your primary domain controller also includes the tools you will use for centralized administration, such as User Manager for Domains, Server Manager for Domains, Dynamic Host Configuration Protocol Server, Windows Internet Name Service Server, and a host of additional tools.

■ Backup domain controller—A backup domain controller is similar in function to a primary domain controller, but with one significant difference. A backup domain does not contain the master copy of the user database. Instead, the master database is replicated from the primary domain controller. Therefore, you cannot make any account changes (global groups, user accounts, or computer accounts) if the primary domain controller is unavailable. The primary reason for using a backup domain controller is to balance the load for authenticating users on the network. In addition, if a primary domain controller goes down, either inadvertently due to a hardware fault or purposely for, say, a hardware upgrade, you can promote a backup domain controller to a primary domain controller. This system enables you to continue authenticating your users and also provides continued network administrative capabilities.

■ Server—A server's primary purpose is to provide optimum resource sharing. Because a server does not authenticate users logging on to the network and does not participate in the user database replication, it can devote all its resources to supporting your network clients. If you have a choice, use a server as your Internet Information Server base platform for optimum efficiency. There is a trade-off for this increased performance, however; you lose the domain administration tools. Instead of User Manager for Domains, for instance, you get a copy of User Manager.

TIP

Another reason to use Windows NT Server operating in server mode is to bypass the Windows NT Workstation limit of 10 simultaneous client user connections. Instead of using Windows NT Workstation, you can use Windows NT Server operating in server mode.

One major item to consider is that in order to create a domain, you must have at least a primary domain controller in your network. You can have one or more backup domain controllers if desired, although they are not required. Keep in mind that a backup domain controller can be useful if you have a primary domain controller failure, particularly because only a primary or backup controller can authenticate your Windows NT clients.

Domain Models

Microsoft has defined four basic domain models, which include the single domain model, the master domain model, the multiple master model, and the complete trust model. However, you should consider this a starting point when it comes time to plan your network implementation. (This topic is discussed in more detail in the next chapter.) You do not have to limit yourself to a specific domain implementation; instead, you can stretch the basic domain model to fit your specific needs. So let's take a look at these different models so we can plan how to make the best network design possible.

The Single Domain Model

The single domain model, as shown in Figure 3.4, includes a primary domain controller and optionally one or more backup domain controllers and servers. It is the basis for all the other domain models. It is the simplest model that Microsoft has to offer and can perform well for you if you meet the following criteria:

- A small network with fewer than 300 users
- Fewer than 15 servers
- An administrative group, like an MIS department, that can administer the network
- No wide area network (WAN)

These criteria do not form a hard and fast rule. You can play with the numbers for the maximum number of users and servers, as long as you keep in mind that the real issue is acceptable performance. If you have fast servers (single or dual CPU Pentiums, for example) and a high-performance backbone (100Mb/sec fiber optic, for instance), you will not see the same performance limitation as a company with 80386-based servers on a 10Mb/sec backbone.

The single domain model provides several benefits. It enables any network administrator to administer all the servers from any server or workstation on the network. Because there is only one user database defined that contains all the user accounts and local and global groups, resource administration is completely centralized. Because there is only a single domain, no trust relationships have to be created to access resources in other domains.

Of course, the single domain model has some limitations. For instance, browsing for resources is based on the domain, and as the number of computers in your domain increases, performance problems may arise. As the number of users in your domain grows, so does the list you have to search through to find an individual user account. And as you make changes to your

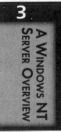

accounts, either by creating or modifying user accounts and groups, these changes have to be replicated to every backup domain controller on the network. That can eat up a lot of your network bandwidth. Finally, if your company has multiple departments that do not want you to administer their network or have access to confidential files, you'll have to split up your domain and choose another domain model.

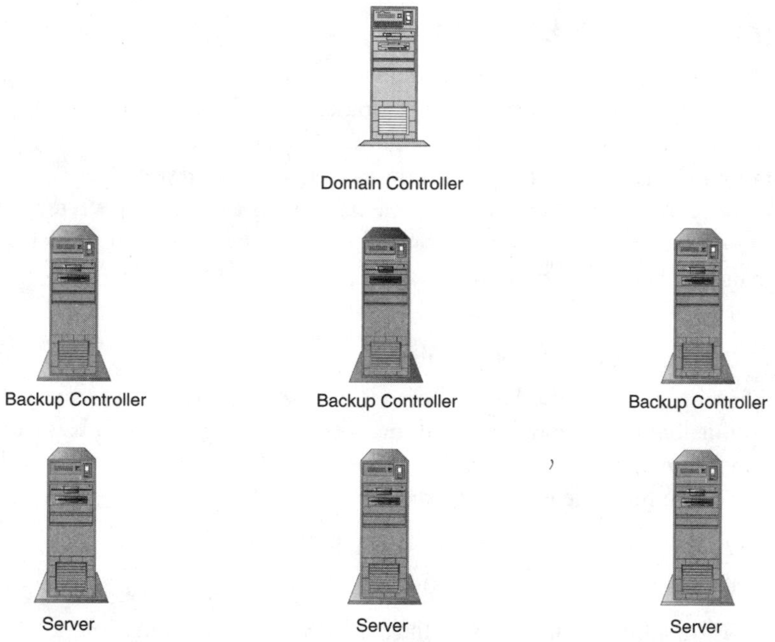

FIGURE 3.4.
The single domain model.

Domain Controller

Backup Controller

Backup Controller

Backup Controller

Server

Server

Server

The Master Domain Model

The master domain model (see Figure 3.5) includes a single master domain with one or more resource domains that trust the master domain. The master domain contains all the user account and global groups; no user accounts or global groups are defined in the resource domains. Because no user accounts exist on the resource domains, all logons and authentications are referred to the master domain.

WARNING

Because all user logons and authentications are processed by the master domain, no users will be able to log on to the network or access shared resources if the primary domain controller fails and you have not included at least one backup domain controller in the master domain.

The master domain model enables you to split your network based on departmental resource allocations, yet still provides for centralized administration of your network. The master domain model is well suited for organizations that have the following specifications:

- Fewer than 1,000 users
- Fewer than 50 servers
- An administrative group, like an MIS department, that can administer the network

FIGURE 3.5.
The master domain model.

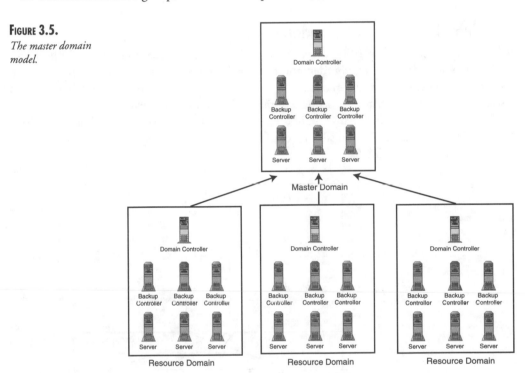

Notice, however, that although each resource domain trusts the master domain, they do not trust each other. Because all the user accounts and groups are defined in the master domain, and each resource domain trusts the master domain and users or groups can be granted access to the resource domain, no additional trust relationships are required. One of the other interesting capabilities of this model is that the central administration group can be limited to just creating user accounts in the master domain. The resource domain administrators can then determine who will be granted access to the resources on their domain by creating global groups that include user accounts from the master domain.

There are, however, a couple downsides to this model that you might want to keep in mind. For instance, a user list that includes 1,000 users can be pretty intimidating to scroll through, and slow to browse. And replicating the entire user list to your backup controllers can generate enough network traffic to make your users scream, which is why I recommend that you do this after normal working hours. The limiting factors here are your network bandwidth and the speed of your servers. If your network bandwidth is insufficient to carry the user logon and authentication requests provided by your servers or your servers cannot process the logon requests quickly enough, then your network performance as a whole will suffer. Consider, for example, a resource domain situated on a WAN. All user logons and authentications will have to travel across the slow WAN link to the master domain, even when they are accessing resources on servers in their local resource domain.

The Multiple Master Domain Model

When you have more than 1,000 users or 50 servers, you really need to think about how you can lessen your administrative burden and provide additional fault-tolerant capabilities. The multiple master domain model may just fit the bill. Like the master domain model, it includes resource domains. But instead of a single domain with all the user accounts defined in it, you have two or more domains that contain all the user accounts, as shown in Figure 3.6. Your MIS department can still administer the entire network as long as accounts are defined in either of the master domains.

FIGURE 3.6.

The multiple master domain model.

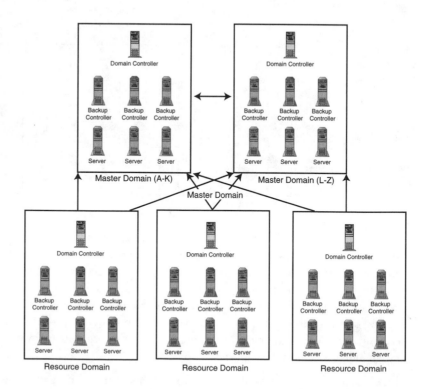

The example in Figure 3.6 shows two domains that have split the user accounts between them. The master domain on the left includes all of the user accounts from A–K, while the master domain on the right includes user accounts from L–Z. Each of these master domains trusts the other, which essentially provides you with one user database, much as the master domain model provides. Continuing with this concept requires that each resource domain trust each master domain to provide all users access to all resources in the resource domains.

This approach increases your logon and user authentication capabilities because a single failure of a primary domain controller (assuming you do not have backup domain controllers) will only prevent half of your network users from logging on to the domain or being authenticated for resource access. If you have a WAN, you can also include a master domain on each side of the wire to give the local users fast access to their local resources and still enable them to access resources anywhere on the network.

However, while I have used this example to split user accounts alphabetically, you will find that this model will work better for large organizations if you split the user accounts by departments or divisions. Each of these departments would have a master domain with all the departmental user accounts. Departmental resource domains would then trust this departmental master domain. This configuration would enable you (the administrator) to create a global group that contains all your users to access a particular resource in only one domain rather than in two or more domains.

For example, suppose you want to create a global group called OFFICE that includes all the users to be granted access to the MSOFFICE sharepoint (which contains the Office installation files). If all of your departmental users are included in the departmental domain, then it is a simple matter of creating the group and including your users. But if you had multiple master domains that split up user accounts alphabetically, you would have to create an OFFICE global group in each of the master domains. Then, in your resource domain, you would have to create a local group that would contain the global groups defined in the master domain in order to accomplish the same task.

The Complete Trust Domain Model

The last domain model is the complete trust model. In this model all the domains trust each other, as Figure 3.7 demonstrates, with each domain having its own user database. This particular model is designed for corporations that do not have a centralized administration group or do not want to have a centralized group dictate who has access to their network resources.

In some cases corporations wind up with the complete trust domain model from lack of prior planning rather than any specific need. While this model works fine, it is much more difficult to administer. And as your network grows, it becomes very time-consuming to create additional trust relationships. You can express the number of trust relationships mathematically as $n(n - 1)$ where n is the number of domains on the network. For instance, if you have 5 domains, as the example in Figure 3.7 shows, and decide to add another domain, you will have to create 30, or 6×5, trust relationships. If you have 20 domains, adding the 21st will require 420 trust relationships. And you thought your life as an administrator was difficult now!

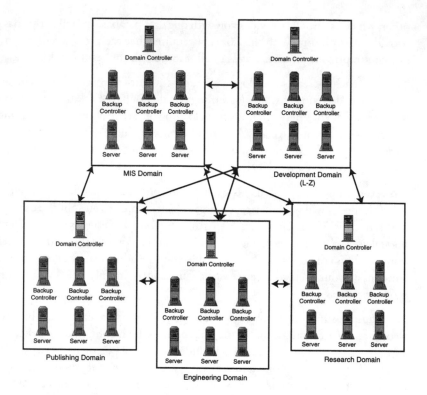

FIGURE 3.7.
The complete trust domain model.

Summary

This chapter looks at some of the features provided by Windows NT Server and the system architecture to prepare you for actually working with Windows NT Server. This information will provide a fuller understanding of the Windows NT Server when you look at future troubleshooting and optimization techniques. It also explains some of the more important features of Windows NT such as the NTFS file system and what it can and cannot do, along with the fault-tolerant features. These fault-tolerant features can be implemented as part of your normal configuration, depending on your needs, available hardware, and budget. Finally, this chapter looks at some of the tools that are available to help you manage your network on a day-to-day basis.

In the next chapter you will learn more about hardware platform choices. Specifically, you will look into items to help you when building a platform to use as your WWW Server. You will learn more about the I/O expansion bus, secondary-level cache options, processor considerations, and how other hardware choices can affect your performance. You will also learn a few tips for configuring your system, via software, to obtain better performance.

Choosing a Platform for Windows NT Server

CHAPTER 4

IN THIS CHAPTER

- Choosing the Right Hardware   71
- Hardware Upgrades   83
- Choosing the Right Server Model   91
- The Software Configuration   92

This chapter focuses on how the choices you make, or that are made for you, affect the performance of your server. Windows NT Server is the foundation that the Internet Information Server (IIS) builds on to provide services to potentially thousands of Internet users, so you should be concerned about these choices. Performance and optimization rely on two key issues: the hardware and the software. How you use these components determines how well your Internet Information Server will perform.

Optimizing your Windows NT Server to provide the most efficient server performance can sometimes be a daunting task. So many options can overwhelm you at times. There is always the option of throwing money at bigger and better hardware, which will always increase some performance aspect, but that's not a very cost-effective solution. It's better to spend some time working with available tools first to determine how to best spend your money to increase performance.

This chapter begins by looking at some of the basic hardware choices. The first section includes a discussion of items that can be useful in planning the initial hardware purchase of the platform you will use as your server. This chapter covers such items as the different processor platforms available for running Windows NT Server, the peripheral I/O expansion buses available on today's computers and when to choose them, and the various disk subsystems and how to best use them. Finally, the chapter covers the options that always increase the performance of your server as compared to the default system configuration provided by a standard Windows NT Server installation. I call these easy performance improvements because these solutions utilize the hardware you have already.

After the chapter explains these basic performance modifications, it examines how you can use some of the hardware-based solutions. You have options such as using hardware like a redundant array of inexpensive disks (RAID) solution, load-balancing your network by adding network adapters and adjusting the network bindings to increase performance, and using additional processors.

The chapter ends with a look at some of the basic software-configuration options to optimize your server. This section helps you determine whether to use a domain controller or server as your IIS server platform choice, and why you want to choose between them.

> **NOTE**
>
> Throughout this chapter you will see references to the BackOffice system files. I expect most of you also will be installing one or more of these components (SQL Server, Exchange Server, System Management Server, or SNA Server) as well as the Internet Information Server. So rather than list these items separately, I have just combined them into a single product to make the reading a little easier to follow.

Choosing the Right Hardware

You can enhance server performance by choosing a faster processor (or using the scalability of Windows NT Server by installing it on an entirely different processor platform), using ISA-, EISA-, PCI-, or VLB-based peripherals (you will learn more about these later in the chapter), or using software RAID solutions. This section examines some options to help you obtain the maximum performance from your server without purchasing additional hardware. You also can use this section as a guide to help make future purchasing decisions.

Choosing a Processor Platform

Windows NT Server (version 4.0) can run on several different processor platforms. These include the Intel processor line and several different reduced instruction set computer (RISC) processors. You currently may use the MIPS, Alpha, or PowerPC RISC processors. The major differences between these platforms, aside from the purchase price, are twofold. First, the Intel processor line is the only processor line that can execute OS/2 16-bit character-mode applications. It is also the only processor line that can be used in a dual-boot mode to boot MS-DOS. If these are not real concerns, you can ignore these options and just consider the second difference: pure performance. Depending on the RISC processor line you choose and the clock speed of the processor, one of these platforms may perform better for you than the Intel processors.

It is becoming very difficult to recommend a RISC processor over the Intel processor line because the Intel processor line keeps improving. For example, the DEC Alpha 275MHz processor is supposed to be about 265 percent faster in integer calculations and up to 600 percent faster in floating-point calculations than a 133MHz Intel Pentium. This means the Alpha also will be faster than a 200MHz Pentium. How do other lines compare (for example, the Intel-clone vendors, the Pentium Pro, or the SMP Pentium platform)? From what I've seen in actual performance, a dual Pentium 133MHz performs about as well as the DEC Alpha. Dual 150MHz or higher processors may be able to exceed the performance of an Alpha processor–based motherboard quite a bit. My server uses dual Pentium 166 MHz processors on a mixed Peripheral Component Interconnect (PCI) and Enhanced Industry Standard Architecture (EISA) bus.

If the primary job of a server is to share resources (generally processor, file, and printer resources, which is pretty much what your WWW and FTP servers do as well), the speed of the processor is not the most relevant issue. Processor performance is a concern, but not a major issue, because Windows NT and the add-on services (like IIS) are more processor-intensive than the same services on other network operating systems. This is due in part to the client/server design of Windows NT Server. This design requires additional overhead to pass messages between the client application (such as the WWW Publishing Service) and the server application (such as the Win32 environmental subsystem). Instead, you should be more concerned with your ability to send information over whatever channel you will be using. If IIS is used to build an intranet, the channel could be a network, in which case a 10MB network adapter would be the limiting factor in how fast you could send information to your clients. In such a case, you could improve the situation by upgrading to a 100MB network adapter. If you are using IIS to build an Internet site, your router could be used as a channel to provide your connection to the Internet. Router bandwidth starts at about 56Kbps, which is a far cry from the bandwidth offered by even a lowly 10MB network adapter. If you need the increased bandwidth, it is possible to use routers that offer bandwidth up to 45Mbps. The primary issues you should be concerned with are the I/O bus performance of your server and the peripherals you choose, because they more noticeably affect your system's overall performance.

Choosing an I/O Bus

The next step after determining which processor platform you will use as your server is to determine the I/O bus architecture. As with processor platforms, several types of I/O buses are available; as summarized in Table 4.1, each has specific capabilities. The main thing to consider here is which bus will perform best for a particular function. For instance, how well will it perform for video, network, or small computer system interface (SCSI) adapters (the most common performance-oriented peripherals). These adapters must function at their peak. Adapters that are not performance intensive are items such as a sound card, a modem card, a parallel port, a mouse adapter, or even a joystick adapter.

Table 4.1. I/O expansion bus summary.

Type	Bus Width	Maximum Bus Speed (MHz)	Maximum Data Transfer Rate (MB/sec)
ISA (XT)	8	4.77	4.5
ISA (AT)	16	8.0	10
EISA	32	8.0	32
MCA	16	8.33–12.5	10–16
MCA	32	16	64
VLB	32	33–50	133–160
VLB	64	33	267
PCI	32	33	133
PCI	64	33	266
PCMCIA	16	N/A	2

TIP

Many Intel-based computers have an advanced BIOS setup option to increase the speed at which the I/O expansion bus operates. Increasing this bus speed above the default of 8MHz can increase performance. Most of today's peripherals are rated for a minimum of 12.5MHz, although some will operate at higher speeds.

WARNING

If you do increase the speed at which your I/O expansion bus operates, make sure you perform a reliability test before placing the unit in service because not all adapters will operate reliably above 8MHz. Make sure when you perform this test that you check for full disk controller, network controller, video adapter, and communication port functionality.

Several I/O bus types are available on computers you have purchased already or that you will purchase in the near future. Each of these I/O buses has good points and bad points to consider. Choosing when and how to use them is where I can help. Consider the following as basic rules for the listed I/O bus:

- Industry Standard Architecture (ISA)—ISA is the original expansion bus that was introduced on the IBM (AT) personal computer. The original PC used an 8-bit I/O bus, which the AT computer extended to 16 bits, although the ISA standard includes both the 8- and 16-bit I/O buses. Most of today's peripherals are 16-bit peripherals and offer excellent value. If performance is not an issue, the ISA bus peripherals are the choice to make when purchasing. This bus should be used for your 8-bit expansion cards (filling up your 8-bit slots first) and your 16-bit expansion cards. It is a good choice for your sound cards, modem cards, and other peripherals, but try to avoid this expansion bus for your network, SCSI, and video cards unless you have no other option. It is an acceptable choice for secondary network and SCSI adapters.

4

CHOOSING A
PLATFORM

NOTE

The ISA expansion bus is able to directly access only the first 16MB of system RAM. If you use a bus master controller (such as a SCSI disk controller) and if your system has more than 16MB of RAM, all disk access will have to be double-buffered. *Double-buffering* refers to data that must first be copied to a buffer within the adapter's addressable range (the first 16MB for a 16-bit adapter) and then copied to the application's data buffer. Copying of data from buffer to buffer will decrease overall performance. Although double-buffering is not a significant performance hit on most systems, on others it is very noticeable, depending on the system architecture.

- Enhanced Industry Standard Architecture (EISA)—This expansion bus is an extension to the ISA bus. It stretches the I/O bus to a full 32 bits and offers software configuration of peripherals through a configuration disk. An EISA expansion slot can also utilize ISA adapters because it utilizes a layered connection mechanism. An ISA adapter fits only halfway down this connection, thus enabling a connection to all the standard ISA expansion pins, while an EISA adapter fits all the way down and can reach the additional I/O and bus connectors. This bus is a good choice for network, video, and SCSI adapters. It performs well in most conditions and offers the ability to have several bus master adapters installed concurrently.

A bus master adapter is one that has its own processor on it and in most cases, one that has its own direct memory access (DMA) controller as well. The idea behind a bus master adapter is that it can use its own processor and DMA controller to pass data between the adapter and system memory, thus letting the processor on the motherboard continue to process data requests instead of spending time passing data between the system memory and the adapter. You can think of it as a poor man's multiprocessor platform.

TIP

Although many people talk about PCI and video local bus (VLB) as the buses to use on the desktop, they tend to forget about performance-oriented servers. These machines can make excellent use of the EISA bus to add additional network adapters, SCSI adapters (there are never enough SCSI channels), and even multiport communications boards, such as those from DigiBoard, to add functionality while maintaining performance. My recommendation for an I/O bus is to find a PCI/EISA bus combination if you can. This solution offers the greatest level of performance and compatibility with a long-term growth potential.

- Microchannel Architecture (MCA)—IBM introduced this I/O bus as a replacement to the ISA expansion bus. It was designed for the PS/2 line of computers. Although MCA offered increased performance compared to the ISA bus, it was completely incompatible with the ISA bus. This led to an increased cost of the adapters and a limited number of peripherals for the consumer to purchase. This bus is a dead end and should be avoided for new purchases.

- Video Local Bus (VLB)—In order to increase performance of video adapters, a method was created to access an adapter by tying it directly to the system memory bus. This increased performance considerably, but limited it to supporting a maximum of three VLB adapters. The current implementation is a 32-bit-wide data bus with an extension to 64 bits on the way. This bus is an excellent choice for your primary video adapter, and in my limited testing, the same adapter in VLB and PCI versions outperforms the PCI bus. Although VLB can be used for multiple purposes, such as a video adapter, disk controller, and network adapter, it is not the best choice for multiple adapters. Use VLB over an ISA bus for these purposes, but realize that you will not obtain optimum performance for simultaneous access. That is, in most cases, a video card as the only VLB adapter will perform better than if both a video card and disk controller are installed.

■ Peripheral Component Interconnect (PCI)—This bus was designed to overcome the limitations of the ISA, EISA, MCA, and VLB expansion buses. It offers true plug-and-play functionality by automatically configuring the adapters (that is, no software-configuration program is needed) and outperforms all other buses in data transfer rates. Current implementations still limit you to three PCI expansion slots, which is why the PCI bus is usually paired with either the ISA, EISA, or even the VLB buses. PCI is an excellent choice for multiple adapters, such as your video card, SCSI (or Integrated Drive Electronics [IDE] disk controller) adapters, and network adapters. Keep in mind, though, that you will probably have only three PCI expansion slots, which can severely limit your performance options. If PCI is your choice as a primary I/O bus, try to find one that is paired with an EISA expansion bus. This configuration enables you to use the PCI bus for your video and two SCSI adapters while utilizing the EISA bus for network adapters. If you need to expand your disk subsystem again, you can always add SCSI adapters to the EISA expansion bus and still be able to maintain adequate performance, compared to a PCI SCSI adapter.

NOTE

Several new high-end servers from HP, Compaq, and other manufacturers have recently been making their way into the market and offer more than three PCI expansion slots. If your budget will support it, take a closer look at these types of servers to obtain the maximum performance possible.

■ Personal Computer Memory Card Industry Association (PCMCIA)—This bus was originally designed to add memory components to handheld and portable computers, but has since become an industry standard I/O bus. This bus is used to connect SCSI adapters, network adapters, video capture cards, miniature hard disk drives, and just about anything else, to portable computers. It is the first plug-and-play device to live up to the name under MS-DOS and Windows 95. Under Windows NT you will still need to choose an IRQ, I/O port and possibly a memory address to configure the device driver. This is because Windows NT does not support the Card and Socket services that provide the plug-and-play functionality. Although this is not a high-performance I/O bus, it still performs relatively well.

4

CHOOSING A
PLATFORM

TIP

If you need to demonstrate a Windows NT Server–based WWW server, such as with IIS, consider installing Windows NT Server on a portable computer. With today's hardware you can find Pentiums with disk drives in the 2.1GB range. Pentium-based portables (the low-end 75MHz models) give excellent runtime (2.5–3 hours), and the high-end 133MHz models, while offering limited runtime (1–1.5 hours), give excellent performance. I use my Toshiba T4600c portable and Windows NT for classes and demonstrations of the various BackOffice components. With the addition of supported PCMCIA network and SCSI adapters, it offers true plug-and-play capabilities. You can just plug your portable computer into your client's network and immediately be fully functional. Not only can you access their resources, but they can access yours as well. Combine this with a fully functional WWW site, and it makes an impressive demonstration. When you have finished your demonstration, you can pack it up and hit the road in minutes.

CAUTION

Avoid an architecture that has a mixture of more than two I/O buses (such as ISA, PCI, and VLB) for your server. Although these platforms offer the capability to use more types of peripherals on a single computer, these mixed bus types (VLB and PCI) do not perform as well. It is better to choose a platform with a dedicated ISA/PCI or ISA/VLB bus and use the faster bus for your video, disk, and network adapters.

Choosing a Disk Subsystem

The most important single component on your system, aside from the processor, is your disk subsystem. If your server cannot access the data fast enough to handle your client requests, it slows down the entire network as your clients wait to access data. On a dynamic WWW site, such as one produced with IIS and SQL Server, this poor performance means you will be notified sooner or later by your superiors, and it will rarely be a happy meeting. Descriptions of the four types of disk subsystems on the market today follow. (See Table 4.2 for a summary.)

■ Antiquated systems—If you have one of these in your server, you're in real trouble. Replace it immediately or suffer the consequences. Antiquated systems are based on the standard disk interface and are all part of the ST-506 family. They include Modified Frequency Modulation (MFM), Run Length Limited (RLL), Enhanced Run Length Limited (ERLL), and Enhanced Small Device Interface (ESDI). All these disk subsystems have since been replaced by more capable and less expensive versions. You should not use computers using these types of disk subsystems as your primary

WWW site. If you are connecting to the Internet on a full-time basis, they could be useful as domain name systems (DNS), WINS, or DHCP servers. The DNS, WINS, or DHCP services are not nearly as I/O intensive as a highly accessed WWW site, but they still can provide a useful service to your network by resolving NetBIOS names (such as the Microsoft Web site www.microsoft.com).

- Integrated Drive Electronics (IDE)—This drive interface is an outgrowth of the ST-506 interface and is designed to replace a dedicated (that is, smart) disk controller with a host (that is, dumb) adapter and a smart disk drive. In this particular scheme, the disk controller is just an interface between the host computer and the smart peripheral. You can add disk drives, tape drives, or even CD-ROM drives to a host adapter. The current limitation includes a maximum of four IDE peripherals in a single system. It accomplishes this by utilizing both the primary and secondary I/O addresses defined for ST-506 hard disk controllers (370-37F and 170-17F), and in some cases it actually provides separate interrupts for each I/O channel. The good news about IDE disk drives is that they are very inexpensive and can offer acceptable performance for a workstation computer. The bad news is that they are not fast enough for a server. The really bad news is that most IDE disk controllers are Programmed I/O (PIO) devices, which means that the host processor (on your motherboard) must transfer the data between the adapter and the system memory. This decreases the efficiency of your server and should be avoided if at all possible.

- Enhanced Integrated Drive Electronics (EIDE)—This is an extension of the current IDE standard and is designed to increase the data transfer rates. It does this by reading multiple sectors of the disk whenever a data access request is specified, as well as supporting various data transfer methods (from PIO to DMA). It also increases the maximum size of a disk drive from 512MB to 8GB, but you are still limited to a maximum of four IDE peripherals in a single system.

- Small Computer Systems Interface (SCSI)—SCSI is my recommendation for a primary disk subsystem, although you can mix and match a SCSI system with any other subsystem mentioned earlier and use it as a secondary disk subsystem. SCSI is another expansion bus, not just a disk I/O bus like IDE. However, like IDE drives, the electronics for controlling the drive and accessing the data are located on the disk drive. You can add SCSI tape drives, SCSI scanners, SCSI printers, and any other SCSI devices to your SCSI host adapter. The standard SCSI interface offers a single disk channel, which can add up to seven SCSI peripherals, while enhanced versions offer the capability to add up to 15 SCSI peripherals on two separate channels (seven on one channel and eight on the other; the remaining SCSI ID on the first channel is used by the host adapter). Most SCSI adapters are also bus masters, which can increase performance quite a bit. Other factors include the capability to attach and detach the SCSI peripheral from the SCSI bus, so that another SCSI peripheral can access the bus while the first is processing a data request, queue multiple disk commands for later processing, and replace bad sectors with spare sectors on command.

4

CHOOSING A
PLATFORM

NOTE

SCSI currently comes in several versions. There is the original SCSI I, which you should avoid when purchasing SCSI peripherals; SCSI II, which is the most used; SCSI III, which is on its way to becoming the new standard; FAST SCSI; and WIDE SCSI. FAST SCSI extends the data transfer rate from 10MB/sec to 20MB/sec, while WIDE SCSI extends the I/O interface from 8 bits to 16 bits. In some cases you can even find a combination of FAST WIDE SCSI (some call this ULTRA WIDE SCSI), which extends the data transfer rate from 40 to 60MB/sec. These types of SCSI adapters obtain their data transfer rates by combining multiple SCSI channels, where each channel can transfer data at 20MB/sec. To obtain the maximum transfer rate, you would need to place a SCSI drive on each channel and then stripe the disks to make a single large logical drive.

TIP

When adding a CD-ROM to Windows NT, always try to choose a SCSI II CD-ROM drive. These types of CD-ROM drives are the easiest to add to an NT system.

Table 4.2. Summary of disk subsystem characteristics.

Type	Data Transfer Rate (MB/sec)	Maximum Number of Peripherals
MFM	2–4	2
RLL	2–4	2
ERRL	2–4	2
ESDI	20	2
IDE	3.3–8.3	2
EIDE	13.5–16.6	4
SCSI I	5	7
SCSI II	10	7
SCSI III	20	15
FAST SCSI	20	15
WIDE SCSI	20	15
FAST WIDE SCSI	40	15
ULTRA WIDE SCSI	60	30

Easy Performance Gains

Increasing the general performance of your Windows NT Server can be accomplished, for the most part, by applying some basic techniques that balance the load of your disk subsystem to increase the I/O performance. You'll concentrate on using SCSI subsystems (because they provides the most benefit), but you could use other disk subsystems, such as IDE or EIDE, as well.

Let's look at this in a couple of steps. First, there is the single disk subsystem, where there is only one disk controller with multiple disk drives. Second, there is the multiple disk subsystem, where you have at least two disk controllers with one or more disk drives per controller. Finally, there is the ultimate disk subsystem where you have multiple disk subsystems with multiple disk drives per disk controller.

The Single Disk Subsystem

The single disk subsystem installation has limited performance-gain options. But that's not to say that there is nothing you can do; it just means that the options for increasing your server's performance are based on the number of physical disk drives you have installed on your system and on how much work you are willing to put in to obtain the maximum benefit. Let's begin with the minimum performance gain option, because it is also the easiest to perform.

This discussion starts with the assumption that you have one disk controller with two disk drives. Each disk drive is 500MB in size and can be an IDE, an EIDE, or a SCSI. Each drive has a single primary partition of 500MB. In this particular case, you have installed Windows NT Server to your C: drive in the WINNT directory (the installation default). This directory is called your SystemRoot. In fact, you have a special environment variable called SystemRoot that equates to the installation directory. For instance, in this example the SystemRoot environment variable is C:\WINNT. Because this drive is where all the system files and paging files are located and where all the print jobs are spooled, it is a heavily used disk drive.

To help balance the load, you can do two things. First, install another paging file on the second disk (drive D:). This solution will enable Windows NT to use both paging files—the one on drive C: and the one on drive D:—when it needs to use virtual memory. If one disk is in use, the other disk can be used to access its paging file to fulfill the virtual memory request. Second, you can place all your BackOffice and support files on the second disk drive. You can even go so far as to split up your user sharepoints (or shared directories) between both drives so that the load is balanced equally. This method will give you relatively good performance with minimum complexity.

4

CHOOSING A
PLATFORM

> **NOTE**
>
> Windows NT Server makes heavy use of its paging file, and the most significant performance gain can be realized by placing your primary paging file on a striped set. The only alternative to paging to disk is to have enough physical memory installed on your system to avoid paging at all. If you have the funds available, a 256MB Windows NT Server can be an outstanding server. Adding processors can increase its capabilities even more as an application server. An application server is a server designed for the client/server environment (such as SQL Server) and not a file server that shares applications (such as Microsoft Office). An application server can make an ideal platform for dynamic WWW sites.

The alternate method of using two disk drives on a single disk controller to gain additional performance requires that you partition your hard disk drives into four equal sizes of 250MB each. You can do this before you install Windows NT Server, or you can partition it as part of the install process, which is the simplest method. If you have already installed Windows NT Server, you can back up your current NT Server installation and repartition, reformat, and reinstall NT and then restore your backed-up version, which is the toughest method. The idea here is to use two partitions (one on each physical disk) and create a striped set of 500MB. You could alternatively create four partitions with two 150MB-partitions and two-350MB partitions to create a 700MB striped set. A *striped set* is the creation of a single logical drive from two or more physical drives. The partitions on the separate physical drives are merged into a single drive by dividing the partitions into discrete blocks (usually 512 bytes per block). These blocks are then combined into a stripe. Multiple stripes are then combined to create the single logical drive. For more detailed information on striped sets and striped sets with parity, you may want to pick up a copy of my other book called *Microsoft Administrator's Survival Guide* by Sams Publishing.

> **NOTE**
>
> I would not recommend less than 150MB—and even that is cutting it close—for the system partition, because the free space available will dwindle as you install additional software. When this partition is filled, you will be required to back up, repartition, reformat, reinstall, and then restore your previous NT installation, which is a lengthy and tedious process, to say the least.

Of course, you cannot create the striped set until you have installed Windows NT, so your first task is to install NT to your first primary partition (drive C:). Once you have installed NT and created the second primary partition (drive D:), you may proceed to create the striped set (drive E:) with the Disk Administrator. Now you can follow a similar process, as mentioned earlier, to install your BackOffice software, and then create your paging files and user directories. In this case, however, you should create small paging files for your C: and D: drives (something in the 10MB to 30MB range) with your largest paging on your E: drive (possibly in the 100MB to 250MB range, depending on your server load). Place the user directories on your D: drive and all other software on the E: drive (the striped set). This will give a moderate increase in system performance and an increased I/O capacity for your shared network files.

CAUTION

Because you are using a striped set without parity, there is no fault tolerance. Your only means of ensuring data integrity is your system backups. So be sure to schedule daily backups. And remember, in order to back up open data files (user files or SQL Server database devices), you must close them first. This can be accomplished by forcing all users off the system (do it gracefully by pausing the service, broadcasting a message to the users of your intentions, and then stopping the Server service) and shutting down SQL Server prior to running your backup.

The Multiple Disk Subsystem

This scenario builds on the previous performance optimizations by assuming that the computer shipped with two disk controllers: one EIDE disk controller and single disk drive and that you have an optional SCSI disk controller with at least two (preferably three to five) SCSI disk drives. In this case, let's install Windows NT Server to the EIDE drive (drive C:) and devote this drive completely to Windows NT and the BackOffice system files. The SCSI subsystem will be used to create a striped set, or if we have enough disk drives (at least three), a striped set with parity.

TIP

When creating a striped set or striped set with parity, the more drives you add, the better performance you will achieve. This is because a striped set stripes the data to the disk drives in a sequential fashion. For instance, if you have three disk drives in a striped set, in theory you can read or write three times as much data. In actuality, the performance is not quite that scalable, but still is significant. A striped set with parity on a three-drive system will achieve only two reads/writes for the same logical drive because a complete stripe includes two data blocks with one error correction code (ECC) block. It is even more important for a striped set with parity to use more than three drives to obtain equal performance with a regular striped set.

Once the striped set (or striped set with parity) has been created (drive D:), you can install the BackOffice system files. These files should be installed on drive C: with all the data files (SQL Server devices, databases, and so on) installed to drive D: (the striped set). All the additional user data files and shared applications also should be installed to drive D: to take advantage of the increase in the I/O subsystem. This gives a significant increase in overall system performance and a noticeable improvement in I/O capacity for your shared network files and SQL Server databases.

The Ultimate Disk Subsystem

To obtain the ultimate in I/O performance without using a hardware RAID solution, you can use multiple disk controllers with multiple disk drives. In this example, let's assume there are three disk controllers: one EIDE disk controller with one disk drive (drive C:) and two SCSI disk controllers. One SCSI controller, SCSI I, will have two disk drives (although more is better), while the other SCSI controller, SCSI II, will have three or more disk drives. The single EIDE drive once again will become the SystemRoot partition, where Windows NT Server and all the BackOffice system files will be installed, along with a small system paging file.

The SCSI I disk controller and disk drives will be used to create a striped set, where the system paging file and alternatively the printer spool files will be installed as well. In this case, use of a striped set will increase system throughput without causing worry about data integrity because print jobs can be resubmitted should an error occur. If an error occurs on this striped set, the small paging file you created on the SystemRoot partition will be used to keep the system up and running.

All your user data files, shared applications, and SQL Server devices and databases will be installed on the striped set with parity, which you will create on the SCSI II disk controller. This installation provides an additional level of fault tolerance for your data files and increased I/O performance to give you the best overall system performance and I/O capacity for your server.

> **TIP**
>
> If you use any of the earlier scenarios with multiple disk controllers in a multiprocessor platform, your performance will increase even more. This is because of the Windows NT symmetric processing model, where any processor can service interrupts and can thereby achieve an additional level of I/O concurrency over a uniprocessor platform.

> **TIP**
>
> In order to really get SQL Server to benefit from the increased I/O capabilities of your striped set with parity, you will need to make a few SQL Server configuration changes. Specifically, you will need to increase the max async I/O from its default of 32. The number will vary based on the number of disk drives and controllers you have available for the SQL Server installation.

Hardware Upgrades

The first rule in maximizing your Windows NT Server performance is to add system memory. The next rule to consider is a hardware RAID configuration to increase your I/O capacity. Then think about adding network adapters and load balancing your system. If your system is very CPU intensive (for example, running SQL Server, Systems Management Server, SNA Server, and Microsoft Mail on the same server), you may want to look at adding processors if your system is capable of being upgraded in this fashion. The following section looks at each of these options and explains some of the benefits each has to offer.

System Memory Upgrades

Memory upgrades can be divided into two types: secondary processor cache upgrades and main system memory upgrades. Your secondary (level 2) cache is used to hold a copy of main system memory that is frequently accessed, pre-read and hold sequential data requests from main memory, or buffer data writes to main memory. All these offer increased memory access times because cache memory operates in the 15-to-20–nanosecond range, while system memory operates in the 60-to-100–nanosecond range. Caches are used because the processor speed has exceeded the speed at which the main memory can be accessed. System memory is based on dynamic random access memory (DRAM) chips, which require a refresh cycle before they can be accessed again. This doubles or even triples, depending on the system architecture and wait cycles, the time between concurrent memory access rates. Secondary cache chips, on the other hand, are based on static random access memory (SRAM) chips, which do not require a refresh between concurrent data access cycles. My recommendation is to increase the size of your secondary processor cache based on the size of your system memory. Use a minimum of 256KB for a 16MB system, a 512KB cache for systems up to 64MB, and at least 1MB of cache for anything larger than 64MB, if possible. Not all systems have upgradable secondary caches.

> **TIP**
>
> Many Intel computers offer an advanced BIOS setup option to configure the secondary cache and main system memory refresh times and wait states. If you can, set your secondary cache to offer write-back functionality, which will buffer writes to system memory, to increase system performance. If data integrity is an issue, set your secondary cache settings to write-thru, which will pass all data writes directly to main memory and cache only memory read requests. If you decrease your refresh times and wait states, you also may increase system performance. Be careful about changing memory refresh rates and wait states, however, because not all memory chips are created equal and they may not be able to function reliably at faster speeds. If you start to see nonmaskable interrupts, which equate to an F002 blue screen error code under Windows NT, you have gone too far.

Upgrading your system memory offers three benefits. It cuts down the requests to page memory to disk, thereby increasing overall performance (memory access is in the nanosecond range, while disk access is in the millisecond range). The additional memory can be used by the Cache Manager to cache both local and network I/O requests, thereby increasing both local disk and remote disk data-access requests. Finally, you can increase the performance of your SQL Server by either preallocating a larger amount of system memory for SQL Server's use, creating the tempdb in RAM, or using both of these options. The tempdb is a temporary database used to process temporary tables created by SQL Server to help you answer a query or to sort your tables.

Windows NT can perform as well as, if not better than, most caching disk controllers with the addition of an equal amount of RAM. For instance, if you compare a caching controller with 16MB of RAM and Windows NT Server with an additional 16MB of RAM, you will find that the performance is about the same. This is because the caching controller is limited by the expansion bus to transfer the requested data, while the Cache Manager utilizes system memory and therefore accesses cached data based on the memory bus speed. If the caching controller has only 4MB of RAM, even the base installation of Windows NT (that is, 16MB of RAM and no caching disk controller) performs as well as, if not better than, the same system with a caching disk controller. Also consider that Windows NT supports very few caching disk controllers. These types of controllers require specific device-driver support in order to use the cache on the disk controller. Most device drivers for caching disk controllers just turn off the cache when used with Windows NT.

> **TIP**
>
> If you have an EISA-based computer, make sure the EISA memory setting, which is based on the EISA setup utility disk application, correctly identifies the amount of physical memory you have installed in your system. If it does not, Windows NT will use the ISA setting (what the computer finds based on the BIOS setting), which may limit the amount of memory that Windows NT will use.

Hardware RAID Alternatives

If you have the budget when selecting a disk subsystem, nothing performs better than a hardware RAID system. A hardware RAID solution generally has an internal battery backed-up memory buffer, in case a power failure occurs during a disk write. This feature adds fault tolerance over a software-based RAID solution. It also has its own processor so that the overhead involved in calculating the ECC stripe is performed by the disk controller rather than by the host processor.

> **NOTE**
>
> Although several RAID levels are currently in use with Windows NT Server, I'll discuss the use of a RAID 5 solution only, which includes RAID 0 (data striping), RAID 1 (disk mirroring), and RAID 5 (striping with parity). RAID levels 2, 3, and 4 are generally used by higher-end mainframes rather than with Windows NT. Each of these is just a slightly different variation of a striped set with parity.

Additional benefits of a hardware RAID solution include the capability to mirror these RAID drives either by using software with Windows NT or by striping multiple RAID drives because NT sees these RAID drives as a single logical drive. If you stripe a hardware RAID device, there is no need to use a stripe set with parity because this already is being performed at the hardware level. Another advantage of the hardware-based RAID solution is that most of them support hot swapping of a failed disk drive. *Hot swapping* is the capability to change a failed disk drive for a new working drive without powering off the entire computer system. After the drive is replaced, the RAID controller begins to rebuild the missing data stripes based on the available data stripes and ECC stripe in the background. Replacing a software-based RAID solution requires powering off the system to replace the drive. Then, once powered back up, you will need to use the Disk Administrator to regenerate the missing data.

> **TIP**
>
> When selecting your disk drives for a RAID solution, either hardware or software based, it is better to choose several small disk drives rather than a few large disk drives to build an equivalent logical drive. For example, suppose you want approximately a 5GB logical drive. You could select either six 1GB disk drives or three 2GB drives for a maximum logical drive of 4.8GB (RAID drives utilize one-fifth of the storage for the ECC stripe). Either solution gives the same logical drive size, but the unit based on the six 1GB drives generally outperforms the unit based on three 2GB drives.

Adding Network Adapters

Even if you have an optimized disk subsystem, multiple processors, and an abundance of physical RAM, your network server will not perform well if it has either a slow network adapter or too many network requests to handle. If you have only one network adapter installed on your server, it better be a 100MB FDDI or Fast Ethernet adapter if you want to get the data out to your network clients as quickly as possible. You may even want to use more than one adapter for a couple reasons.

4

CHOOSING A
PLATFORM

> **NOTE**
>
> Although I mentioned 100MB network adapters earlier, that does not mean you must use them to obtain increased performance. The same benefits can be achieved from techniques you'll learn about later for 10MB network adapters.

First, consider the network transports you will be using. If they are all bound to one network adapter, that adapter will be constantly changing modes to send out a broadcast name to find an associated resource when a network request is received. For example, assume you are looking for a NetWare-based SQL Server database that uses the IPX/SPX transport. In order to find this database, your server probably will send out name requests over the NetBEUI, TCP/IP, and IPX/SPX transport protocols (assuming that this is the default binding order you established) and all through the same adapter. After the SQL Server that contains the database has been found, all further requests will be routed just through the IPX/SPX protocol. The time it takes to switch modes and send out and process these name requests is wasted. This decreases the capability of your server to process additional requests over that same adapter, thereby decreasing overall network throughput.

To increase your network throughput, change your default binding order to use the most-requested network transport. For example, let's assume you are using one adapter with multiple network transports (NetBEUI, TCP/IP, and IPX/SPX). Let's further assume that you have an integrated network with Windows NT Server, UNIX, LAN Manager, and Novell servers, along with Windows NT, Windows for Workgroups, and Novell clients. Approximately 75 percent of these clients use TCP/IP, 15 percent use IPX/SPX, and the remaining 10 percent use NetBEUI as their primary transport. In this case, you can achieve the best client support by changing the binding order for the Server service to TCP/IP, IPX/SPX, and then to NetBEUI.

> **NOTE**
>
> The Server service is used by clients that access your server. This service provides the means to share your network resources. The Workstation service is used by your server to access other servers' shared resources (when the computer is a client, rather than a server).

You modify the binding order through the Control Panel Network applet, as shown in Figure 4.1. After you have selected the Bindings tab, the properties sheet shown in Figure 4.2 will be displayed. To change the binding order for the Server service, follow these steps:

1. Expand the Server entry in the listbox. When you do, the network bindings for the service will be displayed. The properties sheet should look similar to what is displayed in Figure 4.3.

CHAPTER 4

87

FIGURE 4.1.
The Network dialog box.

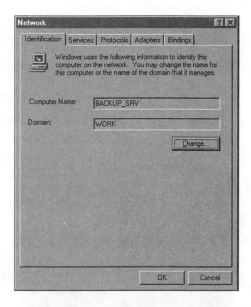

FIGURE 4.2.
The Bindings properties sheet.

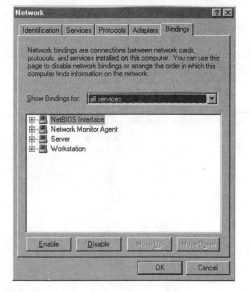

4

CHOOSING A
PLATFORM

2. Notice that the uppermost binding is NWLink IPX/SPX Compatible Transport, because this is Microsoft's default binding order. At this point you want to select the WINS Client (TCP/IP) and then click on the upper arrow to move this protocol to the top, as shown in Figure 4.4. This will change the default binding order to TCP/IP, NWLink IPX/SPX Compatible Transport, NWLink NetBIOS, and then NetBEUI Protocol for the Server service.

FIGURE 4.3.

The Server service bindings for the Bindings properties sheet.

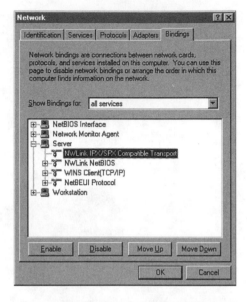

FIGURE 4.4.

The modified Server service bindings for the Bindings properties sheet.

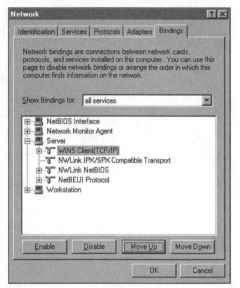

NOTE

If you are not using DHCP and WINS on your Windows NT Server, your binding listing may display TCP/IP instead of WINS Client (TCP/IP).

3. Repeat the earlier steps for the Workstation, NetBIOS Interface, and Remote Access Server service to change their binding order as well.

As an additional performance option, you can use multiple network adapters with each adapter being bound to a single network transport. You follow a procedure similar to the one outlined earlier, but instead of changing the binding order, you can just disable the bindings for the transports you do not want supported on the particular network adapter. Just follow these steps:

1. Select the appropriate protocol, and then expand the item to display the binding for the protocol. In the example shown in Figure 4.5, I have selected the TCP/IP protocol.

FIGURE 4.5.

The WINS (TCP/IP) protocol bindings for the Bindings properties sheet.

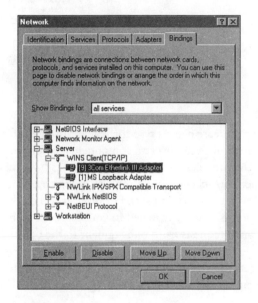

2. Select the network adapter for the appropriate transport protocol.
3. Click the Disable button. Figure 4.6 shows the disabled network transport protocol. Notice that next to the adapter is a little icon of a circle with a diagonal line through it indicating that the binding has been disabled.

> **NOTE**
>
> In this example I have selected the Etherlink III adapter. Because this is my only physical network adapter, if I disable it I will be able to share resources only with the TCP/IP protocol for remote access clients. The Remote Access WAN Wrapper is a wrapper around a logical network adapter (that is, the modem).

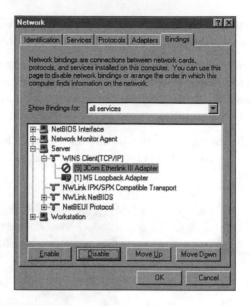

FIGURE 4.6.

The disabled WINS (TCP/IP) protocol bindings for the Etherlink III network adapter in the Bindings properties sheet.

If you want to increase network performance, you may want to use multiple network adapters to split your network into discrete components, commonly referred to as *segments*. This technique limits the impact that these network clients have on each other for accessing resources. Only if the network-client request requires access to a resource outside its default segment will it impact other network client users. However, if you do this on a TCP/IP-based network, each network adapter physically installed in your server must have its own IP address, and in order to route network requests from one segment to the other, you must check the Enable IP Forwarding check box in the Routing properties sheet of the Microsoft TCP/IP Properties dialog box. You access this dialog box by selecting TCP/IP Protocol in the Protocols tab of the Network dialog and then clicking the Routing tab of the TCP/IP Properties dialog box.

Another reason to look into using multiple network adapters and modifying the network bindings is for security. Perhaps you want to use IIS to implement a WWW site, but you want to restrict access to your internal network. You could create a new subnet, which would contain all your servers that are physically connected to the Internet. Your servers (WWW, FTP, Gopher, SQL Server, and so on) would be included on one side of a router and your network on the other. If your router filters all incoming traffic (from your subnet on the Internet), you can prevent a potential breach of security. If you are implementing IIS within your network instead of on another subnet, you can disable certain bindings (such as the NetBIOS Interface for the TCP/IP protocol) to limit access to your network from authorized clients. TCP/IP security issues are discussed in more detail in Chapter 10, "Advanced Security Issues."

Adding Processors

Windows NT Server is more processor intensive than other network operating systems, such as Novell NetWare or UNIX, on identical hardware platforms. So, in most cases, adding a processor to a uniprocessor platform can make a significant difference in network throughput or an application server's performance (such as SQL Server). However, this performance increase is not quite twofold for a dual-processor system. As you increase the number of processors, this performance ratio decreases. As it stands now, four processors give the greatest multiprocessor benefit on standard Intel (Pentium) platforms. This is because most motherboard manufacturers use the Intel multiprocessor support chipset, which supports only four processors. Beyond that, it depends on the proprietary design of the system motherboard.

The problem with multiple processors is that the Windows NT design model requires all processors to have equal access to all system resources. That is what the symmetric multiprocessing model defines. The symmetric multiprocessing model means that the overhead involved in synchronizing access to hardware resources (such as an I/O port on a SCSI controller) increases as you add processors. Even problems with cache management will cause grief because each processor generally has its own secondary cache, and as a thread is moved from one processor to another, the cache must be flushed in order to ensure the integrity of system memory. All these little problems begin to build, until adding processors no longer increases performance or, at best, increases it only a small fraction.

TIP

One of the interesting keys I've found in the registry is the key that specifies how many processors will be supported on a particular multiprocessor Hardware Abstraction Layer (HAL). If you look in

`HKEY_LOCAL_MACHINE\SYSTEM\CurrentControlSet\Control\SessionManager`

you will find the value *RegisteredProcessors*. This entry normally has a maximum setting of four processors for Windows NT Server or two for Windows NT Workstation. However, you can increase this value to support additional processors if your HAL can support them and thereby increase performance on some platforms. The performance increase is based on the architecture of the particular platform. Some platforms will perform better than others, even if they have the same number of processors.

Choosing the Right Server Model

When you install Windows NT Server, you are given a choice between a domain controller or a server, but not both. In this case, a server means that Windows NT is operating in *server mode* and therefore does not participate in *domain authentication*. Therfore, the server does not include a copy of the domain account database; instead it must refer all authentication requests to a domain controller. A domain controller can be either a primary or a backup controller. Only one primary domain controller (PDC), which contains the master copy of the domain account database, is available, but you may have multiple backup domain controllers (BDCs). The master copy of the domain database is periodically replicated from the PDC to each BDC. A PDC or BDC will use resources (processor, memory, storage, or network) to update the account database or to respond to client authentication requests. Because server mode does not provide these services, the resources can be devoted to other tasks (such as the WWW Publishing Service) to improve performance.

The idea is to allocate as many resources as possible to improve IIS performance by choosing server mode. Other aspects of this choice may not have been previously considered. A server loses all domainwide administration tools (such as User Manager for Domains and Server Manager) but keeps the rest of NT Server's capabilities (such as fault-tolerant partitions and no user-connection limit). Two important security considerations are associated with server mode:

- The tools to manage your network, like User Manager for Domains, are not physically available on the server.
- No physical copy of the domain database is available on the server. A local account database is the only one available.

Both of these aspects can aid you in preventing unauthorized access to your server or network from users that connect to your server over the Internet. This factor should be a real concern because by connecting to the Internet, you are in essence connecting your network to probably the largest WAN in the world. There is no telling what is out there that might do you harm, but by taking some precautions you can limit the potential intrusions.

The Software Configuration

You can tune specific components in Windows NT Server in a couple ways, such as by using Control Panel interfaces and the registry. A few of the Control Panel interfaces and what they will do for you are mentioned here, but the registry topics are in Appendix C, "The Registry Editor and Registry Keys." For now, let's consider the Control Panel applets. The System Properties dialog box includes the Performance properties sheet, as shown in Figure 4.7, which has two interfaces for modifying your system and directly affecting your performance.

The first option is the Application slider, as shown in Figure 4.7. This slider sets the runtime percentage of all applications running on your system. The default is to use Maximum setting, but it is a poor choice for a server. This setting steals processor cycles from your background processes (such as your Server service) to provide the best performance for the application you are currently using. This makes the application you are using perform well, but all other processes suffer. It is, however, an excellent choice for Windows NT Workstation because the goal is to provide optimum user interaction. I recommend that you use the middle setting if you plan to use this server interactively (maybe to create user accounts, add computer accounts, or other administrative duties). The middle setting will provide adequate response time but steal fewer processor cycles from the background applications. For optimum IIS performance, you should use the None setting, which gives every process the same priority and distributes the processor time equally among them. This setting generally makes the server a very poor interactive partner because applications take a while to refresh the screen, and any network activity can bring your interactive usage to a crawl. However, this is not a major problem because you can perform all administrative duties from your desktop if you install the client-based administrative tools.

Figure 4.7.

The Control Panel System Properties dialog box Performance properties sheet.

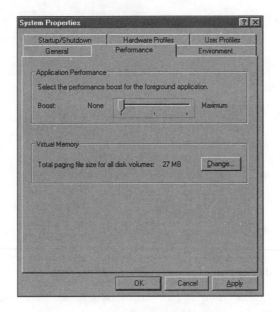

The second option is the Virtual Memory Change button, which will display the Virtual Memory dialog, as shown in Figure 4.8. In this dialog you can create your paging files on a per drive basis. You also can set the minimum and maximum sizes for your paging files. At a minimum, your paging files should total your physical memory plus 12MB, and your maximum should be approximately four times your physical memory size for optimum performance, although you can increase this value if needed (particularly if you do a lot of interactive work).

Changing the Server service properties in the Control Panel Network applet is the other commonly missed performance modification. The way to display this dialog is fairly simple, but it is hidden from casual modification. To get to it, run the Network applet, select the Service tab, and scroll down the Network Services list until the Server entry is visible. Then just double-click it, and the dialog box shown in Figure 4.9 is displayed.

FIGURE 4.8.

The Virtual Memory dialog box.

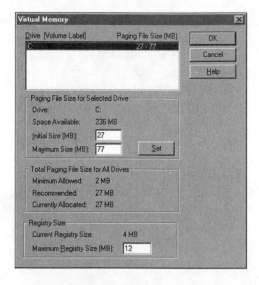

FIGURE 4.9.

The Server dialog box.

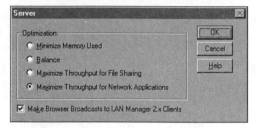

The Server dialog box has four optimization settings:

■ Minimize Memory Used—This setting is best for servers with 10 or fewer clients connected to them, which is a very small network. In most cases, you can just use Windows NT Workstation as your server.

■ Balance—This setting preallocates enough buffers for a maximum of 64 simultaneous network client connections. This setting is the default for networks that support only NetBEUI as their transport protocol.

■ Maximize Throughput for File Sharing —This setting is best used for any network with more than 64 simultaneous network client connections. It not only preallocates buffers but also provides the capability to allocate additional buffers on an as-needed basis. It is the best setting to maximize your network clients' ability to share network resources such as directories, files, and printers.

■ Maximize Throughput for Network Applications —This setting also is suggested for large networks with more than 64 simultaneous clients. However, this case has a trade-off. Rather than maximizing performance for resource sharing, as mentioned earlier, the performance optimization is for RPC buffers, which will increase the performance of an application server (like SQL Server and the Internet Information Server).

TIP

If you have installed multiple network providers, such as the Gateway Service for NetWare, you also may want to step through the Network Provider Search Order dialog accessed via the Networks button, shown in Figure 4.1, so that you can change the default search order to place the network you use most frequently at the top.

Summary

This chapter looks at some of the basic performance tuning issues and trade-offs. Tuning your server consists of several options. One of these options is to pick the right hardware platform and expansion bus to maximize performance of your peripherals. Another option is to optimize your disk subsystem to provide the maximum benefit for virtual memory usage and file sharing. Choosing the correct server model to build a better application server, and configuring your application-tasking options and the Server service to optimize processor time-slicing (the time each process can use before the next process will be scheduled for execution) and server response time are two other options. You can also upgrade your hardware by increasing the amount of physical memory or by adding a hardware-based RAID solution, balance the load of your network subsystem by adding network adapters, or increase processing performance by adding additional processors. The next chapter looks at some of the specific issues involved in preparing your Windows NT Server platform for a successful IIS installation.

Internet Information Server Preparation and Installation

IN THIS CHAPTER

- Determining Where to Install the Internet Information Server *98*

- IIS Preinstallation Requirements *100*

- The Remote Access Service *113*

- Installing the Internet Information Server *123*

CHAPTER 5

Few Windows NT components can stand alone. They generally rely on one or more subcomponents to function properly. The Internet Information Server (IIS) is no different. It, too, requires additional components in order to function properly. While it is possible to install IIS blindly (that is, without consideration of the consequences), you may wind up with a product that does not perform to your expectations or has a possible security breach. In either case, the consequences could be quite severe. A competitor could gain access to proprietary data through your Internet connection, in which case you could lose your job.

> **WARNING**
>
> Internet security is a topic of such importance that I devote an entire chapter to it. Before you install the IIS, I suggest you read Chapter 10, "Advanced Security Issues," to see what you can do about possible security issues that may affect you.

Although Internet security is not the main focus of this chapter, performance considerations certainly are. The performance of IIS is affected by where you plan to install IIS and the associated data you plan to publish with it. This chapter begins with a discussion of where to install IIS and then examines the preinstallation requirements, which can be fairly extensive. I walk you through the mechanics of installing the various components and describe why you may want to use each one. Once you determine which components to use, you can install the IIS and start publishing data for your customers to see, hear, and interact with on the Internet.

Determining Where to Install the Internet Information Server

When planning your installation, you should first consider where to install the IIS and its related components. Do you have a limited budget? Or do you have sufficient funds to carefully plan your installation to obtain maximum performance? Will you place all your data on a single server? Will you use an external database for dynamic publishing? Will you connect to your server to update the data using your local area network (LAN)? Or will you use a dial-up connection? You need to consider all these items because they will make a difference in how and where you will install IIS.

IIS on a Limited Budget

If you are on a limited budget, you may not have many choices. You may have to install everything on a single server. Most publishers with a limited budget have a low-speed Internet connection that includes either a single Basic Rate ISDN interface (BRI) or modem connection. In this case you should consider publishing only static data. If your server is fast enough (a 75MHz or higher Pentium), you may want to consider using an Access database if you plan to provide dynamic publishing capabilities.

With this configuration, you could use the Windows NT Server *Remote Access Service* (RAS) to provide your dial-up Internet connection. You could also use RAS for dial-in clients, and you could create a publishing site without ever connecting to the Internet. You do not have to connect to the Internet to publish data. You only need an Internet connection if you want to reach millions of Internet users. If you are providing local support, however, a non-Internet publishing service may be just what you need. You may be providing local technical support, for example, to your customers. These users could dial up your server for information, software upgrades, and so on and use familiar Internet tools (like the Internet Explorer) to access these services. In most cases, this approach would be less expensive and easier to maintain than a dedicated bulletin board system (BBS). As your client list grows, you could migrate to the Internet, which would certainly be easier than converting a proprietary BBS and all your data.

If you do go this route, you should consider using Windows NT Server, operating in server mode, instead of a domain controller. Windows NT Server provides a more efficient use of local resources without the overhead that a domain controller requires. The only time I would consider recommending a domain controller, instead of a server, is if you also need to migrate a user account list (for your dial-in clients, for example) because any time you upgrade a server to a domain controller, you will lose your account database. You are better off taking the performance hit now, rather than having to reenter each user account, password, and home directory and to reconfigure any file or directory permissions later.

IIS on an Unlimited Budget

An unlimited budget is unrealistic. However, it is quite possible that your budget is sufficient to build a high-performance publishing site. This can include using frame relay, T1, T2, T3, Switched Multimegabit Data Service (SMDS), or Asynchronous Transfer Mode (ATM) as your pipeline to the Internet. Your Internet connection is the main consideration in creating a high-performance publishing site because it doesn't matter how fast your servers are if they cannot quickly pump your data over your Internet connection. If you are a high-performance publishing site, the budget for your hardware should be proportionally higher as well. In most cases, your yearly Internet connection fees will far outweigh your hardware purchases.

You should plan on having multiple Windows NT Server installations. You can use one or more domain controllers with one or more installations operating in server mode (which are referred to as *servers* for the rest of this chapter). You should use these servers as your IIS and SQL Server platforms because they provide the best all-around performance. All your installations should be connected to each other via a 100Mbps network segment for optimum network throughput and the fastest possible publishing site.

Choosing a Location for Your Data

You should carefully consider where you will place the data you plan to publish with one or more servers. You really have two possibilities: You can place the data all on one drive, or you can split it among multiple drives. If you have a choice, use multiple drives. For best performance, consider using a striped set or striped set with parity. Both of these configurations will increase your drive's ability to access your data, which in turn will decrease your client's access times. If you have sufficient funds, consider a hardware RAID alternative, as it will increase your throughput even more.

You should also consider dividing your data based on the service and potential number of clients. If you will be providing a World Wide Web (WWW) and File Transfer Protocol (FTP) site that hundreds or thousands of users will access and a Gopher site that fewer than a hundred clients will access, then devote your resources appropriately. Put your WWW and FTP data on your fastest drive and your Gopher data on your slowest drive. Your drives should also be NTFS, rather than FAT, partitions. An NTFS partition wastes less space resulting from inefficient cluster sizes. Large FAT partitions, for example, use a large cluster size (up to 64KB). A FAT partition is also limited to a maximum of 4GB. An NTFS partition can be as large as 4TB; NTFS provides a faster access time and increases security.

IIS Preinstallation Requirements

Because the IIS is based on providing Internet-related services, which in turn relies on the TCP/IP protocol as the network transport, you should first install the TCP/IP protocol. Installing TCP/IP will also install the various TCP/IP utilities (such as `arp`, `finger`, `hostname`, `ipconfig`, `nbtstat`, `netstat`, `ping`, `rcp`, `rexec`, `route`, `rsh`, `telnet`, `tftp`, and `tracert`). You should *not* install the FTP service, however, as this will conflict with the IIS FTP Publishing service.

If you will be using the IIS as the basis for providing full-time Internet connectivity to your network clients, you may want to install a few additional services. Specifically, you want to include the following:

- Dynamic Host Configuration Protocol (DHCP)—This service provides dynamic IP address allocations to your network clients, rather than statically configuring each client IP address. DHCP can make life much easier for the network administrator. The network clients can be members of your LAN or even dial-in clients.

- Windows Internet Name Service (WINS)—This service provides NetBIOS name resolutions. Rather than locate a computer service by its IP address, you can locate it by the computer name. The WINS service provides this option by maintaining a database of computer names and their corresponding IP addresses.

- Domain Name Service (DNS)—This service also provides NetBIOS name resolution. Rather than being dynamic, like WINS, it utilizes a static list of computer names to IP addresses. The list is maintained in various configuration files, and it requires some additional work, as compared to WINS. However, DNS has the following advantages:

  First, you may need to have one or more DNS servers to fulfill your requirement with the InterNIC to maintain your own domain name. Second, e-mail name resolution is supported only via the use of an MX record type, which is not supported by WINS. If you expect to provide e-mail services (say with Microsoft Exchange Server, for example) for your network clients, you must use DNS and each client must have an MX record. Finally, DNS can be used with WINS to provide dynamic name resolution so that your clients that do not support WINS, which includes many non-Microsoft operating systems, can use DNS instead.

- Simple Network Management Protocol (SNMP)—If you have an SNMP-compatible monitor, such as Hewlett-Packard (HP) OpenView, you can use SNMP to monitor and configure many SNMP-capable hardware items, such as hubs and routers, and most Windows NT services.

- Remote Access Service (RAS)—This service provides dial-out and dial-in connectivity services. You can use RAS to create a simple gateway to the Internet. In this configuration, you connect one server to the Internet; each network client can access the Internet by routing its requests through that server. You can also create a more robust gateway by using RIP for Internet Protocol.

- RIP for Internet Protocol—This service can create a software router. Although not as efficient as a hardware router, RIP is included free with NT Server. You can use RIP to combine multiple network segments into a single logical segment. It dynamically creates routing tables and is preferred over the static routing tables that must be created with the route utility.

NOTE

Even with the RIP for Internet Protocol installed, you must have Internet-routable IP addresses in order to use Windows NT Server as a gateway to the Internet. You cannot assign a random block of IP addresses for your LAN clients to use and expect it to work. Most likely these addresses are already in use on the Internet, which means you will have an IP address conflict and the connection attempt will fail. In order to obtain routable IP addresses, you must request these addresses from either your Internet service provider (ISP) or the InterNIC.

- Simple TCP/IP Service—This service provides support for TCP/IP clients that support the TCP/IP services Character Generator, Daytime, Discard, Echo, and Quote of the Day.

- Microsoft TCP/IP Printing—This service provides printing capabilities to UNIX-based print queues or from UNIX-based clients. When this service is installed, you can use Print Manager to connect to a UNIX-based print queue or to share a printer (in essence, this is the line printer daemon (lpd) service for Windows NT) and have a UNIX-based client connect to the shared printer. It will also install the line printer remote (lpr) and line printer queue (lpq) utilities, which print to a host running the lpd or check the status of a print job on an lpd server.

> **NOTE**
>
> In order to install the above services, you must be a member of the administrator's group on the computer on which you want to install the service.

Installing the TCP/IP Protocol and Utilities

If you did not install all the TCP/IP utilities during your initial Windows NT Server installation, you can add them through the Control Panel Network applet. Follow these steps:

1. Click the Protocols tab in the Network dialog box, as shown in Figure 5.1.

FIGURE 5.1.

Installing a network protocol.

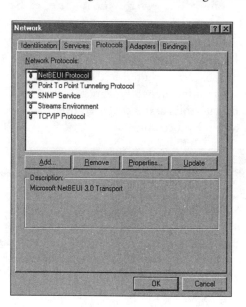

2. Click the Add button to display the Select Network Protocol dialog box, as shown in Figure 5.2.

3. Select TCP/IP Protocol from the Network Protocol list box and click the OK button. The TCP/IP Setup dialog will prompt you to use DHCP to allocate your IP address. If this computer has access to a DHCP server, choose the Yes button; otherwise, choose the No button. This discussion assumes that no DHCP server is available.

FIGURE 5.2.

Installing the TCP/IP protocol.

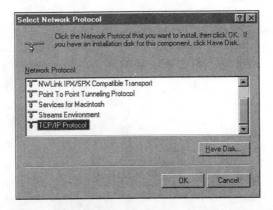

NOTE

Your computer cannot be both a DHCP server and a DHCP client; it must be one or the other. If the computer is a DHCP server, you must manually configure the TCP/IP protocol, as described in step 6.

4. Respond to the prompts in the Windows NT Setup dialog box for the location of your Windows NT source files. Enter the drive and directory and then click the Continue button.

   The source files for the TCP/IP protocol and utilities will be copied to your computer.

5. Do one of the following: Click the Close button in the Network dialog box if you have no additional services to install. Or choose the Services tab and install the additional services as described in the following sections. This option will display the Bindings Review and Configuration dialog box, which will perform an analysis of your network bindings.

6. Specify your IP address, subnet mask, and default gateway in the Microsoft TCP/IP Properties dialog box, as shown in Figure 5.3. If you have more than one adapter, such as a multi-homed system, enter the earlier information for each adapter. If you want to assign multiple IP addresses to your adapter or you have multiple gateways, click the Advanced button to display the Advanced IP Addressing dialog where you can enter the earlier information.

7. Choose the DNS tab, shown in Figure 5.4, and enter your hostname (the name of your computer), your Internet domain name, and the IP addresses of your DNS servers. If you have multiple Internet domains, enter your domain suffix search order.

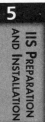

FIGURE 5.3.
Specifying your IP address.

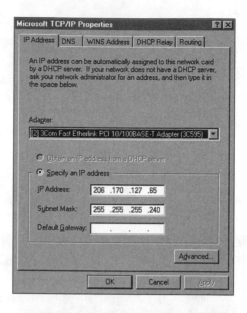

FIGURE 5.4.
Specifying the TCP/IP DNS configuration.

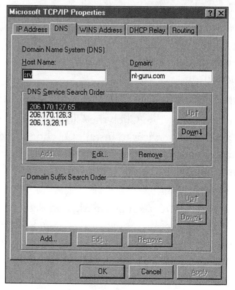

8. Choose the WINS Address tab, shown in Figure 5.5, where you may enter the following information:

FIGURE 5.5.

Specifying the TCP/IP WINS configuration.

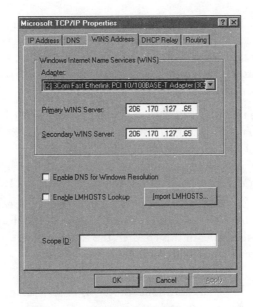

- Primary WINS Server—This entry should be the IP address of the WINS server closest to you.
- Secondary WINS Server—This entry should be the IP address of an alternative WINS server. If you do not have more than one WINS server, enter the same IP address as your primary WINS server.
- Enable DNS for Windows Resolution—This option utilizes a DNS server, in addition to a WINS server, to provide name resolution.

CAUTION

If you will be installing a DNS server on the same computer, you should not enable the Enable DNS for Windows Resolution check box.

- Enable LMHOSTS Lookup—This option is useful if you do not have a DNS server or a WINS server available to provide name resolution. Instead, you may edit the LMHOSTS file located in the SystemRoot\System32\Config\Etc directory to provide a static computer name to IP address mapping. If you have a LMHOST file already configured, say on a network server, you can choose the Import LMHOSTS button to import the file to your computer.

5

IIS PREPARATION
AND INSTALLATION

■ Scope ID—This option provides a mechanism to register a unique NetBIOS name. Multiple computers that use a common scope ID will register broadcast traffic rather than ignore it. If you are unsure as to whether you need to configure your computer with a common scope ID, consult with your network administrator or Internet service provider.

9. Choose the DHCP Relay tab if you have network clients on the other side of a router, with no corresponding DHCP server, that use either DHCP to allocate IP addresses or BOOTTP for diskless workstations. In this tab you may specify the IP addresses of your DHCP server, the number of seconds to wait before a retransmission, and the number of router hops to transmit the DHCP and BOOTTP requests over.

10. Choose the Routing tab and click the Enable IP Forwarding check box to enable forwarding of IP packets on your network. If you install the RIP for Internet Protocol, as described later in this chapter, the routes will be dynamically created. If not, you must create static routes using the route utility.

11. Click the OK button. You will then be prompted to restart your system. If you will not be adding any additional protocols or services, click the Yes button. Otherwise, click the No button and continue to add your additional protocols or services.

Installing the Dynamic Host Configuration Protocol

The DHCP Server service is also installed through the Control Panel Network applet. You can use this service to automate the IP address allocations to your local and remote network clients. I generally recommend that the DHCP Server be installed for even very small networks, as it makes administration easier and provides a means for expansion without a lot of grunt work. Before you install the service on your current server, however, check for the existence of other DHCP servers on the network. These could include other Windows NT Servers, a UNIX server, or possibly even a server provided by your Internet service provider. You want to avoid, at all costs, any conflicts with an existing scope. Creating and managing scopes is covered in Chapter 9, "Using DHCP, WINS, and DNS." To install the DHCP Server service, follow these steps:

1. Launch the Control Panel Network applet to display the Network dialog box and click the Services tab to display the Services page, as shown in Figure 5.6.

2. Click the Add button to display the Select Network Service dialog box, as shown in Figure 5.7.

3. Select the Microsoft DHCP Server and click the OK button.

FIGURE 5.6.
Installing a network service.

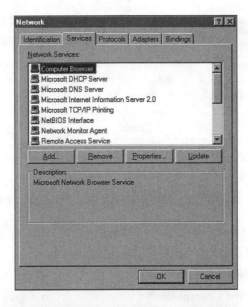

FIGURE 5.7.
Installing the DHCP Server service.

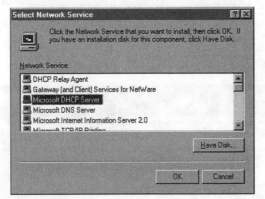

TIP

If you want to use SNMP to configure the DHCP Server service remotely, be sure to install the SNMP service as described in the section "Installing the Simple Network Management Protocol" later in the chapter.

4. Enter the path to the distribution files when prompted and click the Continue button to copy the DHCP Server files to your computer.
5. Choose the Close button if you will not be installing any additional services or repeat steps 2 through 4 for each additional service.

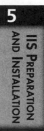

5

IIS PREPARATION
AND INSTALLATION

> **TIP**
>
> Installing the additional services (such as WINS, DNS, RIP, SNMP, and Remote Access Service) at this point will save you time later. Alternatively, you can install the services one at a time, as the following sections describe.

6. Restart your system when prompted. After the system restarts, the DHCP Server service should be activated. If not, check your system event log for any error messages.

Installing the Windows Internet Name Service

Installing the WINS Server service is quite similar to installing the DHCP Server service. Although you can use the DHCP Server service and WINS separately, they function much better when used together. Managing your WINS is covered in Chapter 9. To install WINS, just follow these steps:

1. Launch the Control Panel Network applet to display the Network dialog box and click the Services tab to display the Services page, as shown in Figure 5.6.
2. Click the Add button to display the Select Network Service dialog box, as shown in Figure 5.7.
3. Select the Windows Internet Name Service and click the OK button.

> **TIP**
>
> If you want to use SNMP to configure the WINS remotely, be sure to install the SNMP service as described in the section "Installing the Simple Network Management Protocol."

4. Enter the path to the distribution files when prompted and click the Continue button to copy the WINS files to your computer.
5. Choose the Close button if you will not be installing any additional services or repeat steps 2 through 4 for each additional service.
6. Restart your system when prompted. After the system restarts, the WINS should be activated. If not, check your system event log for any error messages.

Installing the RIP for Internet Protocol Service

If you are not very familiar with TCP/IP routing, you should install the RIP for Internet Protocol service because you can use RIP to build dynamic routing tables. This method is better than building static routes with the route application, as it lessens the administrative burden.

To install RIP, follow these steps:

1. Launch the Control Panel Network applet to display the Network dialog box and Click the Services tab to display the Services page, as shown in Figure 5.6.
2. Click the Add button to display the Select Network Service dialog box, as shown in Figure 5.7.
3. Select the RIP for Internet Protocol and click the OK button.
4. Enter the path to the distribution files when prompted and click the Continue button to copy the RIP for Internet Protocol files to your computer.

> **NOTE**
>
> Although you might expect the RIP for Internet Protocol to be installed in the Protocols property sheet like the WINS service, it will be installed in the Services property sheet. Don't let the name confuse you; RIP really is a service.

5. Click the Close button if you will not be installing any additional services or repeat steps 2 through 4 for each additional service.
6. Restart your system when prompted. After the system restarts, the RIP for Internet Protocol service should be activated. If not, check your system event log for any error messages.

Installing the Domain Name Server Service

The DNS service is based on the UNIX BIND service. It provides a means to map computer names to IP addresses or IP addresses to computer names, much like the WINS service. The primary difference between WINS and DNS is that DNS uses a static mapping mechanism based on host files. Even if you plan to use WINS, you should install the DNS service because it can provide additional functionality when connecting to the Internet. Managing your DNS service is covered in Chapter 9. To install the DNS service, follow these steps:

1. Launch the Control Panel Network applet to display the Network dialog box and click the Services tab to display the Services page, as shown in Figure 5.6.
2. Click the Add button to display the Select Network Service dialog box, as shown in Figure 5.7.
3. Select the Microsoft DNS Server and click the OK button.
4. Enter the path to the distribution files when prompted and click the Continue button to copy the DNS Server files to your computer.
5. Click the Close button if you will not be installing any additional services or repeat steps 2 through 4 for each additional service.
6. Do not restart your system when prompted.

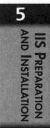

5

IIS PREPARATION AND INSTALLATION

7. Modify your host files, located in the SystemRoot\System32\DNS subdirectory, as described in Chapter 9.

8. Restart your system. After the system restarts, the DNS service should be activated.

9. Check the system event log for any error messages produced by the DNS service. Sometimes an error message is the only indication that you have incorrectly configured a record in one of your host files.

Installing the Simple Network Management Protocol

The SNMP service installation is similar to the installation of other services described in the preceding sections. You may not need to install this service, however, if you do not have an SNMP monitoring and configuration tool. This service only provides a means to monitor or configure your Windows NT services remotely from an SNMP console, such as HP OvenView or a similar product. Although the resource kit provides a simple command-line SNMP console, you will probably find it easier, as I do, to use the Administration tools provided with Windows NT Server for remote administration. But just in case you really need the SNMP service, you can install it by following these steps:

1. Launch the Control Panel Network applet to display the Network dialog box and click the Services tab to display the Services page, as shown in Figure 5.6.

2. Click the Add button to display the Select Network Service dialog box, as shown in Figure 5.7.

3. Select the SNMP Service and click the OK button.

4. Enter the path to the distribution files when prompted and click the Continue button to copy the SNMP Service files to your computer.

5. Follow the prompts to configure the SNMP service, as shown in Figure 5.8, in the Microsoft SNMP Properties dialog box. You should enter the name of the person to contact in case of problems in the Contact text box. You can use the Location text box to specify where the problem has occurred (in building A, for example) or a phone (or beeper) number for the person named in the Contact field. The Service field specifies the types of problems to monitor. You should ask your SNMP manager about these because not every manager will want to see traps for each of these items.

6. Use the Traps property sheet, shown in Figure 5.9, to tell your SNMP service where to send the information. Specify the type of SNMP items you are concerned with, as well as their destination. If you are unsure of the type of SNMP information, just type public in the Community Name text box and click the Add button. Doing so grays out that button and enables the Add button under the Trap Destinations box. At this point, click the Add button and enter the IP or IPX addresses of the computer with the SNMP monitoring console.

FIGURE 5.8.

Configuring the SNMP contact and service properties.

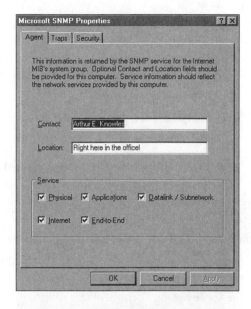

FIGURE 5.9.

Configuring the SNMP traps properties.

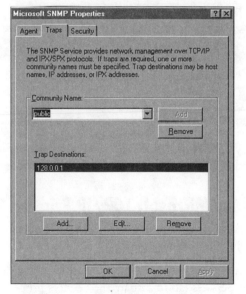

7. Choose the Security tab if you want to limit the SNMP traps you will submit or receive. Once more, you should discuss this setting with your SNMP console manager to determine his requirements.

8. Click the OK button to close the Microsoft SNMP Properties dialog when you have finished configuring the SNMP service.

9. Click the Close button to close the Network dialog if you will not be installing any additional services or repeat steps 2 through 4 for each additional service.

10. Restart your system when prompted. After the system restarts, the SNMP service should be activated. If not, check your system event log for any error messages.

Installing the Simple TCP/IP Service

Installing the Simple TCP/IP Service is very straightforward. Just follow these steps:

1. Launch the Control Panel Network applet to display the Network property sheet and click the Services tab to display the Services property sheet, as shown in Figure 5.6.

2. Click the Add button to display the Select Network Service dialog box, as shown in Figure 5.7.

3. Select the Simple TCP/IP Services and click the OK button.

4. Enter the path to the distribution files when prompted and click the Continue button to copy the DHCP Server files to your computer.

5. Choose the Close button if you will not be installing any additional services or repeat steps 2 through 4 for each additional service.

NOTE

If you actually plan to use these services, and I hope you do because you have installed them, you will need to configure the Quotes file, which is located in the `SystemRoot\ Drivers\Etc` subdirectory.

6. Restart your system. After the system restarts, the Simple TCP/IP Services should be activated. If not, check your system event log for any error messages.

Installing the Microsoft TCP/IP Printing Service

Installing the Microsoft TCP/IP Printing service is also straightforward and requires little user intervention. Just follow these steps:

1. Launch the Control Panel Network applet to display the Network property sheet and click the Services tab to display the Services property sheet, as shown in Figure 5.6.

2. Click the Add button to display the Select Network Service dialog box, as shown in Figure 5.7.

3. Select Microsoft TCP/IP Printing and click the OK button.

4. Enter the path to the distribution files when prompted and click the Continue button to copy the DHCP Server files to your computer.

5. Do not restart your system when prompted. Instead, launch the Control Panel Services applet, as shown in Figure 5.10, and select the TCP/IP Print Server.

FIGURE 5.10.

Configuring the TCP/IP Print Server service.

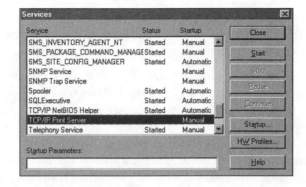

6. Click the Startup button to display the Service dialog, shown in Figure 5.11, to configure the Startup Type from Manual to Automatic. The Automatic option will then start the TCP/IP Print Server service when the server starts instead of requiring you to manually start the service each time you power up the server.

FIGURE 5.11.

Configuring the TCP/IP Print Server service startup values.

7. Choose the OK button to close the Service dialog. Then click the Close button to exit the Services dialog.

All your services should now be installed and configured.

8. Restart your system. After the system restarts, the TCP/IP Print Server service should be activated. If not, check your system event log for any error messages.

The Remote Access Service

The Remote Access Service is a powerful tool that you can use to support your dial-in clients and provide complete network access to your network. You can also use the Remote Access Service to create a wide area network (WAN) or use it as an Internet gateway if desired. Before you can use the software, you must install it. After installing the software, you have to grant

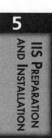

access to your remote clients with the Remote Access Administrator. Otherwise, these clients will be able to connect, but will then be denied access to the network and forcibly disconnected. The Remote Access Administrator is also useful for managing your remote access clients.

One of the most interesting and powerful aspects of the Windows NT Server Remote Access Service is that it can utilize any of the installed network transports (NetBEUI, IPX/SPX, or TCP/IP) for your connection. It can support up to 256 simultaneous client connections on a single server. You can use the Remote Access Service to create a serious communications server to support your entire sales force. It even works quite well with client/server applications because these applications do not send great amounts of data over the wire. However, although you can provide application sharing over the wire, I do not recommend it. You should use the Remote Access Service to provide limited connectivity; that is, you should share only data files, not applications. Rather than share Microsoft Word for Windows, for example, you should install the application directly on the remote user's computer where it will execute quickly. However, you can store the data files on the server and still provide adequate user performance.

> **NOTE**
>
> The Windows NT Workstation and Windows 95 Remote Access Service can support the NetBEUI, IPX/SPX, and TCP/IP protocols. MS-DOS and Windows 3.x Remote Access Service client software are limited to the NetBEUI protocol. If you want to use the IPX/SPX or TCP/IP transports, you will need additional third-party software, such as an Internet SLIP or PPP application, to provide your client with a TCP/IP connection to your Windows NT Server.

Installing the Remote Access Service

Installing the Remote Access Service is a multiple-part process if you want to get the most out of it. Microsoft has configured the default settings to provide more reliable data communications on slower Universal Asynchronous Receiver/Transmitters (UARTs), which is the hardware that is used for your serial port. To obtain a minimum connection of 38,400bps, you must have a 16,450 or better UART. In reality, a 16,450 UART will sometimes drop data, so a 19,200bps connection is a better selection. You will need a 16,550 UART, which contains a 16-byte first-in–first-out (FIFO) buffer to obtain a speed of 57,600bps, and a proprietary UART from DigiBoard, Hayes, or another manufacturer to obtain a 115,200bps connection rate.

Obtaining these higher data rates requires that you set the Maximum Speed field for the modem using the Control Panel Modem applet. I will point out the necessary modifications at the appropriate time during the installation discussion. Before you install the Remote Access Service, you should install your multiport adapter, X.25 adapter, or ISDN adapter. Once the hardware has been added to the system, you will need to install the adapter device driver. Follow these steps:

1. Launch the Control Panel Network applet to display the Network dialog box and click the Adapters tab to display the Adapter page, as shown in Figure 5.12.

FIGURE 5.12.

Adding a network adapter.

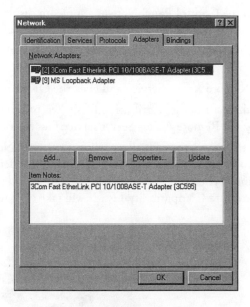

2. Click the Add button to display the Select Network Adapter dialog box, shown in Figure 5.13.

FIGURE 5.13.

Adding an adapter for use by the Remote Access Service.

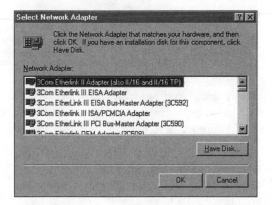

3. Scroll through the list to find your adapter. If it is not listed, choose Have Disk button and insert the OEM disk in your drive A:. Then choose the correct adapter from the list.

4. Install the device driver and configure it if required; then click the OK button. When prompted to restart your computer, select the Restart Now button and restart the server.

You may now install the Remote Access Service software. Use the Control Panel Network applet to perform this task. Just follow these steps:

1. Launch the Control Panel Network applet to display the Network dialog box and click the Services tab to display the Services page, as shown in Figure 5.6.

2. Click the Add button to display the Select Network Service dialog box, as shown in Figure 5.7.

3. Select Remote Access Service and click the OK button.

4. Enter the path to the distribution files when prompted and click the Continue button to copy the Remote Access Server service files to your computer.

5. Install your modem manually or allow the Install New Modem dialog box (see Figure 5.14) to attempt to automatically detect your modem. You should try automatic detection if you do not know what type of modem you have or cannot find it listed in the Hardware Compatibility List. It will take time to detect your modem.

FIGURE 5.14.

The Install New Modem dialog box.

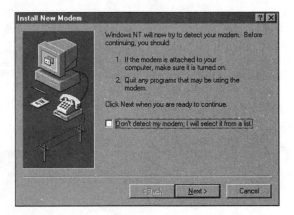

To manually select your modem, enable the Don't detect my modem: I will select it from a list check box. Another version of the Install New Modem dialog box (see Figure 5.15) appears. Select the manufacturer and the specific modem you want to install.

6. Click the Next button and select the port to which the modem is attached. Then click the Next button and enter the location information in the Dialing Properties dialog box. (See Figure 5.16.)

7. Choose your country from the I am in: drop-down list box.

8. Enter the area code for the phone number you will use in the The area code is: field.

9. (Optional) If your phone system requires that you dial a prefix (such as 9) to access an outside line, enter that number in the To access an outside line, 1st dial: field.

FIGURE 5.15.

Installing a modem for use by the Remote Access Service.

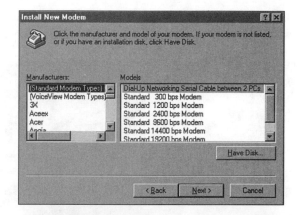

FIGURE 5.16.

Specifying the location properties for use by the Remote Access Service.

10. Choose the appropriate type of phone dialing type (Tone dialing or Pulse dialing radio button) for the phone system in use at your location.

11. Click the Next button; you will be informed that your modem has been set up. Click the Finish button, and the Add RAS device dialog box will be displayed.

12. Select the modem you just installed in the RAS Capable Devices drop-down list box. Then click the OK button to return to the Remote Access Setup dialog box.

13. Click the Configure button to display the Configure Port Usage dialog box. This dialog box enables you to select how your RAS connection will be used. You can choose to support only dial in (Receive calls only), dial out (Dial out only), or both (Receive calls and Dial out).

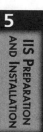

14. Click the OK button to return to the Remote Access Setup dialog box. Then click the Network button to display the Network Configuration dialog box. (See Figure 5.17.)

FIGURE 5.17.

Specifying the Remote Access Service network configuration properties.

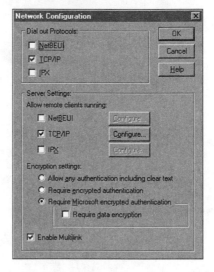

15. This dialog box will let you choose which protocols to support based on the protocols you have installed. You can choose to enable any (NetBEUI, IPX/SPX, or TCP/IP) protocol or only a single protocol for your dial-out and dial-in connections.

16. For each dial in (Server Settings field), you can choose to allow the clients access to your entire network or only to the server they connect to. You may also set a static range of IP addresses for your TCP/IP clients to use or use DHCP to assign IP addresses. I prefer to use DHCP to assign IP addresses. You can also specify a range of IP addresses that your dial-in clients cannot use. For your IPX/SPX clients, you can choose to allocate individual network numbers for each client or assign each IPX client the same network number. If you are integrating your Windows NT Server with a Novell NetWare network and will be providing access to it from your remote connections, you should allocate network numbers. Just enter a number that is not currently in use in the From: field. The To: field will be automatically entered based on the number of remote access ports you have installed. For both your TCP/IP and IPX/SPX connections, you may allow your dial-in clients to allocate a predetermined IP address or network address.

TIP

You may also set encryption settings for your dial-in clients in this dialog. The default is to require Microsoft encrypted authentication. This setting may prevent Point-to-Point Protocol (PPP) and Serial Line Internet Protocol (SLIP) connections from being authenticated if you are not using the Microsoft remote access client. To prevent this situation, enable the Allow any authentication including clear text option. This option will still attempt to encrypt the password, but if all else fails, it will support a clear text password attempt. If you are really concerned about the security of your data when it is sent over the remote access connection, you may enable the Require data encryption setting, which will encrypt all data transmitted over the connection.

TIP

If you will be using more than one PPP connection to the Internet, check the Enable Multilink option, as this setting will merge your separate data streams into a single data stream and can increase throughput. If you will be using two 28,800bps modems, for example, and you connect each one to your Internet service provider—who also has to support multilink PPP connections—RAS will merge these two 28,800bps data streams into a single 57,600bps data stream. This technique can double your network throughput.

17. After pressing the OK button, you will be returned to the Remote Access Setup dialog box. If you have additional ports to add, the quick and easy way is to press the Clone button. This will copy your current configuration to the next available port. Repeat this step for each port you want to install. If you have a different modem on a port, just select it and press the Configure button. You may then pick out the correct modem for it. If you choose another modem, remember to change the modem settings.

18. Once all your modems have been installed and configured, click the OK button in the Remote Access Setup dialog box. Then click the Close button to exit the Network dialog box. You will then be prompted to restart your computer. At this point, be sure to select the Restart Now button.

19. When the system restarts, be sure to check the System event log to look for any possible errors.

Configuring the Remote Access Service

After you have restarted your computer, you can then use the Control Panel Modems applet to configure your modem properties. These properties include the maximum speed at which your computer will transfer data through the modem, whether to use the modem's built-in error correction and hardware compression, and the modem flow control type. The Remote Access Service will use these properties for dial-in clients. To dial up an external RAS server you can use the Dial-Up Networking application, located in the Accessories program group on the taskbar, to connect to other Remote Access Service servers.

The first time you run the Dial-Up Networking application, you will be prompted to create a phone book entry. In the New Phonebook Entry dialog box, enter a name for your connection in the Entry Name text box, a phone number to dial in the Phone Number text box, and a comment for the entry in the Description text box. If you have more than one modem, select it in the Dial using drop-down list box. To use the Telephony service to configure your phone call (such as when an area code or number to access an outside line is used) properties, check the Use Telephony dialing properties.

You can also specify properties for the dial-up server you will connect to in the Server tab. You can specify the type and network protocols (and configure them as well), and enable software compression. If you want to automate your logon sequence, you can do this from the Script tab. You can specify your user authentication type (such as whether you want to encrypt your password or data) in the Security tab. Should you be using an X.25 connection, you can specify the network provider, address, and a few optional properties.

The Remote Access Administrator

The Remote Access Admin application is located in the Administrative Tools program group on your taskbar. You will use this application to grant access to your dial-in users, check the status of the communications port, send messages to your remotely connected users, and stop or start the Remote Access Service on your computer or a remote computer.

Preparing for Client Connectivity

Before your dial-in clients can access your network through the Remote Access Service, grant these users permission to connect through a dial-in connection. Choose Users | Permissions, and the Remote Access Permissions dialog will be displayed. For each user you want to provide dial-in access, follow these steps:

1. Select the username in the Users list box.

2. Enable the Grant dial-in permission to user check box.

> **TIP**
>
> To quickly grant permission to all users to dial in to your network, click the Grant All button. To delete all user permissions, click the Remove All button.

3. Specify a call back option of No Call Back, Set By Caller, or Preset to. This option provides one of two features:

   - It can enhance your system security by using the Preset to field to always call a user back at a specific phone number.

   - It can lower the phone bill of a remote user (such as a member of your sales department who travels a lot) by using the Set By Caller option. The user can then specify the phone number to call back so the client he or she is with will not have to pay the fees for the long-distance call. If you specify Preset to, be sure to enter a complete phone number, including any dial-out codes, calling-card codes, and so on.

4. Click the OK button, and you're done. Your remote access callers may now dial in to your network.

> **TIP**
>
> You can set these same options using User Manager for Domains. Just select the user account; then click the Dialin button to display the Dialin Information dialog box where you can set these values for the user account.

Monitoring Remote Access Connections

To determine who is using your remote access connections, just double-click the server entry or choose Server | Communications Ports, which will display the Communications port dialog. If you have any connected users, the User field will list the connected user, and the Started field will list the time the user connected to your server. If you have an active connection, then the following buttons will be enabled:

- Disconnect User—This button disconnects the selected user.
- Send Message—This button sends a message to the selected user.

> **NOTE**
>
> To send a message to a Windows 3.x or Windows 95 client, the Windows messaging utility (winpopup.exe) must be running on the client computer.

- Send to All—This button sends a message to all connected users. It is extremely useful when you are about to bring down the server or restart the Remote Access Server because you can warn your connected users of the impending shutdown.

If you want to determine the compression rations or errors that have occurred on the selected port, then click the Port Status button.

Using Remote Access as a Gateway to the Internet

In order to use the Remote Access Service to connect to the Internet, you will need either a PPP or SLIP account from an Internet service provider. Once you have obtained an account,

5

IIS PREPARATION AND INSTALLATION

you just need to create a phone book entry with the Dial-Up Networking client. Then follow these steps:

1. Click the Server tab in the Edit Phonebook Entry dialog box to display the Server properties.

2. Choose the PPP:Windows NT, Windows 95 Plus, Internet selection in the Dial-Up server type drop-down box if you will be using a PPP connection to connect to the Internet service provider. If you will be using a SLIP account, choose SLIP Internet.

3. Disable the NetBEUI and IPX protocols in the Network Protocol group.

4. (Optional) Click the TCP/IP Settings button to enter a preassigned IP address or DNS IP address if you have this information from your Internet provider.

NOTE

If you have a choice as to the type of connection your ISP provides, always choose a PPP connection. This connection type is more robust and offers additional functionality.

5. Click the OK button to return to the Edit Phonebook Entry dialog box.

6. Click OK to return to the Dial-Up Networking application main window.

7. Click the Dial button. The first time you dial your connection, a dialog box will be displayed where you can specify the username and password. Leave the domain name field empty unless your ISP requires a specific domain name.

TIP

To save the password so you do not have to enter this information the next time you want to use this connection, check the Save password check box.

After you have completed these steps, you can dial the connection by selecting it from the Phonebook entry drop-down list and clicking the Dial button to connect to the Internet. If you will be using your RAS connection as a gateway to the Internet so that your LAN clients can access the Internet through this same server, you have a bit of additional work to do. Specifically, you need to add the following values to the following keys in the registry:

Key:

```
HKEY_LOCAL_MACHINE\System\CurrentControlSet\Services\RasArp\Parameters
```

Value:

```
DisableOtherSrcPackets
```

Key:

`HKEY_LOCAL_MACHINE\System\CurrentControlSet\Services\RasMan\PPP\IPCP`

Value:

`PriorityBasedOnSubNetwork`

Both of these values are regular double words (`REG_DWORD`). `DisableOtherSrcPackets` should be set to `0`, and `PriorityBasedOnSubNetwork` should be set to `1`. The first entry specifies that network packets should use the IP address of the LAN client. This entry ensures that the data is routed to the proper client. The second entry specifies that the network packets should be sent to the appropriate destination and adapter based on the individual subnet. This information is usually required, for example, when your LAN has a subnet such as `206.170.127.x` and your RAS connection (or your ISP's subnet) is `206.170.126.x`. If `PriorityBasedOnSubNetwork` is not set to `1` (the default is assumed to be `0`), all network traffic would be routed thorough your network adapter. When you set this value, however, your LAN traffic will be passed over your network adapter, and your Internet traffic will be passed over your RAS connection.

> **NOTE**
>
> You must complete one other critical part to this process before your clients can use your server as a gateway to the Internet. Your ISP must create a routing table, and your server and client IP address must be added to the ISP's DNS servers (or your DNS server could be a client of the ISP's DNS server and replicate the information). If you experience problems transmitting or receiving data over the Internet and your ISP has performed the required steps, look at your routing table using the `ROUTE PRINT` command. You may need to modify this information (your ISP should be able to help you through this step) in order to successfully use your computer as a gateway.

Installing the Internet Information Server

After all the work that you had to perform in the preceding sections to prepare for your Internet Information Server installation, you will be happy to know that installing IIS is going to be far easier to accomplish. As IIS 3.0 is an enhancement to IIS 2.0, you must install the base IIS 2.0 components before you can proceed with the rest of the installation. You can order IIS 3.0 on a CD-ROM directly from Microsoft, or you can download it from Microsoft's Web site at `http://www.microsoft.com/iis`.

5

IIS PREPARATION AND INSTALLATION

Installing IIS 2.0 Components

To install IIS 2.0, just follow these simple steps:

1. Look on your desktop for a shortcut called Install the Internet Information Server. Just double-click this shortcut.

2. Click the OK button to continue past the Microsoft Internet Information Server 2.0 Setup dialog box. The dialog box shown in Figure 5.18 will be displayed.

3. Click the Change Directory button to change from the default installation directory SystemRoot\System32\INETSRV. Then specify a different location for your IIS installation in the Select Directory dialog box.

> **NOTE**
>
> You really should choose a different location for the Internet Information Server root directory, as I have done here. Your best choice is to choose an NTFS-formatted partition on another, physically separate drive. This setting will cause less competition for the disk (the SystemRoot disk is heavily used) and enhance the performance of your IIS installation.

FIGURE 5.18.

Choosing the Internet Information Server installation options.

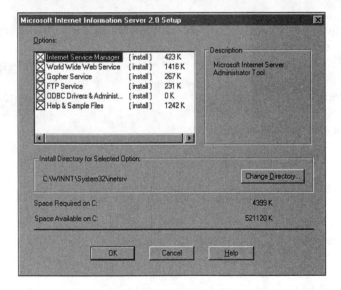

4. (Optional) If you do not want to install all the IIS services, administration tools, help files and documentation, ODBC drivers, or the Internet Explorer, you may uncheck the specific items in the Options box. I recommend, however, that you install all the options for now. When you no longer need them, you can easily execute the IIS setup program to remove specific components. You can also use this application to install components that you may have removed or not installed.

5. Click the OK button to proceed with the installation. If your installation directory does not exist, you will be prompted to create it.

6. Choose a directory to contain your data for the WWW, FTP, and Gopher services in the Publishing Directories dialog box, as shown in Figure 5.19. You should seriously consider putting the data for each service on a separate physical drive (or on a striped set or a striped set with parity), if at all possible, for maximum performance. To specify a different drive or directory, click the browse button and choose a new location.

FIGURE 5.19.

Specifying the root directories for your publishing services.

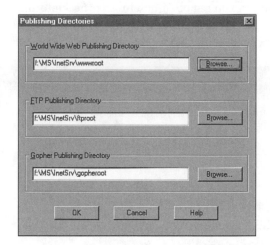

7. Click the OK button when you are done specifying all your data locations. You will be prompted once again to create each directory, if they do not already exist.

   The IIS files will then be copied to your computer in the locations you specified, the publishing services will be started, and a new group will be created on the taskbar.

8. Install the ODBC drivers as prompted. The SQL Server driver is the default and the only driver. Select the driver and choose the OK button.

NOTE

If you will not be using the SQL Server driver, you will need to use the ODBC-32 Control Panel applet to install and configure the alternative driver.

The Internet Explorer will then be installed, and a shortcut will be added to the Microsoft Internet Server group on the taskbar. When this has been completed, a confirmation dialog will be displayed, informing you that IIS was successfully installed.

9. Click the OK button to exit the setup application.

5

IIS PREPARATION
AND INSTALLATION

Installing IIS 3.0 Components

Installing the IIS 3.0 components requires a bit more work than installing the IIS 2.0 components because Microsoft packages the IIS 3.0 components in separate packages. These components include Active Server Pages, Crystal Reports, FrontPage Server Extensions, Index Information Server 1.1, and the NetShow On-Demand Server. At a minimum you should install the Active Server Pages, the NetShow On-Demand Server, and Index Information Server to provide dynamic content, live multimedia, and HTML document search capabilities on your server. However, you can obtain useful statistical information from Crystal Reports, and you will need FrontPage Server Extensions if you plan to support FrontPage 1.1 or FrontPage 97 on your server.

> **NOTE**
>
> The installation process described in this section is based on the downloadable version from the Microsoft Web site. If you obtained your copy on a CD-ROM, the installation process may not follow this exact mechanism.

Installing the Active Server Page Server

To install the Active Server Pages, follow these steps:

1. Execute the self-extracting file that you downloaded from the Microsoft IIS 3.0 Web site.

2. Read the license agreement carefully to understand your rights and the limitations of the software. If you agree to these terms, click the I Agree button; otherwise, click the Exit button.

   If you click on the I Agree button, the Active Server Pages dialog box will be displayed as shown in Figure 5.20.

3. Click the Next button. If any IIS service is currently running, a dialog box will prompt you to stop the service(s) before continuing the installation. Choose the Yes button to stop these services and proceed with the installation. Choose the No button only if you have active users connected to your server or cannot take the server off-line at this time.

   The Select Options dialog box, as shown in Figure 5.21, will be displayed. The ODBC and on-line documentation options are not required components, but I recommend that you install them at this time (by placing a check in the box). The rest of this discussion assumes that you have chosen this option. Later, if you decide you do not need these options, you can rerun the setup program and remove them by unchecking the box.

4. Make your selections and click the Next button.

FIGURE 5.20.
Installing the Active Server Pages.

FIGURE 5.21.
Choosing the Active Server Pages components to install.

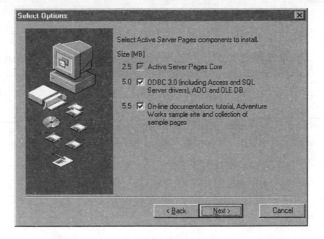

5. Specify the location of the Active Server Page sample files in the Select Paths dialog box. The default directory is `IISRoot\ASPSamp` where `IISRoot` is your IIS root installation directory. To choose an alternative location for these files, click the Browse button and specify another drive and directory. After making your choices, click the Next button.

   The Active Server Page core files, the ODBC, and the on-line documentation will now be copied to your hard disk, and the applications registered in your system registry.

6. Examine the Setup is Complete dialog box carefully, as it will show you the status of the installation. If any part of the installation process failed, it will be noted here so

that you may take corrective action. Once you have finished examining the installation status, click the OK button.

7. Click the OK button to continue past the message box that tells you that a shortcut entry has been created in your program group.

> **NOTE**
>
> If your version of Windows NT does not have Service Pack 1a or later installed, then the Install Windows NT Service Pack 1.1a dialog box will be displayed. Choose the Yes button to install the service pack (the rest of this discussion assumes you chose the Yes button). Choose the No button to skip the service pack installation.

> **NOTE**
>
> If you choose not to install Service Pack 1a, you will be unable to use Active Server Pages. Skip this installation only if you are running a later service pack and the Setup program did not detect this properly.

8. Click the Next button to pass the Welcome dialog box and continue the Service Pack installation. The Service Pack Setup dialog box will be displayed. The first time you run this program only the Install the Service Pack radio button will be enabled. However, if you run this program a second time, the Uninstall a previously installed Service Pack radio button will be enabled. This is a new option for service pack installations and will let you remove a service pack should you later encounter problems.

9. Click the Next button to proceed with the installation. Another Service Pack Setup dialog box will be displayed.

   This dialog box provides you with the option to create, or not create, an uninstall directory. I recommend that you create (the default option) an uninstall directory just in case you encounter problems later.

10. Make your selection and click the Next button. The final Service Pack Setup dialog box will be displayed.

11. Click the Finish button to begin the update. Click the OK button when prompted to restart your computer.

Installing the NetShow On-Demand Server

To install the NetShow On-Demand Server, follow these steps:

1. Execute the self-extracting file that you downloaded from the Microsoft IIS 3.0 Web site. The Microsoft NetShow On-Demand Server Setup message box will appear.

Click the Yes button to install the software. Click the No button to exit the setup program.

Assuming that you chose the Yes button, then the License Agreement dialog box will be displayed.

2. Read the license agreement carefully to understand your rights and the limitations of the software. If you agree to these terms, click the Yes button; otherwise, click the No button.

   Assuming once more that you do want to install the software and that you clicked the Yes button, the Welcome dialog box will be displayed.

3. Click the Continue button to proceed with the installation. The Microsoft NetShow On-Demand Server Setup dialog box, as shown in Figure 5.22, will appear.

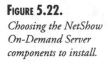

FIGURE 5.22.

Choosing the NetShow On-Demand Server components to install.

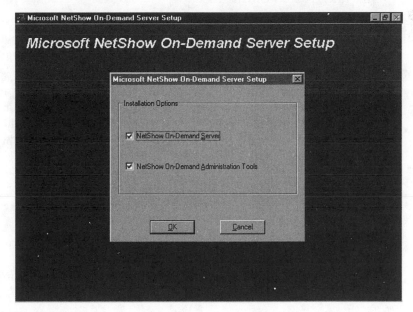

4. Install the NetShow On-Demand Server components by checking the NetShow On-Demand Server check box.

   Although the NetShow On-Demand Administration Tools are optional, I recommend that you install them at this time. To not install the administrative tools, just uncheck the check box. Once you have made your selections, click the OK button.

5. Choose a directory for the NetShow On-Demand Server files and the associated administrative tools when prompted. If the defaults are not acceptable, click the Browse button to choose a different directory. After specifying the directory location, click the Continue button to copy the NetShow On-Demand files to your computer and continue with the installation.

5

IIS PREPARATION AND INSTALLATION

> **NOTE**
>
> Should you encounter an error message stating that some other application is currently using the Database Object Access or JET Engine and the installation cannot continue, use the Control Panel Services applet to shut down the dbWeb Service, DHCP server, and WINS services. You can restart these services when the installation is complete.

6. Enter the maximum number of clients, the maximum network bandwidth, and the maximum file bandwidth to be used by the NetShow On-Demand Server when prompted. For now, just accept the default settings. If these values need to be changed you can do so with the Internet Service Manager as described in Chapter 6, "Using the Internet Service Manager."

7. Choose a directory for the NetShow On-Demand Server content when prompted. If the default is not acceptable, click the Browse button to choose a different directory. Once you have made your selection, click the Continue button to proceed with the installation.

8. Restart your computer by clicking the Restart Now button when prompted. If you will be installing additional IIS 3.0 components, however, you should do so now and restart the computer only after you have finished installing all of these components. To install additional components, click the Exit to Windows NT button to return to your current session and execute the other installation programs.

Installing the Index Information Server

To install the Index Information Server 1.1, follow these steps:

1. Execute the self-extracting file that you downloaded from the Microsoft IIS 3.0 Web site. The Microsoft Index Server v1.1 Setup message box will appear. Click the Yes button to install the software. Click the No button to exit the setup program.

   Assuming that you chose the Yes button, then the License Agreement dialog box will be displayed.

2. Read the license agreement carefully to understand your rights and the limitations of the software. If you agree to these terms, click the Yes button; otherwise, click the No button.

   Assuming once more that you do want to install the software and that you clicked on the Yes button, the Microsoft Index Server v1.1 for Windows NT dialog box will be displayed.

3. Click the Continue button to proceed with the installation.

4. Supply the complete physical path to your IIS scripts directory when prompted. If the directory displayed is incorrect, change it and then click the Continue button.

5. Supply the complete physical path to your IIS World Wide Web root directory when prompted. If the directory displayed is incorrect, change it and then click the Continue button.

6. Supply a complete physical path for the location of the Index Information Server index files when prompted. I prefer to use a subdirectory of the IIS root directory to contain these files, but you may specify any directory for these files. When you have made your selection, click the Continue button.

   The Index Information Server files will be copied to your computer, and a message box will inform you of the location of the sample search page.

7. Click the Exit to Windows NT button to return to your current session and execute the other installation programs.

Installing Crystal Reports for Internet Information Server

To install Crystal Reports, follow these steps:

1. Execute the self-extracting file that you downloaded from the Microsoft IIS 3.0 Web site.

2. Read the license agreement carefully to understand your rights and the limitations of the software. If you agree to these terms, click the Yes button; otherwise, click the No button.

   Assuming that you want to install the software and that you clicked the Yes button, the Select Components dialog box will be displayed as shown in Figure 5.23.

FIGURE 5.23.

Choosing the Crystal Reports components to install.

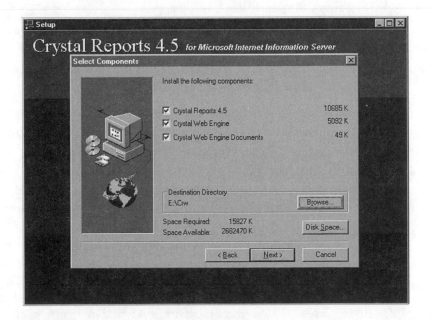

5

IIS PREPARATION AND INSTALLATION

NOTE

If you will be using Crystal Reports on the same server as your IIS installation, make sure that both the Crystal Reports 4.5 and Crystal Web Engine are checked. On the other hand if you will be reviewing these reports from another computer, then you may enable just the Crystal Web Engine to install the core components on the Web server. Then you may rerun this installation program on another computer and enable just the Crystal Reports 4.5 option to install the reporting tools on the remote computer. In either case, I recommend that you enable the Crystal Web Engine Documents to gain a fuller understanding of how to use these components.

3. Enable the Crystal Web Engine Documents.

4. Click the Browse button to choose another directory if the default directory is not acceptable. As usual, I prefer to choose a subdirectory of my IIS root directory rather than the default of \CRW. When you have finished your selections, click the Next button.

   At this point the software will be copied to your system, the program groups and shortcuts will be created, and the default printer will be selected.

5. Follow the prompts to restart your IIS services if your IIS services have not been started (usually because you have installed other software that has stopped these services). If you have no other services to install, choose the Yes button. Otherwise, choose the No button.

   The Setup Complete dialog box will appear.

6. Read the ReadMe file and start Crystal Reports. Make your selections and click the Finish button.

Installing the FrontPage 97 Server Extensions

To install the FrontPage Server Extensions, follow these steps:

1. Execute the self-extracting file that you downloaded from the Microsoft IIS 3.0 Web site.

2. Click the Next button to continue past the Welcome dialog box.

3. Read the license agreement carefully to understand your rights and the limitations of the software. If you agree to these terms, click the Yes button; otherwise, click the No button.

4. Click the Browse button to specify an alternative location if the default directory location in the Destination Path dialog box is not acceptable. Make your selection and click the Next button to proceed with the installation.

   The Installed Servers Detected dialog box will appear. This dialog box enables you to select which WWW Servers to support (if it found more than one).

5. Select the appropriate server to support and click the Next button to continue.

6. Examine the Start Copying Files dialog box to make sure that the actions the Setup program will take are correct. If any of the actions are incorrect, click the Back button to specify a different selection. Otherwise, click the Next button to copy the files to your computer.

   The Administrator Setup for Microsoft Internet Information Server dialog box will be displayed requesting that you enter a username to use for authoring and administering your FrontPage webs.

7. Enter this username and click the OK button to install the server extensions.

> **TIP**
>
> You can enter a local group name, such as Administrators, instead of an individual username. By adding individual users to this group, you can permit multiple users to administer FrontPage webs.

8. Restart the WWW service when prompted. Click the Yes button to complete the installation.

   You will then be informed that earlier versions of FrontPage require that Basic Authentication be enabled.

9. Click the Yes button if you will be supporting earlier versions (1.0 or 1.1). Otherwise, click the No button.

10. Click the Finish button in the Setup Complete dialog box to exit the setup process.

After installing all of the IIS components, you should restart your computer just to make sure everything is in order. After a successful restart, check your event logs for any warning or error messages. Assuming that everything is working properly, you are ready to configure the IIS service, as described in Chapter 6, install the data to be published on your server in the service's root directories, and begin to publish data on the Internet.

Summary

This chapter explains where you should install the Internet Information Server, describes the preinstallation requirements, and discusses the installation of the various components. The chapter even shows you how to install and configure the Remote Access Service. Finally, the chapter covers the basic IIS installation. In Chapter 6 you will learn how to configure the Internet Information Server and begin publishing your content on the Internet.

5

IIS PREPARATION AND INSTALLATION

III

PART

IN THIS PART

- Using the Internet Service Manager   *137*

- Using Internet Explorer   *169*

- Working with Microsoft Exchange   *199*

- Using DHCP, WINS, and DNS   *215*

- Advanced Security Issues   *273*

- Enhancing Internet Information Server   *319*

Administering Your Site

Using the Internet
Service Manager

IN THIS CHAPTER

- **Basic Operations of the Internet Service Manager** *138*

- **Configuring the WWW Service** *141*

- **Configuring the FTP Service** *151*

- **Configuring the Gopher Service** *156*

- **Configuring the NetShow On-Demand Service** *160*

- **Logging Site Access with SQL Server** *163*

CHAPTER 6

One nice aspect of Windows NT is that you can configure almost every service by using an application specifically designed for it, and the Internet Information Server is no different. It includes a tool called the Internet Service Manager (see Figure 6.1), which is installed by default in the Microsoft Internet Service group.

This chapter focuses on managing your Internet Information Server sites using the Internet Service Manager. In this chapter you will learn how to control the basic operations of your IIS sites. You will then learn how to configure the WWW, FTP, and Gopher services. Finally, you will learn how to use the ODBC connector to log all of your IIS site activity to a database. Although you can use any database that has an ODBC driver, this chapter concentrates on using the ODBC connector to connect to a SQL Server database.

FIGURE 6.1.

The Internet Service Manager.

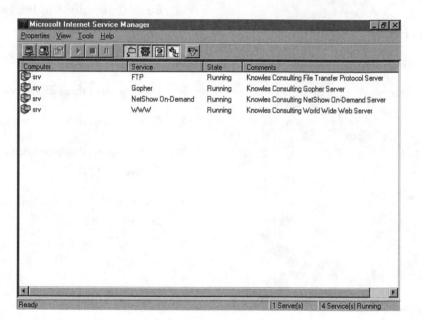

Basic Operations of the Internet Service Manager

The Internet Service Manager has a very simple set of controls. In fact, you can manage your IIS services on a local or remote computer using only the three main menu commands: Properties, View, and Help. Of these commands, only Properties and View offer real functionality. These carefully designed commands make managing your IIS sites quite easy.

This chapter starts by explaining how you can use the Internet Service Manager to control your individual Internet services. After that, you will learn how to manage a single Internet Information Server site. Continuing with this theme, you will then learn how to choose a view that will help you find the appropriate Internet services on multiple sites.

Controlling the Internet Services

One thing a site manager (that's you) needs is the ability to control the operating states of the individual Internet services from either a local or remote server. Before you can control a service, however, that service must be added to the Internet Service Manager. This step should be performed automatically the first time you execute the Internet Service Manager because it will browse the network in an attempt to locate all available sites. However, if the Internet Service Manager failed to add a service, just choose one of the following options:

■ Find All Servers—This option scans the entire network looking for IIS sites. This option is also available by pressing Ctrl+F or by clicking the Find Internet Servers button (second from the left) on the toolbar.

■ Connect to Server—This option displays the Connect to Server dialog, where you can specify the computer name of the server running the Internet Information Server. This option is also available by pressing Ctrl+O or by clicking the Connect to a Server button (first button on the left) on the toolbar.

After you have connected to the appropriate servers, the IIS services will be displayed in the main window of the Internet Service Manager. To start, stop, pause, or continue an IIS service on a connected server, follow these two steps:

1. Select the appropriate service by clicking the server name in the Computer column.

2. Choose either Start Service, Stop Service, or Pause Service from the Properties menu. If you prefer, you can use the Start Service, Stop Service, and Pause/Continue Service buttons on the toolbar. These are the third, fourth, and fifth buttons, respectively.

> **NOTE**
>
> When you pause a service, the Properties | Pause Service menu will be in a checked state to indicate that the service is paused. To continue the service, just choose the Pause Service menu option once more, or use the toolbar Pause/Continue Service button.

Another way to control the state of the Internet services is to use Server Manager, which will display all computers in the domain. To control a service, choose Computer | Services from the menu to display the Services on *ComputerName* dialog box. Then scroll down the list until you find the appropriate service (FTP Publishing Service, Gopher Publishing Service, or WWW Publishing Service). Select the service and then click the Start, Stop, Pause, or Continue button.

> **NOTE**
>
> In order to control the state of a service, you must have administrative privileges on either the local computer or a remote computer.

Managing Internet Information Server Sites

Managing more than a few IIS sites on a network becomes relatively difficult because you have to scroll through the lists of servers and services in order to check the state of each service. The Internet Service Manager makes this chore a little easier because it includes several commands to rearrange the display, allowing you to show the information you are most concerned with at the moment. These commands are accessible through the View menu command and include the following:

■ Sort by Server—This command orders the display based on the computer name. This command is the default sort order.

■ Sort by Service—This command orders the display based on the type of service. You can change the order to FTP, Gopher, and then WWW.

■ Sort by Comment—This command orders the display based on the service description.

■ Sort by State—This command orders the display based on the execution state of the service. This command is particularly useful to determine whether you have any services that are not executing. The default sort order is not alphabetical, however. Instead, the display will show stopped services at the top of the display, running services in the middle of the display, and paused services at the bottom of the display.

Using a View to Manage Multiple Sites

Another useful sorting method for managing multiple sites is to use the various view options accessible from the Views menu. The default view is the Reports view. However, the Servers View and Services View offer benefits not available from the Reports View. First, you can see at a glance the state of the services. The state of each service is represented by the colors of a stop light: red for stopped, yellow for paused, or green for running. Second, you can expand or collapse the display to show just the type of services you want to see. Finally, the right mouse button will activate a pop-up menu to control the state or properties of the service, as shown in Figure 6.2.

If you have many IIS sites, you may find that this view could use a little more room on the display to see the services of interest. If you want to remove a service from the display, you can choose the View | FTP, View | Gopher, or View | WWW commands, or you can choose the seventh, eighth, or ninth buttons on the taskbar to perform the same action. In either case, the commands toggle the current state. With the menu commands, a checked command signifies that the service is visible; if the command is unchecked, the corresponding service is removed from the display. The buttons work in a similar way: A depressed button represents a checked state, and a raised button represents an unchecked state.

FIGURE 6.2.
Using the Service view to manage your IIS sites.

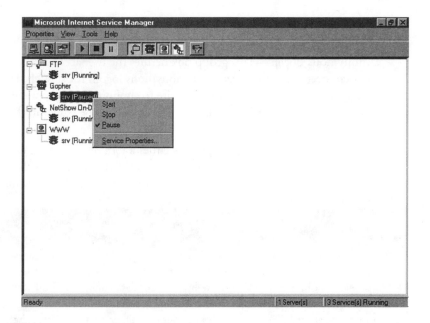

Configuring the WWW Service

Before you make your WWW site available to the world, you should configure it to suit your individual needs. The default configuration provides some protection from Internet hackers, but if Internet security is your primary concern, you should take a look at Chapter 10, "Advanced Security Issues." For the rest of this discussion, I assume you are interested only in the basic options for configuring your WWW Publishing service.

You can configure the four main options of the WWW Publishing service from the WWW Service Properties for *ComputerName* dialog box. You can configure the general properties of the WWW service, specify the WWW directories and create virtual WWW servers, log the activity on your WWW site, and limit access to your WWW site. This dialog box is accessible by choosing Properties | Service Properties from the menu, clicking the Properties button on the toolbar (third button from the left), or right-clicking the service when in the Services View or Server View. The following sections examine the details of the four tabs of the WWW Service Properties for *ComputerName* dialog box.

Configuring the WWW Service

The WWW Service properties sheet includes the following options:

- Connection Timeout—This option specifies the time, in seconds, before an inactive user's connection will be terminated. This setting ensures that even if the Web server fails to close a connection when a user exits the site, eventually it will be closed. The default is 900 seconds, or 15 minutes.

- Maximum Connections—This option specifies the maximum number of simultaneous users who can be connected to your Web server. The default is 1,000.

- Anonymous Logon—This group box defines the user account and password for users that connect to your site using an anonymous logon. Most Web servers support the anonymous logon. If you want your site to support users who are not members of your domain, which most of us do, their access will be based on the user account and password specified in the following fields:

    - Username—This field specifies either a local user account or a domain user account. By default, this account is called `IUSER_ComputerName`, where `ComputerName` is the name of the computer where IIS was installed.

CAUTION

By default, this group is added to the Guests local group. If your server is a member of the domain, the account is also a member of the Domain Users global group. You should verify the privileges of the group to ensure that this account cannot be used to access secure network resources. I prefer to either move the user account to the Domain Guests global group or create a new group for the account. In either case, minimize the privileges associated with the user account or group. (See Chapter 10 for more details.)

    - Password—This field specifies the password to be used with the user account mentioned above. If you change the password here, you must also change the password using User Manager (for a server) or User Manager for Domains (for a domain controller).

TIP

You should change the password for this account every 30 to 45 days to enhance the security of your site.

- Password Authentication—This group specifies the method by which users can attempt to connect to your Web server. It has the following options:

    - Allow Anonymous—When this box is checked, any user may connect to your server using the anonymous logon procedure. When he or she does, the user account and password specified in the Anonymous Logon group is used to supply the user's account privileges. If this box is unchecked, anonymous logons are not allowed and a valid user account and password must be supplied to obtain access to your WWW site.

    - Basic (Clear Text)—When checked, this option specifies that the password associated with a user account be transmitted in an unencrypted format.

Using the Internet Service Manager

CHAPTER 6

143

6

USING THE
INTERNET SERVICE
MANAGER

WARNING

Using the Basic password authentication option opens the possibility of a serious security breach. An Internet user with access to a sniffer might be able to capture network packets sent to your site. This breach could provide the user with a valid user account and password that he or she could then use to access network resources.

■ Windows NT Challenge/Response—When checked, this option specifies that the password be transmitted in an encrypted format when an anonymous logon is denied. Therefore, to secure your site to domain members only (such as for an intranet WWW site) and to support encrypted passwords only, you must also uncheck (disable) the Allow Anonymous and Basic (Clear Text) options.

NOTE

Currently, the only Web browser that supports the Windows NT Challenge/Response authentication mechanism is the Microsoft Internet Explorer version 2.0 (or higher).

■ Comment—This option specifies a description to be displayed on the Internet Service Manager while in report view for the WWW Publishing service.

Configuring the WWW Service Directories

The ability to configure your WWW service's directories offers more flexibility than you might think at first glance. Not only can you configure a few basic operating characteristics, but you can also create virtual directories and virtual WWW Servers. A *virtual directory* is a directory tree that is not physically attached to the parent WWW directory. By default, the parent WWW directory is IISRoot/wwwroot, where IISRoot is the directory where you installed the Internet Information Server (such as F:\MS\InetSrv). When you create a virtual directory, your WWW clients view it as a subdirectory of the parent WWW directory. A virtual directory can be physically present on the same server as the WWW Publishing service, or it can be on a remote computer.

A *virtual server* is a WWW Server that does not exist as a physically separate entity. A physically separate entity, for example, could consist of a new computer with an assigned IP address (for the computer's network adapter), the WWW Server software, and a registered domain name (so that users can find your site using the familiar form of www.*domainname*.com). It is totally self-contained.

Alternatively, you can create a virtual server that uses the WWW Publishing service on your current computer. You will still need to assign an IP address to it and register the domain name, but the mechanism varies just a bit. Instead of assigning an IP address to a new network card, you can add it to your current network card. In essence, your WWW Publishing service would now support two separate WWW sites. Each site would have its own root directory, which could be on the local server or on a remote server. Your clients would not know that the Web site was just one of many Web sites running on the same server. Pretty nifty, isn't it?

Configuring the WWW Service Basic Directory Properties

Selecting the Directory tab on the WWW Service Properties dialog displays the Directories properties sheet, shown in Figure 6.3, which offers two basic configuration options. If you check the Enable Default Document option, you may specify an HTML document name in the Default Document field. Doing so specifies that this HTML document will be loaded as the default document when a client specifies a URL without a specific document name. A client could specify `http://www.nt-guru.com/Company Information`, for example, and the `Index.HTM` document would be loaded automatically. This method is better than specifying `http://www.nt-guru.com/index.htm` because it provides a means for the client to navigate your Web site without having to know the name of each document.

FIGURE 6.3.

The Directories properties sheet.

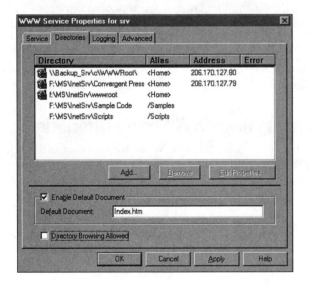

The other basic option is Directory Browsing Allowed. If this option is checked, a client can browse your entire Web site. The client's ability to browse your site, however, depends on the state of the Enable Default Document option. If this option is checked and the default document resides in the directory, the default document will be loaded into the client's Web browser. If the Enable Default Document option is unchecked, or if the option is checked but the default document is not resident in the directory, the client will see a list of files in the directory. This list is a hypertext list. If the user clicks on a document name, the document will be loaded.

The good news about this option is that the client will not be disappointed by seeing an error code on his or her Web browser. This option can also be useful for intranets with a large

Using the Internet Service Manager

CHAPTER 6

145

6

USING THE
INTERNET SERVICE
MANAGER

number of documents. Because the Enable Default Document option allows the user to load a document without creating a master (or *index*) document, it lessens the administrative burden. The bad news about this option is that it opens the door for an unauthorized client to stop by and view information that he or she shouldn't see. Maybe the user got there by mistyping a URL or by using an out-of-date or incorrect URL. To reduce this possibility, you can do one of the following:

■ Disable the Directory Browsing Allowed option.

■ Make sure that every subdirectory of the WWWRoot directory has a default document in it.

■ Install IIS to an NTFS partition; then use File Manager or the Windows Explorer to set permissions on subdirectories with sensitive information. These permissions can be configured to limit access to only those domain members who require it. By default, then, any nonmember of this group will be denied access. You should use this method if you support directory browsing. It enables you not only to control access to the directories but also to audit them to determine who is accessing the directories, their subdirectories, and the files they contain.

How to Create a Virtual Directory

Creating a virtual directory is not a difficult task. The only difference between a virtual server and a virtual directory is that only a virtual server may have an IP address and associated domain name. To create a virtual directory, just follow these steps:

1. Click the Add button in the Directories properties sheet to display the Directory Properties dialog box, shown in Figure 6.4.

FIGURE 6.4.

Creating a virtual directory.

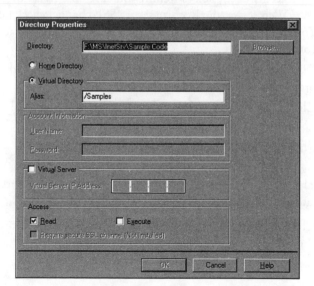

2. To create a virtual directory on the local computer, specify a directory name in the Directory field or click the Browse button to select a directory.

> **NOTE**
>
> If you use the Browse button, the Select Directory dialog box will appear. In it, you can choose an existing directory in the Directories list box. To create a new subdirectory, select an existing directory and enter the name of the subdirectory to create in the New Directory Name text box. After you have entered the requested information, click the OK button. The Directory dialog box closes, and your selected installation directory appears in the Directory field of the Directory Properties dialog box.

3. To create a virtual directory on a remote computer, specify a UNC filename (such as Backup_Srv\C\WWWRoot) in the Directory field.
4. If the Virtual Directory radio button is not enabled, click it to enable it.
5. Enter a name for the virtual directory, such as Samples, in the Alias field.
6. If the virtual directory will reside on a remote computer, enter a username in the User Name field, along with a password for this user account in the Password field. This username and password will be used to connect to the remote share.
7. Specify the type of access your clients will use in the Access group. By default, the Read check box is enabled, specifying that the client will have read-only access to the directory. If this directory will include executable code, such as a CGI script, enable the Execute check box as well. If you have an SSL certificate and have installed SSL on your Web server, the Require secure SSL channel check box will be available as well. You can use this option to provide a secure method for accessing the directory's contents.
8. Click the OK button to create your virtual directory and return to the Directories properties sheet.
9. Click the OK button to exit the Directories properties sheet.

How to Create a Virtual Server

Creating a virtual server is a lot like creating a virtual directory. In fact, a virtual server can use a virtual directory created on the local computer or a virtual directory on a remote computer. To create a virtual server, follow these steps:

1. Click the Add button in the Directories properties sheet to display the Directory Properties dialog box, shown in Figure 6.5.

Using the Internet Service Manager

CHAPTER 6

147

6

USING THE
INTERNET SERVICE
MANAGER

FIGURE 6.5.

*Creating a virtual
server.*

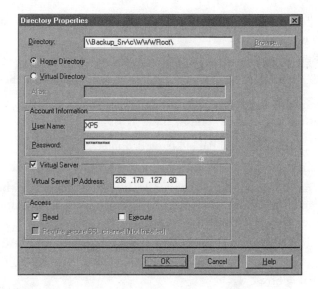

2. To create the virtual directory to be used as the root directory for the virtual server on
the local computer, specify a directory name in the Directory field or click the Browse
button to select a directory.

3. To create a virtual directory to be used as the root directory for the virtual server on a
remote computer, specify a UNC filename (such as `Backup_Srv\C\WWWRoot`) in the
Directory field.

4. If the Home Directory radio button is not enabled, click it to enable it.

5. If the virtual directory will reside on a remote computer, enter a username in the User
Name field and a password for this user account in the Password field. This username
and password will be used to connect to the remote share.

6. Click the Virtual Server check box to enable it.

7. Enter the IP address to be assigned to the virtual server in the Virtual Server IP
Address field.

8. Specify the type of access your clients will use in the Access group. By default, the
Read check box is enabled, specifying that the client will have read-only access to the
directory. If this directory will include executable code, such as a CGI script, enable
the Execute check box as well. If you have an SSL certificate, and have installed SSL
on your Web server, the Require secure SSL channel check box will be available as
well. You can use this option to provide a secure method for accessing the directory
contents.

9. Click the OK button to create your virtual server and return to the Directories properties sheet.

10. Repeat steps 1 through 9 for each virtual server you want to create.

11. Click the OK button to exit the Directories properties sheet.

After you have added all of your virtual servers, you must add the IP addresses and subnet masks to your network adapter. Follow these steps:

1. Open the Control Panel Network applet.

2. Click the Protocols tab to display the Protocols properties sheet.

3. You can display the Microsoft TCP/IP Properties dialog box in one of two ways. You can either double-click the TCP/IP Protocol entry or just click it once to select it and then click the Properties button.

4. Click the Advanced button to display the Advanced IP Addressing dialog box.

5. Click the Add button in the IP Address group to display the TCP/IP Address dialog box.

6. Enter an IP address and subnet mask in the IP Address and Subnet Mask fields. Then click the Add button. This step will add the new IP address and subnet mask to the IP Address and Subnet Mask fields of the IP Address group.

7. Repeat steps 5 and 6 for each virtual server.

8. Click the OK button to exit the Advanced IP Addressing dialog box and return to the Microsoft TCP/IP Properties dialog box.

9. Click the OK button to return to the Network dialog box. The Network Settings Change dialog box will be displayed.

10. Click the Yes button to restart your computer. Once the server reboots, your virtual servers will be available.

NOTE

Your domain name must be registered before your virtual servers are available to the public. Therefore, the IP address and subnet mask you assigned must be the same as those assigned to your domain name. Your ISP should provide you with these names. Your ISP should also configure its DNS servers and set up the necessary routing tables so that clients will be able to find your virtual servers.

Logging WWW Activity

Logging your WWW activity is one way you can determine how active your site is, as well as determine if anyone is accessing data to which he or she should not have access. Two methods are available for logging your WWW site's activity. You can store the information in a standard text file, or you can store it in an ODBC database. If you use an ODBC database, you must create the database and then set up an ODBC data source name (DSN) using the ODBC Control Panel applet. Creating an ODBC database and setting up the DSN is discussed later in this chapter in the section "Logging Site Access with SQL Server." To enable logging, follow these steps:

1. Click the Logging tab in the WWW Service Properties dialog box to display the Logging properties sheet, shown in Figure 6.6.

FIGURE 6.6.

Configuring the WWW service to log activity.

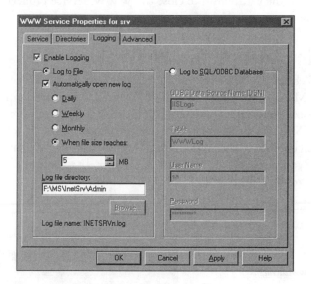

2. Click the Enable Logging radio button.

3. Click the Log to File radio button to log your WWW site's activity to a text file. This step will enable the following options:

   ■ Automatically open new log—This option specifies that a new log will be created based on one of the following criteria:

      ■ Daily—Every day

      ■ Weekly—Once a week

      ■ Monthly—Once a month

      ■ When file size reaches—Whenever the log file exceeds the size specified in the MB field

- Log file directory—This option specifies the location where the log file will reside.

4. Click the Log to SQL/ODBC Database radio button to log your WWW site's activity to an ODBC database. This will enable the following options:

   - ODBC Data Source Name (DSN)—Specifies the name of the data source to use to access the ODBC database

   - Table—Specifies the table within the ODBC database to use for logging

   - User Name—Specifies a username to use to access the table within the ODBC database

   - Password—Specifies a password for the associated user account

5. Click the OK button to close the WWW Service Properties dialog box and return to the Internet Service Manager.

Limiting Access to Your WWW Site

Most Web site administrators are concerned about the security of their WWW site. The Internet Service Manager does provide a limited means of securing your Web site against possible intruders, but these features are not too useful if you expect to provide site access to the public. Using IIS for an intranet is a very useful means of limiting access to sensitive data. To limit potential damage to your system from the public, however, I suggest you look at Chapter 10 to see how you can restrict access to your network. In the meantime, you can limit access to your Web server by following these steps:

1. Click the Advanced tab in the WWW Service Properties dialog box to display the Advanced properties sheet (see Figure 6.7).

FIGURE 6.7.

The WWW Advanced properties sheet.

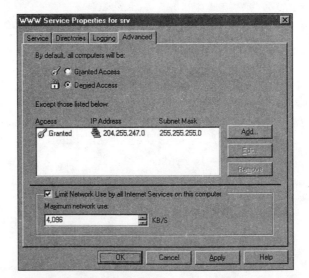

2. Limit access to a specific set of clients by clicking the Denied Access radio button. Then click the Add button to display the Grant Access On dialog box. To specify a single computer to give access to your Web site, click the Single Computer radio button and enter the IP address of the computer in the IP Address field. To specify multiple computers to give access to your Web site, click the Multiple Computers radio button and specify an IP address and subnet mask in the IP Address and Subnet Mask fields. Then click the OK button.

3. Grant access to all but a specific set of clients by clicking the Granted Access radio button. Then click the Add button to display the Denied Access On dialog box. To specify a single computer to deny access to your Web site, click the Single Computer radio button and enter the IP address of the computer in the IP Address field. To specify multiple computers to deny access to your Web site, click the Multiple Computers radio button and specify an IP address and subnet mask in the IP Address and Subnet Mask fields. Then press the OK button.

4. The IP addresses and subnet masks you specified in step 2 or step 3 will then be displayed in the Except those listed below list box. Repeat step 2 or step 3 for each additional set of computers you want to deny, or grant, access to your Web site.

5. Limit the amount of network bandwidth used by your IIS services by clicking the Limit Network Use by all Internet Services on this computer check box. Then specify a value in the Maximum network use field.

6. Click the OK button to close the WWW Service Properties dialog box and return to the Internet Service Manager.

Configuring the FTP Service

Just as you need to configure your WWW Publishing service before making it available to the public, you need to configure your FTP publishing service as well. You have five configuration options. You can configure the general properties of the FTP service, specify the messages users will see when they connect to your FTP site, specify the FTP directories, log the activity on your FTP site, and limit access to your FTP site. The logging and limiting access properties sheets follow the same basic methodology as the WWW service. So rather than repeat this information, I will refer you to the previous sections "Logging WWW Activity" and "Limiting Access to your WWW Site." All of these options, however, are accessed from the FTP Service Properties for *ComputerName* dialog box. This dialog is accessible by choosing Properties | Service Properties from the menu, clicking the Properties button on the toolbar (third button from the left), or right-clicking the service when in the Services View or Server View.

Configuring the FTP Service

The FTP Service properties sheet, shown in Figure 6.8, includes the following options:

FIGURE 6.8.

Configuring the basic FTP publishing service properties.

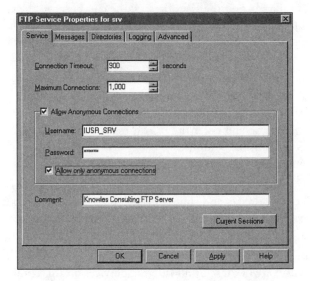

- Connection Timeout—This option specifies the time, in seconds, before an inactive user's connection will be terminated. Connection Timeout ensures that even if the Web server fails to close a connection when a user exits the site, eventually it will be closed. The default is 900 seconds, or 15 minutes.

- Maximum Connections—This option specifies the maximum number of simultaneous users that can be connected to your Web server. The default is 1,000.

- Allow Anonymous Connections—This check box enables you to specify a user account and password for users that connect to your site using an anonymous logon. Most FTP servers support an anonymous logon. If you want your site to support users who are not members of your domain, which most of us do, their access will be based on the user account and password specified in the following fields:

    - Username—This field specifies either a local user account or a domain user account. By default, this account is called IUSER_*ComputerName* where *ComputerName* is the name of the computer where IIS was installed.

CAUTION

By default, this group is added to the Guests local group. If your server is a member of the domain, the account is also a member of the Domain Users global group. You should verify the privileges of the group to ensure that this account cannot be used to access secure network resources. For additional information, see Chapter 10.

■ Password—This field specifies the password to be used with the user account mentioned above. If you change the password here, you must also change the password using User Manager (for a server) or User Manager for Domains (for a domain controller).

TIP

You should change the password for this account every 30 to 45 days to enhance the security of your site.

■ Allow only anonymous connections—When this box is checked, only users that use an anonymous logon may connect to your FTP site

WARNING

Because the FTP protocol does not encrypt passwords, an Internet user with access to a sniffer may be able to capture network packets sent to your site. This breach could provide a user with a valid user account and password that she could then use to access your network resources. Therefore, I recommend that you enable the Allow only anonymous connections check box.

■ Comment—This option specifies a description to be displayed on the Internet Service Manager while in Report view for the FTP Publishing service.

■ Current Sessions—Click this button to display the FTP User Sessions dialog box and see who is active on your FTP site.

Configuring the FTP Service Messages

When a user connects to your FTP site, you can display a greeting message, an exit message, and an error message if the maximum number of clients are currently connected. Not all FTP clients, however, will display these messages—nor will all Web browsers. But it is still a good idea to specify them for FTP clients that support them. To do so, follow these steps:

1. Click the Messages tab to display the Messages properties sheet, shown in Figure 6.9.

2. Enter a greeting message or a warning message (such as when the site is only for authorized users) in the Welcome message field.

3. Enter an exit message to be displayed when the user disconnects from your FTP site in the Exit message field.

4. Enter an error message in the Maximum connections message field to inform users that they cannot connect to your FTP site because the maximum number of simultaneous clients have already connected.

FIGURE 6.9.
Specifying the FTP publishing service messages.

5. Click the OK button to return to the Internet Service Manager.

Configuring the FTP Service Directories

Configuring the directories for the FTP service does not offer as much functionality as the WWW Publishing service does. You cannot create a virtual server, though you can create virtual directories. When you select the Directories tab on the FTP Service Properties dialog box, the Directories properties sheet, shown in Figure 6.10, will be displayed.

FIGURE 6.10.
The FTP publishing service directory properties sheet.

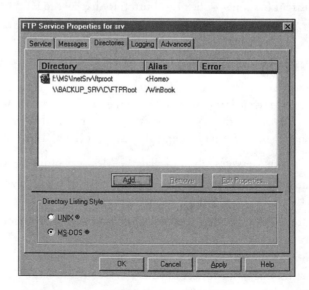

This properties sheet offers two configuration options. You can specify that a directory listing will follow the UNIX or MS-DOS convention by enabling the UNIX or MS-DOS radio button, or you can create virtual directories.

Creating a virtual directory is fairly simple. The only determinate factor is deciding whether the virtual directory will reside on a local computer or a remote computer. To create a virtual directory, follow these steps:

1. Click the Add button in the Directories properties sheet to display the Directory Properties dialog box, shown in Figure 6.11.

FIGURE 6.11.

Creating a virtual directory.

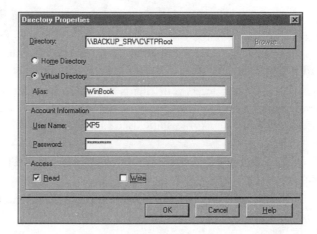

2. To create a virtual directory on the local computer, specify a directory name in the Directory field or click the Browse button to select a directory.

NOTE

If you use the Browse button, the Select Directory dialog box will appear. In it, you can choose an existing directory in the Directories list box. To create a new subdirectory, select an existing directory and enter the name of the subdirectory to create in the New Directory Name field. After you have entered the requested information, click the OK button to close the Directory dialog box. Your selected installation directory will appear in the Directory field of the Directory Properties dialog box.

---

3. To create a virtual directory on a remote computer, specify a UNC filename (such as `Backup_Srv\C\WWWRoot`) in the Directory field.

4. Click the Virtual Directory radio button to enable it if necessary.

> **TIP**
>
> Although you cannot create a virtual server, you can create multiple home directories by enabling the Home Directory radio button. This technique can provide your FTP site with multiple root directories, though your FTP clients will need to know the directory name in order to access them. They could use `ftp://ftp.nt-guru.com/WinBook` to access the files in the `WinBook` home directory, for example, instead of `ftp://ftp.nt-guru.com`, which would put them in the *IISRoot*/FTPRoot directory.

5. Enter a name for the virtual directory, such as `Samples`, in the Alias field.

6. Enter a username in the User Name field and a password for this user account in the Password field if the virtual directory will reside on a remote computer. This username and password will be used to connect to the remote share.

7. Specify the type of access your clients will use in the Access group. By default, the Read check box is enabled, specifying that the client will have read-only access to the directory. If this directory will be used to upload files, enable the Write check box as well.

8. Click the OK button to create your virtual directory and return to the Directories properties sheet.

9. Click the OK button to exit the Directories properties sheet and return to the Internet Service Manager.

Configuring the Gopher Service

As with the WWW and FTP services, you should configure your Gopher site to suit your individual needs before you make it available to the world. You have four options when you configure your Gopher publishing service. You can configure the general properties of the Gopher service; you can specify the Gopher directories; you can log the activity on your Gopher site; and you can limit access to your Gopher site. All of these options are obtained from the Gopher Service Properties for *ComputerName* dialog box. To access this dialog, choose Properties | Service Properties from the menu, click the Properties button on the toolbar (third button from the left), or right-click the service when in the Services View or Server View. Gopher's logging and limiting-access properties sheets follow the same format as the WWW service's. Rather than repeat this information, I refer you to the sections "Logging WWW Activity" and "Limiting Access to your WWW Site."

Configuring the Gopher Service

The Gopher Service properties sheet, shown in Figure 6.12, includes the following options:

FIGURE 6.12.

Configuring the basic options of the Gopher properties service.

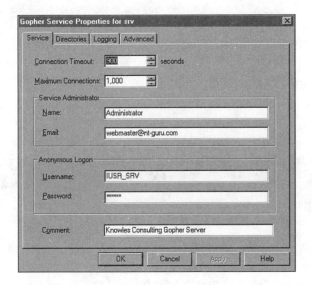

- Connection Timeout—This option specifies the time, in seconds, before an inactive user's connection will be terminated. This option ensures that even if the Gopher server fails to close a connection when a user exits the site, eventually it will be closed. The default is 900 seconds, or 15 minutes.

- Maximum Connections—This option specifies the maximum number of simultaneous users that can be connected to your Gopher server. The default is 1,000.

- Service Administrator—A Gopher client can provide additional information to its user about the administrator of the Gopher service. This information includes the following fields:

   - Name—Specifies a contact name or the administrator of the Gopher site
   - Email—Specifies an e-mail address for the contact name or administrator of the Gopher site

- Anonymous Logon—This group box defines the user account and password for users who connect to your site using an anonymous logon. Most Gopher servers support the anonymous logon. If you want your site to support users who are not members of your domain, which most of us do, their access will be based on the user account and password specified in the following fields:

   - Username—This field specifies either a local-user or a domain-user account. By default, this account is called IUSER *ComputerName*, where *ComputerName* is the name of the computer on which IIS was installed.

> **CAUTION**
>
> By default, this group is added to the Guests local group. If your server is a member of the domain, the account is also a member of the Domain Users global group. You should verify the privileges of the group to ensure that this account cannot be used to access secure network resources. For additional information refer to Chapter 10.

- Password—This field specifies the password to be used with the user account mentioned above. If you change the password here, you must also change the password using User Manager (for a server) or User Manager for Domains (for a domain controller).

> **TIP**
>
> You should change the password for this account every 30 to 45 days to enhance the security of your site.

- Comment—This option specifies a description to be displayed on the Internet Service Manager while in Report view for the Gopher publishing service.

Configuring the Gopher Service Directories

The Gopher service has fewer options for managing directories than the other services: It can only create virtual directories either on the local computer or on a remote computer. Select the Directories tab on the Gopher Service Properties dialog to display the Directories properties sheet, shown in Figure 6.13.

FIGURE 6.13.

The Gopher publishing service directory properties sheet.

Follow these steps to create a virtual directory:

1. Click the Add button in the Directories properties sheet to display the Directory Properties dialog box, shown in Figure 6.14.

FIGURE 6.14.

Creating a virtual directory.

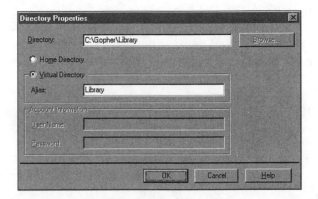

2. To create a virtual directory on the local computer, specify a directory name in the in the Directory field or click the Browse button to select a directory.

NOTE

If you use the Browse button, the Select Directory dialog box will appear. In it, you can choose an existing directory in the Directories list box. To create a new subdirectory, select an existing directory and enter the name of the subdirectory to create in the New Directory Name field. After you have entered the requested information, click the OK button to close the Directory dialog box. Your selected installation directory will appear in the Directory field of the Directory Properties dialog box.

---

3. To create a virtual directory on a remote computer, specify a UNC filename (such as Backup_Srv\C\WWWRoot) in the Directory field.

4. Click the Virtual Directory radio button to enable it if necessary.

5. Enter a name for the virtual directory, such as Library, in the Alias field.

6. Enter a username in the User Name field and a password for this user account in the Password field if the virtual directory will reside on a remote computer. This username and password will be used to connect to the remote share.

7. Click the OK button to create your virtual directory and return to the Directories properties sheet.

8. Click the OK button to exit the Directories properties sheet and return to the Internet Service Manager.

Configuring the NetShow On-Demand Service

The NetShow On-Demand server is probably the easiest IIS service to configure. This service has only three options: the basic service properties, the service directories, or the service logging properties. All of these options are obtained from the NetShow On-Demand Service Properties for *ComputerName* dialog box. To access this dialog box, choose Properties | Service Properties from the menu, click the Properties button on the toolbar (third button from the left), or right-click the service when in the Services View or Server View. The dialog box shown in Figure 6.15 will then appear.

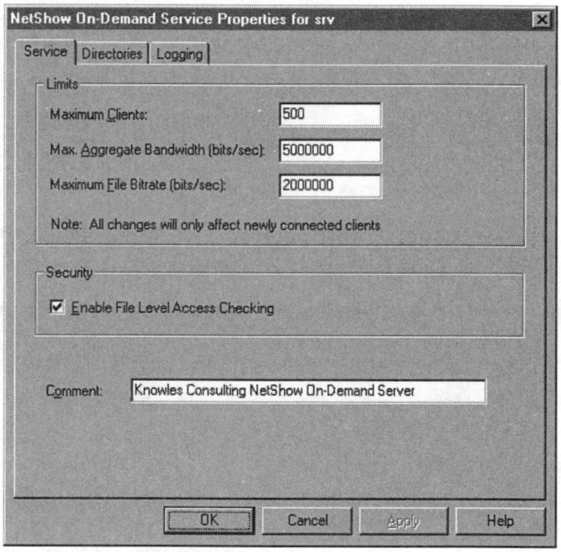

FIGURE 6.15.

Configuring the basic properties of the NetShow On-Demand service.

The following options are available:

- Maximum Clients—Specifies the maximum number of simultaneous clients that can be connected to the server. The minimum value is 0; the maximum value is 10,000.
- Max Aggregate Bandwidth (bits/sec)—Specifies the maximum network bandwidth, in bits per second, that will be used by the server for all streaming multimedia. The minimum value is 0; the maximum value is 100,000,000 (or 100Mb/sec).

> **NOTE**
>
> The max aggregate bandwidth value should be at least 15 percent less than the maximum bit rate of your network adapter. For example, if you have a 10Mb/sec network adapter, then the maximum value for this field should be 8,500,000.

Using the Internet Service Manager

CHAPTER 6

161

6

USING THE
INTERNET SERVICE
MANAGER

■ Maximum File Bitrate (bits/sec)—Specifies the maximum network bandwidth, in bits per second, that will be used by the server for streaming a single multimedia file. The minimum value is 0; the maximum value is 6,000,000 (or 6Mb/sec).

■ Enable File Level Access Checking—Specifies that the Windows NT user account database will be applied to all accesses to the streaming multimedia files. This option, when combined with directory and file permissions, can prevent unauthorized users from accessing files on your server.

■ Comment—Specifies a 260-character comment to be displayed in the Internet Service Manager.

Configuring the NetShow On-Demand Service Directories

Of all the publishing services, NetShow On-Demand has the fewest options for managing directories. It can create virtual directories only on the local computer. Select the Directories tab on the NetShow On-Demand Service Properties dialog to display the Directories properties sheet, shown in Figure 6.16.

FIGURE 6.16.

The NetShow On-Demand publishing service directory properties sheet.

Follow these steps to create a virtual directory:

1. Click the Add button in the Directories properties sheet to display the Directory Properties dialog box, shown in Figure 6.17.

2. Specify a directory name in the Directory field or click the Browse button to select a directory.

FIGURE 6.17.

Creating a virtual directory.

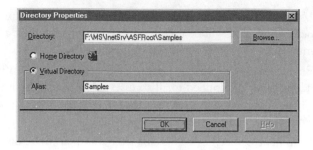

3. Click it to enable the Virtual Directory radio button if necessary.

4. Enter a name for the virtual directory, such as Samples, in the Alias field.

5. Click the OK button to create your virtual directory and return to the Directories properties sheet.

6. Click the OK button to exit the Directories properties sheet and return to the Internet Service Manager.

Logging NetShow On-Demand Activity

Logging your NetShow On-Demand activity is quite useful in determining if your users are making use of your streaming multimedia capabilities. Unlike the other IIS services, however, the NetShow On-Demand server can log this activity only to a standard text file. Perhaps a future version will provide the ability to log this activity to an ODBC database. To enable logging, follow these steps:

1. Click the Logging tab in the NetShow On-Demand Service Properties dialog box to display the Logging properties sheet, shown in Figure 6.18.

2. Click the Enable Logging radio button.

3. Click the Log to File radio button. You can configure the following options:

  ■ Automatically open new log—This option specifies that a new log will be created based on one of the following criteria:

    ■ Daily—Every day

    ■ Weekly—Once a week

    ■ Monthly—Once a month

    ■ When file size reaches—Whenever the log file exceeds the size specified in the MB field

  ■ Log file directory—This option specifies the location where the log file will reside.

FIGURE 6.18.

Configuring the NetShow On-Demand service to log activity.

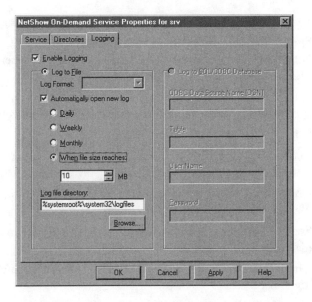

4. Click the OK button to close the NetShow On-Demand Service Properties dialog box and return to the Internet Service Manager.

Logging Site Access with SQL Server

Although you can use any ODBC database to log your IIS site's activity, this section describes how to use SQL Server because it is the most commonly used database engine. Configuring an IIS service to log the activity to an ODBC database is described in the section titled "Logging WWW Activity," so I will not repeat that information here. What you will learn, though, is how to build the database to contain your logs, how to create a user account to access this database, and how to create an ODBC data source to access the logs from your IIS services.

Building the Database

The IIS services actually write their logging information to one or more tables. However, these tables must be contained within a database. While you can create the IIS table(s) in any database, I recommend that you create one specifically for the Internet Information Server. Follow these steps:

1. Create two new devices using the SQL Enterprise Manager. Expand the registered SQL Server in the Server Manager window, select the Database Devices folder, right-click it, and then select New Device from the pop-up menu.

2. Specify a name for the new device (such as IISDatabaseDevice.DAT) in the Name field.

3. Specify the drive where the device should reside in the Location drop-down list box. Next to the drop-down list box is an unnamed field where you may specify the filename to be used for the device.

4. Specify the size of the device in the Size field. If you expect to have a very active Web site and don't want to dump your database too often, you could start with 30MB.

5. Click the Create Now button to create the device.

6. Repeat steps 2 through 5 to create the log device except use a name such as IISLogDevice.DAT and specify a size of 10MB.

7. Create the database by selecting the Databases folder, right-clicking it, and choosing New Database from the pop-up menu.

8. Specify the database name (such as IISLogs) in the Name field in the New Database dialog box.

9. Choose the device you created in step 2 (IISDatabaseDevice) in the Data Device drop-down list box.

10. Choose the device you created in step 6 (IISLogDevice) in the Log device drop-down list box.

11. Click the Create Now button to create the database.

12. Create the table(s) using the following script:

```
USE DATABASE IISLOGS
GO
CREATE TABLE dbo.IISLog (    ClientHost varchar (255) NOT NULL ,
username varchar (255) NOT NULL , LogTime datetime NOT NULL ,
service varchar (255) NOT NULL , machine varchar (255) NOT NULL ,
serverip varchar (50) NOT NULL , processingtime int NOT NULL ,
bytesrecvd int NOT NULL , bytessent int NOT NULL , servicestatus int NOT NULL
➡ ,
win32status int NOT NULL , operation varchar (255) NOT NULL ,
target varchar (255) NOT NULL , parameters varchar (255) NOT NULL)
GO
```

> **NOTE**
>
> This script will create one table called IISLog. If you want to create individual tables for each service, just change IISLog to WWWLog and run the script. Then change it to FTPLog or GopherLog and rerun the script to create the additional tables.

Assigning Permissions to Access the Database

After you have created the devices, the database, and the tables (as described in the preceding section), you will need to assign permission to access the database. You can use an existing user account or create a new one. The method you will use depends on the security model of your SQL Server installation. The following will work for a standard or mixed model:

1. Expand the Databases folder using the SQL Enterprise Manager and then expand the database you want to manage.

2. Select the Groups/Users folder, right-click it, and choose New User from the pop-up menu.

3. Enter a user account in the Name field. The SQL Server uses this name for display purposes.

4. Specify a name in the Login field. This name is usually the name of an existing SQL Server account (such as sa) or a domain account (such as IUSR_SRV).

5. Click the Add button to give the user account permission to access the database. Click Close.

6. Choose Object | Permissions from the top-level menu. Highlight the group or user for which you want to change the permissions. Click the Grant All button and then the Set Button to give full permission for the user to access the objects (such as the tables you created) within the database.

7. Click the Close button to exit the dialog box and return to the SQL Enterprise Manager. You can either leave it running or close SQL Enterprise Manager, but you're done here.

Building the ODBC Data Source

The final step in using an ODBC database to store your IIS logs is to create the link between your ODBC client (the IIS services) and the ODBC server (SQL Server). Follow these steps:

1. Open the Control Panel ODBC applet, which will display the Data Source Administrator dialog box.

2. Click the System DSN tab to display the System Data Sources property sheet.

3. Click the Add button to display the Create New Data Source dialog box.

4. Select the SQL Server entry in the list box. Then click the Finish button. The ODBC SQL Server Setup dialog box will appear.

5. Click the Options button to expand it. (See Figure 6.19.)

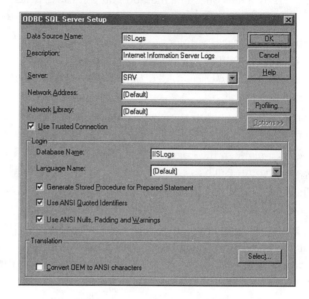

6. Enter a unique name (such as IISLogs) in the Data Source Name field.

7. Enter a comment to describe the DSN in the Description field.

8. Specify the SQL Server to which you want to connect in the Server field.

9. Accept the default configurations for the Network Address and Network Library fields.

   Change these fields only if you will be using a nonstandard connection to a SQL Server installation. You can enable the Use Trusted Connection check box to provide a secure (that is, encrypted) connection between your IIS installation and your SQL Server installation if you are using Microsoft SQL Server 6.0 or higher.

10. Enter the name of the SQL Server database you created (such as IISLogs) in the Database Name field.

11. Leave the rest of the options enabled for optimum performance and compatibility.

NOTE

You can use the Generate Stored Procedure for Prepared Statement option to prebuild and precompile a stored procedure for SQL Server. This option can significantly increase the query performance. The Use ANSI Quoted Identifiers and Use ANSI Nulls, Padding and

> Warnings options are provided for compatibility when the client uses a character set other than the character set used on the SQL Server.

12. Click the OK button to return to the System Data Source Administrator dialog box.

13. Click the OK button to return to the Control Panel.

That's all there is to creating an ODBC data source name. If you are using a different ODBC database, just choose the ODBC driver in step 4 to match your ODBC-compliant database.

Summary

In this chapter you learn to use the Internet Service Manager to manage your Internet Information Server, including the operating state of the services. You also learn to use the various views to sort the IIS sites and services to make managing them easier and how to configure the various options for each type of service. At the end of the chapter you learn how to use SQL Server, or another ODBC-compliant database, for your IIS service activity logging.

In Chapter 7, "Using Internet Explorer," you use the Microsoft Internet Explorer to access your IIS sites. You'll also set the various configuration options to prepare you for those trying times with your network clients.

Using Internet Explorer

IN THIS CHAPTER

■ Installing Internet Explorer   *171*

■ Configuring Internet Explorer   *172*

■ Using Internet Explorer   *195*

CHAPTER 7

To obtain maximum performance from the Internet Information Server, you will need to use a Web browser that supports the complete feature set. Currently, the only Web browser to fit this bill is Microsoft Internet Explorer. Luckily for you, this browser is included with Windows NT 4.0 and Windows 95. It is also available, at no charge from Microsoft, for Windows 3.*x*, as well as for Macintosh. You can download Microsoft Internet Explorer from the Internet at `http://www.microsoft.com/ie`. Because Internet Explorer will also be used as the standard Web browser for Microsoft Network, CompuServe, and AOL, the number of Internet Explorer users will soar in the next couple months.

The prevalence of Internet Explorer means that Internet Explorer users should be your target audience for the Web pages you develop. However, it does not mean that you should ignore users of other Web browsers, such as Netscape Navigator. You should continue to view your Web pages with these other browsers to make sure the content you want to provide is accessible. Nevertheless, you should take advantage of some of the Microsoft HTML extensions for Internet Explorer, such as the `<MARQUEE>` tag, to customize the look of your Web pages and highlight special content areas. Version 3.0 includes a new look and will support ActiveX controls, ActiveX scripts, ActiveX documents, new HTML tags, new security protocols, and a few additional options. For more information on ActiveX scripting, take a look at Chapter 18, "Unleashing the Power of VBScript."

As I write this chapter, Internet Explorer version 3.0 is widely available either directly from Microsoft, downloadable from the Web, or in some retail stores. If you are in charge of a corporate network, you should not rush to implement Internet Explorer version 3.0 at your site until some of the security-related issues have been completely worked out. The "Configuring Internet Explorer Security" section of this chapter covers the basic security options of Internet Explorer version 3.0. One of the main features of Internet Explorer version 3.0 is the ActiveX components that enable you to download executable code or documents.

The potential to download an unfriendly application or document that could run amok on your network is quite real. The same could be said for Java applets supported by other Web browsers. Microsoft is implementing a means to digitally *sign* these executable enhancements to your Web browser. This mechanism means that you will be able to hold accountable whoever created or provided the unfriendly element for your network. This level of accountability is similar to what you can currently obtain for any third-party software that you buy. If you buy an accounting program, for example, and it miscalculates your taxes, you could hold the manufacturer responsible for the error. Nevertheless, in the real world, your data is still very much at risk. Accountability only means that you know who created or provided the enhancement. Getting compensation for your losses is another story.

As a WWW site administrator (Webmaster) or developer, you will be left in the cold if you do not support Internet Explorer 3.0 and ActiveX controls and documents. Therefore, this chapter focuses on Internet Explorer 3.0, rather than the older retail version (Internet Explorer 2.0).

Installing Internet Explorer

The version of Internet Explorer currently included with Windows NT 4.0 is Internet Explorer 2.0. Microsoft may release Internet Explorer 3.0 as part of a newer build of the retail Windows NT 4.0 product. Currently version 3.0 is an add-on product, which may include other applications (such as a mail or news client); therefore, your installation procedure may vary. Version 2.0 is installed through the Control Panel Add/Remove Programs applet. It is normally installed automatically when you install Windows NT 4.0. However, if you performed a custom installation and chose not to include Internet Explorer, you can follow these steps to install it:

1. Launch the Control Panel Add/Remove Programs applet.
2. Select the Windows NT Setup tab to display the Windows NT Setup properties sheet.
3. Select the Accessories item; then click the Details button. This step will display the Accessories dialog box.
4. Scroll down the Components list box and check the Internet Jumpstart Kit item.
5. Click the OK button. You will return to the Windows NT Setup properties sheet.
6. Click the OK button.

    The Add/Remove Properties - Copying Files - Files Needed dialog box will prompt you to supply the path to the installation files.

7. Enter the location of the requested files in the Copy Files From field and click the OK button.

> **NOTE**
>
> If the Add/Remove Programs setup application can find the files without your help, such as when the Windows NT CD-ROM is already in your CD-ROM drive or when the images located on a network server are accessible, the dialog box in step 7 will not be displayed.

At this point the files will be copied to your computer, and you will be prompted to reboot by the Systems Settings Change dialog box.

8. Click Yes to reboot and immediately start using Internet Explorer or click No to continue your current work session.

If you install Internet Explorer version 3.0 using a downloaded copy from the Internet, the installation should follow this basic sequence:

1. Copy the downloaded self-extracting archive file to a temporary directory.
2. Execute the self-extracting archive using File Manager, Windows NT Explorer, or another method of your choice.

The Microsoft Internet Explorer Setup dialog box will appear. This dialog box includes the legal agreement between you and Microsoft. It contains copyright information and rules that specify the usability and suitability of the application to be used by you.

3. Choose the Yes button to install the product. (Choosing the No button will cause the installation to terminate.) The rest of this exercise assumes you have chosen Yes.

   The installation files will be extracted from the archive and placed in the system's default temporary directory, as specified by your TEMP= environment variable.

4. Choose the components to install when prompted by the Microsoft Internet Explorer Setup dialog box. If you click the No button, a full install of all the applications (Internet Explorer, Internet Mail, Internet News, ActiveMovie, and the HTML Layout Control) will occur. If you click Yes, the Optional Components dialog box will be displayed to allow you to select the components you want to install.

   The Installation Status dialog box appears, and the Copying Files dialog box is displayed as the various component files are copied to your hard disk. By default, Internet Explorer files will be copied to the Program Files\Plus!\Microsoft Internet directory. Various other files will be copied to your SystemRoot\System32 directory.

   Finally, the Microsoft Internet Explorer Setup dialog box will prompt you to reboot.

5. Click Yes to reboot and immediately start using Internet Explorer or click No to continue your current work session.

Configuring Internet Explorer

Although you can use Internet Explorer immediately after you install it, you'll get a lot more out of this browser by taking a few moments to configure it. You can customize several options to make Internet Explorer look better, work better, and be safer to use by younger members of your family. This section explains how each option works and steps through the configuration process for each option. When you are finished, Internet Explorer will be ready for use on the Internet.

> **TIP**
>
> If you are a network administrator responsible for rolling out many Internet Explorer installations, you should look into Internet Explorer Administration Kit. You can use this kit to predefine the setup and configuration options for Internet Explorer 3.0. You can download the kit from http://www.microsoft.com/ie/ieak/.

Configuring the Appearance

As the old saying goes, "The clothes make the man." Appearance in your professional and personal life is everything. If you look like a bum, people will think you are a bum. Your Web site is no different. Creating a good-looking text-only Web site or a Web site with attention-grabbing graphics is everyone's goal. However, you must remember that not every Web user will see all your nifty graphics, perhaps because the Web browser your client is using cannot display the images. The client's Web browser may be a text-only browser, or perhaps it cannot support the specific graphic format you used.

Consequently, many Web browsers support a configuration option to disable graphic images. This option can increase the speed at which the Web browser displays the content (text and hypertext links) of the Web page. After all, downloading a graphic over a slow connection can be a time-consuming job. Downloading an AVI or sound file can be a nightmare.

As you develop your Web site, you should view it in text-only mode as well as in graphics mode. You may even want to change the default attributes for displayed text, background, and links just to see how your Web pages will look. If you are configuring multiple installations for your network clients, you may want to standardize on a specific set of attributes. As a network administrator, you may even want to turn off some of these graphics options to limit the amount of network traffic. You can change these attributes by following a few simple steps:

1. Choose View | Options to display the Options dialog box as shown in Figure 7.1. The default property sheet is the General property sheet, and you can use it to configure the basic appearance and behavior of Internet Explorer.

FIGURE 7.1.

Configuring the way Internet Explorer displays a Web page.

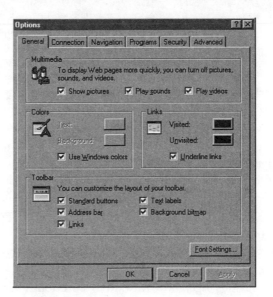

TIP

The General property sheet is also accessible from the Control Panel Internet applet.

---

2. Disable any of the following options in the Multimedia group to increase the speed at which Internet Explorer will display the page:

   ■ Show pictures—Specifies that graphic images (GIF or JPG) will be displayed when checked (the default) or skipped when unchecked.

   ■ Play sounds—Specifies that sounds will be played when checked (the default) or skipped when unchecked.

TIP

If you do not like the background sound of a particular site you visit often, you can disable the Sounds option before you visit the site.

   ■ Play videos—Specifies that audio-video files will be downloaded and played automatically checked (the default) or skipped when unchecked.

NOTE

Audio-video (AVI) files are notorious for eating up network bandwidth. If you have an intranet or are using IIS as a gateway to the Internet, you may want to disable viewing of AVI files.

---

3. Uncheck the Use Windows colors check box to change the default colors for the text and background. Then click either the Text button or the Background button to display the Color dialog box from which you can choose a specific color.

4. Click the Visited or Unvisited buttons, respectively, to change the default colors for the hypertext links you have already viewed or for those that you have not yet viewed. Choose the specific color you want from the Color dialog box. If you do not want your links to be underlined, uncheck the Underline links check box.

5. Check or uncheck the following check boxes in the Toolbar group to remove a toolbar from Internet Explorer or to change its appearance:

   ■ Standard buttons—Specifies to display (checked) or not display (unchecked) the standard toolbar. This toolbar includes menu shortcuts to move backward to the previous page, move forward to a previously viewed page, stop downloading a page, refresh a page, display the home page, display the search page, display your favorite pages, print the current page, change the font, or load your e-mail editor.

■ Address bar—Specifies to display (checked) or not display (unchecked) the address toolbar. This toolbar shows the address of the current page.

■ Links—Specifies to display (checked) or not display (unchecked) the links toolbar. This toolbar includes buttons to jump to various Microsoft sites to show a list of the best pages on the Web, today's links, a Web gallery, a list of product names, and the Microsoft home page.

■ Text labels—Specifies to display (checked) or not display (unchecked) the standard text labels for a button.

■ Background bitmap—Specifies to display (checked) or not display (unchecked) the standard background bitmaps for a button.

6. Click the Font Settings button to specify which fonts to use with Internet Explorer. Use the Fonts dialog box, as shown in Figure 7.2, to make your selection from the fonts installed on your computer.

FIGURE 7.2.

Configuring Internet Explorer for international use.

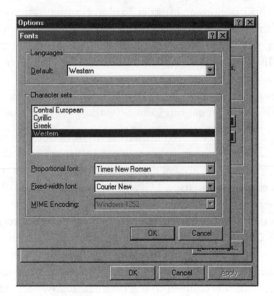

You have the following options:

■ Character sets—Select the desired language to use from the list. This option will set the default MIME encoding scheme as well.

■ Proportional font—To change the default proportional font to be displayed for a character set, choose another font from the Proportional font drop-down list.

■ Fixed-width font—To change the default fixed-width font to be displayed for a character set, choose another font from the Fixed-width font drop-down list.

■ MIME encoding—If you choose a non-Western language, you may choose a character-encoding sequence from the MIME encoding drop-down list. Then click the OK button to return to the General property sheet.

> **TIP**
>
> Internet Explorer can support multiple languages. This feature can be beneficial to Web page developers who create international content. You can also use this option to configure the default proportional-width and fixed-width fonts that will be displayed on the page.

7. Click the OK button to save your changes and return to Internet Explorer.

Configuring the Internet Connection

One of the most important Internet Explorer configuration options is selecting how you will connect to the Internet. You can do so through a dial-up network connection or through a proxy server. If you are not physically connected to the Internet, Internet Explorer can help you access Internet resources more easily. Internet Explorer can sense when you request an Internet resource (such as when you ping an Internet client); then it uses the Dial-Up Networking service to connect to the Internet. Once connected, you can access the Internet resource as if it were part of your local network.

Auto-dial is a great service if your internal network does not use TCP/IP. However, if you do use TCP/IP, using the auto-dial option can be more of a problem than a solution because the auto-dial feature cannot always determine whether you are trying to access a local or remote resource. In essence, if you use a TCP/IP-based client, auto-dial may attempt to dial the Internet to access the resource. Consequently, if you try to ping your server, the Dial-Up Networking service may be invoked in an attempt to resolve the IP address. You could spend a lot of time pressing the Cancel button to terminate the auto-dial attempt. I recommend using auto-dial only when the internal network uses a network protocol other than TCP/IP or when the computer is a standalone computer and not connected to a network at all. To configure the computer to automatically connect to the Internet, follow these steps:

1. Choose Dial-Up Networking from the Accessories menu on the taskbar to display the Dial-Up Networking dialog box.

2. Click the More button to display a drop-down menu list and choose the User Preferences dialog box, shown in Figure 7.3.

3. Check the locations from which you wish to enable auto-dial in the Enable auto-dial by location list.

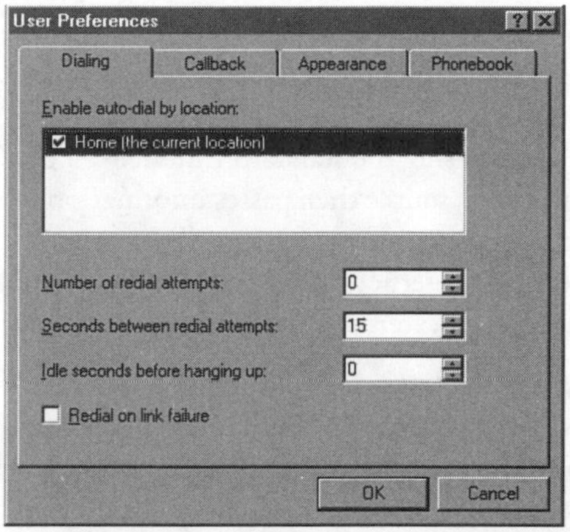

Figure 7.3.

Configuring the computer to connect to the Internet automatically.

> **NOTE**
>
> If this field is empty, you may add one or more locations by using the Control Panel Telephony applet.

4. Specify the number of attempts to make if the number is busy in the Number of redial attempts field.

5. Specify the number of seconds to pause between redial attempts if the number is busy in the Seconds between redial attempts field.

6. Specify the number of seconds to wait on an idle (not being used) connection before the connection is automatically terminated in the Idle seconds before hanging up field.

> **TIP**
>
> To disable the auto-disconnect feature, set the value to 0.

7. Check the Redial on link failure check box if you want the connection to be automatically reestablished if the connection is terminated abnormally.

8. Click the OK button to save your changes and return to Internet Explorer.

A proxy server is a computer on your network that acts as an intermediary between an Internet resource, such as a Web site, and your network client application (in this case Internet Explorer). You can think of a proxy server as a middleman. For example, when you buy a steak at the local market, money passes from you to the local store to the rancher. You do not just go to a ranch and hack a steak off a cow. Well, think of the proxy server as the market and the Internet resource as the rancher.

A proxy server also increases network security by preventing incoming or outgoing network traffic. This condition exists because your network client connects to a specific (nonstandard) port on your proxy server to access an Internet resource. Your proxy server then connects to the Internet resource using the standard Internet resource port address assigned to the Internet service. The Internet resource then passes information to the proxy server, which in turn passes the information to the connected client. This two-way data flow continues until the client disconnects from the Internet resource. By using nonstandard ports on the proxy server, you can prevent internal or external clients from accessing network resources.

However, Internet Explorer does not require that you use a proxy server for all network and Internet access. You can also configure Internet Explorer by domain name, IP address, or port address to bypass the proxy server. This configuration provides faster and more efficient access to intranet resources, which is a good thing considering that a proxy server, like any middleman, consumes resources. Nothing in this world is really free; a proxy server provides increased network security at the cost of network bandwidth and time. To configure Internet Explorer to use a proxy server, follow these steps:

1. Choose View | Options to display the Options property sheet.
2. Click the Connection tab to display the Connection property sheet, shown in Figure 7.4.

FIGURE 7.4.

Configuring Internet Explorer to use a proxy server.

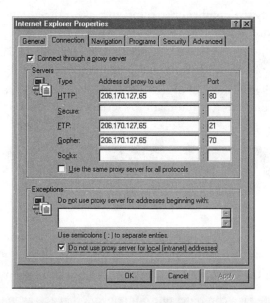

TIP

The Connection property sheet is also accessible from the Control Panel Internet applet.

3. Check the Connect through a proxy server check box. Then enter the IP address and port for the Internet protocols specified in Table 7.1.

Table 7.1. Internet protocols and ports for proxy server configuration.

Internet Protocol	Port	Description
HTTP	80	Hypertext Transfer Protocol. Used for World Wide Web access.
Secure	443	Secure Hypertext Transfer Protocol/Secure Socket Layer protocol. Used for secure World Wide Web access.
FTP	21	File Transfer Protocol.
Gopher	70	Gopher transfer protocol.
Socks	1080	Used to access a Socks-compliant firewall. Note: This type of firewall requires a Socks-modified client such as Internet Explorer or Netscape Navigator. The primary drawback of Socks is that it does not support authentication hooks or protocol-specific logging.

TIP

If your proxy server uses a single port for all Internet services, fill out just the HTTP service entries. Then check the Use the same proxy server for all protocols check box.

4. Enter the DNS name, IP address, or TCP/IP port number in the Do not use proxy server for addresses beginning with list box to bypass your proxy server for specific Internet resources. Each multiple entry should be separated by a semicolon. To bypass a proxy for access to a specific computer or port, for example, you could enter 206.170.127.65;80, which would bypass the proxy server to access the computer with IP address 206.170.127.65 or to access any resource using TCP/IP port 80.

5. Click the OK button to save your changes and return to the Options dialog box.

6. Click the OK button to update your configuration and return to Internet Explorer.

Configuring the Start and Search Pages and History Settings

Internet Explorer will load a default startup page each time it is executed. This default is the Microsoft Corporation home page located at http://www.microsoft.com. This option is fine if you want to check out the Microsoft home page each time you launch Internet Explorer. However, I find this default startup page to be a bit of a nuisance for two reasons. First, if you are not already connected to the Internet, Windows NT will attempt to dial your default connection using the Dial-Up Networking service if you have auto-dial enabled (see the previous section "Configuring the Internet Connection" for further information). Second, I have my own intranet and prefer to view the home page for my WWW site.

Internet Explorer also has a default search page, which connects to the Microsoft site `http://www.microsoft.com/access/allinone.asp`. Although I like this page because it includes shortcuts to several Internet directory listing services (such as Yahoo! and Lycos), it has the same disadvantages as described in the preceding paragraph. To change either of these options, follow these steps:

1. Connect to the Web site you want to use as your start page or your search page.

2. Choose View | Options to display the Options property sheet.

3. Click the Navigation tab to display the Navigation property sheet, shown in Figure 7.5.

Figure 7.5.

Specifying the default start and search pages.

4. To change the start page, make sure that the entry in the Page drop-down list is Start Page and that the entry in the Address field is the URL of the currently displayed page; then click the Use Current button.

5. To change the search page, make sure that the entry in the Page drop-down list is Search Page and that the entry in the Address field is the URL of the currently displayed page; then click the Use Current button.

TIP

To return to Internet Explorer default start or search page, select the appropriate page in the drop-down list and then click the Use Default button.

6. Click the OK button to update your changes and return to Internet Explorer.

Whenever Internet Explorer views a page, it stores a copy of the URL in its history folder. Although this history file can help you find a site you've visited in the past, these stored URLs do take up space on your hard disk. So to save space you may want to limit the storage time for the URLs or remove them from your disk altogether. To do so, just follow these steps:

1. Choose View | Options to display the Options property sheet.
2. Click the Navigation tab to display the Navigation property sheet, shown in Figure 7.5.
3. To specify the number of days to keep a URL, enter a value in the Number of days to keep pages in history field.

> **TIP**
>
> To prevent any URLs from being stored on your hard disk, set the number of days to 0.

4. To clear your disk of all stored URLs, click the Clear History button. When the Internet Properties message box appears asking if you really want to delete all items in the history folder, click the Yes button.

> **TIP**
>
> If you are not sure if you want to delete these stored URLs or if you just want to see what URLs have been stored, click the View History button to display the History folder contents.

5. Click the OK button to update your changes and return to Internet Explorer.

Associating Programs and File Types

Unlike Internet Explorer 2.0, Internet Explorer 3.0 does not incorporate a built-in newsreader, but it does include the option to specify an application to launch whenever a News URI is accessed. It includes this same capability for associating an e-mail application, which is quite useful if you prefer to use Microsoft Exchange, Eudora, or another e-mail client instead of the Microsoft Internet Mail client. At the same time, you can also specify your associated file types.

File type associations should be nothing new to you if you have used any version of Windows before. If not, a file association is nothing more than specifying the name of an application to use with a specific file extension. This file extension is used to launch the application when you open a file with Internet Explorer. Once the application is executing, the file will be loaded into the application. If you do not have a file associated for a specific file type, you will be greeted with a dialog box to specify the application to run. If you choose not to specify an application to run, the hypertext link will fail.

TIP

One of the really neat things about file associations is how Internet Explorer 3.0 works with OLE-enabled applications that support OLE automation, such as Microsoft Word for Windows. If you open a Word document (*.DOC) on a computer with Word for Windows installed on it, Word will be loaded within the main Internet Explorer 3.0 window. Internet Explorer 3.0 menu and toolbars will change, and you can work with the Word document right within Internet Explorer 3.0. If you are using Internet Explorer 2.0, or the associated application does not support OLE automation, Internet Explorer will load Word as a separate application and then Word will load the document.

Normally, each application you install will also install the file associations for you. As you browse the Web, however, you may encounter files for which you have no predefined association. To inform Internet Explorer of the application to run when you want to read a newsgroup message, send e-mail, or when only a data file is selected, you need to specify the news and mail applications or add a new file association.

To view your current news and mail associations, follow these steps:

1. Choose View | Options to display the Options dialog box.

2. Choose the Programs tab to display the Programs property sheet, as shown in Figure 7.6.

FIGURE 7.6.

Specifying program associations for Internet Explorer.

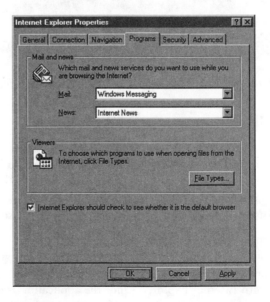

3. Change your e-mail application by selecting the application to run from the Mail drop-down list. By default, this application is Internet Mail. However, if you are using Microsoft Exchange, you should change this setting to Windows Messaging.

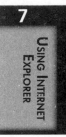

4. Change your news application by selecting the application to run from the News drop-down list.

5. Click the OK button to close the Options dialog box when you are finished.

To view your current file associations, follow these steps:

1. Choose View | Options to display the Options property sheet, shown in Figure 7.1.

2. Choose the Programs tab to display the Programs property sheet as shown in Figure 7.6. Then click the File Types button to display the File Types dialog box, as shown in Figure 7.7.

FIGURE 7.7.

Associating a file type with an application.

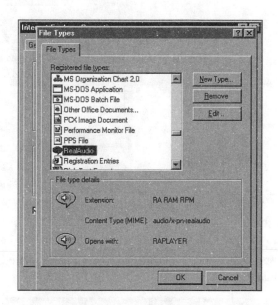

3. Scroll down the list of items displayed in the Registered file types list box.

4. Click a specific file type in the list box.

   The File type details group will then display the relevant information about the file association.

5. Click the OK button when you are done.

To edit a file association, follow these steps:

1. Choose View | Options to display the Options property sheet, shown in Figure 7.1.

2. Choose the Programs tab to display the Programs property sheet as shown in Figure 7.6. Then click on the File Types button to display the File Types dialog box, as shown in Figure 7.7. Scroll through the Registered file types list box until you find the specific file type in which you are interested.

3. Click the item in the list box. The File type details group will update the display to show the current file extensions, MIME content type, and the application associated with the file association.

4. Click the Edit button to display the Edit File Type dialog box, which is shown in Figure 7.8.

FIGURE 7.8.

Editing a file type association.

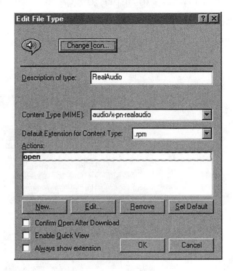

5. Click the Change Icon button to specify a different icon to be displayed with the Windows Explorer. The Change Icon dialog box will appear.

6. Choose an icon in the Current Icon field and click the OK button to return to the Edit File Type dialog box.

TIP

If the icons displayed in the Change Icon dialog box are not acceptable, you can change the name of the icon bank in the File Name field either by manually specifying a path and filename or by using the Browse button to find a file on your computer. You can use any Windows application or DLL that has icons built into the file as a resource or specify an icon file (*.ico).

---

7. Enter a comment in the Description of type field to display a better description of the type of file if the default is not acceptable.

8. Choose a MIME type for the file association in the Content Type (MIME) drop-down list. If the list does not contain a MIME type that fits the type of file, you can manually enter the information for a new MIME type.

9. Choose the file extension to be the default association in the Default Extension for Content Type drop-down list.

10. To change the function of the associated file type, do the following:

    1. Click the function (such as open) in the Actions list box.

    2. Click the Edit button. The Editing Action For Type dialog box will appear.

    3. Specify the application name and command-line parameters, whether the application responds to DDE commands, and the DDE messages to send to the application.

    4. Click the OK button to return to the Edit File Type dialog box when you are finished.

11. Improve performance by disabling the Confirm Open After Download check box. This setting loads files immediately, rather than displaying a dialog box each time a file is downloaded from the Internet with the specified file extension. The Confirmation dialog box requests user confirmation before the execution of the application and the loading of the associated file.

12. Check Enable Quick View if you have a Windows Explorer viewer for the file type. This way, you can quickly display the document using the Windows Explorer rather than by loading the associated application.

13. Check the Always show extension check box to display the filename and file extension in any folder window.

14. Click the OK button to return to the File Types property sheet.

15. Repeat steps 2 through 14 for each file association you wish to edit.

16. Click the OK button when you are finished.

Adding a new file association follows the same general steps as editing a file association except that the name of the dialog changes to Add New File Type and the dialog box is completely empty. You must specify the icon to display the associated file extension, the MIME content type, and the actions you want it to perform.

TIP

If you have multiple Web browsers installed on your computer, you may be tired of seeing the message that Internet Explorer is not the default browser. To disable the check that determines whether Internet Explorer is configured as the default Web browser, uncheck the Internet Explorer Should Check To See Whether It Is The Default Browser check box.

Configuring Internet Explorer Security

In a world full of malicious system hackers, credit card fraud, unfriendly viruses, and poorly written applications, the Internet can be a dangerous place. Although abstinence is the only guaranteed safe option, Windows NT Server and Internet Explorer have options to help you limit the potential dangers of the Internet. In Chapter 10, "Advanced Security Issues," you will learn more about what Windows NT Server can do to reduce the danger involved in connecting to the Internet, but for now the focus is on the security features of Internet Explorer.

WARNING

Internet security is a real problem not so much from what is occurring on the Internet today, but rather from what may occur tomorrow. The first thing you should be concerned about is data snooping. *Data snooping* occurs when an Internet hacker traps information being sent between your computer and a remote site. If you send confidential information (such as your credit card number or user account and password) over an open connection, a hacker can easily obtain this information and use it to your detriment. Another potential security problem is the fraudulent display of a secure site notice or a fraudulent security certificate. In both cases you may think you are using a secure connection, but in reality you are not. The final cause for concern can arise either from a poorly written (but not malicious) ActiveX object or from a malicious ActiveX object. In the first case the poorly written code simply may not function properly; in the second case the ActiveX object may deliberately attempt to damage your system or pass confidential data to its originator.

Internet Explorer can provide three types of basic security.

- You can limit the types of sites to view by enabling the rating options.
- Internet Explorer can check the remote site's security credentials when you are sending or viewing data over a secure connection. You might encounter this type of connection when you purchase a product with a credit card from an electronic store.
- You can configure Internet Explorer to limit the active content that can be displayed on your Web browser. You will encounter active content any time you download and activate an ActiveX object.

The following sections examine these options one at a time.

Configuring the Rating System to Limit Access to Internet Sites

New to Internet Explorer 3.0 is the rating system. This system uses the Platform and Internet Content Selection (PICS)–based rating system and by default uses a rating system defined by the Recreational Software Advisory Council (RSAC). Web authors can obtain an RSAC rating to be applied to their Web site. For additional information check out the Web page at `http://www.rsac.org`. To enable ratings and specify the level of acceptance, follow these steps:

1. Choose Options from the View menu to display the Options property sheet.
2. Click the Security tab to display the Security property sheet. (See Figure 7.9.)

TIP

The Security property sheet is also accessible from the Control Panel Internet applet.

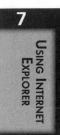

FIGURE **7.9.**

Configuring Internet Explorer security options.

3. Click the Enable Ratings button. The Create Supervisor Password dialog box will be displayed. You must enter and confirm a new password to enable the rating system. When you have done so, click the OK button.

   The Internet Ratings dialog box, shown in Figure 7.10, will be displayed.

FIGURE 7.10.

Configuring the Internet Explorer rating system.

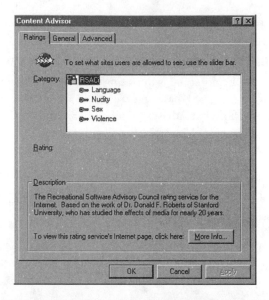

TIP

To turn off the rating system, just click the Disable Ratings button and supply your password. This button will appear after you have enabled ratings. In fact, it replaces the Enable Ratings button.

---

4. Click a category item to display a slider control next to the Rating field.

5. Slide the control to select your restrictions. As each item is selected, the Description field will display a comment for each rating. The ratings are divided into four categories with five subtypes each as follows:

   ■ Language—The five subtypes of this category are Inoffensive Slang, Mild Expletives, Moderate Expletives, Obscene Gestures, and Explicit or Crude Language.

   ■ Nudity—The five subtypes of this category are No Nudity, Revealing Attire, Partial Nudity, Frontal Nudity, and Provocative Display of Frontal Nudity.

   ■ Sex—The five subtypes of this category are No Sexual Activity Portrayed/ Romance, Passionate Kissing, Clothed Sexual Touching, Nonexplicit Sexual Touching, and Explicit Sexual Activity.

   ■ Violence—The five subtypes of this category are No Violence, Fighting, Killing, Killing with Blood and Gore, and Wanton and Gratuitous Violence.

6. Click the General tab to specify that users can see unrated sites, to specify that a user can view restricted sites by entering the supervisor password when prompted, or to change the current password for the rating system.

7. Click the Advanced tab to specify that a different PICS-based rating system be used or to choose a ratings bureau.

8. Click the OK button to update the rating options and return to Internet Explorer.

Using Certificates to Keep Yourself Safe

It's getting tougher and tougher to really know with whom you are communicating over the Web. It's also getting much more difficult for Web servers to know with whom they are really communicating. Why? Because it's just too easy to impersonate another user by learning someone's user identification and password or using someone else's IP address to spoof another site into thinking that it is communicating with him or her.

To deal with these problems, various vendors have recently introduced digital certificates for Web servers, Web browsers, and ActiveX applications. The purpose of these certificates is to positively identify a Web server, a user, or an application. Although digital certificates don't necessarily mean that your connection is 100 percent secure or that the ActiveX application you just installed is 100 percent reliable, at least it does offer some level of security and accountability. You can view an ActiveX certificate, like the one shown in Figure 7.11, whenever an ActiveX application is to be downloaded to your Web browser if your safety level is set to medium (more on this topic in the next section).

FIGURE 7.11.

An ActiveX digital certificate.

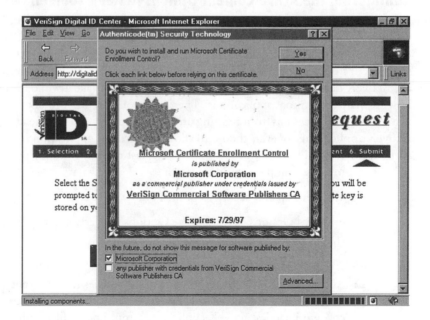

Digital IDs for Web servers and for Web browsers look slightly different and contain different information. These digital IDs are installed when you visit a secured site (that uses a digital ID) or by requesting one from VeriSign at `http://digitalid.verisign.com/ms_client.htm`.

You can view the information for sites you currently trust, your own personal certificate, or ActiveX publisher information by following these steps:

1. Choose View | Options to display the Options property sheet.

2. Click the Security tab to display the Security property sheet. (Refer to Figure 7.9.)

3. View your personal certificate information by clicking the Personal button to display the Client Authentication dialog box. Then select the certificate and click the View Certificate button.

4. View your trusted Web server site certificate information by clicking the Sites button to display the Site Authentication dialog box. To view the specifics for a certificate, select it and click the View Certificate button. To delete a certificate, just select the certificate and click the Delete button.

5. View your ActiveX certificate information by clicking the Publishers button to display the Authenticode Security Technology dialog box. To delete a certificate, select it and click the Remove button.

6. Click the OK button to update the certificate options and return to Internet Explorer when you have finished.

Configuring the Active Content Options to Keep Yourself Safe

As you use Internet Explorer, you will find many Web sites with VBScript, JavaScript, or even ActiveX documents (such as Word or Excel) that are embedded in Web pages. Any of these documents might contain code that could damage your system. These problems do not necessarily occur from malicious developers; they could occur from poorly written applications. After all, ActiveX development is still in its infancy, and it will take a while for developers to learn how to write bulletproof applications. Therefore, you may want to take precautions and prevent ActiveX applications from running on your computer, choose when to download and run ActiveX applications, or even choose to allow any ActiveX application to run on your system. Although I certainly would not recommend the last option, you may prefer it, which is why Microsoft provides multiple security options.

To modify Internet Explorer security options, follow these steps:

1. Choose View | Options to display the Options property sheet.

2. Click the Security tab to display the Security property sheet. (Refer to Figure 7.9.)

3. Specify any of the following options in the Active content group:

   ■ Allow downloading of active content—Specifies that Internet Explorer will automatically download (if checked) active content to your computer. This content includes ActiveX applications, multimedia files, animations, and non-HTML documents.

- Enable ActiveX controls and plug-ins—Specifies that Internet Explorer will automatically enable (if checked) ActiveX controls that display active content (such as a vertical marquee).

- Run ActiveX scripts—Specifies that ActiveX scripts (such as VBScripts) will be automatically executed.

- Enable Java programs—Specifies that Java scripts will be automatically executed.

- Safety Level—Specifies the type of restrictions placed on Web pages with active content. The type can be one of the following:

  - High—Automatically prevents security problems. However, some active content may not be displayed. Recommended.

  - Medium—Provides a warning before displaying any active content that could cause a security problem, but all active content is permissible. Recommended only for ActiveX developers.

  - None—No warnings are displayed, and all active content is permitted. Not recommended—the option opens up the system to potential damage.

4. Click the OK button to save your changes and return to Internet Explorer.

Configuring Internet Explorer Advanced Settings

The Advanced properties are really a set of miscellaneous properties. I think they were placed here because there just wasn't room on some of the previous property sheets or because they just didn't fit into any other category. These advanced options fall into three categories: warnings, caching, and miscellaneous settings. The following sections examine these options.

Configuring Internet Explorer Security Warnings

Internet Explorer provides various warning options to inform you of potentially dangerous actions that you may be about to perform. These warnings give you the opportunity to think about what you are about to do before you do it. Use the following method to access the warnings:

1. Choose View | Options to display the Options property sheet.

2. Click the Advanced tab to display the Advanced property sheet, as shown in Figure 7.12.

Figure 7.12.

*Configuring the
Internet Explorer
Advanced Options.*

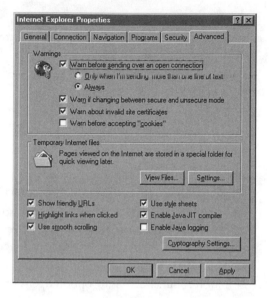

3. Enable (check) or disable (uncheck) the following options from the Warnings group:

■ Warn before sending over an open connection—Checking this option and setting one of the following radio buttons will enable warnings for clear text transmissions.

   ■ Only when I'm sending more than one line of text—You want to be warned about sending clear text data over the Internet if the text is greater than a single line.

   ■ Always—You want to be warned every time you send clear text data over the Internet.

TIP

I recommend choosing the Always radio button so that you are warned each time you transmit information over the Internet. This option reminds you not to send confidential information (such as your credit card number) over the Internet.

■ Warn if changing between secure and unsecure mode—You want to be warned whenever you change from a secure mode to an unsecure mode. You should leave this option enabled to make sure you do not send private information to an unsecure site.

■ Warn about invalid site certificates—Tells Internet Explorer to verify that the security certificate is registered to the correct site and that it has not been tampered with. Internet Explorer will verify the site certificate whenever you are viewing a page at a secure site or whenever you access the site.

■ Warn before accepting "cookies"—This option gives you the opportunity to decide whether you want a cookie to be downloaded and executed on your computer. The default setting is to automatically accept a cookie. A *cookie* is a set of code that can return information to the site server about your configuration. It may contain information that you do not want sent to a server. However, if you do not download and execute the cookie, you may not be able to view the Web pages on the site you are visiting. Cookies are stored in your `SystemRoot\Cookies` directory and may be viewed to see what type of information they are transmitting to the site server.

4. Click the OK button to save your changes and return to Internet Explorer.

Configuring Internet Explorer Caching Options

To decrease the time Internet Explorer needs to display a page on a Web site you visit frequently, this option uses a portion of your hard disk to cache the HTML page and inline graphics. So when you access the Web site, a check occurs to determine whether it has changed. If the site has not changed, the information stored in the cache is used. If the page has changed, the information is downloaded and the cache is updated. The amount of disk space to use for this cache, as well as the update frequency, is configurable. To change any of the cache settings, follow these steps:

1. Choose View | Options to display the Options property sheet.

2. Click the Advanced tab to display the Advanced property sheet; then click the Settings button to display the dialog box shown in Figure 7.13.

FIGURE 7.13.

Configuring Internet Explorer cache options.

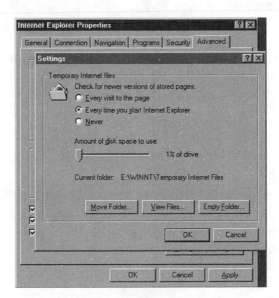

> **TIP**
>
> The Advanced property sheet is also accessible from the Control Panel Internet applet.

3. Select the cache option you prefer. The Check for newer versions of stored pages group has the following three options that can specify when you want to update your cached pages:

   - Every visit to the page—The cached page will be compared to the page on the Web server every time you access the page. Although this setting assures you that the page is always up-to-date, this option does decrease performance slightly.

   - Every time you start Internet Explorer—The cached page will be checked against the page on the Web site only once per session. A session is defined as the period between executing Internet Explorer and closing it. If you visit the Web page twice within a single session and the Web page changes on the server, you will not be aware of it if this option is enabled.

   - Never—The cached page will always be used, regardless of whether it is outdated.

> **NOTE**
>
> The Never option is not a recommended action because it can lead to stale (out-of-date) pages.

4. Move the slider on the Amount of disk space to use control to specify the percentage of your disk that can be used to cache Web pages.

5. View the current contents of your cache by clicking the View Files button.

6. Change the location of your cached Web pages by clicking the Move Folder button.

7. Delete all the cached files by clicking the Empty Folder button.

8. Click the OK button to save your changes and return to Internet Explorer.

Configuring Internet Explorer Miscellaneous Settings

The rest of the settings in the Advanced property sheet are miscellaneous options that control the appearance of URLs, the performance for Java applets, and the types of encryption supported by Internet Explorer. To change any of these options, just follow these steps:

1. Choose View | Options to display the Options property sheet.

2. Click the Advanced tab to display the Advanced property sheet, shown in Figure 7.12. These check boxes enable (check) or disable (uncheck) the following options:

   - Show friendly URLs—Specifies that the URL in the Address bar will appear in simplified form (the default) or in full form. For example, www.nt-guru.com is a simplified URL, whereas http://www.nt-guru.com/ is a full URL.

   - Highlight links when clicked—Specifies that the selected URL or graphic will be displayed with a focus window around it.

   - Use smooth scrolling—Specifies that the page will scroll at a predefined speed rather than at a single leap. Smooth scrolling is a little easier on the eyes but can take a while to get used to. If you prefer the old fashioned scrolling method, uncheck this option.

   - Use style sheets—Specifies whether to enable (checked) or disable (unchecked) the use of style sheets. HTML developers use a style sheet to control the layout of a page. The options specified in the style sheet may override your choices for fonts, background colors, and so on. If you do not want this type of behavior to occur, you may disable support for style sheets.

   - Enable Java JIT compiler—Specifies that the built-in Java compiler be enabled (checked) to increase the performance of Java scripts. Rather than being interpreted line by line, the script is compiled and executed all at once. Although this option may improve performance, it may cause irregular operation of some Java scripts. Should this situation occur, disable this option and restart Internet Explorer before viewing the page again.

   - Enable Java logging—This option, when enabled (checked), keeps a log of all Java activity on your system.

3. Click the Cryptography Settings button to display the Cryptography Protocols dialog box if you want to specify which security protocols to support (SSL2, SSL3, or PCT).

4. Click the OK button to save your changes and return to Internet Explorer when you have finished making your modifications.

Using Internet Explorer

After you have configured Internet Explorer, you are ready to start using it to browse the Internet. To get the most out of Internet Explorer, you can use the toolbars, shown in Figure 7.14, to quickly navigate from site to site.

FIGURE 7.14.

The Internet Explorer toolbars.

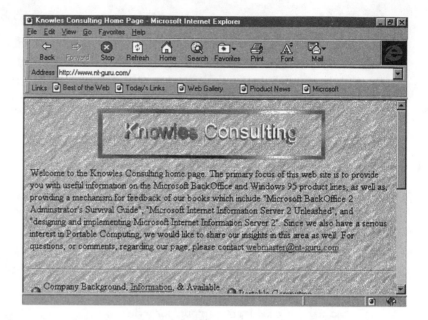

From left to right and top to bottom the toolbar buttons have the following functions:

- Back opens the previous Web page.
- Forward opens the next Web page.

> **NOTE**
>
> The Back and Forward buttons are applicable only when more than one Web page is open.

- Stop halts the downloading of a document, the attempt to activate a hypertext link, or the attempt to access an Internet service.
- Refresh updates the current Web page.
- Home displays the home page.
- Search searches the current Web page for a phrase or word.
- Favorites displays your list of favorite Web sites.
- Print prints the current page using the default printer.
- Font chooses the next font size in a rotating fashion. There are five sizes, and they rotate from smallest to largest.
- Address specifies the current address of a Web page, or you can enter an address of an Internet service to jump to.

- Links provides an additional button bar with predefined links, which include the following:
  - Best of the Web jumps to the Web site at `http://home.microsoft.com/exploring/exploring.asp` that includes predefined links to topics of interest.
  - Today's Links jumps to the Web site `http://www.microsoft.com/default.asp` that includes predefined links to various sites on the Internet.
  - Web Gallery jumps to the Web site `http://home.microsoft.com/gallery` and displays information and links to various Internet-related information, tools, and downloadable objects (including sounds and images).
  - Product News jumps to the Web site `http://home.microsoft.com/ie/default.asp` and displays a list of hypertext links to Microsoft product updates.
  - Microsoft jumps to the Microsoft home page at `http://www.microsoft.com/`.

To manually jump to a Web, FTP, Gopher, or other Internet site, simply enter a URL in the Address field. To access a Web site, for example, you can enter `www.nt-guru.com`, and Internet Explorer will automatically add the resource type of `http://` to build a fully qualified URL that will look like this: `http://www.nt-guru.com`. The same principle applies for the FTP, Gopher, and telnet Internet resources. This technique makes browsing the Internet quite easy because each site you visit will display hypertext links created by Internet Explorer, including the FTP and Gopher services, which are not specifically designed to build such links.

Summary

This chapter describes how to install Internet Explorer. You learn how to tailor Internet Explorer to your tastes and how to configure Internet Explorer to minimize potential security problems.

In Chapter 8, "Working with Microsoft Exchange," you will learn how to configure Microsoft Exchange Server to provide an Internet-based e-mail system. You can use the e-mail addresses you create with your Web pages to provide customer feedback or technical support or to build e-mail lists.

Working with Microsoft Exchange

IN THIS CHAPTER

■ Using Exchange Server on the Internet   200

■ Microsoft Exchange Security Issues   210

CHAPTER 8

There is one feature the Internet Information Server lacks—the capacity to send or receive electronic mail (e-mail) messages. Of course, this is probably by design. After all, Microsoft does include a product to accomplish this task. It is part of the Microsoft BackOffice suite and is called Microsoft Exchange Server. In this chapter, you will learn how to use Microsoft Exchange Server in conjunction with the Internet to provide an SMTP (Simple Mail Transfer Protocol) mail server.

An SMTP mail server is the backbone of Internet e-mail. If you want to allow users who access your Web site to send e-mail to your webmaster, capture information from a guest book, or send a message to your sales staff to follow up on leads from potential customers, you need to provide an SMTP e-mail address. An SMTP mail address uses the form `UserName@DomainName.com`, where `UserName` might be something like `webmaster` or `sales` and the domain name might be something like `nt-guru.com`. Providing Internet mail capabilities to all of your network clients, however, is not something you can do without associated risks, so this chapter also explains some of those risks and, I hope, shows you how to deal with them.

> **TIP**
>
> For best performance, Exchange Server should be installed on a server with no other duties. Exchange Server requires a lot of CPU horsepower and system resources to perform the duties of an enterprise mail server. Unless absolutely required, Exchange Server should not be installed on the same computer as the Internet Information Server. This will ensure that your computer's resources are applied toward your Internet services (such as the WWW, FTP, and Gopher publishing services) rather than your corporate e-mail services.

Using Exchange Server on the Internet

By itself, Microsoft Exchange Server will not provide you with the capability to create an SMTP mail server. Instead you must purchase an add-on product called the *Internet Mail Connector* (IMC). The IMC is used to create a gateway between Exchange Server and the Internet. When installed, the IMC uses the standard Internet Protocol port 25 to provide SMTP mail capabilities. If you are using a firewall with Exchange Server, you must enable this port for two-way access in order to send and receive Internet mail. In this section, you will learn how to install and configure the Internet Mail Connector. You will also learn how to use the Internet Mail Connector to connect multiple Exchange Server sites using the Internet as a backbone.

> **NOTE**
>
> The Internet Mail Connector is included in the Enterprise edition of Exchange Server. For more information on how to install and configure Microsoft Exchange Server, see another

book of mine called *Microsoft BackOffice Administrator's Survival Guide* published by Sams Publishing.

Installing the Internet Mail Connector

Installing the Internet Mail Connector is a snap. It is simply a matter of running the setup program to install the files and update your Exchange Server installation. You perform this same basic process whether you purchase the Internet Mail Connector as a separate product or get it as an integral component when you purchase the Enterprise edition of Exchange Server. Just to make sure you do not have any problems installing the Internet Mail Connector, you can follow these steps:

1. Execute the setup.exe program located on the Exchange Server CD-ROM. Be sure to use the correct version of this program—your CD-ROM may contain several versions. The correct version will be located in the \SETUP\PlatformName directory, where PlatformName will be I386 for Intel processors, ALPHA for DEC Alpha processors, or MIPS for NEC MIPS processors.

2. The Microsoft Exchange Server Setup dialog box appears. Click the Add/Remove button.

3. The Microsoft Exchange Server Setup - Complete/Custom dialog box appears, as shown in Figure 8.1.

FIGURE 8.1.

Installing optional Exchange Server components.

4. Select the Microsoft Exchange Server item in the Options list box. Then click the Change Option button. The Microsoft Exchange Server Setup - Microsoft Exchange Server dialog box, as shown in Figure 8.2, appears.

FIGURE 8.2.

Installing the Internet Mail Connector.

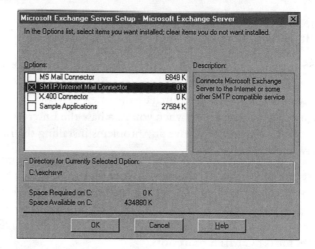

5. Check the SMTP/Internet Mail Connector check box. Then click the OK button.

6. You are then returned to the Microsoft Exchange Server Setup - Complete/Custom dialog box. Click the Continue button.

7. The Site Services Account dialog box then appears. Enter the password for the site (which you chose during your Exchange Server installation) in the Password field and click the OK button.

8. The Internet Mail Connector files are copied to your server, and Exchange Server is reconfigured. Then a message box is displayed informing you that Exchange Server has been successfully set up. Click the OK button to exit the setup program. You may then move on to the next section to configure the Internet Mail Connector.

Configuring the Internet Mail Connector

Configuring the Internet Mail Connector can be either very easy or very complex, depending on how you plan to use it. I know this does not sound very encouraging, but it is true. It's true because of the multitude of property sheets you have available to configure the service. So before you collapse from frustration (or information overload), just configure the following basic properties for the Internet Mail Connector:

■ Specify the administrator's mailbox. This mailbox is used by the Internet Mail Connector to send all error messages that occur.

- Specify MIME (multipurpose Internet mail extensions) or UUENCODE (a conversion scheme to convert 8-bit binary data to a 7-bit format) message encoding for outbound mail messages.
- Specify an SMTP address space. The SMTP address space is used to accept/reject all Internet mail if set to *@* or to accept mail from specific hosts and reject mail from all other hosts (based on their IP address).
- Specify a relay host or internal DNS server for message delivery. The relay host is usually an external host where all of your mail is sent to or received from. It is used for two reasons. First, it can be used internally as a single access point (such as when you have multiple Exchange Server installations but only one has a connection to the Internet) to which you forward all your outbound mail. Second, it can be used to provide an additional level of fault tolerance (for example, when your e-mail server is down, the relay host will continue to receive e-mail from external clients). A DNS server is used to determine the IP address of the destination hosts and supply basic NetBIOS name resolution (such as when you need to convert the e-mail address of webmaster@nt-guru.com to the destination address of webmaster@206.170.126.65).

NOTE

Using a relay host based on an Internet mail server (such as those commonly used by Internet service providers) requires additional support considerations, generally adds complexities to the receipt of your e-mail, and is therefore not recommended unless you need the additional fault tolerance. If you choose to use a relay host, be sure to discuss your requirements with your ISP to determine its methodology for sending stored mail to your Exchange Server installation.

NOTE

If you will not be using a DNS server, you can map the IP addresses using the HOSTS file or WINS or by specifying the outbound servers in the Connections property sheet.

To configure the Internet Mail Connector to use these basic properties, follow these steps:

1. Launch the Microsoft Exchange Administrator, located in your Microsoft Exchange program group.
2. Expand the site folder (for my server, this is WORK, for example) so that the Add-Ins, Addressing, Connections, Directory Replication, Monitors, and Servers folders are displayed. (See Figure 8.3.)

FIGURE 8.3.

*Preparing to configure
the Internet Mail
Connector.*

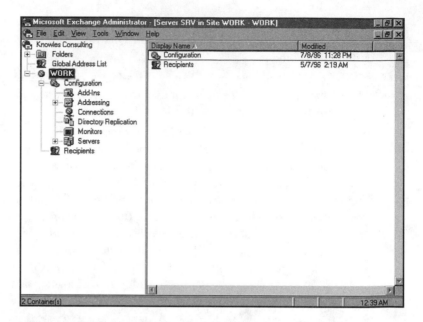

3. Select the Connections folder, and the installed connectors will be listed in the window on the right side. (See Figure 8.4.)

FIGURE 8.4.

*The installed connectors
in the* WORK *site.*

4. Select the Internet Mail Connector. Then choose Properties from the File menu or press Enter to display the Internet Mail Connector Properties dialog box, as shown in Figure 8.5.

FIGURE 8.5.

Configuring the Internet Mail Connector's basic properties.

5. Click the Change button to display the Administrator's Mailbox dialog box, where you may select an e-mail account to use for all administrative messages. After you select an account, click the OK button to return to the Internet Mail properties sheet.

NOTE

Some of the other interesting options, which not everyone will need to change, include the Address Type and Message Content Information group fields and the Enable message tracking check box. This check box is used to create a log file of the routes (or paths) of your e-mail messages to the destination host. The Message Content Information group includes two subgroups called Send Attachments Using and Character Set Translation. The Send Attachments Using subgroup specifies your outbound mail encoding scheme for embedded objects. This encoding scheme can be either MIME, the newer standard with richer content varieties, or UUENCODE, the older but more compatible scheme. When a message is sent, the character set may need to be translated based on the encoding scheme. This choice is configured in the Character Set Translation subgroup. If you want to specify this information on a per domain name basis, click the E-Mail Domain button.

TIP

When you are connected to the Internet, some additional features of Exchange become more of a potential problem than a potential benefit. Having your internal e-mail clients send out-of-office (such as when you are on vacation) or automatically generated replies (such as when you need to time-stamp a message) is a nice feature. Sending confidential information (an address to reach you while you are vacation, perhaps) over the Internet, however, can be a possible security hazard. To prevent this from occurring, click on the Interoperability button to display the Operability dialog box. Then check the Disable Out Of Office responses to the Internet and Disable Automatic Replies to the Internet check boxes.

6. Click the Notifications button to display the Notifications dialog box, shown in Figure 8.6. My preference is to be notified of all non-delivery (when a message could not be sent or received) events, which is accomplished by enabling the Always send notifications when non-delivery reports are generated radio button. You may, however, choose to limit the messages you will receive by enabling the Send notifications for these non-delivery reports radio button. Then you may choose from the following events:

- E-Mail address could not be found—Specifies that a message be sent to the mail administrator when either the sending or receiving party could not be located.

- Multiple matches for an E-Mail address occurred—Specifies that a message be sent to the mail administrator when there are multiple definitions for an e-mail address for either the sending or receiving party. The most common cause of this message is defining the same SMTP address for multiple Exchange Server recipients.

- Message conversion failed—Specifies that a message be sent to the mail administrator whenever an unknown mail format is received. This can be corrected for future messages by updating the MIME mapping in the MIME Types tab.

- Destination host could not be found—Specifies that a message be sent to the mail administrator when the destination mail server could not be located. This can be caused for one of three reasons. First, the destination mail server could be down or otherwise unavailable. Second, the domain name server for the destination server could be down or otherwise unavailable. Third, there may be no definition in the HOSTS file in the SystemRoot\System32\drivers\etc subdirectory.

- Protocol error occurred—Specifies that a message be sent to the mail administrator whenever a transport protocol error occurs.

■ Message timeout exceeded—Specifies that a message be sent to the mail administrator when a message could not be sent to the destination host. This type of failure is called a *time-out error*. (These time-out choices can be specified in the Connections property sheet.)

FIGURE 8.6.

Configuring the Internet Mail Connector message notification properties.

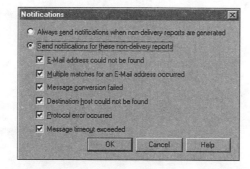

7. Click the Address Space tab to display the Address Space property sheet, as shown in Figure 8.7.

FIGURE 8.7.

Specifying the SMTP address space.

8. Click the New Internet button to display the SMTP Properties dialog box. Enter a value of *@* in the E-Mail domain field. Leave the Cost field as 1. Then click the OK button.

9. Click the Connections tab to display the Connections property sheet, as shown in Figure 8.8.

FIGURE 8.8.

Using the Connections property sheet to specify the SMTP address space.

10. In the Message Delivery field, choose the Use domain name service (DNS) radio button to use your DNS server for NetBIOS name resolution. Or choose the Forward all messages to host radio button and specify a name of the mail server to relay all of your outbound mail to, such as *ServerName* if another Exchange Server is used internally or *ServerName@DomainName*.com if using an external (Internet mail server) mail server.

> **TIP**
>
> I prefer to use the Microsoft DNS service included with Windows NT Server 4.0 rather than a relay host. Although this does add another level of complexity, I consider it a worthwhile effort because it keeps you in control. If you use a relay host, it is up to the administrator of that host to make sure that the DNS service on that site is properly configured. It's easier to use a relay host, but certainly not as satisfying.

11. Click the OK button to close the Internet Mail Connector Properties dialog box.

At this point you might think you are finished, but you're not. You still need to accomplish two steps before you can use the Internet Mail Connector. You need to add your DNS records to your DNS server and configure the Internet Mail Connector's service startup values. To configure your DNS service, follow these steps:

1. Open the file that defines your domain. Mine is nt-guru.dom, and the default file supplied with the Microsoft DNS service is place.dom, but yours will probably have another name. If you are unsure of the file to use, look in the boot file for a primary

entry with the domain name and associated filename (such as `primary nt-guru.com nt-guru.dom`). For additional information, refer to Chapter 9, "Using DHCP, WINS, and DNS."

2. If you left the comments in the file, look for the E-Mail Servers entry. If you did not leave the original comments, you can add the records anywhere in the file. Just make sure not to duplicate the records (in case someone else has already added them). The entries you need to add include an address record (A) and a mail record (MX) and will look like the following:

```
@            IN   MX     10     srv

srv          IN   A      206.170.127.65
```

Be sure to change the value of *srv* to the name of your computer hosting Exchange Server and the IP address (*206.170.127.65*) to the IP address assigned to your server. Otherwise you will not be able to send or receive e-mail from the Internet and I will wind up with a lot of non-delivery messages in my administrator's mailbox.

3. Repeat steps 1 and 2 for each DNS server you have hosting a separate Exchange Server installation. If you will be using only one DNS server, repeat step 2 for each Exchange server installation.

4. Save and close your file.

5. Stop and then restart your Microsoft DNS service using the Control Panel Services applet. Or enter NET STOP DNS and then NET START DNS at a command console prompt.

To configure your Internet Mail Connector's service startup values, follow these steps:

1. Open the Control panel; then launch the Services applet.

2. Scroll down the list until you see the Microsoft Exchange Internet Connector entry in the Service list box. Select the entry and click the Startup button to display the Service dialog box.

3. Choose the Automatic radio button in the Startup Type field.

4. Click the OK button to close the Service dialog box.

5. If you want to get started right away with the Internet Mail Connector, click the Start button to start the service. Then click the Close button to close the Services dialog box.

Using the Internet to Connect Multiple Exchange Server Sites

If your network has multiple sites in external locations (such as a WAN), you are probably using a proprietary means to connect your mail servers so that you can exchange e-mail with all of your network users. This proprietary connection method might be a router, a slow modem, or a similar product. As an alternative to proprietary (and costly) connection schemes, you can use your connection to the Internet to connect your external sites. There is a catch here, however, because you get nothing free. To create an SMTP mail system and connect two Exchange Server sites, you need multiple mail connectors. You can use one of three combinations: one X.400 and one Internet Mail Connector, the Microsoft Exchange Connector (which provides the Site Connector and Dynamic RAS Connector) and the Internet Mail Connector, or two of the same type of connectors (such as two Internet Mail Connectors).

NOTE

If you have the Enterprise edition of Exchange Server or have purchased the Microsoft Exchange Connector, you can use the Site Connector (choose File | New Other | Site Connector) to connect multiple Exchange Server sites. This is a better choice than purchasing multiple Internet Mail Connectors. It is also a more efficient mechanism because it uses Windows NT Remote Procedure Calls over any supported transport protocol that supports NetBIOS or Windows sockets (TCP/IP, IPX/SPX, NetBEUI, and others) to connect the sites. The Site Connector is also required if you want to replicate directories with Exchange Server.

The basic idea is that you will use one Internet Mail Connector to send your SMTP mail to all external e-mail clients (those outside of your organization) and the other connector, whichever one it is, to connect your sites together. You would then set your external sites to forward their SMTP mail to the Exchange Server that provides the outbound SMTP mail service. All outgoing SMTP mail from the external site would be forwarded to this site for final transmission over the Internet. All incoming SMTP mail would be received on this site and then forwarded to all the external sites (using the X.400 Connector, the Site Connector, or the Internet Mail Connector).

Microsoft Exchange Security Issues

The number 1 service most users demand of the Internet is e-mail, which has revolutionized communications. In this section you will examine some of the potential problems and the solutions you can apply to your Microsoft Exchange Server and Microsoft Exchange clients.

Protecting Your Server

Microsoft Exchange Server uses the Windows NT *Remote Procedure Call* (RPC) mechanism as the communication link between the server and client. It uses the Microsoft Challenge/Response security methodology built into the Windows NT RPC to authenticate client/server and server/server connections. Using this methodology, it is possible to not only encrypt the password associated with a user account but also to encrypt the entire communication stream. Therefore, you can provide a secure means for a user to access his mailbox over the Internet, as well as replicate data between Exchange sites. (For more information on site replication and the Internet, refer to Chapter 11 of the *Exchange Administrator's Guide.*) But there is more to protecting your server than just using a secure communications link. The following sections address these issues.

Preventing a Denial of Service

Have you considered what could occur if one of your network clients ticks off someone on the Internet? Suppose this problem occurred on an Internet newsgroup. Your client may just have a nasty message reply (commonly called a *flame*) posted on the newsgroup. If that's all that happens, consider yourself fortunate. Why fortunate? Because it is also possible that this ticked-off Internet user may be so upset, or just malicious enough, to decide to send a flood of e-mail to this network client of yours. There could be a series of small messages, a series of large messages, or possibly a series of huge messages that contain megabytes of embedded junk. Your server will have to deal with them all.

Because each message requires processing time and server storage, a flood of e-mail could cause what is commonly called a *denial of service*. In essence, this means your server could be overloaded, which would prevent all of your e-mail clients (not just the one user) from sending or receiving e-mail. To prevent such an occurrence, you can perform one of the following actions:

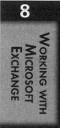

- Warn your network clients about posting inflammatory messages on the Internet. Instigate a policy for users to inform you of high message traffic from an Internet user.

- Configure the Internet Mail Connector Message size parameter in the General tab of the Internet Connector Properties dialog box to limit the size of incoming and outgoing mail. This will prevent large messages from being received by your network client from an irate Internet user.

- Configure the Internet Mail Connector to reject messages sent from the irate Internet user. You do this from the Connections tab of the Internet Mail Connector Properties dialog box. Just enable the Accept or Reject by Host option; then click the Specify Hosts button. You can then specify the IP addresses of the host computers from which to reject messages.

Restricting Access to the Internet

Another problem that could occur with network clients who send or receive e-mail over the Internet is that they could send mail containing sensitive information to someone outside of the organization. This could occur, for example, when an e-mail message is received from an external user. Your very friendly network client, thinking that only someone who works for the company would ask for such information and have access to his e-mail account, sends the requested information back as a reply to the original message. He might not even have been aware that the originating e-mail message arrived from an external source. After all, how many network users do you know who check the properties for each e-mail address they receive?

The enhanced version of the Microsoft Exchange Client included with Microsoft Exchange Server attempts to avoid this possibility by displaying a *friendly name* (the actual name of the sender) along with the e-mail address at the top of each message. A message received from the Internet might appear as Arthur Knowles [webmaster@nt-guru.com]. The e-mail address within the brackets [ ] is a sure sign that this message originated outside of the organization. Messages that are sent within the organization include only the friendly name, such as Arthur E. Knowles, which you define as the display name for the client mailbox.

To prevent such a possibility from occurring in your organization, you can limit the clients who are authorized to send e-mail over the Internet. You do this using the Delivery Restrictions tab on the Internet Connector Properties dialog box. You can specify individual clients to accept e-mail intended for the Internet in the Accept message from list box or reject specific individuals in the Reject messages from list box.

Preventing Auto-Replies to the Internet

One of the really nifty features of the enhanced Microsoft Exchange client is the capability to automatically send a reply to a received message. This is commonly used when a network client will be out of the office for a few days (such as when she is on vacation). It is an appropriate mechanism to inform colleagues at work that you will be unavailable until a specific date, and you might even go so far as to include private data (such as where you can be reached in an emergency). It is not necessarily a good idea, however, to send these types of replies to e-mail received from the Internet.

After all, do you want someone whom you may not know personally to receive private information? Do you want a stranger to know that you will not be at your home for this length of time? Carelessly passing around information like this can lead to trouble. But again, it is easily solved using the Internet Connector Properties dialog box. Just select the Internet Mail tab. Under Message Content Information, choose Interoperability and check the Disable Automatic Replies to the Internet option.

Protecting Your E-Mail Messages from Tampering or Theft

Because anyone with a network packet sniffer can intercept packets sent over the Internet, you may want to ensure that e-mail messages you send cannot be read by just anyone. There are two encryption features you can use with Microsoft Exchange Server to ensure that your e-mail is secure from prying eyes. First, you can encrypt the data contained within a message; second, you can sign a message digitally to verify the authenticity of the sender (to prevent someone else from sending messages in your name, for example).

Performing this task is a twofold process. First you must install the Microsoft Exchange Key Manager components on your Exchange Server. This process is covered in Chapter 6 of the *Exchange Administrator's Guide*, so I will not step through all the details here. Second, you must configure your Microsoft Exchange clients using the Security tab of the Options dialog box (accessed by choosing Tools | Options from the menu). If you do not install the Key Manager, you cannot create the private and public keys for your network clients. Without these keys, the encryption options of the Security tab are disabled.

> **NOTE**
>
> Currently only the enhanced Microsoft Exchange client can support data encryption and digital signatures. If your clients will be sending e-mail to users who do not use the enhanced Microsoft Exchange client, they should not encrypt or digitally sign e-mail to that particular user. If they do, the recipient will not be able to read the message.

Protecting Your Clients from Viruses

In the early days of computing, viruses were transmitted primarily through the sharing of floppy disks. Although this should still be a concern for you, the primary vector for virus transmission has changed. Now, viruses are more easily transmitted by downloading files from an Internet WWW or FTP site. They can also be sent directly to you via e-mail as an embedded object. To prevent the spread of viruses in your organization, you should make sure to instigate a policy to protect your users. At the very least, you should follow these guidelines:

- At system startup, execute a virus-scanning utility such as those provided by the Norton Anti-Virus or McAffees Virus Scan.

- Do not directly activate embedded objects in a mail message that arrives from an external source (such as the Internet). Instead, save the attachment. Then run a virus scanner to verify the contents of the object. Only then should the object be opened.

- If a virus is found within an e-mail message, immediately notify the rest of your e-mail clients who may be the recipient of a broadcast message containing the object. If you want to be friendly about the situation, notify the sender of the e-mail message that a virus was found within the object. (He might not have been aware that his system was infected when he attached the object to the message.) If you want to take a stronger stand about the situation, configure the Internet Mail Connector (via the Accept or Reject by Host group options in the Connections properties sheet) to reject all e-mail messages from the sender of the infected e-mail message. You can reject all new messages from the sender until he proves to your satisfaction that he did not knowingly send you an infected message.

Summary

This chapter focused on installing and configuring the Internet Mail Connector. It also described some of the possible problems you might encounter using Microsoft Exchange and the Internet Mail Connector. For more information on harnessing the e-mail capabilities of Microsoft Exchange Server, consult *Microsoft BackOffice Administrator's Survival Guide* or *Microsoft Exchange Server Survival Guide*, published by Sams Publishing. You have learned some of the techniques you can employ to protect your server, prevent the flow of information to undesired parties, and protect your e-mail clients from viruses. In Chapter 9, you'll learn how to use the Dynamic Host Configuration Protocol (DHCP), Windows Internet Naming Service (WINS), and Domain Name Service (DNS) to make managing your network easier as well as to provide for maximum Internet connectivity.

Using DHCP, WINS, and DNS

IN THIS CHAPTER

- Using the Dynamic Host Configuration Protocol   216

- Using the Windows Internet Name Service   243

- Using the Domain Name System   263

CHAPTER 9

If you have a TCP/IP-based network (at the very least your IIS servers must support TCP/IP) and want to make your administrative life a little easier, the two most important services are the Dynamic Host Configuration Protocol (DHCP) and the Windows Internet Name Service (WINS). These two services enable you to automatically manage your client IP address allocations and NetBIOS name resolution, respectively. However, if you want to connect your network to the Internet or support clients that do not support the Microsoft implementation of DHCP and WINS, you will also be interested in the Microsoft domain name service (DNS). This WINS-aware version of DNS can query the WINS service to resolve any names not included in the static configuration files. You could also use the DNS instead of DHCP and WINS, but I would suggest doing so only for a standalone server or an Internet firewall because DHCP and WINS are much easier to administer.

All these services are client/server applications. You have a service running on your Windows NT Server domain controller, which is the server side of the component, and a service running on a network client, which is, of course, the client component. Currently the supported operating systems that have built-in DHCP and WINS client software include Windows NT Workstation, Windows 95, Windows for Workgroups, and MS-DOS (including Windows 3.1). The MS-DOS and Windows 3.1 network clients must use the Microsoft Network Client 3.0 as their network interface. The various client platforms support the Microsoft DNS implementation as well.

The goal of this chapter is to explain these services so that you can properly implement the DHCP, WINS, and DNS services on your network. The chapter considers the administrative issues of design goals, installation, configuration, and management of these services. Where prudent, the chapter includes specific discussions concerning interoperability with existing UNIX services, tips to get the maximum mileage from these services, and some of the possible problems (gotchas) that you want to avoid.

Using the Dynamic Host Configuration Protocol

The DHCP service is based on the Request for Comment (RFC) document 1541; it is not a newly invented mechanism by Microsoft for managing your IP address allocations. The Microsoft implementation varies a bit from the actual design goals, as specified in RFC 1541, but fulfills the basic design functionality quite well for your Microsoft network clients. A few concerns remain regarding interoperation with your existing TCP/IP-based clients that do not support DHCP, as well as some specific conditions under which you should not use DHCP. Because of these factors, you should either maintain an LMHOST file on your Windows NT Server domain controllers or install the DNS service and configure your network servers and clients properly.

NOTE

For your information I have included RFC 1541 (and other RFCs mentioned in this chapter) on the accompanying CD-ROM in the SOURCE\RFC subdirectory as RFC1541.TXT. It is a rather interesting document, and I highly recommend your reading it for a fuller understanding of the DHCP service.

This chapter's discussion of the DHCP service begins with some of the design goals of the service and then moves on to planning your installation, installing the service, and using the DHCP Manager to administer the DHCP service. Administering your DHCP service consists of creating or deleting scopes and configuring individual scope properties. A *scope* is nothing more than a collection of IP addresses grouped into a single component for ease of administration. A scope can include all the IP addresses in a single subnet if desired, or you can subdivide a subnet into multiple scopes. This section ends with a look at DHCP database management, which will be required from time to time to improve performance, and a look at some of the registry keys that you cannot configure from the DHCP Manager.

The Design Goals for the Microsoft DHCP Protocol

Microsoft's primary goal for its implementation of DHCP was to simplify administration of a TCP/IP-based network. Because TCP/IP is one of the most widely implemented protocols, an easy-to-administer product also reduces the burden on the Microsoft Product Service Support (PSS) technical support groups. The TCP/IP protocol is recommended for medium to large local area networks. TCP/IP is the preferred protocol to use for wide area networks and is required for integration with a UNIX network or the Internet. Some of the goals that Microsoft's DHCP implementation met include the following:

- Centralized administration of your IP subnets. All your IP addresses and their configuration parameters are stored in a central database located on your server.

- Automatic IP address assignment and configuration. As a client computer starts up and accesses the network for the first time, it is automatically assigned an IP address, subnet mask, default gateway, and WINS server IP address. If the client computer then moves between subnets, such as in the case of a portable computer, the original IP address and related configuration information are released back to the original pool of available IP addresses; in addition, the client is assigned a new IP address and related configuration information at system startup.

- The return of unused IP addresses to the available pool of IP addresses. Normally IP addresses are allocated statically by a network administrator, and these IP addresses are stored on a piece of paper or a local database. This list can become outdated when clients move between subnets or when new IP addresses are allocated and the list of IP addresses is not updated. Consequently, some IP addresses will be lost for reuse.

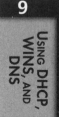

However, DHCP utilizes a time-based mechanism called a *lease*, which a client must renew at regular intervals. If the lease expires and the client does not renew it, the IP address is returned to the pool of available IP addresses.

HOW A DHCP LEASE WORKS

A DHCP client computer steps through six transition states, as shown in Figure 9.1, in the process of establishing a valid IP address for use by the client computer.

Initializing—As the operating system starts, a DHCP client broadcasts a *discover* message on the network that may be received by all DHCP servers on the network. For each DHCP server that receives the discover message, an *offer* message is returned to the client. Each offer message includes a valid IP address and relevant configuration information.

Selecting—The client collects each offer message.

Requesting—The client selects an offer message and then sends a *request* message that identifies the DHCP server for the selected configuration. The DHCP server in turn sends an *acknowledgment* message to the client. The acknowledgment message contains both the IP address that was initially sent in the offer message and a valid lease.

Bound—When the client receives the acknowledgment message, it stores the information locally on the computer (if a local storage mechanism, such as a hard disk, is available), completes the operating system startup, and may then participate as a network member with a valid IP address. Subsequent system startups use this locally stored information.

Renewing—When the lease has reached approximately 50 percent of its expiration time, the client attempts to renew the lease. If the lease is renewed (via an acknowledgment message from the DHCP server), the client enters the bound state once again.

Rebinding—When the lease has reached approximately 87.5 percent of its expiration time, the client attempts to renew the lease once again if it could not be renewed in the previous attempt. If this renewal attempt fails, the DHCP server assigns a new IP address to the client, which then enters the bound state again. Only if the original DHCP server could not provide a valid IP address and lease will the client enter the initializing state to repeat the entire process.

FIGURE 9.1.

The six transition states of a DHCP client.

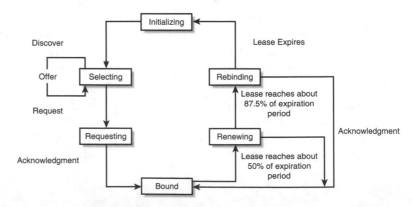

Planning Your DHCP Installation

If you have a small network that does not require any UNIX-based interoperation, you have a fairly easy DHCP server installation. However, even though you have relatively few issues to contend with in your network installation, you still have to do more than just install the DHCP server components.

First you have to decide whether to use a simple network with only one subnet, as shown in Figure 9.2, or a network with multiple subnets, as depicted in Figure 9.3. Because the most common configuration has multiple subnets, that configuration is the focus of most of this chapter.

FIGURE 9.2.

A sample network with a single subnet.

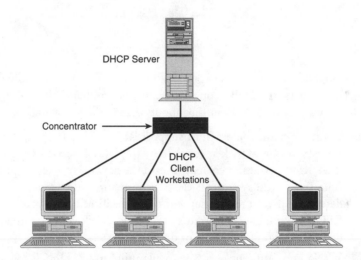

A single subnet is the easiest to work with. It requires very little maintenance because all the DHCP and WINS servers are located on the same subnet. Maintaining the LMHOST files will not be difficult unless you utilize many MS-DOS or Windows 3.x clients using the Microsoft Network Client 3.0 software. In addition, because these computers are all on a single subnet, you can use the B-node node type for name resolution and bypass WINS configuration and LMHOST file maintenance altogether. Nevertheless, applying the techniques described in this chapter to a single-subnet network will pay off in improved performance. It will also pay off if your network grows and must be divided into separate segments.

9

USING DHCP, WINS, AND DNS

FIGURE 9.3.

A network with multiple subnets.

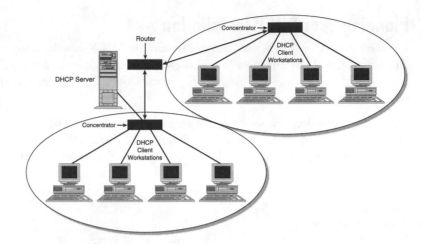

For a multiple-segmented network (that is, one with subnets) you will have to do some planning before installing DHCP on your server and implementing DHCP for your clients. Some of the issues you will need to think about include the following:

- Routers—Your routers must support RFCs 1532, 1533, and 1541, which deal with the forwarding of packets required by the DHCP service. If your routers do not support these RFCs, your routers may discard the network packets required for DHCP operation. In this case, you may need a firmware upgrade. Consult your documentation to determine if your routers support these specifications. If your routers do support these RFCs but you have connectivity problems, check your documentation to see if the default configuration passes or drops these packet types.

- WINS configuration—If you are planning to use DHCP to configure your WINS clients automatically, be sure to set options 44 and 46. (See the section "Working with DHCP Scopes" later in this chapter for details.) Option 44 specifies the WINS Server IP addresses to be assigned to the WINS client, and option 46 specifies the TCP/IP node type to be used. A *node type* specifies the mechanism the TCP/IP protocol uses to resolve NetBIOS name requests and to convert a NetBIOS name to an IP address. The following are the supported node types:

  - B-node—B-node resolves names using broadcast messages. This option is the worst possible option to use because it can flood your network segment with broadcast messages, lowering your network's ability to carry data over the network and effectively lowering your network bandwidth on the segment. Broadcasts are also not forwarded by routers, so if the requested resource is on the other side of a router, it will not be found. I would only recommend B-node for a very small network with a single subnet that does not have a dedicated network administrator to maintain the network. (Using broadcasts can essentially eliminate the need to maintain an LMHOST file or a WINS database, and for a small network very little network bandwidth is eaten by the broadcasts.)

NOTE

A good reason to use B-node is that computers located on the same segment can find each other even if the WINS server or DNS server is down or otherwise unavailable.

■ P-node—P-node resolves names with a name server (WINS or DNS) using point-to-point communications. In point-to-point communications linkages are from one IP address to another IP address. This mechanism is the most efficient but should be used only on networks with a dedicated administrator who will religiously update the various LMHOST files on the network. If these files are not updated, the client may not be able to find a resource by name or the resource computer may not be able to find the client.

NOTE

Unless you are a network client using Microsoft Network 3.0 software, updates should occur automatically if you are using WINS. Clients using Microsoft Network 3.0 software will need their IP addresses added to the LMHOST files of the DHCP servers or added to the configuration files for any DNS server on the network. The domain controller's TCP/IP configuration must also be configured to use the LMHOST file or DNS server.

■ M-node—M-node uses B-node first (broadcasts) to resolve the name and then P-node (name queries) if the broadcast fails to resolve a name. This method works but has the same problem as a B-node because it can flood the network with broadcasts.

■ H-node—H-node uses P-node first (name queries) to resolve the name and then B-node (broadcasts) if the name service is unavailable or if the name is not registered in the WINS server's database. I recommend using this node type because it will first use a point-to-point connection to find a resource's IP addresses, and only if that fails will it use a broadcast to find the resource. This node type is the most efficient to use, and it practically guarantees that the resource will be found even if the LMHOST file or WINS database does not contain the requested resource's IP address.

NOTE

H-node is the default node type when configuring TCP/IP manually unless the WINS IP address field is left empty.

■ Multiple DHCP servers—If you are planning to implement multiple DHCP servers, which is a good way to distribute the load on a large network, each DHCP server must have a statically assigned IP address. You must exclude these IP addresses in the DHCP scope you create.

NOTE

You do not necessarily have to have a DHCP server on each subnet. Your router should be capable of forwarding DHCP requests across subnets. If your router does not support the RFCs mentioned previously, you should not use DHCP.

■ Static IP addresses—Any static IP addresses, such as those used by other non-DHCP servers, non-DHCP computers, routers, and non-Microsoft Remote Access Service (RAS) clients that are using Point-to-Point Protocol (PPP) to connect to your network, must be excluded from the DHCP scope. If you forget to exclude these IP addresses, a name/address conflict is sure to occur, which could prevent your clients from communicating or even cause your network to crash (in the case of a router).

■ DHCP server database replication—This feature doesn't exist in the current implementation, so if you install multiple DHCP servers to support a single segment, you will also have to split the DHCP scope into distinct IP ranges.

■ DHCP server database backup—Because the DHCP database contains all the DHCP scopes for the server and the configuration parameters, you should implement a backup policy. Normally, the DHCP database is backed up automatically, and this backup will be used if the original is corrupted. However, you should not rely on this mechanism as your only backup. Instead, back up the database regularly and then copy the files from the `SystemRoot\System32\DHCP\Backup\Jet` directory.

TIP

If you have a corrupted primary database file that is not detected by the DHCP service, you can force the backup copy to be used by editing the registry. Set the registry key `HKEY_LOCAL_MACHINE\SYSTEM\CurrentControlSet\Services\DHCPServer\Parameters\RestoreFlag` to 1. Then restart the DHCP service by issuing `net stop dhcpserver` followed by `net start dhcpserver`.

■ Lease expiration—The minimum lease expiration should be twice the maximum expected server downtime. For example, if you plan to upgrade the server on weekends, the expiration time should be at least four days. This setting prevents a client from losing his lease and his IP address, which would prevent his computer from communicating on the network.

> **TIP**
>
> A good lease minimum should be based on your network turnaround. If you have many portable computer users, frequent computer upgrades, or many users passing between subnets, you want a lease time of about two weeks. This lease minimum will return the unused IP addresses to the pool of IP addresses, quickly making them available for reassignment. On the other hand, if you have a relatively static network, you can use lease times of six months. The one lease time to avoid is an unlimited lease because these addresses will never be released automatically and returned to the IP address pool.

If you are planning to implement your Microsoft DHCP server service in a mixed environment, such as with a third-party UNIX DHCP server service, you should be aware that the Microsoft client does not support all DHCP configuration options. Specifically, the Microsoft DHCP clients only use the configuration options specified in Table 9.1. The client ignores and discards any other options it receives.

Table 9.1. Microsoft DHCP client configuration options.

#	Name	Data Type	Description
1	Subnet mask	Subnet address	Specifies the TCP/IP subnet mask to be used by DHCP clients. Note that this value can be set only when you create a scope or when accessed from the DHCP Options | Scope Properties menu option.
3	Router	IP address array	Specifies a list, in order of preference, of router IP addresses to be used by the client. A locally defined gateway can override this value.
6	DNS servers	IP address array	Specifies a list, in order of preference, for DNS name servers for the client. Note that a multi-homed computer (a computer with more than one installed network adapter) can include only one IP address, not one IP address per adapter.
15	Domain name	String	Specifies the DNS domain name the client should use for DNS hostname resolution.
44	WINS/NBNS	Address array	Specifies a list, in order of preference, of NetBIOS name servers (NBNSs).

continues

9

USING DHCP, WINS, AND DNS

Table 9.1. continued

#	Name	Data Type	Description
46	WINS/NBT node type	Byte	Specifies the node type for configurable NetBIOS clients (as defined in RFC 1001/1002). A value of 1 specifies B-node, 2 specifies P-node, 4 specifies M-node, and 8 specifies H-node. Note that on a multi-homed computer the node type is assigned to the computer as a whole, not to individual network adapters.
47	NetBIOS scope ID	String	Specifies the Scope ID for NetBIOS over TCP/IP (NBT) as defined in RFC 1001/1002. Note that on a multi-homed computer the scope ID is a global resource and is not allocated on a per network-adapter basis.
50	Requested address	IP address	Specifies that a client's preset IP address be used.
51	Lease time	IP address	Specifies the time, in seconds, from the initial IP address allocation to the expiration of the client lease on the IP address. Note that this value can be set only in the DHCP Options	Scope Properties menu option.
53	DHCP message type	Byte	Specifies the DHCP message type where the message type is 1 for DHCPDISCOVER, 2 for DHCPOFFER, 3 for DHCPREQUEST, 4 for DHCPDECLINE, 5 for DHCPACK, 6 for DHCPNAK, and 7 for DHCPRELEASE.
54	Server identifier	IP address	Used by DHCP clients to indicate which of several lease offers is being accepted. The DHCP accomplishes this by including this option in a DHCPREQUEST message with the IP address of the accepted DHCP server.
58	Renewal (T1) time value	Long	Specifies the time, in seconds, from the initial IP address assignment to the time when the client must enter the renewal state. Note that this value cannot be specified manually because it is based on the lease time as set for the scope.

#	Name	Data Type	Description
59	Rebinding (T2) time value	Long	Specifies the time, in seconds, from the initial IP address assignment to the time when the client must enter the rebinding state. Note that this value cannot be specified manually because it is based on the lease time as set for the scope.
61	Client ID	Word	Specifies the DHCP client's unique identifier.

The Microsoft DHCP client and server do not support option overlays either. An *option overlay* is the process of using free space in the DHCP option packet to contain additional DHCP options. Therefore, if you are using a third-party DHCP server instead of the Microsoft DHCP server, list your important configuration options first to make sure that they fit into the Microsoft 312-byte DHCP network packet allocation. In addition, if you are using the Microsoft DHCP server to support your third-party DHCP clients, follow the same plan: Fit your most important configuration options first. Although you can use the additional configuration options (as listed in Table 9.2) to support your third-party DHCP clients, your Microsoft DHCP clients will not use these options.

Table 9.2. Third-party DHCP client configuration options.

#	Name	Data Type	Description
0	Pad	Byte	Specifies that the following data fields will be aligned on a word (16-bit) boundary.
2	Time offset	Long	Specifies the Universal Coordinate Time (UCT) offset time, in seconds.
4	Time server	IP address array	Specifies a list, in order of preference, of time servers for the client.
5	Name servers	IP address array	Specifies a list, in order of preference, of name servers for the client.
7	Log servers	IP address array	Specifies a list, in order of preference, for MIT_LCS User Datagram Protocol (UDP) log servers for the client.
8	Cookie servers	IP address array	Specifies a list, in order of preference, of cookie servers (as specified in RFC 865) for the client.

continues

Table 9.2. continued

#	Name	Data Type	Description
9	LPR servers	IP address array	Specifies a list, in order of preference, for line printer remote (as specified in RFC 1179) servers for the clients.
10	Impress servers	IP address array	Specifies a list, in order of preference, of Imagen Impress servers for the client.
11	Resource location servers	IP address array	Specifies a list, in order of preference, of RFC 887–compliant resource location servers for the client.
12	Hostname	String	Specifies the hostname (maximum of 63 characters) for the client. Note that the name must start with an alphabetic character; end with an alphanumeric character; and contain only letters, numbers, or hyphens. The name can be fully qualified with the local DNS domain name.
13	Boot file size	Word	Specifies the default size of the boot image file in 512-octet blocks.
14	Merit dump file	String	Specifies the ASCII path of a file where the client's core dump may be stored in case of an application/system crash.
16	Swap server	IP address	Specifies the IP address of the client's swap server.
17	Root path	String	Specifies a path (in ASCII) for the client's root disk.
18	Extensions path	String	Specifies a file that includes information that is interpreted in the same way as the vendor extension field in the BOOTTP response, except that references to Tag 18 are ignored. Note that the file must be retrievable via TFTP.
19	IP layer forwarding	Byte	Specifies that IP packets should be enabled (1) or disabled (0) for the client.
20	Nonlocal source routing	Byte	Specifies that datagram packets with nonlocal source route forwarding should be enabled (1) or disabled (0) for the client.

#	Name	Data Type	Description
21	Policy filter masks	IP address array	Specifies a list, in order of preference, of IP address and mask pairs that specify destination address and mask pairs, respectively, used for filtering nonlocal source routes. The client will discard any source-routed datagram whose next hop address does not match an entry in the list.
22	Max DG reassembly size	Word	Specifies the maximum-size datagram that a client can assemble. Note that the minimum size is 576.
23	Default time to live	Byte	Specifies the time to live (TTL) that the client will use on outgoing datagrams. Values must be between 1 and 255.
24	Path MTU aging time	Long	Specifies the time-out, in seconds, for aging outpath maximum transmission unit values. Note that MTU values are determined by the mechanism defined in RFC 1191.
25	Path MTU plateau table	Word array	Specifies a table of MTU sizes to use when performing Path MTU (as defined in RFC 1191). Note that the table is sorted from minimum value to maximum value, with a minimum value of 68.
26	MTU option	Word	Specifies the MTU discovery size. Note that the minimum value is 68.
27	All subnets are local	Byte	Specifies whether the client will assume that all subnets in the network will use the same MTU value as that defined for the local subnet. This option is enabled (1) or disabled (0), which specifies that some subnets may use smaller MTU values.
28	Broadcast address	IP address	Specifies the broadcast IP address to be used on the client's local subnet.
29	Perform mask discovery	Byte	A value of 1 specifies that the client should use Internet Control Message Protocol (ICMP) for subnet mask discovery, and a value of 0 specifies that the client should not use ICMP for subnet mask discovery.

continues

Table 9.2. continued

#	Name	Data Type	Description
30	Mask supplier	Byte	A value of 1 specifies that the client should respond to ICMP subnet mask requests, and a value of 0 specifies that a client should not respond to subnet mask requests using ICMP.
31	Perform router discovery	Byte	A value of 1 specifies that a client should use the mechanism defined in RFC 1256 for router discovery. A value of 0 indicates that the client should not use the router discovery mechanism.
32	Router solicitation address	IP address	Specifies an IP address to which the client will send router solicitation requests.
33	Static route	IP address array	Specifies a list, in order of preference, of IP address pairs that the client should install in its routing cache. Note that any multiple routes to the same destination are listed in descending order or in order of priority. The pairs are defined as destination IP address/router IP address. The default address 0.0.0.0 is an illegal address for a static route and should be changed if your non-Microsoft DHCP clients use this setting.
34	Trailer encapsulation	Byte	A value of 1 indicates that the client should negotiate use of trailers (as defined in RFC 983) when using the ARP protocol. A value of 0 indicates that the client should not use trailers.
35	ARP cache time-out	Long	Specifies the time-out, in seconds, for the ARP cache entries.
36	Ethernet encapsulation	Byte	Specifies that the client should use Ethernet version 2 (as defined in RFC 894) or IEEE 802.3 (as defined in RFC 1042) encapsulation if the network interface is Ethernet. A value of 1 enables RFC 1042, and a value of 0 enables RFC 894 encapsulation.

#	Name	Data Type	Description
37	Default time to live	Byte	Specifies the default TTL the client should use when sending TCP segments. Note that the minimum octet value is 1.
38	Keep-alive interval	Long	Specifies the interval, in seconds, for the client to wait before sending a keep-alive message on a TCP connection. Note that a value of 0 indicates that the client should send keep-alive messages only if requested by the application.
39	Keep-alive garbage	Byte	Enables (1) or disables (0) sending keep-alive messages with an octet of garbage data for legacy-application compatibility.
40	NIS domain name	String	This ASCII string specifies the name of the Network Information Service (NIS) domain.
41	NIS servers	IP address array	Specifies a list, in order of preference, of IP addresses of NIS servers for the client.
42	NTP servers	IP address array	Specifies a list, in order of preference, of IP addresses of Network Time Protocol (NTP) servers for the client.
43	Vendor-specific info	Byte array	Handles binary information used by clients and servers to pass vendor-specific information. Servers that cannot interpret the information ignore it, and clients that do not receive the data attempt to operate without it.
45	NetBIOS over TCP/IP NBDD	IP address array	Specifies a list, in order of preference, of IP addresses for NetBIOS datagram distribution (NBDD) servers for the client.
48	X Window system font	IP address array	Specifies a list, in order of preference, of IP addresses of X Window font servers for the client.
49	X Window system display	IP address array	Specifies a list, in order of preference, of IP addresses of X Window system display manager servers for the client.
64	NIS + domain name	String	Specifies a list, in order of preference.

9

USING DHCP,
WINS, AND
DNS

continues

Table 9.2. continued

#	Name	Data Type	Description
65	NIS + server	IP address array	Specifies a list, in order of preference.
255	End	Byte	Specifies the end of the DHCP packet.

Installing the DHCP Server Service

The DHCP server service is installed through the Control Panel Network applet. This installation process is described in Chapter 5, "Internet Information Server Preparation and Installation," in the section titled "Installing the Dynamic Host Configuration Protocol." However, before you install the service on your current server, check for the existence of other DHCP servers (either other Windows NT Server servers or a UNIX server) on the network.

Managing Your DHCP Server with the DHCP Manager

The DHCP Manager is your interface for managing the DHCP service. It is installed in the Network Administration Program Manager group, and you need administrative privileges to use it. With the DHCP Manager, you can do everything but stop or start the DHCP service. To stop or start the service you need to use the Control Panel Service applet and specify the Microsoft DHCP service as the service to control. Alternatively, you can issue the net stop dhcpserver or net start dhcpserver commands from a console prompt.

The DHCP Manager's primary function (see the next section) is to create, delete, activate, and deactivate scopes. Following that discussion, you learn how to manage client leases and reservations and how to set individual DHCP properties for a reserved client that differ from those defined for the scope as a whole. Finally, you learn about the DHCP database administration tasks that are required from time to time. This information should provide you with a well-rounded education and prepare you for your duties as a network administrator managing your TCP/IP-based network.

Managing DHCP Scopes

Before you can use the DHCP server to assign IP addresses and relevant configuration options to your DHCP clients, you have to create a DHCP scope. A scope is the heart of your DHCP server service. It is based on an IP address range, or *subnet*. Although a scope can include only a single subnet, within that subnet you can define the IP range to be used as the basis for your DHCP clients' IP address assignment, the subnet mask, any IP addresses to exclude from the scope, a lease duration, a name for the scope, and a comment that describes the scope. The next section discusses how to create, delete, activate, and deactivate DHCP scopes. You also learn how to configure global-scope, local-scope, or default-scope properties.

When you run the DHCP Manager for the first time, it will not have any scopes defined for it. However, it will include a listing in the DHCP server's window for the local machine. Therefore, before you start creating scopes, I suggest you add the additional DHCP servers on your network to the DHCP Manager. When you do, your DHCP Manager lists each DHCP server on your network in the DHCP server window, as shown in Figure 9.4. This step will enable you to manage your other scopes and to use these additional scopes as a reference point when creating new scopes.

FIGURE 9.4.

The Microsoft DHCP Manager with multiple DHCP servers and scopes.

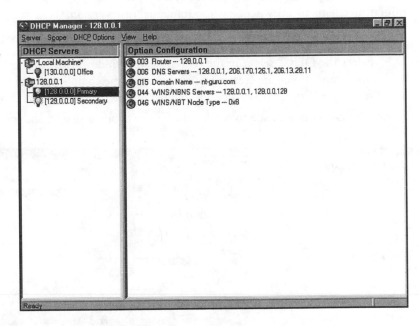

To add DHCP servers to your local DHCP Manager, follow these steps:

1. Select Server | Add or press Ctrl+A to display the Add DHCP Server on the Server List dialog.

2. Enter the IP address of the DHCP server in the DHCP Server field and click the OK button. The IP address will appear in the DHCP server window.

3. Repeat steps 1 and 2 for each DHCP server you want to add to your local DHCP Manager.

9

USING DHCP, WINS, AND DNS

NOTE

Because the DHCP server service does not replicate its database and configuration information to other DHCP servers, you will have to configure the DHCP Manager on each server in order to manage all the DHCP scopes from any computer with the DHCP Manager installed on it.

Working with DHCP Scopes

Creating a scope is the first step to automating your DHCP client TCP/IP configuration. However, before you can use a newly created scope you must activate it. An active scope can assign an IP address and relevant TCP/IP configuration information to your DHCP clients. When you have finished using a DHCP scope you can delete it, but you should deactivate it first. Deactivating a scope prevents a client from renewing its current lease and forces the client to obtain a new lease from another DHCP scope. Thus deactivating a scope is a means of migrating clients to a new scope without manual intervention.

To create a scope, follow these steps:

1. Select the DHCP server in the DHCP server window where you want to create the new scope. If you are creating a new scope on the computer running the DHCP server service, this entry will be Local Machine; otherwise, it will be an IP address.

2. Choose Scope | Create to display the Create Scope dialog, as shown in Figure 9.5.

FIGURE 9.5.

The Create Scope dialog.

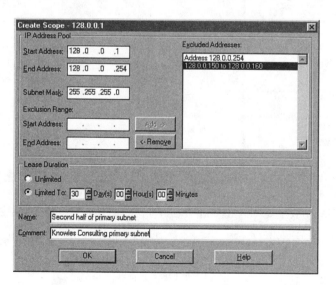

3. Enter the beginning IP address of your subnet in the Start Address field.

4. Enter the last IP address of your subnet in the End Address field.

> **TIP**
>
> If you are not planning to divide your subnet between two DHCP servers, enter the complete IP address range of your subnet. However, if you are planning to split your subnet, as I have, enter only half of your IP address range in the Start Address and End Address fields. This design is easier to work with and will prevent complications with the second DHCP Manager's defined scope.

5. Enter the subnet mask to be assigned to your DHCP clients in the Subnet Mask field.

6. Exclude IP addresses as necessary. If your scope includes statically assigned addresses, such as those assigned to your network adapters in the computer or to the RAS, enter these addresses in the Exclusion Range group. To exclude a single IP address, enter the IP address in the Start Address field and click the Add button. To enter more than one consecutive IP address to be excluded, enter the beginning IP address in the Start Address field, enter the last IP address in the End Address field, and click the Add button. These steps place the IP address range in the Excluded Addresses field.

TIP

To modify or remove an address range, select it in the Excluded Addresses field and click the Remove button. This step places the address range in the Exclusion Range field where you can modify it and later return it to the Excluded Addresses field.

7. Click either the Unlimited or the Limited To radio button in the Lease Duration group to specify the lease type. If you click Limited To, the default, specify how long your DHCP clients can keep their assigned IP address.

TIP

Base your lease time on the frequency with which your computers are upgraded, replaced, or moved between subnets. If your computers change frequently, choose a lease of approximately two weeks. If you have a more stable environment, choose a monthly, trimonthly, or biannual lease.

WARNING

Do not assign the Unlimited lease type unless you are absolutely sure that no computers will ever be upgraded, replaced, or moved. An unlimited lease will never be able to recover IP addresses that have been assigned to a DHCP client.

9

USING DHCP,
WINS, AND
DNS

8. Enter a name for the scope in the Name field. Your name can be a floor, a building location, or a description of the type of subnet. This name, along with the scope address, appears in the DHCP server window.

9. Enter a description for the scope in the Comment field.

TIP

To modify the scope properties of an existing scope, double-click it to display the Scope Properties dialog, which, aside from its name, is identical to the Create Scope dialog. Once the Scope Properties dialog is displayed, you may change any of the options described previously.

10. Click the OK button. Ignore the message box that prompts you to activate the scope unless all your default scope properties are correct.

11. Repeat steps 1–10 for each new scope you want to create.

NOTE

Setting global-scope, local-scope, or default-scope properties is discussed in the following section.

Only after you have configured the scope, as described in the next section, should you activate it. To do so, choose Scope | Activate.

Before you delete a scope, you should deactivate it by choosing Scope | Deactivate. Once the scope lease time has expired and you are sure that no DHCP clients are using a lease from the scope, you may delete it. To delete a scope, follow these steps:

1. Select the DHCP server in the DHCP server window that contains the scope you want to delete. If you are deleting a scope on the computer running the DHCP server service, this entry will be Local Machine; otherwise, it will be an IP address.

2. Once the DHCP server has been connected to, the scopes for the server will be listed. Select the scope you want to delete.

3. Choose Scope | Delete. A message warns you that clients may still have active leases. Click OK to delete the scope.

4. Repeat steps 1 through 3 for each scope you want to delete.

TIP

If you delete a scope with active clients, you can force the client to discontinue using his current lease and obtain one from another DHCP server by issuing the IPCONFIG /RENEW command at a command prompt. For a computer running Windows 95, you can use the WINIPCFG program. Click the Renew button to release the active lease and obtain a new lease.

Configuring DHCP Scope Options

The two classes of scope options are global and local. The global-scope setting applies to all scopes for the DHCP server, and the local-scope setting applies only to the current scope. Locally defined scope properties override globally defined scope properties. This system enables you to define common properties, which apply to all scopes that you create, and then customize the scope properties for each individual scope.

For example, you might define the global router setting to contain the IP addresses for your routers based on subnets. After you create a new scope, you can delete the first IP address entry on your list and tack it on at the end. In effect, you have changed the order of router preference so that the router closest to the user will be used first. You can repeat this sequence to continue moving the router addresses for each subnet you create without having to type in each router address manually. To modify a scope property, follow these steps:

1. Select the DHCP server in the DHCP server window that contains the scope you want to modify. If you are modifying a scope on the computer running the DHCP server service, this entry will be Local Machine; otherwise, it will be an IP address.

2. Once the DHCP server has been connected, the scopes for the server will be listed. Select the scope you want to modify.

3. To set global properties for the scope, choose DHCP Options | Global. The expanded DHCP options dialog appears, as shown in Figure 9.6. Otherwise, choose DHCP Options | Scope to set local properties.

> **NOTE**
>
> Aside from its name, the dialog displayed from selecting the DHCP Options | Scope menu option is identical to the dialog displayed from the Global menu option.

FIGURE 9.6.

The expanded DHCP options dialog.

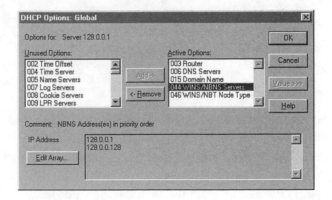

9

USING DHCP, WINS, AND DNS

4. Select the option in the Unused Options field that you want to modify and then click the Add button to move that option to the Active Options field.

5. Click the Value button to expand the dialog and display an edit field. Click the edit button, if available, to modify the existing value.

6. Repeat steps 3–5 for each option you want to modify. When you are finished, click the OK button.

> **TIP**
>
> To modify an existing option, select that option in the Active Options field and then click the Value button to expand the dialog so that you can edit the entry.

Creating New DHCP Scope Options

In addition to being able to modify the predefined scope properties with the DHCP Manager, you can also modify the name, unique identifier, and comment of existing configuration options. And if your DHCP clients can utilize them, you can even create new scope options to be assigned to your DHCP clients. However, just because you can modify an existing configuration option or create new ones doesn't mean you should do so arbitrarily. Do so only if absolutely necessary. To change an existing configuration option default value, follow these steps:

1. Choose DHCP Options | Defaults to display the DHCP Options dialog, which is shown in Figure 9.7.

FIGURE 9.7.

The DHCP Options:Default Values dialog .

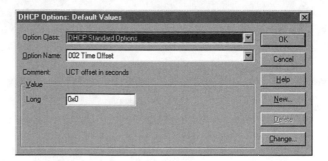

2. Select the class for the option you wish to modify in the Option Class drop-down list box. The default is DHCP Standard Options.

3. Select the DHCP option in the Option Name drop-down list box that you want to modify.

4. Specify the new value for the option in the Value field.

To change a configuration option's name, unique identifier, or description, follow these steps:

1. Repeat steps 1–3 from the preceding series of steps.

2. Click the Change button to display the Change Option Type dialog. You may now change the name of the option in the Name field, the DHCP unique identifier number in the Identifier field, or the description in the Comment field.

WARNING

Changing the name or identifier may prevent a DHCP client from functioning properly. Only an expert who is aware of the consequences should modify any of these settings.

---

3. Click the OK button when you are finished making changes.

4. Repeat steps 1 and 2 for each option you want to change.

To add a new configuration option, follow these steps:

1. Repeat steps 1 through 3 from the list of steps to change an existing configuration option default value.

2. Click the New button to display the Change Option Type dialog.

3. Enter a name for the new option in the Name field.

4. Specify a data type in the Data Type field. This can be binary (an array of bytes), byte (an 8-bit unsigned integer), encapsulated (an array of unsigned bytes), IP address (an IP address in the form of 206.170.127.65), long (a 32-bit signed integer), long integer (a 32-bit unsigned integer), string (an ASCII text string), or word (a 16-bit unsigned integer). If the data type is an array of elements, enable the Array check box.

5. Enter a unique number between 0 and 255 in the Identifier field.

6. Enter a description in the Comment field for the new option.

WARNING

Only an expert who is aware of the consequences and who needs to support non-Microsoft DHCP clients that require the additional options should add a new configuration option as described here.

---

7. Click the OK button when you are finished making changes.

8. Repeat steps 1 through 6 for each option you want to add.

Managing DHCP Clients

Managing your DHCP clients consists of working with client leases and client reservations on the DHCP server and forcing the client to release or renew his lease on the client workstations. I'll talk more about the management options on the server in just a moment; for now, though, I'd like to discuss the options for the command-line program IPCONFIG.EXE. The syntax for IPCONFIG is

```
IPCONFIG [adapter] /all / /release /renew
```

where

```
[adapter]
```

is an optional component that is the specific adapter to list or modify the DHCP configuration. Use IPCONFIG with no parameters, as described below, to obtain the adapter names.

/all lists all the configuration information, which includes the hostname, DNS servers, node type, NetBIOS scope ID, whether IP routing is enabled, whether the computer is a WINS proxy agent, and whether the computer uses DNS (instead of WINS) for name resolution. It also includes per adapter statistics, such as the adapter name and description, the physical address (network adapter Ethernet address), whether the DHCP client is enabled, the IP address, the subnet mask, the default gateway, and the primary and secondary WINS server IP addresses.

/release releases the current DHCP lease. If specified for all adapters (or if there is only one adapter), TCP/IP functionality is disabled.

/renew renews the lease. If no DHCP server is available to obtain a valid lease, TCP/IP functionality is disabled.

> **TIP**
>
> Use the /renew option to manually force a client to obtain a new lease from a new DHCP server or a new DHCP scope.

> **NOTE**
>
> Windows 95 does not include IPCONFIG. Instead, it includes a Windows GUI application called WINIPCFG.EXE.

If IPCONFIG is executed with no parameters, the current DHCP configuration is displayed. This information enables you to determine the installed adapters and IP addresses. For example, the following output is displayed on my WinBook XP:

```
Windows NT IP Configuration

Ethernet adapter Elnk31:

    IP Address. . . . . . . . . : 206.170.127.99
    Subnet Mask . . . . . . . . : 255.255.255.240
    Default Gateway . . . . . . : 206.170.127.78
*******
```

Managing Client Leases

Managing your DHCP client leases, for the most part, consists of informational displays. When you select an active scope and choose Scope | Active Leases, the Active Leases dialog (as shown in Figure 9.8) is displayed. In this dialog you can perform the following actions:

FIGURE 9.8.

The DHCP Manager Active Leases dialog.

■ View the active or reserved leases for the scope. By default, all the leases are displayed in the dialog. However, if you enable the Show Reservations Only check box, only the reserved leases will be displayed.

■ View the Client Properties dialog, as shown in Figure 9.9, by selecting an IP address/ computer name in the Client field and choosing the Properties button. This dialog can be very useful because it displays the Media Access Control (MAC) adapter address in the Unique Identifier field. Several Windows NT Server applications, including the DHCP Manager (when reserving a lease, for example), require a MAC address.

9

USING DHCP, WINS, AND DNS

FIGURE 9.9.

A sample Client Properties dialog.

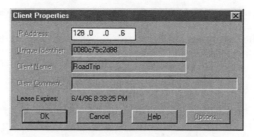

■ Update the DHCP database after a restoration from a backup database copy. If your DHCP database has to be restored from a previous backup, either automatically updated by the system or manually updated by you, you should click the Reconcile button to update the database. This step will add lease entries for any leases that are not in the database.

> **TIP**
>
> You can delete a lease by selecting the lease in the Client field and choosing the Delete button. However, you should not take this action lightly. You may want to move a client to a reserved lease with a new IP address for example. As soon as you delete the lease, reserve it as described in the next section and then force the client to establish a new lease by issuing the IPCONFIG /RENEW command on the client workstation. (For a Windows 95 client, issue the command WINIPCFG and then click the Renew button.) Otherwise, you could wind up with a duplicate IP address on the network if the original lease is used by another computer.

Managing Client Reservations

Client reservations can be more useful than your average lease because you can preassign an IP address for a DHCP client. You can also change the DHCP configuration options for a DHCP client with a reserved lease. This powerful option enables you to define global-scope and local-scope options for the majority of your DHCP clients when you create the scope. This option also allows you to specify DHCP options for those special DHCP clients that are exceptions to the rule. To create a reservation for a client, follow these steps:

1. Select the scope where you want the client reservation to occur.
2. Choose Scope | Add Reservations to display the Add Reserved Clients dialog.
3. Enter an IP address (which must fall within the IP address boundaries of your current DHCP scope) to be assigned to the client in the IP Address field.
4. Enter the MAC address for the client's network adapter in the Unique Identifier field.
5. Enter the client computer's name in the Client Name field.
6. Enter an optional description for the client computer in the Client Comment field.
7. Click the Add button.
8. Repeat steps 3 through 6 for each reservation you want to add to the scope.

Changing the configuration options for a reserved lease requires a little more work. To change a configuration option, follow these steps:

1. Select the scope you want to modify.

2. Choose Scope | Active Leases to display the Active Leases dialog.

3. Select the reserved lease you want to modify and click the Properties button. If there are too many leases to scroll through, enable the Show Reservations Only check box.

4. Click the Options button in the Client Properties dialog to display the DHCP Options dialog. This dialog is exactly the same as the other DHCP Option dialogs (except for its name).

5. Select the option in the Unused Options field that you want to modify and then click the Add button to move the option to the Active Options field. If the option to modify is already in the Active Options field, just select it.

6. Click the Value button to expand the dialog and display an edit field. In this expanded dialog, you may click an edit button, if present, to modify an existing value.

7. Repeat steps 4 through 6 for each option you want to modify. When you have finished modifying options, click the OK button.

8. Repeat steps 3 through 7 for each reservation you want to modify. When you are finished, click the OK button.

Managing the DHCP Databases

As your DHCP server operates day in and day out, and records are added or deleted, the databases may grow. These databases are located in the SystemRoot\System32\DHCP directory and include DHCP.MDB (the DHCP database), DHCP.TMP (a temporary file created by the DHCP server), JET*.LOG files(these files contain transaction records), and SYSTEM.MDB (contains structural information about the DHCP databases). Larger databases will slow down the DHCP server. Therefore, as your DHCP.MDB database approaches the 10MB limit, you should compact it. To do so, follow these steps:

1. Stop the DHCP server service from the Control Panel Services applet or issue the net stop dhcpserver command from a console prompt.

2. Run the JETPACK.EXE program from a console prompt. The program is located in your SystemRoot\System32 directory and the syntax is

   JETPACK *DatabaseName TemporaryDatabaseName*

   where

   DatabaseName, the name of the database to compact, can be a fully qualified pathname.

   TemporaryDatabaseName is a name to use as a temporary database. It, too, can be a fully qualified pathname.

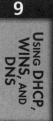

> **CAUTION**
>
> Do not compact the SYSTEM.MDB file. If you do, the DHCP server service will fail to start. If this occurs, restore your configuration from a previous backup or delete all of your files in the SystemRoot\System32\DHCP and SystemRoot\System32\DHCP\backup\Jet directories. Then expand the SYSTEM.MDB file from your source media and restart the DHCP server service. Finally, reconcile your database by selecting Scope | Active Leases and then clicking the Reconcile button.

3. Start the DHCP server service from the Control Panel Services applet or issue a net start dhcpserver command from a console prompt.

> **TIP**
>
> Because the potential for failure and data corruption is possible, you should back up your DHCP databases regularly—and always before you compact them. Just stop the DHCP server service temporarily and copy the files in the SystemRoot\System32\DHCP and SystemRoot\System32\DHCP\backup\Jet directories either to another directory or to another computer.

DHCP Server Registry Keys

Like most Windows NT services, the configuration information for the service is contained in the registry. For the most part, you should use the DHCP Manager to modify your configuration. You cannot configure these listed registry keys from the DHCP Manager; instead, you must use the Registry Editor (REGEDT32.EXE). However, the Registry Editor can be a dangerous tool, and Appendix C, "The Registry Editor and Registry Keys," includes additional information about using it. If you are administering a remote computer with a configuration problem so severe that the service cannot be started, you can modify the registry and restore the database configuration remotely. Once these changes have been made, you can restart the service using Server Manager.

The registry keys are stored in the HKEY_LOCAL_MACHINE\Systems\CurrentControlSet\ DHCPServer\Parameters subkey. If you modify any of these keys (aside from the restore flag), you must restart the computer to apply your changes. The following are keys of interest:

- APIProtocolSupport—This key's value specifies the transport protocol to be supported by the DHCP server. The default is 0x1 for RPC over TCP/IP protocols. However, it can also be 0x2 for RPC over named pipe protocols, 0x4 for RPC over LPC (local procedure calls), 0x5 for RPC over TCP/IP and RPC over LPC, or 0x7 for RPC over all three protocols (TCP/IP, named pipes, and LPC).

- ■ `BackupDatabasepath`—This key specifies the location of the backup copy of the DHCP database. The default is `%SystemRoot%\System32\DHCP\Backup`. For additional fault tolerance, you can specify another physical drive in the system. Note that you cannot specify a network drive because the DHCP Manager does not support remote drives for backup or recovery.

- ■ `BackupInterval`—This key specifies the default backup interval in minutes. The default is `15`.

- ■ `DatabaseCleanupInterval`—This key specifies the interval, in minutes, for the time to remove expired client records from the database. The default is `864,000` (`0x15180`) minutes, or `24` hours.

- ■ `DatabaseLoggingFlag`—This entry specifies whether to record the database changes in the `JET.LOG` file. This file is used to recover the database if a system crash occurs. The default is `1` (enable logging), but if your system is extremely stable you can set this value to `0` to disable logging and slightly increase overall system performance.

- ■ `DatabaseName`—This key specifies the database filename to be used by the DHCP server service. The default is `DHCP.MDB`.

- ■ `DatabasePath`—This key specifies the location of the DHCP database files. The default is `%SystemRoot%\System32\DHCP`.

- ■ `RestoreFlag`—This entry specifies whether the DHCP server should restore the DHCP database from its backup copy. Set this value to `1` to force a restoration; leave it at `0` to continue to use the original database file. Note that if you change this value, you must stop and then restart the service to apply the changes.

Using the Windows Internet Name Service

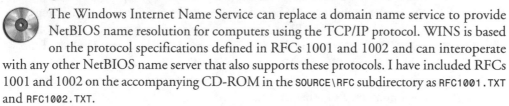

The Windows Internet Name Service can replace a domain name service to provide NetBIOS name resolution for computers using the TCP/IP protocol. WINS is based on the protocol specifications defined in RFCs 1001 and 1002 and can interoperate with any other NetBIOS name server that also supports these protocols. I have included RFCs 1001 and 1002 on the accompanying CD-ROM in the `SOURCE\RFC` subdirectory as `RFC1001.TXT` and `RFC1002.TXT`.

This discussion of WINS begins with some of the service's design goals and some of the concerns you may have while implementing WINS on your network. Then you learn how to plan your WINS server installation; the section includes some guidelines as to the number of WINS servers and WINS proxy agents to install. Following that, you look at the actual installation steps required to install the service and then move on to managing and configuring the WINS service with the WINS Manager. And because a major portion of WINS concerns client-related administration, you learn how to manage your WINS clients with the WINS Manager and find out about some specific quirks for MS-DOS clients using the Microsoft Network Client software. The section ends with a look at managing your WINS database, using the Performance Monitor to monitor your WINS service, and some of the registry keys that control the WINS service behavior.

Design Goals for the WINS Server Service

The primary purpose of the WINS server service is to make an administrator's job easier by automating the process of mapping computer names to IP addresses for NetBIOS name resolution in a TCP/IP-based network. It can replace a UNIX DNS service, which uses a static text file (one or more host files) to define the computer name to IP address mapping. However, WINS is more than just a way to automate the name resolution process. The WINS design also includes the following:

- Centralized management—Along with the WINS server service, Windows NT Server also includes the WINS Manager. With the WINS Manager you can administer other WINS servers and set up replication partners. You'll learn more about replication partners later in this chapter.

- Dynamic address mapping and name resolution—Every time a WINS client starts or whenever the renewal time expires, the WINS client registers its name with the WINS server. When the WINS client terminates, such as when the computer shuts down, the name is released. This feature enables a client computer to change subnets or change its IP address and still be accessible from other computers, thus alleviating the manual modifications to host files that a UNIX DNS service requires. These three stages (registration, release, and renewal) operate in the following manner:

  - Registration—A name registration request is sent to the WINS server to be added to the WINS database. The WINS server either accepts or rejects a client name registration based on its internal database contents. If the database already contains a record for the IP address under a different computer name, the WINS server challenges the registration. A *challenge* is a means of querying the current holder of the IP address to see if that address is still in use. If it is, the WINS server rejects the new client request. If the current holder of the IP address is not using the IP address, the WINS server accepts the new client request and adds it to the database with a time stamp, a unique incremental version number, and other information.

  - Release—Whenever the user shuts down a computer properly (meaning that it did not crash or have a power failure), it informs the WINS server. The WINS server then marks the name entry in the database as *released.* If the entry remains marked as released for a specific period of time, the entry is marked as *extinct,* and the version number is incremented. Version numbers are used to mark a record as changed so that changes to WINS partners are propagated to all WINS servers.

    If a record is marked as extinct and a new registration arrives at the WINS server with the same name but a different IP address, then the WINS server does not challenge the registration. Instead, the new IP address is assigned to the name.

This condition might occur, for example, if a DHCP-enabled portable computer (or other DHCP-enabled computer) is moved to a different subnet.

- ■ Renewal—Periodically, when half of the renewal time has expired, a WINS client reregisters its name and IP address with a WINS server. If the renewal time expires completely, the name is released unless the client reregisters with the WINS server.

■ Domainwide browsing—If you are using WINS servers, your clients (Windows NT, Windows 95, Windows for Workgroups, LAN Manager 2.*x*, and MS-DOS computers using the Microsoft Network Client 3.0) can browse for computer resources on a Microsoft network across a router without needing a domain controller on each side of the router.

■ Reduction of broadcast traffic—A WINS server can reduce the number of broadcast messages. It does so by supplying an IP address when it receives a name query message for a computer name from its local database on a WINS server or from its cache on a WINS proxy agent. A broadcast occurs on the local subnet only if the name query request fails.

■ Interoperation with non-WINS clients—WINS can interoperate with non-WINS clients to provide name resolution, but only if you have one or more WINS proxy agents installed on the subnet. A WINS proxy agent is a computer running the WINS client service that will capture a name query request from, for example, a UNIX client, obtain the IP address from the WINS server, and then pass this address back to the requesting non-WINS client.

Planning Your WINS Installation

For a small Microsoft-based network, all you really need to install are the DHCP and WINS services on each domain controller. This installation provides the means to configure your TCP/IP-based network clients to fully interoperate with any other server or client on the network. This recommendation is based on the fact that a single WINS server can accommodate about 1,500 name registrations and 760 name query requests. In theory, you can use one WINS server, keeping a backup WINS server for every 10,000 clients. However, I prefer to use a WINS server for each logical grouping of computers, such as those within a workgroup or domain, to provide additional fault tolerance and load balancing.

NOTE

You can also route these name query requests to other WINS servers and WINS proxy agents, ensuring that a request will eventually be fulfilled. If you enable replication of your WINS databases, each WINS server will have a complete listing of every WINS client name and IP address. Therefore, when a name query request is received, an IP address will be returned without broadcasting on the network. This mechanism can reduce the amount of broadcast traffic on the subnet.

This logical grouping of computers should be based on the physical layout of your Windows NT Server domain controllers or servers. A logical group could be based on domain controllers or servers in separate physical buildings or floors. It could even be based on domain controllers on the other side of a WAN link or similar property. And for every three to five domain controllers or servers, I like to install the WINS service. This configuration provides fault tolerance in case of required maintenance or a WINS server failure; it also limits the load on a single WINS server. At the very least, you should have a minimum of two WINS servers on your network supplying NetBIOS name resolution in preparation for a failure of the primary WINS server. You should also have a primary and backup domain controller to provide logon authentication in case of a primary domain controller failure.

This scenario works very well for Microsoft-based networks that use the Microsoft TCP/IP protocol stacks. But this scenario will fail if you use third-party TCP/IP protocol stacks that do not support WINS on your network clients. However, you can still use WINS in this situation as long as you also install a WINS proxy agent on each subnet, as depicted in Figure 9.10. These proxy agents provide a linkage between your non-WINS clients and the WINS servers. Your WINS servers should also share their database to provide complete coverage of the entire network. This sharing process is provided by WINS replication, which is discussed in detail a bit further on in this section.

NOTE

To support your non-WINS clients, you can create static mappings that will add a permanent computer name to IP address mapping in the WINS database.

FIGURE 9.10.

Supporting your non-WINS clients in a multiple-subnet network with WINS servers.

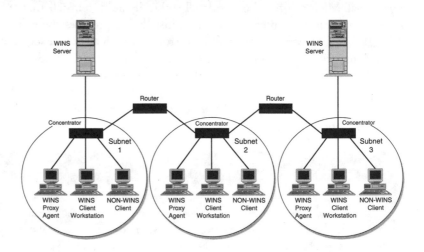

The reason you need to have one WINS proxy agent for each subnet is that broadcast messages are not passed across routers. And when a non-WINS client attempts to find another computer, it will use a broadcast message to obtain the IP address of the requested computer. If this computer is on the same subnet, the request will succeed; but if the computer is on a different subnet, the request will fail (unless you have domain controllers on both sides of the routers). Figure 9.11 shows how the WINS proxy agent comes into play.

In Figure 9.11, client 1 is a WINS client, client 2 is a non-WINS client, and client 3 is a WINS proxy agent. Server 1 is a Windows NT domain controller running the WINS service. When the non-WINS client 2 attempts to access WINS client 1 by broadcasting to obtain client 1's IP address, the request fails because client 1 and client 2 are on different subnets. However, the broadcast is intercepted by client 3, which then caches this name and IP address. Client 3 also returns the IP address for client 1 to client 2 so that a TCP/IP connection can be established. If another WINS client on a different subnet attempts to access client 2 by issuing a name query request, the cached IP address for client 2 that client 3 has stored is returned to the requesting client.

Because a WINS proxy agent does not store information obtained from a broadcast in the WINS server's database, you must have a WINS proxy agent on each subnet that contains nonWINS clients. In this case, the WINS proxy agent can respond to name query requests from WINS clients or WINS servers and will then broadcast on its local subnet to find the non-WINS client. Once the non-WINS client has been found, the IP address can be passed to the WINS client or server that issued the name query request.

FIGURE 9.11.

How a WINS proxy agent interoperates with non-WINS clients.

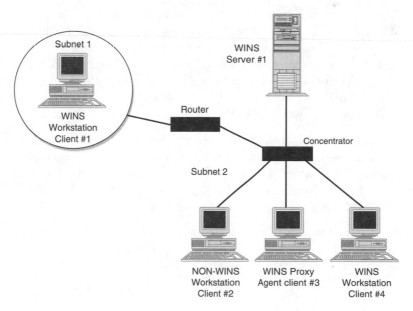

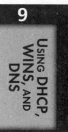

9

USING DHCP, WINS, AND DNS

When a WINS client requires access to another computer, it issues a name query request. This name query request can be routed to WINS servers, but only if the primary or secondary WINS server for the WINS client does not contain a registration for the requested computer. If the routed name query request cannot be resolved by any WINS server, the WINS client issues a broadcast message. Both broadcast messages and routed name query messages eat network bandwidth that could be used to pass data. However, if your WINS servers have a complete listing of the computer names and IP addresses, the primary WINS server can respond to the name query request, limiting the number of routed name query requests and broadcast messages.

This condition leads to the next performance and planning tip, which is that every WINS server on a network should replicate its database to other WINS servers on the network so that every WINS server has a complete listing of every WINS client's name and IP address. This method provides the fastest mechanism for resolving names to IP addresses and for limiting broadcast messages and routed name query messages. WINS servers provide two mechanisms for replication:

- ■ Push partners—A push partner is a WINS server that sends update notifications to its pull partners. When the pull partner receives this update message, it requests the changes from the push partner. The push partner then sends a replica of its database to the requesting pull partner.

- ■ Pull partners—A pull partner is a WINS server that requests updates from its push partner. When the push partner responds, the pull partner receives the database replica.

As you can see, the descriptions of push and pull partners are circular. In order to replicate the WINS database one way, one WINS server must be a push partner and the other must be a pull partner. To completely replicate a WINS database between two or more WINS servers, each WINS server must be a push and pull partner of the other(s). Figure 9.12 shows this two-way nonlinear chain, which can be used to replicate every WINS database to every other WINS database. But you can see from this example that some WINS servers receive update notifications from more than one WINS server, which can lead to increased network traffic.

Although it's a bit slower than a two-way linear chain, a better method is to create a linear chain (as shown in Figure 9.13) where only one WINS server is the push or pull partner of another WINS server. The one pull- or one push-partner rule is broken only at a WAN link. Here, the WINS server at the LAN side is either a push or pull partner of a WINS server on the LAN, and it is also a push or pull partner of a WINS server on a WAN link.

This scenario leads to another question: How often should you replicate? My basic methodology is based on the distance between replication points and the speed of the link. For your local area network, 10 to 15 minutes is a good choice because the network throughput is quite high. For local heavily used WAN links, you should limit your replication period to between 30 and 60 minutes. Only lower the rate if you have a high turnover rate. For longer WAN links, choose a value between 45 and 90 minutes; for intercontinental WAN links, replicate every 6 to 12 hours and schedule the process for off-peak hours. The basic idea is that the more heavily used the link, the higher the replication frequency (or the lower the number of scheduled minutes between replication attempts).

FIGURE 9.12.

WINS server push and pull replication in a nonlinear chain.

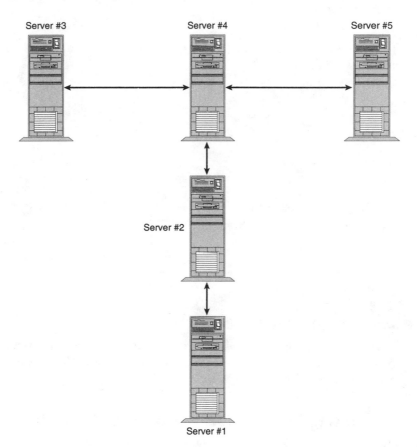

FIGURE 9.13.
*WINS server push and
pull replication in a
linear chain.*

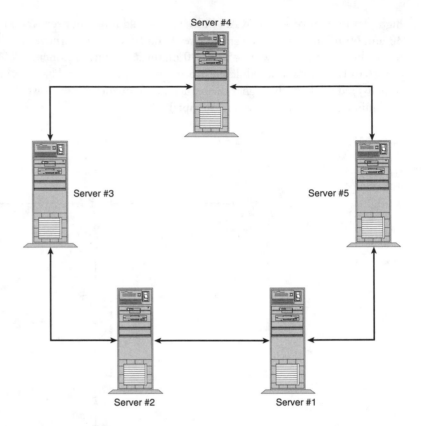

Installing the WINS Service

As with all built-in services, the installation process for the WINS service begins with the Control Panel Network applet. (See the section "Installing the Windows Internet Name Service" in Chapter 5 for detailed installation instructions.)

Configuring the WINS Service with the WINS Manager

The first time you use the WINS Manager, it will display only the WINS server on the local computer. To add WINS servers to the WINS Manager, select Server | Add WINS Server and then supply the IP address or computer name in the Add WINS Server dialog. To delete a WINS server from your WINS Manager list, select it and then choose Server | Delete WINS Server. After adding your additional WINS servers to the local WINS Manager, you will need to configure the local WINS server for optimal performance. This step includes setting your WINS server configuration, replication partners, and preferences. Each of these options performs a slightly different task.

The first recommended option is to choose Server | Configuration, which displays the WINS Server Configuration dialog, as shown in Figure 9.14.

FIGURE 9.14.

*The expanded WINS
Server Configuration
dialog.*

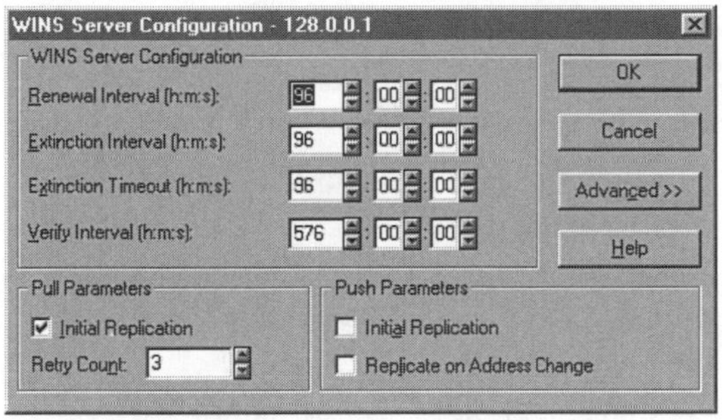

You can set the following options in the WINS Server Configuration dialog:

- Renewal Interval—This selection specifies how frequently a WINS client has to register its name with the WINS server. The default is four days.

- Extinction Interval—This item specifies the time interval between when a record is marked as released and when it is marked as extinct. The default, and maximum time, is four days.

- Extinction Timeout—This item specifies the time interval between when a record is marked as extinct and when it is scavenged from the database. The default is four days, and the minimum is one day.

NOTE

The extinction interval and extinction default for a fully configured WINS server are based on the renewal time and whether the WINS server has replication partners on the replication time interval.

TIP

You can manually scavenge the database by choosing Mappings | Initiate Scavenging. This process will remove outdated records from the database.

- Verify Interval—This entry specifies the time interval within which a WINS server must verify that old names owned by another WINS server are still valid. The default (24 days) is dependent on the extinction interval. The maximum is 24 days.

- Pull Parameters—The pull-partner replication interval is set in the Preferences dialog, as described a little farther on. However, if you want to trigger the replication when the WINS server service starts, enable the Initial Replication check box and specify a number in the Retry Count box.

■ Push Parameters—To configure push-partner configurations, you may enable the following entries:

   ■ Initial Replication—If this setting is enabled, push partners will be informed that a change has occurred when the WINS server service is started.

   ■ Replicate on Address Change—If this setting is enabled, push partners will be informed whenever an entry in the database changes or when a new entry is added.

■ Advanced WINS Server Configuration—These options are accessed when you expand the dialog by choosing the Advanced button:

   ■ Logging Enabled—This option specifies that the WINS server service will log database changes and inform you of basic errors in the system event log. The default is enabled.

   ■ Log Detailed Events—This option specifies that detailed events will be written into the system event log. It should be used only for a limited time, such as when you are troubleshooting WINS server problems, because it can consume considerable resources and will affect system performance. The default is disabled.

   ■ Replicate Only with Partners—This entry, if enabled, will allow replication only with push or pull partners. If it's disabled, you can replicate data from any unlisted WINS server. The default is to enable this setting.

   ■ Backup on Termination—This option will, if enabled, automatically back up the WINS database whenever the WINS server service is shut down. However, it will not perform a backup when the entire system is shut down, such as when you shut down and restart the server from the Start | Shutdown menu. The default is enabled.

   ■ Migrate On/Off—This setting enables or disables the treatment of static or multi-homed records as dynamic whenever they conflict with a new registration or replica (data copied from another WINS server). You should enable this option if you are upgrading a non-Windows NT system (such as a LAN Manager server) to Windows NT Server. The default is disabled.

   ■ Starting Version Count—This option specifies the highest database version number. Normally you will not need to change this value, but if you restore the WINS database from a backup because your primary database is corrupted, you should increment this value to a number higher than any other copy of the WINS server partners to ensure proper replication.

The current value can be displayed by choosing View | Database from the menu. If you want to see the version numbers on other WINS servers, choose the WINS server before making the menu selection.

■ Database Backup Path—This option specifies the full path to use for the backup copies of the WINS server database.

The next suggestion is to set your preferences for the WINS Manager and default settings for the WINS service. Choose Options | Preferences to display the dialog shown in Figure 9.15.

FIGURE 9.15.

Specifying the WINS Manager preferences and WINS server service defaults.

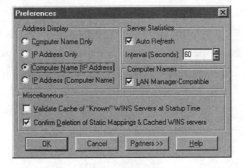

In this Preferences dialog, you can do the following:

■ Specify how the WINS Manager displays the names for the WINS servers it is connected to and, incidentally, the mechanism used for connecting to the service. These options are

■ Computer Name Only—If selected, this item specifies that just the computer name will be displayed. The connection to the WINS server will use named pipes.

■ IP Address Only—If selected, this item specifies that just the IP address of the computer will be displayed. The connection to the WINS server will use a TCP/IP socket.

■ Computer Name (IP Address)—If selected, this item specifies that the computer name will be displayed before the IP address and that named pipes will be used to connect to the WINS server.

■ IP Address (Computer Name)—If selected, this item specifies that the IP address will be displayed first before the computer name. The connection will use a TCP/IP socket to connect to the WINS server.

■ Specify the refresh interval for updating the WINS Manager display. If you enable the Auto Refresh check box, you should also specify a value (number of seconds to wait before updating the display) in the Interval field.

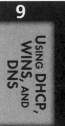

9

USING DHCP, WINS, AND DNS

> **NOTE**
>
> The display will also be refreshed automatically whenever you initiate an action with the WINS Manager.

- Specify the NetBIOS name compatibility. If the LAN Manager-Compatible check box is enabled (the default setting), then NetBIOS names will be limited to 15 bytes to contain the name while the sixteenth byte will be used to contain a special code for static mappings. If you use other applications that require a 16-byte NetBIOS name, such as Lotus Notes, then you should disable this option. The special codes are

  - 0x0—Specifies that a NetBIOS name is used by the redirector.
  - 0x1—Specifies that the NetBIOS name is used by the Master domain browser.
  - 0x3—Specifies that the NetBIOS name is used by the Messenger service.
  - 0x20—Specifies that the NetBIOS name is used by a LAN Manager server.
  - 0x1B—Specifies the master browser name that clients and browsers will use to contact the master browser.
  - 0x1E—Specifies that the NetBIOS name is used for a normal group.
  - 0x1D—Specifies that the NetBIOS name is used for client name resolution when an attempt is made to contact the master browser for server lists.
  - 0x1C—Specifies that the NetBIOS name is an Internet group name. An Internet group name contains the addresses of the primary and backup domain controllers for the domain. This name is limited to 25 addresses.

- Specify the miscellaneous support options. These are

  - Validate Cache of "Known" WINS servers at Startup Time—If this option is enabled, whenever you start the WINS Manager, it will attempt to connect to all WINS servers you have added. If a WINS server cannot be contacted, you will be prompted to remove the WINS server from the list of connected servers. The default is disabled.

  - Confirm Deletion of Static Mappings & Cached WINS servers—This option, if enabled (the default), prompts you with a message box whenever you attempt to remove a static mapping or cached WINS server. I find the constant message boxes a bit annoying and normally disable this setting. However, before you do so, I suggest you become a bit more familiar with the WINS Manager.

If you click the Partners button, the dialog will be expanded and allow you to set defaults for the partner replication. These settings include

- New Pull Partner Default Configuration—The entries in this group specify the default replication settings for new pull partners that you create for the currently selected WINS server. These options include:

■ Start Time—This option specifies the time to start your WINS server database replication. There is no default, although I like to start at 12:00 a.m.

■ Replication Interval—This option specifies the interval for repeating the WINS server database replication. There is no default, although I generally choose a 15-minute interval for local area network WINS servers.

■ New Push Partner Default Configuration—The entry in this group specifies the number of changes that have to occur in the WINS server database before a push notification will be sent to the push partners that you create for the currently selected WINS servers.

■ Update Count—This entry specifies the number of changes that have to occur before a push notification is sent. There is no default, although I recommend a value of 1000.

Next, I suggest you set the replication settings for the local WINS server by choosing Server | Replication Partners, which will display the Replication Partners dialog, shown in Figure 9.16. Once the dialog has been displayed, click the Add button to add the WINS servers to be configured as the local push or pull partners. You can choose to replicate to any, or all, WINS servers in a nonlinear fashion, or you can choose to pull from one WINS server and push to another WINS server in a linear fashion. These techniques are described in more detail in the section titled "Planning Your WINS Installation" earlier in the chapter. After you have added your WINS servers you can do the following:

NOTE

To remove a WINS server from the WINS server list, select it and press the Delete key.

FIGURE 9.16.

Specifying the WINS server replication partners.

- Specify the WINS servers to display in the WINS server list by enabling or disabling the options in the WINS Servers To List field. These options are
  - Push Partners—If enabled, push partners of this WINS server will be displayed. The default is enabled.
  - Pull Partners—If enabled, pull partners of this WINS server will be displayed. The default is enabled.
  - Other—If enabled, any non-partner of this WINS server will be displayed. The default is enabled.
- Specify the individual settings for the currently selected WINS server to be a push, pull, or both partner in the Replication Options box. When you select a WINS server that is already configured as a push or pull partner, the Configure buttons will be enabled:
  - Push Partner—Enable the Push Partner check box to specify that the selected WINS server will be a push partner. You may then click the Configure button to display the Push Properties dialog where you may view or set the Update Count.
  - Pull Partner—Enable the Pull Partner check box to specify that the selected WINS server will be a pull partner. You can then click the Configure button to display the Pull Properties dialog where you may view or set the Start Time and Replication Interval.

> **TIP**
>
> If you specified the default values using the Preferences dialog, these settings will be automatically set for new push or pull partners. However, if you are configuring a push or pull partner across a WAN link, you should set higher values, as described in the previous section titled "Planning Your WINS Installation."

- Initiate a replication trigger immediately rather than waiting for it to occur based on the replication times set in the Configuration dialog. To accomplish this, set the following values in the Send Replication Trigger Now group:
  - Push—Choosing this button sends a push trigger to the selected WINS server.
  - Pull—Choosing this button sends a pull trigger to the selected WINS server.
  - Push with Propagation—Enabling this check box modifies the Push message to indicate that changes sent to the selected WINS server are to be propagated to all other pull partners of the selected WINS servers.

Managing Your WINS Clients

Managing your WINS clients consists of creating static mappings, which are permanent computer names to IP address records, and viewing your current database records. Static mappings are added by choosing Mappings | Static Mappings, which displays the Static Mappings dialog, as shown in Figure 9.17. When you click the Add button, the Add Static Mappings dialog is displayed. Here you may enter a computer name, IP address, and the type of static mapping to add to the WINS server database. Table 9.3 lists the types of static mappings and describes the special names that the WINS server uses and how WINS manages these names. You can delete a static mapping by selecting the mapping and then choosing the Delete button.

FIGURE 9.17.

The Static Mappings dialog.

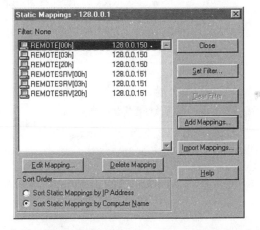

9

Using DHCP, WINS, and DNS

Table 9.3. WINS server special names.

Name	Description
Unique	A unique name is a normal name; it implies that only one computer name will be associated with the IP address.
Group	A group name does not have an associated IP address. Instead, when a group name is registered with the WINS server and a name query request for this name is received, the WINS server returns the broadcast address (FFFFFFFF). The requesting client then issues a broadcast message to find the requested computer.
Multi-homed	A multi-homed name is a name that has multiple IP addresses associated with it. A multi-homed device contains two or more network adapters that can register each individual IP address associated with the computer by sending a special name registration packet. A multi-homed group name can contain a maximum of 25 IP addresses.
Internet	An Internet name is a group name that contains domain controller IP addresses. WINS gives preference to the 25 addresses closest to the name registration request. When a request is received for the domain, the domain controller address and the additional 24 (maximum) IP addresses are returned to the client.

Managing the WINS Databases

Because your WINS server uses the same database format as the DHCP server (a modified Access database), it has the same basic issues as the databases for the DHCP server. As records are added and deleted, the database grows in size. The WINS databases are located in the SystemRoot\System32\WINS directory and include WINS.MDB (the WINS database), WINSTMP.MDB (a temporary file created by the DHCP server), JET.LOG files (this file contains transaction records), and SYSTEM.MDB (which contains structural information about the WINS databases). The database growth affects the performance of the WINS server. Therefore, as your WINS.MDB database approaches the 30MB limit, you should compact it. To do so, follow these steps:

1. Stop the WINS server service from the Control Panel Services applet or issue the net stop wins command from a console prompt.

2. Run the JETPACK.EXE program from a console prompt; the program is located in your SystemRoot\System32 directory. The syntax for this program is

   JETPACK DatabaseName TemporaryDatabaseName

   where

   DatabaseName, the name of the database to compact, can be a fully qualified pathname.

TemporaryDatabaseName is a name to use as a temporary database. It, too, can be a fully qualified pathname.

CAUTION

Do not compact the SYSTEM.MDB file. If you do, the WINS server service will fail to start. If this occurs, restore your configuration from a previous backup.

---

3. Start WINS from the Control Panel Services applet or issue a net start wins command from a console prompt.

TIP

Because the potential for failure exists with the compact utility and because data corruption can occur on your SystemRoot partition, you should back up your WINS databases regularly. Definitely do so before you compact any WINS databases. You can implement a backup choosing Mappings | Backup Database. Make sure to perform a full backup by disabling the Perform Incremental Backup option if you plan to use this copy to restore your configuration.

TIP

Before you back up or compact the database, you should choose the Mappings | Initiate Scavenging command to delete old records that are no longer needed.

Using the Performance Monitor to Monitor the WINS Server Service

The WINS Manager displays the statistics only for the currently selected WINS server. However, the Performance Monitor enables you to monitor multiple WINS servers simultaneously. This information can be of enormous benefit when you are comparing the performance of multiple WINS servers. Table 9.4 list the available WINS server performance object counters that you may use to monitor your selected WINS server. For additional details on how to use the Performance Monitor, see Chapter 27, "The Performance Monitor."

Table 9.4. The Performance Monitor object counters for the WINS server.

Object Counters	Description
Failed Queries/sec	Total number of failed queries per second.
Failed Releases/sec	Total number of failed releases per second.
Group Conflicts/sec	The rate at which group registration received by the WINS server results in conflicts with records in the database.
Group Registrations/sec	The rate at which group registrations are received by the WINS server.
Group Renewals/sec	The rate at which group renewals are received by the WINS server.
Queries/sec	The rate at which queries are received by the WINS server.
Releases/sec	The rate at which releases are received by the WINS server.
Successful Queries/sec	Total number of successful queries per second.
Successful Releases/sec	Total number of successful releases per second.
Total Number of Conflicts/sec	The sum of the unique and group conflicts per second. This value is the total rate at which conflicts are seen by the WINS server.
Total Number of Registrations/sec	The sum of the unique and group registrations per second. This value is the total rate at which registrations are received by the WINS server.
Total Number of Renewals/sec	The sum of the unique and group renewals per second. This value is the total rate at which renewals are received by the WINS server.
Unique Conflicts/sec	The rate at which unique registrations/renewals received by the WINS server result in conflicts with records in the database.
Unique Registrations/sec	The rate at which unique registrations are received by the WINS server.
Unique Renewals/sec	The rate at which unique renewals are received by the WINS server.

WINS Server Registry Keys

The WINS server service stores its configuration information in the registry, just as the DHCP server service does. And once again, you may need to modify the registry in order to modify a configuration setting if you cannot set that configuration setting from the WINS Manager or if you are administering an inactive WINS server. I mention this warning again because, if improperly used, the Registry Editor can damage your system beyond repair. See Appendix C for additional information and tips on backing up your current registry before you attempt to use the Registry Editor (REGEDT32.EXE).

The primary registry keys are located in HKEY_LOCAL_MACHINE\System\CurrentControlSet\ Services\WINS\Parameters and include

- DbFileNm—This item specifies the full pathname to the locations of the WINS database file. The default is %SystemRoot%\System32\WINS\WINS.MDB.

- DoStaticDataInit—If this item is set to 1, the WINS server will initialize its database with records from one or more files in the DataFiles subkey. This initialization is performed at the time the process is executed and whenever a change to a key in the Parameters or DataFiles subkey occurs. If set to the default (0), this initialization will not occur.

- InitTimePause—If this entry is set to 1, the WINS service will start in the paused state. It will stay in this state until it has either replicated with its partners (push or pull) or failed at least once in the replication attempt. If set to 1, the WINS\Partner\ Pull\InitTimeReplication subkey should be set to 1 or removed from the registry for proper operation. A value of 0 (default) disables this option. Note that the InitTimeReplication key value may be set by choosing Options | Preference and choosing the Advanced button to expand the dialog.

- LogFilePath—This item specifies the location for the WINS server log files. The default is %SystemRoot%\System32\WINS.

- McastIntvl—This value specifies the time interval, in seconds, for the WINS server to send a multicast and announce itself to other WINS servers. The minimum and default value is 2400 (40 minutes).

- McastTtl—This value specifies the number of times a multicast announcement can cross a particular router. The default is 6, and the range is 1 to 32.

- NoOfWrkThds—This value specifies the number of worker threads used by the WINS server. The default is one per processor on the system, with a range of 1 to 40. You can change this value and apply the change without restarting the WINS service.

- PriorityClassHigh—Set this entry to 1 to enable the WINS service to run in the high-priority class. This setting prevents other applications and services that are running in lower priorities from preempting the WINS service. The default is 0. Note that if you choose to enable this setting, monitor the system with the Performance Monitor to make sure the WINS service is not using too much processor time and that other applications and services are continuing to function properly.

- UseSelfFndPnrs—Set this option to 1 to enable or 0 to disable the WINS service from automatically finding other WINS servers and configuring them as push and pull partners. The default is 0. If the push and pull partners are configured manually with the WINS Manager, the partnership information will no longer be maintained automatically when a change occurs.

NOTE

If this option is enabled, the WINS service will configure WINS servers as push and pull partners across routers only if the routers support multicasting. Otherwise, only those WINS servers found on the local subnet will be automatically configured as partners.

TIP

Routers that support multicasting can be very useful because you are relieved of the burden of configuring your push and pull partners manually.

The following registry keys can be configured by choosing Server | Configuration and modifying the entries in the WINS Server Configuration dialog:

- BackupDirPath—This item specifies the full pathname to the location to be used to back up the WINS database.

- DoBackupOnTerm—If enabled (1), the WINS database is backed up whenever the WINS service is terminated. If disabled (0), the database is not backed up when the service is terminated. The default is 1. Note that the backup will not occur when the system is shut down. A backup occurs only when the service is stopped manually.

- LogDetailedEvents—If this item is enabled (1), verbose logging of WINS events occurs. The default is disabled (0).

- LoggingOn—If enabled (1), WINS messages are placed in the event log. If disabled (0), no events are placed in the event log. The default is 1.

■ RefreshInterval—This setting specifies the time, in seconds, for the client to register its name with the WINS server. The default is 0x54600 (four days).

■ RplOnlyWCnfPnrs—This setting enables (1) or disables (0) the capability to replicate a WINS server from a WINS server that is not a partner. The default is 1.

■ MigrateOn—This item enables (1) or disables (0) the treatment of unique and multi-homed records as dynamic when a registration conflict is detected. The default is 0.

■ TombstoneInterval—This entry specifies the time, in seconds, between when a client record is released and when it is marked as extinct. The default is 0x54600 (four days).

■ TombstoneTimeout—This setting specifies the time, in seconds, between when a client record is marked as extinct and when it is scavenged from the database. The default is 0x54600 (four days).

■ VerifyInterval—This setting specifies the interval within which the WINS server must verify that old names, which it does not own, are still valid. The default is 0x1FA400 (24 days).

The registry keys for partner replication are located in the HKEY_LOCAL_MACHINE\System\ CurrentControlSet\Services\WINS\Partners key and include the following:

■ PersonaNonGrata—This value specifies IP addresses for WINS servers from which you do not want to replicate data. This key may be very useful for administrators to block replication from WINS servers that are not under their control.

■ Pull\<IPAddress>\MemberPrec—This value specifies the preference order of addresses in an Internet group. Values can be 0 for low precedence or 1 for high precedence. The default is 0. Note that this entry appears under an IP Address (of a WINS server).

Using the Domain Name System

The primary purpose of a domain name system is to supply friendly computer names instead of an IP address to locate a resource. This process is often referred to as *NetBIOS name resolution.* The domain name system uses a hierarchical architecture. If a DNS server is unable to resolve an IP address at the local level, it will query other DNS servers at a higher level to resolve the name. If you do not mind maintaining multiple DNS servers and their associated configuration files, you could use DNS in place of DHCP and WINS. I prefer to use all three components working together because they complement each other to provide ease of administration as well as maximum compatibility.

The Design Goals for the Microsoft DNS Service

Although you can use other DNS servers on your network, they may not support the Microsoft WINS service. In such a case, you may also lose the ability to manage a dynamic network. The real difference between the Microsoft DNS implementation and other DNS servers that run under Windows NT is that the Microsoft implementation fully supports WINS, which in turn is aware of DHCP. If you use DHCP, WINS, and DNS together, you can achieve the following:

- Utilizing DHCP, your clients automatically allocate dynamic IP addresses. This feature allows you, the administrator, to provide dynamic IP addresses to your network clients as they move between subnets (as might be the case with clients who are consultants or temporary employees).

- Utilizing WINS, your clients automatically register their computer name and IP address every time they start up their computer. If the computer moves between subnets, this information is automatically updated as well.

- Utilizing DNS, your clients can find any non–WINS-aware resources through the static mappings maintained in the configuration files. This feature also works in reverse. Any non–WINS-aware client who uses DNS to resolve names and who has a static mapping to your DNS service can locate a WINS client as long as the Microsoft DNS server is configured to use a WINS server for additional name resolution.

This combination of DHCP, WINS, and DNS provides additional benefits as well. Dynamic address allocation also means dynamic address recovery. When a new IP address is allocated to a client on another subnet, the old address is released back to the DHCP scope's address pool. This arrangement can prevent the confusion caused by duplicate IP addresses on the network. The only thing DHCP and WINS will not do is make it easy for you to get on the Internet. One of the requirements for registering your domain (often your company name) with the InterNIC is that you maintain two or more DNS servers on your network so that clients that want to connect to your server, most likely to your WWW page, can find you. Because many Internet service providers (ISPs) don't know how to deal with or support DHCP and WINS, you might as well get accustomed to using a DNS server if you plan to connect to the Internet. But if you also use DHCP and WINS, you don't have to go through all of the hassle of modifying your configuration files every time you move or add a client to your network.

Using a DNS server has some additional benefits as well because it can provide some name resolution capabilities that WINS cannot. A DNS server includes e-mail name resolution by supporting the MX record type that associates an e-mail address with a hostname. And when a DNS server cannot resolve a name locally, it refers the name query to another DNS server higher up the chain in an effort to resolve the name.

Planning Your DNS Installation

This section examines some of the issues you need to consider before you install a domain name system server on your network. If you plan to connect to the Internet, the most important of these is security. For this reason, I suggest you read Chapter 10, "Advanced Security Issues," and consider how security will affect your implementation.

First, consider who will be in charge of maintaining the configuration files. This person will maintain a master copy of all shared configuration files. Everyone else will use a replicated copy of the master copy. Second, if you will have more than one person modifying any configuration file, be sure they are all trained to maintain the files in a standardized manner. Be certain this training includes a standard naming convention for filenames, hostnames, and verification of IP addresses.

> **CAUTION**
>
> A duplicate hostname or IP address on your network can cause serious problems. Make sure your administrators are aware of this situation and that your registration plan allows you to register a name and IP address before it is reassigned. You can use an Access database to maintain information (hostname, IP address, filename, and so on) about your network and then query the database to verify that the hostname and IP address are not in use.

To actually install the Microsoft DNS service, the step-by-step process described in the Chapter 5 section "Installing the Domain Name Server Service" should come in handy. Installing the service is the easy part; configuring the service, which you will learn about next, is the hard part.

The DNS Configuration Files

The configuration files used with the Microsoft DNS server can be replaced by those from a UNIX BIND installation if you are migrating or interoperating with a UNIX system. However, if you are using some outdated BIND commands, you may need to modify the files. The four basic types of configuration files follow.

- ■ BOOT—This file controls the startup behavior of the DNS server. It includes information on the default directory where the configuration files reside, the cache filename, the domain name that the DNS server will service, and the domain name for secondary DNS servers.
- ■ CACHE—This file contains information for Internet connectivity.
- ■ PLACE.DOM—This file contains information on hostnames within the domain. It also includes references to reverse lookup filenames and WINS servers.
- ■ ARPA-###.REV—These files (there should be one per subnet) include information to resolve an IP address to a hostname.

BOOT

The BOOT file does not support very many commands, so the syntax for the commands, as summarized in Table 9.5, is fairly easy to remember. The following is an example of a BOOT file for a simple network, such as the one in my office:

```
;   DNS BOOT FILE - Master configuration for DNS service
directory        %System32%\system32\dns
cache   .        cache
primary    nt-guru.com                  nt-guru.dom
primary  127.170.206.in-addr.arpa   arpa-206.rev
primary    0.0.127.in-addr.arpa     arpa-127.rev
primary  206.170.127.in-addr.arpa       arpa-128.rev
```

Table 9.5. Applicable commands for the BOOT file.

Command	Required	Description
;	No	Starts a comment. Avoid using unnecessary comments because the file is parsed line by line. Each comment added to the file slows down name resolution for any name not in the cache.
directory *PathName*	No	Describes the location of the DNS configuration files where *PathName* is a fully qualified pathname. The default, if not specified, is %SystemRoot%\System32\DNS. If the directory cannot be found, the DNS service will not start.
cache *FileName*	Yes	Describes the location of the cache file, which is used to find additional name servers where *FileName* is the name of the file. If the file cannot be found, the DNS service will not start.
Primary *DomainName FileName*	Yes	Specifies a domain name for which this DNS server is authoritative and a configuration filename that contains information for the domain.

Command	Required	Description
Secondary *DomainName* *HostList* [*FileName*]	No	Specifies a domain name and associated IP address array from which to download zone information. If a filename is specified, the zone information will be downloaded and used if the domain DNS server, or alternate, cannot be located.

CACHE

The CACHE file is used for additional name resolution. When your DNS server cannot resolve a name, it queries the additional name servers listed in this file. If you are using this DNS server to resolve names on the Internet, your file should look similar to the following:

```
;    DNS CACHE FILE
;    Initial cache data for root domain servers.
;    YOU SHOULD CHANGE:
;        - Nothing if connected to the Internet.  Edit this file only when
;          update root name server list is released.
;            OR
;        - If NOT connected to the Internet, remove these records and replace
;          with NS and A records for the DNS server authoritative for the
;          root domain at your site.
;    Internet root name server records:
;        last update:    Sep 1, 1995
;        related version of root zone:    1995090100
; formerly NS.INTERNIC.NET
.                        3600000   IN   NS    A.ROOT-SERVERS.NET.
A.ROOT-SERVERS.NET.      3600000        A     198.41.0.4
; formerly NS1.ISI.EDU
.                        3600000        NS    B.ROOT-SERVERS.NET.
B.ROOT-SERVERS.NET.      3600000        A     128.9.0.107
; formerly C.PSI.NET
.                        3600000        NS    C.ROOT-SERVERS.NET.
C.ROOT-SERVERS.NET.      3600000        A     192.33.4.12
; formerly TERP.UMD.EDU
.                        3600000        NS    D.ROOT-SERVERS.NET.
D.ROOT-SERVERS.NET.      3600000        A     128.8.10.90
; formerly NS.NASA.GOV
.                        3600000        NS    E.ROOT-SERVERS.NET.
E.ROOT-SERVERS.NET.      3600000        A     192.203.230.10
; formerly NS.ISC.ORG
.                        3600000        NS    F.ROOT-SERVERS.NET.
F.ROOT-SERVERS.NET.      3600000        A     39.13.229.241
; formerly NS.NIC.DDN.MIL
.                        3600000        NS    G.ROOT-SERVERS.NET.
G.ROOT-SERVERS.NET.      3600000        A     192.112.36.4
; formerly AOS.ARL.ARMY.MIL
.                        3600000        NS    H.ROOT-SERVERS.NET.
```

```
H.ROOT-SERVERS.NET.       3600000        A     128.63.2.53
; formerly NIC.NORDU.NET
.                         3600000        NS    I.ROOT-SERVERS.NET.
I.ROOT-SERVERS.NET.       3600000        A     192.36.148.17
; End of File
```

> **TIP**
>
> You can find an updated version of this file at the InterNIC FTP site `ftp.rs.internic.net`.
> Log on anonymously, change to the `domain` directory, and download the file called
> `named.root`.

If you are not using this DNS server for Internet name resolution, you should replace the name
server (NS) and address (A) records with the authoritative DNS server for your domain.

PLACE.DOM

This file is the heart of your DNS server's operation. It contains several record types, as summarized in Table 9.6, which are used to provide name resolution for the domain. Since the
sample file that is included with the Microsoft DNS contains information for a nonexistent
domain, you should rename the file and modify it as appropriate for your domain. The following is a copy of my replacement file called `nt-guru.dom`. I use the naming convention
DomainName.dom, and I recommend you do the same. This file is particularly useful when administering multiple domains. The contents I use in my replacement file are as follows:

```
@   IN  SOA    srv.nt-guru.com.  admin.srv.nt-guru.com.
➥( ;source host e-mailaddr
                                 1                              ;
➥serial number of file
                                 10800                          ; refresh interval
                                 3600                           ; retry interval
                                 604800                         ; expiration interval
                                 86400 )                        ; minimum time to live
@              IN  NS    srv.nt-guru.com.                       ;
➥name server for domain
srv            IN  A     206.170.127.65                         ;
➥IP address of name server
@   IN  WINS 206.170.127.65                         ;
➥IP address of WINS servers
localhost      IN  A     127.0.0.1                              ; loop back
@              IN  MX    10      srv                            ; e-mail server
srv     IN  A     206.170.127.65                                ;
➥IP address of e-mail server
ftp            IN  CNAME  srv                                   ;
➥alias name for FTP service
www            IN  CNAME  srv                                   ;
➥alias name for WWW service
gopher         IN  CNAME  srv                                   ;
➥alias name for Gopher service
```

The first entry in the file must be a start-of-authoritative (SOA) record. This record includes parameters that describe the source host (where the file was created), an e-mail address for the administrator of the file, a serial number (or version number) of the file, refresh interval (in seconds) that secondary servers use to determine when a revised file should be downloaded, retry time (in seconds) that secondary servers will wait before attempting to download the file in case of error, and expiration time (in seconds) that secondary servers use to determine when to discard a zone if it could not be downloaded. You should list the name servers (or DNS servers) for the domain and then their IP addresses. Next, include the local host identifier, which is used for loop-back testing, the name and address of any mail servers, and finally hostname aliases. A hostname alias provides a host (such as my server SRV) with more than one hostname. This name is particularly useful when you want your WWW site to be accessible in the commonly used format `WWW.DomainName.COM` (`www.nt-guru.com`, for example), rather than `ServerName.DomainName.COM` (`srv.nt-guru.com`, for example).

> **NOTE**
>
> When you specify a fully qualified domain name, it must be appended with a period. Otherwise, the domain name will be appended to the hostname for resolution and cause the name query to fail.

Table 9.6. Supported domain name records.

Identifier	Record Type	Description
A	Address	Specifies the IP address of the associated hostname.
CNAME	Class name	Specifies an alias for the associated hostname.
MX	Mail	Specifies the e-mail server hostnames.
NS	Name server	Specifies the DNS servers in the domain.
SOA	Start of authority	The first record in any configuration file; used to specify name.
WINS	WINS	Specifies the IP addresses of WINS servers that are used for additional name resolution.

9

USING DHCP,
WINS, AND
DNS

ARPA-###.REV

This file is used for reverse lookups of hostnames within a domain. Instead of resolving a name to an IP address, a reverse lookup resolves an IP address to a hostname. For example, for my domain, which has only one subnet (`206.170.127.0`), the reverse lookup file is as follows:

```
@   IN  SOA     srv.nt-guru.com.  admin.srv.nt-guru.com.
➥( ;source host e-mailaddr
                                  1                          ;
➥serial number of file
                                  10800                      ; refresh interval
                                  3600                       ; retry interval
                                  604800                     ; expiration interval
                                  86400 )                    ; minimum time to live
@               IN  NS      srv.nt-guru.com.                 ;
➥name server for domain
@   IN  NBSTAT      nt-guru.com.                             ;
➥domain name to append for NBSTAT lookups
1       IN  PTR     srv.nt-guru.com.                         ; SRV at 206.170.127.65
99      IN  PTR     winbookxp5.nt-guru.com.                  ;
➥WinBook XP5 at 206.170.127.99
```

Once more, the first record should be an SOA record. The next record lists the name (or DNS) server for the domain, followed by an NBSTAT record, and then the individual PTR records for each host in the domain. Table 9.7 summarizes these records and their usage. Many people find the PTR records confusing. Instead of supplying a complete IP address (such as `206.170.127.65`) for the host, you only supply the last digit of the IP address (such as 1) followed by the fully qualified hostname (host as well as domain name).

Table 9.7. Supported reverse lookup records.

Identifier	Record Type	Description
NBSTAT	NBSTAT	Specifies the domain name to append to any hostname found by an NBSTAT lookup.
NS	Name server	Specifies the DNS servers in the domain.
PTR	Pointer	Specifies an IP address for a host.
SOA	Start of authority	The first record in any configuration file; used to specify name.

Summary

The focus of this chapter is implementing the DHCP, WINS, and DNS services on your network. The major topics are design goals for the services, basic planning issues, and the management options that are available for manipulating your DHCP and WINS clients.

The chapter also mentions specific issues for utilizing DHCP and WINS in a mixed Windows NT and UNIX environment and, where prudent, how to prepare for the possibility of a failure with the services database, some registry keys you can use to configure otherwise nonconfigurable options, and some basic performance tips.

The next chapter looks at some of the security issues involved with connecting to the Internet and how you can configure your server to minimize unauthorized access to your network.

Advanced Security Issues

IN THIS CHAPTER

- Security and the Internet   274

- Security and Windows NT Server   284

- Determining Who Is Using Your System   306

CHAPTER 10

Security is a major issue with Internet connectivity. This chapter teaches you about some of these issues. You start with a look at the two basic types of security: downloaded data and access limitations. Next you look into some of the capabilities provided with Windows NT Server to secure your data and your network. Your final stop is a look into some of the tools you can use to determine who may be using your system, as well as who may be accessing your IIS site.

Security and the Internet

When you connect to the Internet, an entire world of information is available to you. Much of this information is provided by manufacturers to promote or support their products; other times it is provided by an individual to share ideas or provide a useful tool to other members of the online community. Sometimes, however, an object you download from the Internet is provided by someone who gets a sick enjoyment out of causing mental anguish or destroying data. You really need to watch what you download from the Internet, because you never know what it will do until after you try it. Sometimes, that's too late!

The flip side of accessing information on Internet sites is that an Internet client may be accessing your site as well. Not only can you access sites all around the world, but users from the entire world may be accessing your site, too. Of course, this is another reason why you decided to get on the Internet in the first place: You want people all around the world to view your site. This opens up the possibility, however slight it may be, that an external user may attempt to access your site in unexpected—and dangerous—ways.

Because of the damage that can occur, you should seriously consider the possibilities. This section examines two of these subjects. First you learn about some of the security concerns involved with downloading objects from the Internet. Then you learn about some of the issues involved with having external users connect to your site. In both cases you will learn about strategies you can implement to minimize damages.

Application and Document Security Issues

Most new Internet users love the Internet because they can find so much information, or applications, that they can download to their computer free. I will be the first to admit that this is an attractive capability. I will also be the first to mention that this can be a dangerous opportunity, too. Not everyone who provides files for you to download does it out of the goodness of his heart. Some people provide a file without cost only because they want to see how much damage to your system they can cause. This is not necessarily the intention of an Internet site administrator, although in some cases it could be. Take the following scenario, for example.

An Internet administrator creates a Web page to provide an easy-to-use interface to download a nifty shareware, or freeware, utility. This Web page has a hypertext link to an FTP site. This site could be local (on the same computer as the Web site) or remote (on someone else's FTP site). Now suppose some nasty person replaces the file on the FTP site with a copy of the utility that has been infected with a virus. The Web administrator may not even be aware that this has occurred, but he will be aware of it soon after he reads his e-mail from all the users who downloaded and executed the utility!

If you download a file from a private bulletin board system (like the Microsoft Network, CompuServe, or America Online), you have less to worry about, because these services check files for possible viruses before making them visible to their members. Nevertheless, public bulletin board systems and the Internet have a higher security risk that you must be prepared to deal with or you shouldn't be using them. This section addresses some of the types of problems that could occur, and what you can do to prepare yourself for such an eventuality.

Viruses and Trojan Horses

A *virus* is an application that contains code that is usually destructive to your computer system. A virus can also be embedded in a data object that supports a built-in macro language—a Word for Windows document template, for example. Some viruses are not destructive, but rather just cause the loss of a service (such as your ability to receive your e-mail) or user apprehension. A virus is a self-replicating snippet of code. Basically, a virus works like this:

1. An infected application is executed on your computer.

2. The infected application then either modifies the boot sector on your primary hard disk or infects other applications:

   ■ The boot sector on your hard disk contains 512 bytes of executable code, which is called the *master boot record* (MBR). This boot record is used to load the rest of the operating system. If the boot sector is replaced by a virus, as part of this replacement process the original boot sector is copied to a hidden file on your hard disk. After loading the infected boot sector, the rest of the virus's executable code is loaded, and then the virus loads the original boot sector. Because this process happens so quickly, and because the original operating system loads, you may not even be aware that your system has become infected. But any new disk that you load on your system may be infected with the virus. Thereafter, any person who uses one of these disks to boot his system will also infect his boot disk.

   ■ If the virus is not designed to replace your boot sector, when it executes it often looks for other executable programs (most commonly *.EXE or *.COM files) and then infects them with a copy of the virus. Every executable program has a program header that tells the operating system what type of application it is (MS-DOS, 16-bit Windows, 32-bit Windows, OS/2, or POSIX), where the application should be loaded in memory, and the starting point of the

10

ADVANCED SECURITY ISSUES

application's executable code. A virus may add its executable code to the original application, and then change the application's header to point to the virus's startup code. After the virus loads into memory, it will load the application into memory, and you will continue working as you normally would, without realizing the virus is present.

> **TIP**
>
> Windows NT is somewhat protected from most viruses because direct hardware access by MS-DOS applications is not supported except through Windows NT device drivers. For this reason, it is less likely that an MS-DOS application will be able to infect the boot sector, or other applications, if the infected application is executed in a console window under Windows NT. If you boot your system from an infected floppy, however, the boot sector could be infected because at this point Windows NT is not running to protect you. In most cases—in fact, in all that I have encountered to date—the next time you try to boot Windows NT, it won't work. So if your system fails to boot, you should check it immediately for a boot sector virus. For more information, see the section "Recovering an Infected System," later in this chapter.

- A macro virus, such as the Prank macro virus found in a Word for Windows document in 1995, usually infects other data objects by hooking into a macro that is automatically executed whenever the document object is loaded into the source program. Thereafter, any new document that is created will be infected as well. Any user who opens one of these infected documents on a non-infected system will infect her or his system with the virus.

> **WARNING**
>
> One of the really nasty problems with a macro virus is that it is not platform-specific. Most viruses are designed to infect a particular operating-system platform, like MS-DOS, but a macro virus is designed to infect the source application, such as Word. Consequently, the same macro virus could infect installations of the application that run under MS-DOS, Windows, Windows NT, Macintosh, OS/2, UNIX, or any other platform where the source application shares the same macro language capabilities.

3. If the virus is a malicious virus, one day the program may activate and wipe out all the data on your hard disk. If the virus is not malicious, you might just lose control of your system while a message is printed on the screen, or some similar action might take place. To regain control of your system from a nonmalicious virus, you usually will be required to reboot it. This will not remove the virus, but will allow you (in

most cases) to reboot your computer and try to clean your system using a write-protected bootable floppy disk and virus-scanning software.

A *Trojan horse* is an application that is designed to be hidden from the user but to capture sensitive information (like a user account and password) that is then passed to another person for nefarious purposes. A Trojan horse is very unlikely to occur under Windows NT, but it is possible. Windows NT requires that you use a specific mechanism to log on to the system. This is the familiar logon dialog box that is displayed when you press the Ctrl+Alt+Del key combination. This sequence is used only after the system has loaded.

If an MS-DOS Trojan horse was activated at boot time to display the same logon dialog boxes, when the user pressed Ctrl+Alt+Del, one of two things would occur:

1. The system would immediately reboot because the Ctrl+Alt+Del key combination is trapped by the system and is used to perform a warm boot.

2. If the Ctrl+Alt+Del combination was trapped by the Trojan horse, the user account and password could be captured by the application. But then Windows NT would not load afterward.

In either case, you should readily notice if a Trojan horse is present on your system. If either type of activity is noted, immediately notify your system administrator. It will then be up to the system administrator to take corrective action.

Active Content Security Issues

Web browsers that can display active content, such as the Internet Explorer 2.0 or Netscape Navigator, incur additional security risks. These types of Web browsers can create interactive content by utilizing a scripting language, such as VBScript or JavaScript, that executes on the local computer. Even though most of the language constructs (such as direct I/O) that could cause damage to your system have been removed, the potential is still there for damage to your system or loss of confidential data.

Much of this risk is possible because these scripting languages are still in early stages of their life cycle. In an early release of Java-enabled Web browsers, for example, two potential security risks were identified and later corrected. In the first case, it was possible for an invisible window to remain active on the client. This provided the capability for the invisible application to remain in contact with the host Web server and potentially pass data to the Web server. The Web browser user would not even be aware that this was occurring. In the second case, a Java application was able to access any computer on the network where the application was executing. This was a serious issue because it essentially provided a means for the application to bypass the network firewall.

Java-enabled Web browsers from Netscape have been on the market for a little longer than Web browsers from Microsoft that support VBScript or JavaScript, so some of the security leaks have been eliminated. The real problem, however, is that neither of these Web browsers has been available long enough to eliminate all possible problems. (Of course, it's doubtful that they ever will be able to eliminate *all* possible problems.) Consider the following capabilities of an active-content Web browser:

- ActiveX controls—An ActiveX control is a dynamic link library that executes in the context of the current user. Dynamic link libraries can be used to extend the functionality of an application and can call other functions in other dynamic link libraries.

- Scripting—Both VBScript and JavaScript are interpreted languages that are OLE-enabled. They may load additional ActiveX controls or access additional applications using OLE.

- Object linking and embedding—OLE can be used to control the behavior of an OLE-aware application.

By creating an executable package (consisting of your HTML code and scripts) that is downloaded by the user and then executed, it may be possible to create applications that can damage the system. It may even be possible to access shared network resources. This could occur by building a series of dynamic link libraries that would be executed by either an ActiveX control, an interactive script, or a standalone application (like Word for Windows). It may even be possible to execute other functions in dynamic link libraries or even spawn a downloaded application using an OLE-enabled application (like Word for Windows) that could damage your system.

It is really very difficult to say with 100 percent certainty whether this possibility could occur, simply because the products either are still in beta form or are newly released. In either case, they have not been completely tested to ensure that no security breach could occur, and I don't believe that would be entirely possible because the capability to extend the functionality of an application opens up the possibility that someone will do so with the intent to cause harm. One thing I have learned from my years of experience is that if it can be done, someone will find the way to do it.

Recovering an Infected System

When a computer system becomes infected with a virus, you are in trouble unless you can get rid of it. If your computer system uses the FAT file system, you have more options to remove a virus than if your system uses the NTFS file system. This is simply because there are not many tools that operate under Windows NT, and currently only a Windows NT application can access the NTFS file system. In this section you learn a few methods for dealing with viruses that may have infected your system.

- If Windows NT is active, try the following:

  The easiest virus-removal process is to run a virus-scanning tool under Windows NT. Many MS-DOS– or 16-bit Windows–based tools will not work, but the Norton

Anti-Virus and McAffee Virus Scan tools are available as native Windows NT applications. These tools will scan each file on your hard disk, and if a virus is detected, they will either remove the virus or delete the infected file if the virus cannot be removed.

■ If Windows NT is not active, and your boot partition is a FAT partition, try the following:

Boot from a clean, write-protected, MS-DOS system disk. Execute your virus-scanning software. If it succeeds, reboot the computer and run a native Windows NT virus-scanning application to check your NTFS partitions for applications that may contain a virus.

■ If Windows NT is not active, you cannot boot NT, and your boot partition is an NTFS partition, try the following:

This generally occurs when you boot from an infected floppy disk and a boot sector virus replaces the boot sector on your hard disk. The first thing to try in this situation is the set of instructions described in the previous option.

If that option fails to remove the boot sector virus, boot from a clean, write-protected, MS-DOS system disk. Then use the MS-DOS command FDISK /MBR, which will replace the master boot record (MBR). In some cases this will remove the infected boot sector, and Windows NT will then be able to boot normally.

If after using the FDISK /MBR command, the boot sector virus was removed but Windows NT will still not boot, you can try the emergency repair process. This is accomplished by booting your system using the original Windows NT installation disks. During the install process you are prompted to set up Windows NT or repair the current installation. Choose the repair option. When prompted, insert your emergency repair disk. Later you will be prompted as to the actions to take. Choose to verify the startup files, verify the boot sector, and compare the system files. This will restore the system configuration.

NOTE

The only time I have seen the repair process fail to replace the boot sector and system files is when Windows NT can no longer recognize the disk partition. Most times this can be corrected by using the FDISK /MBR option in conjunction with the repair disk process, but if this option fails, your only other option is to wipe the disk (if it is a SCSI drive, you can low-level format it), repartition it, reformat it, and then reinstall Windows NT. Finally, you can restore your last Windows NT configuration using a previous backup.

10

ADVANCED
SECURITY ISSUES

Firewalls, Proxy Agents, and Other Ways to Limit Access

The first thing you should consider when planning your Internet Information Server installation is security of your data. As part of your plan, consider putting the IIS on a network segment that is isolated from your primary network. After all, if the whole world can access your network, there may come a time when someone will decide to try to access more than the information you are making freely available to the public. Preventing an external user from accessing unauthorized areas on your computer (or your entire network) or preventing your internal network clients from accessing external resources (such as Internet resources) is where you will enter the realm of firewalls, proxy agents, and other alternatives.

These topics are discussed in the following sections, but the idea is not to be an all-inclusive reference because there is just too much material to fit into a single chapter. Instead, the discussion is a general reference to describe the technologies that are involved in limiting access to your network. There is one sure statement I can make about this entire process of limiting access to your network: There is no 100 percent guarantee that you can prevent an expert from working his way into your system from the Internet. At best, you can be aware of an intrusion; at worst, the intruder could bypass all of your safeguards and do whatever he wants. These are unlikely propositions, but the longer you are connected to the Internet, the more likely they will become. It is therefore imperative that you do one of two things:

■ Place your server that provides Internet connectivity on a standalone network. This is a guarantee that the worst an intruder can do is damage this particular server. He will not be able to worm his way into your internal network because there is no physical connection between the networks.

■ If you cannot use a standalone server because you are also providing Internet connectivity to your network clients, consider a third-party firewall or proxy agent. At the very least, use the capabilities provided within Windows NT Server 4 to limit the damage that could occur. (See the section "Security and Windows NT Server," later in this chapter.)

TIP

There is one other safeguard you can use that has absolutely nothing to do with limiting access to your computers. It's a pretty simple mechanism, but nonetheless is very important. Just make daily, weekly, and monthly backups of your server and your network client computers! If you have a backup, you can restore your previous configuration.

Using a Firewall to Restrict Access to Your Network

A *firewall* is an intermediary computer that stands between the Internet and your network. (See Figure 10.1.) A firewall basically performs the same task as the security guard at your office. The security guard will check your credentials at the door and then either let you into the building or refuse you access. If your company allows visitors to enter the building, the guard may require the visitor to sign in to a log book and show proof of identity (like a driver's license) to verify that she is who she says she is. These two features—restricting access and logging access—are the fundamental functions that a firewall performs for your network.

FIGURE 10.1.

Using a firewall to protect your network.

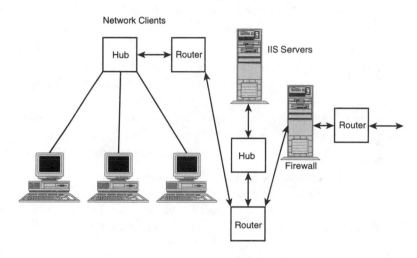

A firewall restricts access to your network by utilizing the information contained within a network packet. For Internet services, which use the TCP/IP protocol, this information can be divided into five basic components, as summarized in Table 10.1. These basic components include the protocol, destination IP address, destination IP port, source IP address, and source IP port.

Table 10.1. The five basic components used by a firewall in an Internet environment.

Component	Description
Protocol	Transmission Control Protocol (TCP) or User Datagram Protocol (UDP).
Destination IP address	Identifies the location of the computer receiving the data transmission.
Destination IP port	Identifies the application on the computer that will receive the data transmission.
Source IP address	Identifies the location of the computer initiating the data transmission.
Source IP port	Identifies the application on the computer that initiates the data transmission.

As a comparison, consider the way you make a phone call. First you pick up the phone, then you dial a 1 (or perhaps you dial 9 first to access an external line if you call from work), the area code, and finally the seven-digit phone number. When the other party hears the phone ring, she picks up the phone and you begin your conversation. You might say something like, "Hello Valda, this is Art." If you want the party (Valda) on the other end of the phone to call you back, you exchange phone numbers. When you have finished your conversation, you hang up the phone.

In this example your area code could be considered as the source address, you would be considered as the source port, the other party's phone number would be the destination address, and Valda would be the destination port. The method you use to dial the number, initiate, and then end the conversation would be considered as the protocol. If your destination party's phone company supports caller ID and your destination party has the appropriate hardware, she can determine who is calling her before she picks up the phone. Some caller-ID hardware devices can even record the number of the calling party (you) and the duration of the call.

A firewall functions in a similar manner. By using the destination and source IP addresses and IP port information contained within the packet, the firewall can either accept or reject the packet. It can also accept or reject packets based on the protocol contained within the packet. The firewall can also log this activity, much as a caller-ID hardware device does, to determine who may be attempting to access the network.

Some firewalls go beyond the basic packet-filtering mechanism and utilize a network session as their key means to accept or reject network requests. A network session occurs at the user or application level rather than at the IP transport level. Each network session will utilize a different IP port, so each session is guaranteed to have a unique identifier consisting of the five basic components previously described. Session-based firewalls offer increased security and more efficient client activity-recording options, so if you are purchasing a firewall, check to see if it supports session-based security.

Many people believe that a firewall is the only protection they need for their network. This is not true, however, because a firewall filters information. If you close the filter completely, you are secure, but this also prevents you from utilizing any of the Internet resources. If you open up the filter to provide access to the Internet, you are also creating a window of opportunity for someone to access your system. This follows the same analogy as the services provided by your security guard on the night shift. If he locks the building, he can prevent thefts from occurring. Of course, he also prevents any employee from entering the building and performing any work (such as cleaning the offices). By opening the doors of the building, the work can proceed. By making his rounds at night, he can help prevent thefts from occurring by his presence, but he cannot prevent all occurrences because he cannot be everywhere at once. All a security guard can do for you is lessen the chance of a theft occurring. All a firewall can do for you is lessen the risk associated with an Internet connection. It cannot entirely remove all risk.

Using a Proxy Agent to Restrict Access to Your Network

A *proxy agent* is really another type of firewall. Rather than working at the packet level, it operates at the application level. This means that it also uses a network session as its primary means of denying access as a session-based firewall, but it includes one additional feature not provided by session-based firewalls: It can mask the address and IP port of the source computer from the destination computer. This can prevent unauthorized access to your network while still providing access to external users. Let's take a look at how this would work in theory.

Assume for the moment that your network includes a server running the IIS on one computer and a proxy agent on another computer, as shown in Figure 10.2. The IIS server and the proxy agent are both connected to a router, which in turn is connected to the Internet. Your network clients' only access to the Internet, however, is through the proxy agent, so all network traffic to or from these network clients and the Internet must go through the proxy agent.

FIGURE 10.2.

Using a proxy agent to protect your network.

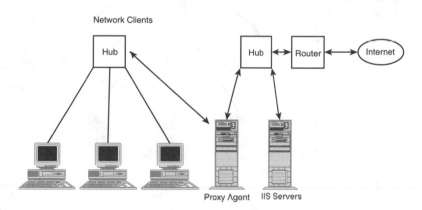

When you create your proxy agent, you also assign an IP port address for the proxy agent to monitor. You may assign one IP port address for all Internet services (such as WWW, FTP, or Gopher) or one port address for each Internet service. Your network clients will then connect to the port on your proxy agent. The proxy agent will then determine the destination IP address and IP port the client wants to use. If the connection is not authorized, it will be terminated. If the connection is authorized, the proxy agent will connect to the external source. As data is received from this external source, it is passed to the network client. Any requests from the network client will be passed to the external source through the proxy agent. In essence, the proxy agent masquerades as the destination computer to the network client and as the network client to the destination computer.

For an external user to gain access to your internal network, he will have to know the IP address of the client computer, the IP address of the proxy agent, and the IP port the proxy agent is monitoring. He will also have to be on the allowed access list (usually based on the external client's IP address). If any of these items are unknown, the external user cannot connect to the client on the other side of the proxy agent.

Using Multiple Network Protocols to Prevent Access to Your Network

A less expensive (and less secure) method to limit access to your network is to use different network protocols on your internal network and your IIS server. You could use the IPX/SPX protocol on your internal networks and both TCP/IP and IPX/SPX on your IIS server. (See Figure 10.3.) This way, your network clients would be isolated from external Internet users, but they would still be able to access the shared directories on the IIS server. In this fashion, you could provide a limited means of accessing data on an FTP site, for example.

FIGURE 10.3.

Using multiple protocols to protect your network.

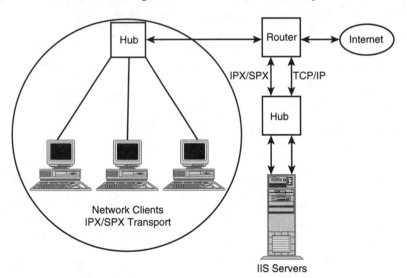

The only drawback to this solution is that your network clients would not be able to access the Internet. A solution does exist for multiple-protocol–based networks, however. It is possible to use a *gateway* (another piece of hardware located between the network clients and the Internet connection) that would convert network requests from your clients using the IPX/SPX protocol to the corresponding TCP/IP protocol. This solution generally requires specially modified Internet utilities that are based on the IPX/SPX protocol rather than on the standard Internet protocols.

Security and Windows NT Server

By now you should be getting the idea that security is a very important issue with any computer connected to the Internet. With Windows NT Server 4, you have several tools in your arsenal that you can apply to limit access to your network and thereby limit the risks associated with the Internet. This section looks into four possibilities. The first item on the agenda is to examine your user-account policies. Your next stop is a look at how you can use the NTFS file system. If you will be supporting dial-up networking clients or connecting to the Internet using a dial-up networking connection, there are a few configuration options you can apply to make it more difficult for someone to cause damage to your network. The last stop is the most important; it shows you how to use the new security features in Windows NT Server to create a miniature firewall.

Using User Accounts to Limit Access

The starting point in securing your server—or your entire network—from unauthorized access is the user accounts that you create. These accounts will be created on your server if it is a standalone computer, or on your domain controller if you are supplying full Internet connectivity to your clients. These user accounts may be used differently, depending on whether you are using the IIS to supply Internet or intranet services. This may be a bit confusing to some of you, so a more thorough discussion may help to clarify the situation.

When you are using IIS to create an intranet site, your network is usually physically secure. The possibility of someone connecting a packet sniffer to your network and capturing clear text password authentication is not very likely. If you use IIS to provide an Internet presence, however, this may change rapidly because anyone with a packet sniffer can capture network packets transmitted over the Internet. It is also possible that someone will go dumpster-diving in an attempt to locate a list of valid user accounts and their associated passwords. It may be that someone is doing this right now in an attempt to obtain a valid user account and password for your network. To prevent these possibilities you need to make sure of three things:

- Protect your user accounts and passwords. Do not leave any lists of user accounts and passwords where they can be easily found. Do not throw out any lists of user accounts and passwords. Instead, lock up any lists in a secure location (not your desk drawer, either) and, if you dispose of any lists, be sure to shred them first.

- Make sure your Internet service provider supports an encryption mechanism for any of your clients that will be connecting to your network over the Internet.

- Make sure your Internet tools support the Microsoft challenge-response authentication mechanism. If this is not possible, because currently only the Microsoft Internet Explorer 2.0 or higher supports this option, consider obtaining a security certificate and using the *Secure Socket Layer* (SSL) to provide access to your server for sites with sensitive data.

Configuring the IIS User Account

If you will be providing Internet access to your IIS site, you will want to make a few modifications to the user account that is created by the IIS setup program. By default, a user account called IUSR_*ServerName*, where *ServerName* is the name of your computer where IIS is installed, is created. This account is added to the Guests local group if you installed IIS on a standalone server. If your server is a member of a domain, the account is also a member of the Domain Users global group. My preference is to move the user account to the Domain Guests global group. If you have modified the privileges for the Domain Guests global group and you will have multiple IIS installations, create a new group, assign the IIS user accounts that are created to this new group, and make sure you remove the IIS accounts from all other global groups. If your IIS sites will be on standalone servers and you have not modified the Guest account, the default IIS user-account privileges should suffice.

> **NOTE**
>
> In order to use the Guest account on a domain, the account must be enabled. The default for the Guest account is for the account to be disabled. You can change this property by double-clicking the Guest account and clearing the Account Disabled check box.

If you create a new global group for the IIS user account, however, make sure that only the Log on locally privilege has been granted to the user account. This can be verified using User Manager (or User Manager for Domains) and choosing Policies | User Rights. This will display the User Rights Policy dialog box. Enable the Show advanced user rights check box so you can view all rights, not just the basic rights. Then in the Right drop-down list box, select each right. As you do, the user accounts and groups that have been assigned the selected right will be displayed in the Grant To list box.

Configuring the User Account Policies

Every network has certain rules for user accounts that can be used to provide additional security for your network. Windows NT Server is no exception. In User Manager (or User Manager for Domains), choose Account from the Policies menu to display the Account Policy dialog box. (See Figure 10.4.)

In the Account Policy dialog box, you can set the following options:

- Maximum Password Age—You can require that a user change his password every so often by specifying a number in the Expires In *x* Days edit field. This is a good idea to implement because it requires that the user change his password and prevents a potential breach of network security.

- Minimum Password Age—By specifying a number in the Allow Changes In *x* Days edit field, you can limit the time period during which the user can change his password. This provides two useful benefits. First, it provides some administrative relief by requiring that a user employ a specific password for a period of time. Second, it provides some network security by preventing a user from setting his password back to a previous password immediately if you have the Password Uniqueness option enabled.

FIGURE 10.4.

Setting user account policies with User Manager.

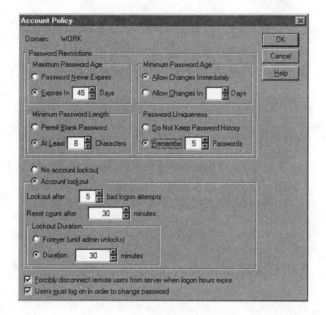

■ Minimum Password Length—This option has a tradeoff that you need to consider before implementing. First, you need to consider that the smaller the password length, the easier it is for the user to remember. However, it also makes it easier for a network hacker to gain access to your network by repeatedly guessing the password for a particular user account. The larger password lengths offer increased network security, but probably will require more intervention from you because your network users will forget their passwords. To specify the minimum length of a password, enter a number in the At Least *x* Characters edit field.

You should require a minimum password length of eight characters. This is a good balance between the ease of user management and potential security breaches.

■ Password Uniqueness—Specifying a number in the Remember *x* Passwords edit field prevents a user from using an older password based on the history list. The *history list* is a record of the user passwords. The number you enter here is used to specify the number of passwords that should be recorded. Any password included in this record cannot be employed by the user when it is time to choose a new password based on the maximum password age.

■ Account lockout—This is your best weapon to fight system hackers because it specifies how many times a user can enter the wrong password to access an account

10

ADVANCED SECURITY ISSUES

before the user account is disabled. This option prevents a hacker from repeatedly attempting to specify a password for a user account to gain access to your network. On the down side, it also can lock out your users who forget their passwords during a logon sequence.

You can specify the number of logon attempts before an account lockout occurs in the Lockout after *x* bad logon attempts edit field. This count is based on the Reset count after *x* minutes edit field. This duration specifies the time frame to determine the count of bad logon attempts. If the number of attempts occurs within the time frame you specify here, the account is locked out. In the Lockout Duration group, you can specify whether the account is locked out for a specific period of time by entering a number in the Duration field, or until an administrator reactivates it by selecting the Forever radio button.

■ Forcibly disconnect remote users from server when logon hours expire—You can enable this check box to force any connected user off the network and close any shared network files (like a SQL Server database) so that you can make system backups.

■ Users must log on in order to change password—You can enable this check box to require that the user log on before he can change his password. This option can prevent a user from using an expired password to gain access to the network for an idle account.

The security of your network is only as good as the policies you implement. You need to balance the aggravation your users encounter due to these policies with reasonable security measures. A good balance between the ease of user management and potential security breaches is to specify a value of 45 to 60 days for the maximum password age, for example. This requires that users change their passwords occasionally to help prevent a hacker from gaining access to your network by using an easily remembered password that never changes.

Using NTFS to Protect Your Data

The *New Technology File System* (NTFS) is another item in your arsenal that, if properly utilized, can aid you in your goal to prevent unauthorized access to your data. You can think of NTFS as your personal security system. In action it is similar to the numerous code-key door-lock systems in use on doors in secure areas. In order to open the door, you must first supply a code, use a badge with a preset code, or wait for someone on the other side of the door to escort you in. All access to this secure area is monitored by security cameras and logged by a security guard. If someone attempts to break in, an alarm is sounded, the guards run to the source of the alarm, and the culprit is taken into custody.

With Windows NT Server, an alarm can be created by using the Performance Monitor in Alert view. (See Chapter 27, "The Performance Monitor.") By monitoring the server object counters Errors Logon and Errors Access Permissions, you can be alerted if the frequency of bad logons or data access attempts are occurring in real time. When informed of the event, if the culprit is a local network client, you certainly can confront him physically, face to face. If the culprit is a remote user, although you cannot take him into custody, you can kick him off of the system. The key to being able to determine who is using your system and what they are doing, however, is based on system resource auditing. Auditing directory or file access is supported only on an NTFS partition. For more specific information on how to configure your system and use this auditing information, refer to the section titled "Determining Who Is Using Your System," later in this chapter. I also recommend that you set permissions on all of your directories and files contained on NTFS partitions because it can help eliminate additional security risks. For more information on how to set directory and file permissions, see the following section.

During the Internet Information Server setup process, the default root installation directory for your WWW, FTP, and Gopher services is SystemRoot\System32\InetSrv. Keeping this directory as the root installation directory is not such a good idea, for at least two reasons.

- This directory is accessible from the Windows NT hidden administration shares ADMIN$ and C$. Although you can delete the sharepoint for the C$ administrative share, deleting the ADMIN$ sharepoint will cause numerous problems with remote administration of the server.

- If your boot partition has a data error, it's possible to lose not only your Windows NT installation but your Internet service's data as well. It is a much better choice to create a new root directory on another physical drive, such as D:\InetSrv. By creating a new root directory, you can control access by deleting the root administration share (D$, for example). You also increase your recoverability options in case your boot partition fails. In the worst case, you can reinstall Windows NT Server and have your Web site back up and running in a couple of hours.

TIP

Wherever you install the IIS files, you should choose an NTFS partition if you have one available. You can then assign permissions to the executable files, as well as all of the root directories for your content files.

Another item in your arsenal is to consider using the fault-tolerant capabilities of Windows NT to limit the downtime that could occur in case of a disaster. You can use a stripe set with parity for increased performance and improved fault tolerance, a mirrored set for additional data redundancy, or both. For maximum fault tolerance, create a mirrored set for your SystemRoot partition to protect you against boot partition errors and a striped set with parity for the partition used as your IIS root directory. But just because you are using a fault-tolerant partition, don't think that you do not need to make system backups.

Plan on daily, weekly, and monthly backups in case all other methods fail. This way, if you install Windows NT Server as a standalone server, you have a way to restore your site. This restoration can occur on the same physical computer that failed (after you replace the failed hardware) or on another computer on your network.

Setting Permissions on a Directory or File

You can prevent unauthorized access to a network resource by setting permissions on a directory or one or more files. Directory- and file-level permissions are divided into the following incremental possibilities:

■ No Access—This permission level prevents any access to the selected directory or files. This includes the parent directory, any subdirectories, and all the files.

CAUTION

Use the No Access option with care because it is exclusive of all other privileges. If you set permissions for directories or files with No Access permissions by user or group, all users or group members are denied access. This occurs even if a different group, which includes selected users of the first group, provides access.

Suppose that you have a group called ChangeAccess that includes the users Bob, Valda, and Mary. You have another group called ExcludeAccess that includes Mary, Joe, and Sally. If you assign the No Access share privilege to the ExcludeAccess group and then assign Change access to the ChangeAccess group, Joe, Sally, and Mary are denied access to the data in the directory, whereas Bob and Valda have change access to the sharepoint.

■ Add—This is an interesting permission level because it denies the user the capability to list the contents of a directory or file. The only thing a user with this permission setting can do is create a subdirectory or file. After he creates the file or subdirectory, he cannot make any changes to it.

TIP

I have found two good reasons to use the Add permission setting. The first is if you want to create an anonymous drop box. You might want to allow a user to send you a data file but prevent some users from seeing it, for example. This is particularly useful for an FTP directory because you can then scan the file with a virus scanner before moving the file to another directory where your users can only read files. This can prevent an Internet user from replacing a file with an infected version. The second good use for this setting is as a backup directory. You can let users drop confidential data files into this directory for backup but prevent any users (including the owner) from accessing it, for example. The only catch for this type of permission setting is that you have to delete directories or files after using them so that the users can add them again later. This is because the user has a one-time option to add a directory or file but cannot replace an existing one.

- Add and Read—This permission is similar to the Add permission, but it also includes the capability to list the directory contents, open a data file, or execute an application.
- Read—Provides read-only access to the parent directory, any subdirectories, and files in a shared directory. Users can connect to the sharepoint, list the directory contents, change subdirectories, read files, and execute applications, but they cannot create subdirectories, add files, or make changes to any data files in the shared directory.
- Change—This permission level includes all the functionality of read access. Users can create subdirectories, add files, and make changes to data files. They also can delete subdirectories and files.
- Full Control—Not only does this level provide the capabilities of the Change share-level permission, it also lets users change the subdirectory- and file-level permissions.
- Special Directory Access—This is a user-specified accumulation of the permissions specified from the list of Read, Write, Execute, Delete, Change, or Take Ownership permissions and applies only to directories.
- Special File Access—This is a user-specified accumulation of the permissions specified from the list of Read, Write, Execute, Delete, Change, or Take Ownership permissions and applies only to files.

NOTE

The capability to change subdirectory- and file-level permissions applies only to network sharepoints that have been created on NTFS partitions.

TIP

Use the Special Directory Access or Special File Access permission if one of the default settings does not provide the restrictions you want. You might want to give someone the capability to use a source code revision program to which you assign the Read, Write, and Delete special file permissions, for example. This assignment lets users make changes to the source code but does not enable them to change any permission settings, take ownership of the files, or execute applications contained in the directory. If you combine this assignment with the special directory permissions, you can even restrict the user from listing or accessing subdirectories.

10

ADVANCED SECURITY ISSUES

Table 10.2 summarizes the directory- and file-level permissions. Table 10.3 contains explanations of the abbreviations.

Table 10.2. Directory- and file-level permissions.

Permission	Directory/Subdirectory-Level Access	File-Level Access
No Access	None	None
Add	(A)	(A)
Add and Read	(L) (R) (W) (E)	(L) (R) (W) (E)
Read	(L) (R) (E)	(L) (R) (E)
Change	(L) (R) (W) (E) (D)	(L) (R) (W) (E) (D)
Full Control	(L) (R) (W) (E) (D) (P) (O)	(L) (R) (W) (E) (D) (P) (O)
Special Directory Access	User Specified	Not Specified
Special File Access	Not Specified	User Specified
List	(L)	(L)

Table 10.3. Directory and file permission attributes.

Attribute	Description
A	Creates a directory or a file once, but you can't make any changes thereafter.
D	Deletes subdirectories and files.
E	Executes applications.
L	Lists subdirectories and files.
O	Takes ownership of subdirectories and files on NTFS partitions.
P	Changes permissions on subdirectories and files on NTFS partitions.
R	Reads files but makes no changes.
W	Creates subdirectories and files and modifies existing files.

To set permissions on directories, follow these steps:

1. Select the directories by using File Manager.
2. Choose Permissions from the Security menu to access the Directory Permissions dialog box. (See Figure 10.5.)

FIGURE 10.5.

The Directory Permissions dialog box.

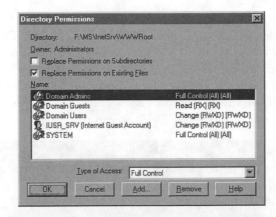

TIP

As a shortcut to the Security | Permissions menu option, you can click the Permissions toolbar button.

---

3. Click the Add button. The Add Users and Groups dialog box appears. (See Figure 10.6.)

FIGURE 10.6.

The Add Users and Groups dialog box.

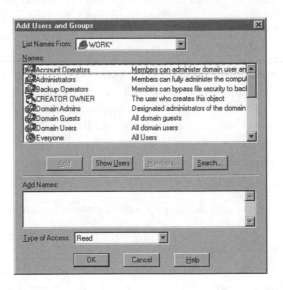

4. By default, the domain you logged on to is displayed in the List Names From drop-down list box. You can use the domain user database from any domain with which you have established a trust relationship. You also can use the local database for a Windows NT Server computer operating in server mode.

5. By default, only groups are listed in the Names drop-down list box. If you want to include user accounts, click the Show Users button. This adds all your user accounts to the end of the list. To add an existing group or user, just double-click on the group or user name displayed in the Names drop-down list box, or select a group or name and click the Add button. This copies the user account or group to the Add Names box. If you mistakenly add a name to the Add Names box, you can highlight the name and then press the Delete key to remove it.

> **TIP**
>
> To display individual user accounts, select a group name in the Names box and click the Members button. If you select a local group and click the Members button, the Local Group Membership dialog box appears, which includes local user accounts and global groups defined in the local group. If you then select a global group and click the Members button, the Global Group Membership dialog appears, which includes a list of users defined in the global group. In either of these dialog boxes, you can select an individual user account (or global groups in the Local Group Membership dialog box) and click the Add button to add users or global groups to the Add Names box in the Add Users and Groups dialog box.

6. After you place the user accounts or groups in the Add Names box, you need to select the directory permission level from the Type of Access drop-down list box. This can be No Access, Add, Add and Read, Read, Change, or Full Control.

7. Click the OK button to return to the Directory Permissions dialog box. All the user and group accounts now are displayed in the Name box of the dialog box.

8. If you want to replace the permissions on all subdirectories of the directory you are setting permissions on, make sure to enable the Replace Permissions on Subdirectories check box. If you do not want to replace the permissions on files currently contained in the directory, be sure to disable the Replace Permissions on Existing Files check box.

9. Click the OK button to assign the directory-level permissions you selected.

10. Click the OK button to continue when you see a confirmation dialog box.

To modify an existing user or group directory-level permission, follow these steps:

1. In the Directory Permissions dialog box, select the user account or group name listed in the Name box.

2. In the Type of Access drop-down list box, select the Share permission level. This can be No Access, Add, Add and Read, Read, Change, Full Control, Special Directory Access, or Special File Access. If you specify Special Directory Access, the dialog box shown in Figure 10.7 appears. If you select Special File Access, the dialog box shown in Figure 10.8 is displayed. You can specify the exact permission settings you want in these dialog boxes.

FIGURE **10.7.**

The Special Directory Access dialog box.

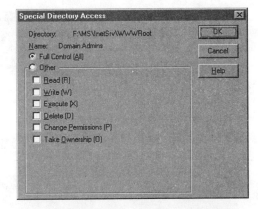

FIGURE **10.8.**

The Special File Access dialog box.

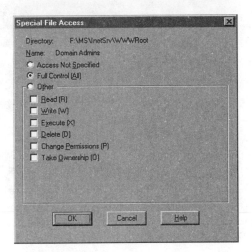

3. Repeat these steps for each user account or group for which you want to change the permissions.

To delete an existing user or group permission, follow these steps:

1. Select the user account or group name listed in the Name box in the Directory Permissions dialog box.

2. Click the Remove button.

3. Repeat these steps for each user account or group you want to delete.

To set file permissions, you follow the same basic steps as outlined earlier, except that when you select files instead of directories, the File Permissions dialog box appears, as shown in Figure 10.9. If you select Special Access in the Type of Access drop-down list box of the File Permissions dialog box, the Special Access dialog box shown in Figure 10.10 is displayed.

10

ADVANCED
SECURITY ISSUES

FIGURE 10.9.

The File Permissions dialog box.

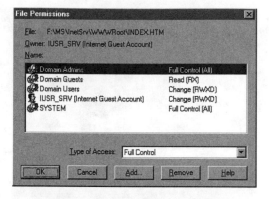

FIGURE 10.10.

The Special Access dialog box.

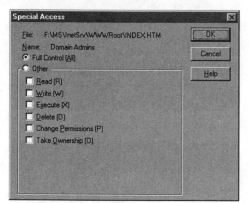

One other interesting feature you can select from the Security menu is Owner. If you select directories or files and then the Security | Owner menu option, you can take ownership of these directories or files. In essence, you replace all the permission settings with those from your current user account. This can be useful if you need to assume ownership of orphaned directories or files so that you later can give this ownership to another user. You can give ownership back to a user by assigning permissions for that user and specifying the Take Ownership permission setting. Then have the new user take ownership by using File Manager. After she takes ownership, only she will be able to access the directories or files. Or you can just assign permissions using his user account.

Security and Dial-Up Networking

The Windows NT dial-up networking service does not provide a high level of security for your network. There are, however, at least two choices you can make that can improve the situation. First, you can configure your dial-out and dial-in connections to use encryption. Second, you can choose to allow all network clients to access either just the computer that is providing the dial-up networking connection or the entire network. The choice as to which encryption setting to use, and whether to provide full access to your network, will be determined by your requirements.

If you are supporting dial-in connections for remote clients that must access the entire network and for those that don't, set up multiple dial-in connections on two or more modems. Each remote client can then access the appropriate modem using a specific phone number that you provide, thus lessening the chance of a security breach. To configure your dial-in connection to enable or disable full access to the network, follow these steps:

1. Open the Network Control Panel applet.

2. Select the Services tab to display the Services properties sheet.

3. Select the Remote Access Service. Then click the Properties button to display the Remote Access Setup dialog box.

4. Select the appropriate connection; then click the Network button. This displays the Network Configuration dialog box.

5. In the Server Settings group, click the Configure button next to the appropriate network protocol under the Allow remote clients running title. This displays the RAS Server *Protocol* Configuration dialog box, where *Protocol* is NetBEUI, TCP/IP, or IPX/SPX.

6. In the Allow Remote *Protocol* clients to access field, where *Protocol* is NetBEUI, TCP/IP, or IPX/SPX, check either the Entire network radio button to grant access to all computers on your network or the This computer only radio button to limit access to just the server providing the dial-in connection.

7. Click the OK button to return to the Network Configuration dialog box.

8. If you will be supporting multiple network protocols, repeat steps 5 through 7 for each additional protocol. When you are finished, click the OK button to return to the Remote Access Setup dialog box.

9. For each additional connection to configure, repeat steps 4 through 8. Then click the OK button to return to the Network dialog box.

10. Click the OK button to close the Network dialog box. You will then be prompted by the Network Settings Change dialog box to restart your system. Click the Yes button to restart your system so that the changes will be applied when the system restarts or click the No button to defer the update until the next time the server is restarted.

To modify your dial-in connections to require password or data encryption for increased security, follow these steps:

1. Open the Network Control Panel applet.

2. Select the Services tab to display the Services properties sheet.

3. Select the Remote Access Service. Then click the Properties button to display the Remote Access Setup dialog box.

4. Select the appropriate connection; then click the Network button. This will display the Network Configuration dialog box.

5. In the Server Settings group, click one of the following options to specify your encryption requirements:

   ■ Allow any encryption including plain text—Specifies that any supported (either MS-CHAP, SPAP, or PAP) encryption method be allowed. A connection will be attempted using the Microsoft password encryption (MS-CHAP) first, then the standard Internet encryption method (SPAP), followed by a plain text (PAP) authentication.

   ■ Require encrypted authentication—Specifies that a connection will be attempted using the Microsoft password encryption (MS-CHAP) first; then, if that fails, the standard Internet encryption method (SPAP) will be used.

   ■ Require Microsoft encrypted authentication—Specifies that a connection will be attempted using only the Microsoft password encryption (MS-CHAP) method. If this item is selected, you can also enable the Require data encryption check box to encrypt your data as well as your password.

NOTE

Many Internet service providers support Microsoft encryption, so you should try this option first. If it fails, try the Require encrypted authentication. Only if both methods fail should you enable the Allow any encryption including plain text check box.

6. Click the OK button to return to the Network Configuration dialog box.

7. If you will be supporting multiple network protocols, repeat steps 5 and 6 for each additional protocol. When you are finished, click the OK button to return to the Remote Access Setup dialog box.

8. For each additional connection to configure, repeat steps 4 through 7. Then click the OK button to return to the Network dialog box.

9. Click the OK button to close the Network dialog box. You will then be prompted by the Network Settings Change dialog box to restart your system. Click the Yes button to restart your system so that the changes will be applied when the system restarts or click the No button to defer the update until the next time the server is restarted.

To configure your dial-out connection (such as when you are using Windows NT Server as a gateway to the Internet), follow these steps:

1. Launch the Dial-Up Networking applet by choosing Dial-Up Networking from the Start | Accessories menu. This displays the Dial-Up Networking dialog box.

2. To create a new connection, click the New button to display the New Phonebook Entry dialog box.

3. Enter a unique name in the Entry name field for the connection.

4. Enter a description in the Comment field for the connection.

5. Specify the phone number to dial in the Phone number field.

6. Specify a modem connection to use in the Dial using drop-down list box.

7. To use the telephony settings for the modem (recommended), check the Use Telephony dialing properties check box.

8. Select the Server tab to display the Server properties sheet.

9. Choose PPP—Windows NT, Windows 95 Plus, or Internet in the Dial-Up server type drop-down list box.

10. Enable the TCP/IP check box in the Network protocols field and disable the NetBEUI and IPX/SPX compatible check boxes.

11. Select the Security tab to display the Security properties sheet.

12. In the Authentication and encryption policy group, specify your encryption requirement. This can be one of the following:

   - Allow any encryption including plain text—Specifies that any supported (either MS-CHAP, SPAP, or PAP) encryption method be used to encrypt the password. A connection will be attempted using the Microsoft password encryption (MS-CHAP) first, then the standard Internet encryption method (SPAP), followed by a plain text (PAP) authentication.

   - Require encrypted authentication—Specifies that a connection will be attempted using the Microsoft password encryption (MS-CHAP) first; if that fails, the standard Internet encryption method (SPAP) will be used.

   - Require Microsoft encrypted authentication—Specifies that a connection will be attempted using only the Microsoft password encryption (MS-CHAP) method. If this item is selected, you can also enable the Require data encryption check box to encrypt your data as well as your password. You may also enable the Use current username and password check box to attempt to connect using the username and password of the active account. This option is rarely used with an ISP, but is often used by clients that will connect directly to your server.

NOTE

Many Internet service providers support Microsoft encryption, so you should try this option first. If it fails, try the Require encrypted authentication. Only if both methods fail should you enable the Allow any encryption including plain text check box.

---

13. Click the OK button to create the new phonebook entry and return to the Dial-Up Networking dialog box.

At this point you are ready to connect to the Internet by just clicking the Dial button on the Dial-Up Networking dialog box. The connection you will dial will be displayed in the Phonebook entry to dial drop-down list box. If you want to dial a different connection, just choose it before you click the Dial button.

Configuring Windows NT Server as a Mini-Firewall

Windows NT Server 4.0 adds two new features that you can use to build a miniature firewall. The first new feature includes PPTP (Point to Point Tunneling Protocol), which can be used to support multiprotocol *virtual private networks* (VPNs). Basically PPTP can be used to provide a secure method of accessing your network over the Internet. It does this by tunneling your network transport protocol (TCP/IP, IPX/SPX, or NetBEUI) over a PPP connection. This also encrypts your network communication linkage so that only the server and network client can make any use of the embedded network packets. To use this option, however, your Internet service provider must also support the PPTP protocol. So check with your service provider(s) before you reconfigure all of your clients to use PPTP. The second feature is the capability to accept or reject specific Internet protocols and specific IP ports that use Transmission Control Protocol (TCP) or User Datagram Protocol (UDP).

To really use these options to obtain the maximum benefit requires that your system fit one of two models. It can be either a standalone server or a multi-homed server. Both of these configurations should use a dedicated router connected to a network adapter in the server. (A *multi-homed server* is just a server with more than one network adapter.)

The reason you need to use one of these two models is because the security and PPTP filtering options, which you will step through shortly, are bound to a specific network adapter. If you have only one network adapter in your computer, use the dial-up networking service to provide an Internet gateway and attempt to restrict access using the TCP/IP security features. This will apply to all computers that are connected to your server. For a standalone server, this does not matter because you want to support only specific ports and protocols. But for a server acting as an Internet gateway, it matters quite a bit because your server's primary purpose is to provide file and print services to your network clients; its secondary purpose is to act as an Internet gateway and pass packets from your clients to the Internet, and vice versa. Your server will not be able to function in both capacities if you use the security features of the TCP/IP protocol and have only a single network adapter.

It would be possible to configure a server with a single network adapter to support multiple protocols such as IPX/SPX and TCP/IP. This way, your network clients would still be able to access the file and print services on the server. If you use the TCP/IP security features to block specific IP ports or protocols, the single network adapter will still affect your network clients' ability to access the Internet service. The TCP/IP security features may also prevent your Internet clients from accessing your IIS services. You will need to be very careful as to which ports and protocols you decide to block if you do not want to have a negative impact on your network functionality.

To configure your server to accept only PPTP packets or to enable the TCP/IP security features, follow these steps:

1. Open the Network Control Panel applet to display the Network dialog box.
2. Select the Protocols tab to display the Protocols properties sheet.
3. Select the TCP/IP Protocol; then click the Properties button to display the dialog box shown in Figure 10.11.

FIGURE 10.11.

The Microsoft TCP/IP Properties dialog box.

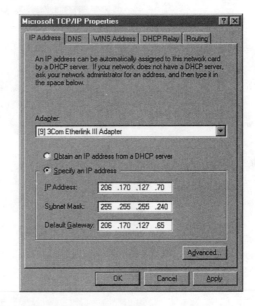

4. Click the Advanced button to display the dialog box shown in Figure 10.12.
5. Select the adapter to configure in the Adapter drop-down list box.
6. To accept only PPTP packets on the adapter, check the Enable PPTP Filtering check box.

NOTE

By enabling the PPTP Filtering check box, you disable all other network protocols for the selected adapter.

7. Repeat steps 5 through 6 for each adapter you want to configure to accept only PPTP network packets.
8. To enable the advanced TCP/IP security features, check the Enable Security check box. Then click the Configure button to display the dialog box shown in Figure 10.13.

10

ADVANCED SECURITY ISSUES

FIGURE 10.12.

The Advanced IP Addressing dialog box.

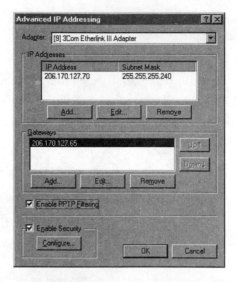

FIGURE 10.13.

The TCP/IP Security dialog box.

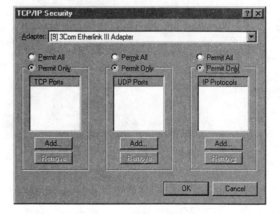

9. Select the adapter to configure in the Adapter drop-down list box.

10. For the TCP Ports, UDP Ports, or IP Protocols, either enable the Permit All (the default) radio button to accept all IP ports or protocols to pass through the network adapter or enable the Permit Only radio button.

    If you select the Permit Only radio button, click the Add button to display the Security Add dialog box for each item.

    In the TCP Port, UDP Port, or IP Protocol field, enter the port or protocol to disable for the specified network adapter. Then click the Add button to add the specified port to the list.

NOTE

Table 10.4 lists the more common IP port addresses and protocols that you may want to disable on the specified network adapter.

11. Repeat step 10 for each additional port or protocol to disable.

12. Repeat steps 9 through 10 for each additional adapter to configure the options for TCP/IP security.

13. Click the OK button to return to the Advanced IP Addressing dialog box.

14. Click the OK button to return to the Network dialog box.

15. Click the OK button to close the Network dialog box. You are then prompted by the Network Settings Change dialog box to restart your computer. Click the Yes button for your changes to go into effect after the system restarts or click the No button to defer your changes until the next system restart.

Table 10.4. Common IP ports and TCP/IP protocols.

Port	Protocol	Description	Note
	ICMP	Internet Control Message Protocol	Used to send error or test messages from a local computer to a remote computer. Commonly used to `ping` Internet hosts. Disabling this protocol will prevent external hosts from probing your network to see what hosts may be available; however, it will also prevent your network clients from `ping`ing external Internet hosts.
	MBONE	Multicast Backbone	This protocol is used to tunnel multicast packets through routers that do not support multicast routing. (*Multicast* is the capability to send a single packet to multiple destinations on the Internet. It is often used for live

continues

Table 10.4. continued

Port	Protocol	Description	Note
			performances, such as radio broadcasts or video feeds.) The threat occurs from the fact that you do not know the protocol and service of the internal IP packet.
21	TCP	File Transfer Protocol (FTP)	This port should be disabled only if you want to prevent your network clients from accessing external FTP sites. If you want to disable your FTP server, it is best to disable the FTP Publishing service in the Control Panel Services applet.
23	TCP	Telnet	Used for remote terminal sessions. There is no Telnet server included with Windows NT Server, so this should not be a concern unless you have installed a third-party Telnet server.
25	TCP	Simple Mail Transfer Protocol (SMTP)	Used by e-mail servers to send/receive e-mail over the Internet.
53	TCP or UDP	Domain Name System (DNS) service	If this port is not blocked for external Internet access, it may be possible for an external DNS server to update the name servers on your network. In addition, your internal DNS servers may share information (such as your host names) that you would prefer to remain only within your internal network.
70	TCP	Gopher	This port should be disabled only if you want to prevent your network clients from accessing external Gopher sites. If you want to disable your Gopher server, it is

Port	Protocol	Description	Note
			best to disable the Gopher Publishing service in the Control Panel Services applet.
79	TCP	Finger service	Used to obtain information about a user on a specified host. Commonly used to probe networks; however, Windows NT Server does not provide a finger server.
80	TCP	World Wide Web (WWW) service	This port should be disabled only if you want to prevent your network clients from accessing external Web sites. If you want to disable your Web server, it is best to disable the WWW Publishing service in the Control Panel Services applet.
111	TCP or UDP	Port Mapper	Used by remote procedure call (RPC) applications to obtain the IP port of a service.
119	TCP	Network News Transfer Protocol (NNTP)	
123	UDP	Network Time Protocol (NTP)	
210	TCP	Wide Area Information Servers (WAIS)	An add-on to the Gopher service. Not provided with Windows NT Server, but may be obtained from third parties.
161, 162	TCP or UDP	Simple Network Management Protocol (SNMP)	Used by SNMP management consoles to monitor or configure services as well as trap errors. It is a good idea to disable the SNMP port unless you need to allow external access to your system or access an external system using SNMP.

continues

10

ADVANCED SECURITY ISSUES

Table 10.4. continued

Port	Protocol	Description	Note
513	TCP	Remote Login (rlogin) service	Used by the remote login, remote copy, remote shell, and other remote services. This should be a concern only for users who have installed either a third-party service or one of these services from the Microsoft Windows NT Resource Kit.
1525	UDP	Archie	An add-on to the Gopher service. Not provided with Windows NT Server, but may be obtained from third parties.
2049	UDP	Network File System (NFS)	Provides the capability to remote mount a file system. This can be a potentially dangerous situation, but will only occur with Windows NT Server if you also install a third-party NFS server because the base package does not include this functionality.
6000+	X11	X graphical interface	Each Xserver can use a port above 6000. The first Xserver would use port 6000, the second port 6001, and so on.
6667	TCP	Internet Relay Chat (IRC)	Used to support text-based online chats.

Determining Who Is Using Your System

Determining who may have accessed your system in the past, or who may be accessing your system now, is very important to anyone connected to the Internet. One of the best methods to determine whether a security breach has occurred or is occurring is to use the security logs created by Windows NT and the Internet Information Server. To determine who may be accessing your system or attempting to access restricted data files, however, the system must be configured to audit events. To restrict access to your sensitive files or enable auditing of your files, you must use File Manager (or the Windows Explorer). To view your system events, you must use the Windows NT Event Viewer, but to view your IIS event logs, you can use a text editor (like Notepad) if you configured the service to write a text file, or you can use an ODBC front end (like Access) to view your logs that were created on an ODBC-compliant database.

Configuring the System to Enable Auditing

If you want to be able to determine who is using your shared network resources, or even who is abusing their privileges on your network, you need to enable the auditing features provided in Windows NT Server. Auditing is divided into several categories, however, and is not enabled in a single application.

To audit a system event related to account usage or modification and the programs running on your server, launch User Manager for Domains and choose Audit from the Policies menu to display the Audit Policy dialog box. (See Figure 10.14.)

FIGURE 10.14.

Enabling system auditing with User Manager.

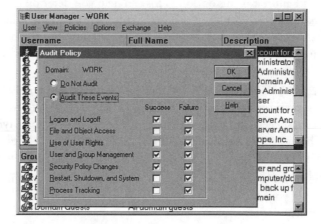

To audit any event, you first need to enable the Audit These Events radio button in the Audit Policy dialog box (even if you select no options here to audit) and then choose the application's audit options. To audit the use of files, use File Manager; for printer auditing, use Print Manager. Both of these have an Auditing option on the Security menu that displays a dialog box similar to the Audit Policy dialog box in which you can specify the events to audit.

When you select an event to be audited, it is entered into the security log, which you can view with the Event Viewer. You can select to audit the successful use of a privilege, failure to obtain access (which indicates a security violation attempt), or both.

10

ADVANCED SECURITY ISSUES

You can audit the following events:

- Logon and Logoff—Determines who has logged on to or off of your network. I recommend that you enable both these check boxes (Success and Failure) to determine who may be using your network.

- File and Object Access—Works with other applications that have been used to specify auditing. You can use File Manager to enable auditing of a directory, for example. You can enable the Success or Failure events for the File and Object Access in order to record any access to the audited directory.

- Use of User Rights—Provides the capability to audit any use of a user right, other than logon and logoff, such as the capability to log on as a service.

- User and Group Management—Gives you the capability to track any user account or group management—whether a new user is added, an existing user password is enabled, or new users are added to a group, for example.

  If you have constant problems with a particular user account or group being modified and cannot determine who is making these changes, you should enable both Success and Failure for this option. This can help you determine who may be making the changes. I've seen a few problems caused by personnel who have been granted administrative privileges but who are not trained in their use, for example. By using this option, you can determine who needs additional training, or even who should have his administrative privileges revoked.

- Security Policy Changes—Helps you determine who may be making changes to your system-audit policies, user-right policies, or trust relationships. Enable this option for both Success and Failure to determine who may be modifying your network policies. This is a good idea, particularly if you have several administrators and find that things have been changing without anyone admitting responsibility.

- Restart, Shutdown, and System—Enables you to determine who may be shutting down your servers or performing any event that affects system security or the security log.

- Process Tracking—Determines which applications are executing on your system.

> **CAUTION**
>
> Auditing the Success events for Process Tracking can fill up your security log in a matter of minutes. Enable this event for Success only when absolutely necessary.

Auditing Directories and Files

If you want to monitor who is using your network resources or if you are concerned about users who consistently attempt to bypass your security restrictions, you can use the auditing features to determine who is doing what with your shared directories or files. Suppose you have an HTML document as a template on your server that is used by many users on your network. Each user should save a copy of the data file under a different name, but suppose someone inadvertently saves a version of the file, replaces the original on the network, and then, to hide the mistake, deletes the file. If you have enabled auditing of the file, you will know which user modified or even deleted it. You then can have a serious talk with him or her about network security. Another possible use of security auditing is to identify an Internet user who may be trying to access restricted data using a stolen user account and password, or maliciously deleting files on your FTP site.

> **NOTE**
>
> Auditing is available only on NTFS partitions.

You can view this auditing information by using the Event Viewer and examining the security log. This topic is covered later in the section "Using the Windows NT Event Viewer." For now, just take a look at what is required to enable auditing of directories and files with File Manager. The first thing to consider is that in order to enable auditing at the system level, you have to use User Manager for Domains and choose Policies|Auditing to turn on the auditing features. (Refer to the section "Configuring the System to Enable Auditing" in this chapter.)

> **NOTE**
>
> I still prefer to use File Manager for my security-related tasks, so this is the tool I will describe how to use. The only difference between File Manager and the Windows Explorer is the means you use to gain access to the Permissions or Auditing dialog boxes. For the Windows Explorer, you can just right-click a directory or file to display a Properties dialog box. Then you just choose the Security tab to display the Security properties sheet. To set permissions on the selected directories, just click the Permissions button. To enable auditing, click the Auditing button. To take ownership, click the Ownership button.

After you enable systemwide auditing, you can follow these steps to audit your directories on your server:

1. Select the directories you want to audit with File Manager. Choose Auditing from the Security menu. The Directory Auditing dialog box appears. (See Figure 10.15.)
2. Select the users or groups you want to audit. To accomplish this task, click the Add button; the Add Users and Groups dialog box appears. (See Figure 10.16.)

10

**ADVANCED
SECURITY ISSUES**

FIGURE 10.15.

The Directory Auditing dialog box.

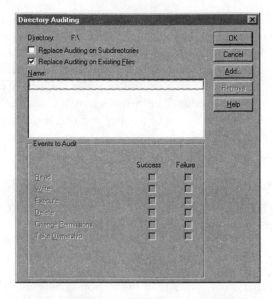

FIGURE 10.16.

The Add Users and Groups dialog box.

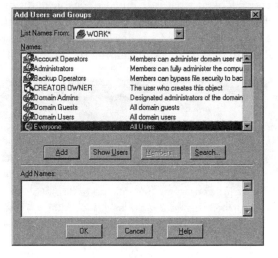

3. By default, the domain you logged on to is displayed in the List Names From drop-down list box. You can use the domain user database from any domain with which you have established a trust relationship, however. You also can use the local database for a Windows NT Server computer operating in server mode or a Windows NT Workstation.

4. By default, only groups are listed in the Names box. If you want to include user accounts, click the Show Users button. This adds all your user accounts to the end of the list. To add an existing group or user, just double-click the group or username

displayed in the Names list or select a group or name and click the Add button. This copies the user account or group to the Add Names list box.

5. After you complete your user and group selections, click the OK button to return to the Directory Auditing dialog box.

6. Determine which events to audit by checking the boxes in the Success or Failure column (see Figure 10.17). Normally, I audit all Failure events, but only the Take Ownership and Change Permissions Success events.

FIGURE 10.17.

Enabling directory auditing.

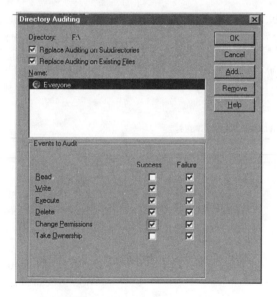

7. If you want to replace the auditing information for all the subdirectories of the parent directory, make sure to enable the Replace Auditing on Subdirectories check box. If you do not want to replace auditing on the files in directories, clear the Replace Auditing on Existing Files check box.

8. Click the OK button to change your current auditing settings.

9. After you receive a confirmation message box, just click the OK button to continue.

To audit files, you follow the same procedure as outlined here. (The dialog box displayed will not have the Replace Auditing on Subdirectories or Replace Auditing on Existing Files check boxes, however.)

10

ADVANCED SECURITY ISSUES

Using the Windows NT Event Viewer

Use the Event Viewer to display status events that occur on your computer. These events are divided into three categories. Each category is contained in a specific log. The *system log* includes events related to the operation of the operating system, the *application log* includes application-specific events, and the *security log* includes auditing events. Of these three, the most important to you is the security log because you can use it to determine whether someone is attempting to access restricted data or whether someone is trying to break into your system by guessing passwords for a known user account. The next log of concern is the system log because it can show, by service, the anonymous logon requests that have occurred on your system. It can also display other publishing-service events. Events are further divided into types that have specific icons associated with them. Table 10.5 summarizes the event types for each log category.

> **NOTE**
>
> You should use the Event Viewer to view your logs on a daily basis for your file servers, and at least once a week for a workstation. If you do not review your logs in this time frame, you might be unaware of system errors that could propagate to a system failure, and you will not be aware of possible attempts to violate the security of your network.

Table 10.5. Event icons and types.

Icon	Type	Description
Stop Sign	Error	Indicates a serious problem that prevents an application, system service, or device driver from functioning properly. Also indicates when a malfunction has been noticed by an application, system service, or device driver.
Exclamation	Warning	Indicates a problem that is troublesome but noncritical to the operation of the operating system or application. Warnings often can propagate errors over time, and therefore should not be ignored.
I Sign	Informational	Does not indicate a problem. This is just a status code to inform you that an application, a system service, or a device driver is functioning properly.

Icon	*Type*	*Description*
Key	Success Audit	Informational events to indicate the success of a security modification or usage of a security-related operation. These event entries are based on the audit events you have selected with User Manager for Domains, File Manager, Print Manager, Clipbook Viewer, Registry Editor, and any other application that supports auditing.
Lock	Failure Audit	Informational events to indicate the failure of a security-related operation. These event entries are based on the audit events you have selected with User Manager for Domains, File Manager, Print Manager, Clipbook Viewer, Registry Editor, and any other application that supports auditing.

Viewing Events

To view the events that have occurred on your system, you first need to select the log to view. Access this information from the Log menu. You can select the application, security, or system log to view. Each event in a log is broken down into components that describe the event. Table 10.6 summarizes these event components. To get the details of an event, just double-click its name and the Event Detail dialog box appears, as shown in Figure 10.18. The description contains a textual message in the Description box that describes the error condition, and if the event has associated data with it, it is included in the Data box. This data list often contains information that you or Microsoft technical support can use to isolate and solve the problem.

Table 10.6. The event components.

Component	*Description*
Icon	A quick indicator to the type of event.
Date	The date the event occurred.
Time	The time the event occurred.
Source	The name of the application, system service, or device driver that reported the event.
Category	A general classification of an event type. In most cases, categories are used only in the security log.

continues

10

ADVANCED
SECURITY ISSUES

Table 10.6. continued

Component	Description
Event ID	An event number specific to the event source and associated with a specific error message.
User	An event can be associated with a specific user that triggered the event. In most cases, this is used only in the security log.
Computer	An event can be associated with a specific computer that triggered the event. In most cases, this is the name of the host computer (the computer where the log resides).

FIGURE 10.18.

The Event Detail dialog box.

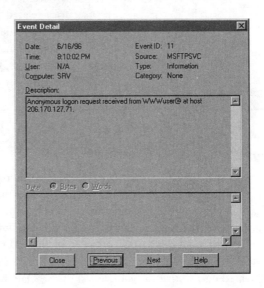

Filtering Events

One of the problems you will notice over time is that so many events occur on your system that finding the trouble spots can be quite time-consuming. And if it takes too much of your time, you probably will stop checking for these problems. Eventually a problem will grow into a system-related failure that could cause you to lose your job. I would like to help you avoid that. The easiest way to minimize the amount of data overload is to use the Event Viewer's filtering capabilities.

Follow these steps:

1. Choose Filter Events from the View menu to display the Filter dialog box shown in Figure 10.19.

FIGURE 10.19.

*The Event Viewer
Filter dialog box.*

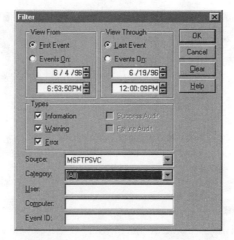

2. In the View From section, select the Events On radio button. Then specify a date and time.

3. In the View Through section, select the Events On radio button. Then specify a date and time.

4. In the Types section, select the type of event to report. For a quick look, I suggest looking only for warning and error conditions.

5. In the Source drop-down list box, select the event source to view. This is useful for limiting the report to a specific application, system service, or device driver to determine how often the error has occurred.

6. In the Category drop-down list box, select the event categories to view. In most systems, there will be only security-related categories, or possibly no subcategories. If you have categories, you can further limit the report to a particular category by selecting it from the list.

7. In the User field, enter the user account you want to use to further limit the report. This can be useful when you are checking events in the security log and have noticed a potential violation. By limiting the report to just this user, you can determine how often the user has attempted to violate your system security.

8. Enter the computer name in the Computer field to further limit events to just events that have occurred on the specific computer.

9. If you are looking for a specific event, enter the event number in the Event ID field. This can be useful to determine how often a specific event has occurred in the past.

10. After you finish entering all your filtering characteristics, click the OK button to engage the filter. When a filter has been engaged, the title bar of the Event Viewer changes to include the word "Filtered."

10

**ADVANCED
SECURITY ISSUES**

> **NOTE**
>
> After a filter has been specified, it remains in effect until you change it. If you enabled the Save Settings on Exit option, the next time you launch Event Viewer, the filter also remains in effect.

To remove a filter that you have created using these steps, just choose the View | All Events menu option, and all the events are displayed in the logs. Select a menu option to refresh the screen.

Archiving Events

Instead of throwing away the events in your event logs when you fill them up, you should archive them. This gives you the ability to load them at a later date for comparison with current logs to isolate any potential problems. You also can use these logs with Excel or any database that can import a comma-separated value or ASCII text file. Use this imported data to spot trends that can indicate a network trouble spot or hardware-related failure.

> **TIP**
>
> You can set the maximum size of the log by choosing the Log | Log Settings menu option to display the Log Settings dialog box. In this dialog box, you also can specify that you want the log to automatically wrap and overwrite events on an as-needed basis, to overwrite events after a specific number of days, or to manually clear the log to free space for further events.

To archive a log, follow these steps:

1. Choose Log Type from the Log menu, where Log Type is the application, security, or system log.

2. Choose Save As from the Log menu to display the Save As dialog box. In the Save File As Type field, select Event Log Files (*.EVT) to save the event file as a binary file that can be reloaded later into the Event Viewer. Or select Text Files (*.TXT), which is a standard ASCII text file, or Comma Delim Text (*.TXT), a comma-separated value text file.

3. Enter a filename in the File Name field and click the OK button. If the drive or directory is not the one you want, change it before clicking the OK button.

The Internet Information Server Logs

Although you can use the Windows NT Event Viewer to look at the security and system logs, these logs do not contain as much information about who is doing what with your Internet services as do the IIS logs. Your IIS logs contain the following fields:

- Clienthost—Specifies the IP address of the connected client.
- Username—Specifies the name supplied by the user to log on to the specified service.
- Logtime—Specifies when the user started the connection in MM/DD/YY HH:MM:SS time format.
- Service—Specifies the service to which the user connected. This will be MSFTPSVC for the FTP Publishing service, W3SVC for the WWW Publishing service, or GopherSvc for the Gopher Publishing service.
- Machine—Specifies the IIS server on which the service is executing.
- ServerIP—Specifies the IP address of the server on which the service is executing.
- Processingtime—Specifies the time the client was connected.
- Bytessent—Specifies the number of bytes sent to the client.
- Bytesreceived—Specifies the number of bytes sent by the client.
- Servicestatus—Specifies a service-specific status code.
- Win32Status—Specifies a Windows NT 32-bit API-specific status code.
- Operation—Specifies the service operation type for the client request.
- Target—Specifies the data object name requested by the client.
- Parameter—Specifies any additional command parameter.

By saving these logs and reviewing them at least once a week, you can obtain performance characteristics such as how many users visited your site. You can also use these logs to determine whether an unauthorized user was trying to access data on your site by looking for user logon failures. If you see several of these from the same IP address, you may want to prevent that IP address from logging on to your site by configuring the advanced options for the service as described in Chapter 6, "Using the Internet Service Manager."

Summary

This chapter covers a lot of material, but it only touches on some of the complex security issues. One key concept you should remember is that a security policy needs to be in place both to protect you from data you download from the Internet and to limit access to your network. You learn how you can configure Windows NT Server to function as a mini-firewall as part of your policy of limiting access, and how to further protect your data by using the NTFS file

10

ADVANCED SECURITY ISSUES

system and applying permissions to directories and files. Finally, you learn about some of the tools you can use to enable system auditing, set auditing on directories and files, and to see if anyone is accessing files on which you enabled auditing.

Enhancing Internet Information Server

IN THIS CHAPTER

- Using the Microsoft Proxy Server 320
- Using the Microsoft Chat Server 345
- Using the Microsoft News Server 363

CHAPTER 11

If all you want to do on the Internet is provide a means for Internet clients to view Web pages, download (or upload) files, or search an index, then the Internet Information Server is all you really need. On the other hand, perhaps you want to do more that just publish files on the Internet. Perhaps you are more concerned about security and want to use the Internet Information Server as the backbone of a proxy server to limit access to your Internet/intranet. Or perhaps you want to add new services to your IIS installation. If so, you're in the right place.

This chapter takes a look at several add-on products for the Internet Information Server. The first is the Microsoft Proxy Server, which can turn your IIS installation into a full-featured proxy server. (For more details on proxy servers, refer to Chapter 10, "Advanced Security Issues.") If you need a feature that the Microsoft Proxy Server cannot accomplish, then you can probably find a third-party proxy server add-on to accomplish the task. The other products you can use to enhance your IIS installation are part of the Commercial Internet Server previously code-named "Normandy." These products include an Internet Relay Chat (IRC) server and a Network News Transport Protocol (NNTP) compliant news server. You can find out more about these components, and download them as well, from the Commercial Internet Server site at http://www.ms-normandy.com/.

Using the Microsoft Proxy Server

To protect your network from potential hackers or to restrict your network clients from accessing specific Internet resources, you need a little more than the basic software included with the Internet Information Server. The Microsoft Proxy Server might be just what the doctor ordered in this situation. You can order the Microsoft Proxy Server directly from Microsoft, or you can download a 60-day trial version from the Microsoft Web site at http://www.microsoft.com/proxy. This proxy server can actually protect your network much better than the mini-firewall option described in Chapter 10 because the granularity is so much finer. You can limit access by user or group to any Internet protocol or TCP/IP port, and you can specify which users on your internal network will be able to browse the Web, chat online, download files, and so on. The Microsoft Proxy Server provides additional benefits as well, for example:

- Caching frequently accessed Web pages, which can add a significant performance boost to networks using a slow Internet connection
- Connecting automatically to the Internet using Dial-Up Networking when an Internet request is detected so you do not need a persistent Internet connection
- Masking your internal IP addresses while providing Internet access for private (commonly called nonroutable) IP addresses

> **TIP**
>
> The key item to understand when using the Microsoft Proxy Server is that you must assign users to groups (using User Manager for Domains) and then use these groups when assigning permissions to specific Internet protocols to really benefit from the software and ease the administrative burden. This methodology to assign permissions works in exactly the same way as assigning permissions to directories or files to restrict access.

The Microsoft Proxy Server actually includes two separate proxy services. The first service, called the *Web Proxy*, supports Web browser clients (such as Internet Explorer, Netscape Navigator, and most other Web browsers) that support the CERN proxy protocol. The second service, called the *WinSock Proxy*, supports WinSock 1.1–compliant applications.

> **TIP**
>
> With third-party software you can enhance the Microsoft Proxy Server to restrict access to specific Web sites, add virus protection, create dynamic Web pages for individual users, and perform other operations. For more information about third-party enhancements check out the Web page at http://www.microsoft.com/proxy/partners.htm.

But enough of this background—let's start with a walk-through of the actual installation and configuration process. That way you will know what is required of you before you download and install the product—no surprises. The walk-through might also help you to determine whether the Microsoft Proxy Server will do the job you really want it to do. Although to be fair, the only way you can really make that determination is to download the software and try it.

Installing the Microsoft Proxy Server

Installing the Microsoft Proxy Server is not a difficult task. Like most Microsoft applications, the installation program provides various user-customizable selections. The installation program also fully supports the software uninstall process. So after you have installed the product, should you decide to uninstall it, just use the Control Panel Add/Remove Programs applet or the built-in uninstall program to remove it. To install the Microsoft Proxy Server, follow these steps:

1. Execute the self-extracting file that you downloaded from the Microsoft Proxy Server Web site or the setup program if you obtained the Microsoft Proxy Server on CD-ROM. The Microsoft Proxy Server Setup dialog box is shown in Figure 11.1.

FIGURE 11.1.

Installing the Microsoft Proxy Server.

2. Click the Continue button.

3. Enter a key to install the software when prompted. The key is on the back of your CD-ROM jewel case. For the downloadable version, the key is 375-1749043, although you should take note of this key when you download the evaluation version, as it might change from time to time.

4. Click the OK button to continue. A product ID dialog box will be displayed. You should write down this number in case you need to call Microsoft for technical support. (You can also obtain this ID by viewing the Service tab for the Proxy Service in the Internet Service Manager.)

5. Click the OK button to continue. Another Microsoft Proxy Server Setup dialog appears. (See Figure 11.2.)

FIGURE 11.2.

Specifying the Microsoft Proxy Server installation options.

6. Click the browse button to specify an alternative location for the Microsoft Proxy Server files if the default location of C:\MSP is not acceptable.

7. Click the Installation Options button to open the Microsoft Proxy Server - Installation Options dialog box shown in Figure 11.3. Specify which components should be installed.

FIGURE 11.3.

*Specifying the Microsoft
Proxy Server
components to install.*

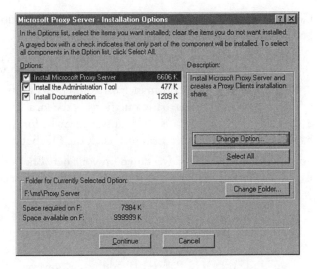

8. Highlight the Install Microsoft Proxy Server option and then click the Change Option button.

9. Specify the types of clients to support in the Microsoft Proxy Server - Install Microsoft Proxy Server dialog box shown in Figure 11.4. Although you could install all the components, you should install only the software for the clients you plan to support on your network. For example, if you will be supporting only Intel platforms for Windows NT and Windows 95, then you should uncheck the Install NT Alpha Client Share, the Install NT PPC Client Share, and the Install Win 3.x Client Share. When you have completed your selections, click the OK button to return to the Microsoft Proxy Server - Installation Options dialog box.

FIGURE 11.4.

*Specifying the clients to
be supported by the
Microsoft Proxy Server.*

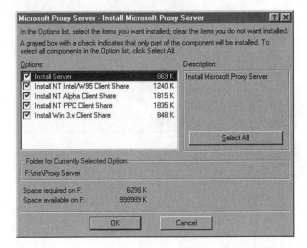

10. Click the Continue button to proceed with the installation. The Microsoft Proxy Server Cache Drives dialog box will appear.

    For each drive detected on your computer, you may specify the number of megabytes that the Proxy Service can use for cached HTML pages. You can use the cache drives option to increase the performance for your clients for frequently accessed pages. This option performs the same basic functions as the local cache used by Internet Explorer except the caching occurs as a global system cache for the entire network. When you have made your drive specifications, click the OK button to continue.

11. Specify the internal IP address used on your network in the Local Address Table Configuration dialog box. (See Figure 11.5.) You can accomplish this task in two ways:

    ■ Specify a starting and ending range of IP addresses in the From and To fields in the Edit group and click the Add button. If you are using DHCP to assign IP addresses, you can enter the DHCP scopes in these fields. Don't forget to include the DHCP server IP addresses, however.

    ■ Click the Construct Table button and have the setup program attempt to locate these internal IP addresses for you. While this option sounds attractive, it can actually require more work as it may detect IP addresses in use outside of your internal network. Should this occur, you will have to remove these addresses manually.

FIGURE 11.5.

Specifying the IP addresses in use on your area network.

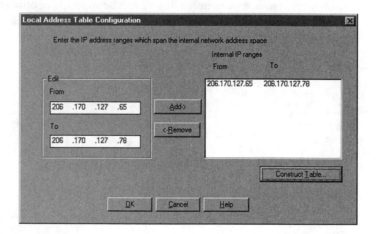

12. Click the OK button to continue and the Client Installation/Configuration dialog box will appear. (See Figure 11.6.)

FIGURE 11.6.

Specifying the client configuration for the Microsoft Proxy Server.

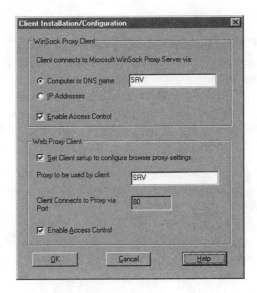

This dialog box is used to configure the proxy client. The defaults should suffice for almost every installation; however, it never hurts to know a little more about the configuration options. These options include

- WinSock Proxy Client group
    - Computer or DNS name—Specifies the NetBIOS name that the proxy clients will use to access the proxy server.
    - IP Addresses—Specifies an IP address that the proxy clients will use to access the proxy server.
    - Enable Access Control—Specifies that only authorized users will be able to access the proxy server and gain access to Internet/intranet resources using a Windows Socket application.

- Web Proxy Client group
    - Set Client setup to configure browser proxy settings—Specifies that the client setup program will attempt to automatically configure the Web browser client.
    - Proxy to be used by client—Specifies the name of the proxy server to be used by the client during an automatic configuration attempt.
    - Client Connects to Proxy via Port—Specifies the TCP/IP port to be used by the client for access to Web services.
    - Enable Access Control—Specifies that only authorized users will be able to access the proxy server and gain access to Internet resources using the FTP, Gopher, WWW, or SSL protocols.

TIP

Enable Access Control is a powerful option. With a single switch you can either limit access to all Internet resources (when enabled in the WinSock Proxy Client group), limit access to all Web browser functions (when enabled in the Web Proxy Client group), or throw the door wide open and allow complete access. Although you can disable this option to make your administrative duties a little easier, I do not recommend doing so, as disabling defeats the "limit access to those who really need it" feature of the proxy server and raises the potential for Internet abuse.

13. Make your proxy client configuration selections and then click the OK button to continue the installation. The proxy server files are copied to your computer.

    The Microsoft Proxy Server Setup dialog box will inform you that the setup completed normally.

14. Click the OK button to exit the setup program.

Configuring the Microsoft Proxy Server

After you have installed the Microsoft Proxy Server, you will need to configure it in order to obtain the maximum benefit. Configuring this server is a multipart process. First you have to configure the Web Proxy and WinSock Proxy services. Then, if you are using Dial-Up Networking as your Internet pipeline, you need to configure the Auto-Dial options. Finally, you need to configure your client Web browsers to use the Proxy Server for all Internet access.

The most important part of the Proxy Server configuration process is assigning permissions (or access rights if you prefer) to restrict access to various Internet protocols/services. The mechanics to assign permissions are actually quite easy and are performed in the Web Proxy and WinSock Proxy service Permissions property sheets that you will step through later in this section. It is the application, or methodology, of applying permissions that requires serious consideration.

You could, for example, assign permissions based on individual user accounts. However, this approach can cause a significant administrative burden. The better methodology is to assign permissions based on groups. Managing groups allows administrators to apply permissions to an object—a directory, file, named pipe, service, and so on—at the highest level. If you utilize groups properly, you can specify permissions to multiple objects. This approach enables the administrator to grant or reject user access to an object easily.

NOTE

I cover the topics of group management and basic network administration in another book, *Microsoft BackOffice 2 Administrator's Survival Guide*, published by Sams. This book covers the basics of network administration and includes plenty of tips and tricks.

The basic method to assign permissions using groups follows this sequence:

1. Create your local groups, using User Manager (if IIS is installed on a server) or User Manager for Domains (if IIS is installed on a domain controller).

2. Assign your users to local groups. You could place the user accounts directly into the local groups. This method works, but it is also more work for your network administrator. The preferred method is to place a global group that contains your domain user accounts into the local group. This way the administrator can assign new user accounts to the appropriate global group, and the correct Internet permissions will be applied automatically. This method works even when you cross domain boundaries—unlike local groups that are relevant only within the domain in which they were created.

3. Utilize these groups to assign permissions to the various protocols specified in the Web Proxy and WinSock Proxy services.

I know, this process sounds a bit confusing. So perhaps an example will help a bit. Let's assume for the minute that you want to limit your network clients ability to use Web browser to access the Internet. You have three basic types of people at your company: administrators (management personnel might be included in this group as well) who require full access to the Internet, technicians who require limited access to the Internet, and all other employees who require Web access only. You could start by creating three local groups called FullInternetAccess, LimitedInternetAccess, and WebAccessOnly. Next assign the global groups containing your domain administrators (Domain Admins) and perhaps a global group containing your upper-level managers to the FullInternetAccess local group. Then assign your global group containing your technicians to the LimitedInternetAccess local group and your regular domain users (Domain Users) global group to the WebAccessOnly local group. Finally, you can use the local groups you've created to actually implement your security restrictions for the Web Proxy as described in a little later in the section "Assigning Web Proxy User Permissions."

To grant Web-only access to your domain users for example, you could grant the WebAccessOnly group permission to the WWW protocol in the Web Proxy Service Permissions property sheet. This permission level would allow your regular domain users to view Web pages on the Internet, but not to access any secure Web sites using the SSL protocol (perhaps to purchase a product), download or upload any files using the FTP protocol, or search a Gopher database. You could grant the LimitedInternetAccess group permission to the WWW, FTP, and Gopher protocols to your technicians so that they can everything except access a secure site. Finally, you could grant the FullInternetAccess group permissions to the WWW, FTP, Gopher, and SSL protocols to your administrators so that they can perform every action.

To restrict access to the Internet even further, you can specify permissions in the WinSock Proxy service, as described later in the section "Assigning WinSock Proxy User Permissions," on a per protocol basis. If an Internet protocol is not specified, you can actually add it. This system allows a great deal of flexibility in granting, or restricting, access to the Internet to your network clients and in preventing Internet hackers from gaining access to your internal network.

Don't let this ability to specify permissions on the proxy server go to your head, however, as it is possible for your network clients to bypass your proxy server by reconfiguring their software (assuming they know how to do so). To prevent these possibilities, the proxy server must be a *chokepoint*—that is, the proxy server must be physically located between your network clients and your Internet connection (router or dial-up server). Furthermore, the server that is executing the Microsoft Proxy Server must not forward (or route) IP packets. Otherwise, your network clients could specify your server's IP address, or your router's IP address, as their default gateway and bypass your proxy server altogether.

Configuring the Web Proxy Service

You can divide the Web Proxy service configuration options into five specific areas. You may do all of the following:

- Set the basic service properties
- Specify permissions for the WWW, FTP, Gopher, and SSL protocols used by Web browsers
- Specify the URL caching options
- Configure the service logging options
- Specify a security filter based on IP address or Internet domain name

Each configuration option is accessible from the Internet Service Manager as a property sheet in the Web Proxy Service Properties dialog box. (See Figure 11.7.) To display this dialog box, highlight the computer name (such as SRV) associated with the Web Proxy service and choose Service Properties from the Properties menu. Alternatively, highlight the service associated with the Web Proxy service, right-click the highlighted service, and select Service Properties from the pop-up menu.

Figure 11.7.

Configuring the Web Proxy Service.

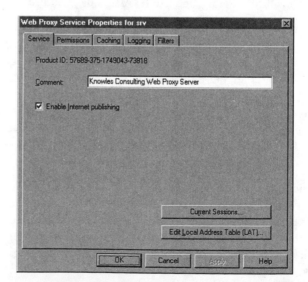

> **TIP**
>
> The fastest method to display the Web Proxy Service Properties dialog box is to double-click the computer (such as SRV) associated with the Web Proxy service.

Configuring the Basic Web Proxy Service Properties

The General property sheet is the default property sheet displayed in the Web Proxy Service Properties dialog box. (Refer to Figure 11.7.) This dialog looks quite simple, and the functionality is accessed easily. However, the power behind these simple check boxes and buttons is very impressive. Within this dialog box you may select the following configuration options:

- Specify a comment to be displayed in the Internet Service Manager in the Comment field.

- Limit the published data to your intranet only or open up your ability to publish data on the Internet and your intranet. If you do not check the Enable Internet Publishing check box, the default, then no external clients will be able to access your Internet Information Server services.

- View the currently connected users by clicking the Current Sessions button. This option will display the Web Proxy Service User Sessions dialog box, which contains the username, IP address, and total connection time for all currently connected users.

- Specify the IP addresses used internally within your network by clicking the Edit Local Address Table (LAT) button. This option will display the Local Address Configuration Table dialog box (refer to Figure 11.5) in which you may enter your IP address ranges. To manually specify an IP address, or range of IP addresses, follow these steps:

    1. Enter the starting IP addresses in the From field.

    2. Enter the ending IP address in the To field.

    3. Click the Add button and the IP address, or range of IP addresses, appear in the Internal IP ranges field.

> **TIP**
>
> If you are using DHCP to assign IP addresses, you can enter the DHCP scopes (or IP address range) in the From and To fields. However, don't forget to include the DHCP server IP addresses.

    4. Repeat steps 1 through 3 for each IP address range used within your internal network.

> **NOTE**
>
> If you'd like to try to automatically build this list of internal IP addresses, click the Construct Table button. Depending on whether all your network clients are currently active, whether you are currently connected to the Internet, and whether any Internet clients are currently connected to your site, the list may be generated properly. If any external IP addresses have been detected, you will have to manually remove them. Because controlling all these variables is difficult, I prefer to create the LAT list manually and suggest you do so as well.

Assigning Web Proxy User Permissions

Assigning permissions, or access rights, is really where the power of the Web Proxy service comes into play. Within this property sheet you get the opportunity to specify which users will have access to the Internet using the World Wide Web (HTTP and S-HTTP), File Transfer Protocol (FTP), Gopher, and Secure Socket Layer (SSL) Internet protocols from their Web browsers. You can assign permissions by following these steps:

1. Select the Permissions tab to display the Permissions property sheet, shown in Figure 11.8.

Figure 11.8.

Specifying Web Proxy service access rights.

2. Check the Enable Access Control check box to enable the rest of the dialog box options.

TIP

If you encounter problems, or need to temporarily disable access control, just uncheck the Enable Access Control check box. The changes will be applied as soon as you either click the Apply button or click the OK button to exit the dialog box.

3. Select the protocol to limit access to by choosing WWW (full World Wide Web access), FTP Read (File Transfer Protocol download capability), Gopher (full Gopher access), or Secure (Secure Socket Layer capability) in the Protocol drop-down list.

4. Click the Add button to display the Add Users and Groups dialog box, as shown in Figure 11.9.

FIGURE 11.9.

Specifying the Web Proxy service users and groups access rights.

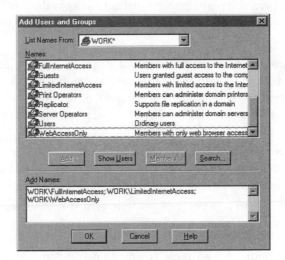

5. Select a group name in the Names field and click the Add button. To select an individual user account, click the Show Users button first. This step updates the Names field to include all user accounts. Then select the user account and click the Add button. As you add each group or user, it will be copied to the Add Names field. When you have completed your selection, click the OK button.

At this point the users and groups with permission to use the selected Internet protocol appear in the Grant Access To field. (Refer to Figure 11.8.) Any user or group not on the list will be denied access to the selected protocol.

> **TIP**
>
> If you have established a trust relationship with other Windows NT domains, you may enter global groups from these domains by selecting the domain name in the List Names From drop-down list. This step will update the Names field with entries from the trusted domain.

6. Repeat steps 3 through 5 for each additional Internet protocol. When you have completed your selections, click the OK button to close the Web Proxy Service Properties dialog box and return to the Internet Service Manager.

Specifying the Caching Options

One of the greatest performance benefits to a network with a slow Internet connection is the proxy server's capability to cache frequently accessed Web objects. This feature provides the following benefits:

- Improved client performance—If an object is in the cache when a network client requests it, it is returned at the speed of your network connection (up to 100Mbps) rather than being limited to the speed of your Internet connection. If the object is not in the cache, it will be retrieved by the proxy server and placed in the cache for the next user.

- Improved storage management—By utilizing the proxy server as a centralized Web object cache, you can save disk space on your network clients. How? By disabling the local caching options of Internet Explorer or Netscape Navigator.

- Objects can be actively or passively cached—An active-caching methodology is proactive. The proxy server will automatically retrieve frequently accessed pages when their TTL (Time to Live) period has expired. This process usually occurs during off-peak hours. A passive-caching methodology, on the other hand, caches objects as they are requested.

This feature can significantly lower your phone bill and may be more valuable to you than the security restrictions if you must access the Internet via a dial-up connection. To obtain the maximum benefit, you will need to experiment with the size of the cache and the timing of cache updates. Follow these steps:

1. Select the Caching tab to display the Caching property sheet, shown in Figure 11.10.

2. Check the Enable Caching check box to enable the rest of the dialog options including the Cache Expiration Policy slider. This slider setting determines how long objects will remain in the cache (the TTL) before being refreshed. You have two choices:

   - Move the slider toward Always request updates to lower the chance of displaying stale data but increase the amount of Internet bandwidth used.

   - Move the slider toward Fewest Internet requests to lower the amount of Internet bandwidth used but increase the chance of displaying stale data.

FIGURE 11.10.

*Specifying Web Proxy
Service caching options.*

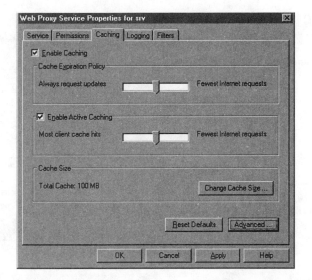

3. Check the Enable Active Caching check box to enable active caching of Web objects, which can improve performance. As with the Cache Expiration slider, the Active Caching Policy slider (though the slider name is not displayed in the dialog box) has a trade-off between Internet traffic and cache performance.

   ■ Move the slider toward Most client cache hits to update the cache more frequently but increase the amount of Internet bandwidth used.

   ■ Move the slider toward Fewest Internet requests to update the cache less often but decrease the amount of Internet bandwidth used.

   ■ Clear the Enable Active Caching check box to disable active caching and perform passive caching instead.

4. To specify a different cache size, click the Change Cache Size button to display the Microsoft Proxy Server Cache Drives. This is the same dialog displayed during the setup process and is used to specify which drives to be used for caching objects and how much space to use on the drive.

5. To specify which Web sites to cache, or to not cache, click the Advanced button. This button opens the Advanced Cache Policy dialog box, shown in Figure 11.11.

6. To specify the maximum size of an object to cache, click the Limit Size of Cached Objects check box and enter the maximum size (in KB).

7. To specify that a cached object which may be a stale object, be returned to the user when the actual site is not available, click the Return expired objects when site is unavailable check box.

8. To specify which Web sites will be cached, or not cached, by the proxy server, click the Add button. This will display the Cache Filter Properties dialog box, as shown in Figure 11.12.

FIGURE 11.11.

Specifying the Web Proxy service advanced caching options.

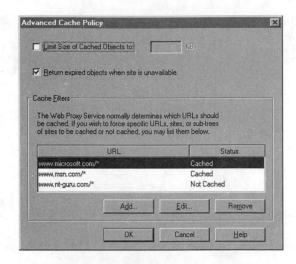

FIGURE 11.12.

Specifying the Web sites to cache.

9. Enter a relative URL in the URL field. A relative URL is a site name (`www.microsoft.com`) or a site name plus a pathname (`www.microsoft.com/inetdev`). You can use the asterisk (*) as a wildcard character; for example, `www.microsoft.com/*` will cache all Web objects within the Microsoft Web site. (If you use a wildcard, make sure you have a lot of space on your Web server.) Then choose a Filtering Status option:

■ Always cache—Specifies that Web objects within this relative path will always be cached by the proxy server.

■ Never cache—Specifies that Web objects within this relative path will never be cached by the proxy server.

10. Click the OK button to add the URL to the Cache Filters list.

11. Repeat steps 8 through 10 for each URL to cache, or not cache. When you have specified all the URLs, click the OK button to return to the Web Proxy Service Properties dialog box.

12. Click the OK button to close the Web Proxy Service Properties dialog box and return to the Internet Service Manager.

Logging Web Proxy Activity

Logging your Web Proxy activity is one way you can determine how active your site is, as well as determine if someone is accessing data he or she should not have access to. You can use two methods you to log your Web Proxy site's activity. You can store the information in a standard text file, or you can store it in an ODBC database. If you use an ODBC database, you must create the database and then set up an ODBC data source name (DSN) using the ODBC Control Panel applet. Creating an ODBC database and setting up the DSN is discussed in Chapter 6, "Using the Internet Service Manager," in the section "Logging Site Access with SQL Server." To enable logging, follow these steps:

1. Click the Logging tab in the Web Proxy Service Properties dialog box to display the Logging properties sheet, shown in Figure 11.13.

FIGURE 11.13.

Configuring the Web Proxy service to log activity.

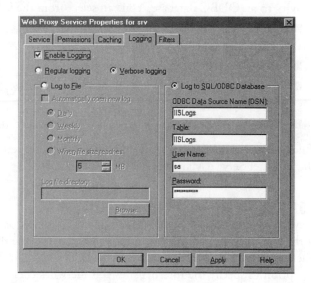

2. Click the Enable Logging radio button to enable the rest of the dialog box.

3. Specify the amount of activity to log. You can choose to log only a subset by enabling the Regular logging radio button, or you can log all activity by enabling the Verbose logging radio button. I recommend that you start with verbose logging; after a month or two, change to regular logging. This process will give you a chance to verify that everything is working as expected.

4. Click the Log to File radio button to log your Web Proxy site's activity to a text file. You can select from the following options:

   ■ Automatically open new log —This option specifies that a new log will be created based on one of the following criteria:

      ■ Daily—Every day

      ■ Weekly—Once a week

      ■ Monthly—Once a month

      ■ When file size reaches—Whenever the log file exceeds the size specified in the MB field

   ■ Log file directory —This option specifies the location of the log file.

5. Click the Log to SQL/ODBC Database radio button to log your Web Proxy site's activity to an ODBC database. You can select from the following options:

   ■ ODBC Data Source Name (DSN)—Specifies the name of the data source to use to access the ODBC database

   ■ Table—Specifies the table within the ODBC database to use for logging

   ■ User Name—Specifies a username to use to access the table within the ODBC database

   ■ Password—Specifies a password for the associated user account

6. Click the OK button to close the Web Proxy Site Properties dialog box and return to the Internet Service Manager.

Limiting Access to Internet Sites and Your Network

Almost everyone is concerned about the security of his or her network. Some companies want to limit the sites their network clients may access to make sure that their employees are working, rather than checking the sport scores on the ESPN Web site. You can use the proxy server's filtering option to specify the Internet sites your network clients may access. You can also use this filtering option to block access to a single computer, a group of computers, or an entire Internet domain by following these steps:

1. Click the Filters tab in the Web Proxy Service Properties dialog box to display the Filters properties sheet. (See Figure 11.14.)

FIGURE 11.14.

*Preventing access to
specific Web sites.*

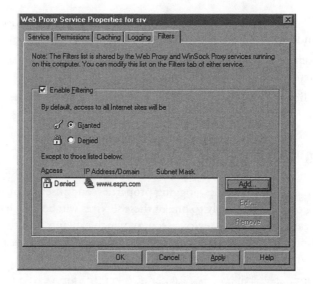

2. To limit access to a specific set of clients, click the Denied Access radio button. Then click the Add button to display the Grant Access On dialog box.

   ■ To specify a single computer to give access to your Web site, click the Single Computer radio button and enter the IP address of the computer in the IP Address field.

   ■ To specify multiple computers to give access to your Web site, click the Multiple Computers radio button and specify an IP address and subnet mask in the IP Address and Subnet Mask fields.

   ■ To specify an entire Internet domain, click the Domain radio button and enter the domain name in the Domain field.

   Click the OK button after making your selection. The domain name or IP addresses and subnet masks you specified will appear in the Except to those listed below list box.

3. To grant access to all but a specific set of clients, click the Granted Access radio button. Then click the Add button to display the Denied Access On dialog box.

   ■ To specify a single computer to deny access to your Web site, click the Single Computer radio button and enter the IP address of the computer in the IP Address field.

   ■ To specify multiple computers to deny access to your Web site, click the Multiple Computers radio button and specify an IP address and subnet mask in the IP Address and Subnet Mask fields.

   ■ To specify an entire Internet domain, click the Domain radio button and enter the domain name in the Domain field.

Click the OK button after making your selection. The domain name or IP addresses and subnet masks you specified will appear in the Except to those listed below list box.

4. Repeat step 2, or step 3, for each additional domain or set of computers you want to deny, or grant, access for your network clients to visit.

5. Click the OK button to close the Web Proxy Site Properties dialog box and return to the Internet Service Manager.

Configuring the WinSock Proxy Service

The WinSock Proxy service shares a bit of functionality with the Web Proxy service, including the basic service properties, logging properties, and filtering properties. In fact, the LAT and filtering options you apply to one of these services will be automatically applied to the other as well. Please refer to the previous section, which explains how to configure the LAT and filtering options, and concentrate now on the WinSock Proxy service options that are different from options in the Web Proxy service.

These differences fall into two related areas. The first is that unlike the Web Proxy service, which is limited to the WWW, FTP, Gopher, and SSL Internet protocols, the WinSock Proxy service supports any Internet protocol or Internet port. If one is not listed, you may add it. This service enables you to grant or deny access to any Internet protocol or port. You can use the WinSock Proxy service not only to prevent your network clients from utilizing one of these protocols or ports to access the Internet but also to prevent external threats (Internet hackers, for example) from gaining access to your corporate network.

In the following sections you will learn how to specify the Internet protocols and ports to monitor and how to grant permission to use these protocols and ports. Each option is accessible from the Internet Service Manager as a property sheet in the WinSock Proxy Service Properties dialog box. To display this dialog box, just highlight the computer name (such as SRV) associated with the WinSock Proxy service and choose Service Properties from the Properties menu; alternatively, highlight the service associated with the WinSock Proxy service, right-click the highlighted service, and select Service Properties from the pop-up menu.

> **TIP**
>
> The fastest method to display the WinSock Proxy Service Properties dialog box is to double-click the computer (such as SRV) associated with the Web Proxy service.

Specifying the Internet Protocols to Monitor

Before you can grant or reject permission to use an Internet protocol or monitor its usage, you must first define it. An Internet protocol definition, such as HTTP (for WWW access) is really just a subset of the Transmission Control Protocol (TCP) or User Datagram Protocol (UDP)

protocol. Most of these Internet protocols use at least one port. The HTTP protocol, for example, is a subset of TCP and uses port 80. Many predefined protocols for the WinSock Proxy service are available; however, at times you may need to add or modify a definition. For example, you may need to expose the TCP port used to access your SQL Server installation, expose the America Online TCP port, or the Microsoft Network TCP port. To add a new protocol follow these steps:

1. Select the Protocols tab to display the Protocols property sheet as shown in Figure 11.15.

FIGURE 11.15.

Specifying the Internet protocols and ports to monitor.

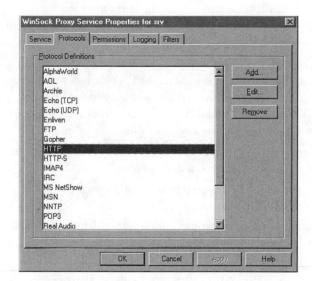

2. Click the Add button to display the Protocol Definition dialog box. (See Figure 11.16.)

FIGURE 11.16.

Adding a new Internet protocol and ports to monitor.

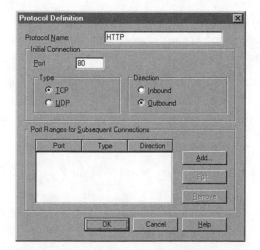

3. Specify a unique name in the Protocol field, such as HTTP for the Hypertext Transfer Protocol.

4. Specify an initial port value in the Port field. By default the HTTP protocol uses port 80. If you have configured your Web server to use another port, you should change this value to match.

5. Specify the type of protocol (either TCP or UDP) in the Type field. The HTTP protocol uses TCP.

6. Specify the direction for the protocol (either inbound or outbound) in the Direction field. For this example you want to monitor, or restrict, access to the HTTP protocol to your network clients (instead of preventing access from Internet clients whom you want to access your Web server), so the direction is outbound.

7. (Optional) If this protocol will use ports other than the primary port listed in the Port field, click the Add button in the Port Ranges for Subsequent Connections group. In the Port Range Definition dialog box, you may specify a port (or range of ports), type (TCP or UDP), and direction (inbound or outbound) to add. Because the HTTP protocol does not use any other ports, skip this step.

8. Complete your protocol definition and click the OK button to return to the WinSock Proxy Service Properties dialog box.

9. Repeat steps 2 through 8 for each additional protocol to add to your list to either monitor or restrict access.

10. Complete all your protocol additions. Click the OK button to close the WinSock Proxy Service Properties dialog box and return to the Internet Service Manager.

Editing an existing protocol or port definition follows a similar sequence of steps. The only difference is that instead of clicking the Add button as described in step 2, you should select an existing protocol definition and then click the Edit button. To delete a protocol definition, select it and then click the Remove button.

Assigning WinSock Proxy User Permissions

Once you have added all the protocols you want to monitor or restrict access to, as described in the previous section, you can move on to apply your user access rights to these protocols.

1. Select the Permissions tab to display the Permissions property sheet as shown in Figure 11.17.

2. Check the Enable Access Control check box. This option enables the WinSock Proxy Service's ability to control access to specified Internet protocols. It will also enable the rest of the dialog options.

3. Select a protocol to grant access to in the Protocol field.

FIGURE 11.17.

*Limiting access to an
Internet protocol.*

CAUTION

The Unlimited Access protocol includes all protocols and all ports on the server. Use this protocol with care, as it essentially bypasses the proxy server restrictions.

4. Click the Add button to display the Add Users and Groups dialog box. (Refer to Figure 11.9.)

5. Select a group name in the Names field and click the Add button. To select an individual user account, click the Show Users button, which updates the Names field to include all user accounts. Then select the user account and click the Add button. Each group or user you add will be copied to the Add Names field. When you have completed your selection, click the OK button.

At this point the users and groups appear in the Grant Access To field, as shown in Figure 11.17. These entries are the users or groups with permission to use the selected Internet protocol. Any user or group not on the list will not be able to use the selected protocol.

TIP

If you have established a trust relationship with other Windows NT domains, you may enter global groups from these domains by selecting the domain name in the List Names From drop-down list. This step updates the Names field with entries from the trusted domain.

6. Repeat steps 3 through 5 for each additional Internet protocol. When you have completed your selections, click the OK button to close the WinSock Proxy Service Properties dialog box and return to the Internet Service Manager.

Configuring the Auto-Dial Options

If you are using your server as a gateway to the Internet, you may find that the Microsoft Proxy Server auto-dial option is quite useful. This option provides an interface between your network clients and a Dial-Up Networking (or Remote Access Session, or RAS) session. When properly configured, the proxy server can automatically connect to the Internet using a pre-defined phone book entry whenever a network client requests access to the Internet. If the network client is using the Web Proxy service (via a Web browser), then the connection will be attempted only if the Web object is not in the proxy server's cache or the cached object TTL has expired. The proxy server can also use the auto-dial connection directly to update its internally cached Web objects. You can use this technique to update the internal cache during off-peak hours and reduce your phone bills. To configure the auto-dial options, follow these basic steps:

1. Select the Auto Dial Configuration applet in your Microsoft Proxy Server program group, which will display the dialog box shown in Figure 11.18.

FIGURE 11.18.

Configuring the auto-dial connection times.

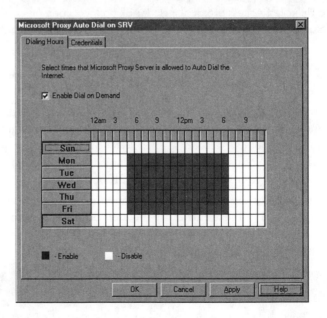

2. Check the Enable Dial on Demand check box to allow the proxy server to connect to the Internet as needed.

3. Specify the times the proxy server may connect to the Internet by clicking each box on the displayed chart. In the example shown, the proxy server may dial up the Internet only between the hours of 5:00 a.m. and 6:00 p.m. Monday through Friday.

> **TIP**
>
> To select all days and any hours quickly, click the gray box in the upper-left corner. To select all hours within a day, click the day button. To select an hour for all days, click the gray button in the appropriate hour column. You can also use the mouse to outline a selection if desired.

4. Click the Credentials tab to display the Credentials property sheet. (See Figure 11.19.)

FIGURE 11.19.

Specifying the phone book entry parameters to use for the dial-up connection.

5. Choose a phone book entry from the Entry Name field. If there are no entries, you must create a new phone book entry using the Dial-Up Networking client.

6. Enter the user account name for your Internet connection in the User Name field.

7. Enter the associated password for the user account in the Password field.

   If this account requires an Internet domain name, enter this value in the Domain Name field. Otherwise, leave this field blank.

8. Click the OK button to close the Microsoft Proxy Auto Dial dialog box. The Microsoft Proxy Server will utilize these settings immediately.

Configuring the Client Software

Okay, so you've install the Microsoft Proxy Server between your Internet connection and your network. All of your Windows 95 and Windows NT clients are using Microsoft Internet Explorer or Netscape Navigator, and you want to configure them to use your proxy server to connect to the Internet. The easy way to make the connection is to connect to the MSPCLNT share on the server where you installed the Microsoft Proxy Server. (For the server named SRV, this share is \\SRV\MSPCLNT.) Once you have connected to the share, run the setup program located in the root directory. This program will install the client software and automatically configure the client Web browser to use the proxy server.

If your Web browser isn't Microsoft Internet Explorer or Netscape Navigator, or you have a Web browser on a non-Windows platform (such as UNIX or the Macintosh), then connecting to the Internet is somewhat more complicated. Although this methodology may differ a bit on where to enter the information, almost all Web browsers include a configuration dialog box in which you may specify the information for a connection via a proxy server. To manually enter this information for Internet Explorer 3.0 for Windows NT, for example, follow these steps:

1. Choose Options from the View menu. The Options dialog box shown in Figure 11.20 will be displayed.

Figure 11.20.

Specifying the Internet Explorer connection properties.

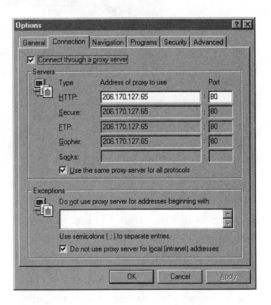

2. Check the Connect through a proxy server check box to enable the rest of the dialog box options.

3. Enter the IP address of the computer running the Microsoft Proxy Server in the HTTP address field. Enter the port number of the HTTP server in the HTTP port field.

4. Check the Use the same proxy server for all protocols check box.

5. Check the Do not use proxy server for local (intranet) addresses check box.

6. Click the OK button to close the Options dialog box and return to Internet Explorer.

That wasn't so hard, was it? However, you need to know a bit more before you try to connect to the Internet on non-Microsoft Web browsers. First, if it is at all possible, use an IP address rather than a DNS name. A DNS name is usually bound to the same IP address as the network card connected to the Internet. Therefore, the proxy server might not accept the name as a valid intranet name, which would cause an "unresolvable name" or "not found" error. You can, however, use a NetBIOS name for TCP/IP and IPX/SPX clients. For example, you could specify the HTTP address field as `http://SRV`, instead of specifying the IP address `206.170.127.65`.

WARNING

Do not insall the Proxy Server client software on a computer running Exchange Server. Doing so also installs the WinSock proxy client software, which will most likely cause Exchange Server to fail. This failure in turn would prevent you from sending or receiving e-mail. If you need to specify a proxy server in such a situation, follow the previous steps and manually specify the connection properties for your Web browser. The Web browser will then use the Web Proxy service, and Exchange Server will continue to operate as expected.

Using the Microsoft Chat Server

Web pages are nice, but for the most part, they are static. Even dynamic Web pages, which can interact with the user, can't provide the interaction that a one-on-one conversation can provide, as shown in Figure 11.21. An Internet Relay Chat (IRC) server can help fill this gap. With an IRC server you can provide the ability for your clients to communicate in real time. An IRC chat server of course requires an IRC chat client. Luckily for you, the Microsoft Chat Server base package includes a chat client, or you can use any standard IRC chat client.

The chat client included with the Microsoft Internet Chat server is called the *Microsoft Internet Chat* (MIC) client. Both the chat server and the chat client have been enhanced to support non-standard IRC functions. So if you want to support both IRC and MIC clients, you need to limit yourself to using standard IRC functions. A chat room accessible from a standard IRC client, for example, must start with a pound sign (#); otherwise, the client will not be able to see the room, much less enter it.

FIGURE 11.21.

*Interacting with
multiple clients in real
time.*

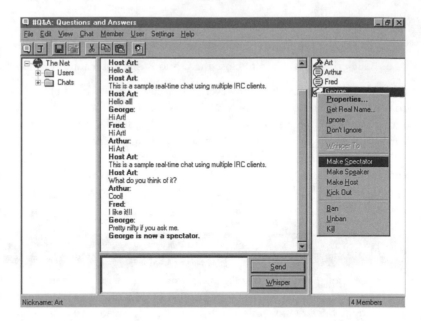

If your clients do not have a MIC or IRC chat client, then you might want to use a Web page–based chat client instead. This chat client is an ActiveX control and requires Microsoft Internet Explorer 3.0 or higher. It is not as feature rich as a regular chat client, but it is much easier to use. You can find the source code for the sample shown in Figure 11.22 on the accompanying CD-ROM in the \SOURCE\Chap11 directory or on my Web site at http://www.nt-guru.com/books/samples/iis/chap11/ChatWithSysop.HTM.

FIGURE 11.22.

*Using a Web-based
chat client for real-time
communications.*

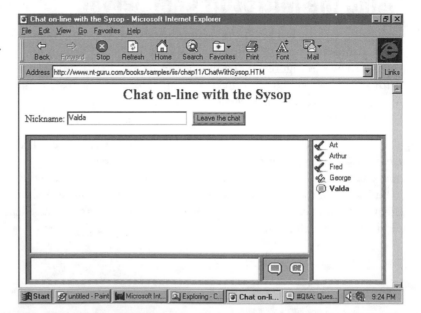

Installing the Microsoft Chat Server

Before you get carried away with the capabilities of the Microsoft chat server, it might be best if you actually installed it. That way you'll get a chance to see it in action, and you'll have the documentation and sample applications. By default, these samples and applications will be installed in the *ChatRoot*\Client (where *ChatRoot* is the root installation directory you chose during the installation) subdirectory. The documentation will be installed in the *ChatRoot*\Docs subdirectory. You'll find both Word documents and on-line HTML documentation in this directory.

1. Execute the self-extracting file that you downloaded from the Microsoft Commercial Internet Server Web site or from the setup program if you obtained the Microsoft Chat Server on CD-ROM.

   The InstallShield Self-Extracting EXE dialog box will be displayed requesting confirmation to install the chat server.

2. Click the Yes button to continue the installation. The Welcome dialog box will appear.

3. Click the Next button to continue the installation.

4. Read the Software License Agreement carefully before you click the Yes button to continue the installation.

   If you do not agree to the terms listed, click the No button and the installation of the chat server will terminate.

5. Enter your name and company name in the Name and Company fields in the Registration dialog box.

6. Click the Next button to display the Choose Destination Directory dialog box. If the default directory (C:\INETPUB\CHAT) is not acceptable, click the browse button to specify an alternative location. I prefer to install these files on an NTFS partition for enhanced security, and I recommend that you do the same.

7. Specify the location for these files and click the Next button. The Select Components dialog box will appear, as shown in Figure 11.23.

   The default software to install is only the Internet Chat Server and Internet Service Manager Extensions. However, I recommend that you install all the available software on your server, including the product documentation, ActiveX components (both client and server), and sample HTML pages.

8. Make your selections and click the Next button to continue.

   If you have active IIS services, the Running Services dialog box will be displayed requesting confirmation to stop these services and install the chat server.

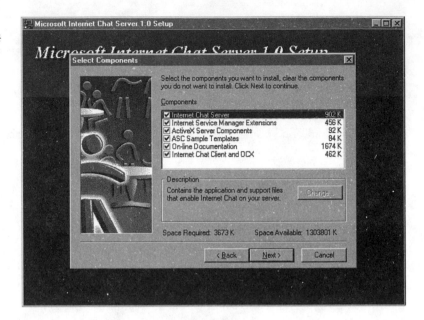

9. Click the Yes button to continue. If you click the No button, you will have to rerun the setup program.

10. Accept the default name and location for the Internet Chat Server shortcuts in the Folder Selection dialog box or enter another name and location; then click the Next button to continue.

11. Review the information in the Confirm Setup Information dialog box. If any information is incorrect, click the Back button until the appropriate dialog box is displayed; make the necessary corrections. If all the information is correct, click the Next button to continue.

    The source files are copied to the location you specified, the chat service is installed, and the IIS services are started. At this point you can read the Internet Chat Server Startup Page (recommended) and start the administration tool.

12. Make your selection and click the Finish button to exit the setup program.

Configuring the Microsoft Chat Server

Although you can use the MIC server as soon as it is installed, you should configure it to perform only the tasks you want to perform. Otherwise, people you don't know might be using your important Internet bandwidth. This section concentrates on the most important options for the MIC server: setting the basic service properties, creating chat rooms, setting your security access rights, and limiting the usage of your chat rooms.

These options are accessible from the Internet Service Manager as a property sheet in the Chat Service Properties dialog box. Just highlight the computer name (such as SRV) associated with the chat service and choose Service Properties from the Properties menu to display the dialog box. Alternatively, highlight the service associated with the chat service, right-click the highlighted service, and select Service Properties from the pop-up menu.

> **TIP**
>
> The fastest method to display the Chat Service Properties dialog box is to double-click the computer (such as SRV) associated with the chat service.

Specifying the Service Properties

When you first install the chat server, there are no restrictions—no options have been specified—which leaves your chat server open to anyone to use. I find this configuration to be unacceptable, so the first thing I recommend is that you configure the basic service properties and apply them immediately. These options are accessible in the Service property sheet of the Chat Service Properties dialog box, as shown in Figure 11.24.

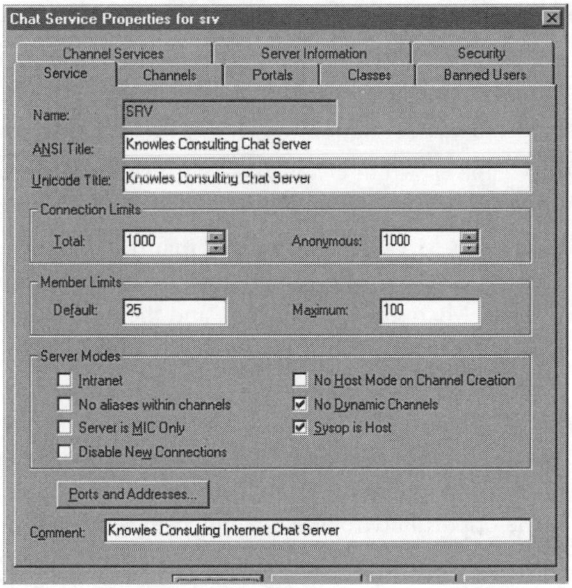

FIGURE 11.24.

Configuring the basic chat server properties.

The service options are global in scope and will override local options specified in other property sheets. You should understand exactly how each option you specify here affects the chat server.

■ Name—This noneditable field displays the NetBIOS name of the computer running the Internet Chat server.

■ ANSI Title—This 63-character space specifies a chat server title to be displayed for ANSI chat clients.

■ Unicode Title—This 63-character space specifies a chat server title to be displayed for Unicode-aware chat clients.

■ Connection Limits—Specifies the number of simultaneous client connections to the chat server. The connection limit is subdivided into two fields:

    ■ Total—The total number of client connections. This value includes both authenticated and anonymous client connections. The default is 1,000, the minimum is 0, and the maximum is 4,096.

    ■ Anonymous—The total number of anonymous client connections. The default is 1,000, the minimum is 0, and the maximum is 4,096.

■ Member Limits—Specifies the number of simultaneous client connections to a specific chat room. The member limit is subdivided into two separate fields:

    ■ Default—Specifies the default number of members to be allowed entrance to a chat room. This default value is applied for any chat room with a member limit of 0 (the default value when creating a new chat room).

    ■ Maximum—Specifies the maximum number of members to be allowed entrance to a chat room.

■ Server Modes—Specifies various behavioral switches for the chat server. For example:

    ■ Intranet—Configures the service to work with internal networks (or intranets).

    ■ No aliases within channels—Specifies that only real names (in the form of *UserName@DomainName*) will be accepted when a member joins a chat room.

    ■ Server is MIC Only—Specifies that the chat server will support only Microsoft Internet Chat–compliant clients. To date, this list includes Microsoft Internet Chat, Microsoft Comic Chat, and the ActiveX chat client for Internet Explorer. I expect many MIC chat clients to be available by the time this book is published.

    ■ Disable New Connections—Specifies that no new client connections will be accepted. This option is useful when you need to perform maintenance on the server, as it prevents new clients from connecting to the chat server. You have the opportunity to warn members in active rooms that you will be closing the chat rooms and to prevent an abrupt disconnection.

    ■ No Host Mode on Channel Creation—Specifies that members cannot become hosts (members with sysop privileges) when they create a dynamic chat room.

CAUTION

If you allow a member to become a host when a chat room is created, the potential exists for that the user to ban you from the room. As an administrator, you might have to kill the entire chat room as your only recourse to regain access to the room.

- No Dynamic Channels—Specifies that no dynamic chat rooms can be created on the chat server.

TIP

This switch is one of the most important for configuring your chat server, as it can prevent any member from creating a dynamic chat room. If you allow dynamic chat rooms, then any member can create a room, which could use a significant amount of resources on your server. To prevent this situation, enable the No Dynamic Channels switch. To allow only authenticated members to create dynamic chat rooms, leave this switch disabled. Then create a new security class (as explained in the next section) and set the Client Logon type to Select Anonymous. In the Restrictions group, check the Cannot Create Dynamic Channels check box.

- Sysop is Host—Specifies that the administrator, or sysop, can be a host in any chat room that he or she can join. The operative word here is *can,* as it is possible for another host to ban the sysop from a chat room. Therefore, I recommend that you enable the No Host Mode on Channel Creation check box to help avoid such problems.
- Ports and Addresses—When this button is clicked, the Ports and Addresses dialog box, shown in Figure 11.25, will appear. It contains the following fields:
  - Server NSID—Specifies the Network Server Identifier (NSID). Each chat server must have a unique NSID. The default is 1, the minimum is 1, and the maximum is 255.
  - Client to Server—This group contains two fields that apply only to chat-client-to-chat-server and to chat-server-to-chat-client communications. These fields include the following:
    - TCP Port—Specifies the TCP port to use for communications between the chat server and chat client. The default is 6,667, the minimum is 1, the maximum is 65,535.
    - UDP Port—Specifies the UDP port to use for communications between the chat server and chat client. The default is 0, which disables communications over a UDP port, the valid range is from 1 to 65,535.

- Server to Server—This group contains two fields that apply only to communications between chat servers. These fields include the following:
    - TCP Port—Specifies the TCP port to use for communications between chat servers. The default is 6,665, the minimum is 1, the maximum is 65,535.
    - UDP Port—Specifies the UDP port to use for communications between chat servers. The default is 0, which disables communications over a UDP port. The valid range is from 1 to 65,535.
- Client IP—Specifies the IP address of the next available MIC chat server. If no server is available, leave this value at 0.0.0.0. If you do not know the IP address of the server, but know its name, click the IP Lookup button and enter the name of the server. If the name is resolvable, the IP address will be entered to the Client IP field.

TIP

If you have multiple MIC chat servers, take the time to link them via the Client IP field and Portals property sheet. By doing so, you can use the dynamic load-balancing features of a MIC server to spread the load among all of your chat servers.

- Reverse DNS Lookup—This group specifies whether a DNS lookup will be performed for clients that connect to your chat server. A DNS lookup can associate a username and domain (such as Arthur@Work or Arthur@nt-guru.com). If you allow aliases on your chat server, I highly recommend that you require reverse lookups. You can then use the returned username with your e-mail program if you encounter a problem with a user. If the problem persists, you can ban the user from your server permanently.

    You can specify the following values for authenticated or anonymous client connections:

    Disable: Disables DNS lookups.

    Attempt: Attempts a lookup; if that lookup fails, the client is still allowed to connect to the chat server.

    Required: Attempts a lookup; if the lookup fails, the client is denied access to the chat server.

- Comment: Specifies the description to be displayed in the Internet Service Manager.

FIGURE 11.25.
*Configuring the chat
server ports, addresses,
and client lookup
properties.*

Creating a Persistent Chat Room

Although you can constantly re-create a dynamic chat room and staff it only as needed, a better approach is to make the room always available and use it only when needed. This method reduces your administrative burden a bit, which is one reason the MIC chat server supports persistent chat rooms. (Anything you can do to reduce the administrative work load is generally worth doing.) You can create a persistent chat room by following these steps:

1. Click the Channels tab to display the Channels property sheet as shown in Figure 11.26. The first character of an IRC chat is either a # or &; any chat that doesn't begin with a # or & is a MIC-only chat room.

2. Click the Add button to display the Channel Properties dialog box, shown in Figure 11.27.

3. Enter a unique name for the chat room in the Name field.

   For an IRC-compatible chat room the following rules apply:

   ■ The first letter of the name must be a # or &.

   ■ The name can be a maximum of 200 ANSI characters in length.

   ■ Any character other than null, bell, CR, LF, space, and comma is acceptable.

   For a MIC chat room the following rules apply:

   ■ The name can be a minimum of 3 and a maximum of 63 ANSI or Unicode characters in length.

   ■ Any character other than null, bell, CR, LF, colon, and backslash is acceptable.

FIGURE 11.26.

*Managing persistent
chat rooms on the chat
server.*

FIGURE 11.27.

*Creating a persistent
chat room.*

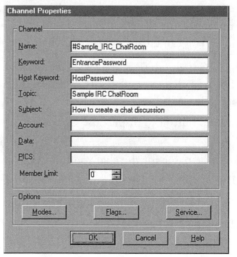

4. To restrict access to the chat room to specific members, enter a password in the
   Keyword field. The password can be up to 31 ANSI or Unicode characters in length.

5. To provide the ability for a member to obtain host (sysop) privileges in a chat, enter a password in the Host Keyword field. The password can be up to 31 ANSI or Unicode characters in length.

TIP

Although this tip is not documented anywhere in the Microsoft Comic Chat client, you can join a password-protected room by entering /join *RoomName Password* where *RoomName* is the name of the chat room and *Password* is the Keyword or Host Keyword.

6. To specify a chat room topic, enter a ANSI or Unicode string of up to 95 characters in the Topic field.
7. To specify a chat room subject, which is used by Web-based finds, enter a ANSI or Unicode string of up to 31 characters in the Topic field.
8. To restrict access to the chat room to members with specific qualifications, enter a security account name in the Account field.

NOTE

I do not recommend specifying a security account for a chat room unless the chat room will be a private chat room to be used by only one type of user. The reason is that you can specify only one account, and the account properties are primarily based on either authenticated or anonymous user accounts and a specific domain name or an IP address range.

NOTE

The Data field should allow you to specify limits to the amount of binary data that a chat client can send to other members. At this time, however, this field is undocumented and undefined.

9. To supply a Platform and Internet Content Selection (PICS) string for client use, enter a string up to 255 characters in length in the PICS field.
10. To specify the maximum number of members allowed in the chat at one time, enter a value from 0 to 4096 in the Member Limit field.

NOTE

If the Member Limit value is set to 0, the default Member Limits value as specified in the Service page, will be used.

11. Click the OK button to return to the Channel Properties dialog box.

12. Click the Mode button to display the Channel Modes dialog box, shown in Figure 11.28. This dialog box is used to specify the basic chat room configuration.

FIGURE 11.28.

Specifying the basic chat room configuration.

The Channel Modes dialog box has the following options:

■ Channel Visibility—Specifies the visibility of the chat room to chat clients. A chat room may be public, private, or secret.

■ Public—Specifies that any member can join the chat, locate the chat room by name, topic, number of members, or by a member list.

■ Private—Specifies that only specific member of a group can join the chat. However, a member may locate the chat room by name or number of members.

■ Secret—Specifies that only specific members of a group can join the chat. The chat cannot be located by nonmembers of the group.

■ Access Options—Specifies various properties for the chat room.

■ Invitation Only—Specifies that members may join the chat room by invitation only.

■ Moderated—Specifies that the chat room is moderated. Only the host has speaker privileges. New members will be spectators.

- Knock Notification—Specifies that a message be sent to the host when a noninvited member attempts to join an invitation-only chat. This option can be useful if the host wants to invite curious members to join the chat.

- Sysop is Host—Specifies that the chat administrator, the sysop, will join the chat room with host privileges.

- Auditorium—Specifies that only the host will be notified when nonhosts enter or leave a chat room.

- Restrictions—Specifies various chat room restrictions.

  - No Alias—Specifies that only the real name (such as Arthur@WORK.COM) will be displayed in MIC-only chat rooms.

  - No Data—Specifies that members will not be allowed to send data to each other while within the chat room.

  - No Whispering—Specifies that members will not be able to whisper (send private messages) to each other.

  - No Remote Users—Specifies that only local (intranet) users may gain access to the chat room.

  - No External Messages—Specifies that nonmember messages will not be passed to members within the chat room.

  - Only Host Changes Topic—Specifies that only the host can change the room topic.

13. Click the OK button to return to the Channel Properties dialog box.

14. Click the Flags button to display the Channel Flags dialog box, shown in Figure 11.29. This dialog box is used to specify various chat room operating modes.

FIGURE 11.29.

Specifying the chat room operating modes.

The following options are available in the Channel Flags dialog box:

- Access—Specifies various chat room access methodologies.
    - Only Authenticated Users Can Join—Specifies that only authenticated users may join the chat.
    - Only Authenticated Users Can Speak—Specifies that only authenticated users will have speaker privileges.
    - Local Channel Only—Specifies that the chat room is available only on this server. That is, the chat room is not replicated to other chat servers on the network.
    - Channel is MIC Only—Specifies that the chat is MIC only, which means that only MIC clients can access the chat room. When this flag is set, the Unicode check box is enabled. If the Unicode check box is enabled, then the chat room will support Unicode characters as well as ASNI characters.
- Channel Services—Specifies various chat room characteristics.
    - Echo to Source—Specifies that member messages will be echoed back to them. This flag is usually used by the chat service.
    - Auto Start—Specifies that the chat room will be automatically created at service startup, even if no members are currently present. This is a useful flag to set, as any room with this flag set will be available in the client's chat room list. This flag makes the room highly visible, and I recommend it for any persistent chat rooms.
    - Allow Impersonation—Specifies that the chat service may impersonate a member.
- Other Options—Specifies various additional properties for the chat room.
    - Template—Specifies that a new copy of the chat room will be automatically created if all currently available chat rooms with the same name are full.
    - Feed Mode—Specifies that no messages be sent to a member when a member enters or leaves a chat room. Any message sent by a host is seen by all members. All members, including hosts, see only themselves in the room. This option is most often used to support a large number of clients when each client receives a very specific set of data, such as a ticker tape stock quote or database feed.
    - Room Chat—Specifies that `from MemberName` prefix will be added to all messages that a member sends. This prefix makes it easier to track conversations within the chat room.

> **NOTE**
>
> The Services button is used for third-party extensions to the MIC chat server. It allows you to specify a custom DLL and GUID to associate with the specific chat room. If you have such an extension, the associated documentation will tell you the required values to be entered into the data fields.

15. Click the OK button to return to the Channel Properties dialog box.

16. Click the OK button to return to the Chat Service Properties dialog box.

17. Click the OK button to return to the Internet Service Manager, which will create the chat room and make it available to members.

Security Considerations for Your Chat Server

As noted in the previous section, you may, at times, want to limit a chat room to a specific type of user. You may even need to restrict access to your chat server to only a specific type of user, such as when you hold a monthly staff meeting chat only members within your organization should attend. Or you may need to prevent a user from using your chat server altogether. You can enforce all these restrictions by configuring the Chat Service. The first two security topics are interrelated. After all, you can't apply a security account when creating a persistent chat room until you have created the security account. Therefore, the first step in this process is to select the Classes property sheet. (See Figure 11.30.) Then just follow these steps:

FIGURE 11.30.

Managing security classes for your chat server.

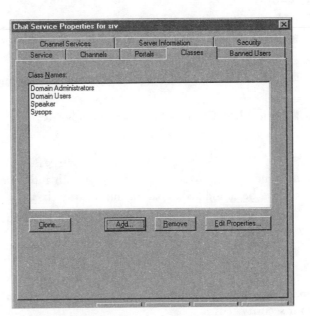

1. Click the Add button to display the Class Properties dialog box, as shown in Figure 11.31.

FIGURE 11.31.

Creating a security class.

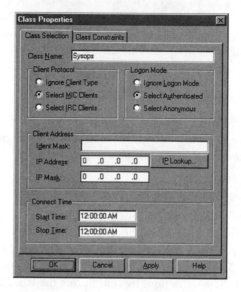

2. Enter a unique name, up to 63 characters in length, in the Class Name field. You can use any alphanumeric character, an underscore, or a hyphen. The first letter cannot be a number.

3. Specify the Client Protocol type as follows:

   - Ignore Client Type—Specifies that both MIC and IRC clients will be part of this security class.

   - Select MIC Clients—Specifies that only MIC clients will be part of this security class.

   - Select IRC Clients—Specifies that only IRC clients will be part of this security class.

4. Specify a Logon Mode type from the following types:

   - Ignore Logon Mode—Specifies that both authenticated and anonymous logons will be considered as part of this security class.

   - Select Authenticated—Specifies that only authenticated logons will be considered as part of this security class.

   - Select Anonymous—Specifies that only anonymous logons will be considered as part of this security class.

5. Specify one or more values in the Client Address group if you want to further restrict your security class.

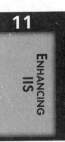

- Ident Mask—Specifies an identification mask such as (*@DomainName.COM*). Any user with this identification mask as part of his or her logon name, who also meets the Client Protocol and Logon Mode specifications, will be considered as part of the security class.

- IP Address—Specifies the IP address of the client's computer. If you do not know the IP address of the client's computer, but know its name, click the IP Lookup button and enter the name of the client computer. If the name is resolvable, the IP address will be entered into the IP Address field.

- IP Mask—Specifies a broader base to use for your restriction to the security class. By logically ANDing the IP address bits and IP mask bits, you can select a group of IP addresses. Any member within this group is considered as part of the security class as long as he or she meets the Client Protocol, Logon Mode, and Ident Mask (if specified) specifications.

6. Specify a start time and an end time to apply the class restriction to in the Start Time and Stop Time fields, respectively, if you want to further limit your security class.

   Once your security class is defined, you can assign restrictions to it.

7. Click the Class Constraints tab to display the property sheet shown in Figure 11.32.

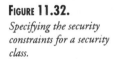

FIGURE 11.32.

Specifying the security constraints for a security class.

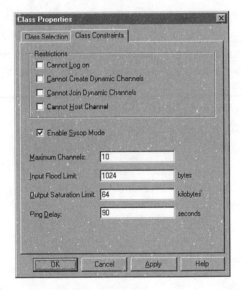

8. Choose one or more of the following entries from the Restrictions group:

   - Cannot Log on—Specifies that any member of this security class cannot log on to the chat server.

> **TIP**
>
> To lock out all anonymous users from your chat server, specify a Client Protocol type of Ignore Client Type, specify a Logon Mode type of Select Anonymous, and enable the Cannot Log on check box. If you want to prevent any authenticated logons (to allow only anonymous logons to the chat server), set the Logon Mode type to Select Authenticated and enable the Cannot Log on check box.

- Cannot Create Dynamic Channels—Specifies that any member of this security class cannot create a dynamic chat room on the server.

> **TIP**
>
> Using the Cannot Create Dynamic Channels switch with the Logon Mode type (set to Select Anonymous) is a good way to prevent anonymous users from creating dynamic chat rooms without denying your authenticated (network users) the ability to create dynamic chat rooms.

- Cannot Join Dynamic Channels—Specifies that any member of this security class cannot join a dynamically created chat room on the chat server.
- Cannot Host Channel—Specifies that any member of this security class cannot host a chat room on the chat server.

9. To allow members of this security class to become sysops of a chat room, check the Enable Sysop Mode check box.

10. To limit the number of chat rooms that can use this security class, specify a number in the Maximum Channels field. The minimum is 0; the maximum (and default) is 10.

11. To prevent members from causing a denial of service and flooding your chat server with garbage, specify a value (in bytes) for unprocessed messages. A member who sends more than this amount of data will be forcibly disconnected. The default is 1,024, the minimum is 256, and the maximum is 4,096.

12. Enter a value (between 4,096 and 262,144) in bytes in the Output Saturation Limit field to specify how much data to send to a client without a response before disconnecting it.

13. To specify the idle time between pings (to verify the client connection), enter a value (in seconds) in the Ping Delay field. The default is 90, the minimum is 15, and the maximum is 3,600.

14. Complete your security class selections. Then click the OK button to create the class and return to the Classes property sheet.

15. Repeat steps 1 through 14 for each security class you want to create. When you are finished, click the OK button to return to the Internet Service Manager.

If you need to ban a user from your server, click the Banned Users tab. From the Banned User property sheet, select the Add button to display the Ban Properties dialog box. Enter the user's alias name (such as BadBoy) in the Nickname field; the user's real name (such as George) in the User Name field; the user's domain name (such as SomeDomain.Com) in the Domain Name field; a comment that will be sent to the user when he or she attempts to log on to the chat server in the Reasons for Ban field; and if you want to limit the ban to specific times, a start and stop time in the Start Time and Stop Times fields, respectively. Then click the OK button.

> **TIP**
>
> To quickly disconnect a user from your chat server, click the Kill a User button. Then enter the user's alias name in the Nickname field, the user's real name in the User Name field, the user's domain name in the Domain Name field, and a comment that will be sent to the user in the Reasons for Ban field. Then just click the Kill button, and the user will be disconnected.

Using the Microsoft News Server

I really like the dynamic interaction with a member connected to a chat server. It's one of the reasons why I host live chats on my forum on the Microsoft Network (http://forums.msn.com/portable). Unless you have someone to monitor the room 24 hours a day, however, you are going to miss a client question now and again. This is one reason why Microsoft has provided a Network News Transport Protocol (NNTP) compliant server. A news server is basically a bulletin board system (BBS) that allows a user to post a message for other members to read. Members can also reply to existing messages posted on the board. Of course, to view a message on a news server, you need a news client like the Microsoft Internet News client included with Microsoft Internet Explorer 3.01. (See Figure 11.33.)

The Internet is home to millions, maybe even hundreds of millions, of news servers. And more are being added every day. What does this proliferation of news servers really mean to you? Two things. First, if you plan on propagating your newsgroups to everyone on the Internet, you need to be able to send your newsgroups to a master server, which will pass them on to its master, which will send them to its master, and so on. This process continues until your newsgroups reach the top of the heap. From that point of view, every news server that connects to the master at the top of the heap is a slave server (including yours), which leads to the second point. A slave news server can pull megabytes of data from its master on a daily basis. Depending on your expiration policy, data can accumulate quite rapidly on your server—which means that you need a lot of disk space! A news server can eat up available free space in a hurry. I wouldn't even think of pulling a news server on a drive with less than 3GB of free space (if you plan a full feed).

FIGURE 11.33.

Browsing messages with the Microsoft Internet News client.

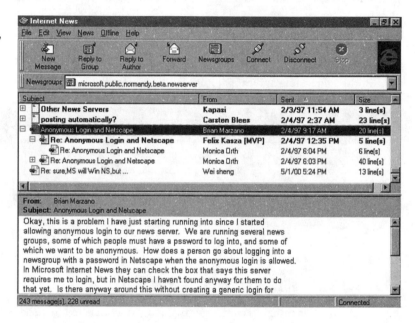

A news server can also eat up a tremendous amount of Internet bandwidth. Unless you have a T1 or higher connection as your Internet pipeline, I recommend that you limit incoming newsgroups as much as possible. But enough of the woes about news servers. I know you are eager to find out just what a news server will do for you, so let's get to it.

Installing the Microsoft News Server

The installation of the Microsoft News Server is really pretty straightforward. The two major considerations are to install the root directory for your newsfeed to an NTFS directory (to protect your newsgroups) and to install it to the largest disk you have available (so you won't run out of storage to process the newsgroups). Follow these steps to install the Microsoft News Server:

1. Execute the self-extracting file that you downloaded from the Microsoft Commercial Internet Server Web site or execute the setup program if you obtained the Microsoft News Server on CD-ROM.

2. Click the Yes button to continue the installation when the InstallShield Self-Extracting EXE dialog box is displayed. The Welcome dialog box will appear.

3. Click the Next button to continue the installation.

4. Read the Software License Agreement carefully. Then click the Yes button to continue the installation. (If you do not agree to the terms listed, click the No button and the installation of the chat server will terminate.)

5. Enter your name and company name in the Name and Company fields in the Registration dialog box. Then click the Next button to continue.

6. Accept the defaults or specify the location for the files in the Choose Destination Directory dialog box. If the default directory (C:\INETPUB\NEWS) is not acceptable, click the Browse button to specify an alternative location. I prefer to install these files on an NTFS partition for enhanced security, and I recommend that you do the same. When you have specified the location for these files, click the Next button.

7. Accept the default or make your selections in the Select Components dialog box. The default is to install all the software at this time, which is also my recommendation. After you have reviewed the documentation, you can rerun the setup program and remove any components that you no longer need. When you have made your selections, click the Next button to continue.

8. (Optional) If you have active IIS services the Running Services dialog box will be displayed requesting confirmation to stop these services and install the news server. Click the Yes button to continue. If you click the No button, you will have to rerun the setup program.

9. Accept the default or enter an alternative in the Choose the NNTP Home Directory dialog box. The default location for your news files is C:\INETPUB\NNTPRoot. If the default is not acceptable, choose another location by clicking the Browse button. Make sure this location has sufficient free space. A full NNTP newsfeed can eat up disk space in a hurry, and it is not unheard of to allocate up to 3GB (or more) for a complete newsfeed. Once you have specified your location, click the Next button to continue.

10. Accept the default or enter an alternative in the Choose the NNTP Database Files Directory dialog box. The default location for the internal database files is C:\INETPUB\NNTPFILES. If the default is not acceptable, choose another location by clicking the Browse button. Once you have specified your location, click the Next button to continue.

11. Accept the default name and location for the Internet News Server shortcuts or make your own selections in the Folder Selection dialog box. Click the Next button to continue.

12. Review the information in the Confirm Setup Information dialog box. If any information is incorrect, click the Back button until the appropriate dialog box is displayed and correct the information. If all the information is correct, click the Next button to continue.

The source files will be copied to the location you specified, the news service installed, and the IIS services will be started. At this point you are offered the opportunity to read the Internet News Server Startup Page (recommended) and start the administration tool.

13. Click the Finish button to exit the setup program.

Configuring the Microsoft News Server

Once you have installed the news server, you might expect to be able to sign on and use it immediately, as you did with the chat server. Unfortunately, you need to do some more work before you can use the news server. The amount of work you have to do depends on whether you will use the server only within your organization or whether you will pull and push a newsfeed to another server.

Rather than step through each property sheet of the Configuration dialog box—and repeat information that is available elsewhere in this chapter or in Chapter 6—this section explores only the following new options: creating newsgroups, setting expiration times for the newsgroup messages, and configuring newsgroup feeds. The starting point is to open the NNTP Service Properties sheet in the Internet Service Manager. To do so, highlight the computer name (such as SRV) associated with the NNTP service and choose Service Properties from the Properties menu to display the dialog box. Or highlight the service associated with the NNTP service, right-click the highlighted service, and select Service Properties from the pop-up menu.

> **TIP**
>
> The fastest method to display the NNTP Service Properties dialog box is to double-click the computer (such as SRV) associated with the NNTP service.

Creating a Newsgroup

If you are like me, the first thing you will probably want to do is create a few newsgroups to make sure your news server is functioning properly. Follow these steps to create your newsgroups:

1. Click on the Groups tab to display the Groups property sheets, as shown in Figure 11.34.

2. Click the Create button to display the Newsgroup Properties dialog box.

FIGURE 11.34.

*Managing newsgroups
for the NNTP service.*

TIP

You can specify all newsgroups by entering a * in the Newsgroup Name field. However, you can also choose a partial name (if the list is a long list) by entering just a portion of the name and the wildcard (for example, `alt.*`). You can also use the Find button to search for a limited group. The Limit Results to field limits the number of returned newsgroup entries to be displayed in the Matching Newsgroups field.

3. Enter the name for the newsgroup in the Newsgroup field. The name can contain ANSI characters, periods, and hyphens.

4. Enter a comment that describes the newsgroup in the Description field.

5. (Optional) Enable the Read Only check box if you want to prevent messages from being posted to the newsgroup.

6. (Optional) Enable the Moderated check box and enter an e-mail address in the Moderator field if the newsgroup will be moderated. This option sends a newsgroup posting to the e-mail address so the moderator can review it prior to posting it on the newsgroup.

7. Click the OK button to return to the Groups property sheet.

8. Repeat steps 2 through 7 for each new newsgroup to create.

Setting Newsgroup Expirations

One thing I can't stress enough is to set realistic limits for the length of time a newsgroup message can remain on your server. As much as I would like to, however, I can't give a universal recommendation. What I can say is that the more messages you have, the sooner you should let them expire. The default expiration time is one week (720 hours) with no newsgroup being able to grow beyond 500MB. But considering the number of newsgroups that are available, this limit may be too optimistic. You can certainly start with these expiration settings and then decrease the time and size by 1/2 if you start to encounter space-related problems. Repeat this process until the you have sufficient free space without losing messages, or increase your storage capacity to avoid deleting messages too soon. Here's how to change these expiration values:

1. Click the Expiration tab to display the Expiration property sheet.

2. Click the Add button to display the Expiration Policy Properties dialog box.

3. Choose one of the following expiration policies:

   ■ Newsgroups older than—Specifies a value (in hours) before a message is automatically deleted from a newsgroup

   ■ Newsgroups bigger than—Specifies a value (in megabytes) before a message is automatically deleted from a newsgroup

   ■ Both—Specifies that messages will be deleted based on time and size

4. Enter an asterisk (*) in the Newsgroups field to apply the expiration values to all newsgroups.

   You may also specify a partial newsgroup name and an asterisk or a specific newsgroup name.

5. Click the OK button to create your expiration rule and return to the Expiration property sheet.

6. Repeat steps 2 through 5 for each expiration policy you want to create. When you have created all your expiration policies, click the OK button to close the NNTP Service Properties dialog box and return to the Internet Service Manager.

Configuring a Newsgroup Feed

The real fun of operating a news server is pulling newsgroups off another news server. Once these newsgroups are available on your server, users may read and reply to them. The replies will need to be replicated back to the server from which you pulled the newsgroups. This process can vary quite a bit from installation to installation, so you need to consult with your ISP. Your ISP will be able to tell you whether or not your news server will be a peer server or a slave

server. (It will rarely be a master.) Your ISP will also be able to tell you what type of feed action is required. Having said all that, the following steps go through the basics of creating a newsfeed:

1. Click the Feeds tab to display the Feeds property sheet.

2. Click the Add button to display the Feed Properties dialog box, as shown in Figure 11.35.

FIGURE 11.35.

Creating a newsgroup feed.

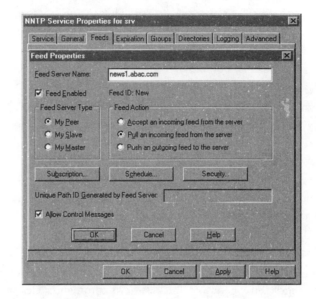

3. Enter the name of the news server to receive/send your newsfeed from/to in the Feed Server Name field.

4. Make sure the Feed Enabled check box is checked. If this check box is disabled, then the feed will not be processed.

5. Specify the type of feed server to contact in the Feed Server Type.

   ■ My Peer—Specifies that the remote server is a peer. Newsgroup messages numbers are not shared between the news servers.

   ■ My Slave—Specifies that the remote server is a client or slave of this server. Newsgroup messages numbers are assigned by the master news servers.

   ■ My Master—Specifies that the remote server is the master of this server. Newsgroup messages numbers are assigned by the remote news servers.

6. Specify the type of feed action to occur in the Feed Action field.

- Accept an incoming feed from the server—Specifies that the remote server will automatically send a feed to the news server as required. When this option is selected, the Schedule and Subscription buttons are disabled.

- Pull an incoming feed from the server—Specifies that the news server will pull a newsfeed from the remote server using the newnews command.

- Push an outgoing feed to the server—Specifies that this server will push a feed to the remote server as required. This option is the complement for the Accept an incoming feed from the server when configuring multiple master/slave configurations.

  If Push an outgoing feed to the server has been selected, the Unique Path ID Generated by Feed Server will be enabled. The unique number specified in this field is used for error reporting to the event log.

7. If you are pulling/pushing a feed from the remote server, specify the newsgroups to receive/send by clicking the Subscription button and entering the names of the newsgroups.

8. If you are pulling/pushing a feed from the remote server, specify the times to receive/send the feed by clicking the Schedule button and specifying the day and times to attempt the connection to the remote server.

9. If the remote server requires a user authentication, specify the valid username and password by clicking the Security button.

10. Leave the Allow Control Messages check box enabled to log and process news control messages. To log, but not process news commands, clear the check box.

11. Click the OK button to save your changes and return to the Feeds property sheet.

12. Repeat steps 2 through 11 for each newsfeed you want to create. In most case you will want to create at least two feeds: one to pull (to receive updates from the remote server) and one to push (to send your message postings to the remote server).

13. Click the OK button to close the NNTP Service Properties dialog box and return to the Internet Service Manager.

Summary

In this chapter you look at several products that you can use to enhance your IIS installation. The Microsoft Proxy Server helps protect you from Internet abuse, the Microsoft Chat Server allows you to establish real-time communications, and the Microsoft News Server supports non–real-time communications. Each product has unique features that may prove beneficial to individual organizations as well as Internet Service Providers. This chapter only touches on the products included in the Commercial Internet System. I expect Microsoft to add more products to this package by the time you read this page. These products should include the Internet

Locator Service (used by Microsoft NetMeeting—a kind of super chat client—to find other NetMeeting users), the Content Replication server (used to copy source material from one server to another), and the Personalization Service (used to provide personalized Web pages for individuals).

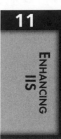

11

ENHANCING
IIS

IN THIS PART

- An HTML Primer   375

- Designing and Managing a Web Site with FrontPage   407

- Publishing on the Web with Microsoft Office   431

- Using Asymetrix Web3D and Corel's Web.Designer   465

- Using Sausage Software's HotDog Pro   479

IV
PART

Web Page Development

An HTML Primer

IN THIS CHAPTER

- What Is an HTML Document?   376
- Basic HTML Styles   380
- Advanced HTML Styles   394

This chapter teaches you how to create basic Hypertext Markup Language (HTML) documents using an American Standard Code of Information Interchange (ASCII) editor such as Notepad. The purpose is to give you the skills you need to build a Web page. This chapter is obviously not a complete tutorial because the subject matter is too broad to cover in a single chapter. As you will learn in the following chapters, you can even use a Web editor, which can write your HTML documents for you using a point-and-click interface. You don't even need to know any HTML to create the documents.

> **TIP**
>
> For a complete description of HTML syntax and more information on how to write HTML documents that fully exploit the HTML specification, check out Laura Lemay's *Teach Yourself HTML in 14 Days* published by Sams.

You will need to know HTML, however, if you have to debug an HTML document. Perhaps the editor is not supplying the correct tags. Or perhaps the editor is using a tag designed for a Web browser other than the Internet Explorer (IE). In either case, solving the problem will require you to know something about the structure of an HTML document. After all, solving a problem is very difficult if you cannot recognize the error when you see it. Appendix B, "HTML Reference," includes additional information on HTML tags supported by the Internet Information Server (IIS).

> **NOTE**
>
> I used Internet Explorer 3.0 for Windows NT to capture the figures in this chapter. If you plan to support other Web browsers, then I cannot stress enough the importance of testing your HTML documents using those specific Web browsers to determine exactly how your documents will appear onscreen. Even the same Web browser on different operating systems may display your document in unexpected ways. The samples provided on the CD-ROM in the SOURCE\CHAP12 directory were coded for use with Internet Explorer 3.0 on Windows NT.

What Is an HTML Document?

Before you actually begin building an HTML document, you should have a good idea of what an HTML document really is. Although the concept is not difficult, it can be a bit confusing to someone who is just beginning to publish content on the World Wide Web (WWW). The first word *World* is especially important to Web publishing because it plays a significant part in the design philosophy behind publishing Web documents.

If you were creating a document for your boss, you could use any word processing document. And as long as your boss has the same word processor, he or she could read, print, or modify your document. On the Web, however, you cannot be sure that everyone is using the same Web browser—which is where HTML comes into play.

What Is a Markup Language?

HTML is based on the Standard Generalized Markup Language (SGML) concept, which is used in the publishing field to describe a document's content. An SGML document is an ASCII document (or plain text file) that uses tags to describe the way the document's content will be displayed. Suppose that you want to use boldface type to highlight one word in a sentence. With Word for Windows, you press Ctrl+B before the chosen word to enable the bold text function and press Ctrl+B after the word to disable the bold text function. In SGML you use a set of tags to place an attribute: one tag to enable text bolding and another to disable text bolding; for example, `<BOLD>` to enable text bolding and `</BOLD>` to disable text bolding. Anything that appears within these tags would have the bold attribute.

> **TIP**
>
> Because these HTML tags are plain ASCII text, almost any Web browser on any platform (Windows NT, Windows 95, Macintosh, MS-DOS, UNIX, and so on) could see the content of your HTML document. Maybe not all your content, since not all Web browsers support every HTML tag, but the basic core of your document would be visible. The platform independence offered by the HTML language provides a means to reach the widest possible audience.

> **NOTE**
>
> In an SGML tag pair, the ending tag is always the same as the beginning tag, except that the ending tag has a ' / ' in front of the actual tag. The previous example, for instance, uses `<BOLD>` as the beginning tag and `</BOLD>` as the ending tag. The two tags and any content within the tags are referred to as an *element*. Sometimes an element is referred to as a *container* because the tag pair acts on the data contained between the two tags.

A tag pair is an essential component of a *markup language*. Marking sections of text with language elements (tags) determines how the document will be displayed. In the SGML language every tag must have an associated end tag. However, this rule is not enforced in HTML. In HTML, most, but not all, tags have an end tag. Like an HTML document, an SGML document is also divided into three parts. The first consists of the SGML declaration, the second is the document type declaration (DTD), which describes the acceptable structure of the document, and the final component is the document instance. In order for an SGML document (the document instance) to be valid, it must follow the rules as specified in the DTD. The DTD is a lexical description of the tags and all acceptable tag attributes. The SGML parser will find any tag that does not have a corresponding end tag. This process is similar to a C compiler examining your source code. If you forget an ending parenthesis, the C compiler generates an error message.

The ability to parse a file to determine if it contains any lexical errors is the feature that makes SGML so useful to publishers. SGML ensures that a document appears as the author intends it to appear. Another advantage of an SGML document is that it is portable. Anyone with an SGML editor and the appropriate DTD can edit, view, or print the document.

HTML to the Rescue

The primary reason that you do not use SGML to edit your documents with Word for Windows is that SGML can be a pain to work with. I'm not knocking SGML, because what it does is important to publications and it does its job very well, but it can be much too complex to use for everyday tasks. Luckily, you can use a subset (as you might like to consider it) of the SGML convention, or HTML. Because HTML utilizes a much smaller set of tags, it is much easier to work with. It is not for the faint of heart, however, because if you do not code your document properly (that is, follow the rules *exactly*), your client's Web browser may not show the page correctly. In fact, HTML does not ensure that your document will appear the same on every Web browser because different computer systems have different display capabilities. However, HTML does ensure that the original content and intent will remain.

> **NOTE**
>
> One of the best tools you can use is a Web editor, which includes an HTML parser that ensures that your HTML documents will follow the rules. (The following chapters examine several Web editors in more detail.)

A typical HTML document is divided into two components—the *head* and the *body*—each of which is enclosed in an <HTML> </HTML> tag pair. Anything outside of these two tags would create an illegal HTML document. Many programmers create skeleton code to use as a foundation to build fully functional programs. A skeleton HTML document follows.

```
<HTML>
<HEAD>
<TITLE>Skeleton HTML Document</TITLE>
</HEAD>

<BODY>
Insert your custom HTML code here!
</BODY>
</HTML>
```

If you opened the document with a Web browser, it would look like Figure 12.1. This document doesn't look like much, but it does illustrate several key points. First, it includes the minimum required information. The required information includes the `<HTML>`, `<BODY>`, `</BODY>`, and `</HTML>` tags, which create a valid HTML document. Nothing else in the document is required, but an HTML document with no other elements would be boring! Therefore, the document also includes the `<HEAD>`, `<TITLE>`, `</TITLE>`, and `</HEAD>` tags, which are used to place a document description (that is, title) on your Web browser's caption bar. The text between the `<BODY>` and `</BODY>` tags is the HTML document content that you want to display. You can base every document you create on the skeleton code in this example.

FIGURE 12.1.
The skeleton HTML document displayed in a Web browser.

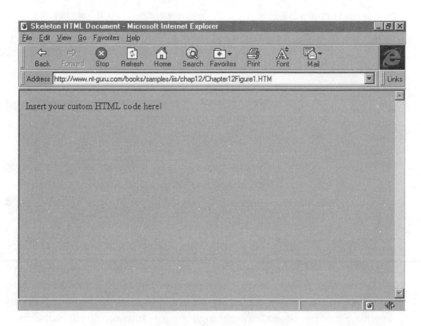

In the next sections, I show you how to use some of the basic tags to make your content look more appealing.

> **TIP**
>
> You should make sure that every HTML document you create includes a descriptive title because most Web browsers use the document title as the default name whenever a user chooses to save the document or to add it to the list of favorite places to visit. A reader is less likely to use a title based on your uniform resource locator (URL) to return to your site. In addition, because various Web automatons search Web sites to index their content, a descriptive title is more likely to attract visitors searching for specific information to your site.

Basic HTML Styles

Because most HTML documents are text based, this discussion begins with the basic HTML styles that you can use to manipulate text. Before you get too involved, however, I should point out a few quirks concerning text manipulation and HTML. Suppose you use the following tabbed table to display your favorite Web sites:

```
WWW Site Description                URL
--------------------                -----------------------
Knowles Consulting                  http://www.nt-guru.com
The Microsoft Network               http://www.msn.com
Microsoft Corporation               http://www.microsoft.com
```

If you place this text in the body of your HTML document, do you think it will appear as it is in the example? Well, if you do, you are mistaken. Instead, it will look something like Figure 12.2.

FIGURE 12.2.

An incorrectly formatted tabbed table displayed on a Web browser.

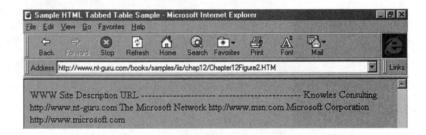

So what happened? Well, two things. First of all, the default font in an HTML document is a proportional font. Proportional fonts are easier to read and appear more natural to the reader, but this format doesn't align easily. Second, an HTML document attempts to collapse all whitespace (or nonprinting characters) into a single space. In the previous example, therefore, everything just runs together, making it almost impossible to read. Obviously, this method of displaying your content is unacceptable. But what can you do about it? Here are three possible solutions.

First, you can add a paragraph tag `<P>` to the beginning and `</P>` to the end of each sentence to force a line break at the end of each sentence. If you do, the display will look like Figure 12.3. Although the result is better than the previous example, the text still doesn't appear correctly on the screen.

Second, you could use one of the HTML tags to force the text to be displayed in a fixed-width font, as shown in Figure 12.4. This example looks quite a bit better. It is easy to read and appears just as the original source code does. This example makes use of the `<LISTING>` and

</LISTING> tags and drops the paragraph <P> </P> tags in each sentence. If you leave the <P> </P> tags, then they would also be displayed on the screen.

FIGURE 12.3.

Displaying a tabbed table with a proportional font.

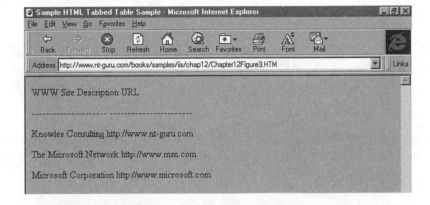

FIGURE 12.4.

Displaying a tabbed table with a fixed-width font.

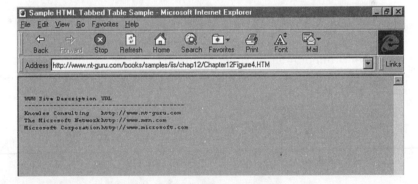

> **NOTE**
>
> Most Web browsers will correctly force a paragraph break whenever they encounter a <P> tag even if no corresponding </P> tag is present. Although the </P> tag is not really required, nor in some cases is it even considered part of the HTML specification (depending on which version you are looking at), I recommend that you use it for consistency.

The third solution is to create a table with each item displayed within a table column, as shown in Figure 12.5. This option is really the best because it utilizes a proportional font, which improves readability. Unfortunately, this option makes writing the code more difficult for the HTML document developer or, in this case, you.

FIGURE 12.5.

Displaying data within a table using a proportional font.

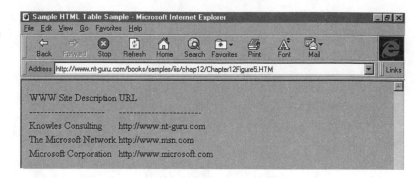

The rest of this section explores the various options available to format your HTML documents. You learn how to change paragraph and text attributes, create document headers, change page attributes, create numbered and unnumbered lists, insert graphics, create tables, and create hypertext links.

Changing Paragraph Attributes

Most word processors enable you to format paragraphs of text within your document. A word processor commonly allows you to align text on the left or right page boundary or to center the paragraph on the page. You can also indent a paragraph or justify the paragraph so that the paragraph margins on the page are as even as possible. HTML also provides this ability, as shown in Figure 12.6.

FIGURE 12.6.

Aligning paragraphs on the screen.

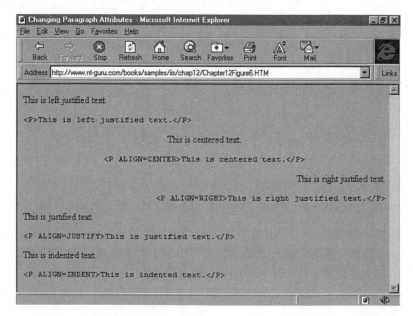

> **NOTE**
>
> To make the discussions a little easier to follow, I have also displayed the source code in Figure 12.6 for each paragraph formatting option. I will continue to do so with future HTML examples when applicable. You'll find the actual samples on the accompanying CD-ROM in the `\SOURCE\CHAP12` subdirectory.

You may notice that not all attributes are supported. The indent and justify options do not seem to appear properly on the screen with Internet Explorer 2.0 or Internet Explorer 3.0. Even though the justify attribute is supposed to be an accepted attribute according to the documentation I have found, it certainly does not appear to function properly. The indent attribute is not supported by Internet Explorer 2.0 or Internet Explorer 3.0. One reason that you should test your HTML documents on various Web browsers is simply that not all Web browsers support the HTML 2.0 specification or the HTML 3.2 draft. Unless you actually test your Web pages on the appropriate Web browsers, you really have no idea what the pages will look like on them.

> **TIP**
>
> You can create sample HTML documents, such as the ones I have created, to test the Web browsers you want to support. (No one really expects you to support them all.) If you choose to support only a single browser, you should say so on your Web page. A nice touch is to include a shortcut to the Web browsers you do support on your Web page. That way, your clients can view your Web pages in all their splendor.

The basic structure for paragraph alignment is

```
<P ALIGN= CENTER¦LEFT¦RIGHT¦JUSTIFY¦INDENT...</P>
```

Other HTML specifications may use variations of this structure. You can also use the `<CENTER>` and `</CENTER>` tags to center text or graphics on the screen, although this tag may disappear from future versions of HTML. You should use the `<P ALIGN=CENTER>` and `<\P>` tags if you want to maintain future HTML source code compatibility.

Changing Text Attributes

Plain text is boring, and most people like to spice it up a bit. To make a word stand out on the screen, make it bold. To call attention to a term you are defining, italicize or underline it. Figure 12.7 illustrates the HTML commands you can use to modify the way your text will appear on the screen. The text *should* look similar on most Web browsers. The important point is that HTML tags define a logical, not physical, representation. The Web browser ultimately determines how the text actually appears to the user.

FIGURE 12.7.

Changing text attributes.

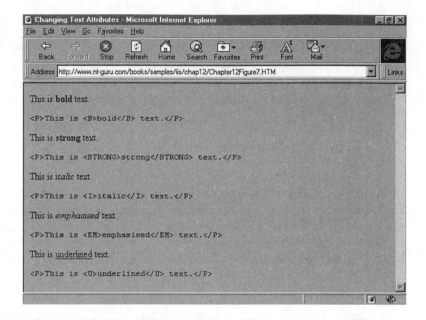

Notice also the `<EM>` `</EM>` and `<STRONG>` `</STRONG>` tag pairs in Figure 12.7. These tags emphasize text and strongly emphasize text, respectively. The HTML specification states that the `<EM>` tags display on the screen with a distinct difference from the `<STRONG>` tag. However, in my experience the `<EM>` tag generally displays as italic text, and the `<STRONG>` tag displays text in bold. I prefer to use the `<I>` `</I>` and `<B>` `</B>` tag pairs when I want to display italic or bold text rather than to use either the `<EM>` `</EM>` or `<STRONG>` `</STRONG>` tag pairs. I prefer the consistency of using specific tags because they give me a better idea of how the text will be displayed.

A couple of other tags, shown in Figure 12.8, are also useful. The `<CITE>` and `</CITE>` tags display a citation (usually used in legal documents). Most Web browsers will display the enclosed text in italic. You can also use the `<STRIKE>` and `</STRIKE>` to display text with a strikeout character, although this tag pair is being replaced with the `<S>` and `</S>` tags. You can use `<KBD>` and `</KBD>` to display text the user should type in exactly as shown on the screen. The `<CODE>` and `</CODE>` tags display source code on the screen. You can use `<TT>` and `</TT>` to display teletype text on the screen. `<KBD>`, `<CODE>`, and `<TT>` all use a fixed-width font.

You can change the size of the font displayed on the screen by using the `<FONT>` and `</FONT>` tags. The full tag is `<FONT SIZE=FontSize COLOR=" DisplayColor" FACE=" TypeFace">`, where *FontSize* is a number from 1 to 7 or the symbols + and - (to increase or decrease the size by one). *DisplayColor* is either `Black`, `Maroon`, `Green`, `Olive`, `Navy`, `Purple`, `Teal`, `Gray`, `Silver`, `Red`, `Lime`, `Yellow`, `Blue`, `Fuchsia`, `Aqua`, or `White`. *TypeFace* is a specific font family to use. Both `COLOR` and

FACE are Internet Explorer 2.0 extensions, so if you do not use Internet Explorer as your Web browser, you may want to avoid using these extensions. Figure 12.9 displays examples of the various fonts and colors you can use.

FIGURE 12.8.

Additional text attribute tags.

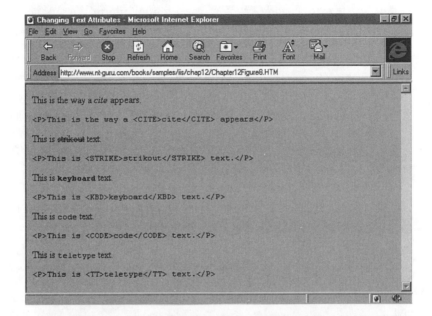

FIGURE 12.9.

Specifying a font size.

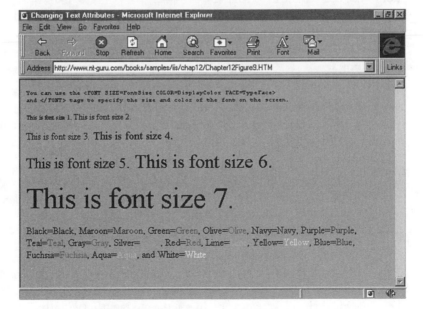

Depending on your Web browser, you may be able to use other HTML tags to specify text attributes. The supported tags seem to change quite rapidly. If you want to keep up-to-date, then you will need to do three things:

- Use the manufacturer's WWW pages to find information on the HTML tags and extensions that your particular Web browser supports. For the MS Internet Explorer, check the Microsoft home page at `http://www.microsoft.com`. For Netscape Navigator, check the Netscape home page at `http://home.netscape.com`. You can find the HTML 2.0 specification and 3.0 draft at `http://www.w3.org`.

- Check for and download the latest version of the Web browser from the manufacturer at least once a month. If you have the time, try once a week. You never know when an update will be available.

- Create a link for your customers to download the latest version of the Web browser and place it on your home page. This way, your customers will be able to take advantage of the HTML extension tags you use.

Displaying Text Using a Fixed-Width Font

As previously mentioned, you can use several HTML tag pairs to display text onscreen in a fixed-width font. They include the `<KBD>`, `<CODE>`, and `<TT>` tags. However, although you can use these tags to display large amounts of text in this fashion, they are really designed for small amounts of text. If you have a large amount of text that you want to display onscreen, you should use the `<PLAINTEXT>` `</PLAINTEXT>`, `<LISTING>` `</LISTING>`, or `<PRE>` `</PRE>` tag pairs. These are unique in that they will display anything within the enclosed tags onscreen; however, this feature also is implementation dependent. The `<LISTING>` tag assumes that a maximum of 132 characters can be displayed onscreen, while the `<PLAINTEXT>` tag does not make this assumption. I used the `<PLAINTEXT>` `</PLAINTEXT>` tag pair around the previous sample HTML source code so that you could see onscreen the behavior of the text attribute tags.

Although I used the tags (once again for consistency) on individual sentences, you could use them to enclose a paragraph or even an entire document. However, your Web browser might not support these tags.

> **NOTE**
>
> HTML is an evolving specification. Previous versions utilized these tags; however, the current specification based on RFC 1866 does not mention them.

You should use the `<PRE>` `</PRE>` tag pairs if you want to maintain maximum compatibility in the future. If your customers are using archaic Web browsers, you can either recommend that they upgrade their software or you can use the old tag pairs with the understanding that your future customers' Web browsers may not support the tag. You really cannot please everyone all the time. I prefer to use the newer tags, and I recommend that you do so as well.

> **NOTE**
>
> Even the same version of the Web browser may have different display characteristics, depending on the operating system. For example, Internet Explorer 2.0 on Windows 95 does not support the `<PLAINTEXT> </PLAINTEXT>` or `<PRE> </PRE>` tags to display embedded HTML tags. Instead, I had to use the `<LISTING> </LISTING>` tags to capture Figure 12.9. Internet Explorer 1.5 under Windows NT does not support the COLOR keyword in the `<FONT>` tag, though Internet Explorer 3.0 does.

The basic formats of these tags are

```
<LISTING WIDTH="MaxNbrOfCharacters"> </LISTING>
<PLAINTTEXT> </PLAINTTEXT>
<PRE WIDTH=MaxNbrOfCharacters> </PRE>
```

MaxNbrOfCharacters is the maximum number of characters to be displayed on the screen. One particular quirk you should be aware of is that some Web browsers will decrease the font size in order to fit the characters on the screen. You should test your Web pages at different resolutions with your Web browser to determine if the effect is acceptable. If not, you should reformat your text if possible.

Creating Document Headers

Most people break their documents into sections when they write. This section of the chapter, for example, uses a level D heading to describe the contents and to help readers to find information. You can do the same with HTML by using the header tags. Figure 12.10 shows the seven header levels you can define in HTML, starting with `<H1> </H1>` and ending with `<H7> </H7>`. As you can see, each header level uses a different size font. Levels 1 through 6 use a bold font, and by the time you reach level 7 you are back to the default font size and characteristics. Once again, you really can't expect the headers to display this way on all Web browsers, but you can expect that each header level will be displayed with a noticeable difference.

You may specify additional information when you define your headers. You can align them on the left side of the page, the right side, center them, or even justify them. The basic syntax is

```
<H# ALIGN=LEFT¦RIGHT¦CENTER¦JUSTIFY NOWRAP> </H#>
```

where # is a value from 1 to 7. (Of course, your Web browser may support additional options.) If printing your Web pages is a concern, you should be aware that if you center a header that utilizes a large font, a page break may be generated after the header.

FIGURE 12.10.

The seven HTML header levels.

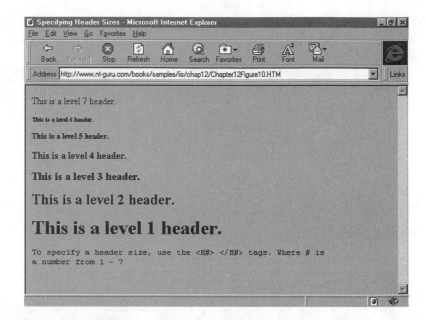

> **NOTE**
>
> You should not use any additional text attribute tags, such as <B>, <I>, <EM>, <STRONG>, and so on, within a header tag; doing so can cause undefined behavior.

Changing Page Attributes

One of the coolest HTML features is the ability to specify a picture to be used as a background for your document. This feature works the same way that a tiled background does for your desktop. Basically, the image is duplicated multiple times to fill the screen, and your document text and images will appear layered on top of the background. You can also specify the default background color and colors for your links. Although Internet Explorer 1.5 does not support, or at least it does not seem to support, color-related tag extensions, it does work fine with background bitmaps.

A background bitmap must be either a Graphical Interchange Format (GIF) or Joint Picture Experts Group (JPEG) file, and you should keep it as small as possible. The smaller the file, the quicker the user can get back to reading your document content. If your backgrounds are too large, then the user will probably give up in disgust and move on to a new Web site. Here's how it works: The Web browser sets the background color, loads the background image, loads the text, and finally displays any images embedded within the document.

You shouldn't specify a background color if you also use a background image that fills the entire screen when tiled, as shown in Figure 12.11, unless your image is an irregular (that is, not square) shape. If you actually load the sample file (Chapter12Figure12.11.HTM) from the CD-ROM, you will see a red flash as the background color is set followed by the background image overlaying the background color.

FIGURE 12.11.

A tiled background image.

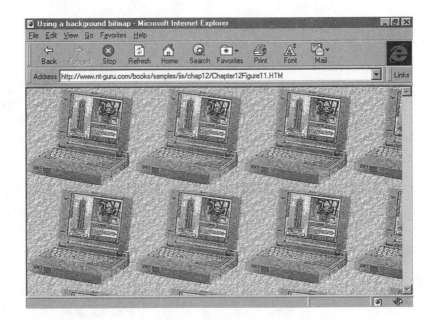

I am particularly fond of using background images, as they provide an easy way to build a great-looking page with minimal impact on downloading the HTML document. You can use a small pattern, such as a square marble image, to create a high-visibility document. Users will say, "Wow! That looks nifty," and they will spread the word to other users, who will then come to visit your pages.

Use <BODY> to specify the page background and color. The basic syntax is

`<BODY BACKGROUND=PathName BGCOLOR=BackGroundColor> </BODY>`

where *PathName* is a relative URL to your background (/images/picture.gif, for example) and *BackGroundColor* is either Black, Maroon, Green, Olive, Navy, Purple, Teal, Gray, Silver, Red, Lime, Yellow, Blue, Fuchsia, Aqua, or White.

Another neat tag to use is

`<BGSOUND SRC="PathName" LOOP="NbrOfIterations"> </BGSOUND>`

where *PathName* is a relative URL that points to the location of your sound file and *NbrOfIterations* is a number or the keyword infinite to play continuously. You need to be aware of two considerations when using this option. First, the size of the audio file will cause a delay in displaying the document. If the wait is too long, the user will go elsewhere. Second, most Web browsers do not currently have a way to turn off the sound. Not everyone will appreciate listening to the same sound over and over (if you use the infinite option). Use this option with care; or if you want to play a sound, create a link to let users play it if they desire.

Creating Numbered and Bulleted Lists

The HTML specification includes the ability to create both a numbered list and a bulleted list, as shown in Figure 12.12. If you want to use fancy bullets, you can load images or specify a different bullet character in your HTML source. You can also use an HTML editor to write the HTML code to insert the image and create the bulleted list. The basic format is <OL> </OL> for an ordered (numbered) list and <UL> </UL> for an unnumbered (bulleted) list. Within these tags you may also specify the list items using the <LI> and </LI> tags and an optional list header using the <LH> and </LH> tags.

FIGURE 12.12.

Creating numbered and bulleted lists.

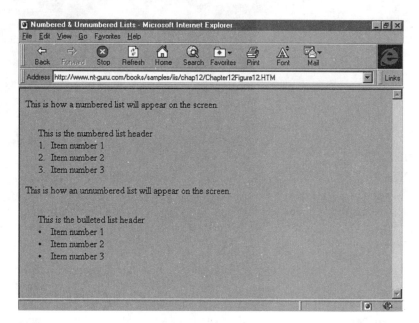

The actual source code for this Web page is as follows:

```
<HTML>
<HEAD>
<TITLE>Numbered & Unnumbered Lists</TITLE>
</HEAD>
```

```
<BODY>
<P>This is how a numbered list will appear on the screen.</P>
<OL>
<LH>This is the numbered list header</LH>
<LI>Item number 1
<LI>Item number 2
<LI>Item number 3
</OL>
<P>This is how an unnumbered list will appear on the screen.</P>
<UL>
<LH>This is the bulleted list header</LH>
<LI>Item number 1
<LI>Item number 2
<LI>Item number 3
</UL>
</BODY>
</HTML>
```

For readability, I always start each item on a separate line. However, doing so is not required. You can generate the same effect by creating a single paragraph (or line) of text. I think you will agree that the previous example is much easier to read than the following:

```
<HTML><HEAD><TITLE>Numbered & Unnumbered Lists</TITLE></HEAD><BODY>
➥<P>This is how a numbered list will appear on the screen.</P><OL>
➥<LH>This is the numbered list header</LH><LI>Item number 1
➥<LI>Item number 2<LI>Item number 3</OL><P>This is how an unnumbered
➥list will appear on the screen.</P><UL><LH>This is the bulleted list
➥header</LH><LI>Item number 1<LI>Item number 2<LI>Item number 3</UL>
➥</BODY></HTML>
```

As with most other textual tags, you can also specify the alignment. The basic syntax for lists is either

```
<OL ALIGN=LEFT¦RIGHT¦CENTER¦JUSTIFY> </OL>
```

or

```
<UL ALIGN=LEFT¦RIGHT¦CENTER¦JUSTIFY> </UL>
```

Additional List Styles

If you have a small amount of information to display within a list, you can use the <MENU> </MENU> tags. You should use these tags with a list of items that have fewer than 40 characters each. The idea is that the Web browser can use a more compact font to display the material, although the result is implementation dependent. You can use the <DIR> </DIR> tags to create a directory that will appear as a single column of items (another list). The <LI> tag precedes each item within a menu or directory. To create a menu of items, you could use something similar to the following:

```
<MENU>
<LI>First menu item.
<LI>Second menu item.
</MENU>
```

To create a directory list, say of files in your File Transfer Protocol (FTP) site, you could use the following:

```
<DIR>
<LI>autoexec.bat
<LI>config.sys
</DIR>
```

The only difference between these tags and those for numbered or bulleted lists is that these tags do not precede the list with either a bullet or a number. Although I do not find much use for these tags unless I am creating custom bullets, the definition list tag pair is quite useful. You can use this set of tags to create a dictionary or glossary of terms for your Web page. Here's the way it works: The outer body uses the <DL> </DL> tags, the term uses a <DT> tag, and the definition uses a <DD> tag. Suppose you want to display a glossary for your Web page for new users. You could use the following code:

```
<DL>
<DT><B>HyperText Transmission Protocol (HTTP)</B>
<DD>Is the common protocol, or language, used by World Wide Web (WWW)
➥servers and web browsers as the communication link between client
➥and server.
<DT><B>HyperText Markup Language (HTML)</B>
<DD>Is a set of rules which utilize ASCII based tags used to format text,
➥display objects, and create links within a document, or web page.
</DL>
```

The result of this code appears in Figure 12.13.

FIGURE 12.13.

A sample glossary for your Web page.

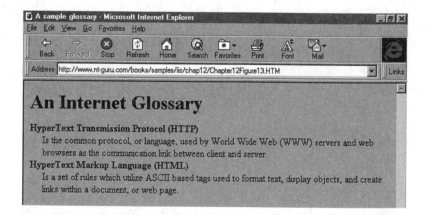

You also might want to change the size of the font for the term, rather than display it in bold as I have done. Another option is to create an index at the top of your page with links to the terms and definitions. A later section of this chapter, "Creating Hypertext Links," contains an example of this particular method.

Miscellaneous Styles

A few additional HTML tags may be useful in your endeavors to design the perfect Web page. To create a visual line break, for example, you can use the horizontal rule tag <HR>. If you are quoting a source on your Web page, you can use the <BLOCKQUOTE> </BLOCKQUOTE> tags. The text enclosed within these tags often appears surrounded by single quote marks or as an indented paragraph of italic text. Another cool tag is the <ADDRESS> </ADDRESS> tag pairs. This set of tags is most commonly used to highlight your name, address, or e-mail address. I often include this type of contact information on the bottom of a page. To give you an idea how these tags will display your text onscreen, take a look at Figure 12.14.

FIGURE 12.14.

Horizontal lines, quoted material, and addresses.

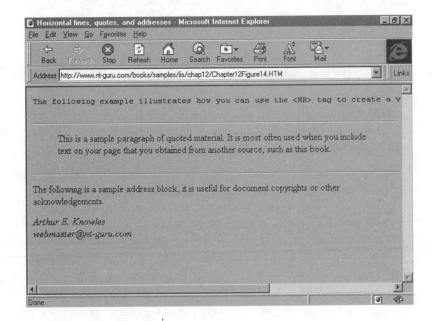

If you look at the source code for this example, you will see another new tag within the <ADDRESS> </ADDRESS> tags. This tag is the line break tag <BR>. Its purpose is to start a new line without creating extra vertical space like when you start a new paragraph. I prefer to use it at the end of a sentence, as shown in the following code; however, you can place it anywhere within your text.

```
<ADDRESS>
Arthur E. Knowles<BR>
Art@MSN.COM
</ADDRESS>
```

Advanced HTML Styles

Once you have mastered the basic HTML tags for text manipulation, you may want to move on to the more advanced tags. You can use these tags to insert graphics into your documents for a more appealing look or to insert tables into your document to more finely control the layout of your page. You can also insert hypertext links to allow a user to point and click to jump to another page, download a file from an FTP server, send e-mail, or execute other supported Internet services. For more fine-tuned control of the displayed page, you can divide your client's pages into sections called *frames*. You can even override the default settings on a client's Web browser by using style sheets, or use a style sheet to specify default attributes for the basic HTML tags. In addition, you can insert invisible meta information into your documents for Web browsers, Web editors, and search engines to use.

Inserting Graphics

Without a doubt, the feature that makes today's Web browsers fun to work with is graphics. Graphics are an integral part of a Web page, and without them life is really boring. The good news is that inserting graphics into your Web page is very easy. You should keep the following rules in mind when using graphics in your documents:

- Never use a 24-bit graphic image. These images, although very nice to view, are just too large. They take an inordinate amount of bandwidth to download, and for most users the wait just isn't worth it. If you do decide to provide 24-bit images, place them on your FTP site. The user can then choose whether to download them. You should also be aware that not every Web browser can display 16-bit or 24-bit images. Most only support 8-bit (or 256 color) bitmaps in GIF or JPEG formats.

- Don't go overboard. Too many graphics cause the reader to collapse from image overload. If your client is using a modem as his or her Internet connection, too many graphic images may try the client's patience. A modem is not a fast connection mechanism, and the client may decide to stop waiting for the slow modem to download all the images and move on to another site.

- Use GIF, instead of JPEG, graphics. Unless you are 100 percent sure that your customers' Web browsers will support JPEG graphic files, stick to the GIF format. Otherwise, your customers may think you don't know how to create a Web page because all they will see is the crossed-out square that their browser uses to represent a missing graphic image.

- Always have a text alternative. If you are using an image as a link, remember that not everyone has a Web browser that supports graphic images. Also, some people disable image viewing entirely in order to decrease access times. So always include a textual reference.

Having said all that, to insert an image on your Web page, you can use the `<IMG> </IMG>` tag pair. The basic syntax is

```
<IMG SRC="ImageURL" ALT="TextAlternative" ALIGN=LEFT ¦ RIGHT ¦ MIDDLE ¦ TOP ¦
BOTTOM ¦ TEXTTOP ¦ ABSBOTTOM ¦ ABSMIDDLE ¦ BASELINE> </IMG>
```

ImageURL is a URL that points to the image to be displayed, and *TextAlternative* is a text description to be used if the graphic cannot be displayed. The Microsoft Internet Explorer can also display video animation. If you choose to do so, the alternate version is as follows:

```
<IMG SRC="ImageURL" ALT="TextAlternative" ALIGN=LEFT ¦ RIGHT ¦ MIDDLE ¦ TOP ¦
BOTTOM ¦ TEXTTOP ¦ ABSBOTTOM ¦ ABSMIDDLE ¦ BASELINE
DYNSRC="VideoURL" START=FILEOPEN ¦ MOUSEOVER CONTROLS
LOOP=number¦INFINITE¦-1 LOOPDELAY=number > </IMG>
```

In this case a static image, as defined by the SRC element, will be used if the browser does not support video files. The DYNSRC element references the actual video file, and the VideoURL defines the location of the video clip. The START element specifies that the image will begin to play when the file is opened; however, if you use the MOUSEOVER option, the video will discontinue playing whenever the mouse is over the image. The CONTROLS option specifies that a set of video controls (stop, start, and so on) should be displayed to control the flow of the video clip. The LOOP element controls how many times the video clip will play. If INFINITE or -1 is selected, the image will play continuously. The LOOPDELAY element defines how long in milliseconds the video clip will pause before restarting.

TIP

Be nice to your customers. If you have a large graphic, video image, or file for them to download when they click a link, place a notice of the object size next to it. This information tells users just how long it will take to download the file and prepares them for the wait.

 I really do wish that this book could display live video because this option is one of the coolest I've seen to date. You can use it to create a marquee of moving textual content, instead of a static banner. It can also display any type of animation, including 3D effects. Chapter 18, "Unleashing the Power of VBScript," will look into this possibility in the context of Asymetrix's WEB 3D product. To give you an idea of how to place an image, see Figure 12.15 and the associated sample code `\SOURCE\CHAP12\Chapter12Figure12.15.HTM` on the accompanying CD-ROM, which displays the Internet Information Server logo in several areas on the screen.

FIGURE 12.15.

*Displaying images on
your Web page.*

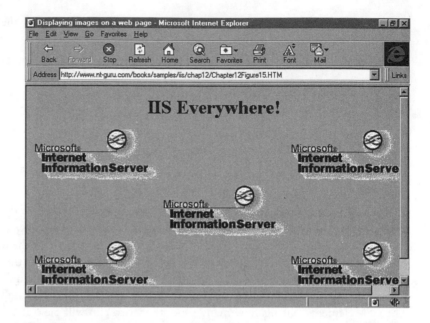

If you look at the sample source code, you will notice that I did not use the ALIGN keyword to align the objects on the screen. I wanted the images to create an X-shaped display. Therefore, I created a 3×3 table (tables are discussed in more detail in the next section, "Creating Tables") with an image inserted in the four corners and in the center element of the table. The ALIGN keyword aligns the image relative to text or other images on the screen. It does not generate an absolute alignment of the viewing area.

TIP

If you want to place an image in a specific location, the best way to do so is to divide your page into logical groupings with a table. Then place each element within a specific column and row, as I have done.

Another cool use for inline graphics is to create custom horizontal rules, banners, mastheads, or even bullet lists. Figure 12.16 demonstrates the creation of custom bullets in a menu list. This bullet is more attractive than the standard bullet. Your users also will see a more attractive bullet unless they have images disabled or are using a text-based Web browser.

FIGURE 12.16.

*Creating custom
bulleted lists.*

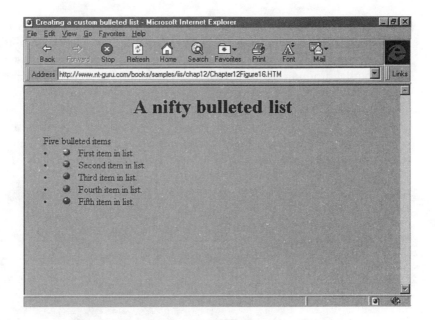

Creating Tables

As previously mentioned, tables are useful for breaking your Web pages into discrete sections. Although you cannot be assured that this method will work in every case, it will work for Web browsers that support the HTML table definitions as described in the HTML 3.2 draft, including the Internet Explorer and Netscape Navigator. Although these Web browsers do not support the full HTML 3.2 draft at this time, they do support the basic implementation that consists of the `<TABLE>` `</TABLE>` tag pair. Within this tag pair you can also include a table header, specified with the `<TH>` `</TH>` tags. A row is defined using the `<TR>` `</TR>` tag pair. An individual column in a row is defined with the `<TD>` `</TD>` tag pair. To create a 2×3 table, for example, you could use the following HTML code:

```
<H1 ALIGN=CENTER>A sample 2 x 3 table.</H1>
<TABLE ALIGN=CENTER BORDER>
<TH>This is the table header for the first column.</TH>
<TH>This is the table header for the second column.</TH>
<TH>This is the table header for the third column.</TH>
<TR>
<TD ALIGN=LEFT>This is the first column in the first row.</TD>
<TD ALIGN=CENTER>This is the second column in the first row.</TD>
<TD ALIGN=RIGHT>This is the third column in the first row.</TD>
</TR>
<TR>
<TD ALIGN=LEFT>This is the first column in the second row.</TD>
<TD ALIGN=CENTER>This is the second column in the second row.</TD>
<TD ALIGN=RIGHT>This is the third column in the second row.</TD>
</TR>
</TABLE>
```

This listing creates the table shown in Figure 12.17. The first line creates a header that will be centered on the screen and displayed before the table. The next line begins the definition for the table. It specifies that the table should be centered on the screen and that the table should have a border around each table element. The following three lines create the table column headers. The subsequent line with the <TR> tag specifies the beginning of the first table row. The next three lines, prefaced with the <TD ...> tag, define the first three columns of the table. Data displayed within these columns are left, right, and center aligned within the column. The very next line, with the </TR> tag, defines the end of the first row. The next five lines define the second row of data, followed by the ending table definition. That's all there is to creating tables!

FIGURE 12.17.

Creating a 2×3 table with table and column headers.

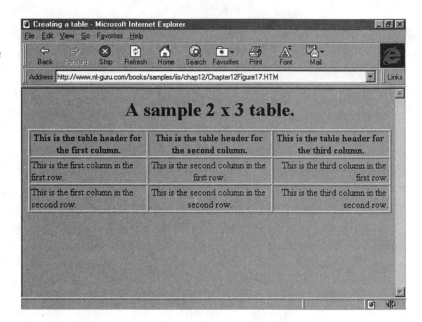

The basic syntax for each table element follows.

```
<TABLE ALIGN=LEFT¦RIGHT¦CENTER¦JUSTIFY BORDER> </TABLE>
<TH ALIGN=LEFT¦RIGHT¦CENTER¦JUSTIFY¦CHAR CHAR=UserSpecifiedCharacter
 VALIGN=TOP¦MIDDLE¦BOTTOM¦BASELINE BGCOLOR=DisplayColor> </TH>
<TR ALIGN=LEFT¦RIGHT¦CENTER¦JUSTIFY¦CHAR¦DECIMAL CHAR=UserSpecifiedCharacter
VALIGN=TOP¦MIDDLE¦BOTTOM¦BASELINE> </TR>
```

The BORDER option specifies that the table should have a border surrounding each cell. The *UserSpecifiedCharacter* option is used with the ALIGN=CHAR option to specify the horizontal alignment of data. It defaults to a decimal point if no other character is specified. The

DisplayColor option can be either Black, Maroon, Green, Olive, Navy, Purple, Teal, Gray, Silver, Red, Lime, Yellow, Blue, Fuchsia, Aqua, or White. The VALIGN option specifies the vertical alignment of items within the table cell.

Creating Hypertext Links

No HTML document is really complete without a link to another document. In HTML terms, a link is defined within an *anchor*. An anchor, <A> </A>, is a relative reference to another object. It can include text or images, and when selected, it will send the user to the specified location. An anchor can either include a HREF, which is a URL to a destination, or a NAME, which is a reference to a specific hypertext link within the associated document. The basic syntax is as follows:

```
<A HREF="PathName"> URLDescription </A>
<A NAME="PathName#LinkName> URLDescription </A>
```

The PathName is a relative URL to the HTML document, and URLDescription is the hypertext link that will be displayed on the screen. For a NAME entry, LinkName specifies a hypertext link within the associated document. With a NAME anchor, the document will be loaded by the Web browser, then a jump will be made to the specified location within the document specified by LinkName.

When you create an anchor, you may specify a graphic image to be loaded by including the <IMG> tag between the beginning <A> and </A> tags. The following code is a link to the IIS Web page:

```
<A HREF="http://www.microsoft.com/infoserv"><IMG ALIGN=LEFT SRC="/samples/images/
➥h_logo.gif></A>
<P ALIGN=CENTER>The Internet Information Server (or IIS) is a new set of tools to
provide Windows NT Server with a WWW, FTP, and Gopher server.
To find out more about the <A HREF="http://www.microsoft.com/infoserv">
Internet Information Server</A> click on the picture to the left, to the link
<A HREF="http://www.microsoft.com/infoserv">here</A></P>
```

Figure 12.18 shows how the previous code appears onscreen. You can create a URL for any of the Internet services as defined in Table 12.1. Of course, to make all of this work properly, you must also have an application associated with the specific service. For example, if you select a URL that includes the mailto URI, then your e-mail client will be launched. If you choose a news uniform resource identifier (URI), then a newsgroup reader will be launched. Unfortunately, version 1.5 of the Internet Explorer for Windows NT does not support news, but news works fine with the Internet Explorer 2.0 for Windows 95 as long as you also have a user account on the Microsoft Network. Internet Explorer 3.0 includes a separate newsreader that is invoked whenever a news URI is selected.

12

AN HTML
PRIMER

FIGURE 12.18.
Creating a hypertext link.

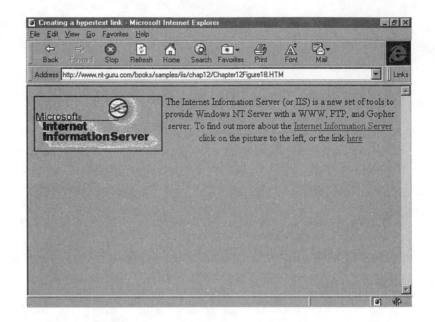

Table 12.1. Acceptable Internet services types.

Uniform Resource Identifier	*Description*
http	Hypertext Transfer Protocol. The most widely used mechanism to retrieve a file; requires that the destination include an application (WWW server) that understands the HTTP protocol.
https	Hypertext Transfer Protocol Secure. A variation on the previous example that includes a secure connection mechanism.
file	Local file access. This option will load a local file.
ftp	File Transfer Protocol. Commonly used to access an FTP server to download a specified file.
mailto	E-mail. Commonly used to load and execute an e-mail form from the host computer on the local computer.
news	Usenet newsgroups. Commonly used to access Internet newsgroups.
wais	Wide area information service. Commonly used to search a Gopher site.
gopher	Commonly used to access large text servers.
telnet	Commonly used to access a telnet server on a remote host.

Creating Frames

Although you can use tables to control the basic layout of your documents, tables just aren't precise enough for the job. Frames, however, enable you to divide a document into discrete components, each of which can be considered as a window with, or without, borders and scrollbars. A frame, or window, can display a complete HTML document within it. It's quite similar to the Windows multiple document interface (MDI) that we have grown accustomed to using. An MDI application can display multiple documents, with each window displaying a single document. A frame cannot be constructed as a standalone entity. It must be contained within a *frameset*. A frameset can contain one or more frameset elements, one or more frame elements, and an optional noframe element, which displays content for Web browsers that do not support frames. The basic syntax to create a frame is

```
<FRAMESET FRAMEBORDER=BorderType FRAMESPACING=SpaceBetweenFrames
➥ ROWS="RowWidths" COLS="ColWidths">
<FRAME SRC="HTMLDocumentPathName" NAME="FrameName"
➥ MARGINWIDTH="MarginWidth" MARGINHEIGHT="MarginHeight" SCROLLING=YES¦NO¦AUTO
➥ NORESIZE></FRAMESET>
<NOFRAME>CharacterData</NOFRAME>
</FRAMESET>
```

The BorderType is a switch that displays a frame border when set to 1 or no border when set to 0. The SpaceBetweenFrames is the additional space, in pixels, between individual frames. The RowWidths and ColWidths are comma-separated values that determine the number and size of the rows and columns. These values can be expressed three ways: as a standalone number that specifies the width in pixels, as a number followed by a percent sign (%) that specifies that the width will be based on a portion of the viewable area of the Web browser, or as an asterisk (*) to indicate a relative size. The HTMLDocument is a relative URL to an HTML document to be displayed within the frame. The FrameName is a name used to reference the frame. Remember, the frame contents can change dynamically, but the frame name is constant. The MarginHeight and MarginWidth are offsets within the frame for the content to be displayed. The SCROLLING parameter specifies that scrollbars will be visible (YES), invisible (NO), or automatically displayed based on the size of the Web browser's viewable area (AUTO). The NORESIZE parameter specifies that the user may not change the size of the frames. The optional NOFRAME element specifies alternate content to be displayed for Web browsers that do not support frames. To get a better feel for these elements, consider the document displayed in Figure 12.19.

This document is divided into four sections. The topmost area is a banner area in which you can display static text such as your company name or the document name. You can display static content such as contact information, an address, or logo at the bottom of the document. The leftmost area usually contains static content as well. I like to use it to display a table of contents with hypertext links. Each time a link is selected, the contents in the main area (the rightmost area) will change. Here's the code to create this document:

```
<HTML>
<HEAD>
<TITLE>Creating multiple frames</TITLE>
</HEAD>
```

```
<BODY>
<FRAMESET ROWS="8%,75%,17%">
<FRAME SRC="Banner.HTM" NAME="banner" MARGINWIDTH="1" MARGINHEIGHT="1">
<FRAMESET COLS="25%,75%">
<FRAME SRC="Content.HTM" NAME="contents" MARGINWIDTH="1" MARGINHEIGHT="1">
<FRAME SRC="Main.htm" NAME="main" MARGINWIDTH="1" MARGINHEIGHT="1">
<FRAME SRC="Bottom.htm" NAME="bottom">
<NOFRAMES>
Your browser does not support frames. To view a non-frame version of this
➥document <A HREF=NoFrame.HTM">click here</A>.
</NOFRAMES>
</FRAMESET>
</BODY>
</HTML>
```

FIGURE 12.19.

A document with multiple frames.

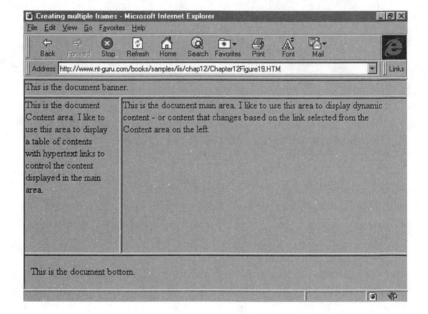

The page is divided into three rows. The banner area is 8 percent, the bottom is 17 percent, and the second row is 75 percent of the viewable area. The second row is further subdivided into columns with the content area set at 25 percent, and the main area set to 75 percent of the row area. Of particular importance in this example is the location of the <FRAMESET COLS> tag. It must be placed before the row you want to subdivide. If you placed this tag element at the beginning as part of the first frameset element, then the entire page would have been divided into two columns. In essence you would have created a document with three rows and two columns, which would not have produced the document layout you wanted.

TIP

Notice that the NOFRAMES element is used to specify an alternate text message for any Web browser that does not support frames.

Using Styles

Sometimes just specifying the document attributes, as you would with the basic HTML elements, is not sufficient to display your document as you intend to. Clients can always override the basic HTML elements to choose their own defaults for text size, text color, hypertext links, and other elements within their Web browser. Client modifications can change the way the document is viewed, and perhaps may even distort the artistic quality of a document.

Fortunately, you can use the power of a style sheet to override a user's default setting. You can also use style sheets to specify global settings for a document or a set of linked documents. Some of these settings include headers, default fonts, the background color, and font colors. Unfortunately, style sheets are currently still under development and therefore the information here may change by the time you read this material. To supplement this glimpse into the potential of style sheets, check out the Web site at `http://www.w3.org/pub/www.style/css`.

The basic syntax for the STYLE element is

```
<STYLE> HTMLElement {HTMLParameter: HTMLValue;...} </STYLE>
```

The HTMLElement parameter specifies the HTML tag to modify. This tag is followed by the HTML parameter, followed by a colon and the value to be associated with this parameter, followed by a semicolon. The final parameter and value tag do not need to be followed by a semicolon. The parameter and value pairs, however, must be enclosed in brackets. Within these brackets you can specify multiple parameters and values. Taken together, this set of elements and parameters is called a *cascading style sheet* (CSS) rule. Many rules are defined by the CSS1 specification—so many, that I would need almost an entire book to show them all. Figure 12.20 shows how some of these style sheet rules work.

The code to display this document is as follows:

```
<HTML>
<HEAD>
<TITLE>Using Style Sheets</TITLE>
</HEAD>
<STYLE>
BODY {BACKGROUND: WHITE; COLOR: BLACK}
H1   {FONT: 24pt "Brush Script MT" Bold}
P    {FONT: 10pt Arial}
B    {FONT: 12pt Arial; COLOR: RED}
</STYLE>
```

```
<BODY>
<H1>This is a level 1 header using the Brush Script MT font</H1>
<p>This is regular text now displayed as 10 point Arial.</p>
<p><b>This is bold text now displayed as 12 point Arial in red.</b></p>
</BODY>
</HTML>
```

Figure 12.20.

Using a style sheet to set document defaults.

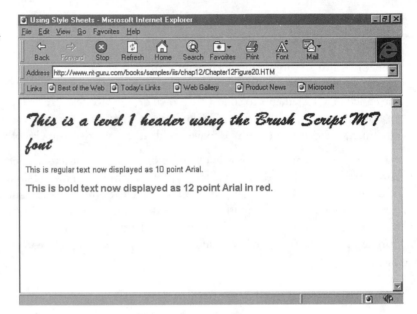

The first rule in this style sheet is for the <BODY> tag. The first parameter (BACKGROUND) sets the Web browser background color to white instead of to the default browser setting of gray. The second parameter (COLOR) sets the default text color to black. The second rule specifies that a level 1 header be displayed using the Brush Script MT font with a 24-point size. The third rule specifies that standard text be displayed using the Arial font with a 10-point size. The final rule specifies that bold text be displayed in red using the Arial font with a 12-point size.

Inserting Meta Information

You can insert a meta tag to provide information about an HTML document to the Web browser, Web editor, search engine, or other application. It can be a very useful tag. You can use a meta tag within your document to perform the following functions:

■ Load a new document, or reload an existing document, at a specified time. This feature is often referred to as a *client pull* because the client's Web browser actually interprets the HTTP header and loads the document.

■ Specify information about the document, such as the content type and character set, to aid the Web browser.

■ Specify information about the document to be used by search engines, such as the Index Information Server. You'll learn more about this option in Chapter 26, "Indexing Your Web Site with Index Information Server."

The meta tag resides within the document header or, if you prefer, it is contained within the `<HEAD>` `</HEAD>` tag pair. The basic syntax for the meta tag is

```
<META HTTP-EQUIV="HTTPResponse" NAME="DocumentDescription"
➥CONTENT="ContentOption" URL="HTMLPathName">
```

HTTPResponse is an HTTP response header. The ContentOption either describes information associated with a given name or is a parameter for an associated HTTP response header. The HTMLPathName is most often used when the HTTPResponse parameter is set to REFRESH to load the associated document. The DocumentDescription is a name to be associated with the document. You can have multiple meta tags with a single name parameter within a document. However, you cannot include a name parameter if you use the HTTP-EQUIV parameter within the same meta tag. Instead, you must create multiple meta tags.

Using the meta tag can be a bit confusing, so perhaps a few examples will help. The following meta tag creates a document that will automatically reload itself after five seconds:

```
<META HTTP-EQUIV="REFRESH" CONTENT=5>
```

To automatically load another document after five seconds, create a meta tag in this form:

```
<META HTTP-EQUIV="REFRESH" CONTENT=5 URL=http://www.domainname.com/
➥documentname.htm>
```

If you change the name of the URL for each page that is loaded, you can load a series of documents one after the other. Cascading a series of documents in this fashion produces a simple animation effect.

The following format specifies a series of keywords for a document about style sheets, which a search engine could use:

```
<META HTTP-EQUIV="Keywords" CONTENT="HTML Reference, Style Sheets, CSS1">
```

Or to inform a Web browser of the specific content type and character set of your document, you could use this form:

```
<META HTTP-EQUIV="Content-Type" CONTENT="text/html; charset=iso-8859-1">
```

Meta tags have other uses as well, but they usually depend on the tools you use (Web browser, Web editor, search engine, and so on). So it pays to spend some time with your documentation for these tools to see how to best use meta tags.

12

AN HTML PRIMER

Summary

Wow, this chapter is intense, and yet it only teaches the basics of HTML programming. This chapter introduces text-manipulation techniques and explains how to create lists, embed images, create links and tables, and use frames and style sheets with your standard ASCII editor.

For more information about the HTML specification, please refer to Appendix B. It includes as much of a description of the current HTML 3.2 specification as I could find on the Internet in an easily digestible format. Keep in mind that HTML is a moving target. It changes rapidly, and the only way to keep up is to use the Internet as an information resource.

Designing and Managing a Web Site with FrontPage

IN THIS CHAPTER

- Installing FrontPage   408

- FrontPage Server   410

- Changing the Default Port of FrontPage Server   411

- FrontPage Server Administrator   412

- FrontPage Explorer   416

- FrontPage To Do List   419

- Verifying Links   420

- FrontPage Editor   421

CHAPTER 13

FrontPage is a powerful Web site development tool. You can use it not only to edit Web pages but also to manage your Web site. The next few sections explain how you can use FrontPage to develop and manage the contents of a Web site. You can obtain more information about FrontPage from Microsoft's Web site.

NOTE

You can find the Microsoft FrontPage Web site at http://www.microsoft.com/frontpage.

Installing FrontPage

Installing FrontPage is as easy as downloading it from Microsoft's Web site and running setup.exe. When the FrontPage installation program is executed, it will display a dialog box similar to the one shown in Figure 13.1. Use this dialog box to specify the directory in which you want to install FrontPage. You can also install three optional FrontPage components from the same dialog box. You should make sure the Client Software component, which consists of the FrontPage Explorer and Editor, is checked. Check the Personal Web Server check box if you want to install the FrontPage Server on your system.

If your Web server is compatible with FrontPage Server Extensions, you do not have to install the FrontPage Web server. Visit the FrontPage Web site for the most up-to-date list of Web servers that FrontPage supports. At the time of this writing, FrontPage Server Extensions are compatible with the Microsoft Internet Information Server, Netscape Commerce Server, Netscape Communications Server, Netscape Enterprise Server, Netscape Fasttrack Server, and WebSite.

NOTE

If you select to install the Personal Web Server component, be sure no other Web server is running on port 80 of your system. If another Web server is using port 80, the FrontPage Web server might have problems binding to port 80 of your server. If you'd like to install the FrontPage Server for testing purposes and have already installed a server such as Internet Information Server, you need to get the FrontPage Server to use a different port. Stop the other server for the duration of the installation process. After FrontPage is installed and its port is changed, you can continue to use the previous server as you did earlier. This process is explained in more detail later in the chapter.

FIGURE 13.1.

FrontPage component selection dialog box.

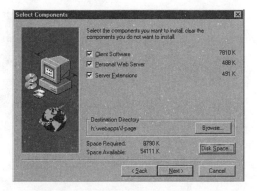

If you wish to install FrontPage extensions for your Web server, place a check mark in the Server Extensions check box and then click the Next button to continue.

Use the Select Program Folder dialog box shown in Figure 13.2 to select the folder in which FrontPage should be installed. When FrontPage is installed, the string of text you specify in Figure 13.2 will become a branch of the Windows NT Start menu. You can use the drop-down list to install FrontPage to an existing Start menu folder.

FIGURE 13.2.

Select Program Folder dialog box.

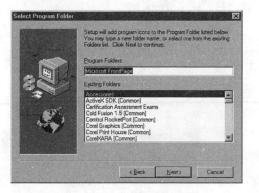

When all the files are copied, the installation program displays a dialog box identical to the one shown in Figure 13.3. FrontPage is now installed on your system. Before the installation program terminates, it might check the IP address of your system and display a confirmation dialog box. As soon as FrontPage is installed on your system, you can start the FrontPage Explorer by checking the check box in Figure 13.3.

FrontPage consists of several separate programs. Depending on the components you selected in Figure 13.1, the FrontPage installation program will install various FrontPage applications and insert them into a Start menu folder as shown in Figure 13.4.

FIGURE 13.3.
Setup Complete dialog box.

FIGURE 13.4.
FrontPage application icons.

FrontPage Server

If your Web server is not compatible with Windows NT, you can use FrontPage Server to experiment with FrontPage and create a Web site. After you create Web pages, you can transfer them to the production Web server. FrontPage Server looks similar to Figure 13.5. You can launch it from the Windows NT Start menu. You may need to edit several configuration files to configure FrontPage Server if you wish to run it on a port other than port 80.

FIGURE 13.5.
FrontPage Server.

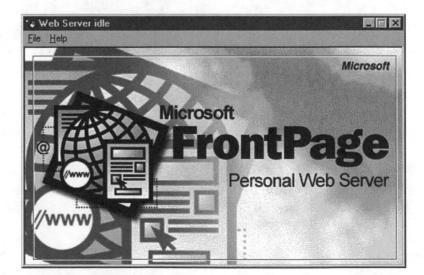

Changing the Default Port of FrontPage Server

By default, FrontPage Server is installed on port 80. If you have another Web server running on port 80, you will have a problem because both servers cannot share the same port. As described shortly, you can solve this problem by changing the default port of the FrontPage Server; to do so, you need to edit several configuration files.

If you've already installed server extensions for the FrontPage Server, invoke the FrontPage Server Administrator application and select Uninstall to remove server extensions from the FrontPage Server. You can reinstall server extensions after you change the port number.

You can change the port that the FrontPage Server uses by editing the file `H:\FrontPageWebs\Server\conf\httpd.cnf`, assuming you installed the FrontPage Server in the `H:\FrontPageWebs` directory. To change the port of the FrontPage Server, locate the line containing the server port information and type in the new port number, as shown in Figure 13.6.

13

DESIGNING A
WEB SITE WITH
FRONTPAGE

FIGURE 13.6.

You can modify the default port of the FrontPage Server by editing the httpd.cnf *file.*

```
# Port: The port the standalone listens to. 80 is the network standard.
#
Port 1200
```

You can now install server extensions for the FrontPage Server and start it in a different port. If you had another Web server running on port 80, you can restart that Web server and use it as usual.

FrontPage Server Administrator

The FrontPage Server Administrator manages server extensions installed on various Web servers managed with FrontPage. You can also use it to make sure Web server extensions are installed properly as well as to enable and disable authoring on a server. The next few sections discuss how you can use FrontPage Server Administrator to manage and administer server extensions. When it is first invoked, the FrontPage Server Administrator dialog box lists Web servers that can be authored with FrontPage as shown in Figure 13.7. By default, if you selected to install the FrontPage Server, only contents of the FrontPage Server can be managed using FrontPage Explorer. As you will learn shortly, managing and authoring the contents of a Web site is easy when you use FrontPage Explorer.

FrontPage Server Extensions have to be installed on a server before you can use FrontPage Explorer to manage the server. Therefore, you should install FrontPage Server Extensions for your Web server as shown in the next section. Make sure FrontPage supports your Web server before attempting to install FrontPage Server Extensions on your Web server. If FrontPage does not support your Web server, you can still use the FrontPage Server to design and manage the contents of your Web site. In the latter case, skip the following section and proceed to the section "Managing Server Extensions."

Installing Server Extensions

Installing server extensions for additional Web servers that FrontPage supports is easy. Click the Install button in the dialog box shown in Figure 13.7 to install server extensions for an existing Web server. Use the dialog box similar to the one shown in Figure 13.8 to select the type of your Web server and press OK to continue. Note that for this demonstration, I am installing FrontPage Server Extensions on a WebSite Web server that is configured to run on port 200. (Again, when changing the port number of a secondary Web server running on your server, do not follow my example and use a port number below 1024. Always use port numbers above 1024 to avoid potential conflicts.)

FIGURE 13.7.

FrontPage Server Administrator dialog box.

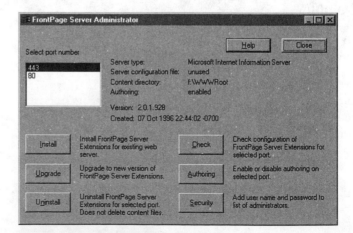

FIGURE 13.8.

Configure Server Type dialog box.

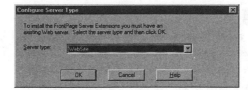

FrontPage will gather information about your Web server and display a confirmation dialog box similar to the one shown in Figure 13.9. Simply click OK to continue, and FrontPage will install server extensions for the Web server you selected earlier. If you are installing FrontPage Server Extensions on a WebSite Web server and it is configured for multiple domain names, enter multiple domain name information when prompted. Otherwise, skip the dialog box asking for multiple domain name information and click OK to continue.

FIGURE 13.9.

Confirmation dialog box.

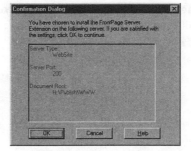

After you install server extensions for a new Web server, its port appears in the FrontPage Server Administrator dialog box, as shown in Figure 13.10. You can then configure server extensions and authoring settings for each server by selecting the server port you want to administer and following the directions given in the next section.

FIGURE 13.10.

The FrontPage Server Administrator dialog box after installing server extensions for an additional Web server.

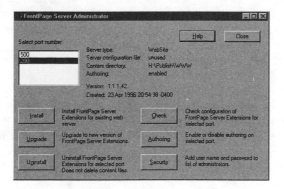

Managing Server Extensions

The Upgrade button of the dialog box shown in Figure 13.10 upgrades server extensions of a Web server to the server extensions of the current version of FrontPage. This feature is particularly useful after upgrading to a newer version of FrontPage. When you click the Upgrade button, the dialog box shown in Figure 13.11 asks for confirmation to upgrade the server extensions of the selected Web server.

FIGURE 13.11.

Server extensions
upgrade confirmation.

The Uninstall button uninstalls server extensions from a Web server. When you click Uninstall, the dialog box shown in Figure 13.12 prompts you to confirm your selection before it begins the uninstall process. As mentioned in Figure 13.12, Uninstall deletes only FrontPage Server Extensions, not the contents of a Web site.

FIGURE 13.12.

Server extensions
Uninstall dialog box.

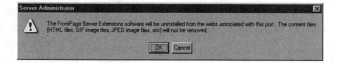

You can verify whether server extensions for a Web server have been installed properly by using the Check button. If server extensions have been installed properly, the dialog box in Figure 13.13 is displayed when you click the Check button. If you do not see this dialog box, you can use the Install button to reinstall FrontPage Server Extensions.

FIGURE 13.13.

The Check button of
the FrontPage Server
Administrator verifies
the status of server
extensions installed on a
Web server.

The Authoring button controls the ability to author a Web server's content using FrontPage. When the Authoring button is clicked, the dialog box shown in Figure 13.14 confirms that you want to change authoring settings on the specified Web server.

FIGURE 13.14.
Enable/Disable
Authoring dialog box.

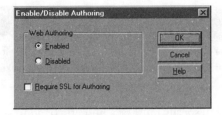

The Security button administers various security settings of FrontPage Server Extensions. You use it to assign a password to a Web site that contains documents managed by FrontPage as well as to limit which computers can manage a Web site using FrontPage Server Extensions.

When you click the Security button, the dialog box shown in Figure 13.15 appears. Specify a username and a password that can be used to author a Web site managed with FrontPage.

FIGURE 13.15.
You can use a username
and password to make
sure unauthorized
people do not make
changes to your Web
site using FrontPage.

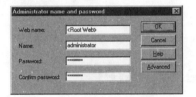

The Advanced button in the dialog box shown in Figure 13.15 controls which computers can use FrontPage to manage the contents of a Web site. If only computers in your domain will manage your Web site, you should change the default setting to match your domain name's IP address. Note that this dialog box accepts numeric Internet IP addresses. You can find your IP address by executing the FrontPage TCP_IP Test icon in the FrontPage Start menu folder. (Refer to Figure 13.4.) When the TCP_IP Test application is executed, it will display your IP address, as shown in Figure 13.16.

FIGURE 13.16.
The FrontPage TCP/IP
Test application finds
the IP address of your
computer.

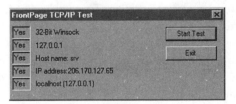

To prevent other computers from using FrontPage to change your Web site, enter your IP address in the dialog box shown in Figure 13.17.

> **NOTE**
>
> Note that even if you do not specify an IP address in Figure 13.17, FrontPage still requests a username and a password before someone can make changes to your Web site.

The IP address you specify must be a numeric IP address that has four digits (1-256) separated by periods. A wildcard character (*) can be used instead of a digit. For example, 128.*.*.* allows all computers whose IP addresses begin with 128 to administer a FrontPage Web site.

FIGURE 13.17.
Internet address restriction dialog box.

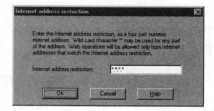

FrontPage Explorer

FrontPage Explorer is a powerful utility that enables you to view your Web site from various perspectives. You can also use File Manager or Windows NT Explorer to view the content of a Web site, but the information you get is limited. For example, although you will probably see several directories and files when you look at your document root directory using Windows NT Explorer, you will not be able to find out what these files are, what they contain, or if they have any URLs that point to your Web site or other Web sites. Most important, you have no way of finding out whether the hyperlinks at your Web site actually work unless you check them individually.

FrontPage Explorer solves all these problems by enabling Web site developers to look at Web sites they create in a new perspective. This section explains how you can use FrontPage Explorer to effortlessly manage the contents of a Web site. When it is first invoked, FrontPage Explorer resembles the window in Figure 13.18. Select File | Open Web from the dialog box shown in Figure 13.18 to invoke the Open FrontPage Web dialog box. (See Figure 13.19.) After selecting a Web using the Open FrontPage Web dialog box, you can manage it with FrontPage Explorer.

After invoking the Open FrontPage Web dialog box, type in the address of your server, as shown in Figure 13.19. If the server you want to manage is not installed in port 80, specify its port name by putting a colon before the port number. When you click the List Webs button, you will see the various Webs installed on the Web server you selected. Select <Root Web> as shown in the Open FrontPage Web dialog box and click OK to continue. You will then have to type in a username and password to administer the Web you selected.

FIGURE 13.18.
FrontPage Explorer.

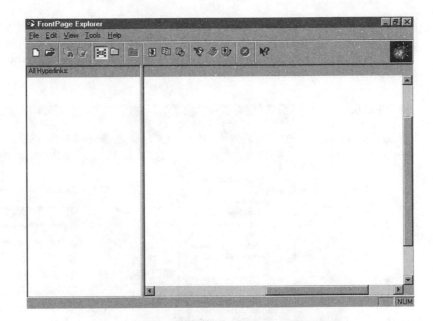

FIGURE 13.19.
Open FrontPage Web dialog box.

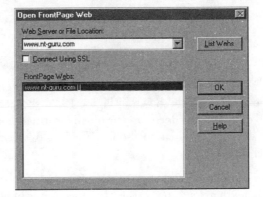

FrontPage Explorer will then extract information about the Web selected in Figure 13.19 and display the information graphically, as shown in Figure 13.20. After you install FrontPage, it defaults to the summary view. Select View | Link View from the Menu bar to change to Link View. As you can see in Figure 13.20, the Outline View pane lists various home pages and the Link View pane graphically displays various URLs that are part of the Web page selected in Outline View.

If you want to edit a Web page shown in Link View, simply double-click it. You will then be able to edit it using the FrontPage Editor. Note the plus and minus buttons that appear to the upper-left corner of some Web pages. Also note how the Web tree of the page selected in

Figure 13.20 is expanded and the minus sign that appears in the upper-left corner of this page. A plus sign in the upper-left corner of a Web page means that the document contains URLs that link to other Web pages. If you click the plus sign, it changes to a minus sign and you will see all the URLs in that page, as shown in Figure 13.20.

FIGURE 13.20.

FrontPage Explorer displays a graphical view of the contents of a Web site.

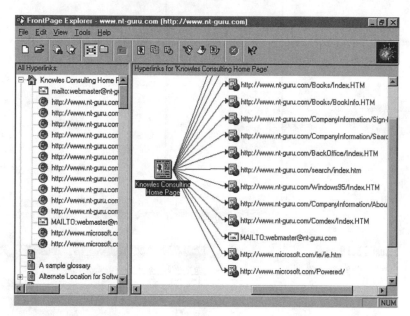

Although the graphical view shown in Figure 13.20 shows how Web pages in a Web site are connected to each other, it does not give much information about files at a Web site. You can obtain more detailed information about a Web site by selecting View | Summary View from the main menu.

As you can see in Figure 13.21, Summary View is ideal for obtaining detailed information about a Web site. Note that you can sort the various columns in Summary View by clicking the description label at the top of each column. This feature is powerful. For example, certain Web pages at your Web site might use graphic files that are too large to be transferred over a POTS link in a reasonable period of time. You can identify these graphic files by clicking the Size column and sorting the files based on their file size.

As you can see in Figure 13.21, FrontPage Explorer is a powerful tool that you can use to graphically manage the contents of a Web site. FrontPage Explorer enables you to exploit the capabilities of FrontPage because it is integrated with various components of FrontPage, such as the To Do List and the program that verifies URLs of Web pages. Be sure to spend some time with FrontPage Explorer to become more familiar with it and realize its potential.

FIGURE 13.21.

Summary View can help you obtain detailed information about various files at a Web site.

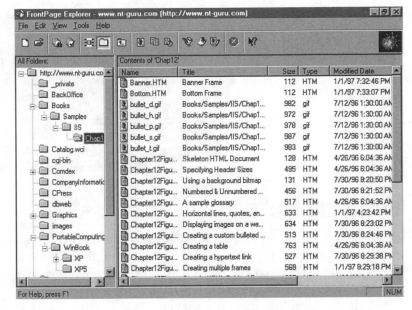

FrontPage To Do List

The FrontPage To Do List keeps track of various tasks, as shown in Figure 13.22. Because it is integrated with other components of FrontPage, such as the program that checks for broken links, the FrontPage To Do List is ideal for keeping track of various tasks that have to be done to maintain a Web site. You can invoke the FrontPage To Do List by selecting Tools | Show To Do List from the main menu.

FIGURE 13.22.

FrontPage To Do List.

Click the Add button to add new tasks to the To Do List. The dialog box shown in Figure 13.23 gathers information (name, description, and priority level) about the task being added to the To Do List.

FIGURE 13.23.

*Adding a task to the
FrontPage To Do List.*

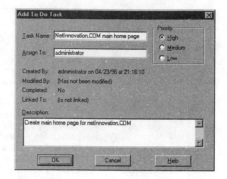

Verifying Links

At some point your Web pages are probably going to contain URLs for objects that no longer exist. You should plan to check your Web site periodically for "broken links." FrontPage includes a utility (select Tools | Verify Links from the main menu) that you can use to verify links at a Web site. As Figure 13.24 shows, the Verify Links utility can locate invalid URLs of a Web site as well as Web pages that contain them.

FIGURE 13.24.

*FrontPage can verify
URLs of a Web page.*

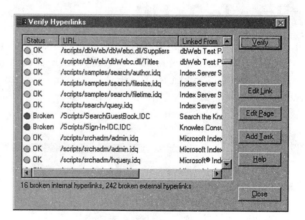

You can add a broken link to the To Do List so you can take care of it another time. (Refer to Figure 13.22.) To add an invalid URL to the To Do List, click the Add Task button, as shown in Figure 13.24. You can correct broken links immediately by clicking the Edit Link button and correcting the URL as shown in Figure 13.25. Also, you can use the Edit Page button to edit the Web page containing the broken URL.

FIGURE 13.25.
FrontPage can verify
URLs of a Web page.

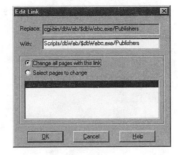

FrontPage Editor

The FrontPage Editor is a powerful WYSIWYG HTML editor that can create Web pages with tables, frames, and other HTML 2.0 enhancements. The purpose of this section is to cover a few key features of the FrontPage Editor and highlight some of its capabilities.

Designing Web Pages Using the FrontPage Editor

The FrontPage Editor is a powerful HTML editor that you can use to create and edit Web pages. Although you can invoke the FrontPage Editor as a stand-alone application or through the FrontPage Explorer, you should open an existing Web before you open the FrontPage Explorer. This method enables you to use features of FrontPage Explorer to create and edit Web pages.

I suggest that you take the time to become familiar with FrontPage Explorer because you can use it to view Web pages at a Web site in a more natural manner. In addition, you can edit Web pages simply by double-clicking them. The next few sections help you get started with FrontPage. First, though, bring up FrontPage Explorer, select a Web, and then select Tools | Show FrontPage Editor from the main menu. These steps enable you to save Web documents edited with FrontPage in an existing Web.

Document Attributes

You can use the FrontPage Editor to define various document-formatting attributes of a Web page. For example, when creating a new document, you might want to assign colors to various elements of the Web page. To do so, select File | Page Properties from the main menu. You can use the Page Properties dialog box, shown in Figure 13.26, to assign a title to a Web page and customize its appearance.

FIGURE 13.26.

Page Properties dialog box.

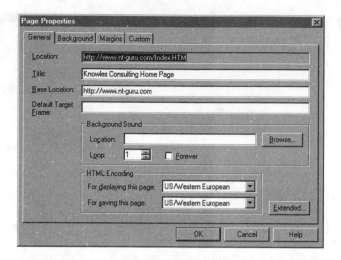

You can format text in a Web page by first selecting the text using the mouse and then selecting Format | Font from the main menu. Use the dialog box shown in Figure 13.27 to format the text you selected; for example, the Color drop-down box enables you to change the color of selected text. This feature is handy for emphasizing a paragraph or heading. After selecting various text-formatting options, click OK to apply them to the selected text.

FIGURE 13.27.

Formatting text using the Font dialog box.

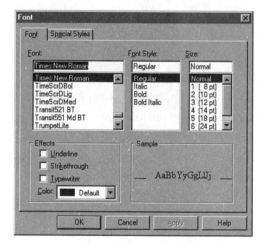

Frames

Frames can make a Web site easier to navigate and more interesting when they are used properly, and FrontPage enables you to create multiframe Web pages with ease. To create a Web page with frames, select File | New from the main menu. Use the scroll-down list in the next dialog box to select Frames Wizard, as shown in Figure 13.28, and click OK to continue.

13

DESIGNING A
WEB SITE WITH
FRONTPAGE

FIGURE 13.28.

*Frames Wizard helps
you create a Web page
with frames.*

The frame creation dialog box, shown in Figure 13.29, enables you to create a multiframe Web page using a custom grid or frames template. Generally, you should create a multiframe Web page using a custom grid if you are familiar with frames and have an unusual frame set in mind. If not, create a Web page using a frames template by selecting Pick a template and clicking the Next button.

FIGURE 13.29.

*The frame creation
technique dialog box.*

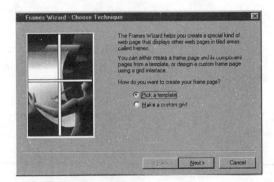

Use the frame layout selection dialog box (see Figure 13.30) to select the layout of various frames on your Web page. Select a layout you like and click OK. When selecting the layout of frames, be considerate of users who might browse your Web site with 640×480 resolution monitors. Always resize your Web browser window to 640×480 pixels and examine every frame set you create to make sure everything is legible.

FIGURE 13.30.

*The frame layout
selection dialog box.*

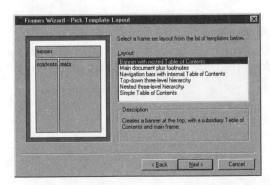

When creating Web pages with frames, be aware that some Web browsers do not support frames. Although the percentage of users using technologically challenged Web browsers is getting smaller, you should make sure a user browsing your Web site with an older browser can still view the contents of your Web site. You can specify an alternate Web page to show to users whose browsers do not support frames in the dialog box shown in Figure 13.31.

FIGURE 13.31.

Alternate content page URL for Web browsers that do not support frames.

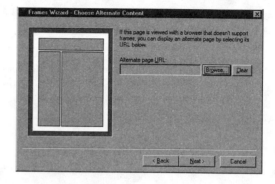

FrontPage will finally ask you for the title and filename of your multiframe Web page, as shown in Figure 13.32. Fill in the information requested and click the Finish button to continue. FrontPage will then create your multiframe Web page.

FIGURE 13.32.

Page information dialog box.

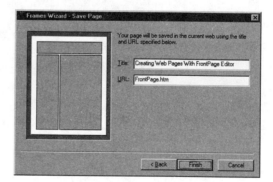

If you go back to FrontPage Explorer, you will see the multiframe Web page that was just created, as shown in Figure 13.33. Note how the new Web page is broken into three separate Web pages, each of which holds the contents of a frame. You can edit a frame by selecting and double-clicking the corresponding file in the Link View pane of FrontPage Explorer.

FIGURE 13.33.

*A new multiframe
document viewed with
FrontPage Explorer.
Double-click various
frames to edit them.*

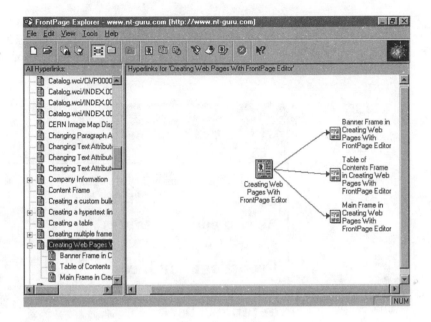

Tables

To insert a table into a Web page, select Table | Insert Table. You can specify the number of
columns and rows for the table, as well as several other attributes, in the Insert Table dialog
box. (See Figure 13.34.)

FIGURE 13.34.

Insert Table dialog box.

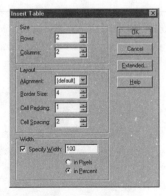

After a table is created, you can insert text and images into various cells the same way you insert
text and images into regular Web pages. To insert images, select Insert | Image from the main
menu. By default, a two-column table has equal-width columns. As shown in Figure 13.35,

this arrangement is not always ideal. The image in Figure 13.35 is small because the left column takes up too much space. You can fix this problem by placing the mouse pointer on the left column and clicking the right mouse button. You will then see the pop-up menu shown in Figure 13.35.

FIGURE 13.35.

You can use the right mouse button to format cells in a table.

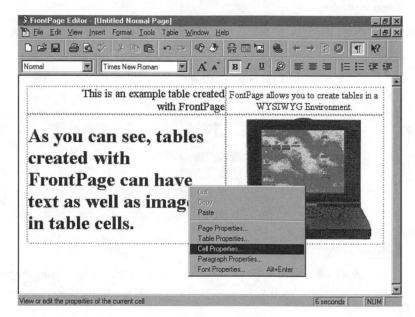

Select Cell Properties to display the Cell Properties dialog box (see Figure 13.36) in which you can define the width of a column. To reduce the width of the left column, specify a lower percentage value. A cell width value of 30 percent is used in this example to reduce the size of the left column.

FIGURE 13.36.

Cell Properties dialog box.

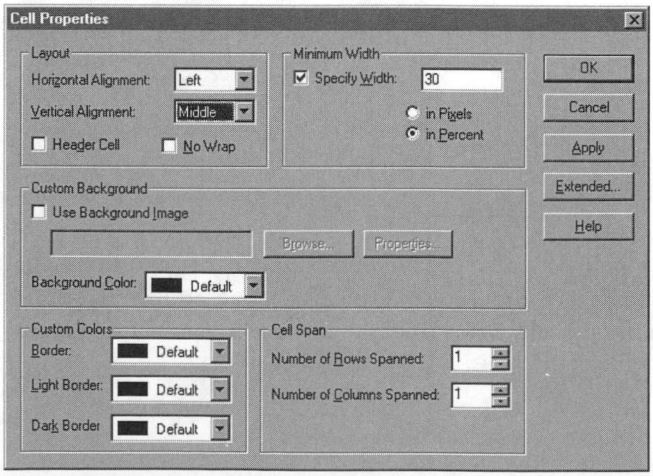

Figure 13.37 shows the results of the modification made in Figure 13.36. Tables are useful for formatting the contents of a Web site. As demonstrated in this example, you can use the right mouse button to format table cells and to have more control over their contents.

FIGURE 13.37.
The table after its left column size is reduced.

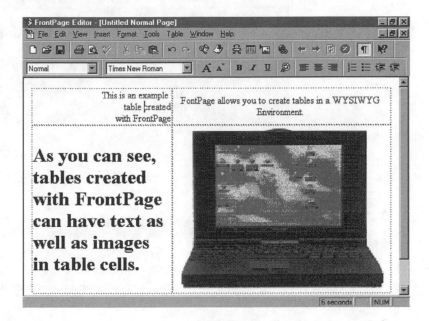

FrontPage Scripts

FrontPage scripts enable you to effortlessly add CGI programs to a Web site. For example, you can use scripts to set up a guest book at your Web site in just a few minutes. Setting up a guest book is as simple as Selecting File | New from the main menu and selecting the Guest Book option as shown in Figure 13.38.

FIGURE 13.38.
Selecting the Guest Book template.

The Guest Book template is loaded into the FrontPage Editor as shown in Figure 13.39. You can customize the Guest Book page by changing the font and maybe adding a few images. Select File | Save from the main menu to save the Guest Book Web page.

FIGURE 13.39.

Editing the Guest Book Web page.

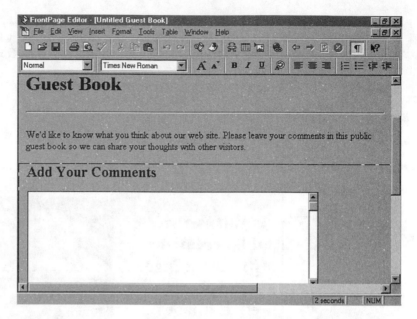

The Save As dialog box, shown in Figure 13.40, is where you save the Guest Book Web page and give it a title. After typing in a title for the Web page and a filename for the guest book, click the OK button to save the file.

FIGURE 13.40.

Saving the Guest Book Web page.

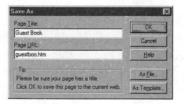

Users can now connect to your Web server and sign your guest book using the filename specified in Figure 13.40. Figure 13.41 shows how a user can connect to your Web server and sign the guest book.

When a user types in a guest book entry and clicks the Submit Comments button, the information is sent to a FrontPage Common Gateway Interface (CGI) program for processing. After the information is processed, FrontPage displays a confirmation message, as shown in Figure 13.42. This message also has a link to the previous page.

When a user either clicks the link to go back to the previous page or manually goes back and reloads the Guest Book Web page, the newly added entry will be displayed, as shown in Figure 13.43. As you can see from this example, CGI applications that are built into FrontPage are powerful. For example, a guest book can be set up using FrontPage—without writing a single line of CGI code—in about five minutes. Experiment with other FrontPage CGI scripts and incorporate them into your Web site to make it more interactive.

FIGURE 13.41.

The guest book you set up using the FrontPage Editor is immediately functional.

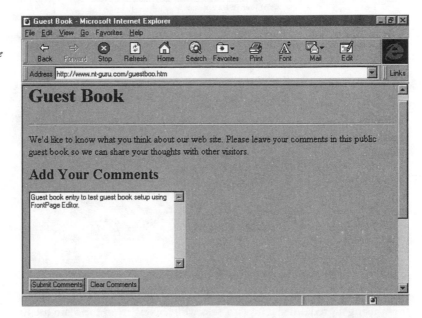

FIGURE 13.42.

Guest book entry confirmation message.

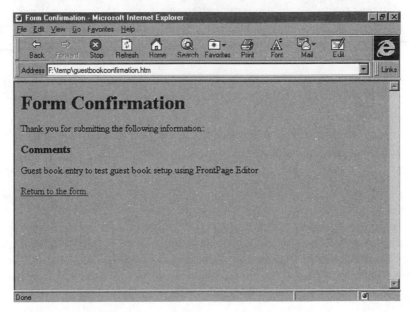

FIGURE 13.43.

Another guest book entry confirmation message.

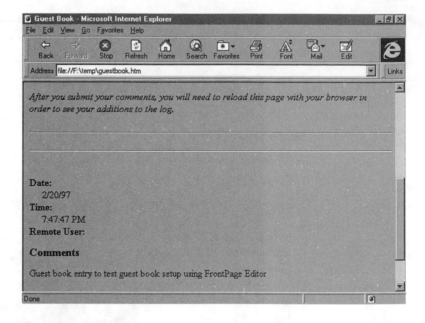

Using Templates to Create Web Pages

Another way to create Web pages is to use predefined document templates. To create a document using a predefined template, select File | New from the main menu and select a template that best resembles the page you wish to create. Experiment with various FrontPage templates and become more familiar with using them. Using templates to create routine Web pages is a great time-saver.

Summary

FrontPage is a powerful, user-friendly Web page development application that you can use to manage the contents of a Web site. Because FrontPage is part of Microsoft Office, it will probably be integrated with various Microsoft Office applications in the future. FrontPage enables you to create interactive Web pages without writing CGI programs or worrying about details of HTML; it is an ideal application for creating content for a Web site.

Microsoft Office is a powerful suite of productivity applications. You can use various Internet Assistants for Microsoft Office to effortlessly publish content for the Web using Microsoft applications. These Internet Assistants are especially useful for converting large amounts of MS Office files into HTML so they can be published on the global Internet or a local intranet. The next chapter demonstrates how to use Microsoft Word, Excel, Access, and PowerPoint to create content for the World Wide Web.

Publishing on the Web with Microsoft Office

CHAPTER 14

IN THIS CHAPTER

- Publishing on the Web with Microsoft Office 97   432

- Publishing on the Web with Microsoft Office 95   446

At the time this chapter was written, the demand for Microsoft Office 97 was extreme to say the least. If you were fortunate enough to have obtained a copy of Microsoft Office 97, then you were one of the lucky ones. Of course, by the time you actually read this, I expect Microsoft to have caught up with the demand, and Office 97 will be available everywhere. One reason for the high demand is that Microsoft Office can convert existing documents, spreadsheets, databases, or slide shows to HTML documents for publishing on the World Wide Web. Someone who puts together a sales report, for example, is probably not a Web developer. Having someone else convert the sales report into an HTML file is not only a waste of resources but also a time-consuming task. On the other hand, using Office 97, the person who created the sales report can easily publish the information on the Internet or an intranet without waiting for someone else to comb through the sales report and add a few funny HTML tags here and there.

Of course, you don't need Office 97 to convert your existing data to HTML documents. Instead, you could use one of the Internet Assistants for Office 95 or Word 6.0. In all fairness, though, I do have to admit that the Internet Assistants are pretty rough and of only limited usefulness when compared to Office 97. The Internet Assistants were precursors to the tools embedded in Office 97. And although I still like to use FrontPage for some of my Web page development efforts, I have found that in some circumstances Microsoft Word 97 is a better WYSIWYG HTML editor. It will display text within the <Marquee> tags, for example, as moving text rather than as a static text string. These little details can make a big difference in the amount of time you spend tweaking a page.

This chapter looks at both of these offerings from Microsoft, starting with the Office 97 products and then moving to the Internet Assistants for the Office 95 products. By demonstrating some of the differences between the products, this information can help you decide if you need to upgrade to Office 97 from Office 95. Not every reader will want, or be able, to upgrade his or her existing Office 95 installed user base.

For more information on using the Internet Assistants to publish content on the Internet, check out the Microsoft Office Web site.

URL

The Microsoft Office Web site is located at http://www.microsoft.com/msoffice/.

Publishing on the Web with Microsoft Office 97

The following sections explain how you can use Word, Excel, PowerPoint, and Access to publish content on the Internet or on your intranet. Before you explore these areas, however, I want to point out some of the key requirements for installing the HTML development tools for Office 97.

Installing Office 97 for Web Development

If you have already installed Microsoft Office 97 and did not choose a custom or a complete installation, then you will need to rerun the setup program to install the Web authoring tools and various HTML converters and wizards. Whether you are installing for the first time or reinstalling, make sure you select the following options:

■ In the Microsoft Office 97 – Custom dialog box, as shown in Figure 14.1, make sure you enable the Web Page Authoring (HTML) check box. This option will install most of the HTML tools for Microsoft Word, Excel, and PowerPoint. Unfortunately, it will not install them all.

FIGURE 14.1.

Installing the Web Page Authoring tools for Microsoft Office 97.

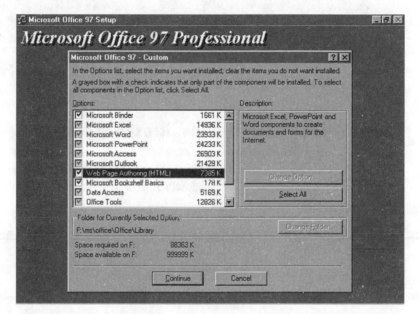

■ Also in the Microsoft Office 97 – Custom dialog box, click the Change Option button to display the Microsoft Office 97 – Converters and Filters dialog box. Then select the Text Converters option and click the Change Option button to display the Microsoft Office 97 – Text Converters dialog box. At this point, scroll down to the last entry in the Options list and enable the HTML Converter entry. This entry installs a converter so that you can import and export HTML documents.

■ Finally, in the Microsoft Office 97 – Custom dialog box, select the Data Access entry and click the Change Option button to display the Microsoft Office 97 – Data Access dialog box. Select the Database Drivers entry and click the Change Option button to display the Microsoft Office 97 – Database Drivers dialog box. Enable the Text and HTML Driver.

If these instructions are too confusing, you can just click the Select All button in the Microsoft Office 97 – Custom dialog box, which installs all of Office 97. All 191MB of it! If you still have some free space and want to consume a few additional megabytes, be sure to check out the Microsoft ValuPack. You will find a few animated GIF files to spice up your Web pages and additional texture files to use as backgrounds. You will also find a tool called WebPost that you can use to package an entire Web site to send to a Web server.

> ## WARNING
>
> If you are installing Office 97 over a previous Office 95 installation with the Internet Assistants installed, I highly recommend that you remove the Internet Assistants first. Otherwise, you might encounter various problems with Word, Excel, PowerPoint, and Access. The Internet Assistant for Microsoft Word 95, for example, stores an HTML.DOT and HTMLVIEW.DOT template in the *OfficeRoot*\Template directory. These templates add menu commands and macros to Word 95 that are not fully compatible with Word 97.

Publishing on the Web with Microsoft Word 97

Publishing on the Web with Microsoft Word 97 couldn't be easier. Really! Word 97 provides a WYSIWYG editing environment for creating and editing HTML documents. It also includes a wizard to help you get started. To actually create an HTML document, choose File | New, which displays the New dialog box, shown in Figure 14.2.

FIGURE 14.2.

Creating a new HTML document with Microsoft Office 97.

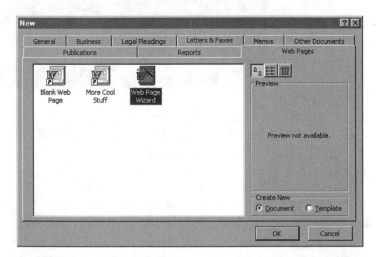

Select the Web Page Wizard and click the OK button. The Web Page Wizard will step you through the process of creating a Web page, as shown in Figure 14.3. One of the most interesting features of the Web Page Wizard is that it interacts with the user. If you double-click an entry in the dialog box, the Web Page Wizard will update the HTML document on the fly so that you can preview the document that will be created.

FIGURE 14.3.

Creating an HTML document using the Microsoft Office 97 Web Page Wizard.

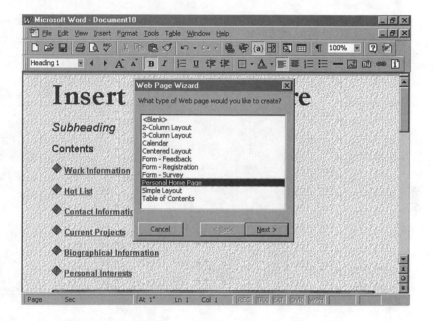

Once you have selected the type of page you want the Web Page Wizard to create, click the Next button. Then select a background for your Web page from the fully interactive dialog box, shown in Figure 14.4. If you double-click an entry, the selected background will be immediately applied to the Web page. You can preview the document and choose a color combination that suits your style.

FIGURE 14.4.

Choosing the background for your Web page with the Microsoft Office 97 Web Page Wizard.

Once you have selected your background, click the Finish button and the HTML document template will be created as shown in Figure 14.5. As you can see, it's not quite ready for publication. Before you can place it on your Web site, you will need to edit the document. Once

14

PUBLISHING ON THE WEB WITH MICROSOFT OFFICE

you have completed your edits, use Save as HTML from the File menu to save it as an HTML document.

FIGURE 14.5.

The home page template created with the Microsoft Office 97 Web Page Wizard.

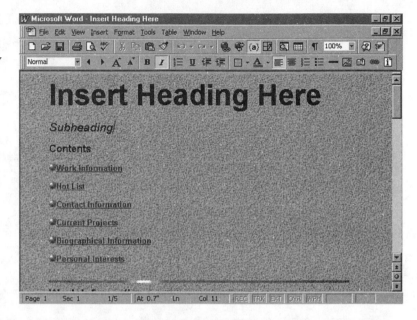

URL

The Microsoft Word Web page is at http://www.microsoft.com/msword/.

Changing Background Colors and Textures

If you don't like the default background for your Web page or you are designing one from scratch, then you'll be happy to know that changing the background is quite easy. Select Format | Background and then choose one of the following:

- ■ No Fill—Removes any background color or texture currently assigned to the document.

- ■ A color—This item is not really a menu option; it is an 8 × 5 color grid. You can select any element on the grid as the document background color.

- ■ More Colors—Displays the Colors dialog box. This dialog box allows you to choose a color from the Standard property sheet or create a custom color using the Custom property sheet. With the Custom property sheet, you may specify a color using the sliders in the Colors list; a color based on the Hue, Saturation, and Luminance; or a color based on specific red, green, or blue values.

- ■ Fill Effects—Displays the Fill Effects dialog box from which you can choose one of the predefined textures. If none of these textures is suitable, you may choose an alternative by clicking the Other Texture button. Other Texture lets you import any graphic image for which you have an import filter and automatically export it as a GIF or JPEG when you save the file. This feature is really cool! I have several very expensive HTML editors that don't have this much flexibility.

Changing Font Attributes

Changing the fonts in your HTML document is just as easy as changing your background. Select Format | Font to change the typeface, size, color, or various attributes including bold, italic, underline, strikethrough, superscript, or subscript. Two other Format menu commands are Text Colors and Change Case. The Text Colors command specifies the default colors for base text, hyperlinks, and a previously selected hyperlink. The Change Case command changes the case of selected text. You can toggle the case, convert upper to lower, convert lower to upper, or perform various other case conversions. Change Case can be quite useful, for example, when you've typed a whole page with the Caps Lock key depressed.

Inserting Objects

Word 97 does not restrict your ability to insert objects into your HTML documents. Not only can you insert any OLE object into your document, but you can also insert any of the following items from the Insert menu:

- Horizontal Line—A line divider used to break a document into upper and lower portions. You can insert just the basic divider as defined by the <hr> tag or insert a predefined graphic image as a divider. You can even insert third-party lines by clicking on the More button and browsing for the line divider. Word will even preview the graphic to make sure you've selected the right image file.

- Picture—Enables you to insert a piece of clip art, any image for which you have an Import filter, an image snarfed from another Web page, a scanned-in image, or a chart.

- Video—Enables you to insert an MPEG or AVI file directly into your Web page. You can also provide an alternative image to be shown for Web browsers that do not support video files, alternative text for Web browsers that do not support graphic images, and various playback options.

- Background Sound—Enables you to specify a background sound (any support file format including, but not limited to, WAV, MID, and RMI) and various playback attributes. This sound file will be downloaded and played on the client's computer.

- Forms—Enables you to insert form controls (check box, option button, drop-down list box, list box, text box, text area, submit button, submit button based on a user-supplied image file, reset button, hidden-text field, or password field) directly into your document.

14

PUBLISHING ON THE WEB WITH MICROSOFT OFFICE

- Scrolling Text—Enables you to insert a marquee directly into your document simply by filling out a dialog box.

- HyperLink—Enables you to link a portion of your document to an external document. When the link is selected, the new page will be loaded.

- Bookmark—Enables you to insert a bookmark (or local link) into your document. Rather than jump to another page outside your document when chosen, the link applies only within the document. It's a fast way of navigating through a lengthy document.

Publishing on the Web with Microsoft Excel 97

Publishing data on the Internet with Excel 97 is even easier than using Word 97, primarily because Excel has fewer formatting options than Word has. To convert a spreadsheet to HTML, just follow these steps:

1. Select the cells in the worksheet to convert to an HTML document as shown in Figure 14.6.

FIGURE 14.6.

Converting a selected region in an Excel spreadsheet to an HTML document.

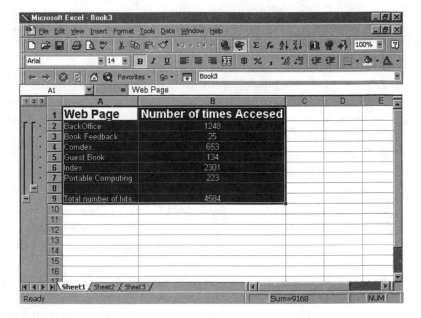

2. Choose Save as HTML from the File menu, and the Internet Assistant Wizard – Step 1 of 4 dialog box, shown in Figure 14.7, will appear. If the selected area—as specified in the Ranges and charts to convert field—is not correct, you may change the cell region by clicking on the Add button to add cells or the Remove button to remove specific cells. Once you have finished your selection, click the Next button.

FIGURE 14.7.

Choosing the region in an Excel spreadsheet to convert to an HTML document.

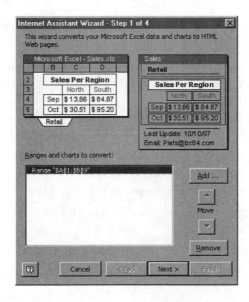

3. Choose an option from the Internet Assistant Wizard – Step 2 of 4 dialog. You can either create a standalone HTML document or use an existing document and insert your table into it. If you choose to insert a table into an existing document, just insert a `<!--##Table##-->` tag as a placeholder for the table. Click the Next button to continue. The rest of this discussion assumes you chose the standalone document option.

The Internet Assistant Wizard – Step 3 of 4 dialog box will appear as shown in Figure 14.8.

FIGURE 14.8.

Specifying additional content for the HTML document.

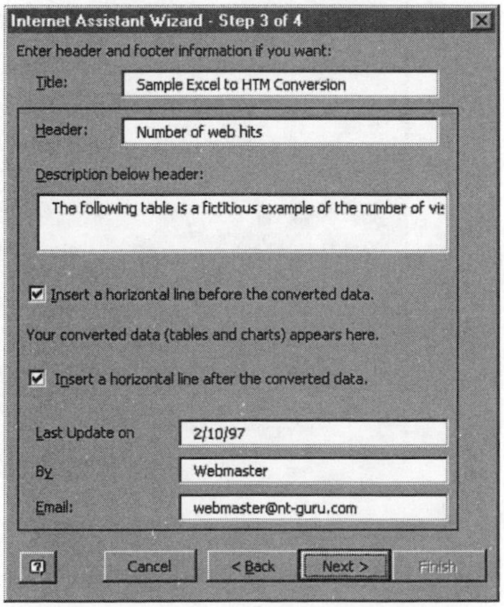

4. Enter a document title, which will be displayed in the Web browser's caption bar, in the Title field.

5. Specify a comment that describes the document in the Header field. This text will be displayed as the first text on the page in a large font, so try not to use more than a few words here.

6. Specify a document comment in the Description field that identifies the table and its content.

7. (Optional) Enable the Insert a horizontal line before the converted data or the Insert a horizontal line after the converted data check box if you want a horizontal line to be placed before or after the converted spreadsheet.

8. Enter today's date in the Last Update on field if it is not already filled out for you by the wizard.

9. Enter the name of the user to be identified with the HTML document in the By field.

10. Enter the e-mail address of the user specified in step 9 in the Email field. Then click the Next button.

11. Specify the code page to use for your document as well as the location to store the created HTML file in the Internet Assistant Wizard – Step 4 of 4 dialog. The location can be either a physical pathname or a relative path on a FrontPage Web.

12. Click the Finish button and the document will be created. (See Figure 14.9.)

FIGURE 14.9.

The converted HTML document.

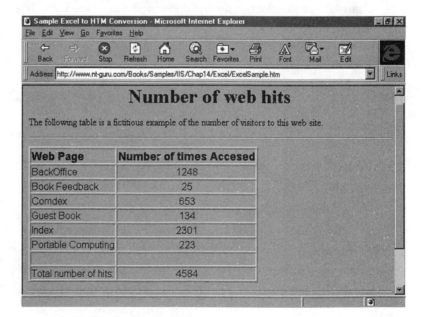

Another interesting wizard in Excel 97 is the Web Form Wizard. You can use this wizard to convert an existing spreadsheet into an HTML-based form to enter data into an ODBC database on your Web server. Like the Internet Assistant Wizard, the Web Form Wizard also steps you through the process of converting your spreadsheet. I expect that Microsoft will offer additional wizards from its Web site in the future.

URL

The Microsoft Excel Web page is at `http://www.microsoft.com/msexcel/`.

Publishing on the Web with Microsoft PowerPoint

Another one of my favorite Office applications is Microsoft PowerPoint. I often use PowerPoint to create slides for my lectures and classes. They provide a little structure for my discussion and help me make sure that I don't forget to cover a particular topic. Converting a set of slides to an HTML document is just as easy as converting an Excel spreadsheet to HTML. Let me show you just how easy it is by stepping though a conversion of a slide show I used for a personalized class I gave to new Windows NT Workstation users at AT&T:

1. Open your slide show and select the slides to convert to an HTML document. Then select File | Save as HTML. The Save as HTML dialog box will appear.

2. Click on the Next button to get started. The dialog will change to display information about the layout of your HTML page. This dialog allows you to select a previously saved layout. Because this is your first time, you don't have any previously saved layouts.

3. Click the Next button. The new dialog, as shown in Figure 14.10, asks you to choose a page style.

FIGURE 14.10.

Choosing a page style with the PowerPoint HTML Wizard.

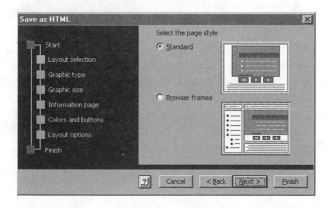

4. Choose either a standard layout—which is what I recommend—or a framed Web page. Click the Next button to continue. The rest of this discussion assumes you chose the Standard layout.

5. Specify the format for your graphic images when prompted for Graphic type information. The format can be GIF, JPEG, or PowerPoint animation—my personal favorite. The reason why I like to use PowerPoint animation is that the slide show doesn't just display an image of the slide. Instead, it follows the same transitions that you used when you created the original slide show. It also plays any associated sound events, so it has more of the look and feel of the original presentation. Click the Next button to continue.

6. Provide the Graphic size information when prompted. You have two options to select. First you can specify the monitor size for playback: 640 × 480, 800 × 600, 1024 × 768, or 1280 × 1024. Second, you can specify the size of the graphic image or slide to be displayed. The default is ½ the width of the screen, but I prefer to use ³⁄₄ of the screen. Make your selections and click the Next button to continue.

At this point the wizard needs to collect additional information from you. (See Figure 14.11.)

FIGURE 14.11.

Specifying user information for the PowerPoint HTML Wizard.

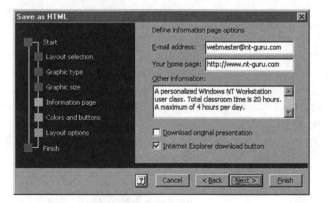

7. Specify the e-mail address of the contact in the E-mail address field, the home page of the Web site in the Your home page field, and an additional comment describing the slide show in the Other information field. If you want to allow the user to download the original slide show, enable the Download original presentation check box. If you create a PowerPoint animation, you should also enable the Internet Explorer download button so the user can download Internet Explorer 3.0 and view the slide show. Once you have made your selections, click the Next Button.

8. Tell the wizard whether to use the Web browser default colors or choose a custom color scheme. I recommend that you use the Web browser color scheme unless you have an overriding reason to specify a color choice. You may need to specify a hyperlink color that will not be the same color as your slide show background, for example. Make your choice and click the Next button to continue.

9. Choose a button style. These buttons are used to navigate through the slide show. Click the Next button to continue.

10. Specify the layout options, including the location of the buttons specified in the previous step (on the top, bottom, left, or right of the graphic image or slide). You may also choose to include any slide notes to be displayed on the HTML page by enabling the Include slide notes in pages check box.

11. Specify a location to create the HTML output in when prompted. After you have entered a path in the Folder field, click the Next button to continue.

12. Click the Finish button. Your HTML pages will be created; they will look similar to the animation shown in Figure 14.12. If you want to reuse these choices some time in the future, enter a name for the conversion settings at the prompt.

FIGURE 14.12.

The finished PowerPoint animation on the Web.

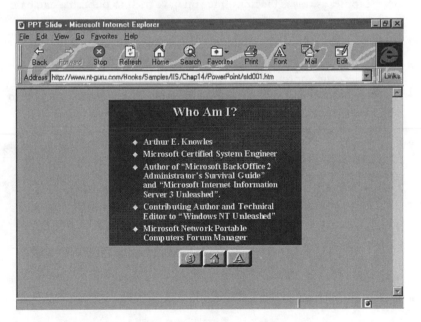

As with the rest of the Office 97 applications, you can check out the Microsoft Web site for additional wizards, tools, and tips. I check the site on a regular basis and recommend that you do so as well.

URL

The Microsoft PowerPoint Web page is at http://www.microsoft.com/mspowerpoint/.

Publishing on the Web with Microsoft Access

Publishing your databases on the Web is also possible with Microsoft Access. You can create both static and dynamic pages. Although you can create dynamic pages using an Access database, I recommend that you use SQL Server databases if at all possible. The ODBC drivers for non–SQL Server databases, such as Access, cannot handle high-usage volumes.

1. Choose File | Save as HTML form and the Publish to the Web Wizard dialog box will appear. This dialog box lets you choose an existing Web publication profile (the saved information from the following steps), which can be useful if you periodically refresh the Web page you'll be creating with the wizard. But first, you have to complete this whole process at least once and then save it. Because you probably do not have a profile, as this is the first time you have tried to publish a database, click the Next button.

   The dialog box now changes, as shown in Figure 14.13, to show tabs for the database tables, queries, forms, reports, and all objects.

2. Select the appropriate tab (I recommend that you write queries or reports to select and format your data) that contains the table, query, form, or report to convert to an HTML document and click the Next button to continue.

FIGURE 14.13.

Choosing the data to be exported to the Web document.

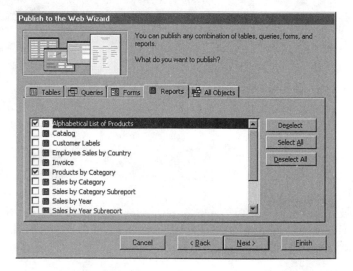

3. Supply a template file when prompted. This file can contain default buttons, background images, text, and so on to be merged with the HTML output the wizard will create. Make your selection and click the Next button to continue.

4. Select the type of HTML document to create. The type can be static (recommended) or dynamic. A dynamic HTML document will always display up-to-the-minute data, but it places a greater load on your server. In addition, a dynamic document can support only a few users (generally less than 64). Make your selection and click the Next button to continue.

5. Enter a location in which to create the documents. Click the Next button to continue.

6. Create a home page for your document by following the prompts. A home page is really just a table of contents that links all of the pages. I suggest you always create a home page. Make your selection and click the Next button to continue.

7. Save your selections as a profile and (optionally) enter a name for the selection in the Profile Name field. Then click the Finish button, and output similar to that shown in Figure 14.14 will be created.

FIGURE 14.14.

The finished HTML document.

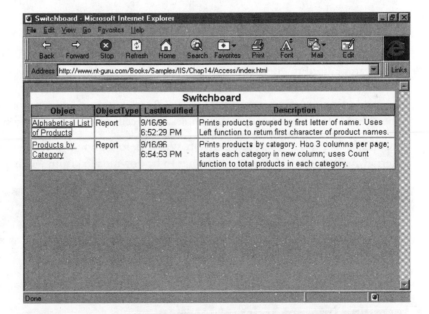

URL

The Microsoft Access Web page is at http://www.microsoft.com/msaccess/.

Publishing on the Web with Microsoft Office 95

The next few sections will demonstrate how you can publish Microsoft Word, Excel, PowerPoint, and Access documents on the Web using various Internet Assistants. Internet Assistants are special add-on programs that can be downloaded from Microsoft's Web site. These applications are designed to seamlessly integrate with various Office applications and extend their functionality by allowing oOffice documents to be saved as HTML documents. Note that most Internet Assistants covered in later sections require Microsoft Office for Windows 95. The exception is the Internet Assistant for Microsoft Word—a version that is available for Microsoft Word 6 has similar functionality.

> **URL**
>
> Microsoft's Internet assistants for Microsoft Office Web page can be found at
> `http://www.microsoft.com/MSOffice/MSOfc/`.

Publishing on the Web with Microsoft Word

Microsoft Word is a feature-rich word processing application. Internet Assistant for Microsoft Word can be used to effortlessly publish Word files on the Internet. As you will see shortly, Internet Assistant can also function as a WYSIWYG HTML editor. At the time of this writing, in addition to various standard HTML 2.0 tags, Internet Assistant for Word also supports various HTML enhancements such as tables, table cell colors, TrueType fonts, and font colors.

Internet Assistant is not part of Microsoft Word. Before using it to create content for the Web, Internet Assistant for Microsoft Word has to be downloaded from Microsoft's Web site.

> **URL**
>
> Microsoft's Internet Assistant for Word information and download site can be found at
> `http://www.microsoft.com/msword/internet/ia/`.

Installing Internet Assistant for Word

After downloading Internet Assistant for Word from Microsoft's Web site, simply run the executable file and specify a directory where Internet Assistant for Word should be installed. Be sure to close all applications before installing Internet Assistant for Word because the installation program might need to copy several shared DLL files. If you get any message boxes similar to the one shown in Figure 14.15 during the installation, simply click the Ignore button. Later, if you encounter problems running Internet Assistant for Word, remove applications from the Windows Start folder, reboot Windows, and then install Internet Assistant for Word soon after logging in.

Figure 14.15.

The Internet Assistant for Word installation program cannot replace shared DLL files that are open and being used by other applications.

After Internet Assistant for Word is installed, you will see a message box similar to the one shown in Figure 14.16. At this point, you can launch Microsoft Word and begin creating documents for the Web using Microsoft Word.

Figure 14.16.

Immediately after Internet Assistant for Word is installed, Microsoft Word is capable of creating content for the Web.

Creating an HTML Document with Word

Once Internet Assistant for Word is installed, creating HTML documents is as easy as creating Word documents. This section demonstrates how you can use various features of Internet Assistant for Word to create an HTML document with TrueType fonts, inline images, a table, and various other HTML attributes. In order to begin creating an HTML document, select File | New. A dialog box similar to the one shown in Figure 14.17 appears. Note the HTML document template that has been added by the Internet Assistant for Word installation program.

From the dialog box shown in Figure 14.17, select the HTML document template and click the OK button. You are now ready to start creating an HTML document using Microsoft Word. Before continuing to create a document, you might want to select Tools | Customize from the main menu to customize the toolbar. Make sure the Font button shown in Figure 14.18 appears in your toolbar because you will learn how to add TrueType fonts to HTML files shortly.

FIGURE 14.17.
You can use the HTML document template to create HTML files with Internet Assistant for Word.

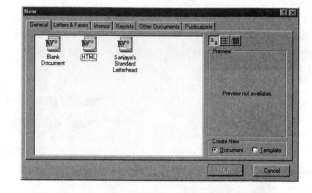

FIGURE 14.18.
You can customize the Microsoft Word toolbar with useful HTML attributes such as TrueType fonts.

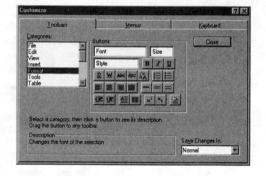

Background Images and Text Colors

You can customize HTML documents created with Word by adding a background image and various text attribute colors. Select Format | Background and Links from the main menu. Then specify various text attributes and colors as well as a background image in the dialog box. (See Figure 14.19.)

When using background images and special text colors, always use either a light-colored background and dark-colored text, or light-colored text with a dark background. Otherwise, users browsing your document will not be able to read the text. Before putting documents created with Microsoft Word on the Internet, use a Web browser to preview the documents to ensure they are legible.

If you wish to specify a background image, click the Browse button to bring up the Insert Picture dialog box shown in Figure 14.20. This dialog box is handy for selecting backgrounds because it displays a preview of the background image in the right column. After selecting the image you wish to use, click the OK button. You should work with a directory structure identical to that of the production Web server to ensure that the directory pathnames in your development environment are compatible with those in the production server.

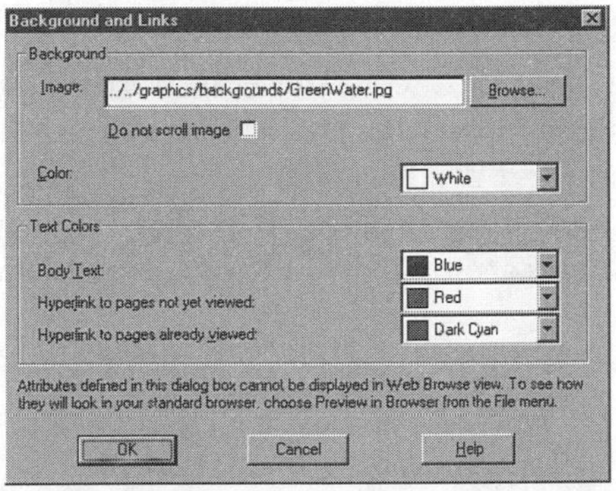

FIGURE 14.19.

Background and Links attribute specification dialog box.

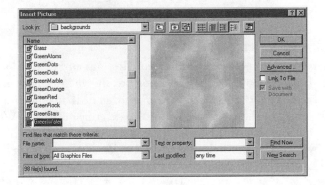

FIGURE 14.20.

You can use the Insert Picture dialog box to add a background image to an HTML document.

Using TrueType Fonts

Microsoft Word supports TrueType fonts in HTML documents. In order to change the font of some text, select the text and select Format | Font. You will then be able to specify a TrueType font for the selected text using a dialog box similar to the one shown in Figure 14.21. You can also use this dialog box to specify the size and color of the selected typeface. Note that not all Web browsers support TrueType fonts.

FIGURE 14.21.

Font specification dialog box.

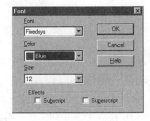

14

PUBLISHING ON
THE WEB WITH
MICROSOFT OFFICE

Inserting Tables

HTML documents created with Word can also have tables. Inserting a table into an HTML document is as easy as inserting a table into a Word document. Simply select Table | Insert Table, and you will see the dialog box shown in Figure 14.22. You can use this dialog box to specify the number of rows and columns the table should have. You can insert, delete, and merge table columns and rows if you have to change a table after it is created.

Figure 14.22.

Insert Table dialog box.

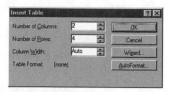

Inserting Inline Images and Video

You can insert inline images and video clips into an HTML document by selecting Insert | Picture from the main menu. The dialog box shown in Figure 14.23 can then be used to select an image or video clip to insert into a Word HTML document. When adding an image, use the data entry field for Alternative Text to describe the image. Web browsers such as Internet Explorer show this text in a balloon if a user rests the mouse pointer on the image. If you click the Browse button shown in Figure 14.23, you can use a dialog box similar to the one in Figure 14.20 to select an image.

Figure 14.23.

Inline picture insertion dialog box.

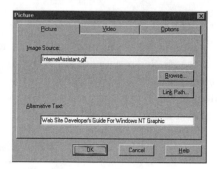

Formatting Table Cells

It is easy to format the table cells of an HTML document. Simply select the cell(s) you wish to format and right-click. You will then see a pop-up menu similar to the one shown in Figure 14.24, which you can use to specify various cell-formatting attributes. For example, if you wish to change the background of a cell, select it and click the Background Color option of the pop-up menu shown in Figure 14.24. You will then be able to define a background color for the selected cell using a Background Color dialog box similar to the one in Figure 14.25.

FIGURE 14.24.

Use the right mouse button to format cells in a table.

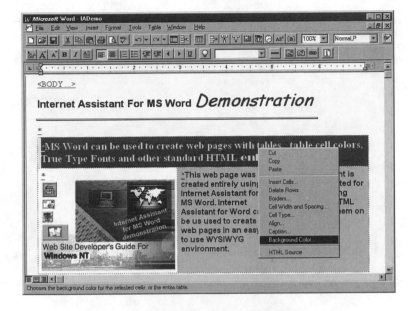

FIGURE 14.25.

You can use the Background Color dialog box to assign a color to one or more selected table cells.

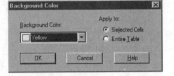

Publishing an HTML Document with Microsoft Word

You can create attractive HTML documents with Microsoft Word using various tips and procedures discussed earlier in this chapter. An example of an HTML document created with various standard HTML 2.0 extensions such as tables and TrueType fonts appears in Figure 14.26. After creating an HTML document with Word, publishing it on the Internet is as easy as saving the document as an HTML file.

HTML documents created with Microsoft Word can be viewed with any Web browser. The HTML document shown in Figure 14.26 looks similar to the Web page in Figure 14.27 when it is viewed with Internet Explorer. As you can see in Figure 14.27, the inline image and text in the table are appropriately formatted by Internet Assistant for Word. As demonstrated in previous sections, Internet Assistant for Word is a powerful Web publishing tool that you can use to leverage the power of Word to the Internet and create richly formatted Web pages.

FIGURE 14.26.
An HTML document created with Microsoft Word.

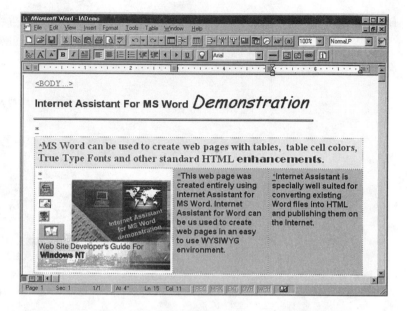

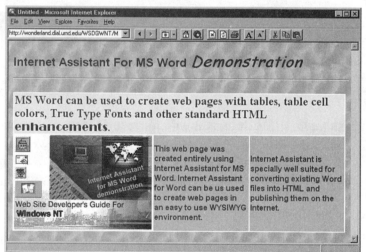

Publishing on the Web with Microsoft Excel

You can use Internet Assistant for Excel to effortlessly convert Excel spreadsheets into HTML documents so they can be published on the Web. You might want to check the Microsoft Excel Web page to obtain the most up-to-date information about Excel and how it can be used to create content for the Web. The next few sections explain how to convert the Excel spreadsheet shown in Figure 14.28 into HTML and publish it on the Web.

Figure 14.28.

You will soon learn how to convert this spreadsheet into HTML.

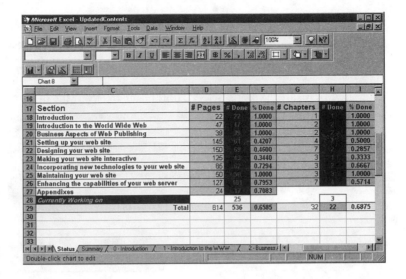

Incidentally, I actually used the spreadsheet shown in Figure 14.28 when I wrote this book. I used Internet Assistant for Excel to regularly update the contents of the spreadsheet in Figure 14.28 to an HTML file so my editor could monitor the progress of the book. The HTML file was stored in a secure Web server directory protected with a password. This application is an example of how you can use Internet Assistant for Excel to share information with selected users through a secure Web server.

URL

Use the following URL to reach the Microsoft Excel home page:

`http://www.microsoft.com/msexcel`

Installing Internet Assistant for Excel

You can install Internet Assistant for Excel by following a few simple steps after downloading it from Microsoft's Web site.

URL

The Internet Assistant for Microsoft Excel download site is `http://www.microsoft.com/msexcel/Internet/IA`.

1. Download Internet Assistant for Excel. This file is named HTML.XLA.

2. Place the file in the \EXCEL\LIBRARY directory if you are running a standalone version of Excel; place it in \MSOFFICE\EXCEL\LIBRARY if you are running the Microsoft Office version of Excel 7.0.

3. Start Microsoft Excel and select Tools | Add-Ins from the main menu. A dialog box similar to the one shown in Figure 14.29 appears.

FIGURE 14.29.

The Microsoft Excel tool Add-Ins dialog box.

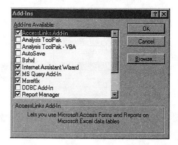

4. Locate the tool Internet Assistant Wizard, place a check mark beside it, and click the OK button.

Internet Assistant for Microsoft Excel is now installed and ready for use.

Publishing a Spreadsheet on the Web with Excel

You can use Internet Assistant for Excel to effortlessly convert a spreadsheet into HTML. As shown in Figure 14.30, simply highlight an area of the spreadsheet you wish to convert into HTML and select Tools | Internet Assistant Wizard from the main menu.

FIGURE 14.30.

You can convert the selected area of a spreadsheet into HTML using Internet Assistant for Excel.

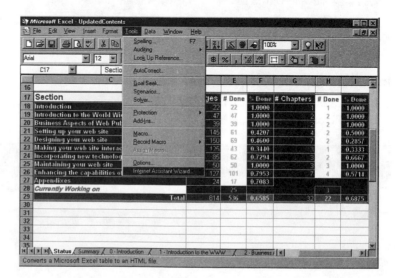

After the Internet Assistant Wizard menu option is selected, a dialog box similar to the one shown in Figure 14.31 will confirm the area selected in Figure 14.30. At this point, you can change the area you wish to convert.

FIGURE 14.31.

Step 1 of Internet Assistant Wizard for Excel confirms the area selected in Figure 14.30.

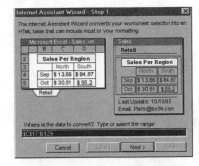

The next dialog box (see Figure 14.32) asks if you want to create a new HTML file or want to insert the data into an existing HTML document. Note that if you want to insert the data into an existing file, the file should contain the string `<!--##Table##-->`. Internet Assistant for Excel will then insert the data from the spreadsheet where it encounters the string `<!--##Table##-->`.

FIGURE 14.32.

The target HTML file selection dialog box.

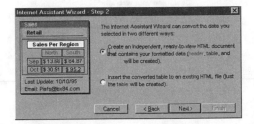

If you selected the option to create a new HTML file, a dialog box similar to the one shown in Figure 14.33 is displayed. You can use this dialog box to customize the HTML file created by Internet Assistant for Excel.

The next dialog box asks if you want to preserve as much formatting as possible. Select this option if you want the HTML file to resemble the original Excel spreadsheet as much as possible. Use the Other option only if you notice other browsers having problems with some of the enhanced HTML tags used by Internet Assistant for Excel. If your users use Internet Explorer or Netscape Navigator, using the option to preserve as much formatting as possible will produce the best results. Afterwards, provide the HTML filename of the new file, and the spreadsheet you selected in Figure 14.30 will be saved as an HTML file. You can view the saved HTML file with a Web browser, as shown in Figure 14.34. Compare the HTML document in Figure 14.34 with the Excel spreadsheet in Figure 14.28 and notice how closely they resemble each other. As this example shows, publishing Excel spreadsheets on the Web using Internet Assistant for Excel is really quite easy.

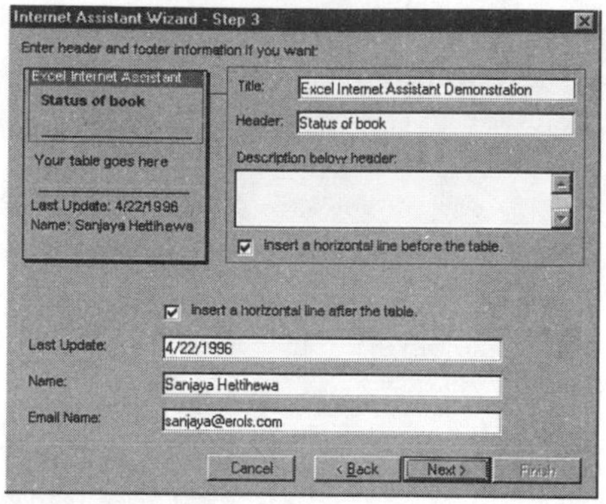

FIGURE 14.33.
The HTML file customizing dialog box.

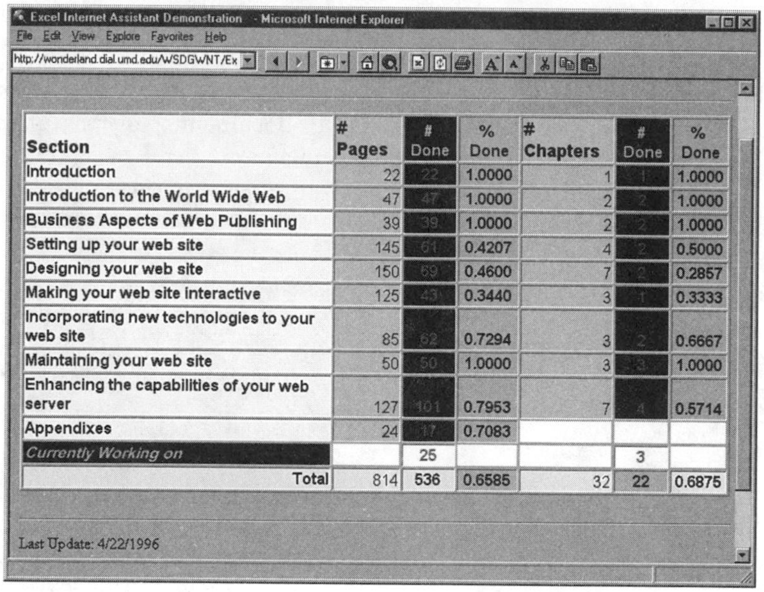

FIGURE 14.34.
The spreadsheet in Figure 14.28 after it is converted into HTML.

Section	# Pages	# Done	% Done	# Chapters	# Done	% Done
Introduction	22	22	1.0000	1	1	1.0000
Introduction to the World Wide Web	47	47	1.0000	2	2	1.0000
Business Aspects of Web Publishing	39	39	1.0000	2	2	1.0000
Setting up your web site	145	61	0.4207	4	2	0.5000
Designing your web site	150	69	0.4600	7	2	0.2857
Making your web site interactive	125	43	0.3440	3	1	0.3333
Incorporating new technologies to your web site	85	62	0.7294	3	2	0.6667
Maintaining your web site	50	50	1.0000	3	3	1.0000
Enhancing the capabilities of your web server	127	101	0.7953	7	4	0.5714
Appendixes	24	17	0.7083			
Currently Working on		25			3	
Total	814	536	0.6585	32	22	0.6875

Last Update: 4/22/1996

Publishing on the Web with Microsoft PowerPoint

PowerPoint is a powerful presentation tool that can be used to create a slide show presentation on the Internet using Internet Assistant for PowerPoint. The next few sections illustrate how easy it to create a PowerPoint presentation and save it as an HTML file. This demonstration shows you how to convert the slides in Figure 14.35 into HTML. Visit the Microsoft PowerPoint Web page for the most up-to-date information about PowerPoint and Internet Assistant for PowerPoint.

URL

The address for the Microsoft PowerPoint Web page is `http://www.microsoft.com/mspowerpoint/`.

FIGURE 14.35.
You will soon learn how to convert these two slides into HTML.

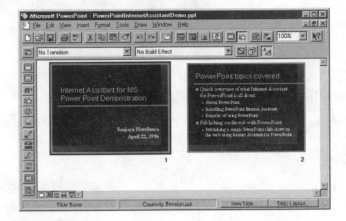

Installing Internet Assistant for PowerPoint

Download Internet Assistant for PowerPoint from Microsoft's Web site, copy it to a temporary directory, and run the executable file to decompress the PowerPoint distribution file. Then execute the file `IA4PPT95.EXE` to install Internet Assistant for PowerPoint. Before executing this file, make sure PowerPoint is not running. The installation program will then install Internet Assistant for PowerPoint and terminate with a message similar to the one shown in Figure 14.36.

URL

The Internet Assistant for Microsoft PowerPoint download site is `http://www.microsoft.com/mspowerpoint/Internet/ia/`.

14

PUBLISHING ON
THE WEB WITH
MICROSOFT OFFICE

FIGURE 14.36.
The Internet Assistant for PowerPoint installation program.

Converting a PowerPoint Slide Show into HTML

You can easily convert PowerPoint slides into HTML by selecting File | Export as HTML from the main menu. A dialog box similar to the one shown in Figure 14.37 will ask you for information about the output that Internet Assistant should generate for PowerPoint.

FIGURE 14.37.
The HTML Export Options dialog box.

Specify whether Internet Assistant for PowerPoint should output the slides in color or grayscale format with the Output style radio buttons. You should select to export your slides in color unless they contain only a limited number of colors or you are concerned about the size of slide files.

Use the next radio buttons to specify the file format of the exported PowerPoint slides. Generally, use the JPEG format for natural-photograph-looking slides that do not have too many sharp edges; use the GIF format for all other slides.

If you are using the JPEG format, you can use the slide bar in Figure 14.37 to define the image quality of JPEG files. Higher image quality results in large files, and lower image quality results in smaller files. You might want to experiment with various settings to determine the ideal level of quality for your slide presentation if you are concerned about bandwidth and file sizes. Note that file size is not an issue in an intranet environment where there is usually an abundance of available network bandwidth.

Finally, specify the folder that will contain the HTML version of the PowerPoint presentation and click the OK button to begin the conversion. Internet Assistant for PowerPoint will then export the slide show presentation and display a message similar to the one shown in Figure 14.38.

FIGURE 14.38.
The HTML conversion dialog box.

You can now view the PowerPoint presentation using a Web browser as shown in Figure 14.39. Note that the first page contains an index in all slides of the presentation.

FIGURE 14.39.
The HTML slide presentation index.

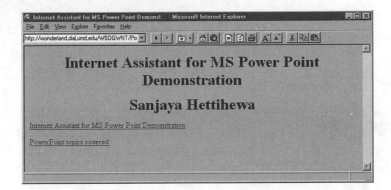

You can use the index shown in Figure 14.39 to view individual PowerPoint slides as shown in Figure 14.40. Note the navigation aids at the bottom of the slide. Internet Assistant for PowerPoint automatically creates these navigation aids to help users browse a PowerPoint presentation with a Web browser.

Publishing on the Web with Microsoft Access

An Internet Assistant is also available for Microsoft Access. As you will see shortly, you can easily publish information in a Microsoft Access database on the Web using Internet Assistant for Access. Visit the Microsoft Access Internet tools Web page for the most up-to-date information about publishing Access databases on the Internet.

FIGURE 14.40.
You can use a Web browser to view PowerPoint slides exported as HTML files.

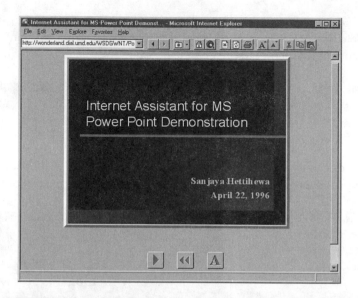

URL

The Microsoft Access Internet Assistant Web page is `http://www.microsoft.com/msaccess/`.

Installing Internet Assistant for Access

Download Internet Assistant for Microsoft Access from Microsoft's Web site, run the executable file, and allow the installation program to detect the Microsoft Access directory. After it detects the Access directory, click the large Install button to install Internet Assistant for Access.

URL

Microsoft's Internet Assistant for Access download site is `http://www.microsoft.com/msaccess/internet/ia/`.

Publishing a Database on the Web with Access

The next few pages explain how to publish a Microsoft Access database on the Web using Internet Assistant for Access. In order to publish an Access database, load the database into Access and select Tools | Add-ins | Internet Assistant from the main menu. (See Figure 14.41.)

Internet Assistant for Access will then begin a welcome message. Click the Next button, and a dialog box similar to the one shown in Figure 14.42 will be displayed.

FIGURE 14.41.

You can invoke Internet Assistant for Access from the Tools menu.

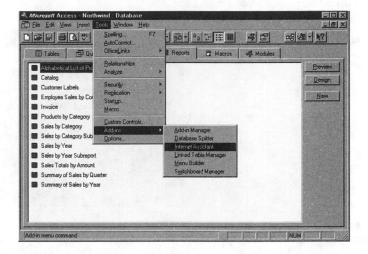

You can use Internet Assistant for Access to export any combination of Microsoft Access tables, queries, reports, and forms into HTML. To do so, select the object type and names of objects in that type from a dialog box similar to the one shown in Figure 14.42. Note that you can select one or more object types and object names. For example, you might want to select several reports and several tables.

FIGURE 14.42.

Various Microsoft Access objects can be exported into HTML.

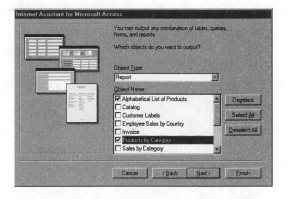

14

PUBLISHING ON THE WEB WITH MICROSOFT OFFICE

After selecting the objects to export as HTML files, click the Next button. Internet Assistant for Access will then present you with a dialog box similar to the one in Figure 14.43 and ask you for a template. You can use a template to enhance the appearance of data exported by Internet Assistant for Access by adding a background image, navigation buttons, and various graphics to its output. You can browse the various templates included with Internet Assistant for Access by clicking the Browse button. Note that templates with filenames ending with the suffix _r are used for reports and those without _r are used for data sheets. When several object types are selected, select the template without the _r suffix, and Internet Assistant for Access will apply the correct template based on its filename.

FIGURE 14.43.

You can use a template to format HTML output generated by Internet Assistant for Access.

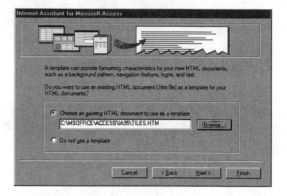

After selecting a template, type in a directory that will contain the exported HTML files. Then click the Finish button to export selected objects as HTML files. Internet Assistant for Access will export selected objects and let you know when it has finished creating the HTML files. You can view the exported data using a Web browser as shown in Figure 14.44.

FIGURE 14.44.

You can use a Web browser to view data exported by Internet Assistant for Access.

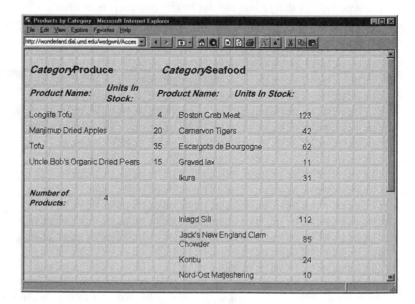

Internet Assistant for Microsoft Access might not always copy all the graphic files that are part of HTML files it creates into the target HTML directory. Use a Web browser to look at the HTML files Internet Assistant for Access creates. If you see any broken links to images, look at the source code to locate the graphic file it refers to and copy the graphic file to the target HTML directory. These graphics files are located in the \MSOFFICE\ACCESS\IA95 directory (assuming you installed Office 95 into the \MSOFFICE directory). Alternatively, you can copy all the graphic files from the \MSOFFICE\ACCESS\IA95 directory to the target HTML directory.

Summary

Microsoft Office is a powerful suite of productivity applications. You can use the various Internet Assistants for Microsoft Office to effortlessly publish content on the Internet. These Internet Assistants are especially useful for converting large amounts of Microsoft Office files into HTML for publication on the global Internet or a local intranet. In the next chapter you will look at a few more Web-based tools from Asymetrix and Corel. These tools include various applications that can enhance your Internet development efforts.

14

PUBLISHING ON
THE WEB WITH
MICROSOFT OFFICE

## CHAPTER 15

Using Asymetrix Web3D and Corel's Web.Designer

IN THIS CHAPTER

- Using Asymetrix Web3D   466
- Using Corel's Web.Designer   473

When you create your initial Web site, your goal is to publish content on the Internet and to get it up and running as quickly as possible. This usually means that the design is strictly functional and text based. If you have a dedicated graphic-design staff, you may also have graphic banners, buttons, backgrounds, rules, or images. If you do not have a dedicated graphic-design staff, however, you have a lot of work ahead of you to create these graphical objects. You can use any graphical application, such as CorelPHOTO–PAINT, which can export GIF or JPEG file formats to create these objects. The alternative to spending days or weeks creating these images is to use a tool specifically designed for WWW site development.

In this chapter you examine two tools for adding pizzazz to your site. The first of these tools is Asymetrix Web 3D, which can be used to create three-dimensional static objects, such as a banner or button, and animated objects, such as a helicopter or a banner where each character of text drops from the top down one at a time until the entire text message is displayed. The second tool is Corel's Web.Designer, which includes three tools to help get you up and running on the Web as quickly as possible. The first tool is CorelWEB.DESIGNER, which is a basic Windows HTML editor. CorelWEB.DESIGNER also includes several HTML templates. The next tool is called CorelWEB.GALLERY, which is a collection of prebuilt banners, buttons, rules, special characters, and clip art. The final tool in the package is CorelWEB.Transit, which is used to convert documents you already have (like Word for Windows documents) into HTML pages.

Although many other tools are available to help you in your Web page development, I chose Web 3D and Corel's Web.Designer for two reasons. First, they are inexpensive. Each costs less than $100. Second, these tools demonstrate the basic types of tools that are available: special effects (like Web 3D) and quick development (like Corel's Web.Designer). Both Web 3D and Corel's Web.Designer also include clip art, or templates, to save you some development time.

Using Asymetrix Web 3D

As the name implies, Asymetrix Web 3D can be used to render a three-dimensional object in a two-dimensional picture. This picture is referred to as a *snapshot* within the application context. A snapshot can be exported as a GIF or JPEG bitmap image. The application, however, does much more than just create static 3D images. It can be used to build animated objects exported as an audio-video interleave (AVI) file. It includes several prebuilt templates that you can use as a starting point for building a very impressive Web page. It also includes many prebuilt objects (such as backgrounds, banners, buttons, and rules) that you can incorporate into your Web pages.

You should be aware of a couple items before you run amok with Web 3D:

- Rendering 3D objects is very resource intensive. For example, when I rendered a 3D revolving welcome sign consisting of 61 frames into an AVI file, it required over 90 percent of both of my 166MHz Pentium processors, maxed out my disk drives, and used about 50MB of paging file space. And it still took over an hour to create the finished AVI file. Rendering simpler static objects requires fewer resources but is still very time-consuming.

■ When you have completed the design of your image, you will need to export the snapshot to either a GIF or JPEG file. You can use this snapshot image as a simple background, but if you want to use the various objects as inline graphics, as a hot-linked button (to jump to another URL, for example), or as an image map, then you will need another graphics application to cut out the individual objects. Finally, you'll need to create the HTML document to include the various objects you created.

■ Too many graphical objects on a single Web page may require more Internet band-width than your user has patience for, particularly on a 14.4Kbps modem connection. Rather than waiting for the nifty Web site to be displayed on his Web browser, your user may just cancel the update and move on to another site. To avoid losing visitors, keep the number of graphics on your Web site low and try to minimize the size of the individual images.

■ Not everyone uses a Web browser that can display a background. In this case the default background will be a light gray rather than the background image you selected. If the user has disabled image rendering on his Web browser, or if his Web browser is incapable of displaying inline images, then all your fancy work is for naught. Be sure to provide text-only alternatives for any banners, buttons, or image maps so your users can navigate through your Web site.

If you keep these items in mind, you, too, can create some pretty spectacular Web pages that incorporate 3D graphics. The two areas of a Web page that you really want to stand out, and that can really benefit from a 3D object, are your home page banner and your shortcut buttons. Usually these are strictly text on an opaque background, so the completed images are relatively small and do not consume a great deal of your user's Internet bandwidth.

How Does Asymetrix Web 3D Work?

Web 3D utilizes a mathematical model of an object to render a 2D picture that appears to exist in three dimensions. Many other applications, such as AutoDesk 3D Studio, can create 3D images. The basic process to create a 3D image follows.

1. A wireframe image is generated. In effect, this is a connect-the-dots image, as shown in Figure 15.1.

2. After the wireframe image has been created, a *surface* (the texture and color of the image's exterior) can be applied. This creates an object that appears to be solid, as shown in Figure 15.2, yet still does not appear very realistic.

3. To apply the finishing touches to the object, lights and shadows are applied. This dramatically improves the illusion of three dimensionality, as shown in Figure 15.3.

FIGURE 15.1.
A wireframe representation of a cube.

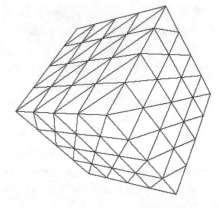

FIGURE 15.2.
A wireframe representation of a cube with a surface applied.

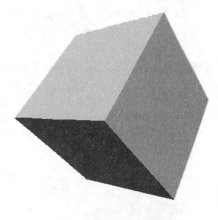

FIGURE 15.3.
A completed representation of a cube with a surface, lights, and shadows applied.

Although these steps seem simple in principle, in reality they are quite complex. That is why it may take hours to generate a finished 3D image. However, this should not deter you from creating 3D text banners, buttons, or other images because the computer will do the tough work of rendering the image for you. What you should be aware of with rendered images is that the higher the color depth, the more realistic the image will appear. The downside to a more realistic image is that it is also much larger in size. This is the reason the publisher asked me to submit the images for this chapter in a 256 (8-bit) color palette instead of a 16 million (24-bit) color palette.

Creating Your Home Page with Web 3D

When you are searching for that special look for your home page, you can use Web 3D's templates. Three of my favorite designs include the Neon style, which provides a flashy color display; the Glass Bubbles style, which provides a futuristic display; and the Polished Wood style, which gives a bit of elegance to your home page.

Follow these steps to create a home page based on a template:

1. Select File | New from the menu, then press Ctrl+N, or click the New button on the toolbar to create a new scene window.

2. If the current catalog is not the WEB3D catalog, open it using the File | Open command. In the List files of type drop-down list box, choose Catalogs (*.cat). The WEB3D catalog can be found in the WEB3D\WEBSTYLE subdirectory. Then click the Styles tab to display the available templates.

3. Click the template of your choice in the Catalog window; then drag it over the Scene Preview window and drop it in place. The Scene Preview window will then display the template with the default objects, as shown in Figure 15.4.

FIGURE 15.4.

Creating a home page using a Web 3D template.

4. Maximize the Scene Contents window. Double-click the icon next to the Picture: Title Plate entry. This will expand the scene and display the individual element list of the composite entry.

TIP

When designing a 3D image, the key ingredients are lighting, shadows, and reflections. These properties are applied based on the common Lights entry in the Scene Contents window. An individual item may also have a Lights entry, which will override the common setting. However, if you override this common light setting, your objects appear out of place with the rest of the objects. It is best to use a common setting, such as that defined within a scene (or template), to provide a more uniform model.

---

5. Double-click the Text: Steve Snyder entry. This will display the Modify Text Model dialog, shown in Figure 15.5, where you may modify the text, model name, font, font size, font justification, and other properties.

FIGURE 15.5.

Modifying an object's text in a default Web 3D template.

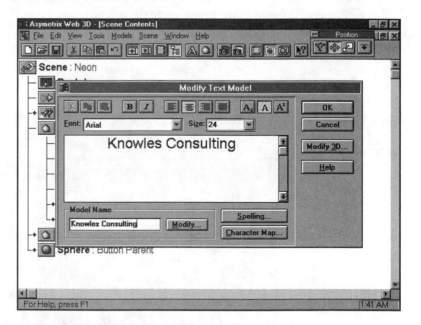

6. Click the OK button after you have finished your modifications. The Scene Preview window will then update the display with your changes.

7. To change the properties for the text face, back, sides, or bevels, expand the text entry by double-clicking on the icon next to the text entry. Then double-click the All Faces, All Backs, All Sides, or All Bevels text description to display the Modify Surface and Color dialog box. Within this dialog box, you may change the name, the color object,

the highlight characteristics, or the effects of the object. When you have completed your changes, click the OK button to update the Scene Preview window.

8. For each additional object you want to modify in the template, repeat steps 5 through 7. To delete an object, just select it in either the Scene Preview or Scene Contents window and press the Delete key. Choose Models | Create Text Models to insert a new text object, Models | Create Picture Model to insert a new object based on a graphic image, or Models | Create Simple Model to insert a new circle, cone, square, or other basic geometric object.

9. Finally, you need to render the image and create your output file. This is accomplished by choosing Scene | Generate Snapshot, which will display the Generate Snapshot dialog box (see Figure 15.6). In this dialog box, you may specify how realistic the image will be by choosing an entry in the Style drop-down list box. A style may be one of the following:

- Wireframes—No shadows, no reflections, no dithering, no custom color palette, and no fog. In essence, this creates an image consisting of lines with no surface and is an unusable image for Web pages.

- Solid models—No shadows, no reflections, no dithering, no custom color palette, no fog. Although similar to the wireframe style, this option does create a solid image that may be used for Web graphics, but the overall quality is very poor.

- Realistic—No shadows or true reflections. This style creates a suitable image for Web page graphics and renders quite rapidly.

- Realistic w/shadows—No true reflections. This style creates more realistic images suitable for Web page graphics.

- Ray traced—No shadows. This style creates a more realistic image with higher overall quality.

- Ray traced w/shadows—Displays shadows, true reflections, dithering, custom color palettes, and fog. This image is the highest quality but also takes the most time to render.

FIGURE 15.6.

Modifying snapshot properties to create your final image.

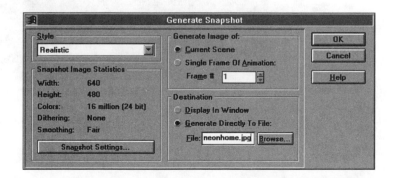

> **TIP**
>
> To create an image suitable for use in your Web page, select the Generate Directly To File radio button in the Destination group and enter a filename in the File edit field.

10. Click the Snapshot Settings button to display the Snapshot and Animation Settings dialog box, where you may specify the image size, quality, default color palette, special effects, or animation settings. Click the OK button to return to the Generate Snapshot dialog box.

11. When you are satisfied with your snapshot options, click the OK button in the Generate Snapshot dialog box to render the image. While this is happening, I suggest you relax and drink a cup of coffee (or a pot of coffee, if you chose a ray-traced style).

12. When the image has been created, you may then import it into your favorite bitmap editor and cut out the individual components you want to use in your Web pages. The final product will look similar to the one shown in Figure 15.7 after you have created the HTML document.

Figure 15.7.

The completed home page using the Neon *template.*

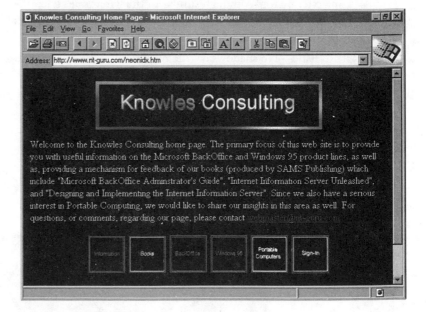

Using Corel's Web.Designer

Corel's Web.Designer is a product recently introduced to the market. Web.Designer is really three separate products on a single CD-ROM. It includes CorelWEB.DESIGNER, a WYSIWYG HTML editor; CorelWEB.GALLERY, a collection of Web-ready clip art; and CorelWEB.Transit, a document-conversion tool.

Using CorelWEB.DESIGNER

The first thing you should know about CorelWEB.DESIGNER is that it is not designed to build Web pages that use the HTML 3.0 tags or the HTML 2.0 tag extensions by Netscape or Microsoft. Nor is it designed specifically to support the Internet Information Server. It is a basic HTML 2.0 editor. I expect this to change with future versions. However, just because CorelWEB.DESIGNER does not support the HTML extensions and the Internet Information Server directly does not mean that it is a worthless product. It works very well as a Web-page forms editor, as you can see in Figure 15.8. It also includes an HTML text editor so that you can add HTML-specific tags that are not supported directly by CorelWEB.DESIGNER. It even includes a built-in spell checker so you can avoid potentially embarrassing spelling errors.

FIGURE 15.8.

Using CorelWEB.DESIGNER to build a Web form.

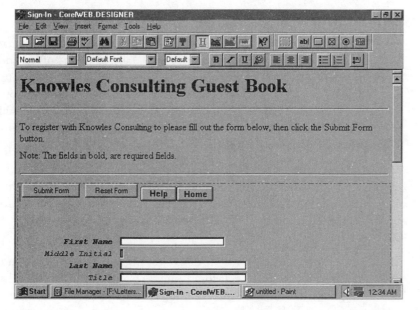

15

USING WEB3D
AND
WEB.DESIGNER

What I like most about CorelWEB.DESIGNER is the user interface. It is a very simple interface with button shortcuts to most of the functions you will want to use to develop the majority of your Web pages. You can insert text, lists, hypertext links, and images. You can even create image maps from any image you insert into your document. You can change paragraph styles, paragraph alignment, fonts, font sizes, and font attributes (bold, italic, and so on) just as you would with any Windows-based word processor. CorelWEB.DESIGNER has more than 100 templates that you can use to get a head start on your Web page development. These include artistic templates, business templates, form templates, and even humorous templates. I also like the capability to use whatever names I want for my form input fields (unlike Microsoft FrontPage), which makes form development for dbWeb a lot easier.

What I do not like, however, is the lack of support for HTML 3.0 and the HTML 2.0 extensions. I also dislike the lack of support for IIS virtual directories. However, I can't fault Corel alone for this, because no product I have used to date supports the Internet Information Server virtual directory structure. All WYSIWYG HTML editors that I have tried have been designed to support one root directory with all subdirectories as physical subdirectories under the root directory. What this means to you is that you will need to manually insert the relative URLs into your HTML documents rather than use the Browse button to create them. You can avoid this problem by making sure that your virtual directory structure matches your physical directory structure.

Using CorelWEB.GALLERY

CorelWEB.GALLERY includes more than 7,500 different images that you can use in your Web pages. These images include arrows, backgrounds, banners, bullets, buttons, clip art, capital letters, dividers (or rules), icons, photos, and themes (which include groups of matching banners, buttons, dividers, and so on that you can use to build a homogenous Web page). These images are either in a GIF or JPEG file format. Regardless of the original file format, you can export them to BMP (Windows or OS/2), JPEG, GIF, PCX (Paintbrush), TGA (Targa), or TIF bitmap file formats.

Many of these objects, like the buttons shown in Figure 15.9, include built-in captions so the objects are ready to be used as inline graphics without any additional effort. There are also blank objects, such as buttons and banners, that you can import into your favorite graphics application. You can then add any text to the object to create a custom object.

Creating a custom object may be just the ticket for your Web page. I found this to be very useful while experimenting with the design for my home page, as shown in Figure 15.10, because it enabled me to create a custom banner. I also created custom bullets to provide a more interesting bulleted list. This was accomplished by exporting the bullet from Web Gallery, importing it into CorelPHOTO–PAINT, modifying the bullet background to match the background of my Web page, saving the final image, and then inserting the image as a custom bullet in my HTML document.

FIGURE 15.9.

A sample of the buttons included with CorelWEB.GALLERY.

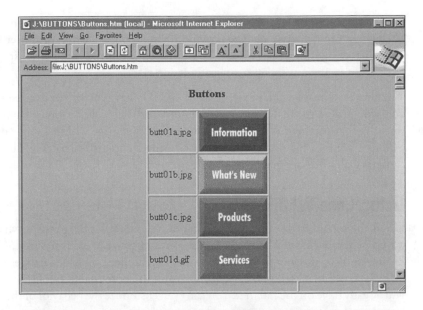

FIGURE 15.10.

Creating a custom banner from an empty banner object.

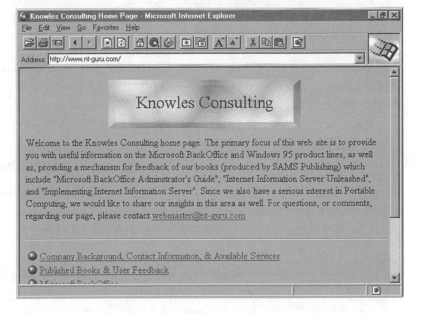

By using these customized objects, I was able to provide a unique look to my document while still keeping the required Internet bandwidth to a minimum. Because my Internet connection uses a single 56Kbps (224Kbps with software compression enabled) ISDN connection, this is an important consideration. If you have the available bandwidth, however, you may be able to take advantage of the numerous other graphic objects provided with Web.Gallery. The icons, in particular, can be very useful. If you are creating an intranet application, for example, your Web pages can use these icons to provide a custom interface that your users are more comfortable with than standard text links or text-based buttons. After all, most users know how to click icons in their Windows applications.

Whichever items you choose to use from Web.Gallery, you can be assured that by using them, you will be able to create a custom look for your Web pages without having to spend days or weeks designing them. You can create your first Web page within a single day, possibly within a couple hours. This time savings is what using a clip-art gallery is all about, particularly because not all of us are graphically inclined.

Using CorelWEB.Transit

Of all the tools provided by Web.Designer, the CorelWEB.Transit is what prompted me to purchase the package. This tool enables you to convert Microsoft Word, Corel WordPerfect, Lotus AmiPro, and any rich-text file to an HTML file. Embedded images will be converted to GIFs (the default) or JPG files. This opens up the potential to publish many documents that you already have on the Internet. You can even customize the behavior of the CorelWEB.Transit conversion process to convert your document styles, paragraph attributes (left, right, and center justification), and font attributes (bold, italic, and so on); set up heading levels; insert address fields and e-mail addresses; and much much more. However, none of these options needs to be assigned to perform a quick conversion. For most of us, the defaults operate quite well. To give you a quick idea of how simple it is to publish your documents on the Internet, here are the steps I used to convert a review of the WinBook XP portable computer to an HTML document:

1. Launch CorelWEB.Transit, and the dialog box shown in Figure 15.11 will appear.
2. Click the Set Up Files button, and the Set Up Files dialog box will appear.
3. Specify the document to be converted in the Select Source File field.
4. Specify the location for the output files in the Output directory field.
5. Specify a name for the output file in the HTML File field.
6. Specify the HTML document title in the Web page title field.
7. Click the OK button to return to the main window.
8. Click on the Translate Publication button, and the document will be generated.

You can find a slightly modified version of this document on my Web site at

```
http://www.nt-guru.com/PortableComputing/WinBook/XP/WinBookXP.HTM
```

The modifications I performed were minor. I moved the table of contents to after the document title. I created a table where I could insert the picture of the laptop, the company information, and the review specifications so I could control the layout of these items. I right-justified the other images and made all the GIFs transparent to mimic the original file as closely as possible. The total conversion time was about 15 minutes.

FIGURE 15.11.

The CorelWEB.Transit dialog box.

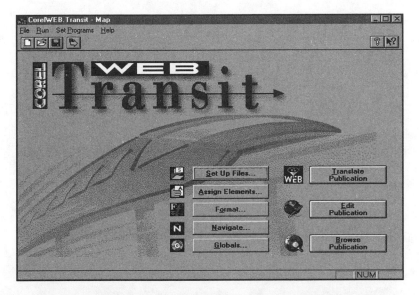

Summary

This chapter focused on two products you can use to provide a custom look for your Web page without a lot of effort. The goal here was not to promote a specific product, as other products perform similar functions just as well. The idea was to provide you with a little exposure to the types of tools that are available and to explain how you can use them to customize your Web page with a little, rather than a lot, of effort. This can give you a head start in creating a Web page that has more user appeal than just a plain text-based Web page.

In the next chapter you will learn about Sausage Software's HotDog Pro. HotDog Pro is a Windows-based Web editor that you can use as an aid in creating and managing a Web site. It provides many functions, such as an HTML syntax checker, that are not included in the Microsoft Internet Assistant.

CHAPTER 16

Using Sausage Software's HotDog Pro

IN THIS CHAPTER

- Why Use HotDog Pro?   480

- Getting Started with HotDog Pro   481

- Working with Documents and Templates   495

- Working with Projects   506

One of the most helpful items for new HTML document developers is a tool that can help them over the rough spots of learning all of the intricacies of HTML coding. HotDog Pro is such a tool. HotDog Pro is not only for beginners, however, because it provides features that the expert HTML document developer may want as well. It includes multiple-language support for its spelling checker, an HTML syntax checker, and even limited project-management capabilities. This chapter explores HotDog Pro, beginning with an in-depth look at its features to understand why you may want to use it. Then I move on to the basics of HotDog Pro, such as how to install it and customize it to fit your needs. Then I explain how to use HotDog Pro to create documents and briefly introduce this tool's project-management capabilities.

> **TIP**
>
> This chapter discusses the retail version of HotDog Pro. A shareware version called HotDog, with slightly fewer features, is available on Sausage Software's Web site at `http://www.sausage.com`.

Why Use HotDog Pro?

In Chapter 13, "Designing and Managing a Web Site with FrontPage," you looked at the Microsoft Office Internet Assistants, which you can download free from the Internet. Microsoft Office Internet Assistants enable you to use familiar tools that you may already own to produce materials for your Web pages. So why should you consider using HotDog Pro? First of all, not everyone has Microsoft Office. You can purchase HotDog Pro for less than $50, whereas Microsoft Office costs between $300 and $400, depending on whether you purchase the standard or professional version. This can be a significant savings, and by itself may make the purchase of HotDog Pro worthwhile. There are, however, some additional compelling reasons to use HotDog Pro:

- Ease of use—HotDog Pro makes it easy for the novice HTML developer to produce Web pages. However, its advanced features make it a productive tool for hard-core HTML enthusiasts as well. There is something for everyone in HotDog Pro!

- Compatibility—HotDog Pro is a Windows application that will execute under Windows 3.*x*, Windows 95, and Windows NT. It provides some of the Windows 95 user interface, such as tabbed dialog boxes, under all versions of Windows. More importantly, the application executes under all versions of Windows without any problems. There is no need to worry about which version of the Internet Assistant template, spreadsheet, or whatever you are using with the correct version of Word, Excel, or some other application. HotDog Pro is a fully self-contained application.

Using Sausage Software's HotDog Pro

CHAPTER 16

481

16

USING SAUSAGE
SOFTWARE'S
HOTDOG PRO

- Customizability—HotDog Pro is fully customizable. You can specify how the application will appear onscreen and how the application will behave. You can configure the button bar and application font, create or modify document templates, assign or change shortcut keys, and take advantage of numerous other options that are described later in this chapter in the section titled "Customizing HotDog Pro."

- Project management—In addition to editing and publishing individual documents, HotDog provides the capability to group multiple documents into a project. You can perform search-and-replace operations on multiple documents, edit individual documents within a project, or even add documents to a project. When all changes have been completed, you can publish the entire project on your Web server with the push of a button.

- Multiple HTML format support—HotDog Pro can be customized to use HTML 2.0 tags, HTML 3.0 tags, Netscape-specific tag extensions, or Microsoft Explorer–specific tag extensions. This makes it quite easy to support different Web browsers. HotDog Pro provides menus and buttons to insert the most common types of tags into your document, as well as tag tables that can be customized to insert a partial or complete tag sequence into your document. As the HTML standard changes, you can use the multiple-file search-and-replace function to update any nonstandard tags to their new formats.

- HTML syntax checker—This feature provides the capability to check an HTML document for syntactical correctness, which, in my opinion, is one of the biggest benefits of HotDog Pro. There is nothing worse than a document with an incorrect tag, or a missing end tag, to cause you embarrassment or grief. This option alone is worth the purchase price of HotDog Pro. An additional benefit of this option is the capability to color-code HTML tags so you know when you are using nonstandard HTML extensions within your document.

- Spell checker—HotDog Pro includes a standard American English language dictionary plus dictionaries for British English, German, Italian, and French. These dictionaries can be used by international content providers to avoid common spelling errors.

- External tools—HotDog Pro includes HotFTP and MapThis. HotFTP is a Windows-based File Transfer Protocol (FTP) application that is far superior to the Windows NT character-mode FTP client. MapThis is used to perform the difficult work of mapping graphical object boundaries for image maps into NCSA or CERN formatted text files.

Getting Started with HotDog Pro

HotDog Pro is one of the easiest applications I've had the pleasure to use. I'm sure you, too, will find it to be as useful as it is easy to use. Before you can use HotDog Pro, however, you have to install it. If you are a new HTML developer, going through the tutorial may be beneficial before you start using the application. On the other hand, you may want to jump right into customizing the application after you have installed it so you can start producing content right away.

Installing HotDog Pro

Installing HotDog Pro is easy. If you are using Windows NT 4.0 or Windows 95 as your HTML development platform, as soon as you insert the CD-ROM you'll be greeted with an installation dialog box. This dialog box is displayed because the CD-ROM includes an autorun script. An autorun script is a file (called `autorun.inf`) in the root directory of your data CD. This file specifies an application to execute whenever Windows NT 4.0 or Windows 95 is notified that a new CD has been inserted into your CD-ROM player. If you are using Windows 3.*x* or earlier versions of Windows NT, you will need to execute the `setup.exe` application located in the root directory of the CD-ROM.

> **NOTE**
>
> HotDog Pro requires Windows enhanced mode to operate. Therefore, it may not run on any software emulation that does not support the 80386 instruction set, including some of the older versions of Windows NT for RISC platforms.

After the setup program has been launched, just follow these steps:

1. The Registration Details dialog box appears. Enter your name and company information in the User Name and Company Name fields, respectively. Then click the OK button.

2. The Select Destination Directory dialog box appears next. Choose the default (`C:\HTDOGPRO`) or change this to the drive and directory of your choice. Then click the OK button.

> **NOTE**
>
> Although the installation program accepts long filenames, I found that when I used long filenames, the installation program failed to create a Program Manager group on a Windows 95 installation. So it is better to stick to the MS-DOS 8.3 filename limitations unless you are willing to create your own Program Manager group.

3. The Select Components to Install dialog box appears. For most users, the default options will suffice. However, if you want to skip the tutorial, additional dictionaries, or other optional components, uncheck the appropriate check boxes. Then click the OK button to continue the installation.

Using Sausage Software's HotDog Pro

CHAPTER 16

483

16

USING SAUSAGE
SOFTWARE'S
HOTDOG PRO

4. You are prompted to have the setup program create backup copies of any files it replaces. Choose Yes to back up these files, or No to skip the backup. If you choose Yes, you are prompted to choose a directory to contain the backed-up files. The default is C:\HTDOGPRO\BACKUP. After you choose whether or not to back up, HotDog Pro files will be copied to your hard drive.

5. The Create HotDog Program Group dialog box appears. Click the Yes button if you want to create the group; click the No button if you do not want to create a Program Manager group. For this discussion, I'll assume you are choosing the Yes button.

6. The Select Folder dialog box appears. In the Folder Name field, enter a name if the default group name (HotDog Pro) is unacceptable or select an available group from the list shown below on the screen. Then click the OK button to create the group.

7. The Installation Complete dialog box appears, and you are prompted to run HotDog Pro now or exit the setup program. Either option will terminate the setup program. So if you are in a hurry to get started, as I was, choose the Yes button. Otherwise, choose the No button.

The HotDog Pro Tutorial

When you first execute HotDog Pro, you are greeted with a cute dialog box. (See Figure 16.1.) It provides the following five options:

- Don't show this screen again—Check this option to disable the Welcome dialog box so it will not appear the next time you start HotDog Pro.

- Use HotDog Now—Click this button to exit the dialog box and start working with HotDog Pro.

- Start an HTML tutorial—Click this button to display the HotDog Pro HTML tutorial. This is a help file that describes the basics to create an HTML document, insert HTML links, and insert graphic images into your HTML document. It also includes an HTML overview and the HTML tag reference. The examples demonstrate both the tag structure and the associated application shortcuts; they are a good place to start if you are unfamiliar with HTML documents.

- Tell me something about HTML—Click this button for a description of HTML. It describes the basic structure of an HTML tag and includes a discussion concerning the various HTML flavors that are available.

- Tell me something about HotDog—Click this button for a working description of HotDog Pro. This option provides you with additional links to an HTML overview, application features, system requirements, and manufacturer-specific information.

All the options, except for the Don't show this screen again check box, are available from the application's built-in help system (just choose Help | Contents). I recommend that you enable the Don't show this screen again check box on the Welcome to HotDog! dialog box to speed up the loading of the application.

Customizing HotDog Pro

The major benefits of HotDog Pro are gained by customizing the application to suit your individual needs. You can customize the button bar, define the application's behavior, and create shortcut keys. Of these three customizable options, I find that the capabilities to create shortcut keys and define the application's behavior to be most beneficial. Creating custom shortcut keys can be used to provide faster access to menu commands. This can save time for a skilled, more proficient user. Defining the application's behavior, however, is useful to everyone. With HotDog Pro you can specify how the application interacts with you, such as by setting display preferences. You can also specify the style of HTML code to be used within your document. There is a pretty wide range of options available to make HotDog Pro suit almost everyone.

Customizing the Button Bar

The HotDog Pro button bar, shown in Figure 16.2, provides easy access to the application's major menu functions. While the button bar is fully customizable, the other bars are not customizable at all. These other bars include the elements bar, the documents bar, and the status bar. These bars can be disabled so they are not displayed on the screen.

To modify button properties on the button bar, follow these steps:

1. Choose Customize Button Bar from the Tools menu to display the Customize Button Bar dialog box, shown in Figure 16.3.

FIGURE 16.2.

The HotDog Pro button, elements, documents, and status bars.

Button bar ┘
Elements bar ┘

Documents bar ——
Status bar ——

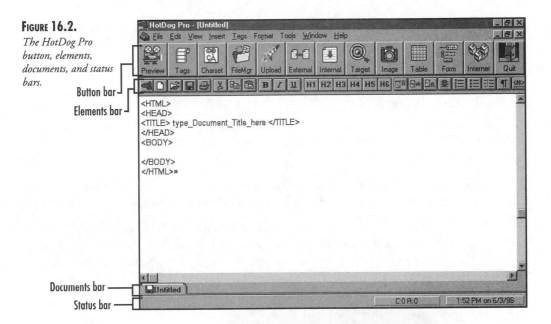

FIGURE 16.3.

Modifying the properties of a button on the button bar.

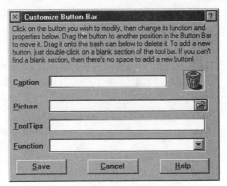

2. Click an existing button to populate the Caption, Picture, ToolTips, and Function fields with the button's current information.

3. To change the button's caption, enter a new description in the Caption field.

4. To change the icon displayed on the button, click the folder icon at the end of the Picture field. This will display the HotDog Pro—Select Picture dialog box, where you can specify any icon (`*.ico`) or bitmap (`*.bmp`) filename. After you have specified a new file, click the OK button to return to the Customize Button Bar dialog box. The new filename will then be displayed in the Picture field.

5. To change the description displayed under the button when the mouse is over the button, enter a new description in the ToolTips field.

6. To change the menu command that is executed when the button is clicked, choose a menu command from the Function drop-down list box.

7. Click the Save button to update the button bar. Click the Cancel button to disregard your modifications.

8. Repeat steps 1 through 7 for each button you want to modify.

To add a new button to the button bar, repeat the above steps, except when you reach step 2, double-click a blank spot on the button bar. The new button will then be inserted into the location of the blank spot when you click the Save button.

To delete a button, click the button on the button bar; then drag it over the trash can in the Customize Button Bar dialog box and drop it. This will leave a blank spot on the button bar.

To move a button to a different location, you must first display the Customize Button Bar dialog box. Then just click and hold the mouse button, which will display a white rectangle (or *button outline*, if you prefer) to illustrate the button. Next drag the outline to the new location on the button bar and then drop it. The button will then be moved to its new location.

Customizing Application Shortcut Keys

Are you a touch typist? If so, customizing the shortcut keys may be one of the ways you can maximize the performance of HotDog Pro and increase your productivity. You do not have to be a touch typist, however, to benefit from shortcut keys. Even a hunt-and-peck typist can use the shortcut keys to access any menu command with a single keystroke. This means you can insert HTML tags or formatting commands with a single keystroke. If you are a touch typist, you can crank out HTML documents quite rapidly. If you are not, just saving the time it takes to manually type the HTML tags, or access them from the menu, is a useful feature. To add a shortcut key sequence to HotDog Pro, follow these steps:

1. Choose Shortcut Keys from the Tools menu to display the Customize Shortcut Keys dialog box. (See Figure 16.4.)

FIGURE 16.4.
Creating shortcut keys.

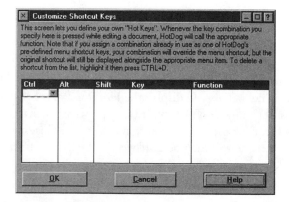

Using Sausage Software's HotDog Pro

CHAPTER 16

487

16

USING SAUSAGE
SOFTWARE'S
HOTDOG PRO

2. To specify a Ctrl+key sequence, choose CTRL from the drop-down list box in the Ctrl column.

3. To specify an Alt+key sequence, choose ALT from the drop-down list box in the Alt column.

4. To specify a Shift+key sequence, choose SHIFT from the drop-down list box in the Shift column.

NOTE

Key-column sequences are cumulative. So if you specify an entry for the Ctrl, Alt, and Shift columns, you must press all three keys plus the key you specified in the Key column to activate the function. This can be a pretty hefty set of keys, so it is best to limit your key sequence to no more than three keys (such as Ctrl+Shift+C).

5. Choose a key from the drop-down list box in the Key column. This key can be a special key (such as the Insert, left-arrow, or pause key), a number, a letter, a function key, or a number-pad key. In fact, from what I have been able to determine, you can use almost any key on your keyboard.

6. Specify a function to execute when the shortcut key is pressed by choosing an entry in the drop-down list box in the Function column.

7. Repeat steps 2 through 6 for each shortcut key you want to create. When all shortcut keys have been entered, click the OK button.

Customizing the Application's Behavior

HotDog Pro has numerous options that you can configure to suit your individual tastes and needs. In fact, there are so many options that I have summarized them in Table 16.1 rather than stepping you through each one. The subheads of the table give the name of the tabbed dialog box, the first column names the option, and the second column describes the option. To set one of these options, follow these steps:

1. Choose Options from the Tools menu to display the Options dialog box, as shown in Figure 16.5.

2. Click a tab to display the appropriate dialog box.

3. Change the options as desired.

4. Click the Save button to save your changes or click the Cancel button to disregard your changes.

FIGURE 16.5.

Customizing the behavior of HotDog Pro.

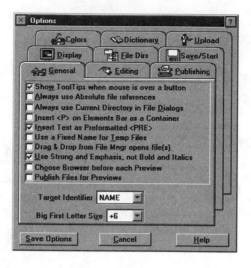

Table 16.1. The customizable options for HotDog Pro.

Option	Description
General Tab	
Show ToolTips when mouse is over a button	Specifies that a description for the button will be displayed when the mouse cursor is over a button.
Always use Absolute file references	Specifies that a file reference will use the complete path and filename to the location of the reference (such as F:\WWW\GRAPHICS \Button.GIF) rather than a relative path and filename (such as ..\GRAPHICS\Button.GIF). Note that while this is a useful option for a locally hosted WWW server (on the computer where HotDog Pro is installed), it may cause a problem for a remotely hosted server when an attempt is made to locate the file.
Always Use Current Directory in File Dialogs	Overrides the directory location defaults as specified in the File Dirs tab and will use the last directory location as the default.
Insert <P> on Elements Bar as a Container	Specifies that the paragraph (<P>) tag be treated as a tag pair (<P>...</P>).
Insert Text as Preformatted <PRE>	Specifies that inserted text be treated as preformatted text. Note that to insert text as a normal part of your document you need to disable this option.

Option	Description
Use a Fixed Name for Temp Files	Specifies that a fixed filename will be used when you preview a document. Note that this should be required only for browsers that do not support DDE commands. After each preview option, you will have to refresh the display in your Web browser to update the contents.
Drag & Drop from File Mngr opens file(s)	Specifies that files dragged from File Manager and dropped on a HotDog Pro window will open the files. Disabling this option may improve performance on slower computers. Note that when this option is disabled you can use the HotDog Pro File Manager to drag and drop files to accomplish the same tasks.
Use Strong and Emphasis, not Bold and Italics	Specifies that the HTML tags `<STRONG>` and `<EMPHASIS>` will replace the `<B>` and `<I>` tags when you choose the bold or italic menu, elements bar, or shortcut key options. Note that this is the preferred method and should be changed only for HTML documents that will be used by Web browsers that do not support the `<STRONG>` or `<EMPHASIS>` tags.
Choose Browser before each Preview	Specifies that HotDog Pro will prompt you for the Web browser to use each time you preview a document. This is a useful feature if you will be supporting multiple Web browsers.
Publish Files for Previews	Specifies that an HTML document will be published (that is, moved to your Web server) before being previewed on your Web browser.
Target Identifier	The HTML 3.0 specification utilizes the `ID` element to specify a target location (such as `<A ID="LocationName">`), whereas previous versions of HTML used a `NAME` element in an anchor tag (such as `<A NAME="LocationName">`). To use the old format, specify `NAME` in the drop-down list box.

continues

Table 16.1. continued

Option	Description
Big First Letter Size	Specifies the size for the Big First Letter option. This is often referred to as a drop caps option, where the first capital letter in a paragraph is a larger size than the rest of the text in a paragraph. The size is specified in a relative format +1 to +6, or -1 to -6.

Editing Tab

Option	Description
Default Font Name	Specifies the default display font.
Default Font Size	Specifies the size of the default font to be displayed.
Color tags after *XX* seconds idle	Specifies that HTML tags will be colorized after the number of seconds you specify. The minimum time is 0, the maximum time is 60 seconds. Note that to color tags, the Quick Color option must be enabled.
Quick Color	Specifies that HTML tags in the edit window will be color coded. This color coding is used only to highlight different types of HTML tags for easier readability. The color coding will not be used by published documents displayed on a Web browser. Nonstandard HTML tags, such as Microsoft or Netscape extensions, will be set to a different color than the base HTML tags.
Convert Extended Characters while typing	Specifies that extended characters (most commonly used by European users) will be converted to the appropriate HTML tag. HotDog Pro could convert the copyright symbol (©) to &copy, for example, while you type. Note that this option may slow down the application, so it may be better to perform this operation when you publish files instead. (See the Convert Extended Characters to HTML codes in the Publishing Tab section later in this table.)

Option	Description
Popup Menu with right mouse button	Specifies that the right mouse button will display an object menu when selected. Note that this option performs the same function as a right mouse click on a computer running Windows 95, Windows NT 4.0, or prior versions of Windows or NT that normally do not support this option.
Tags in lowercase	Specifies that HTML tags be entered in lowercase rather than uppercase (the default). HTML tags are not case sensitive, so this choice is only for readability.
Show spaces	Specifies that spaces will be displayed onscreen while editing.
Show Paragraph Marks	Specifies that paragraph marks be displayed onscreen while editing.
Tab Indent	Specifies the default tab width, in inches.
Undo Depth	Specifies the number of buffers to be used for undo operations. Higher numbers require additional memory. The minimum is 0, the maximum is 99, and the default is 10.

Publishing Tab

Remove All Carriage Returns	Specifies that all CRLF (carriage return line feed) pairs be changed to LF only.
Publish as UNIX text file	Specifies that all CRLF pairs be changed to LF only when the document is published.
Convert Extended Characters to HTML codes	Specifies that extended characters be converted to the appropriate HTML tag when a document is published.
Replace \ with / in filenames	Specifies that the normal directory designator \ be replaced with the HTML directory designator / when the document is published.
Extension for Published Documents	Specifies the published document extension. By default this is .PUB, which is a reminder to change the extension when the document is published. Note that it is best to change this

continues

Table 16.1. continued

Option	Description
	to the .HTM extension so that you can use the default association for your Web browser and preview the document by double-clicking on it in File Manager. It also removes one more step when you publish the document on your Web server.
Replace Words During Publishing	Specifies a set of words to be converted. You may use GP-But\BUTTON.GIF in your document, for example, to specify a relative path to your button. During the publishing phase the GP-But could be automatically changed to ..\GRAPHICS\BUTTONS, which specifies the relative location of your buttons.

Display Tab

Option	Description
3-D Windows	Specifies that the windows will be displayed using the Windows 95 user interface rather than the more traditional Windows 3.*x* interface.
Rounded Tabs	Specifies that tabs on a tabbed dialog will use rounded corners rather than the square corners of the Windows 95 user interface.
Fast Draw	This option may be used to reduce flickering of screen updates on slower systems, but in turn will use additional system resources.
Word Wrap	Specifies that text lines wider than the screen be automatically wrapped to the next line.
Icons Only	Specifies that only the icon be displayed for buttons on the button bar.
Text Only	Specifies that only the text description of a button be displayed on the button bar.
Icons and Text	Specifies that both text and icons be displayed on each button on the button bar.
Refresh document on each keypress	Specifies that the document will be updated after each keypress. Note that use of this option may cause an additional performance degradation on slow computers.

Option	Description
File Dirs Tab	
Preview Browser	Specifies the location of the Web browser to use for a document preview. Note that when this option is enabled, the icon on the button bar will change to the icon of your Web browser.
Documents	Specifies the location of your HTML documents.
Published Files	Specifies the location of your HTML documents in the published format (that is, after any character translation may have occurred).
Graphics Files	Specifies the location of your graphics files.
AutoSave Files	Specifies the location for automatically saved copies of your documents.
.INF Files	Specifies the location of the HotDog Pro initialization files.
Templates	Specifies the location of your HTML document templates.
Temporary Files	Specifies the location to be used for temporary files.
Save/Start Tab	
AutoSave every *XX* minutes	Specifies how often to automatically save your documents, in minutes, where *XX* is the amount of time to wait between saves.
Show Handy Hints when HotDog starts	Specifies whether to display the Handy Hints dialog every time at application startup.
Create Backup Files when saving	Specifies that a backup copy of your document be created with a .BAK file extension whenever a document is saved.
Restore Last Session when HotDog starts	Specifies that the current windows and associated documents be reopened whenever the application starts. This provides the capability to quickly return to your last session status without having to manually open the appropriate files.

continues

Table 16.1. continued

Option	Description
Open New Document when HotDog starts	Specifies that the application always open a new document when the application starts.

Colors Tab

Option	Description
Foreground Color	Specifies the application foreground color.
Background Color	Specifies the application background color.
Default Tag Color	Specifies the default color for HTML tags when used in conjunction with the Quick Color option of the Editing dialog.
Tag Type	Specifies the default HTML tag format to use. This can be Microsoft, Netscape, or HTML 3.0. Note that for optimum usage, you should set this value to Microsoft when designing HTML documents for the Internet Explorer.
Tag Type Color	Specifies the default color for HTML tags you specified in the Tag Type option. This is useful to display any HTML extension tags in a different color than the standard HTML tags.

Dictionary Tab

Option	Description
Custom Dictionary	Specifies a path and filename to be used for additions to the standard dictionary. Note that if you already have a default dictionary created with Word for Windows, you can use it with HotDog Pro.
Standard Dictionary	Specifies the dictionary to use for standard spelling comparisons. This can be american.vtd for an American English, brit.vtd for a British English, french.vtd for a French, german.vtd for a German, and italian.vtd for an Italian dictionary.

Upload Tab

Option	Description
Default Web Server	Specifies the name of your Web server, such as ftp.nt-guru.com.
Directory on Server	Specifies the default directory on your Web server to store the HTML documents.
Default Login Name	Specifies a username to use when logging on to your server via the HotFTP FTP client.

Option	Description
Password	Specifies the password to use with the username specified.
HotFTP Location	Specifies the location of the HotDog Pro FTP client.

Working with Documents and Templates

By now you should have HotDog Pro customized to your satisfaction and be ready to start creating your HTML document. In this section you will learn how to create an HTML document, create a template from an HTML document, and publish your completed HTML document on your Web server. This section focuses on individual document management, and the next section focuses on multiple-document management (or projects). Before you can work with multiple documents, however, you need to learn how to work with individual documents contained within a project. This follows the old adage that says you need to learn how to walk before you can run, which is why we will start with the basics and then move on to the more advanced features.

Creating an HTML Document

Creating an HTML document is the meat of this chapter. Everything else leads up to this point. When you first run HotDog Pro, the default document (shown in Figure 16.6) will be displayed. This default document is based on the Normal template. (We'll talk more about templates in the section "Creating a Template from an HTML Document.") After your default document loads, it's time to customize it to create your finished Web page. Creating a Web page includes such steps as defining the basic properties for the document, adding the document's basic text, and finally adding any HTML tags and associated text. In the following sections, you will look further into creating a Web page using these steps.

Defining the Document Properties

Every HTML document you create will have some unique content, even if it is only the document title. HotDog Pro makes entering this information easy. Just choose Document from the Format menu, press Ctrl+D, or click the Document button on the button bar. This will display the Format Document dialog box, shown in Figure 16.7, with the Document Information tabbed dialog box (the default), where you may specify the following information:

- Document Title—Specifies the title of the document. This title will be displayed on the caption bar of most Web browsers.
- Base URL Address—Specifies the location of the HTML document.

FIGURE 16.6.
Creating an HTML document.

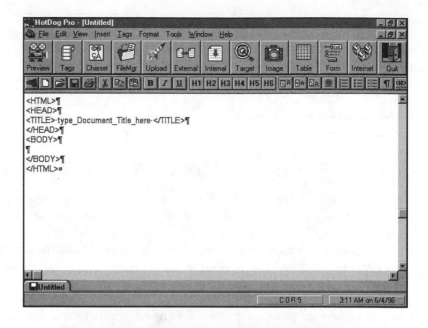

FIGURE 16.7.
Specifying the general document properties.

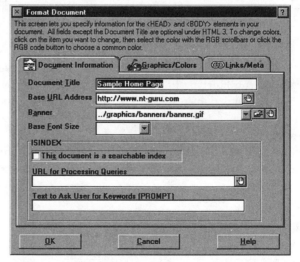

■ Banner—Specifies either an image (GIF or JPEG) to insert into the document as a document banner, or builds an external link to an image. To insert an image, click the folder icon. This will display the HotDog Pro—Select Image File dialog box where you specify a filename. To insert an external link, click the hand icon. This will display the Build External Link dialog box, where you specify the resource type, host address, port, path, filename, target, and description.

- Base Font Size—Specifies the default font size for the document.
- This document is a searchable index—Specifies that this document is a searchable document.
- URL for Processing Queries—Specifies the URL to which the search queries will be forwarded.
- Text to Ask User for Keywords (PROMPT)—Specifies a replacement for the default prompt, `This is a searchable index. Enter search keywords:`, with the message you specify.

If you want to specify additional characteristics for the document, click the Graphics/Colors tab. This will display the dialog box shown in Figure 16.8, where you can display the following information:

Figure 16.8.

Specifying the document colors.

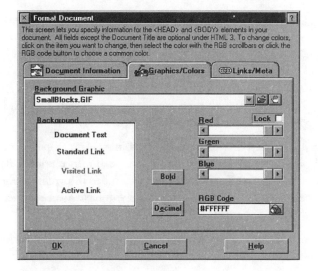

- Background Graphic—Specifies an image to be used as a background image. This image will be tiled across the Web browser.

CAUTION

A background image will prevent anything else from displaying on the Web browser until the image has been downloaded. Therefore, any background image you use should be as small as possible. It should also be a non-interlaced graphic for best results. On the aesthetic side, you might want to consider how the color of your background will affect the readability of the text.

- Background—Specifies the background color of the Web page.

> **NOTE**
>
> Unless your background graphic is a transparent graphic, it makes little sense to use a background color. This is because the background image will be layered over the background.

- Document Text—Specifies the color of regular text on your Web page.
- Standard Link—Specifies the color of a hypertext link that has not been accessed.
- Visited Link—Specifies the color of a hypertext link after it has been accessed.
- Active Link—Specifies the color of a hypertext link while it is being activated and the new document loads.

To change the display color of a link, you can use one of three methods. You can click an entry in the bitmap (such as the Document Text), then change the Red, Green, or Blue sliders until the desired color is achieved. You can click the RGB color icon at the end of the RGB Code field and select a color from the Color dialog box. Or you can specify an RGB entry in decimal or hexadecimal notation in the RGB field. To change from decimal to hexadecimal, click the Decimal button. This will then toggle the button state to Hex. I prefer to use the RGB color icon, because this is the easiest way to select a color.

The final option in this dialog box is the Links/Meta tab. This dialog box has two list boxes for entering link or meta information. This type of information is used to associate links between this document and other documents or to embed information about the document which cannot be performed any other way. Unless you have a specific need to use these fields, you are better off leaving them alone.

Once you have finished entering the document properties, click the OK button. The HTML document will then be updated to include the information you specified.

Formatting Text in a Document

Entering text in your document is a matter of typing it in. Formatting your text, however, is a little more complicated. To format your text, you can use one of the following methods:

- Highlight your text, then choose one of the elements bar buttons (such as the B button to make the text bold, the H1 button to make the text a level-one header, or the Center button to center the text).
- Highlight your text and choose an option (such as Bold) from the Format menu.
- Manually enter your HTML start tags, your text, and then the HTML end tags.
- Use one of the other HotDog Pro methods (choose a menu option, select a tag from the tag dialog box, and so on) to insert an HTML tag pair, and then enter your text between the tag pairs.

> **TIP**
>
> To insert a special character, such as the copyright symbol, select Special Characters from the View menu, click the Charset button on the button bar, or press F7. This will display the Entity list, where you can scroll through the available special characters until you find the one you want. Then just double-click it to insert it into the document.

Inserting HTML Tags in a Document

This is where most of the real work occurs with HotDog Pro. There are so many different HTML tags and methods to insert into your document that it can be a bit confusing. However, no matter which method you use, once you've inserted the tag or tag pair, you will have to insert your text. To make this process easier to understand, I have divided this section into five basic types.

Using the Tag Dialog Box to Insert an HTML Tag

The most versatile method for inserting a tag is to select it from the Tags dialog box. Just follow these steps:

1. Select Tags from the View menu, click the Tags button on the button bar, or press F6. Any of these will display the Tags dialog box, as shown in Figure 16.9.

FIGURE 16.9.

Inserting an HTML tag from the Tags dialog box.

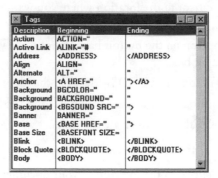

2. Click the scrollbar until the tag you want to insert is visible. Then double-click the tag. This will place it into the document at the current insertion point.

3. Repeat step 2 for each tag you want to insert. When you have finished inserting tags, you can close the Tags dialog box by selecting View | Tags, clicking the Tags button on the button bar, or pressing F6.

> **TIP**
>
> If the tag does not insert all the options you want, you may change this behavior by selecting Tag Information from the Edit menu. This will display the Edit Tag Information dialog box, where you can modify the tag to include the additional options. You can even add new tags.

Inserting a Hypertext Link into a Document

Most, if not all, of your HTML documents will include hypertext links to either a location within the same document or an external document. The format will vary a bit between a link to an internal or external location. However, the method you will use to create these links is quite similar.

To insert a link to an internal point within a document, follow these steps:

1. Move the cursor to the location in your document where you want to jump.
2. Choose Hypertext Target from the Insert menu, press Ctrl+G, or press the Target button on the button bar. Any of these will display the Enter Target ID dialog box.
3. Enter a unique (within the document) identifier in the edit field and press the OK button. This will insert an anchor point at the current insertion point (where the cursor is).
4. Move the cursor to the location where you want the hypertext link to be inserted.
5. Choose Jump Within this Document from the Insert menu, press Ctrl+K, or press the Internal button on the button bar. Any of these will display the Select Hypertext Target dialog box.
6. In the Hypertext Target ID field, select the identifier you want to jump to.
7. Enter a comment in the Description of Link field to identify the link.
8. Click the OK button to create the link.

To insert a link to an external document or service, follow these steps:

1. Move the cursor to the location in your document where you want the link to be created.
2. Choose Jump to Document on Another System from the Insert menu, press Ctrl+H, or click the External button on the button bar. Any of these will display the Build External Hypertext Link dialog box, as shown in Figure 16.10.
3. Select the appropriate type of link (such as http for a WWW document) in the Resource Type drop-down list box.

FIGURE 16.10.

Inserting a link to an external document.

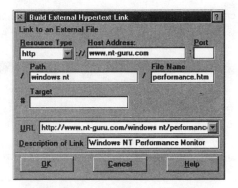

4. Specify the name of the host to which you wish to link (such as www.nt-guru.com) in the Host Address field.

5. If the resource requires a specific TCP/IP port, such as when a proxy agent is used for additional security, enter this number in the Port field.

6. Specify the path to the external document (such as windows nt/performance) in the Path field.

7. Specify the filename you are linking to (such as performance.htm) in the File Name field.

8. If the link will jump to a specific location within the external document, specify the location identifier in the Target field.

9. Specify a comment in the Description of Link field to identify the link.

10. Click the OK button to create the link and insert it at the current insertion point of your document.

Inserting a Graphic Image into a Document

Inserting an image into your document follows a procedure similar to that for inserting a hypertext link into your document. You can insert an image as a static resource, meaning that it is there just for show, or you can insert it as a hypertext link. If you insert it as a hypertext link, when the user clicks it he will jump to the link destination. To insert an image or an image link, follow these steps:

1. Move the cursor to the location in your document where you want the image to be inserted.

2. Choose Image from the Insert menu, or click the Image button on the button bar to display the Insert Image dialog box.

3. Enter the location of the image in the Image File field.

4. Enter the URL of the document to execute when the image is selected in the Document to Launch field. If no document is entered, then the image will be a static resource.

5. Enter a comment in the Alternate Description field to describe the image or link.

6. Click the OK button to create the link and insert it into your document.

TIP

Use the Image Advanced option on the Insert menu to specify additional information about an image. You may specify that the image is an image map or a figure, whether the image is low resolution or high resolution, the image width and height, image border, image alignment, and how much whitespace will be displayed around the image.

Inserting a Table into a Document

Creating tables with HTML can be a real pain. HotDog Pro can make it a lot easier for you. You might be surprised at just how easy it can be to insert a table. Keep in mind, however, that if you insert just a blank table, it will be up to you to populate the rows and columns.

To insert a completed table, follow these steps:

1. Move the cursor to the location in your document where you want the table to be inserted.

2. Choose Table from the Insert menu, press Ctrl+T, or click the Table button on the button bar. Any of these will display the Create Table dialog box (see Figure 16.11).

FIGURE 16.11.

Inserting a table into a document.

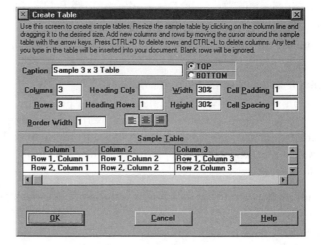

Using Sausage Software's HotDog Pro

CHAPTER 16

503

16

USING SAUSAGE
SOFTWARE'S
HOTDOG PRO

3. To specify a description for the table, enter it in the Caption field. To place the caption at the top of the table, click the TOP radio button. To place the caption at the bottom of the table, click the BOTTOM radio button.

4. Specify the number of columns in the table in the Columns field.

5. Specify the number of rows in the table in the Rows field.

6. Specify the number of heading columns in the Heading Cols field.

7. Specify the number of heading rows in the Heading Rows field.

NOTE

When you specify the size of your table, be sure to include the number of heading rows and columns. For example, if you want to insert three rows with three columns, each with a single header row, you really need to create a table with four rows and three columns.

8. Specify the width of the table in an absolute (generally measured in pixels) value or as a relative value (a percentage of the Web browser's displayable area) in the Width field.

9. Specify the height of the table in an absolute or relative value in the Height field.

TIP

It is usually better to specify relative rather than absolute values. A relative value will give the Web browser more leeway to determine how the table should be displayed for optimum results.

10. Specify the vertical distance between cells of the table in the Cell Padding field.

11. Specify the horizontal distance between cells of the table in the Cell Spacing field.

12. Specify the size of the table border in the Border Width field.

13. Specify a table alignment by clicking the left, center, or right justification button.

14. For each cell in the table where you want to enter text, double-click the cell, and then enter your text.

15. When you have entered all of your text, click the OK button to insert the table at the current insertion point.

The table height, table width, cell padding, cell spacing, and border width are optional components that, if not specified, will be determined by the Web browser.

> **TIP**
>
> One of the features that makes using HotDog Pro so worthwhile is the way it manages tables. If you create a table in the fashion described in this section, you can later select the entire table, click the Table button to display the Create Table dialog box, and modify the table without losing any of your data. You can add columns, change the table width, change the table alignment, or use any other option in this dialog box.

Inserting an Internet Command into a Document

If you want to insert a hypertext link to an Internet service, HotDog Pro makes this a snap as well. The basic method requires four steps:

1. Move the cursor to the location in your document where you want the link to be inserted.

2. Choose Launch an Internet Service from the Insert menu, press Ctrl+Y, or click the Internet button on the button bar. Any of these will display the Create HyperText Link dialog box, as shown in Figure 16.12.

FIGURE 16.12.

Inserting a link to an Internet service in a document.

3. Click the button of the appropriate service (such as Let the User send Mail to someone) to launch (or in this case e-mail a message). This will display a service-specific dialog box.

4. Enter the requested information in the dialog box and click the OK button. The appropriate link will then be inserted into your document.

Creating a Template from an HTML Document

If you will be creating multiple HTML documents, either for yourself or for clients, it is a good idea to create a template. A template is used to create a skeleton HTML document that you can modify as needed. You may want to have a home page button on every document you create, for example. If you create a template that includes the button and the link, every page you create will have this predefined hypertext link to your home page. You can create templates that even include themes. A *theme* might be, for example, a specific color scheme or document layout.

The basic method for creating a template is as follows:

1. Create the basic document. When you create the document, make sure the document properties are correctly set. These properties include the document title, banner, background, base URL, document background, link colors, and link and meta information. If you have any buttons (such as the home page button), copyright information, or other standard items you wish to add, do so now.

2. When the basic framework has been completed, choose Make Template from Document from the Tools menu. This will display the Create Template dialog box. Enter a unique name to describe the template, click the OK button, and the template will be created.

Publishing Your Documents

Publishing your documents is one of the easiest tasks you will perform with HotDog Pro. It requires only the push of a single button to publish your documents, but in order to succeed you must first make sure HotDog Pro is properly configured. So keep the following in mind when it's time to publish your documents:

- Because most Web browsers use the .HTM file extension, you should too. You should either change the default extension of .PUB to .HTM before you upload your documents or be sure to rename them after you upload your documents to your Web server. This is performed in the Publishing tab of the Options dialog box.

- If you do not have a network drive mapped to your Web server, you will need to use the HotFTP client to upload your files to your Web server. You must specify the appropriate URL, directory, user name, and password in the Upload tab of the Options dialog box.

- If you have a mapped network drive, you can specify the location for published files in the File Dirs tab of the Options dialog box.

To actually publish your document, just make sure the active document is the document you want to publish, then choose either File | Publish Document or click the Publish button on the button bar.

Working with Projects

A project provides the ability to group many HTML documents into a single manageable unit. You can create multiple projects, each with different properties. You can use projects to support several different clients, each with their own Web server. Or you can use a project to divide a large Web site into several smaller, easier to manage, subsets. It's up to you to determine whether you will use the project management features, though I do recommend them.

The starting point, of course, is to create a project by choosing Project Manager from the File menu. This will display the Project Manager dialog box, where you can specify the name of the project, the project directory, the Web server, the Web server directory, the username and password, and the document files within the project.

Thereafter you can use the File | Open Project to access all the files defined within the project with one easy step. But more important, you have the ability to check all of the internal and external links contained within the project. The Project Manager Links dialog box enables you to examine individual links or to check all links within a project to verify that the link is correctly formed. This inspection can prevent a flood of e-mail to you about a hypertext link that has been broken.

Summary

In this chapter you learn a bit about HotDog Pro. This discussion gives you a glimpse of its capabilities, perhaps enough to interest you in trying out the shareware version to see how well it suits your needs. HotDog Pro is an easy-to-use tool that can help both the beginner and the expert develop HTML documents.

In the next chapter, you will take a look at the Internet Information Server Software Development Kit (SDK). Although the SDK itself is too much to cover in a single chapter, you will get a look at some ways to extend the Internet Information Server's capabilities by creating ISAPI applications. You will also learn why ISAPI is the best method for developing custom applications.

IN THIS PART

- **The Internet Information Server SDK** *509*

- **Unleashing the Power of VBScript** *527*

- **Introduction to Windows NT CGI Programming** *571*

- **Writing Java Applets** *603*

- **Creating Dynamic Content with Active Server Pages** *627*

- **Using NetShow Live** *637*

V

PART

Advanced Web Page Development

## CHAPTER 17

The Internet Information Server SDK

IN THIS CHAPTER

- What Is an ISAPI Application? *510*

The Internet Information Server SDK is strictly for developers, who will use it in one of two ways:

- ■ To create interactive HTML documents using the ActiveX components, which include VBScript, JavaScript, and OLE (object linking and embedding) controls and documents. Because many of you will be creating HTML documents with active content, you may want to look at Chapter 18, "Unleashing the Power of VBScript," for more in-depth information.

- ■ To create Internet Server Application Programming Interface (ISAPI) applications to extend the capabilities of the Internet Information Server.

This chapter focuses on the latter aspect: how to use the IIS SDK to create ISAPI applications. You start your exploration of the ISAPI interface by defining an ISAPI application. Then you look into the ISAPI interface and ISAPI-specific functions. Finally, you look at a skeleton ISAPI application that you can use to build your own ISAPI applications. In order to successfully build an ISAPI application and to understand the following discussions, you must be a proficient Win32 developer. You need to be familiar with the Win32 API, understand the basic issues in a multithreaded environment (data coherency is one of these issues), and know how to develop a dynamic link library (DLL).

What Is an ISAPI Application?

An ISAPI application is a Windows NT DLL. The primary purpose of ISAPI is to provide an alternative interface to the more commonly used *Common Gateway Interface* (CGI). For more information on CGI development, take a look at Chapter 19, "Introduction to Windows NT CGI Programming." A *CGI application* is an external application that executes in a separate process from the Web server and is commonly used to provide services not provided by the HTTP (or Web) server or defined by the HTML specification. You can use a CGI application to interface to a SQL Server database, to save data from an HTML form, or even to insert a counter on your Web page (such as the hit counters on many Web pages).

Because CGI applications have been around for quite a while, you may be asking yourself why you need (or should care about) another methodology to provide similar functionality. You're probably wondering just what the difference is between ISAPI and CGI. After all, both extend your Web server's capabilities by creating custom extensions, and both allow you to write extensions using your favorite C or C++ compiler. Well, the main difference between these two interfaces can be summed up in one word: performance!

A CGI Application Versus an ISAPI Application

A CGI application executes as a separate process. This means that each time the application is called, it must be loaded into memory, passed the client parameters, and executed. Then it must pass the client data back to the HTTP server. If the application is called multiple times by different clients simultaneously, multiple copies of the application will be resident in memory at the same time, which consumes system resources. An ISAPI application, however, is quite a bit different than a CGI application:

- Rather than executing as an external application in a separate process, an ISAPI application is a native Windows NT application that executes in the same address space as the HTTP server. This is possible because the ISAPI application is a dynamic link library rather than an external program, and it executes as an integral part of the HTTP server.

- A dynamic link library can be loaded or unloaded at will. This means that if the additional functionality provided by the DLL is no longer required, it can be unloaded from memory to conserve system resources. When the service is needed again, it will be reloaded.

- An ISAPI application is a multithreaded shareable image. This means that only one copy of the DLL will be loaded into memory, and this one copy can support multiple simultaneous client requests. Again, this conserves system resources and improves response time.

A Few ISAPI Application Considerations

Although a dynamic link library has its good points (described in the preceding section), it also has a downside that you must consider: Because a dynamic link library executes in the same address space as the parent application, an errant dynamic link library (such as one that references memory indiscriminately) can cause the parent application to fail! That means a poorly written ISAPI application can cause your Web server to choke, spew, and die a cruel and unnatural death. You should prepare yourself for this eventuality by following these suggestions:

- Never perform development or testing on a production server. It may cost you more to maintain a duplicate of your production environment, but this is a necessary requirement if maintaining your server's operation is critical to your business.

> **TIP**
>
> You can reduce the costs associated with ISAPI development by creating a standalone server with all of your development tools and required databases installed on it. You can even use an Access database (or any ODBC database) instead of a SQL Server database to lower costs. However, final testing before installing the ISAPI application on the production server should be performed in an environment that mimics the production environment as closely as possible. If your production server uses an external SQL Server database, your final testing should also use an external (not necessarily the same SQL Server database as your production server) SQL Server installation rather than a local or remote Access database.

■ Never install a third-party ISAPI application on your production server without thoroughly testing the ISAPI application on a different server (such as your duplicate test environment).

■ Stress test the ISAPI application using multiple connections from multiple Web browsers (including the Internet Explorer, Netscape Navigator, and any others you may have available) to make sure your ISAPI application functions as expected.

■ If you develop your own ISAPI applications, make use of the structured exception handling provided by the Win32 API. These exception APIs include the `try except` and `try finally` statements. The `try except` statements are used to capture any exception (such as an invalid memory reference) that occurs in the `try` block and then execute the statements in the `except` block (so you can determine the type of exception and then remedy the situation). The `try finally` statements are used to ensure that no matter what happens in the `try` block (including an exception), your code in the `finally` block will execute (so you can clean up your application by releasing allocated memory, for example).

Even if you do not follow the suggestions described in the preceding section, there is a little extra insurance I can provide for you. If you will stop by my Web site at http://www.nt-guru.com/IIS, you can pick up a copy of my IIS service-monitoring application. This application just monitors the operating state of the IIS publishing services. If it detects a service that is not responding either because it has hung up or has terminated, my service-monitoring application will attempt to restart it. This application cannot solve all of your problems, but it can help keep your IIS services up and running. This will make your Web clients a little happier because they will be able to connect to your site and view all of the wonderful content you are providing.

The Basic ISAPI Interface

If you have performed any Windows or Windows NT development in the past, you may already be aware of the multitude of interfaces (or requirements to implement a desired function) defined by the Windows or Windows NT API. An *ISAPI application*, also commonly called an *Internet Server Application* (ISA), is no different. It too requires that you use a specific interface. The first part of this interface, which is optional, is that the application must support the basic definition of a dynamic link library. Therefore, it can include a function called DLLMain that will be called when the application is loaded or unloaded by the operating system (Windows NT Server). This function provides specific ISA initialization and cleanup.

After the application is loaded into memory, the HTTP server calls the GetExtensionVersion function to obtain version-specific information. If the version numbers are acceptable, the HTTP server then calls the HttpExtensionProc function each time a client makes a request requiring this ISA. Normally, this client request is executed whenever a client selects a URL in the form of

```
http:\\www.DomainName.com/scripts/ExtensionName.DLL?Parameter
```

You can substitute your own domain name, ISA name, and parameters for the values DomainName, ExtensionName.DLL, and Parameter in the URL, respectively. For example, your URL might appear as

```
http://www.nt-guru.com/scripts/skeleton.dll?NoFunction
```

> **NOTE**
>
> The DLLMain, GetExtensionVersion, and HttpExtensionProc functions must be exported in order for the extension to function properly.

To give you a better idea of this required interface, take a look at Figure 17.1, which illustrates the basic ISA architecture.

As you can see in the figure, there is one address space within which the HTTP server and the Internet Server Applications execute. The HTTP server communicates with the ISA using an *extension control block* (ECB). A pointer to the ECB is passed to the HttpExtensionProc function each time a client makes a request. It is up to the HttpExtensionProc function to parse the ECB structure and determine the request by the client and to perform the appropriate processing. The HttpExtensionProc function is similar to the main function of a C application used as a CGI extension, but instead of receiving its input using stdin, as a C application does, the HttpExtensionProc function uses the ECB structure to retrieve its data. Also, instead of using stdout to send the processed data back to the client, the HttpExtensionProc function uses the WriteClient or ServerSupportFunction functions. Within the HttpExtensionProc function, you can use any Win32 API. This provides a means to extend the HTTP server to perform almost any task. Microsoft dbWeb, for example, is an ISAPI application. Microsoft dbWeb is used to provide an ODBC interface to the HTTP server so that your clients can insert, delete, update, or query, your ODBC-compliant databases using their Web browser.

FIGURE 17.1.
*The Internet Server
Application interface.*

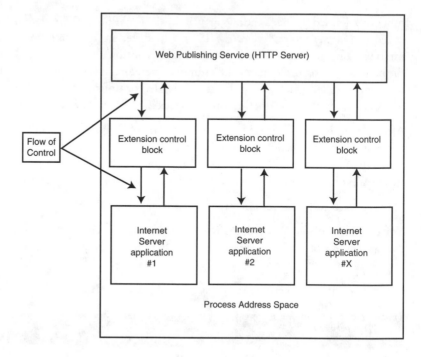

Following are the six functions defined for an ISA:

- GetExtensionVersion—Provides version-specific information to the HTTP server.
- HttpExtensionProc—Performs the real work of the ISA extension.
- GetServerVariable—Provides access to predefined environment variables.
- ReadClient—Obtains additional data from the client when the ECB data buffer cannot contain all the data.
- WriteClient—Sends data back to the client.
- ServerSupportFunction—Provides general-purpose functions as well as HTTP server-specific functions to the ISA.

The GetExtensionVersion Function

The GetExtensionVersion function informs the HTTP server of the suitability of the extension. In essence, when the function is called by the HTTP server, it is passed as a pointer to an HSE_VERSION_INFO structure. This structure contains the major and minor versions of the HTTP server that the extension supports, along with a text description of the server extension. The ISA must populate the HSE_VERSION_INFO structure with this version information when called by the HTTP server. This function is used to prevent an outdated ISA from being loaded on a noncompatible HTTP server. The function definition is as follows:

```
BOOL WINAPI GetExtensionVersion (HSE_VERSION_INFO *pVer);
```

The HSE_VERSION_INFO structure in httpext.h is defined as

```
typedef struct    _HSE_VERSION_INFO {
    DWORD   dwExtensionVersion;
    CHAR    lpszExtensionDesc[HSE_MAX_EXT_DLL_NAME_LEN];
} HSE_VERSION_INFO, *LPHSE_VERSION_INFO;
```

Currently the HSE_MAX_EXT_DLL_NAME_LEN definition is set to a value of 256 characters, which provides you with a 255-character name space because you must leave room for the string's null terminator. When this function is called, it must populate the HSE_VERSION_INFO structure and return TRUE (1) if successful or FALSE (0) if unsuccessful. The dwExtensionVersion element can be populated using the HIWORD and LOWORD macros. The major version number is contained in the high word, and the minor version number is contained in the low word of the dwExtensionVersion element.

The HttpExtensionProc Function

Whenever the client (the Web browser) makes a request requiring the ISA, the HttpExtensionProc function of the ISA is called and passed a pointer to an ECB structure. The ECB structure is defined in the header HTTPEXT.H as EXTENSION_CONTROL_BLOCK and has the elements summarized in Table 17.1. The HttpExtensionProc is defined as follows:

```
DWORD WINAPI HttpExtensionProc (EXTENSION_CONTROL_BLOCK  *pEcb);
```

Table 17.1. The extension control block format.

Element	Type	Used for	Description
cbSize	DWORD	Input	Specifies the size of the ECB structure.
dwVersion	DWORD	Input	Specifies the IIS version number that this extension supports. The major version number is contained in the high word, and the minor version number is contained in the low word. You can use the HIWORD and LOWORD macros to obtain the major and minor version numbers.
ConnID	HCONN	Input	A unique number assigned by the HTTP server. This number should not be modified.
dwHttpStatusCode	DWORD	Output	Specifies the status of the current completed transaction to be returned to the HTTP server.

continues

17
THE INTERNET
INFORMATION
SERVER SDK

Table 17.1. continued

Element	Type	Used for	Description
lpszLogData	CHAR	Output	A null-terminated string of HSE_LOG_BUFFER_LEN (currently defined as 80 characters) to be inserted into the HTTP server log.
lpszMethod	LPSTR	Input	Specifies a null-terminated string containing the method used by the client for this transaction. This is the same value as the CGI variable REQUEST_METHOD.
lpszQueryString	LPSTR	Input	Specifies a null-terminated string containing the query information. This is the same as the CGI variable QUERY_STRING.
lpszPathInfo	LPSTR	Input	Specifies a null-terminated string containing the extra path information given to the client. This is the same as the CGI variable PATH_INFO.
lpszPathTranslated	LPSTR	Input	Specifies a null-terminated string containing the translated path. This is the same as the CGI variable PATH_TRANSLATED.
cbTotalBytes	DWORD	Input	Specifies the total number of bytes received from the client. This is the same as the CGI variable CONTENT_LENGTH.
cbAvailable	DWORD	Input	Specifies the available number of bytes, out of the total as defined by cbTotalBytes, contained within the buffer pointed to by lpbData.
lpbData	LPBYTE	Input	Specifies a pointer to a buffer, of size cbAvailable, containing the data sent by the client.
lpszContentType	LPSTR	Input	Specifies a null-terminated string containing the type of data sent by the client. This is the same as the CGI variable CONTENT_TYPE.

It is up to the HttpExtensionProc function to parse the ECB to determine what the client is requesting. This information will be contained in the ECB lpszQueryString element. Any additional data will be contained in the buffer pointed to by the lpbData element. If the buffer is too small to contain all the data as defined by the cbTotalBytes element, the HttpExtensionProc can retrieve the additional data using the ReadClient function. When the HttpExtensionProc has completed its processing, it must send the resulting data (in HTML format) to the client using the WriteClient or ServerSupportFunction function. It must return a status code to the HTTP server upon completion. The status code can be one of the following:

- HSE_STATUS_SUCCESS—This status code specifies that the ISA completed its task successfully and that the HTTP server can disconnect and free up system resources by unloading the ISA.

- HSE_STATUS_SUCCESS_AND_KEEP_CONN—This status code specifies that the ISA completed its task, but that the HTTP server should keep the ISA active in memory if the client supports persistent connections.

> **NOTE**
>
> The HSE_STATUS_SUCCESS_AND_KEEP_CONN status code should only be used if the ISA has sent a keep-alive header to the client.

- HSE_STATUS_PENDING—This status code specifies that the ISA has queued the request for processing and that it will inform the HTTP server when the request has completed using the ServerSupportFunction with the dwHSERequest parameter set to HSE_REQ_DONE_WITH_SESSION.

- HSE_STATUS_ERROR—This status code specifies that the ISA encountered an error while attempting to complete its task and that the HTTP server can disconnect and free up system resources by unloading the ISA.

The GetServerVariable Function

The GetServerVariable function obtains information about the connection or information about the HTTP server. The function is defined as follows:

```
BOOL WINAPI GetServerVariable (HCONN hConn, LPSTR lpszVariableName,
➥LPVOID lpvBuffer, LPDWORD lpdwSizeofBuffer);
```

The function parameters are defined as follows:

- hConn—Specifies the connection handle.

- lpszVariableName—Specifies the name of the desired CGI variable. These variable definitions are summarized in Table 17.2.

- lpvBuffer—Specifies a pointer to a buffer to contain the data defined by the CGI variable.

- lpdwSizeOfBuffer—Specifies the size of the buffer pointed to by lpvBuffer. When the function returns, this parameter contains the length of the data returned, including the null terminator.

Table 17.2. The `GetServerVariable` variable definitions.

Variable Name	Definition	Note
ALL_HTTP	All HTTP headers that are not parsed into one of the other listed variables in this table.	
AUTH_PASS	Specifies the password supplied by the client.	The password will be a null-terminated string.
AUTH_TYPE	Specifies the authorization type in use.	If the user has been authenticated by the server, the return value will be `Basic`. Otherwise, the entry will not be present.
CONTENT_LENGTH	Specifies the number of bytes the script can expect to receive from the client.	
CONTENT_TYPE	The content type of the information supplied in the `POST` request.	
GATEWAY_INTERFACE	Specifies the revision level of the CGI specification.	
HTTP_ACCEPT	Returns special-case HTTP header information.	
PATH_INFO	Additional path information as given by the client.	This value will contain the trailing part of the URL after the script name, but before the query string (if any query string was supplied).
PATH_TRANSLATED	The same as `PATH_INFO`, but without any virtual pathname translation.	
QUERY_STRING	Specifies the information after the `?` in a script query.	
REMOTE_ADDR	Specifies the IP address of the client.	
REMOTE_HOST	Specifies the hostname of the client.	
REMOTE_USER	Specifies the user name supplied by the client and authorized by the server.	

Variable Name	Definition	Note
REQUEST_METHOD	Specifies the HTTP request method.	
SCRIPT_NAME	Specifies the name of the script being executed.	
SERVER_NAME	Specifies the name of the server (or IP address) as it should appear in self-referencing URLs.	
SERVER_PORT	Specifies the TCP/IP port on which the request was received.	
SERVER_PROTOCOL	Specifies the name and version of the request.	Usually HTTP/1.0.
SERVER_SOFTWARE	Specifies the name and version number of the Web server under which the IIS extension is executing.	

The ReadClient Function

The ReadClient function obtains additional data from the client when the entire block of data will not fit into the buffer pointer by lpdData in the ECB block. The definition of the function is as follows:

```
BOOL ReadClient (HCONN hConn, LPVOID lpvBuffer, LPDWORD lpdwSize);
```

The function parameters are defined as follows:

- hConn—Specifies the connection handle.
- lpvBuffer—Specifies a pointer to a buffer. This buffer will be used to contain the data returned by the read request.
- lpdwSizeOfBuffer—Specifies the size of the buffer pointed to by lpvBuffer. When the function returns, this parameter contains the length of the data returned.

The WriteClient Function

The WriteClient function sends data to the client. The definition of the function is as follows:

```
BOOL WriteClient (HCONN hConn, LPVOID lpvBuffer, LPDWORD lpdwSize,
↪DWORD dwReserved);
```

The function parameters are defined as follows:

- hConn—Specifies the connection handle.
- lpvBuffer—Specifies a pointer to a buffer. This buffer will be used to contain the data sent to the client. Normally, this will be a series of HTML tags and data.
- lpdwSizeOfBuffer—Specifies the size of the buffer pointed to by lpvBuffer. If a null-terminated string is to be sent to the client in its entirety, this value should be set using the value returned by the function call strlen(lpvBuffer). When the WriteClient function returns, this parameter contains the length of the data sent to the client.
- dwReserved—Specifies that the parameter is reserved for future use.

The ServerSupportFunction Function

The ServerSupportFunction sends data back to a client in much the same way as the WriteClient function does. However, it also informs the HTTP server about the status of the operation, which the WriteClient function cannot do. The function definition is as follows:

```
BOOL ServerSupportFunction (HCONN hConn, DWORD dwHSERequest, LPVOID lpvBuffer,
➥ LPDWORD lpdwSizeofBuffer, LPDWORD lpdwDataType);
```

The function parameters are defined as follows:

- hConn—Specifies the connection handle.
- dwHSERequest—Specifies the type of request to be sent to the client. This can be a custom request type, which uses a value greater than that defined by HSE_REQ_END_RESERVED, or it can be one of the following general-purpose predefined values:
  - HSE_REQ_SEND_URL_REDIRECT_RESP—Specifies that a 302 (URL redirect) message be sent to the client. This is similar to specifying URI:<URL> in a CGI script header. If this value is used, the lpvBuffer should point to a null-terminated string containing the URL.
  - HSE_REQ_SEND_URL—Specifies that the data associated with a URL be sent to the client as if he explicitly selected the URL. The lpvBuffer should point to a null-terminated string containing the URL.
  - HSE_REQ_SEND_RESPONSE_HEADER—Specifies that a complete HTTP server response header be sent to the client. The application should append additional information, such as the content type, content length, a \r\n (carriage return–line feed pair), and any other additional information. The skeleton example source code in the section "An Internet Server Application Skeleton" uses this operation to send basic HTML data to be displayed on the Web browser.

- HSE_REQ_MAP_URL_TO_PATH—Specifies that the lpdvBuffer will contain a logical pathname when the ServerSupportFunction is executed, and that the lpdvBuffer will have a physical pathname corresponding to the logical name upon completion.

- lpvBuffer—Specifies a pointer to a buffer containing the null-terminated status string (such as Error 402-Payment required) to be returned to the client. If this value is NULL, the default status code (200 OK) will be sent to the client.

- lpdwSizeOfBuffer—Specifies the size of the buffer pointed to by lpvBuffer. If a null-terminated string is to be sent to the client in its entirety, this value should be set using the value returned by the function call strlen(lpvBuffer). When the ServerSupportFunction function returns, lpdwSizeOfBuffer contains the length of the data sent to the client.

- lpdDataType—This specifies a pointer to a zero-terminated string of data to be appended to the header. This is an optional string, and if this field is NULL, the header will be terminated with an \r\n.

An Internet Server Application Skeleton

To help you to develop an ISA to perform a specific task, I have created a basic skeleton framework for you to use. The source code, including the Visual C++ 4.0 makefile, can be found on the CD-ROM in the \SOURCE\CHAP17 subdirectory. It is printed here to give you an idea of the functional requirements. Basically, an ISA can be divided into three components. The first is an optional application header (shown in Listing 17.1). The second is a required application definition (shown in Listing 17.2). The third is a required application definition file (shown in Listing 17.3), which defines the procedures to export. An exported procedure can be called by another application (such as the HTTP server) by name. This export list allows the HTTP server to execute your ISA.

The source code should be self-explanatory, but I would like to mention two things. First, the DLLMain function is not required to build an ISA, but it can be used to perform per process or per thread initialization or cleanup when called. You can use this function to allocate and deallocate process or thread resources, to maintain state information, or to report performance data that the Performance Monitor can display. This function has numerous possibilities. Second, if you look at the HttpExtentionProc definition in the Skeleton.C code listing, you will see a bare-bones ISA. This function retrieves the query string sent by the client, and then sends this information back to the client along with a very basic HTML document (header, title, and body). This HTML document is created on the fly, so to speak, by the function. If you create an ISA, it will be up to your ISA to create a properly formatted HTML document to display on the Web browser.

Listing 17.1. The source code for Skeleton.H.

```
//------------------------------------------------
// THIS CODE AND INFORMATION IS PROVIDED "AS IS" WITHOUT WARRANTY OF
// ANY KIND, EITHER EXPRESSED OR IMPLIED, INCLUDING BUT NOT LIMITED TO
// THE IMPLIED WARRANTIES OF MERCHANTABILITY AND/OR FITNESS FOR A
// PARTICULAR PURPOSE.
//
//
//    Skeleton.H            -    Sample skeleton code to create an Internet
//                              Server Application (ISA)
//                              multithreaded processor intensive application.
//
//
// Copyright (c) 1996      -    Knowles Consulting. All rights Reserved.
//
//------------------------------------------------

#define    ISA_DESCRIPTION    "Skeleton Internet Server Application"
#define    ISA_TITLE          "<head><title>Skeleton
➥ Internet Server Application \
                              Document Title</title></head>\n"
#define    ISA_HEADER         "<h1>Skeleton Internet Server Application
➥ Document \
                              Header</h1>\n"
#define    ISA_CALL           "<b>This ISA was called passed the '%s' \
                              QueryString.</b>"
#define    ISA_DO_NOTHING     "This is the body of your document. In this
➥ case, \
                              the skeleton application does nothing other
➥ than \
                              print this basic message on your web browser.
➥ You \
                              could do much more, but to do so you will have
➥ to \
                              write the code. You can't get everything for \
                              free. :)"
#define    ISA_CONTENT        "Content-Type: text/html\r\n\r\n"
#define    ISA_BODY_BEGIN     "<body>"
#define    ISA_BODY_END       "</body>"
#define    ISA_HR             "<hr>"
```

Listing 17.2. The source code for Skeleton.C.

```
//------------------------------------------------
// THIS CODE AND INFORMATION IS PROVIDED "AS IS" WITHOUT WARRANTY OF
// ANY KIND, EITHER EXPRESSED OR IMPLIED, INCLUDING BUT NOT LIMITED TO
// THE IMPLIED WARRANTIES OF MERCHANTABILITY AND/OR FITNESS FOR A
// PARTICULAR PURPOSE.
//
//
//    Skeleton.C            -    Sample skeleton code to create an Internet
//                              Server Application (ISA)
//                              multithreaded processor intensive application.
//
//
```

```
// Copyright (c) 1996     -     Knowles Consulting. All rights Reserved.
//
//— — — — — — — — — — — — — — — — — — — — — — — — — — — — — — — — —

#include <windows.h>
#include <httpext.h>
#include <stdio.h>
#include <string.h>
#include "Skeleton.H"

// This function is not required to build an ISA, although it is a
// good idea to include it and perform your initialization and cleanup
// as required by your ISA.
BOOL WINAPI DllMain (HANDLE hModule,ULONG ulReason, LPVOID lpReserved)
    {
    switch (ulReason)
        {
        case DLL_PROCESS_ATTACH:
            { // Insert process specific initalization here
            }
        case DLL_THREAD_ATTACH:
            { // Insert thread specific initalization here
            }
        case DLL_PROCESS_DETACH:
            { // Insert process specific cleanup here
            }
        case DLL_THREAD_DETACH:
            { // Insert thread specific cleanup here
            }
        }

    return (TRUE);
    }

BOOL WINAPI GetExtensionVersion (HSE_VERSION_INFO  *pVer)
    {
    pVer->dwExtensionVersion = MAKELONG(HSE_VERSION_MINOR, HSE_VERSION_MAJOR);
    // Note: Be sure to change ISA_DESCRIPTION in the Skelaton.H header file
➥to define your ISA
    if ((lstrcpyn (pVer->lpszExtensionDesc, ISA_DESCRIPTION,
➥HSE_MAX_EXT_DLL_NAME_LEN)) != NULL)
        {
        return (TRUE);
        }
    else
        {
        return (FALSE);
        }
    }

DWORD WINAPI HttpExtensionProc (EXTENSION_CONTROL_BLOCK  *pEcb)
    {
    DWORD dwStatus = HSE_STATUS_SUCCESS;
    CHAR szBuff[4096];
    CHAR szTemp[80];
    DWORD dwLen;

    // Assign your basic document attributes here
```

continues

Listing 17.2. continued

```
    // Note: These values are defined in Skeleton.H
  wsprintf( szBuff, ISA_CONTENT ISA_TITLE ISA_BODY_BEGIN ISA_HEADER ISA_HR);

    // Insert code to perform the real work here and replace the sample code.
    sprintf (szTemp, ISA_CALL, pEcb->lpszQueryString);    // Build temporary
➥string with query string
    strcat (szBuff, szTemp);                              // Inserts query
➥ string passed
    strcat (szBuff, ISA_HR);                              // Inserts
➥ horizontal rule
    strcat (szBuff,ISA_DO_NOTHING);                        // Inserts do
➥ nothing text
    strcat (szBuff,ISA_BODY_END);                          // Inserts </body>
➥ tag
    dwLen = lstrlen(szBuff);                              // Gets length of
➥ buffer
    //    Sends a completed response header
    if (!pEcb->ServerSupportFunction(pEcb->ConnID,
➥HSE_REQ_SEND_RESPONSE_HEADER, NULL, &dwLen, (LPDWORD) szBuff ))
        {    // If an error occured sending the response header, then sets
➥status code. to error
        dwStatus = HSE_STATUS_ERROR;
        }

    // Returns status code
    return (dwStatus);
    }
```

Listing 17.3. The source code for Skeleton.DEF.

```
LIBRARY    Skeleton

DESCRIPTION    'Internet Server Application Extension DLL'

EXPORTS
    DllMail
    GetExtensionVersion
    HttpExtensionProc
```

Summary

This chapter begins with a definition of an ISAPI application. You learn some of the differences between a CGI application and an ISAPI application, and why you may want to develop ISAPI applications instead of CGI applications. You also learn that not every aspect of ISAPI is a bed of roses, and you are introduced to some of the possible pitfalls associated with ISAPI development. To gain a better understanding of how an ISAPI application works, you look into the basic ISAPI interface and the associated ISAPI functions. The last section contains actual working code to build a functional ISAPI application. You can use this application as a skeleton framework to build your own ISAPI applications. In Chapter 18 you will learn how to create CGI applications for the Internet Information Server. This information should be of particular interest if you already have quite a few CGI applications developed for other HTTP servers and just want to get them up and running with the Internet Information Server.

CHAPTER 18

Unleashing the Power of VBScript

IN THIS CHAPTER

- Introduction to VBScript   528
- How VBScript Works   528
- Hello World!   529
- VBScript Operators   533
- VBScript Control Structures   537
- VBScript Functions   545
- Applications of VBScript   555

VBScript is Microsoft's scripting language for the Internet. Similar in functionality to JavaScript, VBScript has been designed to leverage the skills of millions of Visual Basic programmers to the Internet. Although JavaScript is a powerful scripting language, it is not as easy to learn and use as VBScript. VBScript can be used to easily create active Web pages. Since VBScript is supported by Microsoft, you can expect to see a great deal of VBScript/Windows NT/95/MS Office BackOffice integration. VBScript code is lightweight and fast, and has been optimized to be transmitted via the Internet. You should spend some time with VBScript and learn how it can be used to enhance a Web site by making it easier and more exciting to navigate.

Introduction to VBScript

VBScript is a subset of Microsoft Visual Basic and is upwardly compatible with Visual Basic for Applications (VBA). VBA is shipped with MS Office applications to make it easier for developers to build custom solutions using MS Office applications. The ability to provide scripting, automation, and customization capabilities for Web browsers is a major feature of VBScript. If you are already familiar with Visual Basic, very shortly you will be able to leverage your skills to the Internet using VBScript. Even if you are not familiar with another programming language, after reading this chapter you will be able to create active Web pages using VBScript. However, familiarity with a programming language will make it easier for you to grasp various concepts such as recursion, type casting, and Boolean arithmetic. Visit the Microsoft VBScript home page for the most up-to-date information about VBScript.

> **NOTE**
>
> Visit the Microsoft VBScript information Web site for the latest information about VBScript:
>
> `http://www.microsoft.com/VBScript`

How VBScript Works

VBScript programs are defined between two HTML tags. Browsers that support VBScript read the VBScript program contained between the two HTML tags and execute it after checking for any syntax errors. VBScript works as shown in Figure 18.1.

As you can see in Figure 18.1, a VBScript program is part of a regular HTML file and is enclosed between two HTML tags, `<SCRIPT LANGUAGE=VBS>` and `</SCRIPT>`. When a Web browser that supports VBScript encounters the `<SCRIPT LANGUAGE=VBS>` HTML tag, all text between that tag and `</SCRIPT>` is treated as a VBScript program and is interpreted for syntax errors. If any syntax errors are detected, they are flagged by the VBScript interpreter, as shown in Figure 18.2.

FIGURE 18.1.
How VBScript works.

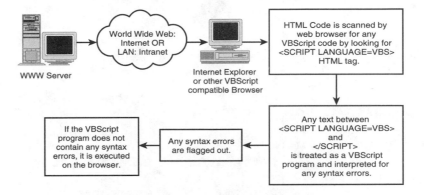

FIGURE 18.2.
Syntax errors in VBScript programs are flagged by the VBScript interpreter.

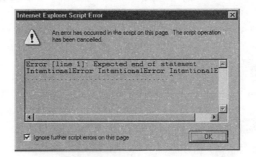

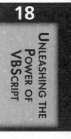

If the code does not contain any syntax errors, it is executed on the Web browser. In order to hide VBScript code from technologically challenged Web browsers, VBScript code can be enclosed in two HTML comment tags, as shown here:

```
<SCRIPT LANGUAGE=VBS>
<!-- To hide VBScript code from technologically challenged browsers
… VBScript code …
!-->
</SCRIPT>
```

Hello World!

Writing the classic Hello World! application with VBScript is very easy. For the purpose of this example, you will be shown how to create a Web page similar to the one in Figure 18.3. This Web page will have three buttons. The first button will display a message box with a greeting, the second button will display the current time, and the third button will display today's date.

FIGURE 18.3.

The classic Hello World! application written with VBScript.

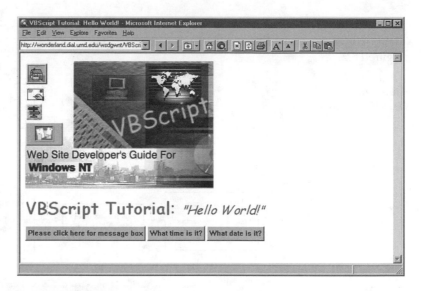

Various key elements of the Hello World! VBScript program are outlined next.

The Hello World! Dialog Box

As shown in Figure 18.4, the Hello World! dialog box is shown each time a user clicks on the `Please click here for message box` button in Figure 18.3. If you look at the HTML page the VBScript program is in, you will see that the command button associated with the Hello World! dialog box is named `BtnHello` (`NAME="BtnHello"`). As you can see from the following listing, the `OnClick` event is associated with the `BtnHello` subroutine. Each time a user clicks on the `Please click here for message box` button in Figure 18.3, the Web browser invokes the `BtnHello_OnClick` subroutine, and any VBScript code defined in that subroutine is executed.

The `BtnHello_OnClick` subroutine is a very simple VBScript subroutine. The first three lines create strings, displayed by the dialog box in Figure 18.4. Note how the string concatenation operator (`&`) is used in line 4 to merge two strings into one and assign the result to a variable. The result is then displayed in a message box, as shown in Figure 18.4.

> **NOTE**
>
> Line numbers in various code segments are not part of the VBScript code. The line numbers are for reference purposes only.

```
1: Sub BtnHello_OnClick
2:   titleString = "Web Site Developer's Guide for Windows NT"
3:   helloString = "Hello world! Welcome to the fun filled "
```

```
4:    helloString = helloString & "world of VBScript programming!"
5:    MsgBox helloString, 0, titleString
6: End Sub
```

FIGURE 18.4.

The Hello World!
dialog box.

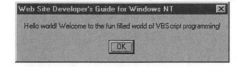

The Time Dialog Box

The `BtnTime_OnClick` subroutine is very similar to the `BtnHello_OnClick` subroutine. The only difference is the fact that, rather than concatenating two strings, it concatenates a string with the result of a function. The `time` function returns the current time. As shown in Figure 18.5, line 3 of the following program listing displays the current time in a dialog box:

```
1: Sub BtnTime_OnClick
2:    timeString = "So, you want to know the time? The time is " & time
3:    MsgBox  timeString , 0, "Time Dialog Box"
4: End Sub
```

FIGURE 18.5.

The Time dialog box.

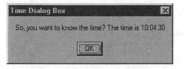

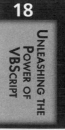

The Date Dialog Box

The Date dialog box displays the current date in a dialog box, as shown in Figure 18.6. As you can see in line 2 of the following code listing, the result of one function (`date`) can be used as an argument of another function (`DateValue`).

```
1: Sub BtnDate_OnClick
2:    dateString = "Today's date is " & DateValue(date)
3:    MsgBox  dateString , 0, "Date Dialog Box"
4: End Sub
```

FIGURE 18.6.

The Date dialog box.

For your reference, the full source code of the Hello World! application appears in Listing 18.1.

Listing 18.1. The Hello World! Web page.

```
<!--
(C) 1996 Sanjaya Hettihewa (http://wonderland.dial.umd.edu)
All Rights Reserved.
!-->

<HTML>
<HEAD>
<TITLE>VBScript Tutorial: Hello World!</TITLE>
</HEAD>

<BODY BGCOLOR="#FFFFFF" TEXT="#0000FF"
      LINK="#B864FF" VLINK="#670000" ALINK="#FF0000">

<IMG SRC="vbscript.jpg"><P>

<B><FONT FACE="Comic Sans MS" SIZE=6 COLOR=RED>
VBScript Tutorial: <FONT></B>
<I><FONT FACE="Comic Sans MS" SIZE=5 COLOR=BLUE>
 "Hello World!" </I><P><FONT>

<form>
<INPUT TYPE=BUTTON VALUE="Please click here for message box"
       NAME="BtnHello">
<INPUT TYPE=BUTTON VALUE="What time is it?"
       NAME="BtnTime">
<INPUT TYPE=BUTTON VALUE="What date is it?"
       NAME="BtnDate">
</form>
<SCRIPT LANGUAGE=VBS>
<!-- To hide VBScript code from technologically challenged browsers

Sub BtnHello_OnClick
 titleString = "Web Site Developer's Guide for Windows NT"
 helloString = "Hello world! Welcome to the fun filled "
 helloString = helloString & "world of VBScript programming!"
 MsgBox helloString, 0, titleString
End Sub

Sub BtnTime_OnClick
 timeString = "So, you want to know the time? The time is " & time
 MsgBox  timeString , 0, "Time Dialog Box"
End Sub

Sub BtnDate_OnClick
 dateString = "Today's date is " & DateValue(date)
 MsgBox  dateString , 0, "Date Dialog Box"
End Sub
!-->
</SCRIPT>

</BODY>

</HTML>
```

VBScript Operators

VBScript supports several operators for various string, Boolean, and number-manipulation tasks. Operators supported by VBScript are listed in the following sections.

The Addition Operator

Syntax: `<operand1> + <operand2>`

The addition operator adds two operands together. If both operands are numeric, the result of the addition operator will also be numeric. However, if they are strings, VBScript will do a string concatenation instead of a numeric addition. To avoid ambiguity, use the string concatenation operator (&) when joining strings and use the addition operator (+) when adding numeric expressions.

The Subtraction Operator

Syntax: `<operand1> - <operand2>`
Syntax: `-<OperandToNegate>`

The subtraction operator is used as a unary minus and the binary subtraction operator. When used as the binary subtraction operator, it subtracts `<operand2>` from `<operand1>` and returns the resulting value. When used as the unary minus, it negates the numeric operand it is used with.

The Multiplication Operator

Syntax: `<operand1> ^ <operand2>`

The multiplication operator takes two numeric operands, multiplies them, and returns the resulting value.

The Exponential Operator

Syntax: `<operand1> ^ <operand2>`

The exponential operator returns the resulting value of `<operand1>` raised to the `<operand2>` power.

The Floating-Point Division Operator

Syntax: `<operand1> / <operand2>`

The division operator divides `<operand1>` by `<operand2>`. Both `<operand1>` and `<operand2>` have to be numeric expressions, and the resulting value is a floating-point number.

The Integer-Division Operator

Syntax: `<operand1> \ <operand2>`

The integer-division operator is somewhat similar to the floating-point division operator. The integer-division operator returns an integer number after dividing `<operand1>` by `<operand2>`. For example:

```
( 23 \ 4 ) = 5
( 4 \ 23 ) = 0
( 4 \ 2 ) = 2
( 5 \ 2 ) = 2
```

The String-Concatenation Operator

Syntax: `<operand1> & <operand2>`

The string-concatenation operator joins `<operand1>` and `<operand2>`.

The MOD Operator

Syntax: `<operand1> MOD <operand2>`

The MOD operator is somewhat similar to the integer-division operator. The only difference is that it returns the remainder of `<operand1>` divided by `<operand2>`. For example:

```
( 23 MOD 4 ) = 3
( 4 MOD 23 ) = 4
( 4 MOD 2 ) = 0
( 5 MOD 2 ) = 1
```

Boolean Operators

VBScript supports a number of Boolean operators. The best way to explain how Boolean operators work is with a truth table. See Figure 18.7 for truth tables of a number of useful VBScript Boolean operators. Various useful VBScript Boolean operators are listed next, along with how they can be used in VBScript programs.

The AND Operator

Syntax: `<operand1> AND <operand2>`

The AND operator returns TRUE if both `<operand1>` and `<operand2>` are true. If not, it returns FALSE. The AND operator can be used with expressions and functions that return a Boolean value.

The OR Operator

Syntax: `<operand1> OR <operand2>`

The OR operator returns TRUE if either `<operand1>` or `<operand2>` is true. The OR operator can be used with expressions and functions that return a Boolean value.

FIGURE 18.7.
Truth tables of VBScript Boolean operators.

AND				
TRUE	AND	TRUE	=	TRUE
TRUE	AND	FALSE	=	FALSE
FALSE	AND	TRUE	=	FALSE
FALSE	AND	FALSE	=	FALSE

OR				
TRUE	OR	TRUE	=	TRUE
TRUE	OR	FALSE	=	TRUE
FALSE	OR	TRUE	=	TRUE
FALSE	OR	FALSE	=	FALSE

XOR				
TRUE	XOR	TRUE	=	FALSE
TRUE	XOR	FALSE	=	TRUE
FALSE	XOR	TRUE	=	TRUE
FALSE	XOR	FALSE	=	FALSE

NOT				
	NOT	TRUE	=	FALSE
	NOT	FALSE	=	TRUE

18

UNLEASHING THE POWER OF VBSCRIPT

The NOT Operator

Syntax: `NOT <operand>`

The NOT operator negates a Boolean value. The NOT operator can be used with expressions and functions that return a Boolean value.

The XOR Operator

Syntax: `<operand1> XOR <operand2>`

The XOR operator is very similar to the OR operator. The only difference is that, in order for the XOR operator to return TRUE, <operand1> or <operand2> has to be true. However, they both can't be true at the same time. The NOT operator can be used with expressions and functions that return a Boolean value.

The Equivalence Operator

Syntax: `<operand1> Eqv <operand2>`

The equivalence operator determines if `<operand1>` is equal to `<operand2>`. If either `<operand1>` or `<operand2>` is NULL, then the resulting value will also be NULL. The truth table of the equivalence operator is listed next:

```
TRUE Eqv TRUE = TRUE
FALSE Eqv TRUE = FALSE
TRUE Eqv FALSE = FALSE
FALSE Eqv FALSE = TRUE
```

(TRUE may be replaced with binary 1 and FALSE may be replaced with binary 0.)

The Object-Reference Operator

Syntax: `<operand1> IS <operand2>`

The object-reference operator compares two object-reference variables. If `<operand1>` refers to the same object as `<operand2>`, the object-reference operator returns TRUE. Otherwise, it returns FALSE.

Comparison Operators

VBScript supports several comparison operators that compare strings as well as numbers. Various comparison operators that can be used in VBScript programs are listed next.

The Equal Operator

Syntax: `<operand1> = <operand2>`

Returns TRUE if both `<operand1>` and `<operand2>` are equal to each other. However, if either `<operand1>` or `<operand2>` is NULL, the equal operator will return NULL.

The Unequal Operator

Syntax: `<operand1> <> <operand2>`

Returns TRUE if both `<operand1>` and `<operand2>` are unequal to each other. However, if either `<operand1>` or `<operand2>` is NULL, the unequal operator will return NULL.

The Less Than Operator

Syntax: `<operand1> < <operand2>`

Returns TRUE if `<operand1>` is less than `<operand2>`. However, if either `<operand1>` or `<operand2>` is NULL, the less than operator will return NULL.

The Less Than or Equal To Operator

Syntax: `<operand1> <= <operand2>`

Returns TRUE if `<operand1>` is less than or equal to `<operand2>`. However, if either `<operand1>` or `<operand2>` is NULL, the less than or equal to operator will return NULL.

The Greater Than Operator

Syntax: `<operand1> > <operand2>`

Returns TRUE if `<operand1>` is greater than `<operand2>`. However, if either `<operand1>` or `<operand2>` is NULL, the greater than operator will return NULL.

The Greater Than or Equal To Operator

Syntax: `<operand1> >= <operand2>`

Returns TRUE if `<operand1>` is greater than or equal to `<operand2>`. However, if either `<operand1>` or `<operand2>` is NULL, the greater than or equal to operator will return NULL.

VBScript Control Structures

Control structures are an important part of any language. They give a language "life" by allowing programmers to add intelligence to programs with conditional and iterative statements. Various VBScript control structures are listed next, along with how they can be used in VBScript programs.

Call

Call is used to transfer program control to another VBScript subroutine. Note that when Call is used to transfer control to another subroutine, if that subroutine has any parameters, they should be enclosed in parentheses. However, if Call is omitted, subroutine arguments do not need to be enclosed in parentheses. Return values of functions are ignored when they are invoked with the Call statement.

Dim

The Dim statement is used to declare variables, such as arrays, and assign them storage space. When variables are declared with Dim, if they are numeric variables, they are initialized with the value 0. Otherwise, they are assigned an empty string. The Dim statement can be used to declare several types of variables. Various types of variables that can be created with the Dim statement are listed next.

Declaring Variant Variables

Syntax: `Dim <VariableName1> , <VariableName2>`

This statement can be used to declare variables of variant type. As shown here, several variables can be defined at the same time by separating them with commas.

Multiple Variables Declarations

Syntax: `Dim <VariableName1> As Integer, <VariableName2>`

One `Dim` statement can be used to declare several variables of more than one type. As in the case of the previous `Dim` command, `<VariableName1>` is declared as an integer variable and `<VariableName2>` is declared as a variant variable.

Declaring Static Arrays

Single Dimension Array Syntax: `Dim <NameOfArray>(50)`

The `Dim` statement can be used to define arrays. In this example, an array of 50 storage locations of type variant is created using the `Dim` statement. If an index range is not specified for an array, VBScript will index the array, starting at zero. For example, in this case, `<NameOfArray>` is indexed from `0` to `49`.

Multi-Dimension Array Syntax: `Dim <NameOfArray>(5,1 To 5)`

The `Dim` statement can also be used to declare multidimensional arrays. For example, the preceding statement can be used to declare a two-dimensional array by the name of `<NameOfArray>`. As shown in this example, the index range of an array can be customized by using a number range (1 to 5). By adding an `As <VariableType>` command to an array declaration, it is possible to define an array of a certain data type.

Declaring Dynamic Arrays

If you are unsure about the size of an array when it is first declared, VBScript allows the creation of dynamic arrays. Dynamic arrays can be expanded or reduced as needed. Dynamic arrays can be created using the following syntax.

```
Dim <NameOfArray>()
```

Storage space for additional elements can be allocated for a dynamic array using the `ReDim` statement, as shown next. (Simply indicate, in parentheses, the number of elements the array should have.)

```
ReDim <NameOfArray>(10)
```

As an added incentive, VBScript dynamic arrays can be expanded while preserving existing array values. As shown in the next example, this is done by adding a `Preserve` statement in between the `ReDim` statement and the array name.

```
ReDim Preserve <NameOfArray>(20)
```

Note that if a data type is defined for a dynamic array using the `As` statement, the array's data type cannot be changed using the `ReDim` statement. Also, if a dynamic array is reduced in size, using the `ReDim` statement, any data stored in the portion of the array that was deleted is permanently lost.

Do...While...Until...Loop

The `Do...Loop` control structure can be used to iterate a group of statements until a certain Boolean expression becomes `TRUE`. The syntax of the `Do...Loop` control structure is listed next. As shown in the following example, the Boolean expression of a `Do...Loop` structure can be placed either at the beginning or the end:

```
Do <condition> <BooleanExpression>
… VBScript statements …
Loop
```

As shown next, the Boolean expression of a `Do...Loop` structure can also be placed at the end of the control structure:

```
Do
… VBScript statements …
Loop <condition> <BooleanExpression>
```

The preceding two examples will repeatedly execute VBScript statements enclosed in the loop structure until `<BooleanExpression>` becomes `TRUE`. In the examples, `<condition>` may be replaced with either `While` or `Until`. As the name implies, if `While` is used, the loop will iterate while `<BooleanExpression>` is `TRUE`. In the like manner, if `Until` is used, the loop will iterate until `<BooleanExpression>` is `TRUE`. Note that within a `Do...Loop` structure, it is possible to transfer control out of the loop using an `Exit Do` statement.

Erase

Syntax: `Erase <NameOfArray>`

The `Erase` statement is used to free memory used by dynamic arrays and reinitialize elements of static arrays. If the array is a dynamic array, all space taken up by the array is freed. Dynamic arrays then need to be reallocated using the `ReDim` statement before they can be used again. If the array is a static array, all array elements are initialized with 0 if its elements are numeric or empty strings otherwise.

Exit

The Exit statement causes program control to be transferred out of the control structure it is used in. The control structure can be a loop or a subroutine. Various forms of the Exit command are listed next:

Exit Do—Exits a Do loop.

Exit For—Exits a For loop.

Exit Function—Exits a function.

Exit Sub—Exits a procedure.

For...Next

The For...Next control structure can be used to iterate a group of VBScript statements a certain number of times. The syntax of the For...Next control structure is listed next:

```
For <LoopCount> = <BeginLoop> To <EndLoop> Step <StepCount>
… VBScript statements …
Next
```

The previous definition can be used to iterate a group of VBScript statements a certain number of times by replacing various labels (enclosed in pointed braces) of the definition, as follows:

<LoopCount>—Name of variable used to keep track of the number of iterations. It's best that your VBScript statements do not alter the value of this variable, because it can easily complicate your code and make it harder to debug.

<BeginLoop>—The first value of the iteration sequence.

<EndLoop>—The last value of the iteration sequence.

Step <StepCount>—Can be replaced with the <LoopCount>, which will be incremented after each iteration of the loop. The Step statement is optional; by default, <LoopCount> will be incremented by one.

Note that the Exit For statement can be used to exit a For loop.

For Each...Next

The For Each...Next control structure is useful for iterating VBScript statements for each object in a collection or each element in an array. The syntax of the For Each...Next loop is listed next.

```
For Each <LoopIndex> In <ArrayOrCollection>
… VBScript statements …
Next <LoopIndex>
```

A For Each...Next loop can be added to a VBScript program by substituting various labels of the preceding example, as follows:

> `<LoopIndex>`—Name of variable that's used to traverse through the elements of an array or objects in a collection.
>
> `<ArrayOrCollection>`—Name of an array or collection of objects.

Note that the `Exit For` statement can be used to exit a `For Each` loop. Also note that `<LoopIndex>` can be omitted in the `Next <LoopIndex>` statement. However, this is not recommended; it can complicate things and cause errors if a `For Each` loop is nested inside another `For Each` loop.

Function

New functions can be defined using the `Function` statement. The syntax of the `Function` statement is as follows:

```
<FunctionType> Function <NameOfFunction> <ArgumentsOfFunction>
… VBScript statements …
<NameOfFunction> = <ReturnValueOfFunction>
End Function
```

A function can be created by replacing various labels of the above definition with the values listed next:

> `<FunctionType>`—Can be left out if it is not needed. By replacing `<FunctionType>` with `Static`, it is possible to preserve values of local variables in between function calls. Unless you have a reason for doing so, `Static` functions are usually not suitable for recursion (a function calling itself).
>
> `<NameOfFunction>`—Used to specify the name of the function.
>
> `<ArgumentsOfFunction>`—Arguments of a function can be specified soon after `<NameOfFunction>`. By using commas, more than one argument can be specified. An argument can be passed either by value or reference. In order to make an argument pass by value, precede the argument name with `ByVal`; to pass by reference, precede the argument name with `ByRef`. When an argument is passed by value, its original value cannot be changed from within the function. However, when it is passed by reference, the variable used in the function is merely a pointer to the original variable. Therefore, any changes made to the value of a variable passed by reference are actually made to the original variable.

Note that the `Exit Function` statement can be used to exit a function. VBScript procedures created with the `Function` statement are very similar to procedures created with the SUB statement. The only difference is that procedures created with the `Function` statement can return values, whereas procedures created with the `Sub` statement cannot.

18

UNLEASHING THE
POWER OF
VBSCRIPT

If...Then...Else

The `If...Then...Else` statement can be used to execute various VBScript statements based on Boolean expressions. The syntax of the `If...Then...Else` control structure is as follows:

```
IF <BooleanExpression> THEN
… VBScript statement …
ELSE IF <BooleanExpression> THEN
… VBScript statement …
ELSE
… VBScript statement …
END IF
```

As shown in the previous example, various VBScript statements can be made to execute using an `If...Then...Else` statement based on various Boolean expressions.

Let

The `Let` command can be used to assign values to variables. The `Let` command is not required to assign a value to a variable. The syntax of the `Let` command is as follows:

```
Let <variableName> = <ValueOfVariable>
```

LSet

`LSet` is used to copy a variable of one user-defined type to a variable of another user-defined type. When a variable is copied with the `LSet` command, it is *left-aligned*. The syntax of the `LSet` statement is listed next.

```
LSet <Variable> = <ValueOfVariable>
```

If the length of `<Variable>` is longer than the length of `<ValueOfVariable>`, after copying `<ValueOfVariable>` to `<Variable>` the remaining space will be filled in with white spaces. In like manner, if the length of `<Variable>` is less than the length of `<ValueOfVariable>`, `<ValueOfVariable>` will be truncated to fit in the space allocated for `<Variable>`. For example, if `<Variable>` can hold only four characters, and `<ValueOfVariable>` contains the string `"ABCDEFG"`, after it is copied to `<Variable>` with the `LSet` command, `<Variable>` will have the value `"ABCD"`.

Mid

`Mid` is a very handy statement for replacing one or more characters of a string with characters from another string. The syntax of the `Mid` statement is listed next.

```
Mid (<Variable>, <Begin>, <NumCharactersToReplace>) = <Replacement>
```

The `Mid` statement can be used by replacing various labels of the preceding example, as follows:

> `<Variable>`—Name of variable containing the string that will be modified.

<Begin>—The position to begin replacing text. For example, if <Variable> contained the string "1234" and you would like "34" to be replaced with "67", <Begin> will be replaced with "3" because the substring "34" begins at the third position.

<NumCharactersToReplace>—Lists the number of characters that should be replaced by <Replacement>. This value can be left out if you wish, in which case the entire <Replacement> string will be copied over.

<Replacement>—Contains string that will be copied over to <Variable>.

On Error

Usually, when a runtime error occurs in a VBScript program, it halts execution of the VBScript program. Using the On Error Resume Next statement, however, it is possible to ignore the error and continue with the program.

Private

By preceding a variable declaration with the Private keyword, it is possible to limit its scope to the script it was declared in.

Public

By preceding a variable declaration with the Public keyword, the scope of a variable can be extended to other scripts.

Randomize

Can be used to initialize the random-number generator. Randomize can be used either with or without a numeric argument. If it is used with a numeric argument, the numeric argument is used to seed the random-number generator. If Randomize is used without an argument, a number from the system clock is used to seed the random-number generator.

Rem

The Rem command is used to document VBScript code. The syntax of the Rem command is listed next:

```
Rem This is a comment
```

Note that the apostrophe (') is equivalent in functionality to the Rem command. The only difference between the Rem statement and the apostrophe is the fact that if Rem is used in the same line with a VBScript statement, it needs to be separated from the VBScript statement with a colon.

18

UNLEASHING THE
POWER OF
VBSCRIPT

RSet

The syntax of the RSet command is listed next:

```
RSet <Variable> = <StringToCopy>
```

The RSet command is similar in functionality to the LSet command. The only difference is the fact that when a variable is assigned a string using the RSet command, it is assigned to the variable right aligned.

Set

The Set command can be used to assign an object reference to a variable or property. The syntax of the Set command is as follows:

```
Set <ObjectVariable> = <Object>
```

When the keyword Nothing is assigned to <ObjectVariable>, system resources consumed by the object are freed when no other variables refer to the <Object>.

Static

By preceding variable and procedure declarations with the keyword Static, it is possible to retain values of variables. When a procedure is declared as a static procedure, all variables in that procedure retain values assigned to them throughout the life of the program. Precede variable declarations of *nonstatic procedures* with the Static keyword to preserve their values. (Variable values of static procedures are automatically preserved.)

Sub

The Sub statement can be used to create VBScript procedures and is identical to the Function statement except for one difference. Procedures created with the Function statement can return values; procedures created with the Sub statement cannot. The syntax of the Sub statement is listed next. Note that the Exit Sub statement can be used to transfer control out of a procedure. The syntax of the Sub statement is listed next:

```
<ProcedureType> Sub <NameOfProcedure> <ArgumentsOfProcedure>
… VBScript statements …
End Sub
```

A procedure can be created by replacing various labels of the preceding definition with the values listed next:

> <ProcedureType>—Can be left out if it is not needed. By replacing <ProcedureType> with Static, it is possible to preserve values of local variables in between procedure calls. Unless you have a reason for doing so, Static functions are usually not suitable for recursion (a function calling itself).

<NameOfProcedure>—Used to specify the name of the procedure.

<ArgumentsOfProcedure>—Arguments of a procedure can be specified soon after <NameOfProcedure>. By using commas, more than one argument can be specified. An argument can be passed either by value or reference. In order to make an argument pass by value, precede the argument name with ByVal, and to pass by reference, precede the argument name with ByRef. When an argument is passed by value, its original value cannot be changed from within the procedure. However, when it is passed by reference, the variable used in the procedure is merely a pointer to the original variable. Therefore, any changes made to the value of a variable passed by reference is actually made to the original variable.

While...Wend

The While...Wend control structure can be used to iterate a group of VBScript statements while a certain Boolean expression is true. The syntax of the While...Wend command is listed next:

```
While <BooleanExpression>
… VBScript statements …
Wend
```

VBScript Functions

Various functions supported by VBScript are listed next. The following functions can be used to add a new level of interactivity to a Web site by creating active Web pages. Shortly, you will be shown how these functions can be used to develop various VBScript programs.

Abs

The Abs function can be used to obtain the absolute value of a number (for example, Abs(-30) = 30 = Abs(30)).

Array

The Array function can be used to quickly create an array because it returns a variant containing an array. An example of how the Array function can be used is given next. The following two commands create an array with three elements. After the two commands are executed, Colors(2) will equal "Blue":

```
Dim Colors As Variant
Colors = Array ( "Red", "Blue", "Green" )
```

Asc

Returns the ASCII character code of a character or the first character of a string. For example, Asc ("A") returns 65 and so does Asc ("America").

Atn

Returns the arctangent of a number.

CBool

Returns the Boolean value of an expression passed into the function. For example, CBool (A = B) will return TRUE if both A and B contain the same value.

CByte

Converts a number passed into the function into a number of type byte and returns it. For example, if CByte is called with the number 123.678, it will return 123.

CDate

If a valid date expression is passed into the function, it is converted into date type and returned. Before passing an expression to the CDate function, it is possible to determine if it can be converted by CDate into date type by using the IsDate function.

CDbl

Converts an expression passed into the function into a variant of subtype double.

Chr

Returns the ASCII character of an ASCII code. For example, Chr(65) returns the character A.

CInt

Converts an expression into a variant of subtype Integer. For example, CInt (1234.567) returns 1235.

CLng

Returns a variant of subtype long after the expression passed into the function is converted into long. For example, CLng (12345.67) returns 12346.

Cos

Returns the cosine of an angle passed into the function.

CSng

Converts a numerical expression passed into the function into a variant of subtype Single. For example, `CSng (12.123456)` returns `12.12346`.

CStr

Converts an expression passed into `CStr` into a string and returns it. For example, `CStr(123.456)` returns the value `"123.456"`.

CVErr

Used to return a user-specified error code. The syntax of `CVErr` is `CVErr(ErrorNumber)`.

Date

Returns the date from the system clock. The value returned by the `Date` command at the time of this writing is `4/1/1996`.

DateSerial

`DateSerial` is a handy function that can be used to calculate various days. By using numerical expressions and using the `DateSerial` function, it is possible to count backward and forward from a date simply by adding and subtracting numbers. The syntax of the `DateSerial` function is as follows:

```
DateSerial (<Year>, <Month>, <Day>)
```

If the current date is `4/1/1996`, for example, `DateSerial(1996,4-2,1+28)` returns the value `2/29/1996`. (Of course, if the year were 1997 (not a leap year), the result would have been `3/1/1996`.)

DateValue

Converts an expression passed into the function into a variant of subtype date and returns it. For example, `DateValue("February 29, 1976")` returns `2/29/1976`. If the year is left out, it will be obtained from the system clock.

Day

The `Day` function returns a value between `1` and `31` and can be used to find the day of a date. For example, `Day("4/1/1996")` returns `1`.

Exp

Returns the value of e raised to a power. For example `Exp(1)` returns `2.71828182845905`.

Hex

Returns the hexadecimal (base 16) value of a numerical expression. For example, `Hex(10)` returns A.

Hour

Returns the number of hours of a time expression. For example, `Hour("12:25:34")` returns 12.

InputBox

The `InputBox` function is used to obtain input from the user by presenting a dialog box. The syntax of the `InputBox` command is as follows:

```
InputBox(<Prompt>,<Title>,<Default>,<X>,<Y>)
```

The arguments enclosed in pointed brackets can be replaced with the following values:

- `<Prompt>`—Dialog-box prompt.
- `<Title>`—Title of dialog box.
- `<Default>`—Default input value.
- `<X>`—Horizontal position, in number of twips, from the left side of the screen. A *twip* is 1/20 of a printer's point, which is 1/1,440 of an inch.
- `<Y>`—Vertical position, in number of twips, from the top of the screen.

InStr

Returns the location of one string in another string. The syntax of `InStr` is as follows:

```
InStr (<BeginPosition>, <String1>, <String2>, <ComparisonType>
```

- `<BeginPosition>`—This argument is optional and specifies the starting position of search.
- `<String1>`—String being searched.
- `<String2>`—String to locate.
- `<ComparisonType>`—This argument is optional. Use 0 for a binary search and 1 for a non–case-sensitive search. The default value is 0.

Int, Fix

Both Int and Fix convert numerical expressions into integers. The only difference is the fact that Int converts a negative number with a fraction into a smaller integer, and Fix converts a negative number with a fraction into a larger integer. The following examples illustrate how Int and Fix handle numbers with fractions:

```
Int(11.75) = 11
Fix(11.75) = 11
Int(12.45) = 12
Fix(12.45) = 12
Int(-17.75) = -18
Fix(-17.75) = -17
Int(-7.25) = -8
Fix(-7.25) = -7
```

IsArray

Returns TRUE if a variable is an array and FALSE otherwise.

IsDate

Returns TRUE if an expression can be converted to a valid date and FALSE otherwise.

IsEmpty

Returns TRUE if a variable has been initialized and FALSE otherwise.

IsError

Returns TRUE if an expression is an error code and FALSE otherwise.

IsNull

Returns TRUE if an expression is NULL and FALSE otherwise.

IsNumeric

Returns TRUE if an expression is numeric and FALSE otherwise.

IsObject

Returns TRUE if an expression references an OLE automation object and FALSE otherwise.

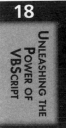

LBound

`LBound` can be used to find the minimum index of an array dimension. For example, if `ArrayVariable` is a three-dimensional array declared with the statement `Dim ArrayVariable(5 To 100, 10 To 200, 20 To 300)`, `UBound(ArrayVariable,1)` returns 5, `LBound(ArrayVariable,2)` returns 10, and of course `LBound(ArrayVariable,3)` returns 20.

LCase

Converts a string expression to lowercase and returns it.

Left

Returns a certain number of characters from the left side of a string. For example, `Left("Windows NT", 7)` returns `"Windows"`.

Len

Returns the number of characters of a string expression.

Log

Returns the natural logarithm of a nonnegative numeric expression.

LTrim, RTrim, Trim

Eliminates spaces from a string and returns it. `LTrim` eliminates preceding spaces, `RTrim` eliminates trailing spaces, and `Trim` eliminates both trailing and preceding spaces.

Mid

Returns a certain number of characters from a string. For example `Mid("Windows NT", 0, 7)` returns `"Windows"`.

Minute

Returns the number of minutes when called with the time. For example, `Minute("23:50:45")` returns 50.

Month

Returns the month when called with a date. For example, `Month("4/1/1996")` returns 4.

MsgBox

A message box can be displayed using the `MsgBox` command. The syntax of the `MsgBox` command is as follows:

```
MsgBox <MessageBoxPrompt>,<ButtonStyle>,<Title>
```

By replacing `<ButtonStyle>` with various values shown in Table 18.1, a message box can be customized using the following table. For example, an OK dialog box with a warning message icon can be created by replacing `<ButtonStyle>` with 48.

Table 18.1. Message box codes.

Button Type	Button Description
0	OK
1	OK and Cancel
2	Abort, Retry, and Ignore
3	Yes, No, and Cancel
4	Yes and No
5	Retry and Cancel
16	Critical Message icon (See Figure 18.8)
32	Warning Query icon (See Figure 18.9)
48	Warning Message icon (See Figure 18.10)
64	Information Message icon (See Figure 18.11)
256	Second button is default
512	Third button is default
4096	All applications are stopped until the user responds to the message box

FIGURE 18.8.
The Critical Message box.

FIGURE 18.9.
The Warning Query box.

FIGURE 18.10.
The Warning Message box.

FIGURE 18.11.
The Information Message box.

Now

Returns the current date and time from the system clock. The return value is followed by the date and then the time. For example, the Now command returned the string 4/1/1996 23:08:31 at the time of this writing.

Oct

Returns the octal value (base 8) of a numeric expression. For example, Oct(10) returns 12.

Right

Returns a certain number of characters from the right side of a string. For example, Right("Windows NT", 2) returns NT.

Rnd

Returns a random number between 1 and 0. Be sure to seed the random number generator by calling Randomize before using the Rnd function.

Second

Returns the number of seconds of a date expression. For example, Second("18:23:57") returns 57.

Sgn

Returns the sign of a numerical expression. If the expression is 0, 0 is returned. If it is less than 0, -1 is returned. Otherwise, 1 is returned.

Sin

Returns the sine of an angle. For example, Sin (Pi) returns 0.

Sqr

Returns the square root of a nonnegative, numeric expression.

Str

Converts a numeric expression into a string and returns it.

StrComp

The syntax of the StrComp function is as follows:

```
StrComp (<String1>, <String2>, <ComparisonMethod>)
```

After StrComp compares both strings, it returns 0 if both strings are identical, -1 if <String1> is less than <STRING2>, and 1 otherwise. The <ComparisonMethod> argument is optional. If it is 0, a binary comparison is performed, and if it is 1, a non–case-insensitive comparison is performed. If <ComparisonMethod> is left out, a binary comparison is performed.

String

The String function is handy for repeating a character a certain number of times. For example, String(5,"*") can be used to create a string of five asterisks.

Tan

The Tan function can be used to calculate the tangent of an angle. For example, Tan (0) returns 0.

Time

Returns the current time from the system clock. For example, the value 01:23:48 was returned by the Time function at the time of this writing.

TimeSerial

This handy function can be used to perform various time calculations. For example, if the current time is 12:30, TimeSerial can be used to calculate the time 25 minutes ago. For example, TimeSerial(12,30-25, 0) returns 12:05:00.

TimeValue

Returns an expression passed into the function after converting it into a variant of subtype Date. For example, TimeValue ("2:35:17pm") returns 14:35:17.

UBound

UBound can be used to determine the maximum size of an array dimension. For example, if ArrayVariable is a three-dimensional array defined with the statement Dim ArrayVariable(100,200,300), UBound(ArrayVariable,1) returns 100, UBound(ArrayVariable,2) returns 200, and, of course, UBound(ArrayVariable,3) returns 300.

UCase

Converts strings passed into the function into uppercase and returns them. For example, UCase("Windows NT") returns WINDOWS NT.

Val

The Val function can be used to obtain a number contained in a string. The function scans the string until it encounters a character that is not part of a number. For example, Val("1234 567 in a string") returns the number 1234567.

VarType

The type of a variable can be determined using the VarType function. For example, if IntVariable is an Integer variable, VarType(IntVariable) will return 2. The type of a variable can be determined by examining the return value of VarType according to Table 18.2.

Table 18.2. Variable type codes.

Value Returned	Type of Variable
0	Empty
1	Null
2	Integer
3	Long integer
4	Single-precision, floating-point number
5	Double-precision, floating-point number
6	Currency
7	Date
8	String
9	OLE Automation object

Value Returned	Type of Variable
10	Error
11	Boolean
12	Variant
13	Non-OLE Automation object
8192	Array

Weekday

The `Weekday` function returns a number between 1 and 7. The numbers returned by the `Weekday` function correspond to the days of the week, as shown in Table 18.3.

Table 18.3. Day codes.

Day Code	Day of Week
1	Sunday
2	Monday
3	Tuesday
4	Wednesday
5	Thursday
6	Friday
7	Saturday

For example, `Weekday("April 2, 1996")` returns 3—which is, indeed, a Tuesday.

Year

Returns the year of the expression. For example, `Year("February 29, 1976")` returns 1976.

Applications of VBScript

Various control structures and commands that can be used to create VBScript programs were outlined in preceding sections. The last few sections of the chapter are devoted to applications of these commands and control structures to demonstrate how VBScript can be used to create active Web pages.

Simple Calculator

You can use various functions and control structures described earlier to create a simple calculator using VBScript. (See Figure 18.12.)

FIGURE 18.12.

The Simple Calculator application.

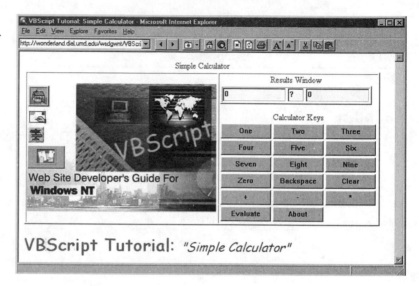

Operators and numbers can be entered into the calculator either by using numeric buttons shown in Figure 18.12 or simply typing them into one of the three text boxes. Before proceeding any further, it is recommended that you experiment with the calculator program and find out how it works. When the Simple Calculator Web page is first invoked and numbers are typed in using various command buttons, they appear in the left-hand text box. After a valid operator is entered into the operator text box, numbers entered next appear in the right-hand text box. At this point, if the Evaluate button is clicked, the VBScript program will evaluate the expression entered and return its value in a dialog box, as shown in Figure 18.13.

After the OK button in the dialog box shown in Figure 18.13 is pressed, the result of the calculation will be copied to the first text box, as shown in Figure 18.14. The user can then keep on performing calculations using the results of previous calculations.

The following VBScript subroutine displays a dialog box similar to the one shown in Figure 18.15 when a user clicks the About button. Note how the string-concatenation operator is used in line 4 to merge two strings:

```
1: Sub BtnAbout_OnClick
2:   titleString = "Web Site Developer's Guide for Windows NT"
3:   helloString = "Simple VBScript calculator by "
```

```
4:  helloString = helloString & "Sanjaya Hettihewa."
5:  MsgBox helloString, 64, titleString
6: End Sub
```

FIGURE 18.13.

When the Evaluate button is pressed, the VBScript program calculates the expression entered and returns its value in a dialog box.

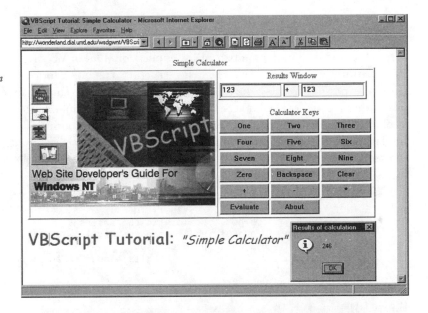

FIGURE 18.14.

The result of a calculation is copied to the first text box so that it can be used as part of another calculation.

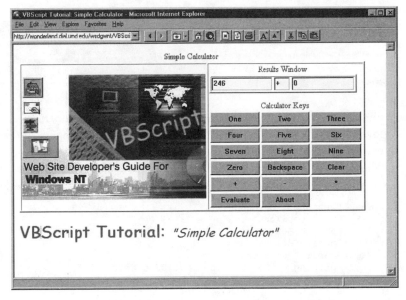

18

UNLEASHING THE POWER OF VBSCRIPT

FIGURE 18.15.

The About dialog box.

Error checking is an important part of any application. One of VBScript's strengths is its ability to perform various error checks when users enter data into a form. By using the OnChange event, it is possible to check the value of a text box that was recently changed by the user. The subroutine shown next makes sure the user entered a valid number into a text box that is used to obtain an operand from the user. The error-checking subroutine of the second operand is similar to the one shown next. Note how chr(10) is used to create a multiline string. As you can see in Figure 18.16, when a user enters an invalid number, the following subroutine informs the user and resets the text box:

```
 1: Sub Operand1Box_OnChange
 2:  IF (NOT IsNumeric(Operand1Box.Value)) THEN
 3:     MsgBoxString = "Do not type invalid characters "
 4:     MsgBoxString = MsgBoxString & "into the Results Window! "
 5:     MsgBoxString = MsgBoxString & chr(10)
 6:     MsgBoxString = MsgBoxString & "Results Window will now be reset."
 7:     MsgBox MsgBoxString , 48 , "Invalid input detected!"
 8:     Operand1Box.Value = 0
 9:  END IF
10: End Sub
```

FIGURE 18.16.

The Operand1Box_OnChange *subroutine detects invalid entries.*

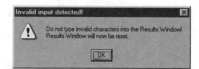

A similar subroutine checks that operators entered into the operator text box are valid. The following code listing verifies that operators entered into the operator text box are valid. Note how the underline character (_) is used to join a long expression that spans several lines. If an invalid operator is entered, it is detected by OperatorBox_OnChange subroutine, the text box is reset, and the user is informed of the invalid input, as shown in Figure 18.17:

```
 1: Sub OperatorBox_OnChange
 2:  IF (NOT((OperatorBox.Value = "+" ) OR _
 3:     (OperatorBox.Value = "-" ) OR _
 4:     (OperatorBox.Value = "*" ) OR _
 5:     (OperatorBox.Value = "?" ))) THEN
 6:     MsgString = "Do not type invalid characters "
 7:     MsgString = MsgString & "into the operator text box! "
 8:     MsgString = MsgString & chr(10)
 9:     MsgString = MsgString & "The operator text box will now be reset."
10:     MsgString = MsgString & chr(10) & chr(10)
11:     MsgString = MsgString & "Valid input: +, -, *"
```

```
12:     MsgBox MsgString , 48 , "Invalid input detected!"
13:     OperatorBox.Value = "?"
14:  END IF
15: End Sub
```

FIGURE 18.17.

The
OperatorBox_OnChange
subroutine detects
invalid entries.

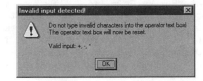

The Delete button deletes characters entered into one of the operand text boxes. The subroutine associated with the Delete button, BtnDelete_OnClick, is a *smart function* subroutine. As shown in line 2 of the following code listing, the subroutine first examines the operator text box and determines if a calculation has already been performed. If so, it knows that any numbers added appear on the text box to the right and deletes a digit from that text box. If not, a digit from the left text box is deleted:

```
 1: Sub BtnDelete_OnClick
 2:  IF (OperatorBox.Value = "?") THEN
 3:     IF ((Len (Operand1Box.Value) > 0) AND (Operand1Box.Value <> 0)) THEN
 4:        Operand1Box.Value = Left (Operand1Box.Value,  Len (Operand1Box.Value)
               ➡-1)
 5:     IF (Len (Operand1Box.Value) = 0) THEN
 6:        Operand1Box.Value = 0
 7:     END IF
 8:     END IF
 9:  ELSE
10:     IF ((Len (Operand2Box.Value) > 0) AND (Operand2Box.Value <> 0)) THEN
11:        Operand2Box.Value = Left (Operand2Box.Value,  Len (Operand2Box.Value)
               ➡-1)
12:     IF (Len (Operand2Box.Value) = 0) THEN
13:        Operand2Box.Value = 0
14:     END IF
15:     END IF
16:  END IF
17: End Sub
```

The Evaluate button calculates two operands using an operator and returns a value as shown in Figure 18.13. As you can see in line 2 of the following program listing, the BtnEvaluate_OnClick subroutine first checks the Operator text box. If a valid operator is found, it performs a calculation and displays it using a dialog box. If not, a dialog box similar to the one shown in Figure 18.18 is displayed. Afterwards, as shown in lines 17 and 18, the operand text boxes are reset so that additional calculations can be performed. Note that the result of the calculation is copied in line 17 to the left operand box so that the result of the calculation can be used as part of another calculation:

```
 1: Sub BtnEvaluate_OnClick
 2:  IF (OperatorBox.Value = "?") THEN
 3:     MsgBoxString = "A valid operator is required to carry out "
```

18

UNLEASHING THE
POWER OF
VBSCRIPT

```
 4:     MsgBoxString = MsgBoxString & "an evaluation."
 5:     MsgBoxString = MsgBoxString & chr(10)
 6:     MsgBoxString = MsgBoxString & "Valid operators are: +, -, *"
 7:     MsgBox MsgBoxString , 48 , "Invalid operator!"
 8: ELSE
 9:     IF (OperatorBox.Value = "+")  THEN
10:         answer = CDbl(Operand1Box.Value) + CDbl(Operand2Box.Value)
11:     ELSEIF (OperatorBox.Value = "-")  THEN
12:         answer = CDbl(Operand1Box.Value) - CDbl(Operand2Box.Value)
13:     ELSEIF (OperatorBox.Value = "*")  THEN
14:         answer = CDbl(Operand1Box.Value) * CDbl(Operand2Box.Value)
15:     End IF
16:     MsgBox answer , 64 , "Results of calculation"
17:     Operand1Box.Value = answer
18:     Operand2Box.Value = 0
19: END IF
20: End Sub
```

Figure 18.18.

The operands are evaluated only if a valid operator is found.

The AddDigit subroutine adds a digit selected via one of the calculator buttons into one of the operand text boxes. As shown in line 4 of the following program listing, if a valid operator is not present, digits are added to the left text box. However, if a valid operator is present, this means that the user has either entered a valid number to the left text box or that it contains the result of a previous calculation (in which case, the digit selected by the user is added to the right text box). When adding digits, the user might try to add too many digits. This is taken care of in lines 9 and 16, where a separate subroutine is used to inform the reader by displaying a dialog box similar to the one shown in Figure 18.19:

```
 1: Sub AddDigit ( digit )
 2: REM Just in case there are any preceding zeros or spaces
 3: Operand1Box.Value = CDbl (Operand1Box.Value)
 4: IF ( OperatorBox.Value = "?") THEN
 5:     IF ( Len ( Operand1Box.Value ) < 14 ) THEN
 6:         Operand1Box.Value = Operand1Box.Value & digit
 7:         Operand1Box.Value = CDbl (Operand1Box.Value)
 8:     ELSE
 9:         TooManyDigits
10:     END IF
11: ELSE
12:     IF ( Len ( Operand2Box.Value ) < 14 ) THEN
13:         Operand2Box.Value = Operand2Box.Value & digit
14:         Operand2Box.Value = CDbl (Operand2Box.Value)
15:     ELSE
16:         TooManyDigits
17:     END IF
18: END IF
19: End Sub
```

FIGURE 18.19.

The `AddDigit`
subroutine prevents
users from entering too
many digits into a
text box.

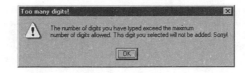

For your reference, the full source code of the Calculator application is given in Listing 18.2.

Listing 18.2. The Calculator Web page.

```
<!--
(C) 1996 Sanjaya Hettihewa (http://wonderland.dial.umd.edu)
All Rights Reserved.
Permission is hereby given to modify and distribute this code
as you wish provided that this block of text remains unchanged.
!-->

<HTML>
<HEAD>
<TITLE>VBScript Tutorial: Simple Calculator</TITLE>
</HEAD>

<TABLE COLSPEC="L20 L20 L20" BORDER=2 WIDTH=10 HEIGHT=10>
<CAPTION ALIGN=top>Simple Calculator</CAPTION>
<TR><TD>
<BODY BGCOLOR="#FFFFFF" TEXT="#0000FF"
      LINK="#B864FF" VLINK="#670000" ALINK="#FF0000">
<IMG ALIGN=TOP SRC="vbscript.jpg">
<TD>

<TABLE BORDER=2 >
<CAPTION ALIGN=top>Results Window</CAPTION>
 <TD>
 <input type=text size=14 maxlength=14 name="Operand1Box" value="0">
 <input type=text size=1 maxlength=1 name="OperatorBox" value="?">
 <input type=text size=14 maxlength=14 name="Operand2Box" value="0">
 </TD>
</TABLE>

<TABLE COLSPEC="L20 L20 L20" >

<CAPTION ALIGN=top>Calculator Keys</CAPTION>
<TR>
 <TD><INPUT TYPE=BUTTON VALUE="One" NAME="BtnOne"></TD>
 <TD><INPUT TYPE=BUTTON VALUE="Two" NAME="BtnTwo"></TD>
 <TD><INPUT TYPE=BUTTON VALUE="Three" NAME="BtnThree"></TD>
</TR>
<TR>
 <TD><INPUT TYPE=BUTTON VALUE="Four" NAME="BtnFour"></TD>
 <TD><INPUT TYPE=BUTTON VALUE="Five" NAME="BtnFive"></TD>
 <TD><INPUT TYPE=BUTTON VALUE="Six" NAME="BtnSix"></TD>
</TR>
<TR>
```

continues

18

UNLEASHING THE POWER OF VBSCRIPT

Listing 18.2. continued

```
 <TD><INPUT TYPE=BUTTON VALUE="Seven" NAME="BtnSeven"></TD>
 <TD><INPUT TYPE=BUTTON VALUE="Eight" NAME="BtnEight"></TD>
 <TD><INPUT TYPE=BUTTON VALUE="Nine" NAME="BtnNine"></TD>
</TR>
<TR>
 <TD><INPUT TYPE=BUTTON VALUE="Zero" NAME="BtnZero"></TD>
 <TD><INPUT TYPE=BUTTON VALUE="Backspace" NAME="BtnDelete"></TD>
 <TD><INPUT TYPE=BUTTON VALUE="Clear" NAME="BtnClear"></TD>
</TR>
<TR>
 <TD><INPUT TYPE=BUTTON VALUE="+" NAME="BtnPlus"></TD>
 <TD><INPUT TYPE=BUTTON VALUE="-" NAME="BtnMinus"></TD>
 <TD><INPUT TYPE=BUTTON VALUE="*" NAME="BtnMultiply"></TD>
</TR>

<TR>
 <TD><INPUT TYPE=BUTTON VALUE="Evaluate" NAME="BtnEvaluate"></TD>
 <TD><INPUT TYPE=BUTTON VALUE="About" NAME="BtnAbout"></TD>
</TR>

</TABLE>

</TR>
</TABLE>

<P>

<B><FONT FACE="Comic Sans MS" SIZE=6 COLOR=RED>
VBScript Tutorial: <FONT></B>
<I><FONT FACE="Comic Sans MS" SIZE=5 COLOR=BLUE>
 "Simple Calculator" </I><P><FONT>


<SCRIPT LANGUAGE=VBS>
<!-- To hide VBScript code from technologically challenged browsers

Sub BtnAbout_OnClick
 titleString = "Web Site Developer's Guide for Windows NT"
 helloString = "Simple VBScript calculator by "
 helloString = helloString & "Sanjaya Hettihewa."
 MsgBox helloString, 64, titleString
End Sub

Sub Operand1Box_OnChange
 IF (NOT IsNumeric(Operand1Box.Value)) THEN
    MsgBoxString = "Do not type invalid characters "
    MsgBoxString = MsgBoxString & "into the Results Window! "
    MsgBoxString = MsgBoxString & chr(10)
    MsgBoxString = MsgBoxString & "Results Window will now be reset."
    MsgBox MsgBoxString , 48 , "Invalid input detected!"
    Operand1Box.Value = 0
 END IF
End Sub

Sub Operand2Box_OnChange
```

```
      IF (NOT IsNumeric(Operand2Box.Value)) THEN
          MsgBoxString = "Do not type invalid characters "
          MsgBoxString = MsgBoxString & "into the Results Window! "
          MsgBoxString = MsgBoxString & chr(10)
          MsgBoxString = MsgBoxString & "Results Window will now be reset."
          MsgBox MsgBoxString , 48 , "Invalid input detected!"
          Operand2Box.Value = 0
      END IF
  End Sub

  Sub OperatorBox_OnChange
   IF (NOT((OperatorBox.Value = "+" ) OR _
       (OperatorBox.Value = "-" ) OR _
       (OperatorBox.Value = "*" ) OR _
       (OperatorBox.Value = "?" ))) THEN
       MsgString = "Do not type invalid characters "
       MsgString = MsgString & "into the operator text box! "
       MsgString = MsgString & chr(10)
       MsgString = MsgString & "The operator text box will now be reset."
       MsgString = MsgString & chr(10) & chr(10)
       MsgString = MsgString & "Valid input: +, -, *"
       MsgBox MsgString , 48 , "Invalid input detected!"
       OperatorBox.Value = "?"
   END IF
  End Sub

  Sub BtnOne_OnClick
   IF (IsNumeric(Operand1Box.Value)) THEN
       AddDigit ( 1 )
   ELSE
       ResetResultsWindow
   END IF
  End Sub
  Sub BtnTwo_OnClick
   IF (IsNumeric(Operand1Box.Value)) THEN
       AddDigit ( 2 )
   ELSE
       ResetResultsWindow
   END IF
  End Sub
  Sub BtnThree_OnClick
   IF (IsNumeric(Operand1Box.Value)) THEN
       AddDigit ( 3 )
   ELSE
       ResetResultsWindow
   END IF
  End Sub
  Sub BtnFour_OnClick
   IF (IsNumeric(Operand1Box.Value)) THEN
       AddDigit ( 4 )
   ELSE
       ResetResultsWindow
   END IF
  End Sub
  Sub BtnFive_OnClick
   IF (IsNumeric(Operand1Box.Value)) THEN
       AddDigit ( 5 )
```

18

UNLEASHING THE
POWER OF
VBSCRIPT

continues

Listing 18.2. continued

```
ELSE
    ResetResultsWindow
 END IF
End Sub
Sub BtnSix_OnClick
 IF (IsNumeric(Operand1Box.Value)) THEN
    AddDigit ( 6 )
 ELSE
    ResetResultsWindow
 END IF
End Sub
Sub BtnSeven_OnClick
 IF (IsNumeric(Operand1Box.Value)) THEN
    AddDigit ( 7 )
 ELSE
    ResetResultsWindow
 END IF
End Sub
Sub BtnEight_OnClick
 IF (IsNumeric(Operand1Box.Value)) THEN
    AddDigit ( 8 )
 ELSE
    ResetResultsWindow
 END IF
End Sub
Sub BtnNine_OnClick
 IF (IsNumeric(Operand1Box.Value)) THEN
    AddDigit ( 9 )
 ELSE
    ResetResultsWindow
 END IF
End Sub
Sub BtnZero_OnClick
 IF (IsNumeric(Operand1Box.Value)) THEN
    AddDigit ( 0 )
 ELSE
    ResetResultsWindow
 END IF
End Sub

Sub BtnDelete_OnClick
 IF (OperatorBox.Value = "?") THEN
    IF ((Len (Operand1Box.Value) > 0) AND (Operand1Box.Value <> 0)) THEN
       Operand1Box.Value = Left (Operand1Box.Value,  Len (Operand1Box.Value) - 1)
    IF (Len (Operand1Box.Value) = 0) THEN
       Operand1Box.Value = 0
    END IF
    END IF
 ELSE
    IF ((Len (Operand2Box.Value) > 0) AND (Operand2Box.Value <> 0)) THEN
       Operand2Box.Value = Left (Operand2Box.Value,  Len (Operand2Box.Value) - 1)
    IF (Len (Operand2Box.Value) = 0) THEN
       Operand2Box.Value = 0
    END IF
    END IF
 END IF
End Sub
```

```
Sub BtnClear_OnClick
 Operand1Box.Value = 0
 Operand2Box.Value = 0
 OperatorBox.Value = "?"
End Sub

Sub BtnPlus_OnClick
 OperatorBox.Value = "+"
End Sub

Sub BtnMinus_OnClick
 OperatorBox.Value = "-"
End Sub

Sub BtnMultiply_OnClick
 OperatorBox.Value = "*"
End Sub

Sub BtnEvaluate_OnClick
 IF (OperatorBox.Value = "?") THEN
    MsgBoxString = "A valid operator is required to carry out "
    MsgBoxString = MsgBoxString & "an evaluation."
    MsgBoxString = MsgBoxString & chr(10)
    MsgBoxString = MsgBoxString & "Valid operators are: +, -, *"
    MsgBox MsgBoxString , 48 , "Invalid operator!"
 ELSE
    IF (OperatorBox.Value = "+")  THEN
       answer = CDbl(Operand1Box.Value) + CDbl(Operand2Box.Value)
    ELSEIF (OperatorBox.Value = "-")  THEN
       answer = CDbl(Operand1Box.Value) - CDbl(Operand2Box.Value)
    ELSEIF (OperatorBox.Value = "*")  THEN
       answer = CDbl(Operand1Box.Value) * CDbl(Operand2Box.Value)
    End IF
    MsgBox answer , 64 , "Results of calculation"
    Operand1Box.Value = answer
    Operand2Box.Value = 0
 END IF
End Sub

Sub AddDigit ( digit )
 REM Just in case there are any preceeding zeros or spaces
 Operand1Box.Value = CDbl (Operand1Box.Value)
 IF ( OperatorBox.Value = "?") THEN
    IF ( Len ( Operand1Box.Value ) < 14 ) THEN
       Operand1Box.Value = Operand1Box.Value & digit
       Operand1Box.Value = CDbl (Operand1Box.Value)
    ELSE
       TooManyDigits
    END IF
 ELSE
    IF ( Len ( Operand2Box.Value ) < 14 ) THEN
       Operand2Box.Value = Operand2Box.Value & digit
       Operand2Box.Value = CDbl (Operand2Box.Value)
    ELSE
       TooManyDigits
    END IF
 END IF
End Sub
```

18

UNLEASHING THE
POWER OF
VBSCRIPT

continues

Listing 18.2. continued

```
Sub ResetResultsWindow
 MsgBoxString = "Do not type invalid characters "
 MsgBoxString = MsgBoxString & "into the Results Window! "
 MsgBoxString = MsgBoxString & chr(10)
 MsgBoxString = MsgBoxString & "Use Calculator keys instead. "
 MsgBoxString = MsgBoxString & "Results Window will now be reset."
 MsgBox MsgBoxString , 48 , "Invalid input detected!"
 Operand1Box.Value = 0
 Operand2Box.Value = 0
 OperatorBox.Value = "?"
End Sub

Sub TooManyDigits
 MsgBoxString = "The number of digits you have typed "
 MsgBoxString = MsgBoxString & "exceed the maximum"
 MsgBoxString = MsgBoxString & chr(10)
 MsgBoxString = MsgBoxString & "number of digits allowed. "
 MsgBoxString = MsgBoxString & "The digit you selected will "
 MsgBoxString = MsgBoxString & "not be added. Sorry!"
 MsgBox MsgBoxString , 48 , "Too many digits!"
End Sub

!-->
</SCRIPT>

</BODY>
</HTML>
```

Labeling an Image

VBScript can be used to label a graphic when the mouse is moved over it. The VBScript program in Listing 18.3 can be used to label an image. When the Web page containing the VBScript program is first invoked, it looks similar to Figure 18.20. Note the string Hello! Select a link, please. is contained in the description text box.

At this point, if the mouse is moved over the graphic in Figure 18.20, the value of the text box changes, as shown in Figure 18.21.

As you can see in Figure 18.22, four icons appear in the graphic to the left of the browser window. When the mouse is moved over any of these icons, the text box will list the description of the text box. For example, when the mouse is over the bulletin-board icon, the value of the text box in Figure 18.21 changes to Post messages on an online discussion forum.

In order to detect mouse movement over the graphic in Figure 18.22, a special identification code needs to be assigned to the graphic. This is done in line 1 of the following code listing:

```
1: <A ID="ImageMapGraphic" HREF="ImageMap.Map">
2: <IMG  ALIGN=TOP SRC="vbscript.jpg" ALT="Sample Graphic" ISMAP BORDER=0>
3: </A>
```

FIGURE 18.20.

Text box contains the string Hello! Select a link, please. *when the VBScript Web page is first invoked.*

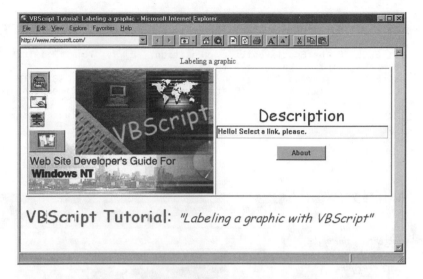

FIGURE 18.21.

When the mouse is moved over the graphic, the value of the text box changes to No link selected. Please select a link!.

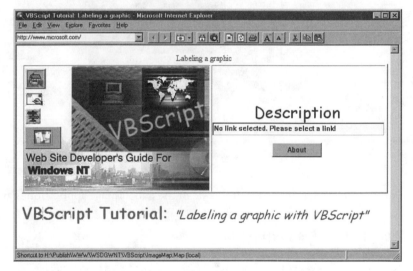

The `ImageMapGraphic_MouseMove` is the heart of the VBScript shown in Figure 18.22. When the mouse is moved over the graphic, the following subroutine is activated. When the mouse pointer falls in a predetermined region of the graphic, the text box is updated with the description of the region the mouse pointer is over, as shown in line 4 of the following program listing. The `HotSpot` subroutine simply returns TRUE if the mouse coordinates passed into the `HotSpot` subroutine fall within a certain region of the graphic:

```
1: Sub ImageMapGraphic_MouseMove(keyboard,mouse,xPosition,yPosition)
2:
3: IF (HotSpot(xPosition, yPosition,  2, 5, 70, 41)) THEN
```

```
 4:    Description.Value = "Main Homepage"
 5: ELSE IF (HotSpot(xPosition, yPosition,  2, 49, 70, 82)) THEN
 6:    Description.Value = "Send Feedback"
 7: ELSE IF (HotSpot(xPosition, yPosition,  2, 84, 70, 117)) THEN
 8:    Description.Value = "Site Map"
 9: ELSE IF (HotSpot(xPosition, yPosition,  2, 119, 70, 164)) THEN
10:    Description.Value = "Post messages on an online discussion forum"
11: ELSE
12:    Description.Value = "No link selected. Please select a link!"
13: END IF
14: END IF
15: END IF
16: END IF
```

FIGURE 18.22.

When the mouse is over one of the icons of the image, the value of the text box changes the icon's description.

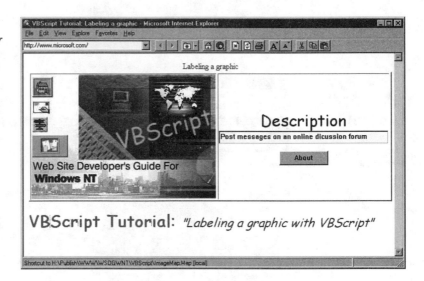

For your reference, the full source code of the Label Image application is given in Listing 18.3.

Listing 18.3. Labeling a graphic.

```
<!--
(C) 1996 Sanjaya Hettihewa (http://wonderland.dial.umd.edu)
All Rights Reserved.
     Permission is hereby given to modify and distribute this code as you wish
provided that this block of text remains unchanged.
!-->

<HTML>
<HEAD>
<TITLE>VBScript Tutorial: Labeling a graphic</TITLE>
</HEAD>

<BODY BGCOLOR="#FFFFFF" TEXT="#0000FF"
           LINK="#B864FF" VLINK="#670000" ALINK="#FF0000">
```

```
<TABLE COLSPEC="L20 L20 L20" BORDER=2 WIDTH=10 HEIGHT=10>
<CAPTION ALIGN=top>Labeling a graphic</CAPTION>
<TR><TD>

<A ID="ImageMapGraphic" HREF="ImageMap.Map">
<IMG  ALIGN=TOP SRC="vbscript.jpg" ALT="Sample Graphic" ISMAP BORDER=0>
</A>

</TD><TD>

<CENTER><FONT FACE="Comic Sans MS" SIZE=6 COLOR=Black>
Description<FONT></CENTER>
<input type="text" name="Description"
       Value="Hello! Select a link, please." size=45><P>

<CENTER><INPUT TYPE=BUTTON VALUE="About" NAME="BtnAbout"></CENTER>

</TD><TD>

</TR>
</TABLE>

<P>

<B><FONT FACE="Comic Sans MS" SIZE=6 COLOR=RED>
VBScript Tutorial: <FONT></B>
<I><FONT FACE="Comic Sans MS" SIZE=5 COLOR=BLUE>
 "Labeling a graphic with VBScript" </I><P><FONT>
</TD></TR>
</TABLE>

<SCRIPT LANGUAGE="VBS">
<!-- To hide VBScript code from  technologically challenged browsers

Sub BtnAbout_OnClick
  titleString = "Web Site Developer's Guide for Windows NT"
  helloString = "Labeling a graphic with VBScript by "
  helloString = helloString & "Sanjaya Hettihewa."
  MsgBox helloString, 64, titleString
End Sub

Sub ImageMapGraphic_MouseMove(keyboard,mouse,xPosition,yPosition)

IF (HotSpot(xPosition, yPosition,  2, 5, 70, 41)) THEN
  Description.Value = "Main Homepage"
ELSE IF (HotSpot(xPosition, yPosition,  2, 49, 70, 82)) THEN
  Description.Value = "Send Feedback"
ELSE IF (HotSpot(xPosition, yPosition,  2, 84, 70, 117)) THEN
  Description.Value = "Site Map"
ELSE IF (HotSpot(xPosition, yPosition,  2, 119, 70, 164)) THEN
  Description.Value = "Post messages on an online discussion forum"
ELSE
  Description.Value = "No link selected. Please select a link!"
END IF
END IF
END IF
END IF
```

18

UNLEASHING THE
POWER OF
VBSCRIPT

continues

Listing 18.3. continued

```
End Sub

Function HotSpot ( mouseX, mouseY, TopX , TopY, BottomX, BottomY)
 HotSpot = (mouseX >= TopX) AND _
           (mouseX <= BottomX) AND _
           (mouseY >= topY) AND _
           (mouseY<=bottomY)
End Function

!-->
</SCRIPT>

</BODY>
</HTML>
```

Summary

VBScript, a subset of Visual Basic, is an easy-to-use scripting language that can be used to create active Web pages. It enables Web-site developers to create various client-side solutions that make Web sites easier and more interesting to navigate.

CHAPTER 19

Introduction to Windows NT CGI Programming

IN THIS CHAPTER

- Introduction to CGI   572

- Applications of CGI   574

- CGI Basics   574

- CGI Issues   577

- CGI Environment Variables   580

- CGI Perl Scripts   584

- CGI C Scripts   586

- "Content Type" Returned by CGI Applications   586

- A Few Things to Note About Developing CGI Applications   587

- Hello World! CGI Scripts   588

- Accessing Environment Variables Available to CGI Scripts   592

- Using CGI to Provide Customized Content   594

- Setting Up a Feedback Form   599

One of the best things about the World Wide Web is that you can use it to exchange information with potentially millions of users. However, static HTML pages do not allow you to adequately display dynamic content to people surfing your Web site for specific information. On the other hand, Common Gateway Interface (CGI) is a mechanism that enables you to interact with browsers of your Web site and exploit the World Wide Web to its fullest potential. After you set up your Web site and create some Web pages, you are ready to set up CGI scripts on your Web server.

Feedback forms, e-mail forms, database query interfaces, database update mechanisms, Web page counters, and search engines are all applications of CGI. Thanks to the user-friendly development environment of Windows NT, by the end of this chapter you will be able to develop CGI scripts, experiment with them, and harness the power of interactive Web interfaces.

This chapter starts with an introduction to CGI and explains how CGI works. Then you examine some practical applications of CGI and learn how to utilize CGI scripts to enhance your Web site. Next you begin to develop CGI programs in two programming languages, C and Perl. When you finish this chapter, you will be able to utilize CGI to interact with your Web site browsers.

Introduction to CGI

Before going any further, an introduction to CGI is in order. CGI is a standard for various programs that you can use to interact with users surfing your site. Because CGI is a standard, it is not browser or server dependent and can be moved from one Web server to another while still retaining its full functionality.

Just like application programs, CGI programs can be written in almost any programming language that will let you either create an executable program or interpret it in real time with another program (as in the case of AWK and Perl). Here are a few languages that you can use to create CGI applications under Windows NT:

- AWK
- C/C++
- FORTRAN
- Pascal
- Perl
- Visual Basic
- NT batch scripts

Depending on your expertise, what's available, and the nature of your CGI projects, you can choose the language that best suits your needs. Customarily, CGI scripts are stored in the CGI-BIN directory of the Web server's document root directory. All files and pathnames of a Web site are relative to this directory.

Benefits of an Interactive Web Site

Plain text HTML files retrieved by Web clients are static. The information contained in these files never changes unless you edit them manually. However, by utilizing CGI scripts, your Web pages can be created dynamically each time a client accesses them. To the client, the page looks as if it has been specially created for him or her based on the information needed. Obviously, this tool is a very powerful way to interact with Web surfers. You should utilize CGI to make your Web site interactive so that you can provide customized content and enable those browsing your Web site to interact with the information you provide.

The benefits of CGI are invaluable to any Web site. They range from having a customized input form for feedback to allowing someone browsing your Web site to update and retrieve information from a database on your server. By setting up a customized e-mail feedback form, you get all the information you need. Furthermore, you can be sure that your e-mail feedback form will always work because it does not depend on the e-mail capability of your client's Web browser. In the section "Setting Up a Feedback Form," you learn how to use CGI to set up an e-mail feedback page. Furthermore, if you want to set up a database that collects data from users browsing your Web site, you can use a CGI script to update the information they provide to a database. CGI enables you to update a database on your server without direct human intervention. As you can see, the possibilities and applications of CGI are endless.

One of CGI's best features is that it allows Web surfers to interact with databases on your server. For example, you might have a Microsoft Access database on your server that needs to be updated with user-provided information. You might also need to make parts of this database available to authenticated users for querying. Although you can use standard e-mail to correspond with people and manually perform database queries and updates, this method is not very practical when you start getting more and more visitors. Eventually, you will end up spending the whole day answering and responding to e-mail. (Maybe you do so already, but just imagine how much worse it will be!) By setting up a simple form, you can use a CGI script to perform updates to your database. Keep on reading, and soon you will find out how easy it is to use CGI to interact with people browsing your Web site.

You can also port the dynamic content that is output by CGI programs across other Web servers. For example, if in the output of a CGI script, you need to create a hypertext link to the main home page of a Web server, you can use the CGI environment variable SERVER_NAME. By using this CGI variable, as opposed to hard-coding the home page in the CGI program, the CGI script will be portable across various Web servers.

19

WINDOWS
NT CGI
PROGRAMMING

TIP

Whenever possible, you should use CGI variables to make moving scripts from one Web server to another as effortless as possible.

The power of CGI enables you to make your Web site interactive so that your visitors will be able to find the information they need easily. If your Web site is easy to navigate, users will visit it again and again for more information. Because CGI provides dynamic content, you can customize what people see when they browse your Web site. Furthermore, you can use a CGI script to provide content that's customized for the Web browser being used to access the information.

Applications of CGI

Many organizations and individuals are using CGI for a variety of tasks, for example, having a simple counter on a Web page to count the number of accesses or using a CGI script to manage the front end of an entire store. A CGI script can allow Web site visitors to examine merchandise and even place orders. In addition, various Web sites offer search capabilities to help users find information.

You can use CGI whenever you want to interact with those browsing your Web site, to get feedback from those browsing your Web site, or to provide dynamic content. Here are a few CGI applications that you can use to enhance the capabilities of your Web site:

- Setting up a guest book
- Setting up a feedback form
- Adding a counter to a Web page
- Designing a database front end for the Web
- Allowing Web surfers to visit various Web pages via a pull-down list
- Enabling those browsing your Web site to e-mail comments
- Customizing Web pages based on a client's Web browser
- Enabling those browsing your Web site to search your Web site

This chapter demonstrates how to add most of these capabilities to your Web site. Before moving on to more advanced topics, it's time to cover the basics of CGI.

CGI Basics

A CGI script is typically used to provide dynamic content to the client that called the CGI script. CGI scripts communicate with Web browsers, as shown in Figure 19.1. If the CGI script is an interactive script, typically a form with various input controls is sent to the Web client. After filling in the form, the user submits it to the Web server. The Web server then uses CGI to call the CGI script with data from the Web client. The CGI script processes the data, possibly accessing a database on the server, and sends a message to the client that made the request. If the CGI script is noninteractive, the output of the script is sent directly to the client that called the CGI script with its URL.

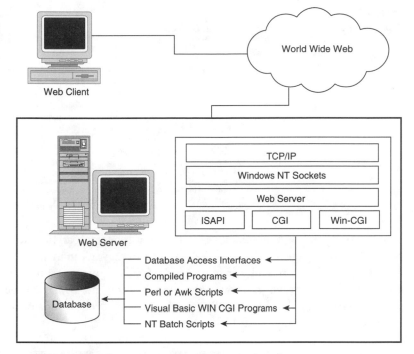

FIGURE 19.1.
Architecture of a typical Web server with CGI scripts.

When a CGI script is called, the Web server first examines the REQUEST_METHOD used to call the script to determine how the Web client is sending data to the CGI script. This process is shown in Figure 19.2. If the REQUEST_METHOD used to call the CGI script is GET, any data supplied by the Web client for the CGI script is found immediately following the URL name of the CGI script. Therefore, this information is stored in the environment variable QUERY_STRING. On the other hand, if the REQUEST_METHOD used is POST or PUT, the size of input for the CGI script is stored in CONTENT_LENGTH. CONTENT_LENGTH contains the size (in bytes) of data supplied to the CGI script. The CGI script can then read from standard input the number of bytes returned by CONTENT_LENGTH. If you are confused about all these strange environment variables, don't worry—they are all discussed later in the chapter.

How CGI Works

Although a major use of CGI is to provide dynamic content to people browsing your Web site, CGI programs do not always need to be interactive. You can use noninteractive CGI scripts to provide dynamic information that does not require user input. For example, to take advantage of various features offered by Web browsers such as Netscape Navigator and Microsoft Internet Explorer, you can write a CGI program to determine which browser the client is using and then send a page specially designed to take advantage of that browser's capabilities. (See the section "Using CGI to Provide Customized Content" later in the chapter.)

19

WINDOWS
NT CGI
PROGRAMMING

FIGURE 19.2.

How Web servers determine and handle the REQUEST_METHOD, *which calls the CGI scripts.*

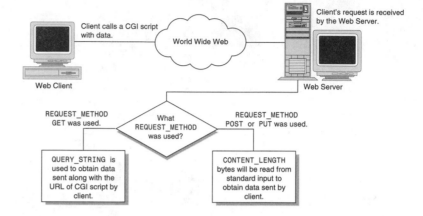

The execution of this noninteractive CGI script can be transparent to the user. For example, if the default Web page of a Web server is welcome.html, you can map the main Web page of the Web server to a CGI script by creating a URL-CGI mapping, as shown in Figure 19.3. Such a script can determine which browser the client is using and display a page with dynamic content optimized for that browser. Please refer to your Web server's documentation for more information on creating URL-CGI mappings.

FIGURE 19.3.

You can map a Web page URL to a CGI script to provide dynamic content.

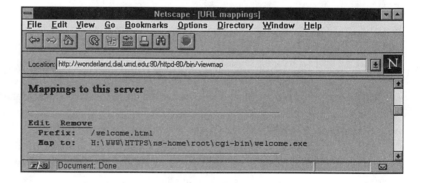

If the type of CGI script described in the preceding section does not need to prompt the user for input, the sequence of events that occur when a client accesses the page is very simple.

1. The client connects to the Web server and requests a Web page that is linked to a CGI script.
2. The Web server executes the CGI program that the page is linked to.
3. The output of the CGI program is sent to the client that requested the page.
4. The connection between the Web server and the Web client is closed.

This interaction is shown in Figure 19.4.

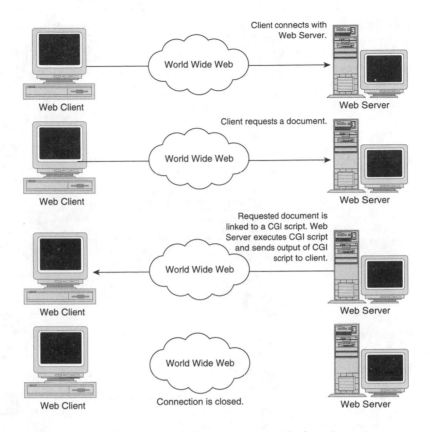

FIGURE 19.4.
You can use a noninteractive CGI script to provide dynamic content.

One of the most powerful aspects of CGI is its capability to interact with those browsing your Web site. You can ask a user to fill in a form and then submit the form. The CGI script can then validate the user's input, ask the user to complete any incomplete information, and process the user's input, as shown in Figure 19.5.

When a CGI script interacts with a Web client to display dynamic content, first it sends a Web page with various controls to the Web browser. The user submits the filled-in form to the Web server to be processed. Depending on the REQUEST_METHOD used to communicate with the CGI script, the CGI script obtains data sent from the client, processes the data, and displays its output to *standard output*. Everything written to standard output by the CGI script will be visible to the client that called the CGI script.

CGI Issues

When you are setting up CGI scripts, you need to be aware of several important issues:

- Security
- Processing time
- Multiple instances of the same script

19

WINDOWS
NT CGI
PROGRAMMING

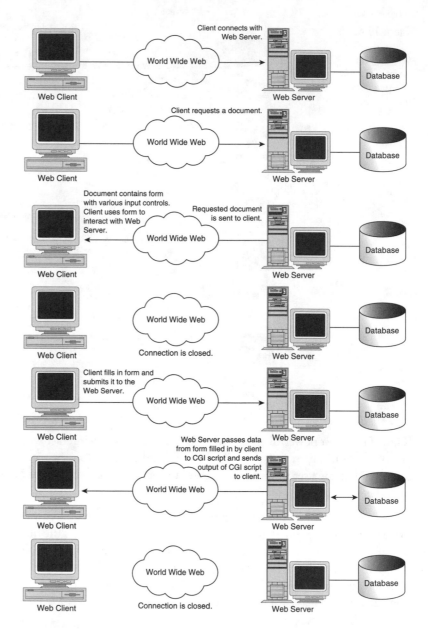

Figure 19.5.

You can use an interactive CGI script to provide dynamic content.

Security

The first thing you should be concerned about is security. Each time you allow someone surfing your Web site to execute a CGI script, you are allowing that person to execute a program on your server, which opens the door to security breaches. Fortunately, you can reduce the risk by following a few guidelines. CGI is very safe when you use it properly.

You should be particularly careful about CGI scripts that take input from a Web client and use that data (without checking) as a command-line argument, for example, using an e-mail address supplied by a Web client to call Blat, a command-line e-mail program. When using such an e-mail address, make sure there is no possibility of it being interpreted as a command-line command. Your CGI scripts should always check for special control characters to avoid potential security breaches.

If you protect various sections of your Web site with a password, you might want to disable directory browsing of your Web server to prevent people from "snooping around" your Web site directories as they browse. Only a person who knows the URL of a certain page or is transferred to a page from one of your own pages should have access to that page.

Processing Time

Another issue is the time it takes for a CGI script to fulfill a client's request. If you will be providing data to those browsing your Web site in real time, you should ensure that, at most, no one has to wait longer than about 5 to 10 seconds; otherwise, the user might think something is wrong with your site and simply stop waiting. If you need more time to process a request, you should obtain the e-mail address of the person requesting the information and simply e-mail the information when it is ready.

> **PERFORMANCE**
>
> If you need to provide data in real time and your CGI scripts take longer than about 10 seconds to execute, you are probably outgrowing your server and need more processing power, more RAM, or both. Slow processing can also indicate a bottleneck such as an inefficient database access driver or a poorly written CGI script.

Multiple Instances of the Same Script

Because of the nature of HTTP, two or more clients might call a CGI script at the same time. A script that locks various files or databases when it is processing data can cause you problems, potentially resulting in lost data. Therefore, you should make sure that your CGI application does not lock databases or files that another instance of the same application might need to access.

Controlling Access to Your CGI Directory

You should be cautious about who has access to your Web server's CGI directory. You should carefully control who has access to your CGI directory via FTP or any other method. Anyone with a little programming knowledge can write a potentially malicious program, upload it to the CGI directory, and execute it with a Web browser.

19

WINDOWS NT CGI PROGRAMMING

Transmitting Sensitive Data

You should never set up CGI applications to distribute potentially harmful personal information unless the Web server is configured to encrypt the data before it is transmitted over the Internet. If you will be distributing financial information or credit card numbers, you should not use CGI unless you have configured your Web server to encrypt data before it is transmitted over the Internet. If you need to transmit sensitive data and your Web server does not encrypt data before transmitting, you should consider a medium such as Pretty Good Privacy (PGP) protected e-mail to transmit such data.

Validating Users

If you validate users who access parts of your Web site, you should never use the IP address returned by the Web server as the real IP address of the Web client. The Web server can be tricked into believing that the client making the HTTP request is requesting the data from a site other than the site the Web client is connecting from. Even if you protect a certain area of your Web server with a password and a user ID, a third party might be able to intercept this data. Someone might be able to intercept a valid user ID and password when a legitimate user uses it to access your Web site.

If your Web server supports data encryption, this type of interception won't be a problem; however, it will be a problem if you are not using any Web server–based encryption. If your server is vulnerable, you should use a one-time password (OTP) mechanism to validate users. An OTP authorizing mechanism makes sure that a password cannot be reused.

An OTP typically sends a "challenge string" to the client that wants to gain access. The client then uses a special program to find the correct "response string" to respond to the server's challenge. (The client types the user's secret password and challenge string, and the program returns a response string.) The response string is then sent to the server. The server then validates the user and remembers the response string so that it can't be used again. The next time the user wants to gain access, the server sends a different challenge string to the client that can be decoded only with the user's secret password.

Because the user's secret password never travels across the Internet, this process is a safe way of authorizing users. However, unless an encryption technology is used, a clever person with too much free time might still be able to intercept the content. You can find more information on OTP mechanisms at `http://www.yahoo.com/Computers_and_Internet/Security_and_Encryption/S_KEY/`.

CGI Environment Variables

Each time the Web server executes a CGI script, it creates a number of environment variables to pass information to the CGI script. These variables tell the CGI script how it is being invoked and provide information about the server and the client's Web browser. Depending on how the CGI script is invoked, some environment variables may not be available.

Environment variables supplied to CGI scripts are always all uppercase. When they are being accessed by a C program, Perl script, or any other language, be sure to use all uppercase letters.

This section discusses the environment variables available to CGI scripts. By accessing these variables, CGI scripts can obtain certain information, such as the browser used to invoke the script. Following the discussion of environment variables, you learn how to access these variables from a Perl script as well as from a C program via CGI.

AUTH_TYPE

Some Web servers can be configured to authenticate users. If the server has authenticated a user, the authentication type used to validate the user is stored in the AUTH_TYPE variable. The authentication type is determined by examining the Authorization Header the Web server might receive with an HTTP request.

CONTENT_LENGTH

Sometimes CGI scripts are invoked with additional information. This information is typically input for the CGI program. The length of this additional information is specified by the number of bytes taken up by the additional information in this variable. If a CGI script is called with the PUT or POST method, CONTENT_LENGTH is used to determine the length of the input.

CONTENT_TYPE

MIME content types are used to label various types of objects (HTML files, Microsoft Word files, GIF files, and so on). The MIME content type for data being submitted to a CGI script is stored in CONTENT_TYPE. For example, if data is submitted to a CGI script using the GET method, this variable will contain the value application/x-www-form-urlencoded. Responses to the form are encoded according to URL specifications.

GATEWAY_INTERFACE

The CGI specification revision number is stored in the GATEWAY_INTERFACE environment variable. The format of this variable is CGI/revision. By examining this variable, a CGI script can determine the version of CGI that the Web server is using.

HTTP_ACCEPT

Various Web clients can handle different mime types, which are described in the HTTP_ACCEPT variable. MIME types accepted by the Web client calling the CGI script appear as a list separated by commas. This list takes the format *type/subtype, type/subtype*. For example, if the Web client supports the two image formats GIF and JPEG, the HTTP_ACCEPT list will contain the two items image/gif, image/jpeg.

HTTP_USER_AGENT

This value determines which Web browser the client is using. For example, if the client is using Netscape 2.0 beta 4, the HTTP_USER_AGENT variable will contain the value Mozilla/2.0b4 (WinNT; I). The general format of this variable is *software/version library/version*.

PATH_INFO

The PATH_INFO variable is usually used to pass various options to a CGI program. These options follow the script's URL. Clients may access CGI scripts with additional information after the URL of the CGI script. PATH_INFO always contains the string that was used to call the CGI script after the name of the CGI script. For example, PATH_INFO will have the value /These/Are/The/Arguments if the CGI script FunWithNT.EXE is called with the following URL:

http://your_server.your_domain/cgi-bin/FunWithNT.EXE/These/Are/The/Arguments

PATH_TRANSLATED

In the event the CGI script needs to know the absolute path name of itself, the CGI script can obtain this information from PATH_TRANSLATED. For example, if the CGI script being invoked is HelloNTWorld.EXE, all CGI scripts are stored in H:\www\http\ns-home\root\cgi-bin, and the CGI script is accessed with the URL http://your_server.your_domain/root/cgi-bin/ HelloNTWorld.EXE. PATH_TRANSLATED will contain the value H:\www\http\ns-home\root\cgi-bin\HelloNTWorld.EXE. If the CGI program needs to save or access any temporary files in its home directory, it can use PATH_TRANSLATED to determine its absolute location by examining this CGI variable.

QUERY_STRING

You may have noticed that when you submit some forms, a string of characters appears after a question mark, followed by the URL name of the script being called. This string of characters is referred to as the *query string* and contains everything after the question mark. When a CGI script is called with the GET method, QUERY_STRING typically contains variables and their values as entered by the person who filled in the form. Various search engines sometimes use QUERY_STRING to examine the input when a form is submitted for a keyword search. For example, if a CGI application is executed using the URL http://www.server.com/cgi-bin/ application.exe?WindowsNT=Fun, QUERY_STRING will contain the string "WindowsNT=Fun".

REMOTE_ADDR

The IP address of the client that called the CGI program is stored in the REMOTE_ADDR environment variable. For security reasons, you should never use the value of this variable to authenticate users. Someone can easily trick your Web server into believing a client is connecting from a different IP address.

REMOTE_HOST

If the Web server can do a DNS lookup of the client's IP address and finds the alias of the IP address, the REMOTE_HOST variable will contain the alias name of client's IP address. Some Web servers allow you to turn DNS lookups on or off. If you will be using this variable to find the IP address alias of clients, be sure to turn on the DNS lookup option. The Web server can find the IP address alias of most clients, but it might not be capable of getting the alias of some clients. In this case, the REMOTE_HOST variable will not be assigned the client's DNS alias value; it will contain the client's IP address only. Never use this value for user-authentication purposes.

REMOTE_IDENT

If the Web server being used supports RFC 931 identification, this variable will contain the username retrieved from the server. Unfortunately, this value cannot be trusted when transmitting sensitive data. Typically, a Web server obtains this value by contacting the client that initiated the HTTP request and by speaking with the client's authentication server. Visit `http://www.pmg.lcs.mit.edu/cgi-bin/rfc/view?number=931` for additional information about RFC 931 and the Authentication Server Protocol.

REMOTE_USER

Some Web servers support user authentication. If a user is authenticated, the CGI script can find out the username of the person browsing the Web site by looking at the value of the REMOTE_USER environment variable. The REMOTE_USER CGI variable is available only if the user has been authenticated using an authentication mechanism.

REQUEST_METHOD

A client can call a CGI script in a number of ways. The method used by the client to call the CGI script is in the REQUEST_METHOD variable. This variable can have a value like HEAD, POST, GET, or PUT. CGI scripts use the value of this variable to locate data passed to the CGI script.

SCRIPT_NAME

All files on a Web server are usually referenced relative to its document root directory. SCRIPT_NAME contains the virtual path name of the script called relative to the document root directory. For example, if the document root directory is `c:\www\http\ns-home\root`, all CGI scripts are stored in `c:\www\http\ns-home\root\cgi-bin\`. When the CGI script `HelloNTWorld.EXE` is called, the SCRIPT_NAME variable will contain the value `\cgi-bin\HelloWorld.EXE`. The advantage of this variable is that it allows the CGI script to refer to itself. This technique is handy if somewhere in the output, the script's URL needs to be converted to a hypertext link.

19

WINDOWS
NT CGI
PROGRAMMING

SERVER_NAME

This variable stores the domain name of the Web server that invoked the CGI script. This domain name can either be an IP address or a DNS alias.

SERVER_PORT

Typically, Web servers listen to HTTP requests on port 80. However, a Web server can listen to any port that's not in use by another application. A CGI program can determine this port number by looking at the value of the SERVER_PORT environment variable. When displaying self-referencing hypertext links at runtime by examining the contents of SERVER_NAME, be sure to append the port number of the Web server (typically port 80) by concatenating it with the value of SERVER_PORT.

SERVER_PROTOCOL

Web servers speak *Hypertext Transfer Protocol* (HTTP). You can determine which version of HTTP the Web server is using by examining the SERVER_PROTOCOL environment variable. The SERVER_PROTOCOL variable contains the name and revision data of the protocol being used. This information is in the format *protocol/revision*. For example, if the server speaks HTTP 1.0, this variable will have the value HTTP/1.0.

SERVER_SOFTWARE

The SERVER_SOFTWARE environment variable stores the name of the Web server that invoked the CGI script. This environment variable is in the format *name/version*. If a CGI script is designed to make use of various special capabilities of a Web server, the CGI script can determine the Web server being used by examining this variable before those special capabilities are used.

CGI Perl Scripts

This section introduces you to Perl and explains how you can set up CGI Perl scripts on Windows NT Web servers. The Internet contains many CGI Perl scripts. You can easily improve a Web site by customizing these scripts to suit your needs. A comprehensive tutorial of Perl is beyond the scope of this book, so this chapter discusses only the basics of writing CGI Perl scripts.

Perl stands for Practical Extraction and Report Language. With the growth of the World Wide Web, Perl is being used increasingly to write CGI programs. Because Perl incorporates most of the best features of C, sed, awk, and sh (and avoids reinventing the wheel for fundamental tasks such as string manipulation), Perl scripts can be developed in a very short time.

The expression syntax of Perl corresponds quite closely to the expression syntax of C programs, which makes Perl an easy language to learn if you are already familiar with C. One of the best things about Perl is its portability. Perl is an interpreted language that is available for a number of hardware platforms including PC, Mac, and various flavors of UNIX. Unlike most languages and utilities, Perl does not impose limits on the size of data. As long as you have enough system resources, Perl will happily read the contents of an entire file into a string. Thanks to various optimizing algorithms built into Perl, scripts written in Perl are robust and fast.

Before proceeding any further, you need to obtain Perl for Windows NT and install Perl on your Web server. Perl for Windows NT is provided free of charge on the Internet. You can obtain it from `http://info.hip.com/ntperl/`. Once you have Perl for NT, create a directory for Perl and copy the Perl distribution file to this directory. Then uncompress the distribution file. When uncompressing the distribution file, be sure to use the option to use stored directory names in the archive. If you don't use this option, all files will be extracted to the Perl directory you created and you'll find yourself in a mess! After the archive is uncompressed, run `install.bat` to install Perl on your server. Then copy `Perl.EXE` to the root CGI directory of your Web server, which enables your Web server to execute Perl CGI scripts.

> **NOTE**
>
> When uncompressing the ZIP file, be sure to use a 32-bit unzipping program that supports long filenames. Otherwise, the distribution files may not be properly installed. WinZip is a fine file uncompressing program that supports long filenames and a variety of file compression formats. You can obtain WinZip from `http://www.winzip.com/WinZip/download.html`.

After installing Perl, you need to reboot your server for the installation directory paths to become effective. Failing to reboot will cause Perl to greet you with an `Unable to locate DLL` message. (Yes, I was naïve and tried it!) If you don't feel like rebooting your server, there is another alternative (and I found a way around the problem!). You can simply copy all files in the `Perl\bin` directory to the CGI directory of your Web server. However, you *should not* use this workaround in a production Web server because this technique opens several security holes.

Before creating CGI applications, you should check your Web server settings and find the name of its CGI directory. The remainder of this chapter assumes this directory is `CGI-BIN`.

Perl Resources on the Internet

When you are comfortable with CGI and using CGI Perl scripts, you can get more information about Perl and sample CGI Perl scripts from the following URLs:

Yahoo!—Computers and Internet:Internet:World Wide Web:Programming:Perl Scripts

`http://www.yahoo.com/Computers_and_Internet/Internet/World_Wide_Web/Programming/Perl_Scripts/`

19

WINDOWS
NT CGI
PROGRAMMING

Yahoo!—Computers and Internet:Languages:Perl

`http://www.yahoo.com/Computers_and_Internet/Languages/Perl/`

To keep up-to-date with the latest news on Perl for Windows NT, you might also want to consider joining the following mailing lists:

Perl-Win32—Perl discussion list

To subscribe, send e-mail to

`majordomo@mail.hip.com`

Include the following in the message body:

`subscribe Perl-Win32`

Perl-Win32_announce—Perl announcements

To subscribe, send e-mail to

`majordomo@mail.hip.com`

Include the following in the message body:

`subscribe Perl-Win32_announce`

The Perl discussion list is a relatively high-volume mailing list. However, many Windows NT Perl programmers read this list and will answer any questions you might have.

CGI C Scripts

C is a general-purpose language that imposes very few restrictions on the programmer. It is also a portable language that can be moved from one computer to another as long as only standard POSIX/ANSI C function calls are used. Many CGI programs written in C are available on the Internet; you can use them to enhance the capabilities of your Web site. For more information on C CGI programs, please look up `http://www.yahoo.com/Computers_and_Internet/Internet/World_Wide_Web/Programming/`.

By using various Windows API calls from C programs, you can further exploit the capabilities of C and Windows NT. Although a command-line C compiler for Windows NT is available at `ftp://ftp.cygnus.com/pub/sac/gnu-win32/`, consider investing in a C compiler with a GUI development environment such as Microsoft Visual C++ or Borland C++.

"Content Type" Returned by CGI Applications

All CGI scripts have one thing in common: The first two lines displayed by all CGI programs that display text output are the same. The first line displayed by all CGI programs that display text is `Content-type: text/html`. This line of text is always followed by two blank lines. Typically, ASCII character 10 is used twice, immediately after this line of text, to create the blank lines.

For example, the first line of output for all CGI C programs with text output is

```
printf("Content-type: text/html%c%c",10,10) ;
```

The first line of output for all CGI Perl scripts with text output is

```
print "Content-type: text/html\n\n";
```

A Few Things to Note About Developing CGI Applications

A small note about programming in CGI is in order before moving into writing CGI programs. Sooner or later, when you write your own programs or try out examples, you'll get error messages generated by your Web server when you call the CGI script. Although things might get somewhat frustrating for you, don't give up! Most likely, the error message you receive from your Web server is the result of a small oversight on your behalf. After a while, if you're still not getting anywhere with debugging your CGI script, you can start printing everything you can think of to standard output. Perhaps a variable you thought contains a value contains nothing but a null string. Perhaps an environment variable that you thought would be available to your script is not available. Or perhaps you left out the most important element: the first line of all CGI scripts, as mentioned in the preceding section.

Rather than trying to debug CGI scripts by executing them on your Web server, you can execute them from the command prompt to find out what really happens. By manually setting various CGI environment variables, you can make the CGI program believe that it's really being invoked by a Web server. Environment variables can be defined by using the SET command, with the following syntax:

```
SET VARIABLE_NAME=VARIABLE_VALUE
```

For example, you can create a batch file with the following variable declarations to test CGI programs when running them from the command prompt. Please note that you may need to change the value of QUERY_STRING if your CGI script makes use of arguments.

```
SET SERVER_SOFTWARE=Netscape-Communications/1.12
SET SERVER_NAME=your.host.name
SET GATEWAY_INTERFACE=CGI/1.1
SET SERVER_PROTOCOL=HTTP/1.0
SET SERVER_PORT=80
SET REQUEST_METHOD=GET
SET SCRIPT_NAME =/cgi-bin/ScriptName.exe
SET QUERY_STRING=ArgumentsToCGIScript
SET REMOTE_HOST =000.000.000.000
SET REMOTE_ADDR =000.000.000.000
SET CONTENT_TYPE=application/x-www-form-urlencoded
SET HTTP_ACCEPT=image/gif, image/x-xbitmap, image/jpeg, image/pjpeg, */*
SET HTTP_USER_AGENT=Mozilla/2.0b4 (WinNT; I)
```

Hello World! CGI Scripts

It's customary for the first program written in a new language or programming interface to display the string "Hello World!". Although this application of CGI is very simple, it will teach you the basics of CGI scripts as well as how Web browsers call CGI scripts. The following sections create the Hello World! script in Perl as well as in C.

The Hello World! CGI script will simply display the current day, time, arguments passed in, the browser being used by the client to access the CGI script, and of course, the string "Hello World!".

Hello World! CGI Script in Perl

The script that displays "Hello World!" and the additional information is very simple to write in Perl. The code for this Perl script follows, and the output appears in Figure 19.6.

> **SECURITY**
>
> Do not place PERL.EXE in your CGI directory. A user with malicious intent can potentially use PERL.EXE to execute commands on your NT Server. Rather than place PERL.EXE in your CGI directory, create a CGI extension mapping and place PERL.EXE in a directory that's not accessible via your Web server. Refer to your Web server documentation for information about creating CGI extension mappings.

```perl
# Sanjaya Hettihewa, http://wonderland.dial.umd.edu/
# December 31, 1995
# "Hello World" CGI Script in Perl
# Display content type being outputted by CGI script
print "Content-type: text/html\n\n";

# Label title of contents being outputted
print "<TITLE>Perl CGI Script Demonstration</TITLE>\n";

# Display text
print "<H1>Hello World!</H1>\n";
print "<H3>Welcome to the fun filled world of<BR>\n";
print "Windows NT CGI programming with Perl!</H3><BR><BR>\n";
print "The Web browser you are using is:";

# Display value of the environmental variable HTTP_USER_AGENT
print $ENV{"HTTP_USER_AGENT"} , "<BR>\n" ;
print "Arguments passed in: ";

# Display value of the environmental variable QUERY_STRING
print $ENV{"QUERY_STRING"} , "<BR>\n" ;

# Obtain date and time from the system
($sec, $min, $hour, $mday, $mon, $year, $wday, $yday, $isdst) = localtime(time);
```

```
# display time
print "\nThe current time is: ";
print  $hour, ":", $min, ":", $sec , "<BR>\n";

# display date
print "\nThe current date is: ";
print $mon + 1 , "/", $mday , "/", $year, "<BR>\n";
```

FIGURE 19.6.

Output of the Hello World! CGI Perl script.

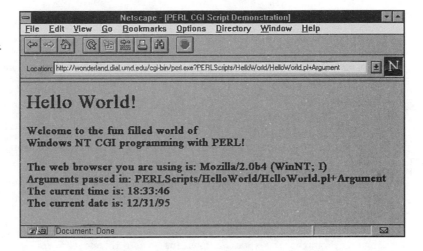

Pay particular attention to how the Perl CGI script is invoked. In this example, the URL that invokes the CGI script is `http://wonderland.dial.umd.edu/cgi-bin/perl.exe?PERLScripts/HelloWorld/HelloWorld.pl+Argument`.

When calling a Perl script on a Windows NT Web server, the general syntax of the URL is

`http://A/B?C+D`

where

    A is the hostname of the Web server; in this example, it is `wonderland.dial.umd.edu`.

    B is the relative path to `PERL.EXE`; in this example, it is `cgi-bin/perl.exe`.

    C is the location of the Perl script. This path is relative to the location of `PERL.EXE`.

    D contains any arguments passed into the Perl script.

You can find these arguments by examining the contents of the CGI environment variable `QUERY_STRING`.

As you can see from the preceding example, when Perl scripts are called with arguments, URLs can become quite long. You can avoid this situation by creating aliases for Perl scripts on your Web server. (Please consult your Web server's documentation for more information on creating aliases for URLs.) For example, if an alias called `Hello` was created for `http://wonderland.dial.umd.edu/cgi-bin/perl.exe?PERLScripts/HelloWorld/HelloWorld.pl`, the URL to call the preceding Perl CGI script becomes

```
http://wonderland.dial.umd.edu/Hello+Argument
```

Whenever you have complex URLs for CGI scripts, create an alias for the CGI script. Your Web site will look friendlier and you will have to do less typing whenever you refer to such CGI scripts from one of your Web pages. If you're still not convinced, an alias is much easier to remember. For example, remembering

```
http://wonderland.dial.umd.edu/Hello+Argument
```

is easier than remembering

```
http://wonderland.dial.umd.edu/cgi-bin/perl.exe?PERLScripts/HelloWorld/
HelloWorld.pl+Argument
```

Hello World! CGI Script in C

The following code lists the C program that displays the same information as the Perl example. The output of the C script appears in Figure 19.7.

```c
/* Sanjaya Hettihewa, http://wonderland.dial.umd.edu/
 * December 31, 1995
 * "Hello World" CGI Script in C
 */

/* Libraries containing special functions used in program */
#include <stdio.h>
#include <stdlib.h>
#include <time.h>

main ( )
{

/* Obtain current time */
   time_t      currentTime ;
   struct tm   *timeObject ;
   char        stringTime[128] ;
   currentTime = time ((time_t *) NULL ) ;
   timeObject  = localtime (&currentTime) ;

/* Display content type being outputted by CGI script */
   printf ("Content-type: text/html\n\n");

/* Displaying simple text output */
   printf ("<TITLE>C CGI Script Demonstration</TITLE>\n");
   printf ("<H1>Hello World!</H1>\n");
   printf ("<H3>Welcome to the fun filled world of<BR>\n");
   printf ("Windows NT CGI programming with C!</H3><BR><BR>\n");

/* Display value of the environmental variable HTTP_USER_AGENT */
   printf ("The Web browser you are using is: ");
   if ( getenv ( "HTTP_USER_AGENT" ) != NULL )
     printf ( "%s%s" , getenv ( "HTTP_USER_AGENT" ) ,"<BR>\n") ;
```

```
/* Display value of the environmental variable QUERY_STRING */
  printf ("Arguments passed in: ");
  if ( getenv ( "QUERY_STRING" ) != NULL )
    printf ( "%s%s", getenv ( "QUERY_STRING" ) ,"<BR>\n") ;

/* Display date and time using strftime() to format the date */
  strftime ( stringTime, 128, "%H:%M:%S", timeObject ) ;
  printf  ("\nThe current time is: %s<BR>\n", stringTime );
  strftime ( stringTime, 128, "%m/%d/%y", timeObject ) ;
  printf  ("\nThe current date is: %s\n", stringTime );

  return   ( 0 ) ;
}
```

FIGURE 19.7.

Output of the Hello World! CGI C script.

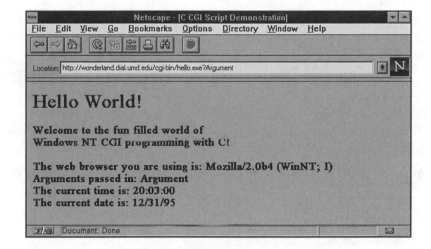

CGI C programs are accessed differently than Perl CGI scripts. C programs can be directly executed by the Web server. However, Perl scripts have to be interpreted using the Perl interpreter. After you compile the C program into an executable program, you should place it either in the CGI directory of your Web server or in a directory that is a child of the CGI directory. In this example the executable program was placed in the cgi-bin directory. The URL used to invoke the CGI script is http://wonderland.dial.umd.edu/cgi-bin/hello.exe?Argument.

When a CGI program on a Windows NT Web server is called, the general syntax of the URL is

```
http://A/B?C
```

where

> A is the hostname of the Web server; in this example, it is wonderland.dial.umd.edu.
>
> B is the relative path to the executable program from the Web server's document root directory; in this example, it is cgi-bin/hello.exe.
>
> C contains any arguments passed into the C program.

19

WINDOWS NT CGI PROGRAMMING

You can obtain these arguments by examining the contents of the CGI environment variable `QUERY_STRING`.

Accessing Environment Variables Available to CGI Scripts

A thorough introduction to various programming languages and how you can utilize them to develop CGI applications is beyond the scope of this book; therefore, most CGI applications in this chapter are developed using the C programming language. However, to give you a feel of how you can use various programming languages to write CGI applications, the next sections show you how to access various environment variables by using Perl and C.

Accessing CGI Environment Variables from a C Program

The following C program displays all CGI variables that have been set by the Web server. Note that all environment variables may not be defined, depending on how the script is called. The following CGI program will display all CGI variables that have been defined by the Web server before invoking the CGI script:

```c
/* C Program to display CGI environment variable values defined by the Web server
before the CGI program is invoked */

#include <stdio.h>
#include <stdlib.h>
#define  NUM_ENVIRONMENT_VARIABLES 19

main ( )
{
/* Define the data structure that stores all the CGI variable
   names   */
   char* environmentVariables[] =
        { "SERVER_SOFTWARE",    "SERVER_NAME",
          "GATEWAY_INTERFACE", "SERVER_PROTOCOL",
          "SERVER_PORT",        "REQUEST_METHOD",
          "PATH_INFO",          "PATH_TRANSLATED",
          "SCRIPT_NAME",        "QUERY_STRING",
          "REMOTE_HOST",        "REMOTE_ADDR",
          "AUTH_TYPE",          "REMOTE_USER",
          "REMOTE_IDENT",       "CONTENT_TYPE",
          "CONTENT_LENGTH",     "HTTP_ACCEPT",
          "HTTP_USER_AGENT" } ;
   int  count ;

   printf("Content-type: text/html%c%c",10,10) ;
   printf("%s%s" ,
        "<PRE>\n",
        "<TITLE>CGI Environmental Variables Demonstration</TITLE>\n") ;
```

```
/* Loop through all CGI variables that were defined earlier */
  for (count = 0; count < NUM_ENVIRONMENT_VARIABLES; count++)
/* Check if a certain CGI variable has been defined by the Web server
   and print its value if the CGI variable has been defined */
  if ( getenv ( environmentVariables[count] ) != NULL )
    printf   ( "%17s = %s\n" , environmentVariables[count] ,
               getenv ( environmentVariables[count] ) ) ;

  printf("</PRE>\n") ;
  return   ( 0 ) ;
}
```

The output of the preceding CGI script appears in Figure 19.8. As you can see from the URL, the URL of the CGI script is followed by additional arguments to the CGI script. Notice how the Web server has passed the arguments following the URL to the CGI script by using an environment variable.

FIGURE 19.8.

Output of a CGI program written in C when called with an argument after the URL of the CGI program.

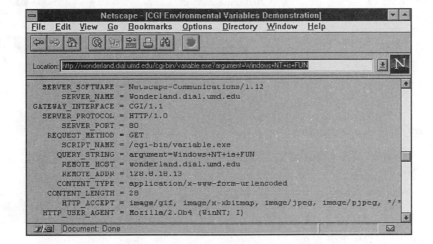

Accessing CGI Environment Variables from a Perl Script

Similarly, CGI scripts can be accessed very easily from a Perl script. The CGI Perl script that displays values of various CGI variables is listed here:

```
# Print the first line of all CGI scripts
print "Content-type: text/html\n\n";
print "<TITLE>PERL CGI Variable Demonstration</TITLE>\n";

printf( "<PRE>\n" );

foreach $EnvVar ( SERVER_SOFTWARE, SERVER_NAME, GATEWAY_INTERFACE,
                  SERVER_PROTOCOL, SERVER_PORT, REQUEST_METHOD,
                  PATH_INFO, PATH_TRANSLATED, SCRIPT_NAME, QUERY_STRING,
                  REMOTE_HOST, REMOTE_ADDR, AUTH_TYPE, REMOTE_USER,
                  REMOTE_IDENT, CONTENT_TYPE, CONTENT_LENGTH, HTTP_ACCEPT,
                  HTTP_USER_AGENT )
```

19

WINDOWS
NT CGI
PROGRAMMING

```
# Loop through all environment variables and display the values of all
  CGI variables that have been defined by the Web server.

{
  if ( $ENV{"$EnvVar"} ) {
    printf( "%17s = %s\n",  $EnvVar, $ENV{"$EnvVar"} );
  }
}

printf( "</PRE>\n" );
exit( 0 );
```

The output of the preceding Perl script appears in Figure 19.9. Note again how the Perl script is being called. The URL of the Perl script is made up with the URL of PERL.EXE and the location of the Perl script with respect to the location of PERL.EXE.

FIGURE 19.9.

Output of the CGI script written in Perl to display CGI variables.

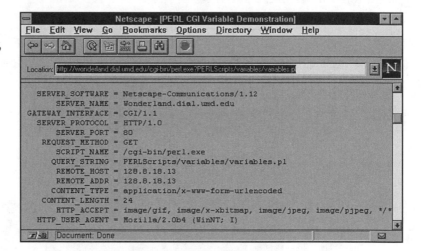

Using CGI to Provide Customized Content

With the expansion of the World Wide Web, more and more Web browsers are being invented. Although many Web browsers are available for Windows NT, their capabilities differ greatly. Although at the time this book was written, Netscape accounted for about 70 percent of all Web browsers being used, this situation will probably change when Microsoft's Internet Explorer becomes more widely used. If the appearance of your Web site is very important to you, you might want to consider setting up a CGI script to provide a customized Web page, depending on the browser being used. Clearly, this process is not practical for a very large Web site. However, by setting up a very simple CGI script as shown next, you can find out which Web browser the person browsing your Web site is using. If the browser being used is Netscape Navigator or Microsoft's Internet Explorer, you can provide a richly formatted Web page with various HTML enhancements; otherwise, you can provide a basic page with the same content.

Most Web pages that make use of special HTML tags (such as Netscape enhancements to HTML) look very attractive when viewed with a browser that supports those tags. However, these pages tend to look less attractive when viewed with browsers that do not support the enhancements. The percentage of people with Web browsers that do not support various enhancements to HTML can be as high as 40 percent. For these Web browsers, you can set up a CGI script that will display the same content formatted by using standard HTML. Such a CGI script can display customized content, as shown in Figure 19.10, based on the CGI variable HTTP_USER_AGENT.

Figure 19.10.

Using a CGI program to provide customized content based on the Web browser being used.

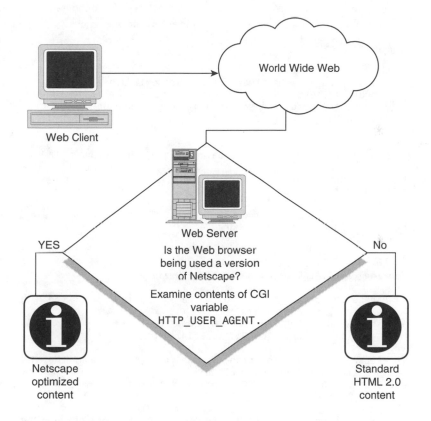

The CGI script in the following listing is very simple. It first determines the Web server being used by looking at the environment variable HTTP_USER_AGENT. Depending on the value of this variable, a page with Netscape enhancements to HTML can be displayed if the browser being used is Netscape Navigator. Otherwise, a page that contains only standard HTML 2.0 can be displayed. By modifying the script, you can always add more customized pages for other browsers. You can use this type of script for important pages like the main home page for your organization. By utilizing CGI to provide dynamic content, you will give a good impression to someone browsing the contents of your Web site. You can ensure that a user with an advanced Web browser will see richly formatted Web pages. It is not feasible to support more than two custom Web pages. Both Internet Explorer and Netscape Navigator interpret HTML tags more or less the same way. You might want to create one page with Netscape Navigator and Internet Explorer extensions and another that uses only standard HTML 2.0.

PERFORMANCE

Please note that the following program is not optimized for speed of processing but for ease of reading. Because it is written to demonstrate how a CGI program can be written to provide customized content, it focuses on teaching CGI fundamentals and not on optimizing the code. You can make it more efficient by reading chunks of the file at a time rather than reading and outputting the file character by character.

```c
/* (C) 1995 Sanjaya Hettihewa http://wonderland.dial.umd.edu/
 * January 1, 1996
 * Program to output a customized Web page based on
   Web browser being used.
 */

/* Special function libraries being used by this program */
#include <stdio.h>
#include <stdlib.h>
#include <string.h>

/* Please note the use of double quotes. This is because a single quote is
   used to quote the next character */

/* If you provide content specially formatted for a different browser, please
   change the following */
#define  SPECIAL_BROWSER_SUB_STRING "Mozilla"

/* Please change the following to the full path name of the HTML file that's
   specially formatted */
#define  SPECIAL_BROWSER_PAGE "H:\\www\\https\\ns-
home\\root\\documents\\WSDGNT\\special.htm"

/* Please change the following to the full path name of the HTML file that's
   formatted using standard HTML */
#define  OTHER_BROWSER_PAGE   "H:\\www\\https\\ns-home\\root\\documents\\
➥WSDGNT\\regular.htm"

/* Please change the following to the e-mail address of your Web site
   administrator */
#define  WEBMASTER            "mailto:Webmaster@wonderland.dial.umd.edu"

static int DisplayPage ( char *pageName ) ;

main ( )
{

/* The "First Line" of all CGI scripts... */
  printf("Content-type: text/html%c%c",10,10) ;
```

```
/* Find out what Web browser is being used */
  if ( getenv ( "HTTP_USER_AGENT" ) == NULL ) {
    printf("FATAL ERROR: HTTP_USER_AGENT CGI variable undefined!\n") ;
    return   ( 0 ) ;
  }

/* Display apropriate page based on browser being used by client */
  if (strstr (getenv ("HTTP_USER_AGENT" ), SPECIAL_BROWSER_SUB_STRING)!=NULL)
    DisplayPage ( SPECIAL_BROWSER_PAGE ) ;
  else
    DisplayPage ( OTHER_BROWSER_PAGE ) ;
  return   ( 0 ) ;

}

/* Contents of file passed into this function will be displayed to standard
   output. The Web server will transmit what's displayed to standard output
   by this CGI script to the client that called the CGI script */
int DisplayPage ( char *pageName )
{

  FILE *inFile   ;
  char character ;

/* Check to ensure a valid file name is given */
  if ((inFile = fopen(pageName, "r")) == NULL) {
      printf ( "FATAL ERROR: Content file can't be opened! %s<BR>", pageName);
      printf ( "Please contact the  <A HREF=%s>Webmaster.</A><BR>",
             WEBMASTER );
      return ( 0 ) ;
  }

/* Displaying contents of file to standard output
   Please note that this can be done more efficiently by reading chunks of the
   file at a time */
  fscanf ( inFile  , "%c" , &character ) ;
  while ( !feof(inFile) ) {
    printf ( "%c" , character ) ;
    fscanf ( inFile  , "%c" , &character ) ;
  }
  fclose(inFile);
  return ( 1 ) ;

}
```

Because the purpose of this program is to provide customized content based on the browser being used to browse your Web site, you need to create two separate Web pages. The first Web page is sent to any non-Netscape browser, assuming it does not parse various HTML-enhanced tags as does Netscape Navigator. This Web page can be very simple. For the purpose of this demonstration, assume that you need to display a number of options inside a table. Because browsers that do not support the <TABLE> tag might interpret this tag differently, you will have no control over how your Web site will look when viewed with a different browser. To remedy this situation, you can use the preceding CGI program. For Web browsers that do not support enhanced HTML tags, you can create a nontable version of the same page using only standard HTML. In this way you can control the appearance of your Web site regardless of the browser that is being used to access your Web pages.

19

WINDOWS
NT CGI
PROGRAMMING

The following is the standard HTML Web page designed for non-Netscape browsers. In case you're interested in knowing where this Web page is referenced in the CGI program, this file will be saved at `H:\\www\\https\\ns-home\\root\\documents\\WSDGNT\\regular.htm`.

The location of the preceding file is defined in the C program so that its contents can be displayed for non-Netscape browsers. In the C program, the location of the preceding file is defined in `OTHER_BROWSER_PAGE`.

```
<TITLE>Standard HTML page</TITLE>
<BODY>
Welcome to the standard HTML page for technically challenged Web browsers.
<P>
Option One<BR>
Option Two<BR>
Option Three<BR>
</BODY>
```

The following is the Netscape-enhanced HTML Web page that is specially designed for those browsing your Web site with Netscape Navigator. The following HTML code displays the same three options that are displayed by the standard HTML page. However, the options are displayed inside a table with some additional Netscape enhancements. Because the C program needs to know the location of this file for the purpose of this example, the following page is located at `H:\\www\\https\\ns-home\\root\\documents\\WSDGNT\\special.htm`.

In the C program, the full path name of the preceding file is stored in `SPECIAL_BROWSER_PAGE`. The contents of this file are displayed by the CGI program whenever Netscape Navigator is used. You will need to change this variable depending on where you store the Netscape-enhanced Web page.

```
<TITLE>Netscape Enhanced page</TITLE>
<BODY>
<CENTER>
<TABLE BORDER=15 CELLPADDING=10 CELLSPACING=10 >
<TR>
<TD >
Welcome to the
<FONT SIZE=4>Ne</FONT><FONT SIZE=5>ts</FONT><FONT SIZE=6>ca</FONT><FONT SIZE=7>pe
➡</FONT>
<FONT SIZE=6>En</FONT><FONT SIZE=5>ha</FONT><FONT SIZE=4>nc</FONT><FONT SIZE=3>ed
➡</FONT>
 Web page!
</TD>
<TD>Option One<BR></TD>
<TD>Option Two<BR></TD>
<TD>Option Three<BR></TD>
</TR>
</TABLE>
</CENTER>
</BODY>
```

After compiling the preceding program and placing it in your Web server's CGI directory, the page that is displayed will correspond to the browser being used to call the CGI script. When compiling the C program, please be sure to change `SPECIAL_BROWSER_PAGE`, `OTHER_BROWSER_PAGE`, and WEBMASTER. The output of the CGI program to provide customized content appears in Figures 19.11 and 19.12. For the purpose of this example, the two Web browsers Netscape Navigator and Mosaic were used. Note how the enhanced HTML page is displayed when accessing the script with Netscape Navigator and the standard HTML page is displayed when accessing the script with Mosaic.

FIGURE 19.11.
Output of a CGI program when it is invoked with Netscape Navigator.

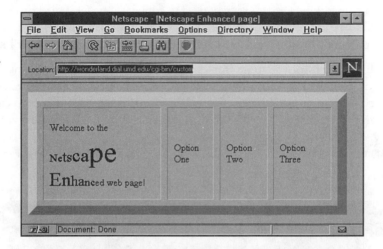

FIGURE 19.12.
Output of a CGI program when invoked with a non-Netscape browser such as Mosaic.

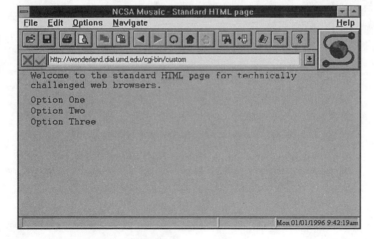

Setting Up a Feedback Form

One of the best things about CGI is that it lets you interact with people browsing your Web site. What better way is there to interact with them than ask for their feedback? By using a Windows NT command-line mail utility called Blat and another CGI program that can be used to e-mail the contents of a form, you can set up a feedback form at your Web site in just a few minutes.

After setting up Blat, you need to create a feedback form for users who want to e-mail their feedback to you. Before setting up the form, you need to download the program that will process the contents of the form after it's submitted. The programs you need to download are wwwmail.exe and blat15i.zip, which you can download from http://www.nt-guru.com/books/software.htm.

After downloading wwwmail.exe, you need to copy it to the CGI directory of your Web server. Then you need to create a page that appears after the user submits his or her feedback. This page can thank users for the feedback and allow them to choose another link to follow.

Now all that's left for you to do is to create a feedback form and a response page. Refer to the following code listing for a simple feedback page. You can utilize a similar page to set up a feedback form at your Web site. You will need to change a few values to customize the feedback form, depending on how your Web site is organized. These values are

```
name="mailto"          value="user_ID@your.site"
name="WWWMail-Page"    value="<Full Path of page to display after submitting the
➥form">
action="<your CGI Directory>/wwwmail.exe/cgi-bin/feedback.hfo">
```

TIP

In order to provide the user with a set of predefined selections, you can have a pull-down list using the <SELECT/OPTION> tag, as shown in the following listing.

```
<HTML>
<HEAD>
<title>Feedback Form Demonstration</title>
</HEAD>

<BODY>
<FORM  method=POST
       action="/cgi-bin/wwwmail.exe/cgi-bin/feedback.hfo">
<INPUT TYPE=hidden name="mailto"
       value="Webmaster@wonderland.dial.umd.edu">
<INPUT TYPE=hidden name="WWWMail-Page" value="H:\www\netscape_commerce\
➥ns-home\root\documents\feedback\ThanksForFeedback.html">

<PRE>
<b>Subject:</b> <SELECT name="subject">
  <OPTION> I have some Feedback
  <OPTION> I have a comment...
  <OPTION> I have a suggestion...
  <OPTION> I need assistance with...
  <OPTION> Other
</SELECT>
<B>Your E-mail address please:</B>    <INPUT name="sender" SIZE=30>
<b>Your name Please:</b>              <INPUT name="name" SIZE=30 >
<b>Your phone # (If you wish)</b>    <INPUT name="phoneno" SIZE=20 >
<b>Would you like a reply from me?</b> <SELECT name="Reply">
```

```
   <OPTION> If you wish
   <OPTION> Yes, please
   <OPTION> No thanks
</SELECT>
<b>Is this message urgent?</b>          <SELECT name="Urgency">
   <OPTION> Not particularly
   <OPTION> Yes, very urgent
   <OPTION> Not at all
</SELECT>

<b>Please type your message and press the submit button:</b>
<TEXTAREA name="comments" cols=65 rows=3> </TEXTAREA>
<input type=submit value="Please click here to send message">
</FORM>
</PRE>
</BODY>
</HTML>
```

The preceding code generates a feedback form that looks like the form shown in Figure 19.13.

FIGURE 19.13.

A generic feedback form.

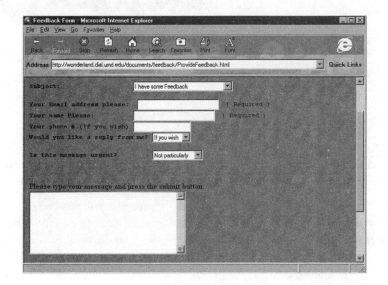

Finally, you need to create a page like the one shown in Figure 19.14. After the feedback form is submitted, the CGI script will display this page to thank the user for the feedback. The location of this page is defined in the variable WWWMail-Page of the HTML form. After the form is filled in and submitted, the page defined in WWWMail-Page should let the user know that you received the feedback and will get in touch with the user soon. (You might also want to let users know how soon you will be contacting them.) This page should also contain a hypertext link to another page at your Web site so the users can continue to browse your Web site with ease.

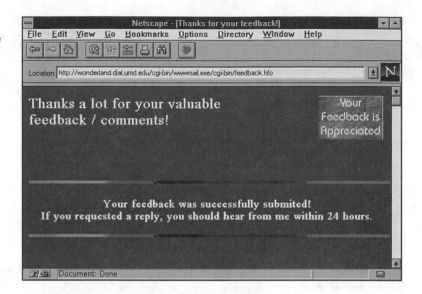

Summary

One of the best things about the World Wide Web is that you can use it to distribute information to millions of people. CGI allows you to interact with this large audience. This chapter explains how to use CGI to enhance the capabilities of your Web site as well as how to write CGI scripts in Perl and C. This chapter also covers various aspects of setting up CGI scripts, including security issues. Various practical applications of CGI appear along with the source code so that you can modify the examples to enhance your Web site.

In order to become more familiar with these topics, you need to spend some time with either C or Perl. After writing some CGI programs and experimenting with the effects of modifying them, you will discover how CGI scripts work and gain more experience in debugging and developing CGI scripts. You will then be able to create various CGI applets to perform many specialized tasks. As you gain experience, writing CGI programs that you once thought were very complicated will be easy. By utilizing CGI and unleashing its potential to make the contents of your Web site easier to navigate, you will have an outstanding Web site that attracts many repeat visitors.

CHAPTER 20

Writing Java Applets

IN THIS CHAPTER

- Java Break   604
- Understanding Java   605
- Creating a Java Applet   608
- Compiling Java Applets   624
- Embedding Java Applets in HTML   625

As exciting as the World Wide Web is, its frequent users are always expecting more from it. Simple presentation of information and form-processing capabilities for a Web site are acceptable and the norm, but the Web lacks true interactive communication with a user. As a result, most Web sites are quite dull. A site may have spiffy graphics and loads of good information, but no sites are interactive in real time.

The reasons for this situation are numerous. First, the Web is painfully slow for most users. People accessing the Web at modem speeds have built up a tolerance for slowly painting graphics. When they submit forms for further information, they are accustomed to the time necessary to route this information to a site, have the server perform work based on the information, and return the results. This slowness truly inhibits the idea of real-time interactive communication with the user.

A second reason for the lack of interactive sites is that most Web pages are treated as client/server applications in the very lightest of definitions. Most site developers view client/server technology simply as a client accessing data on the server. In a true client/server relationship, data should be passed back and forth between the client and server machines, but neither machine should do all the work itself. Data-intensive, time-consuming functions should be performed on the server, which is typically a robust machine that has vast access to databases. A local PC can handle the simpler functions. Having the client do some of the processing minimizes the amount of traffic between the user's computer and servers on the Internet, resulting in quicker access. In addition, because the many functions are being performed on a local computer, the speed of the overall Web site appears to be much faster.

Finally, and most important, the ability to write interactive applications that run on a user's computer was not widely available until now. But thanks to the work of developers at Sun Microsystems (www.sun.com), a new technology is becoming wildly popular.

Java Break

Sun's Java is the answer to the dilemma regarding how to run truly complex Internet applications on your computer. It solves the mystery of writing a single application that can work on any machine. Because Java applications run on your computer, they are fast and highly interactive. Because the resulting applications are small, they come across the Internet as fast as most graphic files. Because Java was written especially for the Internet and is based on C++, it is extremely powerful and robust.

This chapter takes an introductory look at how to create Java applications. It does not cover every feature of Java or Java programming. It is meant to serve as an introduction to writing your own Internet applications. You learn how to write a basic Java application and some of the necessary, related functions. Coverage of each method and function of the entire Java programming language clearly extends beyond the scope of this book, but a couple of good Java books are on the market, such as *Presenting Java* and *Teach Yourself Java in 21 Days*, both from Sams.net Publishing. This chapter examines a simple Java application and disseminates each function of it and every line of significant code. Through this process, you will learn enough to write your own Java applications.

To write Java applications, you should have an adequate understanding of C/C++ and the concepts of object-oriented development. Of course, experience with Windows development or a similar graphical user interface helps. This chapter works off this base of knowledge to present Java application development. For more information on C/C++ and object-oriented programming, check out *Teach Yourself C++ in 21 Days* from Sams Publishing.

Understanding Java

If you searched for Java on the Internet with a search engine, chances are you would find two types of results. The first would be links to gourmet coffee stands, and the second would be links to a new language for the Web. This chapter deals with the latter.

Java has grown from its roots at Sun Microsystems and was developed primarily as a language for creating software for electronic consumer products. Normally C++ was the language of choice for creating embedded software in such systems, but as the developers worked, they discovered numerous disadvantages with C++. Therefore, they decided to create a language that was extremely similar to C++, but without the complexity of C++ that often caused more havoc than good for the developer. The result is a language that enables application developers to easily create object-oriented programs that are very secure, portable across different machine and operating system platforms, and dynamic enough to allow for easy expandability. Because C++ is a common development language, there is little need for the vast amounts of training an entirely new language would require; therefore, Java can be more easily adopted.

Applets Work on Any Computer

But what *exactly* is Java? The Java language is a compiler-based language. That is, once a developer has written the Java code, that code must be passed through another program called a *compiler*. The compiler translates the textual code a programmer writes into something the machine understands. In the world of C++ and similar languages, the compiler creates an executable program that can run on a computer. However, that executable program has been compiled for a particular machine and cannot also be run on a different machine. Computers may look similar on the outside or even in the way they work, but the very core of the machine can be drastically different. This difference is why an application written and compiled on a Macintosh cannot run on a Windows PC or a UNIX machine.

Although Java is a compiler-based language like C++, it has been modified so that a single compiled application may work on any type of computer. How is this possible? Java code is compiled into a compact and optimized program called an *applet*. The applet consists of instructions called *bytecodes* that are then fed to a program called a *runtime module*. The runtime module translates the bytecodes into machine instructions for a particular computer.

Sun Microsystems has created a Web browser for Java applications called HotJava. This browser works like typical Web browsers, but it includes the runtime program that reads Java instructions and translates them into machine instructions. Other browsers such as Netscape Navigator 2.0 also offer a Java runtime module in its browser so that Netscape users can view Java applets as well. The runtime program is the only Java-related program written specifically for each type of computer.

To illustrate how Java works, assume that there is a Java application on a Web page that you want to view with Windows 95 and Netscape Navigator. When you view that page with Netscape Navigator, Netscape Navigator retrieves the Java applet and passes that applet to a Java runtime program that is bundled with Netscape Navigator. That runtime program, in this case written specifically for Windows 95, reads the Java applet's instructions and translates them to function appropriately with Windows 95. It's similar to being able to put any brand of coffee into any brand of coffeemaker.

Object-Oriented Programming

Java, because of its roots with C++, is even more tightly integrated with object-oriented concepts. Object-oriented languages enable developers to create Windows-type applications with less effort than with traditional techniques. Object-oriented languages rely on the concepts of objects, properties, and methods. These concepts can be related to a coffeemaker and the process of making coffee.

Clearly, in this case the coffeemaker is the object you are working with to perform a task. Properties of the coffeemaker might include the color of the plastic and where it is located in your kitchen, things that are attributes of the coffeemaker. Methods are actions that an object can perform. For instance, the Make Coffee button triggers the process of making coffee. There also may be events associated with this coffeemaker. *Events* are the triggers that cause an object do something. For example, if the coffeemaker has a timer built into it and the capability to start coffee at a particular time, the clock triggers the brewing process when the correct time occurs.

With object-oriented technology, a Java applet can react differently according to different types of input. Also, because pieces of the object are treated as components, you can replace components easily. This component approach of object-oriented programming also enables Java to handle multiple things at once, independently of each other. A Java applet can have multiple components working on continuously updating live information from a variety of sources while another component is available to handle user interaction. Each independently running task is referred to as a *thread* in Java. You can think of the thread as a series of events that occur in a line. The lines run parallel to each other, but the threads do not necessarily affect each other.

Secure and Robust

You cannot listen to a coffee commercial without hearing about its robustness, and you should expect no less from computerized Java. When Java applications are compiled, they are heavily scrutinized to avoid possible problems. The language itself removes many of the error-prone functions associated with C++, and Java even does dynamic checking for errors while the applet is running. This checking helps protect the developers from creating errors and forces them to not use ambiguous declarations that a language like C++ would allow. As an example, programs written in languages such as C++ historically had to remember to free resources that they had allocated during execution. A Java application does not need to explicitly release memory; the Java interpreter automatically handles this function.

The way Java implements this robustness also indirectly heightens security on the applet. Because Java forces developers to be more structured, there are fewer chances for information to be illegally altered in the applet. Security is also heightened with the use of encryption and compression. Java can squeeze and scramble the contents of its applets to limit the threat of tampering.

What Can You Do with Java?

The capabilities of Java outlined in the preceding sections allow for more dynamic, animated, and interactive Web pages in the future. To make you fully appreciate what these features can offer to the Web and you, the section examines an example of a Java application.

> **TIP**
>
> Earlier, alpha versions of Java applets may not run on newer Web browsers that support Java. To determine whether a Web page is using an older version of Java, examine the HTML source for the Web page. Newer versions of Java use the <APPLET> tag to indicate a Java application; older versions use the <APP> tag.

Netscape offers a daily crossword puzzle at its site. You can access this page by jumping to Netscape (http://www.netscape.com). Then choose to view Java information on Navigator 2.0. A list appears with a few sample Java applications.

One nice feature of Java is that you do not have to explicitly invoke a Java application. Most Web browsers will automatically display the application—in this case, a screen similar to that in Figure 20.1. This crossword puzzle applet is an excellent example of a Java application that is very graphic in nature and requires user interaction. It also stresses the importance of adding instructions or creating clearly intuitive interfaces for Java applets. Each Java applet may behave entirely differently than other Java applets, and users require instruction the first time they use an applet.

20

WRITING JAVA
APPLETS

FIGURE 20.1.

This crossword puzzle application demonstrates how Java applets support enhanced interaction between a user and a Web page.

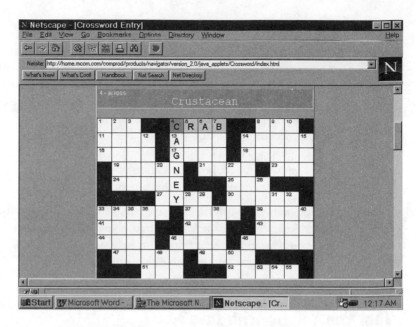

Notice that when you view the crossword puzzle page, the crossword puzzle itself is embedded in the Web page, just like an inline GIF image. From the HTML source code, you can control where the Java application appears, just as you would images.

To work on the crossword puzzle, click any row or column in the puzzle to highlight that row or column. The hint for that row or column is then displayed at the top of the puzzle. To toggle between horizontal row selections and vertical column selections, press the spacebar. When you're ready, you can enter the word you think is the answer into the currently highlighted area. Incorrect letters are highlighted in red.

As you can see, this Java application is accepting many different types of events from the user: the keyboard for text entry, the space bar for row/column selection, and the mouse for selecting rows or columns in the puzzle. This application also demonstrates how Java can produce very graphical results by drawing the board, highlighting appropriate sections, and adding multicolor text.

Creating a Java Applet

So now that you have an idea of what a Java applet is and what it can do, how do you write your own specific Java applet? This chapter examines the coding and creation of a single Java applet, which will help you further understand the technology so that you can create your own custom applets. The applet that this chapter examines is the Marquee applet. At times, you may want scrolling text to appear on your Web page. For instance, if you were designing a Web site that tracked stock prices, you might want to implement the familiar ticker symbol line. The ticker line consists of a solid rectangle in which text and numbers are scrolled. The information in the ticker scrolls off the left side of the ticker line and returns on the right side of the ticker area. This applet is also very similar to the Windows Marquee screen saver, which has been aptly renamed in Windows 95 as Scrolling Marquee. The idea is the same; text you enter is scrolled across the screen until it disappears, and then it scrolls back onto the screen from the opposite side.

Writing this effect in Java ensures that the applet can run on a plethora of operating systems and hardware platforms. The computer that the application is running on must simply have the Java interpreter software installed on it. If the computer is using Netscape Navigator 2.0, HotJava, or a similar Web browser to view Java applications, then this interpreter is included.

Choosing Java as the development tool also enables you to use graphics for smoother scrolling and have greater font and color control. You can also set the applet to run continuously in the background, which is essential for the effect as well. The text should continuously loop around the marquee area instead of just scrolling once. Java offers support for these requirements.

Parameters for the Marquee Applet

The Marquee applet exists as a Java applet embedded in a Web page. Because it is embedded, it takes on all of the typical attributes of Java applets. It exists within a window as defined by the HTML code and is loaded/unloaded appropriately as the Web page is loaded and unloaded from the Web browser. The applet will also accept additional parameters from the Web page, defining the nature of the applet.

For this applet, the HTML document for a Web page can set several options:

- ■ text—This text is scrolled within the applet's window. The default is `Scrolling Marquee`.

- ■ direction—The marquee's text may scroll either to the left or to the right. This parameter may be set to `right` to indicate that direction; otherwise, the default is `left`.

- ■ speed—The scrolling text may be sped up or slowed down by modifying this value. Speed is measured in milliseconds; therefore, a value of 1000 is equivalent to a one-second delay. The default is one tenth of a second (100 milliseconds).

- ■ bgcolor—This parameter indicates what the background color of the applet's window should be. The value must consist of a nine-digit number. The number represents three separate three-digit numbers. These individual numbers represent values between 000 and 255. Each three-digit number represents the amounts of red, blue, and green color, respectively. This parameter is similar to the `#00` to `#FF` values typically found in the HTML `<BODY>` tag for setting colors. Instead of using hexadecimal values, however, this Java applet is expecting decimal numbers. The default is white (`255255255`).

- ■ fgcolor—Just as the background color for the marquee may be determined through HTML, so can the text color. This value expects the same nine-digit color format as explained in the `bgcolor` value. The default is dark blue (`000000128`).

20

WRITING JAVA
APPLETS

Assuming that this Java applet is correctly embedded within your Web page, the result may be a screen similar to the one in Figure 20.2.

FIGURE 20.2.

A sample of the Marquee Java applet within the Netscape browser window.

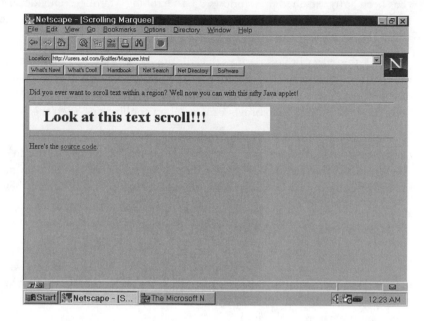

The Marquee Applet's Code

Listing 20.1 shows the complete code listing for the Marquee Java applet.

Listing 20.1. The code for Marquee.java.

```
// *******************************
//    Application: MARQUEE.JAVA
// *******************************

import java.awt.*;

public class Marquee extends java.applet.Applet implements Runnable {
  Thread   appThread;
  Font     fFont;
  String   sMsg;
  int      speed=100;
  int      direction=-1;
  int      x=0;
  int      bg_red=255,bg_green=255,bg_blue=255;
  int      fg_red=0,fg_green=0,fg_blue=128;

  // Bunch of setup stuff, read in values from HTML
  public void init() {
    String sParam;

    // Use the Times Roman font, BOLD 32pt.
```

```
fFont = new java.awt.Font("TimesRoman",Font.BOLD,32);

// Get the text to scroll from HTML
sParam = getParameter("text");
if (sParam==null)
  sMsg="Scrolling Marquee";
else
  sMsg=sParam;

// Default is to scroll left, can specify right
// Set from HTML
sParam = getParameter("direction");
if (sParam!=null){
  if (sParam.equalsIgnoreCase("right"))
    direction=1;
}

// How fast to scroll
sParam = getParameter("delay");
if (sParam!=null)
  speed=Integer.valueOf(sParam).intValue();

// Find background color for Marquee window
// Like <BODY> tag's #FFFFFF format, but uses
// Decimal:
//     255255255 is white
//     000000000 is black
sParam = getParameter("bgcolor");
if (sParam!=null){
  // Check that the string looks long enough
  if (sParam.length()==9){
    // Get the Red value (0-255)
    bg_red=Integer.valueOf(sParam.substring(0,3)).intValue();
    // Get the Green value (0-255)
    bg_green=Integer.valueOf(sParam.substring(3,6)).intValue();
    // Get the Blue value (0-255)
    bg_blue=Integer.valueOf(sParam.substring(6,9)).intValue();
  }
}

// Find foreground color for Marquee text
// Works same as background above
sParam = getParameter("fgcolor");
if (sParam!=null){
  if (sParam.length()==9){
    fg_red=Integer.valueOf(sParam.substring(0,3)).intValue();
    fg_green=Integer.valueOf(sParam.substring(3,6)).intValue();
    fg_blue=Integer.valueOf(sParam.substring(6,9)).intValue();
  }
}
}  // End of INIT


// Paint to the applet's Window within Web browser
// "g" represents that window's canvas
public void paint(Graphics g) {
  Dimension      d = size();
  FontMetrics    fm;
```

continues

Listing 20.1. continued

```java
    // We have a pointer to the font we want to use from above,
    // now we have to set it.
    g.setFont(fFont);
    fm=g.getFontMetrics();

    // Use rectangle to paint background color
    // drawRect is the border, fillRect is interior
    g.setColor(new java.awt.Color(bg_red,bg_green,bg_blue));
    g.drawRect(0,0,d.width,d.height);
    g.fillRect(0,0,d.width,d.height);

    // Set text color and draw it
    g.setColor(new java.awt.Color(fg_red,fg_green,fg_blue));
    g.drawString(sMsg,x,fFont.getSize());

    // Update text position
    x+=(10*direction);
    // If we're scrolling right and outside window, then wrap
    if (x>d.width-1 && direction==1)
      x=-fm.stringWidth(sMsg);
    // If we're scrolling left and outside window, then wrap
    if (x<-fm.stringWidth(sMsg) && direction==-1)
      x=d.width-1;
}   // End of PAINT

public void start() {
    // Create a thread to run in background
    appThread = new Thread(this);
    appThread.start();
}

public void stop() {
    appThread.stop();
}

public void run() {
    while (true){   // While applet is running on page...
      repaint();    // update graphics
      try {
        // Pause the thread, which pauses the animation
        Thread.currentThread().sleep(speed);
      }

      // Exception handling for interrupted thread
      catch (InterruptedException e) {
      }
    }
  }   // End of RUN
}   // End of MARQUEE Class
```

At first glance, the code certainly appears daunting. However, it is really not as confusing as it may seem. The following sections explain each line of this applet.

> **NOTE**
>
> A single comment line for a Java code listing begins with the double forward slash (//).
> Comments may span multiple lines by beginning the comment block with /* and ending it
> with */.

Imported Java

If you are familiar with other languages such as C and C++, you may quickly realize that the
first line of the Java code, `import java.awt.*`, resembles the familiar `#include` statement in C.
Like the `#include` statement, Java's `import` statement allows the application you are writing to
import code from other sources. In this case Java can retrieve code from other Java classes.

One of the nice features of the `import` statement is that it can import multiple classes using the
wildcard (*) notation. Because this applet draws results to the applet window, it requires several classes from the AWT (Abstract Window Toolkit). This toolkit serves as the mediator between the Java applet and the operating system. Because every computer system uses different
operating systems and supports different hardware, translating GUI functions appropriately is
necessary in order for Java to maintain its cross-platform advantage. The AWT takes requests
for drawing information to the screen or managing windows and associated controls. The Java
interpreter translates these requests to draw information correctly onto your computer's screen,
whatever type of computer it may be.

You probably will include the AWT in one way or another in most of your Java applets. The
`import` statement in Listing 20.1 imports all of the AWT classes. Some of these classes include
support for drawing windows, buttons, graphics such as rectangles and polygons, fonts, and
colors, for instance.

When importing classes, all those related to Java specifically begin with `java`. If you have your
own custom classes, you may reference them as well. A Java applet is built on dozens of classes
that you invoke within your own program. It is important that you include all of the Java
methods that your program will require.

Because the Java language is built on classes, there is a class hierarchy. (For a complete description of these classes, their properties and methods, and their relationships, see Sun's Java site at
`www.javasoft.com`.) Therefore, you can specify a particular class to use in your applet instead
of using them all through the * notation. You must separate the levels along the hierarchy with
a period (.). The period is essential to identifying objects and methods and specifying relations
within the Java language. Suppose that you were going to place a button somewhere within
your Java applet. To use the appropriate class to handle the buttons, you would use the following line:

```
import java.awt.button;
```

Because you usually import many classes into your final Java applet, using the wildcard notation (*) to import all classes within the group of classes may be convenient.

Head of the Class

Whether or not you realize it, you are creating a class when you create an applet. The Java language uses a truly object-oriented approach, and your applet is treated as a leaf on the end of the object-oriented tree. So it should be no surprise that the first thing you must do when creating a Java applet is create its class. The Marquee applet declares itself using the following syntax:

```
public class Marquee extends java.applet.Applet implements Runnable
```

This line creates a Java applet or class with a particular name and options. This example creates the class `Marquee`, which will become a Java *interface*. An interface is similar to subclassing or inheriting another class with one important difference: Interfaces do not inherit all the excess baggage from the superclass. An interface implements only the methods of the class that are specific for the applet.

The `extends java.applet.Applet` code instructs this class to inherit the capabilities of the main Java applet class, which allows this `Marquee` class to be used as an applet by the Java interpreter. The actual definition of the applet is defined by the methods that you implement within your applet, as you will see in a moment. The `implements Runnable` portion of this line instructs Java to use threads to control this applet.

As mentioned earlier in the chapter, threads are processes that run independently of other processes. They can be thought of as a series of instructions that execute without interfering with each other. This concept is similar to multitasking, which is found in many operating systems. In fact, operating systems use threads for tasks in one fashion or another.

Because you want the text within the marquee window to scroll continuously in the background, you need to implement a thread for this Java applet. You may argue that you do not have to implement a thread to scroll the text. This is true, but if you did not use a thread, the Java interpreter would end up spending all its time processing this single application. This approach is not effective when more than one Java applet exists on a page.

Now that the class is defined, any code that exists between the starting brace ({) and the ending brace (}) is implemented in that class. On the first line past the first starting brace, notice that a number of variables are declared. If you have experience with C or C++, you should recognize some familiar data types. Some of the types, such as `Font` or `Thread`, are specific Java data types. Also, notice that these variables are defined before any additional methods are introduced to the class. This order causes the variables to have a wider scope. Each variable is available to any method within the `Marquee` class.

The `init` Method

Every Java applet must be initialized. Because Java is an object-oriented language, it is important to remember that there may be multiple instances of a class that you design. For example, you may use this Marquee applet on the main page of your Web site as well as in an additional page deeper in the site. Therefore, you must initialize each instance of this applet if each instance is to contain different data and display different results. The Java interpreter triggers the `init` method automatically. Typically this triggering occurs after the Java applet is first retrieved from the network. Once the applet is created on the client computer, the applet is started and this is the first function that is executed.

You can use the `init` method for many different purposes. Often it is used to allocate resource memory, retrieve additional resources from the Internet, retrieve the parameters sent to the applet from the Web page, and set properties of the applet, such as color or position. In the Marquee applet, the `init` method sets the font to be used in the applet and retrieves the parameters passed into the applet from the HTML document for a Web page. The `init` method is actually a function within the `Marquee` class and is defined appropriately. It is a simple method that accepts no arguments and returns no value. It is also made public so that other applets or the interpreter may invoke the method.

Getting the Right Font

The first line after the string declaration within the `init` method uses the `Font` class from the Java AWT:

```
fFont = new java.awt.Font("TimesRoman",Font.BOLD,32);
```

Because fonts are drawn to the computer screen, each system may handle this function differently. In addition, each system may have different names that identify a Times Roman font. Therefore, it is up to the AWT to process this request and set up a pointer to the correct font type to use when drawing the text later in the applet. As you can see from the line of code, the `new` instruction allocates memory for the new font object that is created from the `Font` class. That memory is assigned to the `fFont` variable for future reference within the applet.

Parameters

The next four sections of the `init` method retrieve variables passed in from the HTML document of a Web page. This capability allows Java applets to be more generic. Suppose you want to scroll text to the right on one Web page and to the left on another. You could write two separate applets—one that scrolls text to the left and another that scrolls text to the right—but that would be foolish. Instead, you could pass a parameter from the HTML document for a Web page that determines the direction: left or right. That parameter would then be read by a single Java applet, which would take the appropriate action. This capability to pass information between the Web page and an applet allows for even greater dynamic Web pages when coupled with the JavaScript language. JavaScript can control what parameters to pass to the Java applet based on criteria that you specify. Later in this chapter you learn how to embed Java applets and pass parameters to those applets.

Each parameter that is passed into a Java applet is named, which makes it much easier to parse through the arguments and retrieve the correct ones. The sParam is a temporary string used to hold the results of an argument. The getParameter method retrieves the argument that is specified within the method's parentheses:

```
sParam = getParameter("text");
```

In the preceding line, the "text" parameter is passed in from the HTML for the page. For example, the HTML source for a Web page could include the following tag for a Java applet:

```
<param name=text value="Look at this text scroll!!!">
```

This tag indicates to the Java applet that the "text" parameter is to be set to "Look at this text scroll!!!". Therefore, the getParameter would set the string sParam to "Look at this text scroll!!!".

Testing the Strings

After reading in a parameter, you may want to perform some tests on the data that is returned. Most Java applets accommodate Web page developers who may neglect to include all of the parameters for the applet. When a parameter is not yet specified in HTML retrieved in the Java applet through the getParameter method, the result of the getParameter method is null.

On the surface this result appears to be harmless. However, it can prove to be quite disastrous. What if an applet is reading a parameter to be converted to a number to be used in an equation and that parameter is not specified? The applet may encounter an error. Although error handling is built into Java, it is good practice to catch errors before they occur. In the Marquee applet, each parameter is tested to determine whether it was set to null. If so, a default value is substituted.

The second parameter read by the applet specifies the direction in which text is to scroll within the Marquee applet. After the parameter is read and guaranteed not to be set to null, the applet checks the value of the parameter. The default direction for scrolling is to the left; therefore only the "right" condition needs to be considered:

```
if (sParam.equalsIgnoreCase("right"))
```

Your first inclination may be to test the string returned by getParameter using the == notation. Experienced C developers quickly realize that this notation is not suitable for strings. The equivalence test (==) is appropriate only for testing logical equivalence between numbers or Boolean values. Strings must be compared using a dedicated method that is a member of the string class.

Strings defined within Java inherit the string class, which contains many methods. Examples of these methods are length, substring, and append. The method for comparing strings is inherited as well. The equalsIgnoreCase method tests whether two strings are equivalent. The string sParam in the preceding line of code is tested via its equalsIgnoreCase method with the data passed into that method ("right"). If the result is true, appropriate action is taken to change the direction of the scrolling text. As the method clearly indicates, the strings are compared, but the case of individual letters in those strings is ignored.

Converting Strings to Numbers

One of the requirements for this applet is to be able to specify parameters other than text from within a Web page. These parameters include background and foreground colors to use for the marquee, as well as the speed at which the text scrolls. The actual parameters that are read from the HTML document for a Web page are treated as strings. In the applet, however, these values must be treated as numbers.

Java offers numerous class conversion methods for converting between strings and numbers and vice versa. In the case of the Marquee applet, several values are to be read in from the Web page and processed as integer values, or more specifically, int values:

```
speed=Integer.valueOf(sParam).intValue();
```

You must use the Integer class to process a string and convert it appropriately. This class contains the valueOf method that converts the string (which sParam holds the value for from the Web page) to an Integer object format. However, because the Java application requires int values and not objects, you must also invoke the intValue method. The intValue method is invoked for the integer object that is a product of the valueOf method. The result is an int value that is returned to the speed variable.

Substrings and Lengths of Strings

Values are passed from the Web page to the Marquee applet that indicate the colors to use for the background of the window, as well as the text that scrolls within that window. For simplicity, the requirements defined these color numbers to be nine digits long. Each number actually consists of three separate numbers, each three digits long, which are concatenated. These three numbers represent the amount of red, green, and blue to mix respectively to form a color. These individual components may range in value between 000 and 255. This format is similar to the one that the HTML <BODY> tag uses to indicate colors; however, the numbers are represented in decimal as opposed to hexadecimal. Table 20.1 shows examples of valid colors for the Marquee applet.

Table 20.1. Sample color values for the Marquee Java applet.

Value	Color
000000000	Black
255000000	Red
000255000	Green
000000255	Blue
255255000	Yellow
255128000	Orange
255000255	Purple
255255255	White
128128128	Medium Gray

Because a color number is passed as a nine-character string, this string must be separated into three components, each with three characters. The easiest approach to this process is to use the `substring` method. This method retrieves only a particular number of characters from a main string. As with the `equalsIgnoreCase` method, the `substring` method comes with any string you create in Java.

The `substring` method accepts two parameters. The first specifies the starting position within the string from which you would like to begin reading. The second parameter indicates the position immediately after the last character in the string that you would like to read.

```
sParam.substring(0,3)
sParam.substring(3,6)
```

The preceding two lines return two separate pieces of the string `sParam`. Assume that `sParam` holds the value `255196000`. In this case, `sParam.substring(0,3)` would return the value `255`, and `sParam.substring(3,6)` returns `196`. You may notice that the `substring` method retrieves the characters starting at and including the first parameter of the method and ending at the character just before the second parameter of the method.

> **NOTE**
>
> You can identify each character of a string by a number in Java methods such as `substring` or `charAt`. The numbering of these characters begins at zero and ends at one less than the length of the string.

The `substring` method returns a particular range of characters from the string between zero and one less than the length of the string. But how do you determine the length of a string? Java strings also inherit another method: `length`. This method determines the number of characters that a string consists of and returns that number for you to use.

Painting Applets

Any Java applet that draws to the applet window or uses buttons, windows, or other objects that the AWT offers, requires the paint method. This method may be triggered either through your own code or automatically by the Java interpreter. For instance, the interpreter may trigger the method when the Web browser window is resized.

If you are familiar with GUI development, you already know the unparalleled importance of the paint method. This method is triggered any time a window is to be repainted. This method has the appropriate source code for drawing graphics or controlling the placement of GUI objects. In the Marquee applet, this method is the appropriate place for painting the background color of the applet's window and for drawing the text within that window at a particular location.

The paint method, like the init method, is a public method, which means that other applets or the Java runtime module, not just other methods within the Marquee class, can call this method. The paint method does not return a value, but it does accept one argument, the Graphics class. You can think of this class as the canvas that is linked to the Java applet. The Java applet may then paint on this canvas by using methods associated with this class.

In the Marquee applet, this canvas is painted with the appropriate background color, and new text is drawn on the canvas in the correct color at a particular location. On subsequent paint events, which are triggered later in the applet by a thread, the location of this text is updated to give the illusion that it is scrolling. To prevent text streaks, the background must first be painted each time the text is drawn. Painting the background clears the window, which removes the text that was already drawn at the old position, before the text is drawn at the new position.

Setting the Current Font

The applet sets the font to use when drawing the text. Earlier in the init method, the font object was prepared and stored as fFont. The setFont method uses that font class and sets the current font for drawing text on the canvas using that class. At the same time the font metrics—information such as the width and height of the font—are retrieved for use later in the method:

```
g.setFont(fFont);
fm=g.getFontMetrics();
```

> **NOTE**
>
> Remember to use the setFont method to set the current font to draw with on the canvas. A common mistake is to expect that when an instance of the font class is created that it also sets the font for drawing.

After the font object has been initialized, the background of the window is painted to the appropriate colors found earlier by the `init` method. This process involves drawing an opaque rectangle that occupies the entire width and height of the Java applet window. In order to know how big a rectangle to paint, the applet must be able to determine the size of its own window. Fortunately, Java offers a `Dimension` object that holds information regarding the dimensions of the applet's window after its `size` method is invoked.

Three steps are used to draw the rectangle. First, the current drawing color must be set to the background color specified by the Web page and read by the `init` method. Because this is a custom color, you must create a new object to hold it. The color of the object is determined by using the `Color` method in the AWT class. This method accepts three integer values that represent the amount of red, green, and blue to mix together to create the final color. Only after the new color object has been created may the current drawing color for the canvas be set by the `setColor` method:

```
g.setColor(new java.awt.Color(bg_red,bg_green,bg_blue));
```

The rectangle is then drawn to fill the window, effectively painting the applet's window. AWT supports two methods for drawing rectangles: `drawRect` and `fillRect`. The difference is that `drawRect` draws a transparent rectangle, and `fillRect` draws an opaque rectangle. The border of the rectangle is drawn in the current color when `drawRect` is used, and the solid rectangle is painted with the current color when `fillRect` is used. The Marquee applet uses both methods to explicitly draw the opaque rectangle with a border of the same color. This approach was used so that both the `fillRect` and `drawRect` methods would be demonstrated. It is more efficient to use the `fillRect` by itself and to stretch its coordinates wide enough to compensate for the border typically drawn with `drawRect`. The following is the code for these methods:

```
g.drawRect(0,0,d.width,d.height);
g.fillRect(0,0,d.width,d.height);
```

As you can see, both `drawRect` and `fillRect` expect four parameters. Each parameter specifies the coordinates to use when drawing the rectangle. These coordinates designate the left position, top position, width, and height of the rectangle, respectively.

Writing Text

After the background of the applet window has been painted, the Marquee application is ready to draw text on top of it. As with most drawing methods of the `Graphics` class, text is drawn using the current color. If the current color is not appropriate, a new color object must be chosen. If the current color was used for drawing text in the Marquee applet, the color would be the same as the background color, effectively not painting text at all. The applet must therefore create a new color to use:

```
g.setColor(new java.awt.Color(fg_red,fg_green,fg_blue));
g.drawString(sMsg,x,fFont.getSize());
```

The current color to use for drawing text is set in the same fashion as the rectangle's drawing color. A new color object is created using the parameters passed in from the Web page to the applet and is assigned as the current color. The drawString method then draws a line of text using the current color. This method expects three parameters: the text to display, the horizontal position of the text, and the vertical position of the text. The positions describe where the text is to be drawn, starting at the first character in the text.

Reading Font Information

After the text is drawn to the canvas, the variable representing the horizontal position of the text is updated appropriately for the direction in which it is to scroll. Immediately following this update, two conditionals check to see whether the text has scrolled completely outside of the applet's window. The first condition determines whether the text has scrolled past the right side of the window if it is scrolling to the right. The second condition determines whether the text has scrolled past the left side of the window when it is scrolling left. In both instances, the space that the text occupies when drawn is required. This size is necessary to ensure that the entire length of the text has scrolled beyond the bounds of the window, not just the starting point of the text:

```
if (x>d.width-1 && direction==1) x=-fm.stringWidth(sMsg);
if (x<-fm.stringWidth(sMsg) && direction==-1) x=d.width-1;
```

If the current horizontal position of the text (x) is greater than the width of the window and the text is scrolling to the right, the text should reappear on the left. However, if the horizontal position (x) was merely reset to zero, the effect would not appear correctly. The text would scroll beyond the right side of the window and then reappear in full on the left side of the window. Instead, the text should scroll on from the left, starting with its last character. To accomplish this effect, the horizontal position of the text must be as far to the left as the amount of space that the entire text string occupies. This same theory works for text that scrolls to the left, only the parameters are different.

So how is the amount of space required by the drawn text calculated? Java provides this feature for the applet developer. Earlier in the paint event, the FontMetrics object was introduced. This object allows the applet to query particular information regarding the font being used. In the Marquee example, the applet must determine how much space the text in a particular font requires. The FontMetrics class features a method stringWidth that performs this calculation. Most fonts consist of individual characters that require different widths, depending on the character. For example, the *W* character may be four times wider than the *I* character. Therefore, for the stringWidth to return an accurate measurement for the width of the text, you must pass the text to be measured into the method.

Threads

Earlier in this chapter you were introduced to threads. Threads are vital in operating systems for processing multiple tasks at once. Threads are equally as important in order for the Java interpreter to work with several applets at once. A *thread* is basically a series of instructions that define the nature of the applet. Typically, threads have a start point and an end point, but these points are not required. For instance, in the Marquee applet, a single thread is used to instruct the application to continuously scroll text. This task is accomplished by constantly forcing the applet window to be repainted. The thread instruction to repaint the window is continuously looped and is started or stopped as determined by the interpreter.

The Java runtime program starts the applet when the Web page that the applet exists on is loaded and stops the applet when the page is unloaded. Note that the applets are either started or stopped; they are not unloaded from memory. Therefore, they are still available. If an applet uses threads, those threads are still running. For performance, it is important to prepare appropriate `start` and `stop` methods within your Java applet that control the threads within your applet.

The start Method

Each time the Marquee applet is started, the `start` method is triggered, which in turn starts a thread that scrolls the text:

```
public void start() {
    appThread = new Thread(this);
    appThread.start();
}
```

These lines of code in the `start` event create the thread object and start it. You may notice the keyword `this` in the line that creates the thread object. You can use the `this` keyword to refer to the current object within your Java applet. In the case of the preceding `start` method, `this` refers to the current applet.

The stop Method

An equivalent to the `start` method is triggered when the applet is stopped. You need to *stop* running threads when the applet is stopped for performance reasons:

```
public void stop() {
    appThread.stop();
}
```

The `stop` method for the Marquee applet is fairly basic. It is triggered when the applet is stopped, and its sole responsibility is to stop execution of the application's thread.

The run Method

Because the Marquee applet has `implements Runnable` in its class definition, a `run` method is available that may be used for thread execution. The `run` method constructs the instructions that a thread is to follow. The requirements of the Marquee example indicate that the text should be continuously flowing. Therefore, the first thing that is implemented in the `run` method is an infinite loop. Now you are probably wondering why you would ever want to implement an infinite loop. The fact of the matter is that threads may be interrupted by other threads or by the Java interpreter. When the applet is stopped or closed, this loop is stopped because the thread is halted.

The loop implements two simple tasks: repainting the window to update the scrolling text and causing the thread to pause momentarily for effect. The `repaint` method forces the window of the applet to be redrawn, triggering the `paint` event discussed earlier. The `sleep` method for the current thread delays the thread for a predetermined number of milliseconds. As you can see from Listing 20.2, the `sleep` method belongs to the object `Thread`. To clarify which thread should be stopped (particularly useful with multithreaded applets that use several threads at once), the `currentThread` method is used.

Listing 20.2. The run method implements the instructions for a thread in a Java applet.

```
public void run() {
    while (true){
        repaint();
        try {
            Thread.currentThread().sleep(speed);
        }

        catch (InterruptedException e) {
        }
    }
}
```

Exception Handling

Although you should always try to avoid errors, some errors cannot be detected through your code. These types of errors are often referred to as *exceptions*. Java handles these exceptions more elegantly than most languages and allows your code to perform based on the occurrence of an exception. Java cannot do it all for you, however. It will handle exceptions gracefully for you, but in order for your program to do something about an exception, you must specify the portion of code where the error may occur. You must also create code that handles what happens when the exception occurs.

Java uses the keywords `try` and `catch` in this process. Each of these keywords is followed by a set of opening and closing braces (`{}`) that indicate the block of code to be applied to each keyword. In Listing 20.2, the Marquee applet instructs Java to be wary of exceptions that may occur while the thread is paused. A typical exception that may be raised while a thread is paused is `InterruptedException`. The fact that a thread was sleeping when another thread interrupted it may cause an error.

The `catch` keyword indicates the block of code to execute when a particular exception is raised. In the Marquee application, an `InterruptedException` error may occur. When it does, the `catch` keyword will trap that error and safely prevent the applet from crashing. Although the applet could have performed some action based on this event, it is not necessary in this case, and therefore no code exists in the `catch` section of the Marquee applet.

Because you are specifying to the Java interpreter what section of code may raise exceptions, you must also indicate which type of exception to expect. The `catch` keyword accepts one argument, the type of exception to catch. If you specify a different type of exception than the one actually raised, the block of code following the `catch` statement may not be executed.

The block of code following the `catch` statement that handles exceptions is aptly called an *exception handler.* This is one method by which exceptions may be trapped. As with most any language, there is more than one way to accomplish the same thing. Another approach is to use the `throws` statement, which triggers a specific Java class when an exception is raised.

Compiling Java Applets

Sun Microsystems offers the Java Developer's Kit (JDK) at its Web site. The JDK includes several binary programs for compiling, disassembling, and debugging Java applets. To compile an applet like the Marquee applet shown in Listing 20.1, you first need to create a new file called `Marquee.java` and key in the code. I recommend that you create a special subdirectory for your Java applet. In this case a `Marquee` subdirectory would suffice. The `Marquee.java` file that you create should be in this subdirectory as well.

Once you are ready to compile the applet, you must use the `javac` program that is included with the JDK. Run the `javac` compiler program from the directory that holds the applet you want to compile.

The result of this compilation is a `.class` file that you may embed into your HTML documents for Web pages. When you compile the Marquee applet, a `Marquee.class` file is generated in the current working directory.

Most developers who write applications experience errors. Some experience more errors than others. Because the `javac` program is a console-based application, the results are pumped to the screen. And if you have more errors than there are lines of text, those error messages will zip by. I recommend that you make a quick batch file to help you compile your Java project. For the Marquee applet, I wrote the simple batch file shown in Listing 20.3 on a Windows 95 PC. It served two purposes: It paused the output of errors so that I could actually read them, and it made invoking the compiler easier because I named it JC.BAT. One word of caution, though; remember to change the name of the applet you are compiling if you plan on using this batch file for additional applets in the future.

Listing 20.3. A DOS batch file for compiling Java applets.

```
@echo off
c:\java\bin\javac Marquee.java > results
type results ¦ more
```

Embedding Java Applets in HTML

Now that you know how to create an applet, how do you use it with your Web page? Java-enabled browsers support the embedding of applets with the <APPLET> tag. One of the greatest advantages to Java applets is that you can place them anywhere on a page, just as you would inline graphics. The <APPLET> tag has a corresponding ending tag </APPLET>. Between these two tags, you may use additional <PARAM> tags to specify parameters for the Java applet. Listing 20.4 shows a simple HTML document for embedding the Marquee applet.

Listing 20.4. Embedding the Marquee applet.

```
<HTML>
<HEAD>
<TITLE>
Scrolling Marquee
</TITLE>
</HEAD>

<BODY>
Did you ever want to scroll text within a region?
Well now you can with this nifty Java applet!
<HR>

<APPLET CODE="Marquee.class" WIDTH=500 HEIGHT=50>
<param name=text value="Look at this text scroll!!!">
<param name=direction value="left">
<param name=delay value="250">
<param name=bgcolor value="255255255">
<param name=fgcolor value="000000128">
</APPLET>

<HR>
Here's the <A HREF="Marquee.java">source code</A>.
</BODY>

</HTML>
```

The <APPLET> Tag

As you can see from Listing 20.4, the Java applet and pertinent information are embedded in the HTML document within the <APPLET> and </APPLET> tags. The <APPLET> tag requires three parameters: CODE, WIDTH, and HEIGHT:

```
<APPLET   CODE = "classname.class"
         WIDTH = width in pixels
        HEIGHT = height in pixels>
```

CODE—This parameter specifies the applet to be embedded on the Web page. In the case of the Marquee example, the code would be "Marquee.class".

WIDTH—This parameter specifies the width of the applet's window in pixels. The Marquee applet reads this information using the size method discussed in the "Painting Applets" section of this chapter.

HEIGHT—Just as WIDTH determines the width of an applet's window, HEIGHT determines its height in pixels.

The <PARAM> Tag

By now you are well aware that Java applets accept parameters from the Web page into which they are embedded. Parameters are optional, and default values should always be used for Java applets. However, when parameters are specified by the Web page, they are identified by single <PARAM> tags. Each parameter passed to the Java applet must have its own <PARAM> tag. The <PARAM> tag accepts two parameters of its own—NAME and VALUE:

```
<PARAM  NAME = Java parameter to change
       VALUE = "Java parameter's value">
```

NAME—A Java applet may accept multiple parameters. To indicate which parameter the Web page is changing, the Web page must specify the parameter's name within the <PARAM> tag.

VALUE—Once the parameter to be changed has been identified, the actual value it is to be changed to must be passed from the Web page. The value must be enclosed by quotation marks because it is treated as a string by Java.

Summary

In this chapter you take the first steps toward learning Java. It may not seem like much, but these skills are used repeatedly when coding Java. With the advent of new powerful scripting languages, such as JavaScript and VBScript, these skills are more important than ever.

Creating Dynamic Content with Active Server Pages

IN THIS CHAPTER

- What Is an Active Server Page? 628

- Additional Considerations for Active Server Pages 635

CHAPTER 21

You will find two basic types of documents on the Internet today: static documents that are basically standalone products that never change and dynamic documents that can change their appearance and even interact with the user. This chapter focuses on the latter type of document and explores some of the possibilities of dynamic documents created with the Active Server technology. As you read, though, keep in mind that this chapter only touches on these technologies. The subject is so rich it needs a complete book to fully explore all the possibilities.

> **NOTE**
>
> You will find the full documentation for active server pages on your Web server, assuming you choose to install the documentation as recommended previously in Chapter 5, "Internet Information Server Preparation and Installation." If you did not install the documentation, you will need to rerun the setup program to install it. The URL to use to access the documentation is `http://YourServerName.YourDomainName/IasDocs/RoadMap.ASP`.

What Is an Active Server Page?

An active server page (ASP file) is a unique type of HTML document. It is unique because the processing actually occurs on the Web server, rather than on the Web browser (the client). The final product that is passed to the Web browser is a series of HTML codes, but the document is not necessarily the same as the source document(s) on the server. In the next sections you will learn more about how this transformation occurs, but for now, just take my word on it.

One of the really interesting characteristics of ASPs is that they support three scripting languages. I bet that right about now you are thinking, What does he mean three scripting languages? There were only two the last time I looked—VBScript and JavaScript. Well, now there are three because Microsoft recently licensed the technology from Sun to create its own version of JavaScript called JScript. JScript has been optimized for the Microsoft platforms and includes functionality not available from JavaScript.

> **NOTE**
>
> If you plan to use any server-side components of the JScript language, you will need to download and install Microsoft VM for Java™ on your Web server. You can download these files for the Intel platform at `http://www.microsoft.com/java/jvmi386.cab`, for the Alpha platform at `http://www.microsoft.com/java/jvmalpha.cab`, and for the PowerPC platform at `http://www.microsoft.com/java/jvmppc.cab`.

In Chapter 18, "Unleashing the Power of VBScript," you learned how to utilize some of the features of the VBScript language. In Chapter 20, "Writing Java Applets," you learned how to use some of the scripting capabilities of the JavaScript language. The JScript language is primarily a superscript of the JavaScript language. If you already know JavaScript, you will have no difficulty with JScript. All these languages can still be used to develop ASPs. You can even mix and match VBScript and JScript or VBScript and JavaScript within the same document. But you cannot mix JavaScript and JScript within the same document. If you do, you will wind up with a compile-time error message. Having said all that, here's a look at how an active server page is created and how it works.

Creating a Simple Active Server Page

The first thing you need to do is to actually write an active server page. While you can perform this task using VBScript, I decided to use JScript for my examples. Although VBScript can perform the same tasks, I decided to use JScript because I do not think Microsoft provided enough JScript samples with the documentation. Maybe one more will help you understand the process a little better. Before turning to the code, however, take a look at the actual output displayed on the Web browser. (See Figure 21.1.)

FIGURE 21.1.

The sample active server page displayed in Internet Explorer.

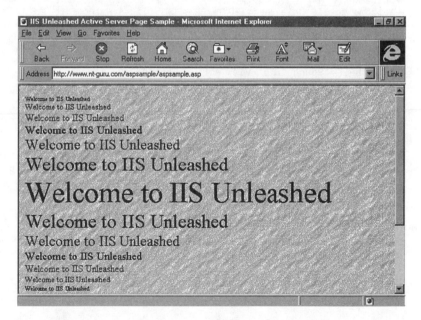

What you are looking at is the phrase *Welcome to IIS Unleashed* shown in a series of font sizes—from 1 to 7 and then back again to size 1. If you select View | Source, you'll see the corresponding HTML code, which also appears as Listing 21.1.

Listing 21.1. The HTML code used to display the document in Figure 21.1 on the Web browser.

```
1.  <HTML>
2.  <HEAD>
3.  <META NAME="Author" CONTENT="Arthur E. Knowles">
4.  <META NAME="Description" CONTENT="Welcome to IIS Unleashed Active Server Page
➥Sample">
5.  <META NAME="Subject" CONTENT="Active Server Page - JScript Sample">
6.  <TITLE>IIS Unleashed Active Server Page Sample</TITLE>
7.  </HEAD>
8.  <BODY BACKGROUND="blulight.gif" BGCOLOR="#C0C0C0">
9.  <FONT Size=1>Welcome to IIS Unleashed</FONT><BR><FONT Size=2>Welcome to IIS
➥Unleashed</FONT><BR><FONT Size=3>Welcome to IIS Unleashed</FONT><BR><FONT Size=4>
➥Welcome to IIS Unleashed</FONT><BR><FONT Size=5>Welcome to IIS Unleashed</FONT>
➥<BR><FONT Size=6>Welcome to IIS Unleashed</FONT><BR><FONT Size=7>Welcome to IIS
➥Unleashed</FONT><BR><FONT Size=6>Welcome to IIS Unleashed</FONT><BR><FONT Size=5>
➥Welcome to IIS Unleashed</FONT><BR><FONT Size=4>Welcome to IIS Unleashed</FONT><BR>
➥<FONT Size=3>Welcome to IIS Unleashed</FONT><BR><FONT Size=2>Welcome to IIS
➥Unleashed</FONT><BR><FONT Size=1>Welcome to IIS Unleashed</FONT><BR>
10. </Script>
11. <HR>
12. <A HREF="Source.HTM">View Active Server Page Source</A>
13. <P>
14. <table border="0" width="100%">
15.     <tr>
16.         <td valign="top" width="50%"><font size="2"><em>Copyright
17.         © 1996 Knowles Consulting. All rights reserved</em></font><font
18.         size="2"><em><br>
19.         </em></font>For comments or suggestions send e-mail to:<br>
20.         <a href="MAILTO:webmaster@nt-guru.com">webmaster@nt-guru.com</a></td>
21.         <td align="right" valign="top" width="50%">This page was
22.         last modified on:<br>
23.         <!--webbot bot="Timestamp" startspan s-type="EDITED"
24.         s-format="%A, %B %d, %Y" -->Tuesday, February 11, 1997<!--webbot
➥bot="Timestamp"
25.         i-checksum="60550" endspan --></td>
26.     </tr>
27. </table>
28. </BODY>
29. </HTML>
```

The preceding code looks just like regular HTML code that anyone could have created. So what's so special about it? Well, the HTML code in Listing 21.1 was created by the code in Listing 21.2, which you can find in the SOURCE\CHAP21 directory on the

CD-ROM. The first file to look at is ASPSample.ASP. This file is the root page, or the page that ties the entire document into a single product.

Listing 21.2. ASPSample.ASP—An active server page sample.

```
1.  <%@ Script RunAt=Server Language=JScript %>
2.  <HTML>
3.  <HEAD>
4.  <META NAME="Author" CONTENT="Arthur E. Knowles">
5.  <META NAME="Description" CONTENT="Welcome to IIS Unleashed Active Server Page
➥Sample">
6.  <META NAME="Subject" CONTENT="Active Server Page - JScript Sample">
7.  <TITLE>IIS Unleashed Active Server Page Sample</TITLE>
8.  </HEAD>
9.  <BODY BACKGROUND="blulight.gif" BGCOLOR="#C0C0C0">
10. <%
11. var WelcomeString;
12. WelcomeString = "Welcome to IIS Unleashed";
13. for (i=1; i <= 7; i++)
14.     {
15.     Response.Write("<FONT Size=");
16.     Response.Write(i);
17.     Response.Write(">");
18.     Response.Write(WelcomeString);
19.     Response.Write("</FONT>");
20.     Response.Write("<BR>");
21.     }
22. for (i=6; i > 0 ; i--)
23.     {
24.     Response.Write("<FONT Size=");
25.     Response.Write(i);
26.     Response.Write(">");
27.     Response.Write(WelcomeString);
28.     Response.Write("</FONT>");
29.     Response.Write("<BR>");
30.     }
31. %>
32. </Script>
33. <HR>
34. <!--#include file ="CopyRight.INC"-->
35. </BODY>
36. </HTML>
```

Obviously, the code in Listing 21.2 is quite different from the HTML output shown in Listing 21.1. In fact, only a few lines (2 through 9, 33, 35, and 36) can be matched to lines in the previous source listing. The second listing might be a bit confusing, even if you know C++ or JavaScript, because some of the functions may not be familiar. You can examine the code a bit more closely while I explain how it works.

The first thing to note is line 1. This line includes the command <%@ Script RunAt=Server Language=JScript %>, which tells the compiler that the scripting commands contained within the document are JScript commands and that they should be executed on the server. If you choose to use VBScript instead, you can skip the Language element, as VBScript is the default and will be assumed by the compiler. Like most HTML tags, `<Script>` has a corresponding end tag shown in line 32 (`</Script>`), although in this example the end tag really isn't required. I've used it only for clarity. By using the `<SCRIPT>` and `</SCRIPT>` tags, you can mix and match both VBScript and JScript in the same document. This feature allows you to reuse an existing code base, or perhaps to use a third-party code base, within your documents.

The next item to notice is the text contained within lines 10 through 31 where the heart of the script comes into play. These lines (10 and 31) delimit (mark) the starting and ending points of the script. Everything within these delimiters must be JScript code; otherwise, a compile-time error will occur. Line 11 creates a string variable WelcomeString, which is assigned the value Welcome to IIS Unleashed in line 12. Line 13 begins a loop that will count up from 1 to 7 and is delimited by the braces in lines 14 and 21. Line 22 begins a loop that will count down from 6 to 1 and is delimited by the braces in lines 23 and 30.

Lines 15 to 20 and 24 to 29 also loop to change the font size. The task is repeated each time the loop condition is true. The important feature about these lines of code is the Response.Write portion of the statement. This portion of code actually writes the HTML output you saw in Listing 21.1. What you are seeing here is the use of the Write method for the Response object. Each statement writes a portion of the HTML code into the HTTP data stream. Lines 15 and 24 write "<FONT SIZE=", lines 16 and 25 write the loop counter, and lines 17 and 26 write ">" (the end of the tag). Lines 18 and 27 write the actual "Welcome to IIS Unleashed" string. Lines 19 and 28 write the end tag "</FONT>", while lines 20 and 29 write a "<BR>" tag into the output stream. The result is line 9 of Listing 21.1.

> **NOTE**
>
> Make sure you remember the Response object, as it can be difficult to find in the Microsoft documentation. If you have the Index Information Server installed on the same site, then you can use the Search option (within the Active Server Page Roadmap) and perform a search on the phrase Response object. This search should get you to the page where the Response object methods will be documented and explain how to use this object to write information into the HTTP data stream.

If you have never encountered a *server side include* (SSI) before, then line 34 should prove interesting. It inserts a complete file into the HTTP data stream. The inserted file is called CopyRight.INC. The source code is shown in Listing 21.3.

Listing 21.3. CopyRight.INC—The included file in the active server page example.

```
1. <A HREF="Source.HTM">View Active Server Page Source</A>
2. <P>
3. <table border="0" width="100%">
4.     <tr>
5.         <td valign="top" width="50%"><font size="2"><em>Copyright
6.         © 1996 Knowles Consulting. All rights reserved</em></font><font
   ➥size="2"><em><br>
7.         </em></font>For comments or suggestion send e-mail to:<br>
8.         <a href="MAILTO:webmaster@nt-guru.com">webmaster@nt-guru.com</a></td>
9.         <td align="right" valign="top" width="50%">This page was last modified
   ➥on:<br>
10.        <!--webbot bot="Timestamp" startspan s-type="EDITED"
11.        s-format="%A, %B %d, %Y" -->Tuesday, February 11, 1997<!--webbot
   ➥bot="Timestamp"
12.        i-checksum="60550" endspan --></td>
13.    </tr>
14. </table>
```

Notice that the HTML code here is exactly the same as the HTML code generated in the original listing. Server side includes can be very useful for your development efforts, as they can cut down on the amount of code you need to generate and improve usability. The subject of the next section is the many ways in which you can include files.

Including Files in an Active Server Page

Now that you know that you can include files within your HTML documents, you need to know more about how to accomplish the task. Before you start to insert files, however, I'd like you to consider that you can also include other objects. You could, for example, insert the file size into the HTML output stream. Or perhaps you'd like to execute a CGI application and send its output into the HTML output stream. All of this, and more, is possible.

The basic format of the HTML insert statement is `<!--InsertTagHere PathType=PathName-->` where *InsertTagHere* is a directive that determines the type of information to be inserted into the HTML output stream, *PathType* specifies the type of path to use (either VIRTUAL or FILE), and *PathName* is the actual path to the object. These directives are summarized in Table 21.1.

> **NOTE**
>
> A file path is assumed to be relative to the directory of the parent document (the document with the #include directive), whereas a virtual path is assumed to be relative to the IIS WWWRoot directory.

Table 21.1. Include directives to insert files and application information into the HTML output stream.

Directive	Description	Example

#include	Inserts a file into the HTML output stream.	`<!--#include file="CopyRight.INC"-->`
		`<!--#include virtual="/Books/Samples/`
		`CopyRight.INC"-->`

#flastmod	Inserts the file's last modification date into the HTML output stream.	`<!--#flastmod virtual="/Books/` `Samples/CopyRight.INC"-->`
#fsize	Inserts the file's size into the HTML output stream.	`<!--#fsize virtual="/Books/Samples/` `CopyRight.INC"-->`
#echo	Inserts the output of a CGI variable into the HTML output stream.	`<!--#echo var=CONTENT_TYPE-->`

#config	Specifies how error messages, the date time format, and the file size format will be issued to the client.	`<!--#config errmsg="An error`
		`has occurred attempting to`
		`include a file. Please e-mail`
		`the administrator " -->`

#exec	Executes a given CGI application, command shell, or ISAPI application and outputs the result into the HTML output stream.	`<!--#exec cmd="DIR"-->`

TIP

One of the really neat features of server side includes (STM files) is the ability to include ASPs within the HTML document. However, you can't use the #include directive to insert an ASP file. If you do, the file contents will be embedded into the document, but they will not be executed on the server. Instead, to include an ASP file, use the #exec directive. You could, for example, use `<!-- #exec cgi="/PageInfo.ASP" -->`, which would insert the HTML output generated by the `PageInfo.ASP` file into the HTML data stream.

TIP

You can use your Web browser to find more information on how to use server side includes. Just use the URL http://*YourServer*.*YourDomain*/iasdocs/aspdocs/ssi/isiall.htm where *YourServer* is the name of the IIS server and *YourDomain* is your Internet domain name.

Additional Considerations for Active Server Pages

Before ending this chapter, I need to discuss some of the more basic administration issues. Otherwise, you might find that although you can write JScript code, use server side includes, and generate tons of ASP files, you can't actually execute any of them. I bet that raised an eyebrow or two. So here's your chance to examine some of the issues for using ASPs before you get too deeply involved.

The first thing to consider is that an active server page is neither a normal HTML document nor a regular script file. A normal HTML document is only read by the client. A normal script file is only executed by the client. The standard permissions applied to a home directory, or virtual directory, with the Internet Server Manager is read only for HTML directories and execute only for scripts.

These permissions will work fine for HTML documents and script files. If you place ASP files into either of these directories when they are loaded into the client's Web browser, however, you are not going to like the results. Instead of being interpreted by the Web server and converted into a standard HTML output stream, the documents will be loaded *as is* into the Web browser if the directory is marked as readonly. Consequently, the client will see any HTML code you might have, but it will ignore all the scripting commands and display the script commands as regular text. In most cases the client will see an empty page! If the directory is marked as execute, but not read, then the client will get an access violation when he attempts to load the file. To avoid these problems, just make sure that any directory you use for ASP files has both read and execute permissions—which leads to the second item to consider: security. How can you prevent users from loading all your ASP pages? You may have created various private active server applications for use only within your intranet, for example. If these pages access sensitive data, you obviously do not want to allow just anyone to run them. One way to prevent unauthorized access is to use permissions to limit access to the files. However, this method requires that the documents be stored physically on an NTFS partition and that you use File Manager or Windows Explorer to assign permissions to limit access to the files.

Summary

This chapter demonstrates some of the basic functionality provided by ASPs. The most important concept to remember is that ASPs are executed on the server, rather than on the client. As a script is processed, it is converted to HTML, which in turn is sent to the client. This technique is very different from processing scripts locally on the client. It also opens up new ways for developers to take advantage of the server's computational horsepower. In the next chapter you will explore some of the options for streaming multimedia over the Internet.

Using NetShow Live

IN THIS CHAPTER

- What Is Microsoft NetShow Live? *638*

- Building a Streaming Audio-Video File *641*

- Putting It All Together *643*

The introduction of Microsoft's Internet Information Server 3 puts streaming multimedia capability within financial reach of almost anyone. Streamed multimedia differs from regular multimedia in that a streamed multimedia file is sent over the wire in packets. Each packet is then played on the client's computer as it is received. This process is quite different from the usual method of playing an AVI or WAV file in which you must first download the complete file. Only then can you play it using the Media Player or another application. Therefore, you must wait until after you have downloaded the file before you can enjoy it; in contrast, a streamed multimedia file plays as it downloads.

This new streaming technology is called NetShow Live. In this chapter, you will explore some of the capabilities of NetShow Live and learn about some of the issues you have to deal with before implementing this technology on your network.

What Is Microsoft NetShow Live?

Microsoft NetShow Live is a client/server tool that has several components. The core component is the Microsoft Internet Information Server (IIS). You need to use IIS 2.0 or higher before you can install NetShow Live. You must also be using Windows NT Server 4.0 or higher, as you cannot install the NetShow Live components on a Windows NT Workstation. NetShow Live consists of the following components:

- NetShow On-Demand Server—This component executes as a Windows NT 4.0 Server service. It can supply multiple-bit-rate audio, video, or interleaved audio-video multimedia streams to Windows NT and Windows 95 clients. I expect this capability will be added to other clients soon.

- NetShow On-Demand Server Administration Utilities—This component consists of the Internet Service Manager Add-In, the Trace Facility, and the Log Facility.

- NetShow On-Demand Player—This component includes the client-side tools required to view a streamed multimedia file: a standalone player and an ActiveX control that can be embedded in an HTML document. You can also use the ActiveX control within Visual Basic or Visual C++ applications.

- ActiveX Streaming Format (ASF) Editor—You can use this editor to assemble your audio, video, or audio-video files into a streamable data file. It is a crude tool with but one purpose—the assembling of files into an ASF file—which it seems to do well enough. However, I expect the third-party manufacturers to hop on the bandwagon and create some much better tools.

- Various conversion tools—These tools include `vidtoasf.exe`, which converts AVI and MOV files to ASF file format, and `wavtoasf.exe`, which converts WAV files to the ASF file format. The sample file that I built used `vidtoasf.exe` to convert an AVI file into an ASF file. All I can say about the tools is that they work—I have included them here only to get you started in developing ASF files.

You might have noticed a few disparaging remarks in the preceding descriptions, but I'm not faulting Microsoft, or its developers, in any way. I've been a developer for many years, and I understand that new technologies introduce new requirements into the industry. If we, as developers, had to wait until all the tools were written before the products were introduced, then we would never get anything done. Third-party manufacturers need a little time before they can get their tools out on the market, and this rule applies to Microsoft as well. First, the underlying product is developed. Then and only then do the development teams (both from Microsoft and third parties) get involved.

What this sequence of events means to you is that you will need to use other tools that are currently available, which (at this time) include a tool to record and edit audio files. You'll also need a tool capable of capturing, editing, and assembling audio-video files. Luckily many of these types of tools are already available. The bad news is that none of them can work with the native ASF file format; therefore, you will have to edit your files, convert your files, assemble your files, and then use the ASF editor to build the ASF file. If you are unhappy with the result, you must repeat the entire cycle.

What Is a Stream?

If you have ever listened to a RealAudio presentation on the Internet, then you might already have used streamed audio. But perhaps you want to know a bit more about how a stream works. Essentially a stream is an assemblage of audio only, video only, or audio and video files that are synchronized to a common timeline. These files are interleaved in the data stream so that when an image needs to be rendered, or an audio file played, it can be assembled from the various bits and displayed, or played, at the correct time.

With NetShow Live you can stream audio, video, or any mixture of the two to your target audience on your intranet or on the World Wide Web via the Internet. This feature is potentially powerful. It could also be the death of your network if misused. Why? Simply because any network has a limited bandwidth. Only so many bits can be sent over the network wiring before the network chokes and then dies a cruel death.

Nothing, and I mean nothing, is more bandwidth intensive then multimedia files. Or perhaps I should clarify that statement a bit and say that high-quality audio-video files can consume bandwidth faster than you would believe. The good news with NetShow Live is that it has some pretty impressive codecs (a piece of software used to compress/decompress audio-video files) that you can use to compress your audio and video files. Without this capability to compress your data streams, even 100Mbps networks would be unable to cope with the demands put upon it. Even with compressed data, however, you will still need to limit the number of simultaneous connections and users on your network. Otherwise, the same problems could occur.

If you choose to provide a more open connection standard, then you will need to use less video and more audio. Audio is far less intensive then video in its bandwidth requirements. But let's look a bit more into the supported stream types.

NetShow Live Stream Types

There are three basic types of streamed data you can assemble with the ASF editor and then play back using an ASF player (like the NetShow player). The benefits and drawbacks of each type of data are summarized in Table 22.1. You should consider each format carefully to make sure it suits your needs before implementing it. At all times you must consider the bandwidth requirements; that is, you can support only a limited number of clients based on your available network bandwidth. If you have a high-quality audio-video file, then the number of simultaneous clients who can access the file will be far fewer than the number of clients who can access an audio-only file. If you need to support many simultaneous clients, you should consider using a less-bandwidth-intensive format.

Table 22.1. The supported streamed file types.

File Type	Descriptions	Comment
Audio Only	High-quality audio-only data. You can use any supported WAV file format as your input file format. These formats include mono or stereo from 11.025 to 44.1KHz.	The higher the frequency, the better the quality. The higher frequencies also require an increased network bandwidth to render properly. You should use the higher frequencies (44.1KHz) only for sound sources that require it, for example, CD-quality music uses 44.1KHz.
Illustrated Audio	A mixture of static images and interleaved audio.	This format is an excellent choice for narratives, such as PowerPoint slide shows. Although it uses more bandwidth than an audio-only format, it can provide more information.
Interleaved Audio-Video	A high-quality audio and video interleaved file that can display full-motion video. It can basically provide the same quality as broadcast television right on your network.	Requires an extreme amount of network bandwidth for full (24-30 frames per second). Using fewer frames (15 fps) can significantly lower the bandwidth requirements and still provide acceptable animation.

Building a Streaming Audio-Video File

Okay, you've finally made it to the fun part of this chapter—creating a streamed multimedia file to use on your network. You will need to use one of three tools: the ASF Editor, the video-to-ASF converter, or the WAV-to-ASF converter. Because the ASF converters are simpler to use than the other tools, you should start with them. The command-line arguments for the ASF converter tools follow.

> **NOTE**
>
> Some of the options you will see for the following command-line arguments are not displayed when you use the /? argument on the application, even though they are supported.

Command-line arguments for `VIDTOASF.EXE`:

```
VIDTOASF -IN FileName.EXT -OUT FileName.ASF -WAVESPAN MSSpan -LEADTIME MSTime
-VIDEO StreamToUse -AUDIO StreamToUse -ECCSPAN ECCValue -SCRIPT ScriptName -
SEEKABLE SeekValue -AUDIOFILE AudioFileName -BITRATE BitRate -BUFFERTIME
BufferTime -OPTIMIZE OptimizeValue -PACKETSIZE PacketSize
```

where

FileName.EXT is the filename and extension of the input file you want to convert. This file can be an AVI file or a QuickTime movie, although not all QuickTime movie file formats are currently supported.

FileName.ASF is the output filename.

MSSpan is the wave span in milliseconds. The wave span is the time frame in which an audio file will be smeared in the file. It is used to compensate for lost data packets. If you have a highly reliable network, you can disable spanning by setting this value to 0.

MSTime specifies the time to wait to play an input file after buffering it. The default is 1000 milliseconds.

StreamToUse specifies which data stream in the file to convert. This argument is applicable only for source files with multiple audio or video data streams.

ECCValue enables (ON) or disables (OFF) error correction.

ScriptName specifies a script file used to insert URLs and markers into the output file.

SeekValue specifies that the file will include seekable frames (ON) even when there are not enough key frames. The default is OFF.

AudioFileName specifies the name of an audio file to be used instead of the audio file in the original audio-video source file.

BitRate specifies the bit rate to convert the file to use. The default is to allow the application to determine the bit rate.

BufferTime specifies the maximum time to use for buffering the input file when played on the client.

OptimizeValue specifies a percentage (the default is 5) for the application to maintain when calculating the maximum bit rate.

PacketSize specifies the network packet size to use.

Command-line arguments for WAVTOASF.EXE:

```
WAVTOASF -IN FileName.WAV-OUT FileName.ASF LEADTIME MSTime --ECCSPAN ECCValue
-SCRIPT ScriptName
```

where

FileName.WAV is the filename of the input file to convert. This file must be a WAV file.

FileName.ASF is the output filename.

ECCValue enables (ON) or disables (OFF) error correction.

ScriptName specifies a script file used to insert URLs and markers into the output file.

Using the ASF Editor, as shown in Figure 22.1, is actually much easier than using the command-line conversion programs—mostly because it is a Windows application. Figure 22.1 shows the sample ASF file included with the NetShow Creation Tools. It displays images in green and yellow (on the top of the timeline) and the associated sound file in blue (on the bottom of the timeline). Adding images and sounds is as simple as dragging them from the bottom window (the source window) of the application and dropping them into the timeline. You can drag files from Windows Explorer into the source window, or you can use the Add Files command from the File menu.

The important feature to note about the ASF Editor (which is really very basic in its capabilities) is that it can convert various graphics formats into a format that is more presentable for streamed media. I've found that the most compressible option is the VDONet/VDOWave format. It converted the sample file from 1.5MB to 140KB—more than a 10 to 1 ratio! You can also select a targeted bit rate for your streamed media—14,400 or 28,800 or 112,500 bits per second—right from the toolbar. Just remember to pick the bit rate before you start working with the ASF Editor to import your media because this setting has a significant affect on the timeline.

The timeline specifies how long it will take for an image to be downloaded and rendered on the client computer. I've found that audio files are rendered quickly, whereas video files take quite a bit longer. Therefore, if you decide to mix audio and video in the same file, you should make sure your audio stream is long enough to cover the time it takes to download and render the video images. The Stream | Test menu option can help you with this calculation.

FIGURE 22.1.
The ASF Editor in action.

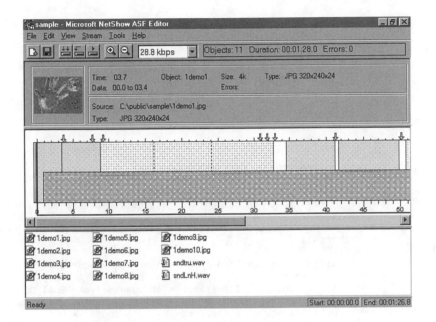

Putting It All Together

Once you have created your ASF file, you need to find a way to display it on the client's computer. You can accomplish this goal in two ways. First, you can just let clients download the ASF file and play it on their computer. This file functions much like any other multimedia file, however, and defeats the purpose of streaming the file. The second method is to provide an HTML page with the Microsoft NetShow On-Demand Control embedded within it. This task is really easier than you might think because Microsoft provided a very nice sample that I have modified slightly. The source code (located in SOURCE\CHAP22 on the CD-ROM) minus the associated comments for ASFSample.HTM follows.

```
<!DOCTYPE HTML PUBLIC "-//IETF//DTD HTML//EN">
<html>
<head>
<meta http-equiv="Content-Type"
content="text/html; charset=iso-8859-1">
<meta name="GENERATOR" content="Microsoft FrontPage 2.0">
<title>NetShow Sample Page</title>
</head>
<body background="blulight.gif">
<h1 align="center">A leopard on the move!</h1>
<hr>
<div align="center"><center>
<table border="3">
    <tr>
        <td><object id="NSOPlay"
        classid="clsid:2179C5D3-EBFF-11CF-B6FD-00AA00B4E220"
        codebase="http://www.microsoft.com/netshow/download/
```

```
    ➥nsoplay.exe#version=1,0,0,475"
    align="baseline" border="0" width="260" height="62"><param
    name="_ExtentX" value="18574"><param name="_ExtentY"
    value="22410"><param name="AutoRewind" value="-1"><param
    name="AutoStart" value="-1"><param name="ControlType"
    value="2"></object></td>
    </tr>
</table>
</center></div>
<hr>
<table border="0" width="100%">
    <tr>
        <td valign="top" width="45%"><address>
            <font size="2"><em>Copyright © 1997 Knowles
            Consulting. All rights reserved<br>
            </em></font>For comments or suggestion send e-mail
            to:<br>
            <a href="MAILTO:webmaster@nt-guru.com">webmaster@nt-guru.com</a>
        </address>
        </td>
        <td align="right" valign="top" width="40%"><address>
            This page was last modified on:<br>
            <!--webbot bot="Timestamp" startspan s-type="EDITED"
            s-format="%A, %B %d, %Y" -->Thursday, February 13, 1997<!--webbot
            bot="Timestamp" i-checksum="999" endspan -->
        </address>
        </td>
    </tr>
</table>
<address>
    <script language="VBScript"><!--
Sub window_OnLoad()
    dim servername 'create a variable
    servername=Location.Hostname
    SetNetShowFileName( "leopard.asf" )
end sub
sub SetNetShowFileName( szNSOFile)
    Dim dwTruncPoint, GetCurrentPath
    dwTruncPoint = 1
    while( InStr( dwTruncPoint, window.location, "/" ) )
        dwTruncPoint =  InStr( dwTruncPoint, window.location, "/" ) + 1
    wend
    while( InStr( dwTruncPoint, window.location, "\" ) )
        dwTruncPoint =  InStr( dwTruncPoint, window.location, "\" ) + 1
    wend
    GetCurrentPath = Left( window.location, dwTruncPoint - 1 )
    dwTruncPoint = instr( GetCurrentPath, "///" )
    if( Not( IsNull( dwTruncPoint ) ) And ( 1 < dwTruncPoint )  then
        GetCurrentPath = Left( GetCurrentPath, dwTruncPoint ) &
        ➥Right(GetCurrentPath, Len( GetCurrentPath) - dwTruncPoint - 1 )
    end if
    On Error Resume Next
    NSOPlay.FileName = GetCurrentPath & szNSOFile
    if( 2 < Len( Err.Description ) ) then
        Res = Msgbox( Err.Description, 16, "NetShow On-Demand Player" )
        exit sub
    end if
    Err.Clear
```

```
end sub
--></script>
</address>
</body>
</html>
```

> **NOTE**
>
> You must use Internet Explorer 3.0 or Netscape 3 with an ActiveX plug-in to view any HTML document with an embedded NetShow Live ActiveX control.

When executed, the HTML page shown in Figure 22.2 displays the streamed file with the control. Users have full control of how the object is played on their computers. All they need to do to specify an action is to either click one of the buttons or right-click the control to specify various properties.

FIGURE 22.2.

A streamed audio-video file using NetShow Live.

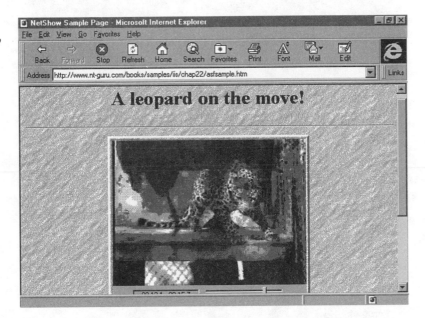

The document includes the ActiveX embedded object (within the `<OBJECT>` `</OBJECT>` tags) and an associated Visual Basic script. You could do without the Visual Basic script entirely if you were to set the `FileName` property for the object to the full URL of the ASF file. You could set the `NSOPlay.FileName` property to `http://www.nt-guru.com/books/samples/iis/chap22/leopard.asf`, and then you would not need any script at all. However, if you were to do so, you would not be able to use a relative pathname, and this example requires a relative pathname. Otherwise, you could not run this sample from the companion CD-ROM.

I would also like to point out that working with embedded objects and VBScripts within FrontPage 97 is much easier than using an ASCII editor. With FrontPage 97 you may insert objects, specify object properties, and write your scripting code (VBScript or JScript) without ever leaving the GUI environment. Believe me, writing code this way is much easier than writing code in an ASCII editor (like Notepad)!

Summary

In this chapter you explore some of the basic features of Microsoft NetShow Live. You also learn a bit about streamed multimedia and the various formats that NetShow Live supports. The chapter also briefly examines the ASF Editor and associated conversion tools. The next chapter explains how to interface the Internet Information Server and your ODBC-compliant databases.

IN THIS PART

- Interfacing Internet Information Server with ODBC Databases 649

- Building Dynamic Web Pages with SQL Server 693

- Using Crystal Reports for Internet Information Server 719

- Indexing Your Web Site with Index Information Server 727

VI

PART

Using Internet Information Server with Databases

Interfacing Internet Information Server with ODBC Databases

IN THIS CHAPTER

- Installing Microsoft dbWeb   650

- Using the Miscrosoft dbWeb Administrator   655

- Creating a Custom Guest Book Using Microsoft dbWeb   687

At one time or another, you will probably want to either capture data from or display information in databases to Internet clients who access your Web sites. With the Internet Information Server, you can accomplish this task using one of three methods:

- Use the Internet Database Connector (an ISAPI dynamic link library), included with the Internet Information Server, to create custom HTML documents.
- Write a custom CGI application and create custom HTML documents.
- Use Microsoft dbWeb to provide a point-and-click interface to your ODBC databases.

Of these three options, I think you'll find that dbWeb is the easiest because both the Internet Database Connector and CGI applications require much more technical experience and custom development of C (or C++) applications. Microsoft dbWeb version 1.1 executes as a Windows NT service. It is a multithreaded ISAPI dynamic link library that has been written to provide customizable access to any Open Database Connectivity (ODBC) database for which you have a 32-bit ODBC driver. Microsoft dbWeb takes advantage of the multithreaded capabilities of Windows NT to provide superior performance and usability. It includes another program, called the dbWeb Administrator, that you use to define a database schema. (A *schema* is nothing more than the interface between your ODBC database and dbWeb and is maintained in an Access database.) The schema defines the ODBC database system name (DSN) and the fields to display for query by example (QBE), tabular (multiple rows of records), freeform (a single record), or insert/update/delete database forms. You can even create customizable forms using handwritten HTML documents to provide a different look and feel.

You can currently obtain Microsoft dbWeb from the Microsoft WWW site at `http://www.microsoft.com/intdev/dbweb/`. In this chapter you learn how to install Microsoft dbWeb and how to use the Microsoft dbWeb Administrator. You also learn how to interface Microsoft dbWeb to an ODBC database by creating HTML forms that allow visitors to your Web site to leave information about themselves (a guest book, in other words).

Installing Microsoft dbWeb

You can use Microsoft dbWeb 1.1 with Internet Information Server version 1.0 or later. To use dbWeb with Windows NT Server 3.51 and IIS 1.0, however, you must update your Windows NT Server installation to Service Pack 4, and you must have ODBC 2.5 or later installed on your server. As part of the dbWeb installation, the setup program offers to copy the ODBC 2.5 setup files to your computer. After installing dbWeb, you can install the ODBC 2.5 drivers. Just make sure you install the ODBC drivers as described in the following steps, or dbWeb will fail to function. Microsoft dbWeb works best with Windows NT Server 4.0 and the Internet Information Server 2.0. The rest of this discussion assumes that you are using NT Server 4.0 and IIS 2.0.

To install Microsoft dbWeb, follow these steps:

1. Copy `dbweb11.exe` to an empty directory on the computer where you want to install Microsoft dbWeb. I commonly use the temporary directory `C:\TEMP` for my installations and recommend that you do the same.

2. Execute the self-extracting archive `dbweb11.exe`. You will then be prompted by the Installshield self-extracting EXE message box to install dbWeb (press the Yes button) or to Exit (press the No button). Click the Yes button.

3. A message box informs you that the files will be extracted from the archive. Another message box informs you of the delay while the Installshield wizard is being set up to guide you through the rest of the installation. At this point the dialog shown in Figure 23.1 is displayed.

FIGURE 23.1.

The first screen of the Microsoft dbWeb Setup wizard.

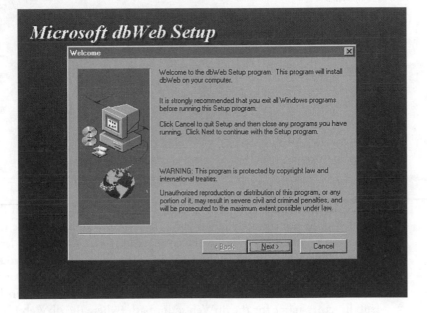

4. Click the Next button to display the Microsoft dbWeb License Agreement dialog. After reading the agreement, click the Accept button to continue. If you do not agree to the license terms, click the Exit button to exit the Setup program.

5. The Choose Destination Location dialog is displayed after you click the Accept button.

   The default directory is `C:\DBWEB`, but I prefer to install all of my IIS-related files in the IIS root directory (the default is `%SystemRoot%\System32\InetSrv`). To change the location where the dbWeb source files are installed, click the Browse button. This will display the Change Directory dialog, where you can specify an alternate location.

After you have specified the new location, click the OK button. If the directory does not exist, you will be prompted to create it; after you do that you are returned to the Choose Destination Location dialog.

6. Click the Next button to display the dialog shown in Figure 23.2. You should leave the dbWeb Server and dbWeb Administrator checked, but the Microsoft ODBC 2.5 and Examples are optional components. Because you are a new user of dbWeb, I recommend that you install the examples—they are the only tutorial files available. If you are using Windows NT Server 3.51, you should install the ODBC 2.5 files so you can install them later, as described at the end of this step-by-step list.

FIGURE 23.2.

Selecting the Microsoft dbWeb components to install.

7. Click the Next button; the dialog shown in Figure 23.3 appears. If the directories displayed do not correctly identify the IIS wwwroot directory or the IIS script directory, you should change them to list the correct directories. Otherwise, leave them as they appear. The IIS script directory is a virtual directory in which all your executable files reside. These executable files can include ISAPI DLLs, Internet Database Connector IDC and HTX files, CGI scripts, or other executable code. The final choice is the subdirectory name for the dbWeb script path (where the dbWeb ISAPI DLL will reside). It will be created under the IIS script directory. It is not necessary to change this directory unless your IIS installation uses nonstandard directory names.

TIP

When you install the Internet Information Server, I recommend that you choose an alternative installation directory (like D:\InetSrv) on a physically separate drive from where you installed Windows NT Server for enhanced performance and data integrity. Furthermore, this new drive should be an NTFS partition so you can use the capability to assign permissions and audit access to these directories. For more information, refer to Chapter 5, "Internet Information Server Preparation and Installation."

FIGURE 23.3.

Specifying the Microsoft dbWeb component directories.

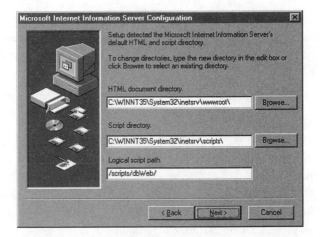

8. Click the Next button. The Microsoft dbWeb source files, the sample files, and the ODBC files will be copied to the destination directories you specified in step 7.

9. The Information message box informs you of the successful installation of Microsoft dbWeb. Click the OK button to close this message box.

10. If you choose to copy the ODBC setup files, another Information message box is displayed. Click the OK button to close the message box.

11. The registry will then be updated, and a new item will be added to your program group for the dbWeb Administrator. Following this, another message box is displayed asking if you would like to review the readme file. Click the Yes button (a good idea) to read the file or click the No button to exit the Setup program.

12. At this point you might think you are ready to roll, but you are not finished yet. Instead, you must configure the dbWeb service to start at system bootup. This is similar to the modifications you made for the TCP/IP Printing service, described in Chapter 5 in step 5 of the section titled "Installing the Microsoft TCP/IP Printing Service." The only difference is that the name of the service changes to dbWeb Service.

13. If you want to get to work with dbWeb now, click the Start button to start the dbWeb Service. Otherwise, the service will start automatically the next time you reboot.

14. Click the OK button to close the Services applet. Then close the Control Panel dialog, and you are ready to get to work as described in the next section, "Using the Microsoft dbWeb Administrator."

23

INTERFACING IIS WITH ODBC DATABASES

NOTE

If you are using a version of ODBC older than version 2.5, remember that you must install the new version as described below before you can use Microsoft dbWeb.

15. After a successful installation you may delete the dbweb11.exe file located in your temporary installation directory, although you should keep a copy of this file available on a network drive or a tape backup in case you need to reinstall dbWeb sometime in the future.

To install the Open Database Connectivity version 2.5 drivers, follow these steps:

1. Change to the ODBC32 subdirectory of your dbWeb installation. By default, this is %SystemRoot%\System32\InetSrv\dbWeb\ODBC32.

2. Execute the installation program, setup.exe. This displays the ODBC Driver Pack 3.0 Setup dialog.

3. Click the Continue button. A search will occur for previously installed components. Another ODBC Driver Pack 3.0 dialog is displayed that contains three buttons: Complete, Custom, and Change Folder.

4. The default installation directory for all files is the %SystemRoot%\System32. You should not change this setting unless you have previously installed ODBC files in another directory. To change the installation directory, click the Change Folder button. This displays the Change Folder dialog, where you may specify an alternate installation directory. Click the OK button to return to the ODBC Driver Pack 3.0 dialog.

5. Choose the Complete (recommended) button to install all components or the Custom button to specify which components to install. If you choose the Custom button, the ODBC Driver Pack 3.0–Custom dialog is displayed. You can choose which desktop ODBC drivers to install (MS Access, FoxPro and dBASE, Paradox, Text, or Excel), which server ODBC drivers to install (either SQL Server or Oracle), and various other components. When you have completed your modifications, click the Continue button.

6. The ODBC Driver Pack 3.0—Choose Program Group dialog is displayed. Choose an existing Program Manager group in the Existing Groups list box or enter a name for a new group in the Program Group field. Then click the Continue button.

7. A check is made to ensure that you have enough free space, that the files will be copied to your installation directories, and that the new icons and/or program group will be created.

8. The Data Sources dialog is displayed so that you can immediately add a new ODBC data source for use by any ODBC-compliant application. This topic is discussed later in this chapter in the section titled "Creating the ODBC Data Source"; for now, just click the Close button.

9. Finally, you are greeted with a successful setup confirmation message box. Just click the OK button to close the message box and exit the Setup program.

> **TIP**
>
> If you will be developing ODBC-compliant applications (Visual C++, Visual Basic, and so on), be sure to read the various readme files (located in the ODBC program group) for changes in using the ODBC 2.5 drivers.

Using the Microsoft dbWeb Administrator

Before you can actually create HTML documents to take advantage of Microsoft dbWeb, you must use the dbWeb Administrator to create your dbWeb schema. This means you must become familiar with the dbWeb Administrator, which is located in the Programs group. This is not really very difficult. In this section you will learn how to configure the dbWeb Administrator to tailor it for your use, how to create a dbWeb data source, and how to create a dbWeb schema so that you can access your ODBC database.

You might want to consider this as a discussion of the basic functions of the dbWeb Administrator, because you will not actually create a product you can use. Rather, this section is devoted to describing the various dialoges, data types, and dbWeb methods to give you an understanding of how to use dbWeb with your custom ODBC databases. In the section "Creating a Custom Guest Book Using Microsoft dbWeb," you learn, by example, how to use dbWeb to create a form-driven guest book that uses a SQL Server database.

Configuring dbWeb Preferences

You should set basic configuration options before using the dbWeb Administrator to actually create your ODBC data source and database schema. By setting these properties beforehand, you will not need to change the individual properties for your dbWeb data sources and database schemas later. These properties are divided into two sections. First, you can specify the basic properties for the dbWeb Administrator. Second, you can specify the properties that define how the dbWeb server (the actual service that performs the real work) will operate.

Specifying the dbWeb Administrator Properties

To set the dbWeb Administrator options, choose Preferences from the Edit menu to display the Administrator Preferences dialog. (See Figure 23.4.) Then follow these steps:

1. If the default Access database (dbWeb.MDB)is not suitable to hold your dbWeb schemas, you can change the name in the Default Schema Database field. The only real reason to change this entry, however, is if you will be sharing a schema database. You might have multiple IIS servers on your network and want to share a single schema database, for example.

FIGURE 23.4.

Specifying the Microsoft dbWeb preferences.

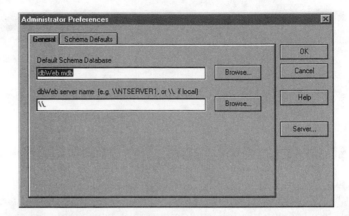

> **NOTE**
>
> If you share a single schema database, you must also make sure that all ODBC data source names match on each computer. Otherwise, dbWeb will be unable to access the ODBC database and will generate error messages instead of the expected HTML code.

2. If you will be using dbWeb with a remote IIS server, you should also change the name in the dbWeb server name field to correspond to the computer name of the IIS server (\\SRV, for example).

3. Click the Schema Defaults tab to display the properties sheet shown in Figure 23.5.

FIGURE 23.5.

Specifying the default schema properties.

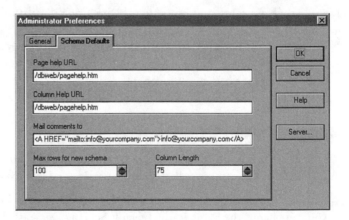

4. Each dbWeb HTML page may have an HTML Web page associated with it to display information concerning how to use the displayed page. To assign a default help page,

you can specify a relative path and filename in the Page help URL field. This page is accessed from the Help button inserted onto the page by dbWeb.

5. Each column of information displayed on a dbWeb HTML page may also have an HTML Web page associated with it to display information describing the columns of data on the displayed page. This is another help file for the page but is accessed any time a column header is selected on a page created by dbWeb. In essence, each column will have a hypertext link associated with it to access a specific HTML help document. If there is no specific document, the default document will be displayed. To assign a default column help page, you can specify a relative path and filename in the Column Help URL field.

> **TIP**
>
> Because the information displayed by the default page and column is used for any dbWeb page where you have not given specific instructions, you should create generic page and generic column HTML help files. You might, for example, want to create HTML pages that will inform the user that the help pages have been inadvertently omitted. This help page could include a bit of text with a hypertext link to e-mail the Web administrator. After receiving the message, the Web administrator can create the custom page and column help files.

6. To enable users who access your Web pages to send you e-mail, change the references in the Mail comments to field to your e-mail address. For users to send e-mail to me, for example, I have changed the tag

```
<A HREF="info@yourcompany.com"> info@yourcompany.com</A>
```

to the tag

```
<A HREF="mailto:webmaster@nt-guru.com">webmaster@nt-guru.com</A>
```

7. To specify the default maximum number of rows to be displayed by a query, just change the number in the Max rows for new schema field.

8. To specify the default width of a column, which will also determine the size of the edit box displayed on a form, enter a new value in the Column Length field. This field can be overridden on a column-by-column basis as you create your forms, but you should choose a value that represents the most commonly used field size in your databases to save a little time editing the various properties sheets.

9. Click the Close button to save your changes and return to the dbWeb Administrator.

Specifying the dbWeb Server Properties

After you have specified the default configuration options for the dbWeb Administrator, turn your attention to the default behavior of the dbWeb service. To specify these properties, choose

Preferences from the Edit menu to display the Administrator Preferences dialog. Click the Server button to display the Server Preferences dialog. (See Figure 23.6.)

FIGURE 23.6.

Specifying the dbWeb server properties.

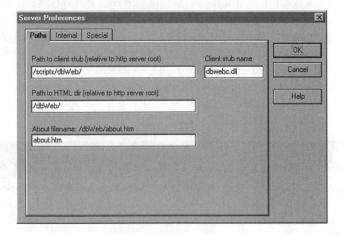

Then follow these steps:

1. Check the Paths properties. (You should not have to change any of these options unless you experience problems with the dbWeb service finding its files or finding your HTML files, or you have created a custom dynamic link library to replace the default client stub.)

   ■ Path to client stub—Specifies the relative (to the IIS WWWRoot directory) path of the dbWeb client stub.

   ■ Client stub name—Specifies the name of the dbWeb client stub. The client stub is an ISAPI DLL (dbwebc.dll). This DLL is responsible for connecting to the ODBC database, for processing the ODBC query, and for building the HTML pages that are eventually displayed on your client's Web browser.

   ■ Path to HTML dir—Specifies the relative (to the IIS WWWRoot directory) path for your HTML files.

   ■ About filename—Specifies the name of the HTML file used to describe dbWeb.

2. Click the Internal tab to display the Internal properties sheet, shown in Figure 23.7, where you can configure the following options:

   ■ Beep on error—Specifies that when a dbWeb error occurs, a beep sound should be played. This can be used to notify a site administrator (at the computer where dbWeb is installed) that errors are occurring in real time. The site administrator can then look at the application event log to determine the cause.

   ■ Maximum concurrent users—Specifies the maximum number of users who can access dbWeb at one time. Unless you expect to support only a maximum of five users at a time, you should change this value. This setting really requires a bit of trial and error to set properly. A starting value of 10 is sufficient for most sites. If you have a very active site, however, you will want to increase this value to support anywhere from 25 to 100 concurrent users.

FIGURE 23.7.

Specifying the dbWeb server internal properties.

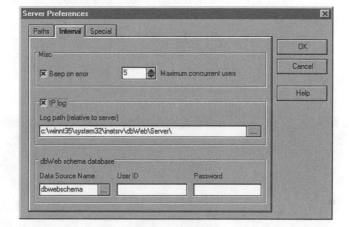

- IP log—Check this box, and the Log path field will become active. The file specified in the log path will be used to capture information from your connected clients, such as their TCP/IP addresses, and store it as a text file.

TIP

If you manage a high-volume site, you can improve performance by disabling the IP log check box. However, by disabling IP logging, you will lose the ability to track your database activity based on an IP address.

- dbWeb schema database—This group field includes the following fields that can be used to define the characteristics of the ODBC data source used by dbWeb:
  - Data Source Name—Specifies the data source name used by dbWeb to access the schema database. By default, this is dbwebschema.
  - User ID—Specifies the username to be used to access the schema database.
  - Password—Specifies the password to be used in conjunction with the user name to access the schema database.

3. Click the Special tab to display the properties sheet shown in Figure 23.8, where you can specify the following options:
   - HTML header type—This drop-down list box includes two choices: Full and Custom. The default is Full, and when selected, dbWeb will display its own default HTML headers. If this is not acceptable, you can choose Custom. If you

choose the Custom setting, the information you enter in the following fields will be used:

- Custom access header—Specifies custom HTML code to be displayed as the document header whenever a client accesses an ODBC database using dbWeb.

- Custom secure header—Specifies custom HTML code to be displayed as the document header whenever a client accesses an ODBC database that requires a user account and password as defined by the custom properties for the ODBC database using dbWeb.

FIGURE 23.8.

Specifying the dbWeb server special properties.

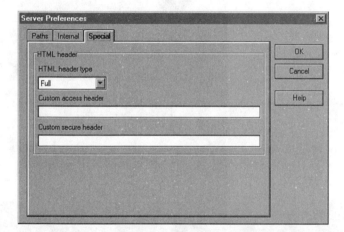

TIP

One of the many reasons to use a custom access header or a custom secure access header is to display a user-customized greeting message. When a user connects to an ODBC database that requires user authentication (meaning a valid user account and password), your HTML-secure custom header could display his name as part of the document header. You could display similar greetings, warnings, or other textual content with the custom access header.

---

4. Click the OK button to return to the Administrator Properties dialog. Then click the OK button to return to the dbWeb Administrator.

Creating the ODBC Data Source

The first step in the chain to getting the dbWeb server to actually create Web pages for you is to define the ODBC data source. The ODBC data source specifies information to access the actual database and displays information about the database as well. For an Access database, for example, this could include the actual path and filename of the database and of the system database (used for record locking), and other options. Each ODBC data source may have unique properties associated with it, so you'll have to play it by ear when configuring the data source and fill out the information requested by the dialogs for each type of ODBC driver you choose.

Defining the ODBC System Data Source

A SQL Server database is the most likely type of database to be used. This is because SQL Server includes much more functionality and increased performance in a multiuser environment. Before you can create the ODBC data source, you must create an ODBC-compliant database. (For this discussion, I'll assume you have already created the database.) The next step is to create the link between the dbWeb Administrator and your ODBC database by performing the following steps:

1. Select the Data Sources and Schemas entry in the Data Sources window of the dbWeb Administrator.
2. The buttons on the top of the window now include a New Datasource button. Click this button to display the Data Source dialog.
3. Click the Manage button to display the Data Sources dialog.
4. Click the System DSN button to display the System Data Sources dialog.
5. Click the Add button to display the Add Data Source dialog.
6. Select the SQL Server entry in the Installed ODBC Drivers list box. Then click the OK button.
7. The ODBC SQL Server Setup dialog appears. Click the Expand button to expand the dialog. (See Figure 23.9.)

FIGURE 23.9.

Specifying the dbWeb system data source name.

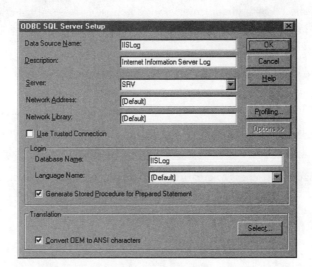

8. In the Data Source Name field, enter a unique name (such as IISLogs).

9. In the Description field, enter a comment to describe the DSN.

10. Specify the SQL Server to connect to in the Server field.

11. Normally, the default Network Address (for Microsoft SQL Server this is a named pipe that, by default, uses the form of *ServerName*\\pipe\\sql\\query, where *ServerName* is the computer name of the SQL Server installation) and Network Library (for Microsoft SQL Server, this is DBNMPTW.DLL, which will use named pipes) fields should be left as they appear. If you will be using more than one type of connection to SQL Server databases, you may need to change these values. To determine the correct entries, you should consult with the SQL Server administrator of the SQL Server installation to which you want to connect.

12. To ensure the integrity of your connection to SQL Server, you can enable the Use Trusted Connection check box. This check box is applicable only to Microsoft SQL Server 6.0 or higher. A trusted connection is a means of authenticating the connection between dbWeb and your SQL Server database based on the supplied user name and password. This option is applicable only when you utilize named pipes or the multi-protocol, SQL Server network libraries.

> **NOTE**
>
> The Generate Stored Procedure for Prepared Statement check box is an ODBC performance enhancement and should be left enabled. This option will create and precompile any SQL Server procedures that may be used. If this option is disabled, the procedure will be created and compiled on demand. The Convert OEM to ANSI characters check box provides translations of the IBM-PC OEM character set to the Windows ANSI character set and should be enabled unless your database makes use of high-order (above character 128) graphics characters in the PC OEM character set.

13. In the Database Name field, enter the name of the SQL Server database you created (such as IISLogs).

14. Click the OK button to return to the System Data Source dialog.

15. Click the Close button to return to the System Data Source dialog.

16. Click the Close button to return to the Data Source dialog.

And that's all there is to creating an ODBC data source name. If you will be using a different ODBC database, just choose the ODBC driver in step 4 to match your ODBC-compliant database.

Specifying the Data Source Profile Properties

After you have created the ODBC data source, you need to configure the dbWeb Administrator to use the data source. This consists of three configuration steps and one informational step. They are as follows:

1. Select the Data Sources and Schemas entry in the Data Sources window of the dbWeb Administrator.

2. The buttons on the top of the window now include a New Datasource button. Click this button to display the Data Source dialog, as shown in Figure 23.10.

FIGURE 23.10.

Creating a dbWeb system data source.

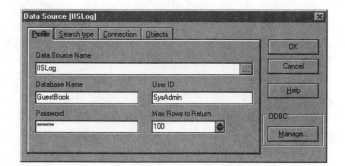

3. In the Profile properties sheet, fill out the following fields:

   ■ Data Source Name—Specifies the name of the ODBC data source to use. This should be the same name as the database you specified in step 8 of the section "Defining the ODBC System Data Source."

TIP

If you click the ... button, the ODBC Data Sources dialog will appear. You can select an ODBC data source from the list, and when you click the OK button, the data source name will be automatically entered in the Data Source Name field.

   ■ Database Name—Depending on the type of ODBC database used, this field may not be relevant. For a SQL Server database, however, this should be the name of the table contained within the SQL Server database to be accessed.

   ■ User ID—Specifies the user account to be used to access the specified database.

   ■ Password—Specifies the password to be supplied with the user account to authorize access to the database.

   ■ Max Rows to Return—Specifies the maximum number of rows to be returned in a single query.

4. Click the Search type tab to display the Search type properties sheet, where you can choose between using the default search order as defined by your database or to always perform case-insensitive searches.

5. Click the Connection tab to display the Connection properties sheet, where you can specify a timeout value between concurrent connections, to always disconnect between concurrent queries, and to use a secure connection. A secure connection specifies that the Web browser display a login screen on which you can specify a user name and password. This user name and password will be used to access the ODBC database.

6. Click the Objects tab to display the Objects properties sheet, where the objects in your database (tables, views, and procedures) will be displayed. This is an informative display only.

7. Click the OK button to create your data source and return to the dbWeb Data Source window.

Creating the Database Schema

Creating your database schema is where the real work of using the dbWeb Administrator occurs. But it is not going to be as bad as you think, because Microsoft has utilized the Wizard technology introduced with Windows 95 to make creating a database schema easier. After you create the schema, however, you will need to fine-tune it to meet your specifications. The basic process to create your database schema is as follows:

1. Select your data source in the Data Sources window. Then click the New Schema button.

2. The New Schema dialog appears, as shown in Figure 23.11. Click the Schema Wizard button.

FIGURE 23.11.

Creating a new schema.

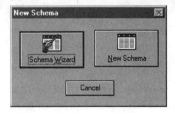

3. The Choose a table dialog appears, as shown in Figure 23.12. Select the desired table in the Tables field and click the Next button.

4. The Choose the data columns to query dialog appears, as shown in Figure 23.13. Select the column you want to use in your query by example form in the Available fields list.

5. Click the > button to move the selected field to the Fields on QBE form list.

FIGURE 23.12.

Choosing tables for the new schema.

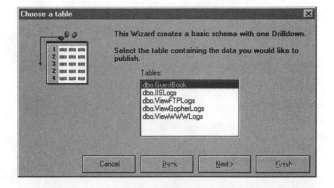

FIGURE 23.13.

Choosing columns to use in the query by example form.

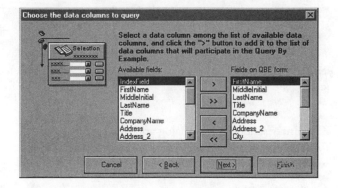

6. Repeat steps 4 and 5 for each field in the table you want to use. Then click the Next button.

TIP

Click the >> button to move all of the columns listed in the Available fields list to the Fields on QBE form list.

---

7. The Choose tabular form data columns dialog appears. Select the column you want to use in your query by example form in the Available fields list.

8. Click the > button to move the selected field to the Fields on Tabular form list.

9. Repeat steps 7 and 8 for each field in the table you want to use. Then click the Next button.

10. The Specify a Drilldown Automatic Link dialog appears, shown in Figure 23.14.

11. Choose a column in the Fields list to use as the link to jump to the next item (drilldown) in the hierarchical level of your table. Then choose the Next button. By default, this drilldown link will be specified as a zoom to the same schema, meaning that it will display multiple records with the same field.

FIGURE 23.14.

Specifying the drilldown link.

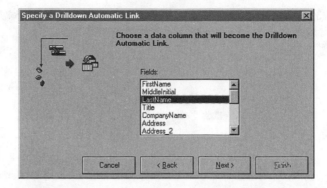

NOTE

You can change this property to specify no drilldown, a static link to a URL, a dynamic link specified in the table column, a zoom to the same schema, or a jump to another schema by specifying the property for the field in the Tabular properties sheet.

---

12. The Enter schema name dialog appears, as shown in Figure 23.15. Enter a unique (within the schema) name and click the Finish button to return to the Data Sources window of the dbWeb Administrator.

FIGURE 23.15.

The final touch to building the schema.

Repeat steps 1 through 12 for each table within the database for which you want to create a schema. After you create all of your schemas, you can fine-tune the individual properties, which include

- Database schema properties
- Schema tables
- Schema joins and constraints

- Schema query-by-example properties
- Schema tabular form properties
- Schema freeform properties
- Schema insert/update/delete form properties
- Schema custom HTML form properties

Specifying the Database Schema Properties

The default properties you specified when you configured the dbWeb Administrator are used to set some of the default properties for your schemas. These defaults are useful because, if you forget to define a specific Web help page for your page (or column) help pages, the defaults will be used instead. This way, your Internet clients will not see an error message. Instead, they'll be greeted by your custom help file that verifies the omission of a specific help page and requests the client to e-mail the Web administrator to correct the omission. There are other useful tidbits of information you may want to define for each schema as well. To do so, follow these steps:

1. Double-click a data source (such as IISLogs) to expand it and display the schemas below the data source name.

2. Select the schema (such as GuestBook) and click the Modify Schema button. The dialog shown in Figure 23.16 then appears.

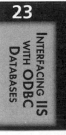

FIGURE 23.16.

Configuring the database schema properties.

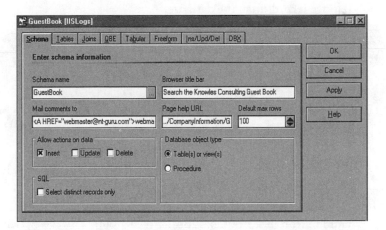

3. The name of the schema is displayed in the Schema name field. If you decide that your original schema name is unsatisfactory, you can change it by clicking the unnamed button to the right of the Schema name field. This displays the Schema Name dialog. Enter the new name in the Schema name field and click the OK button to return to the Schema properties sheet.

4. To specify a title to be displayed in the caption bar of the client Web browser, enter a value in the Browser title bar field.

5. To specify an e-mail address to be displayed on the bottom of the Web page created by dbWeb, change the HTML tag in the Mail comments to field. The default tag may not be applicable for all schemas, and you may need to change it based on the page content. You might have a Web page to sell products and want any e-mail to be sent to `sales@yourcompany.com`, for example.

6. To specify a custom help file to be accessed from the Help button created by dbWeb, enter a relative URL in the Page help URL field. A relative URL is based on the default directory of `WWWRoot\DbWeb`, so if you place your help file in a different subdirectory, such as `WWWRoot\CompanyInformation`, your entry should look something like

   `../CompanyInformation/GuestBookQBEPageHelp.htm`

   You can also use an absolute URL, such as

   `http://www.nt-guru.com/CompanyInformation/GuestBookQBEPageHelp.htm`

7. To specify the maximum number of rows to be returned in a single query, enter the value in the Default max rows field.

8. To specify the types of actions an Internet client can perform on your database, enable the appropriate check box in the Allow actions on data group. This can be Insert to add records to the database, Update to modify records in the database, or Delete to remove records from the database.

> **CAUTION**
>
> Allowing someone to update or delete records in your database could be asking for trouble. A malicious user could stop by and have a bit of fun if you allow just anyone to update or delete information. If you do support these options, you should also use the Secure Connection option (accessible from the Data Source Connection tab) to validate the user.

9. To limit the returned rows to single instances of a record, enable the Select distinct records only option in the SQL group.

10. To specify the type of database objects the schema will define, enable the appropriate radio button in the Database object type group. This can be Table(s) or view(s) to define access to tables, views, or querydefs contained within the database. It can also be Procedure if you want to define access to executable functions contained within the database.

11. When you have completed your definitions, click the OK button to accept your modifications and return to the Data Sources window, or click the Apply button to immediately update the schema with your changes. This is useful when you are making continuous modifications and testing each action.

Specifying the Schema Tables

Most databases include more than one table, and many of these tables are related to one another. In order to define how the schema will display data in such a situation, you might need to configure it to include multiple tables. This can be accomplished by following these steps:

1. Double-click a data source (such as dbpubs) to expand it and display the schemas below the data source name.

2. Select the schema (such as Author_Titles) and click the Modify Schema button. Click the Tables tab to display the properties sheet shown in Figure 23.17.

FIGURE 23.17.

Specifying the tables for the database schema.

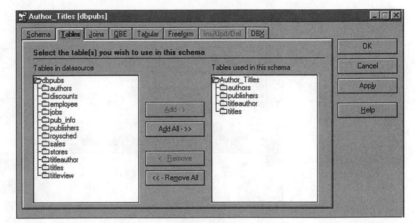

3. The tables contained within the database will be displayed in the Tables in datasource list box. To specify an individual table to use with your schema, select it and click the Add button to copy the table definition to the Tables used in this schema list box.

4. Repeat step 3 for each table to add to the schema. To add all of the tables, click the Add All button. To remove a table definition, select the table in the Tables used in this schema list box and click the Remove button.

5. When you have completed your definitions, click the OK button to accept your modifications and return to the Data Sources window, or click the Apply button to immediately update the schema with your changes. This is useful when you are making continuous modifications and testing each action.

Specifying the Schema Joins and Constraints

If you have multiple tables that you want to combine into a single table, you must define a join. A *join* is where two or more tables have records with a common field. This common field is used to link these records. The dbWeb sample pubs database, for example, uses the author_id field to define a relationship between the author table and the titles table. The pubs database also uses the pub_id field to define a relationship between the titles table and the publishers

23

INTERFACING IIS
WITH ODBC
DATABASES

table. This relationship is used to combine the three tables to display the author, title, publisher, and other relevant information. If these tables were accessed separately, the information would not be nearly as useful to the reader. To create a join, you must first have defined multiple tables for the schema, as described in the previous section, "Specifying the Schema Tables." When that has been accomplished you can define your joins by following these steps:

1. Double-click a data source (such as `dbpubs`) to expand it and display the schemas below the data source name.

2. Select the schema (such as `Author_Titles`) and click the Modify Schema button. Click the Joins tab to display the properties sheet shown in Figure 23.18.

FIGURE 23.18.

Specifying the table joins for the database schema.

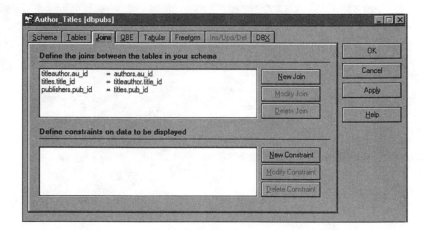

3. To define a new join, click the New Join button and the Joins dialog will be displayed. (See Figure 23.19.)

FIGURE 23.19.

Creating a new join.

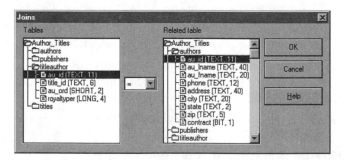

4. Select a table in the Tables list. Double-click the table to expand it and display the individual table columns. Select the appropriate column (such as `au_id`).

5. Select a table in the Related table list box. Double-click the table to expand it and display the individual table columns. Select the appropriate column (such as `au_id`).

6. Specify the join type using the drop-down list box.

7. Click the OK button to create the join and return to the Joins properties sheet. To modify an existing join, select the join and click the Modify Join button. To delete an existing join, select the join and click the Delete Join button.

> **NOTE**
>
> Modifying or deleting a join will affect the query by example, tabular, freeform, insert/update/delete, and custom forms you create. So use care when designing and creating your joins. Otherwise, you may spend more time rebuilding your forms than you do accomplishing any useful work.

8. When you have completed your definitions, click the OK button to accept your modifications and return to the Data Sources window or click the Apply button to immediately update the schema with your changes. This is useful when you are making continuous modifications and testing each action.

You can also specify a constraint on the returned records. A *constraint* is a set of rules that defines a set of values that the record must follow in order to be included in the result set returned by the query. You may want to make sure that no author records with a null (or empty) au_id field will be returned. This is accomplished by following these steps:

1. Follow steps 1 and 2 in the section about specifying the schema joins and constraints to create a new join. Then click the New Constraint button to display the Constraints dialog. (See Figure 23.20.)

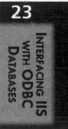
23

INTERFACING IIS
WITH ODBC
DATABASES

FIGURE 23.20.

Creating a table constraint.

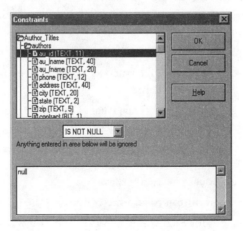

2. Select a table and double-click the table to expand it and display the individual table columns. Select the appropriate column (such as au_id).

3. Specify the constraint type using the drop-down list box.

4. A default specification will be entered in the lower list box, with a brief description of the requirements below the drop-down list box. Change the default specification to meet your constraint requirements.

NOTE

Even if your constraint does not require a specification, such as in this example, you must enter a value in the lower list box. Otherwise, the OK button will remain disabled, and you will be unable to create the constraint.

---

5. Click the OK button to create the constraint and return to the Joins properties sheet. To modify an existing constraint, select the constraint and click the Modify Constraint button. To delete an existing constraint, select the constraint and click the Delete Constraint button.

6. After you have completed your definitions, click the OK button to accept your modifications and return to the Data Sources window or click the Apply button to immediately update the schema with your changes. This is useful when you are making continuous modifications and testing each action.

Specifying the Schema Query-By-Example Properties

The *query-by-example* (QBE) form is the most useful form provided by dbWeb. It is used to search your database based on user-supplied search criteria. You can define the search fields, the types of searches the user may perform, column heads, and other relevant information. Before you do so, however, you must first have defined the tables, joins, and constraints as described in the previous sections. Otherwise, you will not obtain the desired results. To define your QBE form, follow these steps:

1. Double-click a data source (such as IISLogs) to expand it and display the schemas below the data source name.

2. Select the schema (such as GuestBook) and click the Modify Schema button. Click the QBE tab to display the properties sheet shown in Figure 23.21.

3. Select a table in the Data columns in selected tables list box. Double-click the table to expand it and display the individual table columns. Select the appropriate column (such as dbo.GuestBook.FirstName).

4. Click the Add button to add the column to the QBE data columns list box.

5. Repeat step 3 for each column in the table you want to display in your QBE form.

FIGURE 23.21.
Specifying the columns to be used in the query-by-example form.

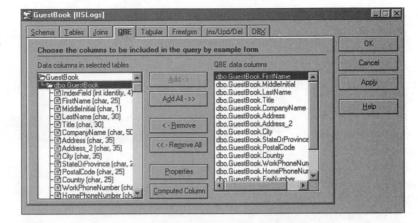

6. Repeat steps 3 and 4 for each table. If you will use all the columns in all of the tables, click the Add All button to copy all of the table and column definitions to the QBE data columns list box.

TIP

The order in which tables and columns are added to the QBE data columns list box also defines the order in which they will be displayed on the QBE form. If you need to modify the order later, you can change the sequence by setting the `Col` sequence and `Row` sequence properties.

---

7. To create a column to be displayed on the QBE form based on a computed value, click the Computed Column button to display the Computed Column Expression Builder dialog. This will let you select the columns to use as the base, the expression that will create the computed column, and the resulting data type.

8. To modify the column properties, select the column in the QBE data columns list box and click the Properties button.

9. A Properties dialog, as shown in Figure 23.22, is displayed.

10. At the top of the dialog is a drop-down list box that determines which properties for the columns and QBE form will be displayed. This can be All properties to include both column and form properties, Column Properties to display just column properties, or QBE Form Properties to display just the form-related properties. These properties are summarized in Table 23.1.

11. After modifying the properties for the column, click the Close button in the Properties dialog to return to the QBE properties sheet.

12. Repeat steps 8 through 11 for each column.

13. When you have completed your definitions and modified the column properties, click the OK button to accept your modifications and return to the Data Sources window or click the Apply button to immediately update the schema with your changes. This is useful when you are making continuous modifications and testing each action.

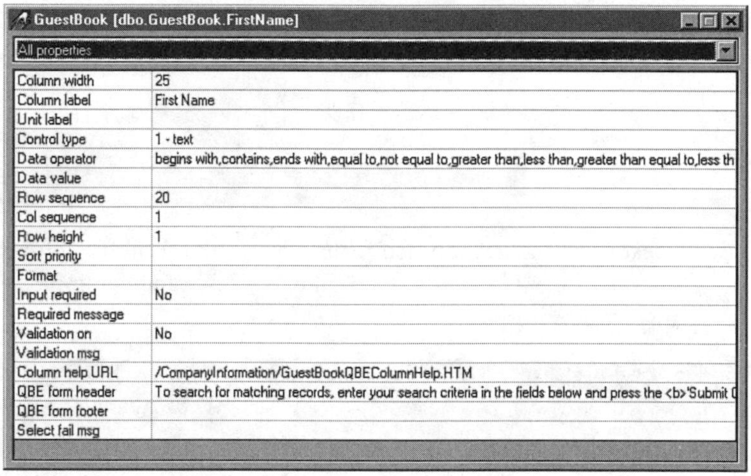

FIGURE 23.22.

Specifying the column properties.

Table 23.1. The QBE properties.

Name	Description	Note
Column width	Specifies the maximum width for data entry.	
Column label	Specifies a label, to the left of the form input field, to be displayed for the column.	By default, this value is the actual name of your column. To provide a more intuitive look to your form, you should change this value.
Unit label	Specifies a label to be displayed to the right of the form input field.	
Control type	Specifies the type of data.	This value can be 1 for text, 2 for a radio button, 3 for a list box, 4 for a combo box, or 5 for a check box.

Name	Description	Note
Data operator	Specifies the search methods to be employed.	This can be begins with, contains, ends with, equal to, not equal to, greater than, less than, greater than or equal to, less than or equal to, >, >=, <, <=, =, or <>.
Data value	Specifies a default value to be displayed for the column.	
Row sequence	Specifies the row order of the column.	
Col sequence	Specifies the column sequence to be displayed on the form.	By default, this value is always 1.
Row height	Specifies the height of the input form to be displayed on the form.	By default, this value is always 1.
Sort priority	Specifies a sort order.	
Format	Specifies a format mask for the data.	
Input required	Specifies that the field must have a value to be accepted.	Values can be No or Yes. The default is No.
Required message	Specifies the message to be displayed if the field is a required field and the user does not enter a value.	
Validation on	Specifies that the data must match the format specified in the Format property to be accepted.	Values can be Yes or No. The default is No.

23

INTERFACING IIS WITH ODBC DATABASES

continues

Table 23.1. continued

Name	Description	Note
Validation msg	Specifies a message to be displayed if the column does not match the valid format.	
Column help URL	Specifies a relative URL, or an absolute URL if desired, to be displayed when the column hot link is activated.	
QBE form header	Specifies a custom header to be displayed on the top of the Web page instead of the default dbWeb header.	
QBE form trailer	Specifies a custom message to be displayed on the bottom of the Web page in addition to the default dbWeb trailer.	
Select fail msg	Specifies a custom message to be displayed if the query fails.	

Specifying the Schema Tabular Form Properties

The tabular form is used to display the database result set returned by the query as a series of records. Before you can create a tabular form, however, you must have defined the tables, joins, and constraints as described in the previous sections. To define your tabular form, follow these steps:

1. Double-click a data source (such as IISLogs) to expand it and display the schemas below the data source name.

2. Select the schema (such as GuestBook) and click the Modify Schema button. Click the Tabular tab to display the properties sheet shown in Figure 23.23.

3. Select a table in the Data columns in selected tables list box. Double-click the table to expand it and display the individual table columns. Select the appropriate column (such as dbo.GuestBook.FirstName).

FIGURE 23.23.

Specifying the columns to be used in the tabular form.

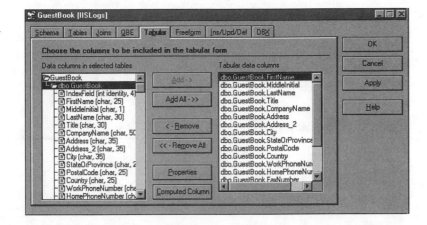

4. Click the Add button to add the column to the Tabular data columns list box.

5. Repeat step 3 for each column in the table you want to display in your tabular form.

6. Repeat steps 3 and 4 for each table. If you will use all the columns in all of the tables, just click the Add All button to copy all of the table and column definitions to the Tabular data columns list box.

> **TIP**
>
> The order in which tables and columns are added to the Tabular data columns list box also defines the order in which they will be displayed on the tabular form. If you need to modify the order later, you can change the sequence by setting the Col sequence property.

7. To create a column to be displayed on the Tabular form based on a computed value, click the Computed Column button to display the Computed Column Expression Builder dialog. This will let you select the columns to use as the base, the expression to create the computed column, and the resulting data type.

8. To modify the column properties, select the column in the Tabular data columns list box and click the Properties button.

9. A Properties dialog, similar to that shown in Figure 23.22, will be displayed.

10. At the top of the dialog is a drop-down list box that determines which properties for the columns and tabular form will be displayed. This can be All properties to include both column and form properties, Column Properties to display just column properties, or Tabular Form Properties to display just the form-related properties. These properties are summarized in Table 23.2.

11. After modifying the properties for the column, click the Close button on the Properties dialog to return to the Tabular properties sheet.

12. Repeat steps 8 through 11 for each column.

13. When you have completed your definitions and modified the column properties, click the OK button to accept your modifications and return to the Data Sources window or click the Apply button to immediately update the schema with your changes. This is useful when you are making continuous modifications and testing each action.

Table 23.2. The Tabular properties.

Name	*Description*	*Note*
Display when	Specifies when to display the column.	Value can be Always, Default on, or Default off.
Column width	Specifies the maximum width for data entry.	
Column label	Specifies a label, to the left of the form input field, to be displayed for the column.	By default, this value is the actual name of your column. To provide a more intuitive look to your form you should change this value.
Col sequence	Specifies the column sequence to be displayed on the form.	By default, this value is always 1.
Row height	Specifies the height of the input form to be displayed on the form.	By default, this value is always 1.
Sort priority	Specifies a sort order.	
Format	Specifies a format mask for the data.	
Column help URL	Specifies a relative URL, or an absolute URL if desired, to be displayed when the column hot link is activated.	

Name	Description	Note
Automatic Link URL	Specifies the type of link to execute when the column is selected.	Choosing this property will display the Automatic Link From dialog where you may specify the type of link (None, Static, Dynamic, Drilldown, or Schema link) and the link properties.
Tabular page header	Specifies a custom header to be displayed on the top of the Web page instead of the default dbWeb header.	
Tabular page trailer	Specifies a custom message to be displayed on the bottom of the Web page in addition to the default dbWeb trailer.	

Specifying the Schema Freeform Properties

The *freeform* form is used to display the database result set returned by the query in series of records displayed in a column-, rather than row-, oriented fashion. It is usually invoked when the user enables the Use full-screen output even if more than one row is returned check box on the QBE form. Before you can create a freeform form, however, you must first have defined the tables, joins, and constraints as described in the previous sections. To define your freeform form, follow these steps:

1. Double-click a data source (such as IISLogs) to expand it and display the schemas below the data source name.

2. Select the schema (such as GuestBook) and click the Modify Schema button. Click the Freeform tab to display the properties sheet shown in Figure 23.24.

3. Select a table in the Data columns in selected tables list box. Double-click the table to expand it and display the individual table columns. Select the appropriate column (such as dbo.GuestBook.FirstName).

4. Click the Add button to add the column to the Freeform data columns list box.

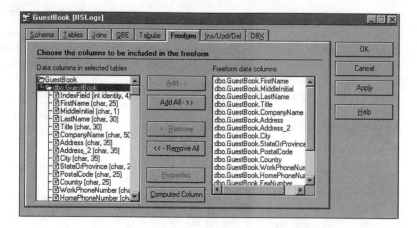

5. Repeat step 3 for each column in the table you want to display in your freeform form.

6. Repeat steps 3 and 4 for each table. If you will use all the columns in all of the tables, click the Add All button to copy all of the table and column definitions to the Freeform data columns list box.

TIP

The order in which tables and columns are added to the Freeform data columns list box also defines the order in which they will be displayed on the freeform form. If you need to modify the order later, you can change the sequence by setting the Row sequence and Col sequence properties.

7. To create a column to be displayed on the freeform form based on a computed value, click the Computed Column button to display the Computed Column Expression Builder dialog. This will let you select the columns to use as the base, the expression to create the computed column, and the resulting data type.

8. To modify the column properties, select the column in the Freeform data columns list box and click the Properties button.

9. A Properties dialog, similar to that shown in Figure 23.22, will be displayed.

10. At the top of the dialog is a drop-down list box that determines which properties for the columns and freeform form will be displayed. This can be All properties to include both column and form properties, Column Properties to display just column properties, or Freeform Form Properties to display just the form-related properties. These properties are summarized in Table 23.3.

11. After modifying the properties for the column, click the Close button on the Properties dialog to return to the Tabular properties sheet.

12. Repeat steps 8 through 11 for each column.

13. When you have completed your definitions and modified the column properties, click the OK button to accept your modifications and return to the Data Sources window or click the Apply button to immediately update the schema with your changes. This is useful when you are making continuous modifications and testing each action.

Table 23.3. The Freeform properties.

Name	*Description*	*Note*
`Column width`	Specifies the maximum width for data entry.	
`Column label`	Specifies a label, to the left of the form input field, to be displayed for the column.	By default, this value is the actual name of your column. To provide a more intuitive look to your form you should change this value.
`Row sequence`	Specifies the row order of the column.	
`Col sequence`	Specifies the column sequence to be displayed on the form.	By default, this value is always 1.
`Row height`	Specifies the height of the input form to be displayed on the form.	By default, this value is always 1.
`Sort priority`	Specifies a sort order.	
`Format`	Specifies a format mask for the data.	
`Column help URL`	Specifies a relative URL, or an absolute URL if desired, to be displayed when the column hot link is activated.	

continues

23

INTERFACING IIS
WITH ODBC
DATABASES

Table 23.3. continued

Name	Description	Note
Automatic Link URL	Specifies the type of link to execute when the column is selected.	Choosing this property will display the Automatic Link From dialog where you may specify the type of link (None, Static, Dynamic, Drilldown, or Schema) and the link properties.
Freeform page header	Specifies a custom header to be displayed on the top of the Web page instead of the default dbWeb header.	
Freeform page trailer	Specifies a custom message to be displayed on the bottom of the Web page in addition to the default dbWeb trailer.	
Freeform record header	Specifies a custom header to be displayed at the top of each record.	

Specifying the Schema Insert/Update/Delete Form Properties

The Ins/Upd/Del (Insert/Update/Delete) form is used to insert, update, or delete records in your database. This form is accessed by choosing a radio button (Insert, Update, or Delete) next to the Submit or Reset form buttons displayed at the bottom of the Web page for a tabular result set or a Web page with a freeform record layout. After the radio button has been selected and the user clicks the form Submit button, the Ins/Upd/Del form is displayed. Before you can create an Ins/Upd/Del form, however, you must first have defined the tables, joins, and constraints as described in the previous sections. To define your Ins/Upd/Del form, follow these steps:

1. Double-click a data source (such as IISLogs) to expand it and display the schemas below the data source name.

2. Select the schema (such as GuestBook) and click the Modify Schema button. Click the Ins/Upd/Del tab to display the properties sheet shown in Figure 23.25.

FIGURE 23.25.

Specifying the columns to be used in the Insert/ Update/Delete form.

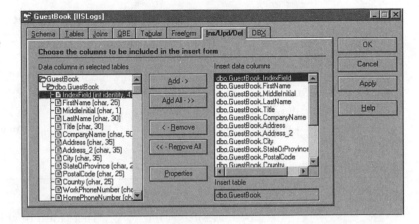

3. Select a table in the Data columns in selected tables list box. Double-click the table to expand it and display the individual table columns. Select the appropriate column (such as `dbo.GuestBook.FirstName`).

4. Click the Add button to add the column to the Insert data columns list box.

5. Repeat step 3 for each column in the table you want to display in your Ins/Upd/Del form.

6. Repeat steps 3 and 4 for each table. If you will use all the columns in all of the tables, click the Add All button to copy all of the table and column definitions to the Insert data columns list box.

> **TIP**
>
> The order in which tables and columns are added to the Insert data columns list box also defines the order in which they will be displayed on the Ins/Upd/Del form. If you need to modify the order later, you can change the sequence by setting the Row sequence and Col sequence properties.

7. To modify the column properties, select the column in the Insert data columns list box and click the Properties button.

8. A Properties dialog, similar to that shown in Figure 23.22, will be displayed.

9. At the top of the dialog is a drop-down list box that determines which properties for the columns and Ins/Upd/Del form will be displayed. This can be All properties to include both column and form properties, Column Properties to display just column properties, or Ins/Upd/Del Form Properties to display just the form-related properties. These properties are summarized in Table 23.4.

10. After modifying the properties for the column, click the Close button on the Properties dialog to return to the Ins/Upd/Del properties sheet.

11. Repeat steps 8 through 10 for each column.

12. When you have completed your definitions and modified the column properties, click the OK button to accept your modifications and return to the Data Sources window or click the Apply button to immediately update the schema with your changes. This is useful when you are making continuous modifications and testing each action.

Table 23.4. The Ins/Upd/Del properties.

Name	*Description*	*Note*
Key	Specifies whether the field is an index field.	There must be at least one unique index field in order to update or delete a record. The key property can be set to none, non-updatable, updatable, or counter.
Column width	Specifies the maximum width for data entry.	
Column label	Specifies a label, to the left of the form input field, to be displayed for the column.	By default, this value is the actual name of your column. To provide a more intuitive look to your form you should change this value.
Unit label	Specifies a label to be displayed to the right of the form input field.	
Control type	Specifies the type of data.	This will be 1 for text, 2 for a radio button, 3 for a list box, 4 for a combo box, or 5 for a check box. It cannot be changed on this form.
Data value	Specifies a default value to be displayed for the column.	

Name	Description	Note
Row sequence	Specifies the row order of the column.	
Col sequence	Specifies the column sequence to be displayed on the form.	By default, this value is always 1.
Row height	Specifies the height of the input form to be displayed on the form.	By default, this value is always 1.
Sort priority	Specifies a sort order.	
Format	Specifies a format mask for the data.	
Input required	Specifies that the field must have a value to be accepted.	Values can be No or Yes. The default is No.
Required message	Specifies the message to be displayed if the field is a required field, and the user does not enter a value.	
Validation on	Specifies that the data must match the format specified in the Format property to be accepted.	Values can be Yes or No. The default is No.
Validation msg	Specifies a message to be displayed if the column does not match the valid format.	
Column help URL	Specifies a relative URL, or an absolute URL if desired, to be displayed when the column hot link is activated.	

23

INTERFACING IIS WITH ODBC DATABASES

continues

Table 23.4. continued

Name	Description	Note
Insert form header	Specifies a custom header to be displayed on the top of the Web page instead of the default dbWeb header.	
Insert form trailer	Specifies a custom message to be displayed on the bottom of the Web page in addition to the default dbWeb trailer.	
Insert success msg	Specifies a custom message to be displayed if the insert succeeds.	
Insert fail msg	Specifies a custom message to be displayed if the insert fails.	

Specifying the Schema Custom HTML Form Properties

If the default tabular or freeform forms are not to your liking, you can create custom forms and invoke them from your HTML pages. The best example on how to do this is the North Wind Traders sample database installed by the dbWeb Setup program. I'm not really very impressed with the custom forms option because it requires that you build a custom HTML document, which is a lot of work. Another reason you may decide to use custom forms, however, is to insert graphics on your Web page. But you should know that to do this, the graphics files cannot be part of your ODBC database; they must reside as separate images on your WWWRoot path. I decided, and I think you will too, that if you are going to go to this much trouble you'll want to use the Internet Database Connector (IDC) that ships with the Internet Information Server. But for a small database that you want to customize, it may be worth the trouble. So just to give you an idea on how to interface your custom forms with dbWeb, follow these steps:

1. Double-click a data source (such as IISLogs) to expand it and display the schemas below the data source name.

2. Select the schema (such as GuestBook) and click the Modify Schema button. Click the DBX tab to display the properties sheet shown in Figure 23.26.

3. Enter the relative or absolute URL for the form to be used in place of the default tabular form in the Multi record result output custom format file field.

FIGURE 23.26.

Specifying a custom form to be used with dbWeb.

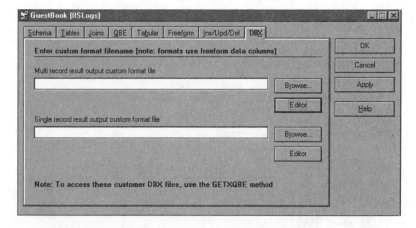

4. Enter the relative or absolute URL for the form to be used in place of the default freeform form in the Single record result output custom format file field.

> **NOTE**
>
> Clicking the Editor button will display the DBX Editor dialog. You can use this dialog to select the columns you want to add to your form. After you have done so, save the file by selecting File | Save from the menu. Then you will have to edit the file to create a real HTML document that you can use. To invoke these forms from an HTML file, you need to create a link with the following syntax:
>
> ```
> /scripts/dbweb/dbwebc.dll/SchemaName?getxqbe
> ```
>
> where *SchemaName* is the name of your schema with the custom forms.

5. When you have completed your definitions and modified the column properties, click the OK button to accept your modifications and return to the Data Sources window or click the Apply button to immediately update the schema with your changes. This is useful when you are making continuous modifications and testing each action.

Creating a Custom Guest Book Using Microsoft dbWeb

Now that you have learned the basic operations of dbWeb, you probably want to get to work and actually use it. This section walks you through the basic process of creating a guest book that you can use on your Internet Information Server site. The first step in this process is to create a database; then you create the guest book table. The following SQL Server script is what I used to create the sample guest book:

23

INTERFACING IIS
WITH ODBC
DATABASES

```
CREATE TABLE dbo.GuestBook (
    IndexField int IDENTITY (1, 1) NOT NULL ,
    FirstName char (25) NULL ,
    MiddleInitial char (1) NULL ,
    LastName char (30) NULL ,
    Title char (30) NULL ,
    CompanyName char (50) NULL ,
    Address char (35) NULL ,
    Address_2 char (35) NULL ,
    City char (35) NULL ,
    StateOrProvince char (25) NULL ,
    PostalCode char (25) NULL ,
    Country char (25) NULL ,
    WorkPhoneNumber char (14) NULL ,
    HomePhoneNumber char (14) NULL ,
    FaxNumber char (14) NULL ,
    E_Mail char (25) NULL ,
    URL char (255) NULL ,
    Note text NULL ,
    Contact char (1) NULL
)
GO
```

Although you can use another ODBC-compliant database such as Microsoft Access, I used SQL Server. I chose this route because SQL Server can execute procedures automatically. These procedures will be used to check the contact field and send me e-mail whenever new users request that I contact them. As part of the procedure, the contact field will be reset so that I will not receive duplicate e-mail messages. Another reason I chose SQL Server is because it was easy to assign a key field. (This is the `IndexField` specified in the second line of the script.) This field uses the `identity` property to automatically insert a unique counter whenever a user inserts a record into the database. This field is not displayed on my dbWeb pages, but dbWeb uses this field as the unique key for updates or deletes. If you do not specify a unique key, it is possible that dbWeb will update or delete multiple rows of data in your table.

After you create the database, you need to create the ODBC data source as described in the section titled "Creating the ODBC Data Source." After that, it is a simple matter of creating the dbWeb data source and the schema, and setting the various column properties, as described in the preceding sections. Although these operations do take a bit of time, they are not complex tasks. The fun part really comes into play when you have to create your custom forms. Fun, you say? Am I joking, you ask?

Well, the truth is, I am joking. As part of this experiment I decided to use Microsoft FrontPage 1.1 to create my forms. But I found out the hard way that FrontPage does not support the dbWeb interface. FrontPage assumes that a form name must start with a character, and dbWeb requires a name using the syntax of *ControlType,SchemaName,ColumnName* (such as `1,GuestBook,FirstName`), although you can also use the format *ControlType, TableName,ColumnName* (such as `1,dbo.GuestBook,FirstName`). But FrontPage has such a nice user interface for form creation that I decided I would use it anyway. Therefore, I had to create the form with bogus names for each form control and then edit them manually using a text editor. The result was well worth it, though, and can be seen in Figure 23.27.

FIGURE 23.27.

A guest book form inserting data into a SQL Server database using dbWeb.

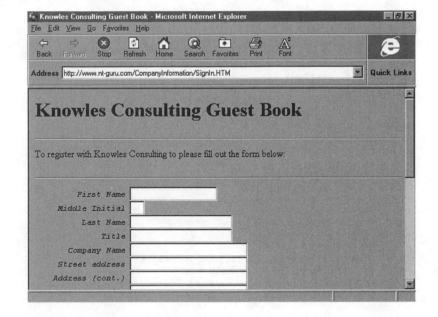

The HTML code used to create this form follows.

```
<html>
<head>
<title>Knowles Consulting Guest Book</title>
</head>
<body>
<h1>Knowles Consulting Guest Book</h1>
<hr>
<p>To register with Knowles Consulting to please fill out the form below:</p>
<hr>
<form action="/scripts/dbweb/dbwebc.dll/GuestBook?insert" method="POST">
<blockquote>
<pre><em>      First Name </em><input type=text size=25 maxlength=25
name="1,dbo.GuestBook,FirstName">
  <em>Middle</em> <em>Initial</em> <input type=text size=1 maxlength=1
name="1,dbo.GuestBook,MiddleInitial">
      <em>Last</em> <em>Name</em> <input type=text size=30 maxlength=30
name="1,dbo.GuestBook,LastName">
<em>           Title </em><input type=text size=30 maxlength=30
name="1,dbo.GuestBook,Title">
<em>    Company Name </em><input type=text size=35 maxlength=50
name="1,dbo.GuestBook,CompanyName">
<em>  Street address </em><input type=text size=35 maxlength=35
name="1,dbo.GuestBook,Address">
<em> Address (cont.) </em><input type=text size=35 maxlength=35
name="1,dbo.GuestBook,Address_2">
<em>            City </em><input type=text size=35 maxlength=35
➥ name="1,dbo.GuestBook,City">
<em>  State/Province </em><input type=text size=25 maxlength=25
name="1,dbo.GuestBook,StateOrProvince">
<em> Zip/Postal code </em><input type=text size=25 maxlength=25
name="1,dbo.GuestBook,PostalCode">
```

23

INTERFACING IIS
WITH ODBC
DATABASES

```
<em>          Country </em><input type=text size=25 maxlength=25
name="1,dbo.GuestBook,Country">
<em>        Work Phone </em><input type=text size=14 maxlength=14
name="1,dbo.GuestBook,WorkPhoneNumber">
<em>         Home Phone </em><input type=text size=14 maxlength=14
name="1,dbo.GuestBook,HomePhoneNumber">
<em>               FAX </em><input type=text size=14 maxlength=14
name="1,dbo.GuestBook,FaxNumber">
<em>            E-mail </em><input type=text size=25 maxlength=255
name="1,dbo.GuestBook,E_Mail">
<em>   Home Page URL </em><input type=text size=25 maxlength=255
➥name="1,dbo.GuestBook,URL">
              <em>Note</em> <textarea name="1,dbo.GuestBook,Note" rows=2
cols=44></textarea></pre>
<pre><input type=checkbox name="5,dbo.GuestBook,Contact" value="Y">
➥ Please contact me as soon as possible regarding this matter.
</pre>
</blockquote>
<p><input type=submit value="Submit Form"> <input type=reset
➥ value="Reset Form"> <a
href="/CompanyInformation/GuestBookPageHelp.HTM">
➥<img src="/Graphics/Buttons/help.gif"
align=absmiddle border=0></a> <a href="http://www.nt-guru.com"><img
src="/Graphics/Buttons/home.gif" align=absmiddle border=0></a></p>
</form>
<hr>
<table width=100%>
<tr><td width=50%><address><font size=2><em>Copyright &#169; 1996 Knowles
➥ Consulting. All
rights reserved</em></font> </address>
</td><td align=right width=50%><div align=right>
<address><font size=2><em>Last Updated: June 21, 1996</em></font> </address>
</div>
</td></tr>
</table>
</body>
</html>
```

I've highlighted a few of the nonstandard areas of this text in bold to point out these areas of particular interest. The first item is the form action. Rather than call a custom FrontPage CGI script, I've converted this form to use dbWeb. It was rather easy, too. All that was needed was to change the URL to

```
/scripts/dbweb/dbwebc.dll/GuestBook?insert
```

When the Submit button is invoked, the Insert method is activated and the data contained in the form is inserted into the database defined by the GuestBook schema. There are other dbWeb methods you can use as well; they are described in the dbWeb help file under the Developer Reference topic. A few that I would like to point out as particularly useful when creating custom forms to use with dbWeb are as follows:

- getqbe—Displays the dbWeb query by example form on the Web browser.
- getresults—Obtains the results set and displays the data using the tabular form if more than one record is returned, or the freeform form if only one record is returned.

- getinsert—Obtains the insert form and displays it on the Web browser.
- getupdate—Obtains the update form and displays it on the Web browser.
- insert—Inserts the data specified by the column tags into the database.
- update—Updates the data specified by the column tags in the database.
- delete—Deletes the data specified by the column tags from the database.

You can use these dbWeb methods with your custom Web pages to access and control the behavior of dbWeb. On my home page, for example, I've created a link to the dbWeb QBE form using the syntax

```
http://www.nt-guru.com/scripts/dbweb/dbWebc.dll/GuestBook?getqbe
```

This invokes the query by example form, shown in Figure 23.28, that I use to search my guest book. To make my custom guest book form a little more consistent with the Web pages produced by dbWeb, I inserted the same help and home buttons that will invoke a custom help page and jump to my home page, respectively.

FIGURE 23.28.

The dbWeb query by example form for the guest book.

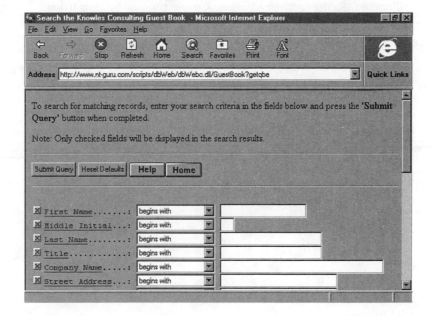

Summary

This chapter explores some of the features of dbWeb. It explains how to install dbWeb and how to configure the dbWeb Administrator and the dbWeb Server. You learn how to create an ODBC data source and a dbWeb schema. You also learn how to configure the various properties for your QBE, tabular, freeform, and insert/update/delete forms. Finally, you have seen how it all comes together with dbWeb by taking a look at the HTML source code for a sample guest book. In Chapter 24, "Building Dynamic Web Pages with SQL Server," you'll learn how to build dynamic Web pages using the Internet Database Connector and how to build semistatic Web pages with Microsoft SQL Server 6.5. Before moving on to the next chapter, consider the following:

- dbWeb has a built-in graphical user interface to its core functionality, which means that you can use a point-and-click methodology to design your schema.

- dbWeb provides the ability to design table joins, or set table constraints, to modify the query dbWeb sends on your behalf dynamically.

- dbWeb can be used to build quick and easy-to-use forms to search your database with built-in links to help files.

- dbWeb does not assume you know much about HTML, but does provide customization for HTML-proficient users.

dbWeb is a tool designed for rapid development of interactive HTML documents. If you need more control, the Internet Database Connector may be your ticket.

Building Dynamic Web Pages with SQL Server

IN THIS CHAPTER

- **Using the Internet Database Connector** 694

- **Using the SQL Server Web Assistant** 712

The Internet Information Server gives you several ways to build dynamic Web pages. A *dynamic* Web page is one that interacts with the user or changes periodically. Most people think of ActiveX technologies and Internet Explorer 3.0 when the word *interactive* is mentioned, but this chapter will focus on interacting with ODBC-compliant databases. In Chapter 23, "Interfacing Internet Information Server with ODBC Databases," you learned how to build interactive Web pages using an add-on tool called Microsoft dbWeb. In this chapter, you explore some of the other options for making dynamic Web pages that are provided with the Internet Information Server base product and with Microsoft SQL Server 6.5.

Some of the reasons to use the Internet Database Connector (IDC) instead of dbWeb include

- Query control—If you are an experienced database developer with knowledge of your database's query language, the IDC offers finer levels of control. The IDC requires you to specify a query rather than supplying one for you. This requirement should be considered a blessing rather than a burden because it provides fine-tuned control of what will be returned by your query.

- Layout control—If you are an experienced HTML developer, the IDC offers finer control over how the user will interact with your Web page. Since you create the input forms used to obtain the query and the Web pages to display the query result, you also get to determine exactly how the Web page will look.

- Reusability—You can copy the basic components of an IDC skeleton (the source code consisting of the Web pages, HTX, and IDC files) to quickly build a variant input form or query result page. Microsoft dbWeb requires that you build an entirely new data source and schema. There is no code reusability.

Using the Internet Database Connector

The Internet Information Server has the built-in capability to interface with any ODBC-compliant database for which you have a 32-bit ODBC driver. There is more work involved in developing an interactive Web page using the IDC than there is using Microsoft dbWeb, but the IDC provides more fine-tuned control. Another good thing about the IDC is that unlike dbWeb, the IDC does not require form names to start with a number. Therefore, you can use Microsoft FrontPage to develop your forms from start to finish.

In this section you learn how to use the IDC to create an interactive guest book, which looks a lot like the guest book created with dbWeb in Chapter 20. There are three steps for the creation of this or any other interactive IDC Web page. First, you must create the Web page form. Next, you must create an IDC interface file. Finally, you must create another HTML file to use as a template for the resulting output created by your query.

Creating the Web Page Forms

You can use any text editor to create your forms, but I prefer a what-you-see-is-what-you-get (WYSIWYG) editor such as Microsoft FrontPage. (See Figure 24.1.) Microsoft FrontPage makes it easy to build your form using the familiar Windows GUI. It is not imperative that you know how to write HTML documents, although knowing syntax for HTML helps considerably if you have to edit a document manually or if a problem crops up during the development stage.

FIGURE 24.1.

Creating your form with Microsoft FrontPage.

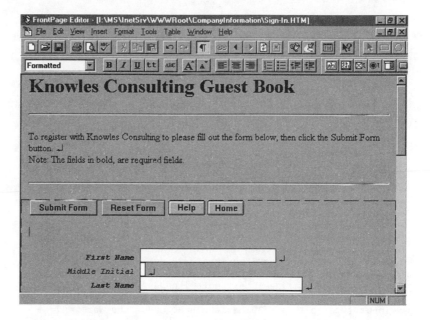

You must create two forms to build a working guest book. First, you need a form to insert information into your ODBC database. Second, you need a form to query your database. This form is optional because you may not want to allow your Internet clients to browse your database. However, I am including it here because it does illustrate the basic techniques that are required to query your database and to display the resulting data on a Web page. The ability to query and to display the data is what really makes a form interactive.

> **TIP**
>
> If you look closely at the HTML source code in the next few sections, you will see a reference to a database column called Hide. This variable prevents the display of a client's information on the Web. While you may still view the data by using another ODBC frontend, such as Access, the queries used to find and display the guest book specifically exclude any information for which the Hide column is set to Y. The client sets this variable by checking the Do not post this information on the Web for others to see check box at the end of the form.

Creating the Input Form

I used the following HTML code to build the basic form I created to enter information into my guest book:

```
1.      <html>
2.      <head>
3.      <title>Knowles Consulting Guest Book</title>
4.      </head>
5.      <body>
6.      <h1>Knowles Consulting Guest Book</h1>
7.      <hr>
8.      <p>To register with Knowles Consulting to please fill out the form
below, then click the Submit Form button.</p>
9.      <p>Note: The fields in bold, are required fields. </p>
10.     <hr>
11.     <form action="/Scripts/Sign-In-IDC.IDC" method="get">
12.     <p><input type=submit value="Submit Form">
<input type=reset value="Reset Form">
<a href="/CompanyInformation/GuestBookPageHelp.HTM">
<img src="/Graphics/Buttons/help.gif" align=absmiddle border=0></a>
<a href="http://www.nt-guru.com">
<img src="/Graphics/Buttons/home.gif" align=absmiddle border=0></a></p>
13.     <blockquote>
14.     <pre><em>        </em><em><b>First Name</b></em><em> </em>
<input type=text size=25 maxlength=25 name="FirstName">
15.        <em>Middle</em> <em>Initial</em>
<input type=text size=1 maxlength=1 name="MiddleInitial">
16.             <em><b>Last Name</b></em>
<input type=text size=30 maxlength=30 name="LastName">
17.     <em>          Title </em>
<input type=text size=30 maxlength=30 name="Title">
18.     <em>     Company Name </em>
<input type=text size=35 maxlength=50 name="CompanyName">
19.     <em>  Street address </em>
<input type=text size=35 maxlength=35 name="Address">
20.     <em> Address (cont.) </em>
<input type=text size=35 maxlength=35 name="Address_2">
21.     <em>            City </em>
<input type=text size=35 maxlength=35 name="City">
```

```
22.     <em>   State/Province </em>
➥<input type=text size=25 maxlength=25 name="StateOrProvince">
23.     <em> Zip/Postal code </em>
➥<input type=text size=25 maxlength=25 name="PostalCode">
24.     <em>           Country </em>
➥<input type=text size=25 maxlength=25 name="Country" value="US">
25.     <em>        Work Phone </em>
➥<input type=text size=14 maxlength=14 name="WorkPhoneNumber">
26.     <em>        Home Phone </em>
➥<input type=text size=14 maxlength=14 name="HomePhoneNumber">
27.     <em>               FAX </em>
➥<input type=text size=14 maxlength=14 name="FaxNumber">
28.     <em>            E-mail </em>
➥<input type=text size=25 maxlength=255 name="E_Mail">
29.     <em>   Home Page URL </em>
➥<input type=text size=25 maxlength=255 name="URL">
30.                  <em>Note</em>
➥<textarea name="Note" rows=2 cols=44></textarea></pre>
31.<pre><input type=checkbox name="Contact" value="Y">
➥Please contact me as soon as possible regarding this matter.
32.     </pre>
33.     <pre><input type=checkbox name="Hide" value="Y">
➥Do not post this information on the web for others to see.</pre>
34.     </blockquote>
35.     <p><input type=submit value="Submit Form">
➥<input type=reset value="Reset Form">
➥<a href="/CompanyInformation/GuestBookPageHelp.HTM">
➥<img src-"/Graphics/Buttons/help.gif" align=absmiddle border=0></a>
➥<a href="http://www.nt-guru.com">
➥<img src="/Graphics/Buttons/home.gif" align=absmiddle border=0></a></p>
36.     </form>
37.     <table width=100%>
38.<tr><td width=50%><address><font size=2>
➥<em>Copyright &#169; 1996 Knowles Consulting. All rights reserved</em>
➥</font> </address>
39.</td><td align=right width=50%><div align=right><address>
➥<font size=2><em>Last Updated: June 21, 1996</em></font>
➥</address></div></td></tr>
40.     </table>
41. </body>
42.     </html>
```

NOTE

The preceding HTML code should not include the line numbers. These numbers are included in the text to make the discussion easier to follow.

The first two and last two lines of the text are required for any HTML document. Line 3 specifies the title of the document, which will be displayed on the caption bar of the Web browser. Line 5 specifies the beginning of the document body. Line 6 is the document header. Lines 7 and 10 insert a horizontal rule (line break) into the document to divide the instructions on how to use the form (lines 8 and 9) from the header and the form. Line 11 is the beginning of the form, and includes the IDC definition as well as the type of action to be performed (a GET rather than the more commonly used POST).

This definition (/Scripts/Sign-In-IDC.IDC) file is associated with the IDC ISAPI dynamic link library HTTPODBC.DLL, which can be found in your InetSrv\Server subdirectory. You'll learn more about the IDC definition files in the next section, "Creating the IDC Interface File." For now, just mark this spot in your HTML file as the executable file to which your form's output will be passed.

Moving on, lines 12 and 35 are the form's Submit, Reset, Help, and Home buttons. These buttons submit the information entered into the form by the user, clear the form, display a help file, and return to the home page, respectively. You should notice that both the Help button and the Home button are image files. When the user selects one of these buttons, the page associated with the hypertext link will be displayed. This is a different action than that performed by the Submit and Reset buttons, which are really form controls. This is because there are only two basic form buttons supported in the HTML definition. One button submits the form, and one button clears the form.

Line 13 (the <blockquote> tag) indents the form's Input fields (lines 14 through 33). Line 36 is the end of the form. Lines 37 through 40 include a table definition, the copyright information, and a form last-update notification.

That's about all it takes to create the form that sends an entry to your database. To create a form that allows a user to query your guest book and view the resulting data, use the following:

```
 1: <html>
 2: <title>Search the Knowles Consulting Guest Book</title>
 3: <BODY>
 4: <hr>
 5: <h1>Search the Knowles Consulting Guest Book</h1>
 6: To search for matching records, enter your search criteria in the fields
➥ below and press the 'Submit Query' button
➥ when completed.
 7: <p>Type in any of these boxes to match against people in the guestbook.
➥Use the '%' symbol as a wildcard. A blank field here will match any entry.<br>
 8: <form action="/Scripts/SearchGuestBook.IDC" method=get>
 9: <p><input type=submit value="Submit Form">
➥<input type=reset value="Reset Form"> <a href="/CompanyInformation
➥/GuestBookPageHelp.HTM">
➥<img src="/Graphics/Buttons/help.gif" align=absmiddle border=0></a>
➥<a href="http://www.nt-guru.com">
➥<img src="/Graphics/Buttons/home.gif" align=absmiddle border=0></a></p>
10: <blockquote>
11: <pre><em>      First Name </em>
➥<input type=text size=25 maxlength=25 name="FirstName">
12:    <em>Middle</em> <em>Initial</em>
➥<input type=text size=1 maxlength=1 name="MiddleInitial">
13:       <em>Last</em> <em>Name</em>
➥<input type=text size=30 maxlength=30 name="LastName">
```

```
14: <em>          Title </em>
➥<input type=text size=30 maxlength=30 name="Title">
15: <em>     Company Name </em>
➥<input type=text size=35 maxlength=50 name="CompanyName">
16: <em>  Street address </em>
➥<input type=text size=35 maxlength=35 name="Address">
17: <em> Address (cont.) </em>
➥<input type=text size=35 maxlength=35 name="Address_2">
18: <em>             City </em><input type=text size=35 maxlength=35 name="City">
19: <em>  State/Province </em>
➥<input type=text size=25 maxlength=25 name="StateOrProvince">
20: <em> Zip/Postal code </em>
➥<input type=text size=25 maxlength=25 name="PostalCode">
21: <em>          Country </em>
➥<input type=text size=25 maxlength=25 name="Country">
22: <em>       Work Phone </em>
➥<input type=text size=14 maxlength=14 name="WorkPhoneNumber">
23: <em>       Home Phone </em>
➥<input type=text size=14 maxlength=14 name="HomePhoneNumber">
24: <em>              FAX </em>
➥<input type=text size=14 maxlength=14 name="FaxNumber">
25: <em>           E-mail </em>
➥<input type=text size=25 maxlength=255 name="E_Mail">
26: <em>   Home Page URL </em><input type=text size=25 maxlength=255 name="URL">
27:           <em>Note</em> <textarea name="Note" rows=2 cols=44></textarea>
➥</pre>
28: <p><input type=submit value="Submit Form">
➥<input type=reset value="Reset Form"> <a
href="/CompanyInformation/GuestBookPageHelp.HTM">
➥<img src="/Graphics/Buttons/help.gif" align=absmiddle border=0></a>
<a href="http://www.nt-guru.com">
➥<img src="/Graphics/Buttons/home.gif" align=absmiddle border=0></a></p>
29: </form>
30: <hr>
31: <table width=100%>
32: <tr><td width=50%><address><font size=2>
➥Copyright &#169; 1996 Knowles Consulting. All rights reserved</em>
➥</font> </address>
33: </td><td align=right width=50%><div align=right><address><font size=2>
➥<em>Last Updated: June 21, 1996</em></font>
➥</address>
34: </div></td></tr>
35: </table>
36: </body>
37: </html>
```

24

BUILDING
DYNAMIC
WEB PAGES

Although this form looks similar to the form used to enter information into the ODBC data-base, there are a few differences. First, the form title (line 2), header (line 5), and instructions (line 7) are different. This is not too surprising, since this Web page's purpose is to provide a mechanism for the user to query or search your guest book. The previous HTML document's purpose is to request that the user fill out a form so she or he can enter the information into your guest book. Second, the form calls the /Scripts/SearchGuestBook.IDC IDC interface file (line 8) rather than the Scripts/Sign-In-IDC.IDC IDC interface file used with the input form.

This is because I wanted to perform a different action—a database query instead of a database insert. Lines 10 through 29 define the actual form that will be displayed on the Web browser. The rest looks almost the same except for the Contact and Hide database columns, which are not included on the query form because a user has no need to search your guest book using these fields as search criteria. After all, although you may want to provide a listing of people who have visited your Web site as a service, you do not want users to know who you may have contacted or who does not want his or her information made public.

As you can see, creating the forms to insert data into your database or to query and display the results seems quite easy. Unfortunately, you also need to create the IDC interface and HTML template files before you can actually use the forms to enter information into your database or to query and display the result set on the Web.

Creating the IDC Interface File

The next step in building your guest book using the IDC is to build the IDC definition files. These files contain information about the ODBC data source, the template file used to display the result set, and most important, the database query to execute. You will need to create three IDC files.

The first file will be called `Sign-In-IDC.IDC`. It is used by the `Sign-In.HTM` form you created earlier. The source code follows:

```
1.    Datasource: IISLogs
2.    Username: sa
3.    Template: Sign-In-IDC.HTX
4.    RequiredParameters: FirstName, LastName
5.    SQLStatement:
6.    + if exists (
7.    +    select * from GuestBook
8.    +    where FirstName='%FirstName%' and MiddleInitial = '%MiddleInitial%'
➥and
9.    +    LastName='%LastName%' and Address = '%Address%' and
➥Address_2 = '%Address_2%' and
10.   +    City = '%City%' and StateOrProvince = '%StateOrProvince%' and
11.   +    PostalCode = '%PostalCode%' and Hide = '%Hide%'
12.   +    )
13.   +       select result='duplicate'
14.   +else
15.   +    INSERT INTO GuestBook
16.   +    (FirstName, MiddleInitial, LastName, Title, CompanyName, Address,
17.   +    Address_2, City, StateOrProvince, PostalCode, Country,
➥WorkPhoneNumber, HomePhoneNumber,
18.   +    FaxNumber, E_Mail, URL, Note, Contact, Hide)
19.   +    VALUES('%FirstName%', '%MiddleInitial%', '%LastName%', '%Title%',
20.   +    '%CompanyName%', '%Address%', '%Address_2%', '%City%',
➥'%StateOrProvince%',
21.   +    '%PostalCode%', '%Country%', '%WorkPhoneNumber%', '%HomePhoneNumber%',
22.   +    '%FaxNumber%', '%E_Mail%', '%URL%', '%Note%', '%Contact%', '%Hide%');
```

Line 1 specifies the ODBC system DSN used to access the ODBC database. Line 2 specifies the username. If you are using SQL Server with the mixed (or integrated) security model, as I am, this option is ignored. Instead, the user account is validated using the IUSR_*ServerName* account (where *ServerName* is the name of the server on which IIS is installed), which is created by the IIS setup program. However, depending on your ODBC database, you may need to supply the password option and specify a valid password to access your ODBC database. Line 3 specifies the HTML template file, which informs the user either that the data was entered into the database successfully or that a duplicate entry has been found. Line 4 specifies that the first name (FName) and last name (LName) fields must be entered on the form; otherwise, the record will not be entered into the database.

> **NOTE**
>
> Other defined parameters that you can use in an IDC file are summarized in Table 24.1.

Lines 5 through 12 are a series of SQL select statements that, when executed, will return a result set containing the first name, middle initial, last name, address lines, city, state, postal code and Hide flag. If all of these fields match the data that is entered by the user, line 13 is executed and the result is determined to be a duplicate entry. A duplicate entry will not be accepted, and the user will be informed of this fact via the message defined in the HTML template (more on this in the next section). If the record is not a duplicate, the insert statement after line 14 (the else clause) is executed and the record is inserted into the database. The user will see a success message, as defined by the HTML template.

The query for the guest book requires two IDC definition files. The first one, called SearchGuestBook.IDC, is used to define the search parameters. The source code is

```
Datasource: IISLogs
Username: sa
Template: SearchGuestBook.HTX
SQLStatement:
+SELECT FirstName, LastName,
+FROM GuestBook
+WHERE FirstName like '%FirstName%'
+and LastName like '%LastName%'
+and Hide <> 'Y'
DefaultParameters:FirstName=%,LastName=%
```

This source code looks very similar to the Sign-In-IDC.IDC file. Indeed, the only real difference is that SearchGuestBook.IDC does not search for duplicate records. Instead, it executes a query to find records based only on the first and last names specified by the user. If the user does not specify one or both of these fields, a wildcard (% character) will be substituted in the empty field (as specified by the DefaultParameters entry). The DefaultParameters entry is used to create a substitution mechanism to supply default values for a field in the query if the user does not explicitly enter a value. When this query is executed, the template file SearchGuestBook.HTX will be used to display the result set, which consists of first and last names. At this point, the user can click one of these entries to expand it and display more detail. This will execute the final IDC file called GuestBookDetails.IDC. The source code for this file follows.

```
Datasource: IISLogs
Username: sa
Template: GuestBookDetails.HTX
SQLStatement:
+SELECT FirstName, MiddleInitial, LastName, Title, CompanyName, Address,
Address_2,
+City, StateOrProvince, PostalCode, Country, WorkPhoneNumber, HomePhoneNumber,
 FaxNumber,
+E_Mail, URL, Note
+FROM GuestBook
+WHERE FirstName = '%FName%' and LastName = '%LName%' and Hide <> 'Y'
```

NOTE

Notice in both of these queries that the Hide column is used to make sure that only records that do not contain a Y will be displayed. This is to prevent you from displaying information that a user requests remain confidential on the Web.

This IDC definition file uses the GuestBookDetails.HTX template file to display the result set on the Web browser. The IDC definition file will display the matching records using the detail form in the template file. The query that is executed will select all of the fields that match the user-specified FName and LName fields. These fields are actually specified in the SearchGuestBook.HTX template file, which you examine in the next section.

Table 24.1. The IDC parameters.

Parameter	Description	Note
Datasource	Specifies the data source name (DSN) used to connect to the ODBC-compliant database.	This is a required field.
DefaultParameters	Specifies a default value to be used in the query if the user does not explicitly supply a value for a field.	

Parameter	Description	Note
Expires	Specifies a time, in seconds, to wait before refreshing a cached page.	By default, an output page is not cached by `httpodbc.dll`. It will be cached only if the `Expires` parameter is used.
MaxFieldSize	Specifies the maximum buffer size to be allocated per field by `httpodbc.dll`.	
MaxRecords	Specifies the maximum number of records to be returned by `httpodbc.dll`.	
Password	Specifies a password to be used with the associated username to access an ODBC database.	
RequiredParameters	Specifies the parameters that must be supplied by the user.	
SQLStatement	Specifies the SQL select statement (or query) to be executed.	This is a required field.
Template	Specifies the HTML template file that will be used to display the result set.	This is a required field.
UserName	Specifies a username that will be used to access the ODBC database.	
Content-Type	Specifies a valid MIME type describing the returned result set.	

Creating the IDC HTML Template

Well, you made it to the last step of the process: the creation of the HTML template files. It's important to understand how these files work because these files determine just what the user will see on his or her Web browser. Before you look at the files, however, it may pay off to learn a bit about what an HTML template (or HTX) file contains. Basically, an HTX file contains extensions to the HTML language. These extensions will be enclosed in a `<%' '%>` tag pair. The returned result set will be merged with the HTML document between the `<%begindetail%>` and `<%enddetail&>` tag pairs. There are also several HTX variables, summarized in Table 24.2, which, when combined with the `if...else...endif` flow-control statement, determine how your output will appear.

Table 24.2. The HTX extensions.

Extension	Description	Note
ALL_HTTP	All HTTP headers that are not parsed into one of the other listed variables in this table.	
AUTH_TYPE	Specifies the authorization type in use.	If the user has been authenticated by the server, the return value will be `Basic`. Otherwise, the entry will not be present.
BeginDetail	Specifies the beginning of a detail record block.	
CONTAINS	String includes the specified character.	Can be used only in an `if...else...endif` statement.
CONTENT_LENGTH	Specifies the number of bytes the script can expect to receive from the client.	
CONTENT_TYPE	The content type of the information supplied in the `POST` request.	
CurrentRecord	Specifies the current record number.	Can be used only in an `if...else...endif` statement.
else	Else.	The `else` clause of an `if...else...endif` statement block.
endif	Endif.	The end of `if...else...endif` statement block.

Extension	Description	Note
`<%EndDetail%>`	Specifies the end of the detail record block.	
`EQ`	Equal to.	Can be used only in an `if...else...endif` statement.
`LT`	Less than.	Can be used only in an `if...else...endif` statement.
`GATEWAY_INTERFACE`	Specifies the revision level of the CGI specification.	
`GT`	Greater than.	Can be used only in an `if...else...endif` statement.
`HTTP_ACCEPT`	Returns special-case HTTP header information.	
`if`	If.	The `if` clause of an `if...else...endif` statement block.
`MaxRecords`	Specifies the maximum number of records that can be returned.	Can be used only in an `if...else...endif` statement.
`PATH_INFO`	Additional path information as given by the client.	This value will contain the trailing part of the URL after the script name but before the query string (if any query string was supplied).
`PATH_TRANSLATED`	The same as `PATH_INFO`, but without any virtual path name translation.	
`QUERY_STRING`	Specifies the information after the `?` in a script query.	
`REMOTE_ADDR`	Specifies the IP address of the client.	
`REMOTE_HOST`	Specifies the hostname of the client.	

continues

Table 24.2. continued

Extension	Description	Note
REMOTE_USER	Specifies the username supplied by the client and authorized by the server.	
REQUEST_METHOD	Specifies the HTTP request method.	
SCRIPT_NAME	Specifies the name of the script being executed.	
SERVER_NAME	Specifies the name of the server (or IP address) as it should appear in self-referencing URLs.	
SERVER_PORT	Specifies the TCP/IP port on which the request was received.	
SERVER_PORT_SECURE	Specifies a 0 or 1, where 1 is an encrypted (such as a secure) port.	
SERVER_PROTOCOL	Specifies the name and version of the request.	Usually HTTP/1.0.
SERVER_SOFTWARE	Specifies the name and version number of the Web server under which the IIS extension is executing.	
UNMAPPED_REMOTE USER	Specifies the username before an authentication filter mapped the username to a Windows NT username.	
URL	Specifies the URL of the request.	

The first file is called Sign-In-IDC.HTX and contains the following code:

```
1.   <html>
2.   <title>Knowles Consulting Guest Book</title>
3.   <BODY>
4.   <hr>
5.   <h1>Knowles Consulting Guest Book</h1>
6.   <hr>
7.   <%begindetail%>
8.   <%enddetail%>
```

```
9.     <%if CurrentRecord EQ 0 %>
10.    <h2>Information registered. Thanks!</h2>
11.    <p>
12.    <table border="1" width="100%">
13.    <caption align="top">Details for <%idc.FirstName%> <%idc.LastName%>
       ➥</caption>
14     <tr>
15.    <td><%if idc.FirstName EQ ""%>
16.    <%else%>
17.    First Name:</td><td><%idc.FirstName%><td><tr>
18.    <%endif%>
19.    <tr>
20.    <td><%if idc.MiddleInitial EQ ""%>
21.    <%else%>
22.    Middle Initial:</td><td><%idc.MiddleInitial%><td><tr>
23.    <%endif%>
24.    <tr>
25.    <td><%if idc.LastName EQ ""%>
26.    <%else%>
27.    Last Name:</td><td><%idc.LastName%><td><tr>
28.    <%endif%>
29.    <tr>
30.    <td><%if idc.Title EQ ""%>
31.    <%else%>
32.    Title:</td><td><%idc.Title%><td><tr>
33.    <%endif%>
34.    <tr>
35.    <td><%if idc.CompanyName EQ ""%>
36.    <%else%>
37.    Company Name:</td><td><%idc.CompanyName%><td><tr>
38.    <%endif%>
39.    <tr>
40.    <td><%if idc.Address EQ ""%>
41.    <%else%>
42.    Street Address:</td><td><%idc.Address%><td><tr>
43.    <%endif%>
44.    <tr>
45.    <td><%if idc.Address_2 EQ ""%>
46.    <%else%>
47.    Address (cont):</td><td><%idc.Address_2%><td><tr>
48.    <%endif%>
49.    <tr>
50.    <td><%if idc.City EQ ""%>
51.    <%else%>
52.    City:</td><td><%idc.City%><td><tr>
53.    <%endif%>
54.    <tr>
55.    <td><%if idc.StateOrProvince EQ ""%>
56.    <%else%>
57.    State/Province:</td><td><%idc.StateOrProvince%><td><tr>
58.    <%endif%>
59.    <tr>
60.    <td><%if idc.PostalCode EQ ""%>
61.    <%else%>
62.    Postal Code:</td><td><%idc.PostalCode%><td><tr>
63.    dif%>
64.    <tr>
65.    <td><%if idc.Country EQ ""%>
66.    <%else%>
67.    Country:</td><td><%idc.Country%><td><tr>
```

```
68.     <%endif%>
69.     <tr>
70.     <td><%if idc.WorkPhoneNumber EQ ""%>
71.     <%else%>
72.     Work Phone Number:</td><td><%idc.WorkPhoneNumber%><td><tr>
73.     <%endif%>
74.     <tr>
75.     <td><%if idc.HomePhoneNumber EQ ""%>
76.     <%else%>
77.     Home Phone Number:</td><td><%idc.HomePhoneNumber%><td><tr>
78.     <%endif%>
79.     <tr>
80.     <td><%if idc.FaxNumber EQ ""%>
81.     <%else%>
82.     Fax Phone Number:</td><td><%idc.FaxNumber%><td><tr>
83.     <%endif%>
84.     <tr>
85.     <td><%if idc.E_Mail EQ ""%>
86.     <%else%>
87.      E-Mail Address:</td><td><%idc.E_Mail%><td><tr>
88.     <%endif%>
89.     <tr>
90.     <td><%if idc.URL EQ ""%>
91.     <%else%>
92.     Home Page URL:</td><td><%idc.URL%><td><tr>
93.     <%endif%>
94.     <tr>
95.     <td><%if idc.Note EQ ""%>
96.     <%else%>
97.     Note:</td><td><%Note%><td><tr>
98.     <%endif%>
99.     </table>
100.     <p>
101.     <%else%>
102.     <h2><I><%idc.FirstName%> <%idc.LastName%></I> is already registered.</h2>
103.     <%endif%>
104.     <hr>
105.     <table width=100%>
106.     <tr><td width=50%><address><font size=2>
        ➥<em>Copyright &#169; 1996 Knowles Consulting. All rights reserved</em>
        ➥</font> </address>
107.     </td><td align=right width=50%><div align=right>
108.     <address><font size=2><em>Last Updated: June 21, 1996</em></font> </
        ➥address>
109.     </div>
110.     </td></tr>
111.     </table>
112.     </body>
113.r</html>
```

Although this code is longer than you might expect, it is not really as complex at it seems. When the page displays the confirmation message that the client data was accepted, it also creates a table containing the submitted data. If the data was not accepted, an error message stating that the user is already registered is displayed. The important parts of this record are contained between lines 9 and 101. Line 9 is the start of the major if...else...endif statement block. If the CurrentRecord parameter is equal to 0, which will be true if the IDC returns a record in the result set, then the record was accepted. If a result set consists of multiple rows, then the

`CurrentRecord` parameter will be 0 the first time the `<%begindetail%>` `<%enddetail%>` block is executed. Each subsequent time the `<%begindetail%>` `<%enddetail%>` block is executed the CurrentRecord counter will be incremented by one. Each row statement includes an `if...else...endif` statement block to check if the column is a nonnull value. If it is, the `else` statement is executed, which builds the row. Each row contains a tag and the value of the column. The rest of the document contains the standard copyright and update information that you've already seen.

The next HTX file is the `SearchGuestBook.HTX` file. The source code follows.

```
<html>
<title>Guest Book Query Results</title>
<BODY>
<h1>Selected Guest Book Contents</h1>
<%begindetail%>
<%if CurrentRecord EQ 0 %>
<h2>Here are the selected contents of the guest book.
Click a name to get details:</h2>
<p>
<%endif%>
Name: <a href="/Scripts/
GuestBookDetails.IDC?FName=<%FirstName%>&LName=<%LastName%>">
<b><%FirstName%>
<%LastName%></b></a>
<p>
<%enddetail%>
<%if CurrentRecord EQ 0 %>
<h2>Sorry, no entries in the guest book match those criteria.</h2>
<%endif%>
<p>
<hr>
<table width=100%>
<tr><td width=50%><address><font size=2>
<em>Copyright &#169; 1996 Knowles Consulting. All rights reserved</em></font>
</address>
</td><td align=right width=50%><div align=right>
<address><font size=2><em>Last Updated: June 21, 1996</em></font> </address>
</div>
</td></tr>
</table>
</body>
</html>
```

This is a very simple HTX file. Between the `<%begindetail%>` and `<%enddetail%>` tags, you'll find the statement

```
Name: <a href="/Scripts/GuestBookDetails.IDC?FName=<%FirstName%>&
LName=<%LastName%>"><b><%FirstName%>
<%LastName%></b></a>
```

This is how the hypertext link is created between the search results page and the `GuestBookDetail.HTX` file. I mentioned in the previous section that the `GuestBookDetails.IDC` file uses the parameters passed to it in the `FName` and `LName` parameters to search the database for matching records to display. Well, this is where they are set and converted to a hypertext link all in one step. What's interesting about this line of code is that a form is not used; instead, the `GuestBookDetails.IDC` script is executed by the IDC directly, which then passes the `FName` and `LName` parameters to the `GuestBookDetails.IDC` script. Kind of nifty, isn't it? The final file is the detail form used by the `GuestBookDetails.IDC` file to display the result set. It is called `GuestBookDetails.HTX` and is quite similar to the `Sign-In-IDC.HTX` file. In fact, they share the same table definition code:

```
<html>
<title>Guest Book Entry Details</title>
<BODY>
<h1>Guest Book Entry Details</h1>
<hr>
<%begindetail%>
<p>
<table border="1" width="100%">
<caption align="top">Details for <%FirstName%> <%LastName%></caption>
<tr>
<td><%if FirstName EQ ""%>
<%else%>
First Name:</td><td><%FirstName%><td><tr>
<%endif%>
<tr>
<td><%if MiddleInitial EQ ""%>
<%else%>
Middle Initial:</td><td><%MiddleInitial%><td><tr>
<%endif%>
<tr>
<td><%if LastName EQ ""%>
<%else%>
Last Name:</td><td><%LastName%><td><tr>
<%endif%>
<tr>
<td><%if Title EQ ""%>
<%else%>
Title:</td><td><%Title%><td><tr>
<%endif%>
<tr>
<td><%if CompanyName EQ ""%>
<%else%>
Company Name:</td><td><%CompanyName%><td><tr>
<%endif%>
<tr>
<td><%if Address EQ ""%>
<%else%>
Street Address:</td><td><%Address%><td><tr>
<%endif%>
<tr>
<td><%if Address_2 EQ ""%>
<%else%>
Address (cont):</td><td><%Address_2%><td><tr>
<%endif%>
<tr>
<td><%if City EQ ""%>
<%else%>
City:</td><td><%City%><td><tr>
<%endif%>
<tr>
<td><%if StateOrProvince EQ ""%>
```

Building Dynamic Web Pages with SQL Server

CHAPTER 24

711

24

**BUILDING
DYNAMIC
WEB PAGES**

```
<%else%>
State/Province:</td><td><%StateOrProvince%><td><tr>
<%endif%>
<tr>
<td><%if PostalCode EQ ""%>
<%else%>
Postal Code:</td><td><%PostalCode%><td><tr>
<%endif%>
<tr>
<td><%if Country EQ ""%>
<%else%>
Country:</td><td><%Country%><td><tr>
<%endif%>
<tr>
<td><%if WorkPhoneNumber EQ ""%>
<%else%>
Work Phone Number:</td><td><%WorkPhoneNumber%><td><tr>
<%endif%>
<tr>
<td><%if HomePhoneNumber EQ ""%>
<%else%>
Home Phone Number:</td><td><%HomePhoneNumber%><td><tr>
<%endif%>
<tr>
<td><%if FaxNumber EQ ""%>
<%else%>
Fax Phone Number:</td><td><%FaxNumber%><td><tr>
<%endif%>
<tr>
<td><%if E_Mail EQ ""%>
<%else%>
E-Mail Address:</td><td><%E_Mail%><td><tr>
<%endif%>
<tr>
<td><%if URL EQ ""%>
<%else%>
Home Page URL:</td><td><%URL%><td><tr>
<%endif%>
<tr>
<td><%if Note EQ ""%>
<%else%>
Note:</td><td><%Note%><td><tr>
<%endif%>
</table>
<p>
<%enddetail%>
<p>
<hr>
<table width=100%>
<tr><td width=50%><address><font size=2>
<em>Copyright &#169; 1996 Knowles Consulting. All
rights reserved</em></font> </address>
</td><td align=right width=50%><div align=right>
<address><font size=2><em>Last Updated: June 21, 1996</em></font> </address>
</div>
</td></tr>
</table>
</body>
</html>
```

Notice that the table definition is between the `<%begindetail%>` and `<%enddetail%>` tags. This will display one or more records on the page, depending on the number of records returned in the result set. The only real difference between this page and the others you have examined is that no check occurs to verify that at least one record was found. However, this check is not needed. After all, to get to this page in the first place, you must have clicked on a hypertext link created in the previous page (`SearchGuestBook.HTX`), which would have been created only if a record had been found. You can also use other tags, like the `<%begindetail%>` and `<%enddetail%>` tags, in your HTX files.

Using the SQL Server Web Assistant

While you can use the IDC to build dynamic Web pages that interact with the user, you can also use the Web Assistant. The main difference between the IDC and the Web Assistant is that the Web Assistant is not designed to interact with the user. Instead, it is designed to publish a database online. It does this by creating static Web pages; but perhaps *static* is the wrong word. Most people consider a static page to be a Web page that does not change its contents. However, with the Web Assistant, these Web pages can be automatically refreshed when a new record is inserted into the database or when a specific time interval is reached. Therefore, the Web page contents could change, and you have the ability to create a dynamic Web page. If you combine the IDC with the Web Administrator, you can build a fully interactive online order system, for example.

Creating an interactive online order system would require an event-driven processing methodology, where you would respond to actions that occur, rather than a hierarchical methodology, where you would control the data flow in a step-by-step process. Let me show you how this could work. First, let's lay a few rules for the groundwork:

- You have an ODBC database containing your product inventory. This inventory database contains the quantity, price, and a description of the items.
- You want to publish an online catalog using this information.
- You want to accept client orders from the online catalog.

To bring these three basic ideas together and build an interactive order-entry database, you'd have to build the following constructs:

- Online catalog—You could use the Web Administrator to build this Web page using a query designed to select all items from your product inventory database whenever the item quantity is greater than one. Anytime the database changes, you could have the Web Administrator rebuild the page. The Web page could include a hypertext link to another Web page containing the order form.
- Order form—The order form will use the IDC to insert an order record into the Order databases.

■ Order database—This database would contain information about the client and about the product ordered. It might contain order number, date, name, address, payment, and product fields. For optimum results, this would be a client/server database (such as SQL Server) rather than an application database (such as Access) so that you could benefit from the ability to execute code automatically (like triggers or scheduled procedures). In this fashion, whenever an order record is entered into the database, your code could automatically decrement the quantity for the item contained in your product inventory database. This same code could automatically notify a sales or shipping representative and update other databases. These databases could be used by applications within your company to automate the shipping and billing processes.

The basic work flow, then, to obtain an order would follow these steps:

1. The client connects to your Web site.

2. The client selects your catalog to browse through it.

> **TIP**
>
> You could create a custom query form using the IDC to search for specific items in your catalog. The description field could be used as a searchable text field, for example, so the client could specify the type of items of interest. The returned result set, based on this query, could be displayed on another custom IDC HTML page. The user could then follow the same order process once she selects the item to order.

3. The client selects an item and clicks a link to order the item.

4. An order form appears. The user fills out the relevant data fields and submits the form. This submission inserts a record into the Order database.

5. The Order database insert trigger is activated. This could send an e-mail message requesting manual intervention to continue the order and shipping process. Or the trigger could cause a cascade of events to occur in which one or more databases are updated (like the quantity field for the item in the product inventory database), applications are executed, and finally the product is shipped to the user.

6. When the product inventory database is updated to reflect that there is one fewer of the ordered item, the Web Administrator could update the online catalog page so the next user will see an accurate count for the item. If the current user purchases the item, then attempts to reorder the item based on his cached online version of the catalog, your IDC order form would report an error, since the query executed by the IDC would return real-time results. (The query would return no records as the quantity field in the product inventory database would be 0.)

To use the Web Assistant to build your Web pages, follow these steps:

1. Launch the SQL Server Web Assistant, located in the SQL Server 6.5 program group, to display the SQL Server Web Assistant - Login dialog box (see Figure 24.2).

FIGURE 24.2.

Specifying the SQL Server parameters for the Web Assistant.

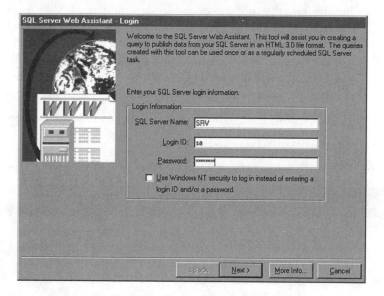

2. Enter the name of your SQL Server installation in the SQL Server Name field.
3. Enter a username in the Logon ID field.
4. Enter a password for the username in the Password field.

NOTE

If you are using the mixed, or integrated, security models, you can enable the Use Windows NT security to log in instead of entering a login ID and/or a password check box. This way, your current credentials will be used.

5. Click the Next button to display the dialog shown in Figure 24.3.
6. In the How do you want to select data for the Web page? group, specify one of the following:

   ■ Build a query from a database hierarchy—This option specifies that the database table you select will be posted on the Web in its entirety, unless you specify additional restrictions in the query window at the bottom of the dialog.

■ Enter a query as free-form text—When selected, the dialog box will change to let you choose a database and enter a free-form query. This free-form query will be used to return a result set. This result set will be displayed on the Web page created by the Web Assistant.

■ Use a query in a stored procedure—When selected, the dialog box will change to allow you to choose a database, choose a stored procedure in the database, and enter any command-line arguments for the stored procedure.

FIGURE 24.3.

Specifying the SQL Server database for the Web Assistant.

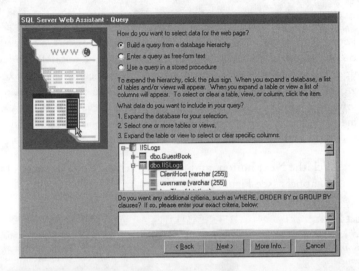

TIP

You can publish multiple tables simply by selecting the list box. If you only want to publish part of a table, you can expand the table item and select the specific fields you want to publish.

---

7. When you have made your selection, click the Next button. For this discussion, I will assume you have chosen the Build a query from a database hierarchy option and selected a single table.

8. The SQL Server Web Assistant - Scheduling dialog will appear. Choose one of the following from the Scheduling Options drop-down list box:

■ Now—This option specifies that the Web page will be created immediately.

■ Later—This option specifies that the Web page will be created one time at a user-specified date and time.

■ When Data Changes—This option specifies that the Web page will be re-created automatically whenever the database changes.

■ On Certain Days of the Week—This option specifies that the Web page will be re-created on specific days at specific times.

■ On a Regular Basis—This option specifies that the Web page will be re-created at scheduled time intervals.

> **TIP**
>
> For high-traffic sites, the On Certain Days of the Week or On a Regular Basis options can be particularly useful. Although the data would not be updated in realtime, it could be updated frequently enough to promote a sense of continuity (for example, new products would constantly be added to the database) to the client. This could benefit you by lowering the system resource demands on your server during peak activity periods, which means that your server could support more simultaneous user connections.

9. Click the Next button, and the SQL Server Web Assistant - File Options dialog box will appear (see Figure 24.4).

FIGURE 24.4.

Specifying the Web Assistant Web page parameters.

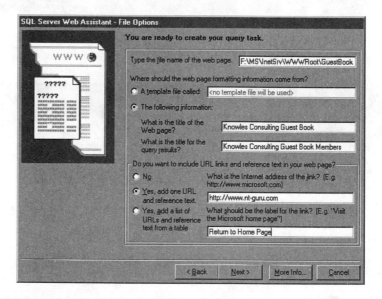

10. Specify a path and filename for the Web page in the Type the file name of the web page field.

11. Choose the A template file called radio button and enter the name of the HTML template file to be used to format your output. Or choose The following information radio button and specify the Web page title in the What is the title of the web page? field, and then enter a subtitle in the What is the title for the query results? field.

12. If you want to add an HTML hypertext link, enable the Yes, add one URL and reference text radio button, and supply a single URL and description. Or enable the Yes, add a list of URLs and reference text from a table radio button and specify the table name containing this information.

13. Click the Next button to display the SQL Server Web Assistant - Formatting dialog box, shown in Figure 24.5.

FIGURE 24.5.

Specifying the formatting parameters.

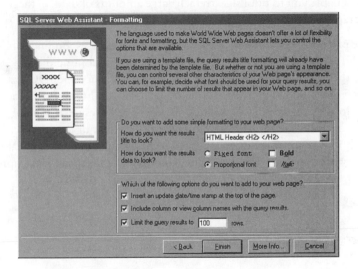

14. Specify the size of the HTML header to be used for the result columns in the How do you want the results title to look? field.

15. Specify how the result rows will be displayed by enabling the Fixed font radio button to use a fixed-width font or the Proportional font radio button to use a proportional-width font.

16. To make the results rows more visible, enable the Bold check box. To emphasize the result rows, enable the Italic check box.

17. To insert a time/date time stamp at the beginning of the page, enable the Insert an update date/time stamp at the top of the page check box.

18. To include column name headers on the output, enable the Include column or view column names with the query results check box.

24

BUILDING
DYNAMIC
WEB PAGES

19. To limit the number of rows on a single Web page, enable the Limit the query results to check box and enter a value in the rows field.

20. Click the Finish button to build your Web page.

Summary

In this chapter you learn by example how to build a guest book using the IDC. You learn how to build the HTML forms, how to build the IDC definition files, and how to build the HTML template files. You also learn how to use the SQL Server Web Assistant to build Web pages to display data from your database in a semistatic form. Although it is not interactive, this method does enable you to publish extremely large amounts of data on the Web. If combined with the interactive capabilities provided by the IDC, an interactive online system can be built.

The primary reason to use the IDC rather than a corresponding Microsoft dbWeb implementation is for enhanced control over the behavior (including the look and feel) of the Web page and the query used to return the resulting data. Since the IDC is a predefined interface that uses HTML documents, HTX, and IDC files to interface with a database, it is easier than developing a custom CGI application, which requires development with a compiler. Since the IDC is an ISAPI application, it runs in the context of the Internet Information Server. This method is more efficient than a corresponding custom CGI application, which runs in a separate process address space, meaning you have less overhead and improved user response time.

CHAPTER 25

Using Crystal Reports for Internet Information Server

IN THIS CHAPTER

- What Is Crystal Reports for Internet Information Server?   720

- Creating a Report   721

- Using Crystal Reports Live on Your Web Server   723

When you installed the Internet Information Server (IIS), you had the opportunity to install Seagate Software's Crystal Reports for the Internet Information Server. This special version of Crystal Reports is specifically designed to generate reports using your IIS log files. You can use Crystal Reports to view IIS-formatted log files, NCSA-formatted log files, and IIS logs stored on an ODBC-compliant database. Crystal Reports can also generate live activity reports using active server pages. In this chapter you will explore some of these capabilities to help prepare you to use these tools.

> **NOTE**
>
> The version of Crystal Reports you will be using may not be a 100 percent complete product. (In the version—4.5—that I downloaded from the Internet, the help file is missing many related topics, the online documentation is scanty, and the application has a few bugs.) Its primary purpose is to provide you with an evaluation copy of the product. If you like it, you can upgrade to the complete product (version 5.0). Keep this information in mind as you work with the product and try not to fault it for its inadequacies. After all, you did get it for free.

What Is Crystal Reports for Internet Information Server?

Crystal Reports for the Internet Information Server consists of several components. Not all of these components are accessible directly by the user, however, as you will see once you start working with the product. The product has the following components:

- Crystal Web Publishing Interface—This component is a Windows application that uses a WYSIWYG interface to aid you in generating presentation-quality reports. You can print these reports to your printer, or by using the Crystal Web Application Interface, you can print your reports directly to the Web.

- Crystal Web Activity DLL—This component provides the interface between the Crystal Reports Engine and the Web server log. It treats all log files as a common database with standard fields, which can then be used to create in-depth reports.

- Crystal Reports Engine—This component retrieves selected data from the database. The data is then sorted, summarized, grouped as specified by the report, and then presented in a presentation-quality format. Web developers can use the Crystal Reports Engine to add reporting capabilities to their Web pages with minimal coding.

- Crystal Web Application Interface—This component provides the interface between your Web pages and the Crystal Reports Engine. It provides a mechanism to allow parameters to be passed to the Crystal Reports Engine to specify report information.

Creating a Report

If you will be using Crystal Reports on log files rather than on ODBC-compliant databases, then the samples provided with the product should get you up and running in no time. The first thing you will need to do for each report is to specify the location of your IIS log files using the Crystal Reports application. (See Figure 25.1.)

FIGURE 25.1.

Using Crystal Reports with IIS log files.

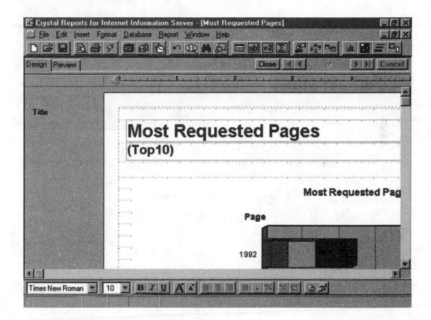

Just follow these steps to change the log file location:

1. Choose Set Location from the Database menu. The Set Location dialog box will appear.

2. Make sure the in960628 entry in the Databases field is selected. Then click the Set Location button and wait for a few minutes. Why the wait? Because the default location for the log files is on a shared directory called LogFiles on a remote server called VADER, you will have to wait for the request to connect to this server to fail before you can change the default locations.

   The Select IIS Log Files and Dates dialog, shown in Figure 25.2, will then appear.

3. Enable the Standard (in*.log) radio button.

4. Specify the correct location for your log files in the text box below the radio buttons. The default log file location for an IIS installation should be %SystemRoot%\InetSrv\LogFiles.

25

**USING CRYSTAL
REPORTS FOR IIS**

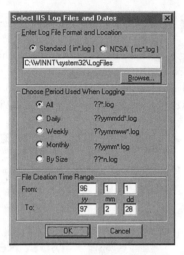

FIGURE 25.2.

*Specifying the location
of the IIS log files.*

5. Choose a file format type by enabling one option in the Choose Period Used When Logging. These types directly relate to the naming convention used when you enabled logging using the Internet Service Manager.

6. Specify a file creation date to help eliminate files by specifying a start and end date in the From and To fields.

7. Click the OK button. The Choose SQL Table dialog box will be displayed. Do not be concerned by the name of this dialog. It is configured to use the database files that you specified rather than a SQL Server table. (See Figure 25.3.) Click the OK button to continue.

NOTE

If you are using ODBC databases instead of IIS log files, then you have another step or two to complete. When you get to step 7, click the Log On Server button to display the Log On Server dialog box. In the Server Type list, select the Microsoft SQL Server entry or the ODBC DSN that you are using to connect to your IIS log database. Then click the OK button. The Select Data Source dialog box will then appear. Just select the DSN you use to connect your database and click the OK button. If a logon dialog box appears, enter the user identification and password and continue. Then select the appropriate table and database to use in the Choose SQL Table dialog box and click the OK button.

The previous dialog boxes will then close, and you will return to the Set Location dialog box. The location information displayed on the bottom of the dialog box should now reflect the correct location of your IIS log files.

8. Click the Done button to close the Set Location dialog box and return to the Crystal Reports editor.

Figure 25.3.
Specifying the IIS log files for Crystal Reports to use.

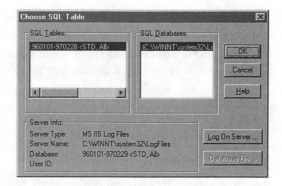

If your reports have a few errors relating to data types when they are executed, you might want to use the modified reports that I have created. You can find the modified reports on the CD-ROM in the SOURCE\CHAP25 directory. They are basically the same report files, but they log on to an ODBC database and have been modified to eliminate the type-related errors that occurred. I hope I didn't add any new errors, but if I did, it will be up to you to fix them. Do let me know if you encounter any problems in this area, as I would like to fix them.

> **NOTE**
>
> If you come across type-related error messages while using Crystal Reports, check the report options using Report Options from the File menu. If the Convert Date-Time to Date field is enabled (checked), then you should disable it. If this change solves your type-related error messages, then you may want to perform this action on a global scope as well. The global change will prevent this problem from occurring in any new reports you build. You can accomplish this task by choosing Options from the File menu. Then click the Reporting tab to display the Reporting properties sheet, uncheck the Convert Date-Time field to Date check box, and click the OK button to save your changes.

You also need to modify several bits and pieces of the sample HTML documents to work with an ODBC database. The following discussion explains some of the modifications.

Using Crystal Reports Live on Your Web Server

It is possible to use the same reports you created using Crystal Reports within an HTML page on your Web server. If you used an ODBC or Microsoft SQL Server data source, then you can also generate a logon screen automatically. The samples that are included with Crystal Reports are designed for use with the IIS log files. I've modified these samples (with appropriate comments) to work with an ODBC database. Here's how the process works:

1. Make sure you have installed the Microsoft active server pages software before trying to run the sample applications. The samples require active server pages (ASP).

2. Use the Internet Service Manager to create a new virtual directory for your ASP files. This directory must have both read and execute permission.

3. Copy all the source files from the SOURCE\CHAP25 directory on the CD-ROM to this virtual directory.

4. Change the database location to point to your IIS log files. (You can use the previous section, "Creating a Report," as a guide.) These log files can be either a local file or tables in an ODBC database.

5. Execute your Web browser and load the file index.htm. You must supply a URL in the form of http://yourservername.yourdomainname/YourVirtualDirectory/Index.HTM in order for this process to work correctly.

   The Web page shown in Figure 25.4 will appear. It is a bit different from the samples provided by Seagate. It is a live page, and I will leave it on my server for a while for you to try. The URL to access this page is http://www.nt-guru.com/aspsample/chap25.

FIGURE 25.4.

Generating a report on the Web using Crystal Reports.

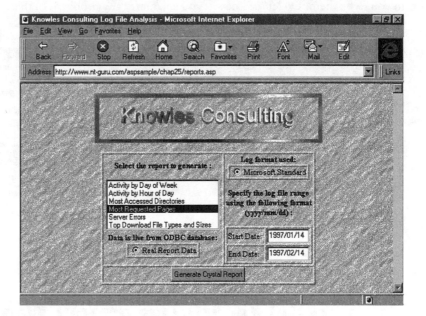

6. Select the report type to view in the Select the report to generate field.

7. Enter a start and end date to use as the base data for the report in the Start Date and End Date fields, respectively.

> **TIP**
>
> You might notice that my page automatically sets the start date to be one month less than the end date (the current date). I modified the source code to do this step automatically so you can obtain a status report for the last month.

8. Click the Generate Crystal Report button. A page will be displayed asking you to wait while the report is generated. Then the logon dialog box shown in Figure 25.5 appears.

FIGURE 25.5.

Logging on to the database.

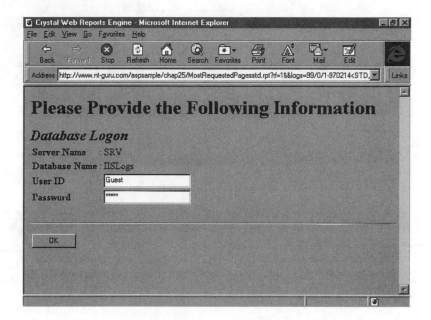

9. Enter a valid username with access to the database and click the OK button. For my live reports, I have created a user account with only select (that is, read) permissions for you to use. It has access only to the IISLogs database. The username is Guest and the password is guest.

   Feel free to try out the reporting capabilities. Just remember that I can't promise how long this feature will remain on my site.

After you click the OK button in step 9, you will have to wait for the query to execute and the report page to be created. The larger the time period (specified by the start and end dates), the longer the wait. The report will be similar to that shown in Figure 25.6.

FIGURE 25.6.

A live report on the Web server.

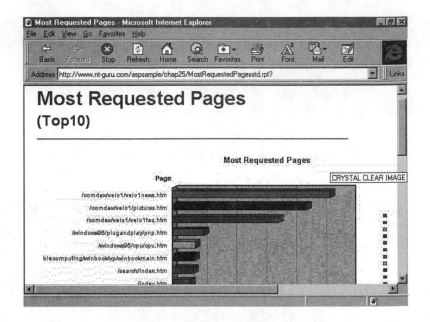

FIGURE 25.6.

A live report on the Web server.

Don't bother to click on the URLs within the reports. From what I could tell, the reporting module has a bug in the HTML code it outputs. The URLs will not work properly. We can only hope that this problem is fixed in version 5.0.

> **NOTE**
>
> If I can obtain a copy of Crystal Reports 5.0 from Seagate Software, I will let you know if these problems have been fixed. Just check out http://www.nt-guru.com/books/ occasionally for any updated information.

Summary

In this chapter you explore some of the possibilities of Crystal Reports for Internet Information Server. If you decide to continue using the product, you should consider upgrading to the full version. The product is extremely useful for generating the type of high-quality reports you would be proud to present at weekly staff meetings. You should also examine the source code carefully to see how the ASP file is used to call the Crystal Reports Engine as well as to inspect the modifications I made to support ODBC databases. The next chapter describes the Index Information Server and shows you how to tailor it to your requirements.

Indexing Your Web Site with the Index Information Server

IN THIS CHAPTER

- Using the Index Information Server   *728*

CHAPTER

26

The Index Information Server is an add-on component to the Internet Information Server. You can use it to provide full-text search capabilities of your Web site. Consequently, any user who stops by your site can easily search your site to find the information he or she wants to look at—which translates into the user spending more time at your Web site. The documentation included with the Index Information Server provides a basic understanding of what the product is and how it works. However, the documentation does neglect some of the more useful information, such as, how to customize the Index Information Server for use at your site. Therefore, this chapter focuses on some of these issues to prepare you to use the Index Information Server on your site.

NOTE

To access the Index Information Server documentation, just choose the Index Server Online Documentation shortcut in the Microsoft Index Server program group.

Using the Index Information Server

The following sections show you how to successfully index your entire Web site with the Index Information Server. You can start using the Index Information Server sample query form on your Web site almost immediately after you install the Index Information Server. (For additional information on installing the Index Information Server, refer to Chapter 5, "IIS Preparation and Installation.") You may need to spend some time modifying your installed base of HTML documents, however, to obtain the maximum benefit, which is the topic of the next section.

Next you learn how to create a custom search page. This section contains the real meat of the chapter because the process involves many components. First is the HTML document you will use as the search page, which is basically an HTML document with various form controls. This form will send information to an Internet Data Query (IDQ) file. The IDQ file is where the actual interaction with the Index Information Server ISAPI (formally known as the Internet Server Application Programming Interface) application occurs. Once the result set (the data returned by the user query) has been created, it will be displayed (on the user's Web browser) using the HTML Extension (HTX) file.

Creating these files is not very difficult, but understanding and using the variables for the IDQ and HTX files can be difficult at times. Although I cannot explain every detail in this chapter, I've tried to provide the basic information you need to begin working with and customizing the Index Information Server.

Preparing Your Documents for the Index Information Server

Preparing your documents for the Index Information Server is probably not going to be as bad an experience as you might expect. Then again, it might be even worse than you expect if you have a very large installed base of HTML documents and did not use the standard meta tags to describe your documents. Adding meta tags to all of your documents retroactively could be quite a task to accomplish. Should you be in this position, I hope you can develop an application to automate the task for you. If not, you might want to forget about applying the meta tags to old documents and concentrate on adding the meta tags to new documents.

The Index Information Server uses the following meta tags:

- Description—Specifies an abstract comment that describes the contents of the document. If this tag is used within the document, the Index Information Server will use it as the abstract to be displayed to the user. If this tag is not present, the Index Information Server will automatically generate an abstract using various portions of text from the document title, headings, and plain text.

- Author—Specifies the author who created the document. This tag can be quite useful if you have multiple writers for your site.

- Keywords—Specifies a series of keywords to be used by the Index Information Server. Even though the Index Information Server will automatically generate a word list for the document, you may want to create a keyword list to make sure the document is found. If you wrote a document on the Windows 95 Plug-and-Play features, for example, but never included the acronym PnP, then you could include PnP in the keyword list. That way when a user performed a query on PnP, he or she would receive your Plug-and-Play document in the result set.

- Subject—Specifies a small comment that describes the subject matter. You can use this tag to describe the contents of the document or to organize your documents into a group to make searching easier for the user.

- MS.Category—Specifies a higher-level grouping of the document. Not everyone uses this option because there is no friendly name mapping for the associated property. Instead, it requires a complex globally unique identifier (GUID) number to access the value in the IDQ file. This terminology may sound like Greek to you, but what it boils down to is that you cannot specify a named object, such as CiCatalog, to access this property. Instead you must create the friendly name by specifying a name to map to a long series of numbers in the IDQ file. This process can be extremely tiresome, which is why not everyone uses this option.

- MS.Locale—Specifies the locale or language of the document. This option is quite useful for a Web site that supports customers in several countries. By specifying the locale, you can return information to the user in a language he or she can actually understand!

- Content-type—Specifies the character set identifier, or code document, of the document. The function of this option is similar to the function of the MS.Locale tag, which is used on the Web server, but Content-type is more often used by Web browsers. The Web browser can read this tag and use it to specify the character set to use when displaying the document.

Of course, you can't just stick these tags anywhere in your document. You must place meta tags between the <HEAD> and </HEAD> tags of your HTML document. Also, each tag consists of two parts: a NAME= component, where the just-mentioned tags are appended, and a CONTENT= tag, which specifies the actual value to be associated with the meta tag. The completed tags will look like the following code:

```
<META NAME= "DESCRIPTION" CONTENT= "Describes how the Windows 95 Plug and Play
features work. The document includes diagrams of the various components and is
suitable for intermediate to advanced readers.">
<META NAME= "AUTHOR" CONTENT= "Arthur E. Knowles">
<META NAME= "KEYWORDS" CONTENT= "PnP, BIOS, PCI">
<META NAME= "SUBJECT" CONTENT= "Windows 95 Plug and Play">
<META NAME= "MS.CATEGORY" CONTENT= "BOOKS">
<META NAME= "MS.LOCALE" CONTENT= "EN-US">
<META NAME= HTTP-EQUIV= "CONTENT-TYPE" CONTENT = "text/html; charset=iso-8859-1">
```

These meta tags are associated with variables used in the IDQ file. You will learn more about how to access the information contained within these tags throughout the chapter.

Creating the Search Page

In the previous section, you learned about some of the meta tags that the Index Information Server can use to supply specific information to its search engine. These tags are quite useful, but only if you have a search form to use. The samples supplied by Microsoft are a good starting point. The forms on my Web site are based on these forms, as shown in Figure 26.1, although I have modified them a bit to reduce the Internet bandwidth requirements. I've also changed the samples to use other locations.

> **CAUTION**
>
> If you make significant changes to the sample files for use in a production environment without changing the location and then upgrade the Index Information Server, you will lose all your changes when the setup program replaces these sample files.

Now that you know why you want to change these sample files if you plan to use them, you are ready to learn more about how to create a search page by examining a working model. The source code for my search page (Index.HTM) appears as Listing 26.1.

FIGURE 26.1.

*A working Index
Information Server
search page.*

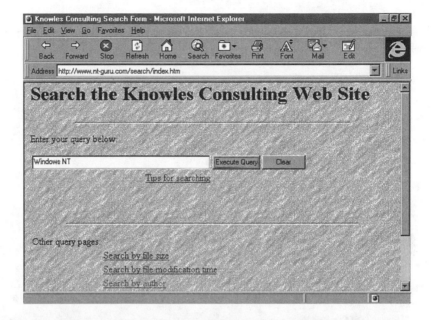

> **NOTE**
>
> The numbers in this example are for clarity and discussion purposes only. They are not part
> of the HTML file.

Listing 26.1. The HTML code to create the sample search page for the Index Information Server.

```
1.  <!DOCTYPE HTML PUBLIC "-//IETF//DTD HTML//EN">
2.  <html>
3.  <head>
4.  <meta http-equiv="Content-Type"
content="text/html; charset=iso-8859-1">
5.  <meta name="Author" content="Arthur E. Knowles">
6.  <meta name="Description"
content="Search the Knowles Consulting web site using the Microsoft Index
Information Server">
7.  <meta name="Subject" content="Search page">
8.  <meta name="FORMATTER" content="Microsoft FrontPage 2.0">
9.  <meta name="GENERATOR" content="Microsoft FrontPage 2.0">
10. <title>Knowles Consulting Search Form</title>
11. </head>
12. <body stylesrc="../Index.HTM" topmargin="0">
13. <h1>Search the Knowles Consulting Web Site</h1>
14. <hr size="3" width="75%">
15. <form action="/scripts/query.idq" method="GET">
16.     <input type="hidden" name="CiMaxRecordsPerPage" value="10"><input
17.     type="hidden" name="CiScope" value="/"><input type="hidden"
```

continues

Listing 26.1. continued

```
18.        name="TemplateName" value="query"><input type="hidden"
19.        name="CiSort" value="rank[d]"><input type="hidden"
20.        name="HTMLQueryForm" value="/search/index.htm"><p>Enter your
21.        query below: </p>
22.        <table border="0">
23.            <tr>
24.                <td><input type="text" size="55" maxlength="100"
25.                name="UserRestriction"></td>
26.                <td><input type="submit" value="Execute Query"></td>
27.                <td><input type="reset" value="Clear"></td>
28.            </tr>
29.            <tr>
30.                <td align="right"><a href="/search/tipshelp.htm">Tips
31.                for searching</a></td>
32.            </tr>
33.        </table>
34.  </form>
35.  <p> </p>
36.  <hr size="3" width="80%">
37.  <table border="0">
38.      <tr>
39.          <td>Other query pages:</td>
40.      </tr>
41.      <tr>
42.          <td> </td>
43.          <td><a href="/search/filesize.htm">Search by file size</a></td>
44.      </tr>
45.      <tr>
46.          <td> </td>
47.          <td><a href="/search/filetime.htm">Search by file
48.          modification time</a></td>
49.      </tr>
50.      <tr>
51.          <td> </td>
52.          <td><a href="/search/author.htm">Search by author</a></td>
53.      </tr>
54.  </table>
55.  <hr size="3" width="80%">
56.  <table border="0" width="100%">
57.      <tr>
58.          <td width="50%"><address>
59.              <font size="2"><em>Copyright © 1996 Knowles
60.              Consulting. All rights reserved<br>
61.              </em></font>For comments or suggestion send e-mail
62.              to:<br>
63.              <a href="MAILTO:webmaster@nt-guru.com">webmaster@nt-guru.com</a>
64.          </address>
65.      </td>
66.      <td align="right" valign="top" width="50%"><div
67.      align="right"><address>
68.          This page was last modified on:<br>
69.          <!--webbot bot="Timestamp" startspan s-type="EDITED"
70.          s-format="%A, %B %d, %Y" -->Tuesday, February 11, 1997<!--webbot
71.          bot="Timestamp" i-checksum="60550" endspan -->
```

```
72.          </address>
73.          </div></td>
74.      </tr>
75.  </table>
76.  </body>
77.  </html>
```

As you can see, the search page is really nothing more than a form. The real work occurs elsewhere, but everything has to start somewhere. Right? So, notice the meta tags in lines 4 through 7. These entries specify the character set the Web page was designed with, the author of the document, the description for the document, and the document subject. The real meat of the document occurs between lines 15 and 34, which is where I specified the actual form the user will interact with. The following discussion focuses on these lines.

Line 15 begins the actual form definition. The form will send the information submitted by the user to the IDQ file (more on these in the next section) Query.IDQ located in the virtual Scripts directory. Lines 17 through 20 include several hidden variables that will also be passed to the IDQ file. Each variable has a specific purpose:

- CiMaxRecordsPerPage—Specifies the maximum number of records to be displayed on a single result set page. The current value is 10, which does not require too many mouse clicks to scroll through the document. You could create another field on the form, if desired, and let the user specify the total number of records to display on the page.

- CiScope—Specifies the starting directory to search through for the query. The current value specified here is to use the root directory and search the entire site. By specifying a different directory, you could effectively limit the search.

- TemplateName—Specifies the name of the file to use to display the result set. This field is used by the other files to specify the name of detail file without hard-coding in a value.

- CiSort—Specifies the sort order for the result set. The current value is rank[d], which means to rank (sort) the records in descending order. To change this value to ascending order, change the value to rank[a].

- HTMLQueryForm—Specifies the name of the current HTML document. This field is also used by the other files to return to the search page without hard-coding in a value.

Lines 24 and 25 create the actual input field where the user enters his query. The data in the input field is stored in the variable UserRestriction and passed to the IDQ file. Lines 26 and 27 create Submit and Reset buttons for the form. Line 34 ends the form definition. The rest of the document is not essential, though I would like to point out that lines 37 through 54 create a table of links to alternative search pages. These links are nice options and can be to the user. Although I won't be discussing these pages here, you can find the source code for them in the SOURCE\CHAP26 directory on the CD-ROM or on my Web site.

Creating the Internet Data Query File

The IDQ file is similar to an Internet Database Connector (IDC) file. The IDC file (`Query.IDQ`) that my search page uses appears as Listing 26.2.

> **NOTE**
>
> The numbers in this example are for discussion purposes only. They are not part of the HTML file.

Listing 26.2. The HTML code for the IDQ file used to create the sample search page.

```
1. [Query]
2. # CiCatalog=f:MS\INetServ\
3. CiColumns = filename, size, rank, characterization, vpath, DocTitle, write
4. CiFlags=DEEP
5. CiScope=%CiScope%
6. CiRestriction=(%UserRestriction%) &! #vpath *\_vti_*
7. CiMaxRecordsInResultSet=300
8. CiMaxRecordsPerPage=%CiMaxRecordsPerPage%
9. CiTemplate=/Scripts/%TemplateName%.htx
10. CiSort=%CiSort%
11. CiForceUseCi=true
```

Line 1 specifies the block section for the query. It must be present in the file, or you will receive an error message. Line 2, which is commented out, specifies the location of the Index catalog. I've included it for reference because it can be very useful, particularly if you have several catalogs and want to override the default location specified in the registry. Line 3 specifies the fields to be gathered for the result set. This result set will then be displayed using the HTML extension file (HTX) that you will learn more about in the next section. Line 4 specifies that the search should include any subdirectories of the directory specified by the variable `%CiScope%` in line 5. Line 5 assigns the value (\) passed by the search page (line 17 of `Index.HTM`) to `CiScope`. You can look at this as passing a local value on from one page to another. Line 6 specifies the query—in this case, it is the data contained within the `%UserRestriction%` variable, and the result set must not include any records with the phrase `#vpath *\_vti_*`. The phrase just makes sure the user does not see data from the FrontPage informational files. These files are used only by FrontPage and really do not include any useful data. Line 7 specifies the maximum number of records to return in the result set, and line 8 specifies the maximum number of records to display on a page (the HTX file). Line 9 specifies the location and name of the HTX file to be used to display the result set. (The value for `%TemplateName%` was specified in the `Index.HTM` form.) Line 10 specifies using the sort order passed to it by the `Index.HTM` form to sort the result set. Line 11 specifies using the content index even if it is not current. Otherwise, the user might not get a returned result set.

26

You can use other variables within your IDQ file as well. Table 26.1 lists the user-configurable variables, Table 26.2 lists the various locale definitions, and Table 26.3 lists the standard CGI variables that you may use within both IDQ and HTX files.

Table 26.1. User configurable variables.

Parameter	Description	Note
CiCatalog	Overrides the default location for the catalog.	If not specified, the registry value for CiCatalog is used. If the registry value is not specified, the CiScope is used instead. If neither is available, an error message wil be displayed.
CiColumns	Specifies a list of output column name to use in the HTX file.	
CiDeferNonIndexedTrimming	When set to TRUE, specifies that the result set will be limited to a trimmed version of the CiMaxRecordsInResultSet.	When this value is set to TRUE, the number of records returned to the user may be less than that defined by CiMaxRecordsInResultSet.
CiFlags	Specifies the query flags to determine the depth of the search. When set to DEEP, the directory specified in CiScope and all subdirectories will be searched. When set to SHALLOW, only the directory specified in CiScope will be searched.	
CiForceUseCi	Specifies that the content index will be used even if it is out of date.	
CiLocale	Specifies the locale used to issue the query.	See Table 26.2 for a complete listing of locale codes.

continues

Table 26.1. continued

Parameter	Description	Note
CiMaxRecordsInResultSet	Specifies the maximum number of query results to return from a query.	
CiMaxRecordsPerPage	Specifies the maximum number of records to be displayed on the page.	
CiRestriction	Specifies the query or what to search for.	
CiScope	Specifies the staring directory for the search.	
CiSort	Specifies the sort order. This entry is a list of column names separated by columns.	Using this option may force a nonsequential query to be used.
CiTemplate	Specifies the output template (HTX file) to be used to display the result set.	

Table 26.2. Locale codes and their associated language.

Language	Locale code
Chinese	ZH, ZH-CN, ZH-TW
Bulgarian	BG
Croatian	HR
Czech	CS
Danish	DA
Dutch	NL
English (Great Britain)	EN-GB
English (US)	EN, EN-US
Finnish	FI
French	FR, FR-FR
French (Canadian)	FR-CA
German	DE

Language	Locale code
Greek	EL
Icelandic	IS
Italian	IT
Japanese	JA
Korean	KO
Neutral (uses built-in word wrapping)	NEUTRAL
Norwegian	NO
Polish	PL
Portuguese	PT
Portuguese (Brazilian)	PT-BR
Romanian	RO
Russian	RU
Slovak	SK
Slovenian	SL
Spanish	ES, ES-ES
Swedish	SV
Turkish	TR

Table 26.3. Variables available from standard CGI parameters.

Parameter	Description	Note
ALL_HTTP	All HTTP headers that are not parsed into one of the other listed variables in this table.	
AUTH_TYPE	Specifies the authorization type in use.	If the user has been authenticated by the server, the return value will be Basic. Otherwise, the entry will not be present.
CONTENT_LENGTH	Specifies the number of bytes the script can expect to receive from the client.	

continues

Table 26.3. continued

Parameter	Description	Note
CONTENT_TYPE	The content type of the information supplied in the POST request.	
GATEWAY_INTERFACE	Specifies the revision level of the CGI specification.	
HTTP_ACCEPT	Returns special-case HTTP header information.	
MaxRecords	Specifies the maximum number of records that can be returned.	Can be used only in an if...else... endif statement.
PATH_INFO	Additional path information as given by the client.	This value will contain the trailing part of the URL after the script name but before the query string (if any query string was supplied).
PATH_TRANSLATED	The same as PATH_INFO, but without any virtual pathname translation.	
QUERY_STRING	Specifies the information after the ? in a script query.	
REMOTE_ADDR	Specifies the IP address of the client.	
REMOTE_HOST	Specifies the hostname of the client.	
REMOTE_USER	Specifies the username supplied by the client and authorized by the server.	
REQUEST_METHOD	Specifies the HTTP request method.	
SCRIPT_NAME	Specifies the name of the script being executed.	
SERVER_NAME	Specifies the name of the server (or IP address) as it should appear in self-referencing URLs.	

Parameter	Description	Note
SERVER_PORT	Specifies the TCP/IP port on which the request was received.	
SERVER_PROTOCOL	Specifies the name and usually the HTTP/1.0. version of the request.	
SERVER_SOFTWARE	Specifies the name and version number of the Web server under which the IIS extension is executing.	

Creating the HTML Extension File

Well, you made it to the last step of the process: the creation of the HTML extension files. Understanding how these files work is important because they determine just what the users will see on their Web browsers. Before you look at the files, however, it may pay off to learn a bit about what an HTML extension (or HTX) file contains. An HTX file contains extensions to the HTML language, which are enclosed in a `<%'  '%>` tag pair. The returned result set is merged with the HTML document between the `<%begindetail%>` and `<%enddetail&>` tag pairs. Tables 26.4 and 26.5 summarize several HTX variables, which, when combined with the `if...else...endif` flow control statement, determine how your output will appear. As an example, Listing 26.3 shows portions of the Query.HTX file used by my search page.

Listing 26.3. A partial HTML code snippet from the HTX file used to generate a user-specified control flow.

```
<table border="0" width="80%">
<tr>
<td> <a href="<%HTMLQueryForm%>"> New query </a> </td>
<%if CiContainsFirstRecord eq 0%> <td> <form action= "/scripts/query.idq"
method="GET">
<input type="hidden" name="CiBookMark" value="<%CiBookMark%>">
<input type="hidden" name="CiBookmarkSkipCount" value="-<%CiMaxRecordsPerPage%>">
<input type="hidden" name="CiMaxRecordsInResultSet"
value="<%CiMaxRecordsInResultSet%>">
<input type="hidden" name="CiRestriction" value="<%CiRestriction%>">
<input type="hidden" name="CiMaxRecordsPerPage" value="<%CiMaxRecordsPerPage%>">
<input type="hidden" name="CiScope" value="<%CiScope%>">
<input type="hidden" name="TemplateName" value="<%TemplateName%>">
<input type="hidden" name="CiSort" value="<%CiSort%>">
<input type="hidden" name="HTMLQueryForm" value="<%HTMLQueryForm%>"> <p>
<input type="submit" value="Previous <%CiMaxRecordsPerPage%> documents"> </p>
</form>
</td>
```

continues

Listing 26.3. continued

```
<%endif%>
<%if CiContainsLastRecord eq 0%>
<td align="right"><form action="/scriptsearch/query.idq" method="GET">
<input type="hidden" name="CiBookMark" value="<%CiBookMark%>">
<input type="hidden" name="CiBookmarkSkipCount"  value="<%CiMaxRecordsPerPage%>">
<input type="hidden" name="CiMaxRecordsInResultSet"
value="<%CiMaxRecordsInResultSet%>">
<input type="hidden" name="CiRestriction" value="<%CiRestriction%>">
<input type="hidden" name="CiMaxRecordsPerPage"  value="<%CiMaxRecordsPerPage%>">
<input type="hidden" name="CiScope" value="<%CiScope%>">
<input type="hidden" name="TemplateName" value="<%TemplateName%>">
<input type="hidden" name="CiSort" value="<%CiSort%>">
<input type="hidden" name="HTMLQueryForm" value="<%HTMLQueryForm%>"> <p>
<input type="submit" value="Next <%CiRecordsNextPage%> documents"> </p>
</form>
</td>
<%endif%> </tr>
</table>
```

You'll find a copy of this code in the following places within the HTX file, at the top of the detail section and below the detail section of the file. The reason is that this code provides a flow of control to the user. This code allows the user to browse forward or backward through the result set by creating a form with two buttons: Previous 10 Documents and Next 10 Documents. When the user selects one of these buttons, the query is executed but the result set is skipped by the number of records specified by the `CiBookmarkSkipCount` variable.

> **TIP**
>
> If you need more than the basic options provided by the HTX scripting commands, you can use either VBScript or JScript scripting languages.

The detail section of the HTX file is built from the HTML code shown as Listing 26.4.

Listing 26.4. Another partial HTML code snippet from the HTX file used to display the output records to the user.

```
<%begindetail%> <dd> </dd>
<dt><%CiCurrentRecordNumber%>. <%if DocTitle isempty%> <a href="<%EscapeURL
vpath%>"> <b> <%filename%> </b> </a> <%else%> <a href="<%EscapeURL vpath%>"> <b>
<%DocTitle%> </b> </a> <%endif%> </dt>
<dd> <b> <i> Abstract: <%characterization%> </i> </b> <br>
<a href="<%EscapeURL vpath%>"> <cite> http://<%server_name%> <%vpath%> </cite> </a>
<cite>
</cite> <font size="2"> <cite>- </cite> </font> <%if size eq ""%> <p> <font
size="2"> <cite> (size and time unknown) </cite> </font> </p>
<%else%> <p> <font size="2"> <cite> size <%size%> bytes - <%write%> GMT </cite>
</font> </p>
<%endif%> </dd>
<%enddetail%> </dl>
```

This detail section verifies that each returned field contains some data. If the field does contain data, then the it will be displayed. Otherwise, it will be skipped. The fields that will be displayed include the record number, filename, abstract, full URL, file size, and date-time stamp.

Table 26.4. Variables and control flow commands used only within HTML extension files.

Parameter	Description	Note
`<%BeginDetail%>`	Specifies the beginning of a detail record block.	
`<%Else%>`	Else	The `else` clause of an `if...else...endif` statement block.
`<%EndDetail%>`	Specifies the end of the detail record block.	
`<%Endif%>`	Endif	The end of `if...else... endif` statement block.
`<%EscapeHTML VariableText%>`	Specifies that the text specified in the value `VariableText` be formatted as HTML.	The default formatting.
`<%EscapeRAW VariableText%>`	Specifies that the text specified in the value `VariableText` not be formatted or changed in any way.	
`<%EscapeURL VariableText%>`	Specifies that the text specified in the value `VariableText` be formatted as relevant to text contained within a URL or anchor.	
`<%If%>`	If	The `if` clause of an `if...else...endif` statement block.

continues

Table 26.4. continued

Parameter	Description	Note
`<%Include VariableText%>`	Specifies that the text specified by the filename in the value `VariableText` be inserted into the output at execution time.	
`CiBookmarkSkipCount`	Specifies the number of rows to skip for the next page.	A positive value will jump x amount of records forward in the result set, whereas a negative number will jump x amount of records backward in the result set.
`CONTAINS`	String includes the specified character.	Can be used only in an `if...else...endif` statement.
`CiCurrentRecord`	Specifies the current record number.	
`CiMatchedRecordCount`	Specifies the total number of records matched by the query.	Using this variable will force a nonsequential query.
`EQ`	Equal to	Can be used only in an `if...else...endif` statement.
`GT`	Greater than	Can be used only in an `if...else...endif` statement.
`ISEMPTY`	Specifies that the variable is empty or null when set to 1.	Can be used only in an `if...else...endif` statement.
`ISTYPEEQ`	Provides a method to determine the type (`VT_TYPE`) or a particular variable.	Can be used only in an `if...else...endif` statement.
`LT`	Less than	Can be used only in an `if...else...endif` statement.

Table 26.5. Read-only variables used in HTX files.

Parameter	Description	Note
CiBookmark	Specifies a reference to the first row of the page.	
CiContainsFirstRecord	Set to 1 if the page contains the first record of the result set. Otherwise, it is set to 0.	
CiContainsLastRecord	Set to 1 if the page contains the last record of the result set. Otherwise, it is set to 0.	For a sequential query, this value cannot be assumed to be true unless it is placed after the <%enddetail%> section.
CiCurrentPageNumber	Specifies the current page number of the result set.	
CiCurrentRecordNumber	Specifies the number of the currently displayed record.	
CiErrorMessage	An error message.	Available only for error pages.
CiErrorNumber	An error number associated with an error message.	Available only for error pages.
CiFirstRecordNumber	Specifies the number for the first record on the page.	
CiLastRecordNumber	Specifies the number for the last record on the page.	For a sequential query, this value cannot be assumed to be true unless it is placed after the <%enddetail%> section.

continues

Table 26.5. continued

Parameter	Description	Note
CiMatchedRecordCount	Specifies the total number of records returned by the query.	
CiOutOfDate	Set to 1 if the catalog index is out of date. Otherwise, it is set to 0.	
CiQueryComplete	Set to 1 if the query could not be resolved by using the content index. Otherwise, it is set to 0.	Only applicable if CiForceUseCi set to 1.
CiQueryDate	Specifies the date, at the Web server, when the query was executed.	
CiQueryTime	Specifies the time, at the Web server, when the query was executed.	
CiQueryTimedOut	Set to 1 if the query failed to complete within the specified time limit. Otherwise, it is set to 0.	
CiQueryTimeZone	Specifies the time zone of the Web server.	
CiRecordsNextPage	Specifies the number of records to be placed on the next page.	Using this variable within a HTX file will force a nonsequential query to occur.
CiTotalNumberOfPages	Specifies the total number of pages to contain the query result set.	Using this variable within a HTX file will force a nonsequential query to occur.

Summary

This chapter contains a lot of information, and I hope you will continue to use it as a reference. But it cannot be a complete guide to developing search pages. The only real guide is experience based on experimentation. Therefore, I suggest that you play around a bit with the samples to get a feel for how things work. The good news in this area is that FrontPage 97 does support the creation of HTML and HTX files. Although FrontPage 97 does not support the development of IDQ files, you can use Notepad to create these files. The next chapter shows you how to use the Windows NT Performance Monitor, which can be useful in determining how well your server is working.

IN THIS PART

- The Performance Monitor   749
- Tuning the Server   767

Performance-Tuning and Optimization Techniques

The Performance Monitor

IN THIS CHAPTER

■ Using the Performance Monitor 750

CHAPTER 27

The Performance Monitor can monitor almost everything that is happening on your system, so gaining a basic understanding of its usage is quite important. In the next chapter you will learn about specific performance counters you can use to tune various system components. In this chapter you will learn the basic functions of the Performance Monitor, including how to create and configure charts, logs, reports, and alerts. Keep in mind that performance tuning can be very complex, and entire books are devoted to just this particular program and its usage, so it may take some time for you to get the hang of using the Performance Monitor and the associated performance counters.

Using the Performance Monitor

The Performance Monitor is used to monitor a system in real time. That is, the event objects you monitor are occurring right now, and the value you see for the event object reflects the actual value of the event object with a minimal time lag. You can use the Performance Monitor on the computer you want to monitor, which will affect the performance on that computer slightly, or you can use it remotely from another computer, which will impact your network bandwidth more than it will the performance of the computer you are monitoring. The amount of performance-tuning degradation will vary from unnoticeable to appreciable, depending on the number and frequency of monitored events.

The Performance Monitor defines events, as I put it, as *objects*. An object is an item such as a system, a processor, a process, a thread, or a similar item. Objects are further divided into *counters*. For example, the system object includes counters for % Total Processor Time (the total amount of processor usage on the system), % Total Interrupt Time (the total number of interrupts generated on the system), and % Total Privileged Time (the total amount of processor time spent in the kernel on the system). Within a counter, you may also have one or more *instances*. For example, if you have more than one processor on your system and view the Processor Counter % Processor Time (the total amount of processor utilization for a particular processor), then you will find multiple entries in the Instance field. Instance counts start with 0 and increase by one for each additional item. If you have two processors, then your Instance field will include 0 for the first processor and 1 for the second processor. You could also have multiple named instances, rather than numbers. If you monitor the RAS Port object counter, for example, the Instance field could include COM1, COM2, and COM3, up to as many RAS connections as you have installed.

The Performance Monitor supports four types of views, each of which displays the performance object counters in a different format to provide you with unique capabilities. These include the following:

- Chart—This view can display values for performance counters in either a line (Graph) or bar (Histogram) chart. The most useful view to quickly display performance data over a period of time is the line chart and for performance peaks is the histogram chart. It can become cluttered and difficult to read if you attempt to view more than 10 active performance counters.

■ Log—This view can capture all the performance counters for a particular object to a file. This captured file may be read in to the Performance Monitor at a later date for in-depth analysis. You can load in a log file and then chart it, for example.

TIP

When using this option, you should remember that you can view only object counters that you have previously captured. However, you do not have to view all the object counters that you captured. You may select a subset of these counters to view, which is one way to start with the big picture and then narrow it down to a specific incident. It is always better to capture any performance counters that you think you may need, rather than to limit the capture to a few specific performance counters that you know you will need.

■ Report—This view can display a large series of performance object counter values in real time. It is an instantaneous view of the performance counters, so you may only view the current value. This value will change at the next update interval, which means the value you are monitoring may be reset to 0 before you can evaluate it.

■ Alert—This view can set conditions based on performance object counters and alert you when this condition is met. For example, you may want to be informed when your server's paging file grows beyond its current minimum allocation so that you can increase the minimum allocation size and increase overall system performance. Any time a paging file grows beyond the minimum, there is a significant amount of overhead involved in expanding the page file. Additionally, any page-file expansion may be fragmented, which will slow down retrieval of paged data.

The Performance Monitor Toolbar

The Performance Monitor toolbar, as shown in Figure 27.1, provides quick access to the Performance Monitor feature set.

FIGURE 27.1.
The Performance Monitor toolbar.

From left to right, the toolbar buttons perform the following functions:

■ View a chart—Changes the default view to the chart view.
■ View the alerts—Changes the default view to the alert view.
■ View output log file status—Changes the default view to the log view.
■ View report data—Changes the default view to the report view.

- Add counter—Displays the Add To *Item* dialog where *Item* can be either a chart, an alert, a log, or a report. Use this as a quick mechanism to add performance object counters.

- Modify selected counter—When you select an object counter in the legend and press this button, the Edit *Item* Entry dialog displays; in it you may change the item's color, scale, line width, and line style if viewing a chart, or other attributes for alerts, logs, and reports.

- Delete selected counter—Deletes the object counter selected in the legend from a chart, alert, log, or report.

- Update counter data—Updates the display when you have set the Update Time to Manual Update.

- Place a commented bookmark into the output log—Bookmarks insert a comment into a log file to refresh your memory of the usage of captured object counters.

- Options—Displays the Options dialog for the selected view.

Creating Charts

Creating a chart consists of selecting the performance objects, configuring the view, and then saving the chart for future use. You can follow these steps to create a chart:

1. Make sure the default view, as shown in Figure 27.2, is for a chart. If a different view is displayed, you can click the View a chart button on the toolbar, choose View | Chart, or press Ctrl+C.

FIGURE 27.2.

The Performance Monitor Chart view.

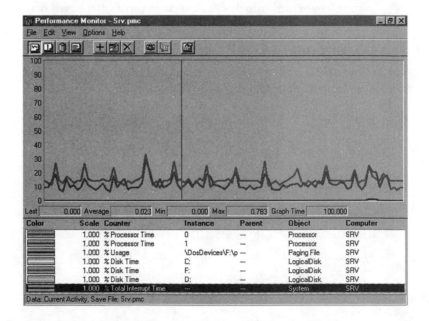

2. Choose Edit | Add to Chart, press the Add counter button on the toolbar, or press Ctrl+I. All these will display the Add to Chart dialog, as shown in Figure 27.3. This dialog is used to select the performance object counters to monitor.

FIGURE 27.3.

The Add to Chart dialog.

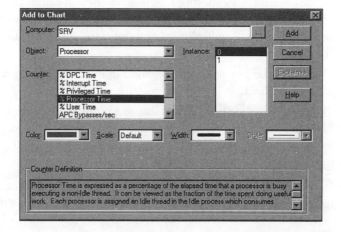

3. Choose the event type (performance object) to monitor in the Object: field.
4. Choose the event subtype (object counter) to monitor in the Counter: field.

TIP

If you are unsure of the object counter's properties, click the Explain button to expand the dialog and see a short description of the counter.

5. Choose an instance of the object counter if applicable. An *instance* differentiates between one or more occurrences of an object counter. Not all object counters include an instance number.

TIP

You can select a different source to monitor by specifying the name of a remote computer in the Computer: field, or you can click the button at the end of the field to display the Select Computer dialog where you can browse the network for the computer you wish to monitor. Once you have selected the computer you wish to monitor, repeat steps 3 through 5. This can be particularly useful if you want to monitor multiple servers simultaneously for comparison.

6. To specify a different color for the performance object counter to use for its display, select a color from the Color: field.

7. To change the default scale for the object counter, select a multiplier or divisor from the Scale: field. By choosing a smaller divisor you can force all of the chart to be visible when a performance counter's maximum value is at the top of the chart. By choosing a higher multiplier you can force the counter to be visible when the counter is too low to be readily visible.

8. To change the line thickness displayed in the chart, choose a different selection from the Width: field.

9. To change the line from a solid line to a series of dashes or dots to differentiate chart lines of the same color, select a pattern from the Style: field.

10. Click the Add button to add the object counter to the Performance Monitor's display list.

11. Repeat steps 2 through 10 for each object counter you want to monitor. When you have finished, click the Done button to return to the Performance Monitor Chart view.

TIP

To select a range of object counters, select the first counter in the range; then while holding the Shift key, select the last counter in the range. To select noncontiguous items, select the first counter and then, while holding the Ctrl key, select the next counter. Repeat this for each counter. Repeat these same steps for the Instance field if you want to monitor multiple object counters for multiple instances. The Performance Monitor automatically selects a color and line width for each item.

To modify the chart configuration, choose Options | Chart to display the Chart Options dialog, as shown in Figure 27.4.

FIGURE 27.4.

The Chart Options dialog.

You can select the following items:

- **Legend**—This item displays a map legend at the bottom of the chart, which contains each monitored item. This includes the color of the item, the item name, the instance, parent, object, and computer.

- **Value Bar**—This item is displayed just above the legend and contains the last value, average value, minimum value, maximum value, and graph time of a selected legend item. The graph time is the time it takes in seconds for a performance counter to completely fill the display area.

- **Vertical Grid**—Use this item to subdivide the vertical chart axis. When selected, vertical reference lines are drawn on the displayed window.

- **Horizontal Grid**—Use this item to subdivide the horizontal chart axis. When selected, horizontal reference lines are drawn on the displayed window.

- **Vertical Labels**—This item enables or disables the vertical scale numbers displayed to the left of the chart window.

- **Gallery**—This item selects the chart type. It can display either a line chart by selecting the Graph option or a bar chart by selecting the Histogram option.

- **Vertical Maximum**—Use this item to specify a different maximum scale for the vertical axis. The default is 100.

- **Update Time**—Use this item to specify the time when the chart should be updated. You can specify to automatically update the chart by specifying a value (in seconds) for the Periodic Update option or specify a manual chart update by choosing the Manual Update option. If you select the Manual Update option, the chart will be updated only when you choose Options | Update Now, the Update counter now toolbar button, or Ctrl+U.

After all this work, you should save the chart in case you want to use it again. Do this by choosing the File | Save Chart Settings from the File menu. This displays the familiar File | Save As dialog, where you may specify the filename and directory in which to store the file, the first time you save the chart and updates the file thereafter. To load a previously saved chart, choose File | Open.

TIP

To save all Performance Monitor views (Chart, Log, Report, and Alert), choose File | Save Workspace. This saves all Chart views and the selected performance counter objects along with the window placement to a file.

Creating Logs

Creating a log consists of selecting the performance objects, configuring the log options, and then starting the log capture. Once performance data has been captured to a log, you may load this data back into the Performance Monitor for analysis. Follow these steps to create the log:

1. Make sure the default view, as shown in Figure 27.5, is for a log. If a different view is displayed, you can click the View output Log file status button on the toolbar, choose View | Log, or press Ctrl+L.

FIGURE 27.5.

The Performance Monitor Log view.

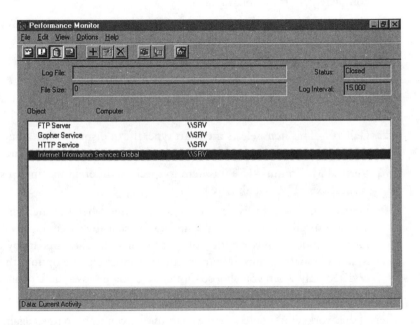

2. Choose Edit | Add to Log, press the Add counter button on the toolbar, or press Ctrl+I. Any of these commands will display the Add To Log dialog, as shown in Figure 27.6.

FIGURE 27.6.

The Add To Log dialog.

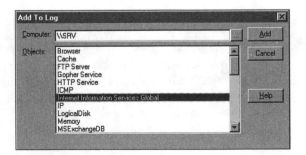

3. This dialog is used to select the performance object to monitor. To select an object, highlight the object in the Objects: field, and then press the Add button. To select a range of object counters, select the first counter in the range; then hold the Shift key and select the last counter in the range. To select noncontiguous items, select the first counter and then, while holding the Ctrl key, select the next counter.

TIP

If you are unsure of the events to monitor for your first-time use, select them all, but only capture these events for a maximum of five minutes because the log file can become quite large. The log file then can be used with the Chart, or Report, view to look at specific object counters. As you view these different object counters and become familiar with their use, you can then limit your logs to just those counters of interest.

---

4. After you have made your choices, the Cancel button will change to the Done button. Press this button to return to the Performance Monitor's main window.

5. At this point all the performance objects will be listed in the Log window. However, you are not ready to capture data yet. First, you have to modify the log options to specify a file to place the captured data in and specify an update interval. These features are accessible from the Log Options dialog. To display this dialog, choose Options | Chart, press the Options button on the toolbar, or press Ctrl+O.

NOTE

To automatically update the log, specify a value (in seconds) for the Periodic Update option. To manually update the log, select the Manual Update option. If you select the Manual Update option, the chart will be updated only when you choose Options | Update Now, the Update counter now button on the toolbar, or press Ctrl+U.

---

6. To start your data capture, press the Start Log button in the Log Options dialog. Once this option is enabled, the Status: field changes from Closed to Open and the File Size: field displays the size of the data-capture file. The longer you capture data, the larger this file will be, so you should not capture data on a drive containing your network client files because this could prevent a client from being able to save his data files. Of course, this assumes that you are capturing a large amount of data over a significant amount of time.

Once you have captured all the data you want for analysis, open the Log Options dialog and click the Stop Log button. This closes the log file. To use this captured data, choose Options | Data From to display the Data From dialog where you may load a log file. Once you load a log file, you may then chart it (to create a new chart, just choose New Chart from the File menu) or use it to generate alerts or reports. You can also change the object to log by redisplaying the Add To Log dialog and adding objects. However, before you can append these new objects, be sure to select the Options | Data From menu option and change the setting from Log File to Current Activity. You may then use the Start button in the Log Options dialog to append your data to the capture file.

> **TIP**
>
> Don't forget to save your log options by choosing the File | Save Log Setting As menu option.

Creating Reports

The Report view is useful for viewing large amounts of performance object counters simultaneously. The only hitch is that the counter value displayed is always the last known value of the counter. You cannot view a series of values over a period of time. Only a Chart view in line-graph mode can display a series of counter data over a period of time. You will find the Report view most useful for monitoring complex items, such as your entire network.

For example, network-related counters include objects such as AppleTalk, Browser, FTP Server, ICMP, IP, Gateway Services for NetWare, MacFile Server, NBT Connections, NetBEUI, NetBEUI Resource, Network Interface, Network Segment, NWLink IPX, NWLink SPX, NWLink NetBIOS, RAS Port, RAS Total, Redirector, Server, Server Work Queues, TCP, UDP, and WINS Server. That's a lot of object counters to monitor, and if you have installed other network components or third-party products, you may have even more object counters.

To create a report, follow these steps:

1. Make sure the default view, as shown in Figure 27.7, is for a report. If a different view is displayed, you can click the View Report data button on the toolbar, choose View | Report, or press Ctrl+R.

2. Choose Edit | Add to Report, press the Add counter button on the toolbar, or press Ctrl+I. All these selections will display the Add to Report dialog, as shown in Figure 27.8. This dialog is similar to the Add to Chart dialog and is used to select the performance object counters to monitor.

3. Choose the event type (performance object) to monitor in the Object: field.

4. Choose the event subtype (object counter) to monitor in the Counter: field.

FIGURE 27.7.

The Performance Monitor Report view.

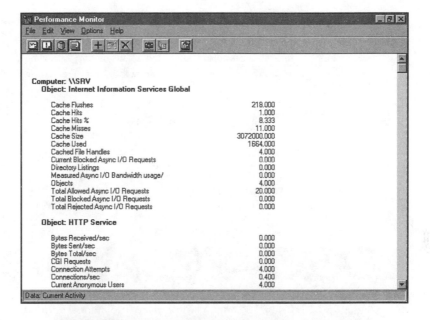

FIGURE 27.8.

The Add to Report dialog.

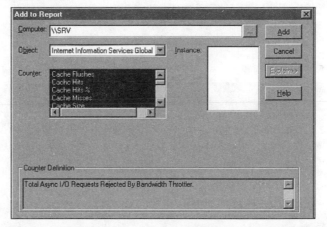

> **TIP**
>
> If you are unsure of the counter's properties, click the Explain button to expand the dialog and see a short description of the counter.

5. Choose an instance of the object counter if applicable.

> **TIP**
>
> You can select a different computer to monitor by specifying the name of a remote computer in the Computer: field. Once you have selected the computer, repeat steps 3 through 5. This is useful for monitoring multiple servers simultaneously to quickly check the load of a particular server.

6. Click the Add button to add the object counter to the Performance Monitor's display list.

7. Repeat steps 2 through 6 for each object counter you want to monitor. When you have finished, click the Done button to return to the Performance Monitor Report view.

> **NOTE**
>
> To change the update interval for an automatic update, specify a value (in seconds) for the Periodic Update option. To change from automatic to manual updates, select the Manual Update option. Just remember, if you choose the Manual Update option, the chart will be updated only when you select Options | Update Now, click the Update counter now button on the toolbar, or press Ctrl+U.

> **TIP**
>
> Don't forget to save your report configuration by choosing the File | Save Report Settings As menu option. You never know when you may want to use this configuration again.

Creating Alerts

The Alert view is the best way to automatically inform you of a problem with your server. It can inform you of low disk space, high processor utilization, network errors, or other items that might concern you. Keep in mind that an alert can be sent only if the Performance Monitor is running. If you want to automate specific alerts, then you should obtain the Windows NT Resource Kit or check the Microsoft FTP site (ftp.microsoft.com) for a downloadable copy. This includes the DATALOG.EXE program that can perform the same alerting and logging features of Performance Monitor but runs as a service. The MONITOR.EXE program installs the service and stops and starts the alert or logging features.

> **NOTE**
>
> In order to use the alert service, you must first create a Performance Monitor workspace file that contains your alert and log settings. If you will be monitoring any activity on a remote computer, be sure to create a user account with sufficient network privileges. When configuring the service startup values, configure the service to use the This Account option in the Log On As group.

To create an alert, follow these steps:

1. Make sure the default view, as shown in Figure 27.9, is for an alert. If a different view is displayed, you can click the View the Alerts button on the toolbar, choose View | Alerts, or press Ctrl+A.

FIGURE 27.9.

The Performance Monitor Alert view.

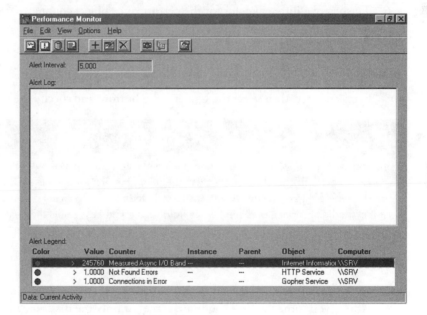

2. Choose Edit | Add to Report, click the Add counter button on the toolbar, or press Ctrl+I. This will display the Add to Alert dialog, as shown in Figure 27.10, which you can use to select the performance object counters to monitor.
3. Choose the event type (performance object) to monitor in the Object: field.
4. Choose the event subtype (object counter) to monitor in the Counter: field.

FIGURE 27.10.

The Add to Alert dialog.

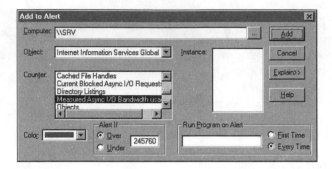

5. Choose an instance of the object counter if applicable. An instance differentiates between one or more occurrences of an object counter, and not all object counters include an instance number.

6. To specify a different color for the performance object counter to use for its display, select a color from the Color: field.

7. In the Alert If field, choose either Over or Under and specify a value in the data field for the alert condition. For example, if you want an alert sent when your disk drive has less than 10MB free, you would choose the LogicalDisk object and the Free Megabytes counter, then select the Under radio button, and specify the value as 10.

> **TIP**
>
> To specify the same alert condition for multiple instances (such as two or more logical disks), select a range of instances by highlighting the first instance in the range; then, while holding the Shift key, select the last instance in the range. To select a noncontiguous range, select the first instance and then, while holding the Ctrl key, select the next instance. Repeat this for each instance. The Performance Monitor will automatically select a color for each instance.

8. In the Run Program on Alert field, you can specify a command line to be executed either every time the alert condition is met or only the first time the alert condition is met by enabling either the Every Time or First Time radio button.

> **TIP**
>
> The preceding option is particularly useful if you have a pager and a command-line program, which can be used to dial your pager and send you a notification message.

9. Click the Add button to add the object counter to the Performance Monitor's display list.

10. Repeat steps 2 through 9 for each object counter you want to monitor. Click the Done button to return to the Performance Monitor alert view.

To modify the alert configuration, choose Options | Alert, which will display the Alert Options dialog, shown in Figure 27.11.

FIGURE 27.11.
The Alert Options dialog.

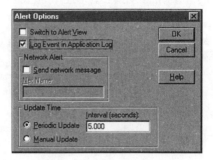

You may select the following items:

■ Switch to Alert View—This option automatically switches the Performance Monitor to the Alert view when an alert condition is met.

■ Log Event in Application Log—Use this option to log the alert condition in the computer's application log.

■ Network Alert—This option broadcasts a message to the domain users, specifying the alert condition. To send a message to a specific user, enter a user name in the Net Name: field. This name can specify a name from a different domain by prefacing the user name with the domain name like *DomainName\UserName* where *DomainName* is the name of the external domain, and *UserName* is the name of the user in the external domain (SRV\Administrator, for example).

■ Update Time—Use this item to specify the alert update interval. You can specify an automatic update interval by specifying a value (in seconds) for the Periodic Update option or a manual alert update interval by choosing the Manual Update option. If you select the Manual Update option, then the alert conditions will only be checked when you choose Options | Update Now, the Update counter now toolbar button, or Ctrl+U.

> **TIP**
>
> Save the alert settings by choosing File | Save Alert Settings As and specifying a file to save your settings.

Not all performance object counters are useful for specifying alert conditions. The object counters I find most useful, and which you may find useful as well, are summarized in Table 27.1.

Table 27.1. Performance object counters for alerts.

Counter	Instance	Condition	Description
Logical Disk Object			
% Free Space	Per drive	Under	Useful for notification in a low free-space situation. Specify the minimum percentage of free space per drive in the Alert If value field. Set this value to 10 or higher for useful warnings. Any value below this may notify you too late for your users' comfort.
Free Megabytes	Per drive	Under	Useful for notification in a low disk-space situation. Specify the minimum free space in MB per drive in the Alert If value field. On a large drive (over 1GB) set this value to 100 or less if you want to run on the ragged edge.
Memory Object			
Pages/sec.	5 to 10	Over	Set this to 5 for a notification that the system is paging too often and as an indication that a memory upgrade may improve performance if consistent alerts are sent. Set this value to 10 to be notified that a memory upgrade is required, as the system is definitely paging too much.
Network Interface Object			
Current Bandwidth	Per network transport protocol	Over	Set this value to 50000000bps for a notification that your network transport protocol has reached 50 percent capacity.

Counter	Instance	Condition	Description
		Network Segment Object	
%Network Utilization	Per network adapter	Over	Set this value to 50 for a notification that your network segment has reached 50 percent of its carrying capacity.
		Redirector Object	
Network Errors/sec	N/A	Over	If you have any errors, you should spend more time isolating them. This value should be set to 1.
		Server Object	
Errors System	N/A	Over	Any value over 1 indicates a problem with the server. If detected, you should examine the system log for the cause of the error or spend some time with the Performance Monitor, as specified in the "Finding Network Bottlenecks" section of Chapter 28, to help isolate the error.
Errors Logon	N/A	Over	This item notifies you that someone is attempting to hack into your system. A good threshold value is from 3 to 10.
Errors Access Permissions	N/A	Over	This item informs you of potential users trying to access files they should not be, in order to gain access to privileged data. A good threshold value is from 3 to 10.
Pool Nonpaged Failures	N/A	Over	This item should be set to 1, as this counter indicates a lack of nonpageable memory for the server service. An error indicates that the server is unable to process a client request for lack of resources. This value also indicates a physical memory shortage.
Pool Paged Bytes		Over	This item should be set to 1, as this counter indicates a lack of pageable memory for the server service. An error indicates that the server is unable to process a client request for a lack of resources. This value also indicates a physical memory shortage or that the page file setting is too low.

continues

27

THE PERFORMANCE MONITOR

Table 27.1. continued

Counter	Instance	Condition	Description
Server Work Queues Object			
Work Item Shortages	Per network adapter	Over	This value should be set to 0, as any indication represents a problem with the server service. If errors are encountered, the MaxWorkItems value should be increased.

Summary

This chapter discusses the basics of using the Performance Monitor to create charts, logs, alerts, and reports to give you an idea of how to use these features. The goal in this chapter is not to explain every detail of the Performance Monitor, but instead to give you a good understanding of the features and enable you to use the Performance Monitor in your day-to-day activities. In the next chapter, you will use the Performance Monitor to tune your server, the Internet Information Server, and SQL Server.

Tuning the Server

IN THIS CHAPTER

- Performance Tuning with the Performance Monitor   768

- Configuring SQL Server   793

CHAPTER 28

Whether you are using the Internet Information Server for Internet or intranet publishing, your goal is to obtain the maximum performance from it. Tuning the base platform (Windows NT Server) is an excellent starting point. However, depending on your IIS implementation, you may need to tune other components as well. For example, if you are using SQL Server to store your IIS logs or for dynamic Web pages, then you will need to tune SQL Server. In this chapter, you will learn how to tune Windows NT Server, Internet Information Server, and SQL Server using some Performance Monitor examples. Along the way, you will work with a few programs I wrote to illustrate the types of bottlenecks you may encounter. If you need additional information on how to use the Performance Monitor, you may want to refer back to Chapter 27, "The Performance Monitor."

Keep in mind that the Internet Information Server basically provides the same services as a file server. It consumes processor cycles, as an application server does, and it provides shared resources (files, Web pages, and so on) to network clients. You can think of the Internet as a large WAN connected to your internal network. The methods you use to tune for optimum IIS performance are the same methods you would apply to any application or file server.

Performance Tuning with the Performance Monitor

Performance tuning is based on finding your *bottleneck* (the item causing a performance limitation) and doing something to correct it. The primary goal with performance tuning is to provide adequate performance in four categories: processor, memory, disk subsystem, and network. If these components are performing well, users will not complain about poor system performance. This section looks at each component and provides sample Performance Monitor workspaces to illustrate the process of finding bottlenecks in these areas.

> **NOTE**
>
> The sample Performance Monitor charts, alerts, reports, logs, and workspace files can be found in the \SOURCE\CHAP22 subdirectory on the CD-ROM.

It's unavoidable. After you find and eliminate one bottleneck, another will always be exposed. Say you have a server with a 100MHz Pentium processor, 32MB of main memory, a lightning-fast pair of EIDE disk drives, an EIDE disk controller, and a 16-bit network adapter, and your primary concern is providing a fast user response time for shared files and SQL Server access.

Where do you think the performance bottleneck would be? In the processor? The memory? The disk subsystem? The network adapter? Based on my experience, it would probably turn out to be the disk subsystem. This would be caused by the EIDE, which would use the standard ATDISK driver provided with Windows NT Server; this driver can support only one pendingI/O request at a time. It's not really the fault of the driver, but the hardware the driver supports. Almost all IDE (and EIDE) disk controllers use programmed I/O (or PIO). A PIO controller uses the processor to move data from the disk, through the disk controller, to system memory. This process requires a high percentage of processor time and limits the device to one I/O request at a time.

The solution would be to replace the EIDE disks and controller with SCSI disk drives and a SCSI controller that supports direct memory access (DMA). A controller that supports DMA will move data from the disk to system memory without processor intervention.

But even here you need to exercise good judgment. Don't choose an 8-bit or a 16-bit SCSI controller if you have a 32-bit expansion bus; instead choose a 32-bit SCSI controller. The basic idea is to choose a disk controller with the largest I/O bus that your expansion bus supports for the fastest data transfer rate. Otherwise, the process requires copying data from the disk drive to memory below 1MB for an 8-bit controller and below 16MB for a 16-bit controller. The data will then have to be copied to the application or system buffer above 16MB if you have more than 16MB installed in your system. This copying of data is referred to as *double-buffering* and can severely hamper system performance.

Now that you have increased the performance of your I/O subsystem compared to the base system, another performance bottleneck may be exposed. Most likely, this is the processor because SQL Server can be very processor intensive. Adding an additional Pentium processor and dedicating this processor to SQL Server will increase SQL Server performance. Once this has occurred, you'll probably find that replacing your current network adapter with a 32-bit network adapter and adding memory can increase performance even more. This sequence can go on and on. Eventually, you will have to draw the line based on your budget and your acceptable performance requirements.

Finding Processor Bottlenecks

Finding processor bottlenecks on your server is not an easy task, but it is possible. To start, use the performance counters I have included in Processor.PMW on the CD-ROM. This workspace file includes processor chart, alert, and report view settings. These object counters are listed in Table 28.1, which includes a description of each object counter.

Table 28.1. Processor performance object counters.

Counter	Instance	Parent	Description
			System Object
% Total Processor Time	N/A	N/A	The percentage of processor time that is currently in use on your system. The basic formula for calculation is [(% CPU in use on CPU 0) + (% CPU in use on CPU 1) ... + (% CPU in use on CPU x)] / Total number of CPUs.
System Calls/sec	N/A	N/A	The number of system service calls that are executed per second. If this value is lower than the number of interrupts/sec, a hardware adapter is generating excessive interrupts.
Context Switches/sec	N/A	N/A	The frequency of switches between executing threads. A high value indicates that a program's use of critical sections or semaphores should have a higher priority to achieve a higher throughput and less task switching.
Processor Queue Length	N/A	N/A	The number of threads waiting in the processor queue for processor cycles. A consistent value of 2 or higher indicates a processor bottleneck. This value will always be 0 unless at least one thread is being monitored.
Interrupts/sec	Per processor	N/A	The number of interrupts the system is servicing.
			Thread Object
% Processor Time	Per processor	Idle	The percentage of processor time the thread is using.

Using a baseline chart, as shown in Figure 28.1, will help you become familiar with your system in an idle state. You should then use the same counters to obtain a baseline in a normal working state, which will help locate the processor bottleneck.

FIGURE 28.1.

Using Performance Monitor to isolate processor bottlenecks.

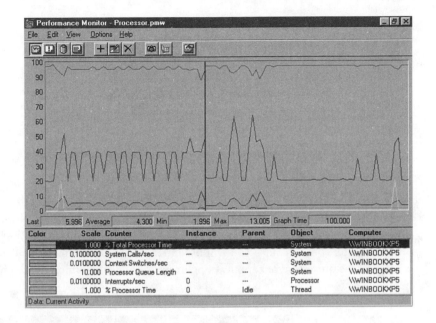

28

TUNING THE
SERVER

Next, use these counters on an active system. Examine the % Total Processor Time counter. If this value is consistently above 90 percent, you have a processor bottleneck. It is then time to examine each process in the system to see which one is using more of the processor than it should. If you have too many processes to view in a chart, you can use the report view. To select these processes, choose Edit | Add to Chart and select Process as the object type. Then select % Processor Time for the Counter. Next, select each application listed in the Instance field. The process that has the highest peak is generally your performance bottleneck. Let's take a look at this process in a little more detail, with an example performance hog.

In a multithreaded environment, such as Windows NT Server, a processor shares CPU cycles among multiple threads. Each of these threads can be running or waiting for execution. For example, while an application is waiting for user input or is waiting for a disk I/O request, it is not scheduled for execution. That means other threads that can perform work will execute instead. However, this is based on the application design, and in this regard not all applications are created equal. Many applications have been ported from a different application environment and may not make efficient use of the Win32 APIs. If you have ported an MS-DOS application to a Win32 console application, for example, you may have left programming constructs that consumed processor cycles indiscriminately. These constructs may have constantly polled for user input, incremented a counter, or something similar. Here's an example of such a programming construct:

```
#include <stdio.h>
#include <stdlib.h>
```

```c
int main (void)
{
unsigned long uMaxNumber,x;
char chUserInput;

for(x=0;x=4294967295;x++)
{
uMaxNumber=x;
}
printf("Counter = %d", uMaxNumber);
chUserInput=getchar();

return (0);
}
```

When this application executes, it utilizes from 80 to 98 percent of the processor, as shown in Figure 28.2. This is the definition of a *processor-intensive application*. Notice that I have the process object selected for the BadExample.EXE application (or instance). You will use this same object counter (but of course you will use different process instances) to determine what percentage of the processor your applications are using and to determine which process is the bottleneck.

FIGURE 28.2.

An example of a processor-intensive application displayed with Performance Monitor.

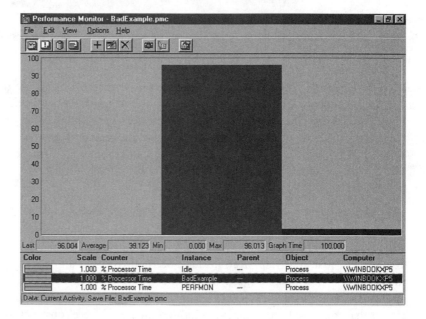

The Visual C++ project file, source code, and executable for this application are included in the \SOURCE\CHAP28\BADEXP subdirectory on the CD-ROM and are called BadExp.mak, BadExp.C, and BadExp.EXE, respectively. On a uniprocessor system, this code snippet will use most of your available processor cycles. However, on a multiprocessor system, the other processors will remain available to process other application requests. If you have a multiprocessor system, try the BadExample.EXE application and add the %Total Processor Time for each processor to your chart. One of these processors will show 80 to 98 percent utilization, while the other processors will continue to function normally.

To see how a multithreaded processor-intensive application affects performance on a multiprocessor system, take a look at BadExp3.mak, BadExp3.C, and BadExp3.EXE. These are multithreaded versions of the application. Each will spawn three threads and will equally distribute the load among them. (See Figure 28.3.) My system is only a uniprocessor machine, so the load per thread is between 30 and 33 percent. But if you have three or more processors, then three of these processors should show 80 to 90 percent processor utilization. Notice in this example that the thread object has been selected. You will use this object counter to determine which thread of a process is the bottleneck in your processor.

FIGURE 28.3.
A multithreaded example of a processor-intensive application displayed with Performance Monitor.

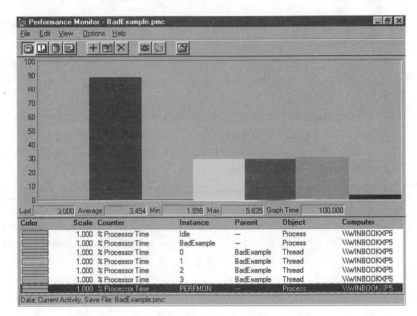

When you have isolated a processor-intensive application, what can you do about it? Well, there are several things you can do depending on your resources and the application.

If you have access to the source code, you can

■ Use a profiler to modify the application to be less processor intensive. This could include making more efficient use of critical sections or semaphores. For example, if your application spawns multiple threads, you should set the thread priorities to make more efficient use of these control mechanisms. That way, the threads are not constantly being switched in and out of the processor queue and performing less work than the overhead involved in switching them in and out of the processor queue. The processor cycles consumed by switching the thread in and out of the processor queue (which occurs whenever the thread cannot access a data construct protected by a critical section) can be used by the thread to perform real work instead.

■ Rewrite the application to spread the load by distributing it among several computers.

■ Rewrite the application to use thread affinities so that the application uses a specific processor (or processors) in a multiprocessor system. This allows for higher system performance because the threads will not be constantly switched to different processors. As a thread is switched, it often requires that the processor cache be flushed to maintain data coherency. That slows down the overall system performance.

If you do not have access to the source code, you can try the following:

■ Inform the manufacturer of the problem and try to get them to fix it.

■ Run the application at off-peak times by using the Scheduler service.

■ Start the application from the command line with the `start` command at a lower priority. For example, `start AppName /low`, where *AppName* is the name of the application to execute.

■ Add additional processors. This will only benefit the system if you have multiple threads/processes to execute. For the Microsoft BackOffice products, this can provide significant benefits because these applications are designed with multithreading/multiprocessing concepts.

■ Upgrade the processor. Change from an 80486 to a Pentium, a Pentium to a Pentium Pro, or from an Intel processor to a RISC processor.

■ Upgrade the processor to one with a larger internal cache. For example, the 486/DX4 (75MHz and 100MHz) models include a 16KB cache over the default 8KB cache of the other 486 models.

■ Upgrade the secondary system cache. This item is quite important when adding additional memory to the system. As you increase system memory, the cache has to map a larger address space into the same size cache. This can increase the cache miss ratio and degrade performance.

Finding Memory Bottlenecks

If you do nothing else to your system, adding memory will almost always increase system performance. This is because Windows NT Server will use this memory instead of virtual memory and thus decrease paging. It will also be used by the cache manager to cache all data accesses.

This includes remote (that is, network) or local resource access. The other Microsoft BackOffice components can also benefit from this increased memory. For example, SQL Server can use some of this memory for its data cache, its procedure cache, and for the temporary database.

Start with the big picture and then narrow down the search to a specific application to find the memory resource hog. A good starting point is to use the performance counters listed in Table 28.2 to see if you have a problem. If a problem is found, then you can use the process object's memory-related counters to see which application is the resource hog.

Table 28.2. Memory performance object counters.

Counter	Instance	Description
		Memory Object
Pages/sec	N/A	The number of pages read from or written to disk to resolve memory references to pages that were not in physical memory at the time.
Available Bytes	N/A	The amount of free virtual memory.
Committed Bytes	N/A	The amount of memory that has been committed to use by the operating system as opposed to memory that has been merely reserved for use by the operating system.
Page Faults/sec	N/A	The number of virtual memory page faults that occurred on the system because the physical page was not in the process's working set or main memory. A page may not need to be read from disk if the page is available on the standby list or is in use by another process that shares the page and has it in its working set.
Cache Faults/sec	N/A	The number of page faults that occur in the cache manager in reference to a memory page that is not in the cache.
		Paging File Object
% Usage	Per page file	The amount of use of a specific page file.
% Usage Peak	Per page file	The maximum use of a specific page file.

> **TIP**
>
> You can use the Windows NT Task Manager, accessible by right-clicking the taskbar and selecting Task Manager, to get a quick indication of your memory usage. Just click the Performance tab to display the Memory dialog. Check the Available value in the Physical Memory group to see if it is higher than 1MB for a Windows NT Server computer or 4MB for a Windows NT Workstation. If you don't have this much memory, you will have a performance degradation due to excessive paging.

The first step in isolating the memory bottleneck is to load the Memory.PMW workspace file into the Performance Monitor. This workspace includes basic counters for the chart, alert, and re-port views. Again, you want to obtain one baseline for an inactive system and one for your normally active system. If you have a memory-intensive process, then your chart will look similar to the one shown in Figure 28.4. This particular chart is based on a log file (Memory.LOG) I cap-tured while running the MemHog.EXE program. However, the same basic object counter activity will be displayed in real time for a memory-intensive application as well.

FIGURE 28.4.

An example of a systemwide memory shortage displayed with the Performance Monitor.

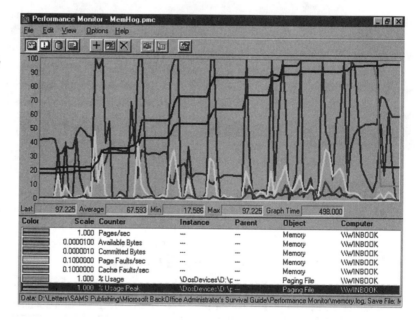

You should watch the behavior of these counters. The behavior displayed in the chart shown in Figure 28.4 is an indication of memory-related problems. Specifically, you should note the following behaviors:

- Pages/sec—Notice the high peaks for this counter. This indicates a great deal of paging activity, generally because your system does not contain enough physical memory to handle the demands placed on it by the application. If you see such activity on your system, you should look closer to see which application is placing such a load on the system. It may be normal behavior for the application, in which case you should add more physical memory to increase system performance.

- Available Bytes—This counter indicates the amount of virtual address space available to your system. As applications utilize memory and page to disk, this value will decrease. When it drops below 10MB, you will most likely see a message warning you that virtual memory is running low and urging you to close some applications or increase your virtual memory settings. If this counter is consistently low after running an application, it generally indicates a system memory leak.

- Committed Bytes—As the Available Bytes counter decreases, the Committed Bytes counter increases. This demonstrates that the process is allocating memory from the virtual address space, but is not necessarily using it. Still, your virtual address space is a limited resource, and you should watch this counter to check for applications that allocate memory, but do not use it. This behavior should be noted, and you should discuss it with the manufacturer. Notice in my example that this counter steps up as the paging file activity steps up. This is an indication that the application is making use of the memory it is allocating. Consistently high values are an indication that adding physical memory will increase system performance. You should also note the counter value when an application ends. If this counter does not return to the original value, the application has a memory leak or a hidden process that is not terminating properly.

- Page Faults/sec—Notice that the peaks here follow the peaks for the Pages/sec counter. That, too, is an indication that your system is paging heavily. A consistent value over 5 indicates that your system is paging more than it should; a consistent value of 10 or higher is a desperate cry for help. Adding physical memory is the only cure. In my example, these counters only peak to a high value and then drop back to a normal level. But on an active file or application server, the activity should be more linear.

- Cache Faults/sec—This counter should be compared with Page Faults/sec to determine whether you actually are paging too much in a normal system. If this counter reads less than the Page Faults/sec counter, you are definitely paging too much and should add physical memory.

- Usage—This counter indicates your current paging file activity. If this value is consistently larger than your minimum paging file size, you should increase your minimum paging file size. A significant amount of system overhead is involved in growing the page file, and any page file growth is not *contiguous*, which means that more overhead is involved in accessing pages stored in this section of the page file. Notice here that the paging file use is incremental in steps of 10MB, and when the application terminates, the usage counter drops back to the original (or slightly smaller) value. If your usage counter does not return to the original value after running an application, then it has either a memory leak or a hidden process that is not terminating.

■ Usage Peak—This counter indicates the maximum use of your page file. If this value consistently reaches 90 percent, your virtual address space is too small and the size of your paging file should be increased. When the counter hits above 75 percent, you will generally notice a significant system performance degradation.

> **NOTE**
>
> The MemHog.EXE program and make file can be found in theSOURCE\CHAP28\MEMHOG subdirectory. This program allocates up to 100MB of memory, in 1MB allotments. For every 10MB of memory allocated, the program sleeps for 30 seconds. The program suspends execution for 30 seconds per 10MB so that the system will use quite a bit of the processor to grow the page file and allocate the memory during heavy use of the paging file. This high-volume processor utilization will mask the memory utilization curve of the application.
>
> The purpose of this program is to simulate an application that is making heavy use of your system memory. You will not find many commercial programs that actually allocate 100MB in less than 10 seconds. Also, the program uses the memset command to populate each 1MB memory block with a series of asterisks. This is so the memory is actually accessed. If you do not perform this step, the memory will be merely allocated, but not used. The Committed Bytes object counter will then max out momentarily as the virtual memory address space is increased, but no paging activity will take place because no memory was physically used.

The previous example, shown in Figure 28.4, illustrates a general systemwide memory-related problem. But in the real world, you need to find the specific cause of the problem. This, too, can be achieved with the Performance Monitor. Instead of looking at systemwide object counters, you want to narrow the search to the process object counters to find the process that is using your system memory.

Note that this looks quite similar to the display shown in Figure 28.4. You should see the same basic peaks for Memory Page Faults/sec as for Process Page Faults/sec, although if you directly overlay the Memory Page Faults/sec with the Process Page Faults/sec, you will notice that the Memory counter is a bit higher than the Process counter. This is because the Memory counter is a systemwide counter and includes other paging activity from other processes. The corresponding system to process counters are displayed in Table 28.3 to aid you in your analysis.

Table 28.3. Corresponding system to process object counters.

Counter	*Process Counter*
	Memory Object
Page Faults/sec	Page Faults/sec
Available Bytes	Virtual Bytes
Committed Bytes	Private Bytes
	Paging File Object
Usage	Page File Bytes
Usage Peak	Page File Bytes Peak

Because I knew which process was the problem, my chart only includes the MemHog application. In order to find a real-world application problem, you should select all the process instances except for the system processes unless you are looking for a system process memory leak. A couple other process object counters you may find useful in your diagnosis of a memory intensive application are

■ Pool Nonpaged Bytes—The nonpaged pool is a system resource area devoted to system components. Allocations from this area cannot be paged out to disk. This is a finite resource; if you run out of nonpaged pool bytes, some system services may fail.

■ Pool Paged Bytes—The paged pool is also a system resource area devoted to system components, but allocations from this area may be paged to disk. However, it is also a finite resource, so if you run out of paged pool bytes a system service may fail.

NOTE

Both the Pool Paged Bytes and Pool Nonpaged Bytes counters are very useful in tracking down a process that is incorrectly making system calls and using all the available pool bytes.

■ Virtual Bytes Peak—This counter is the maximum size of the virtual memory address space used by the process.

■ Working Set—This counter indicates the size of the application's working set (the amount of memory assigned by the operating system for use by the application) in bytes. The working set includes pages that have been used by the process's threads. When memory is low, pages will be trimmed from the working set to provide additional memory for other processes. As the pages are needed, they will be pulled from main memory if the page has not already been removed or read from the paging file.

■ Working Set Peak—This counter indicates the maximum working set size in bytes.

28

TUNING THE
SERVER

> **TIP**
>
> By monitoring the working set for a particular process and comparing it to the Working Set Peak, you can determine whether adding memory will increase the performance of the process. The idea here is to add memory until the working set and Working Set Peak values are equal. This will provide the maximum benefit to the process. You should consider that this may prove to be an unrealistic goal if your budget is limited.

Finding Disk Bottlenecks

Finding disk bottlenecks is easier than finding processor or memory bottlenecks because disk bottleneck performance degradations are readily apparent. There are only four performance counters to monitor for bottlenecks:

- % Disk Time—This counter is the percentage of elapsed time that the disk is servicing read or write requests. It also includes the time the disk driver is waiting in the disk queue.

- Disk Queue Length—This counter indicates the number of pending I/O service requests. A value greater than 2 indicates a disk bottleneck. On a multidisk subsystem, such as a striped set or striped set with parity, a little calculating is needed to determine the presence of a disk bottleneck. The basic formula is

  Disk Queue Length - Number of Physical Disk drives in the multidisk configuration

  If this value is greater than 2, it indicates a disk bottleneck. For example, if you have a queue length of five, and a striped set with three disk drives, you get an acceptable value of 2 (5 − 3 = 2).

- Avg. Disk sec/Transfer—This counter is the time in seconds of the average disk transfer. However, it is not used just to gain this information; rather, it is used in connection with the Memory Pages/sec counter.

- Memory Pages/sec—Use this counter with the Avg. Disk sec/Transfer counter in the following formula to determine how much of your disk bandwidth is used for paging:

  Percent Disk Time Used for Paging = (Memory Pages/sec × Avg. Disk sec/Transfer) × 100.

When I perform disk diagnostics, I break my Performance Monitor charts into two different settings. I use the % Disk Time, Disk Queue Length, and Avg. Disk sec/Transfer counters previously mentioned, plus the Memory Pages/sec from the logical disk object, to determine the performance of the disk on a drive-letter basis. I then use the same counters from the physical disk object to determine my hardware disk performance. If you look in the SOURCE\CHAP28 subdirectory on the CD-ROM, you will find the LogicalDisk.PMW and PhysicalDisk.PMW Performance Monitor workspace files. These files include basic chart, alert, and report examples for you to use as a starting point.

To see these examples in action, run two copies of the Performance Monitor, loading LogicalDisk.PMW into one copy and PhysicalDisk.PMW into the other. Then run the DiskHog.EXE program. This program takes one command-line argument—the drive letter to write its data file to (for example, DiskHog H:). The default, if no drive letter is specified, is drive C:. This program will write up to 1,000 1MB blocks of data to the file DumpFile.DAT, which can total almost 1GB.

The purpose of this program is twofold. First, it can be used to demonstrate disk activity on logical drives (as shown in Figure 28.5) and disk activity on physical drives (as shown in Figure 28.6). Second, the program can be used to test your alert conditions for low disk space. When the program finishes writing the data file, it informs you of how much data was written and prompts you to press a key to continue. At this point, it will delete the data file it created.

FIGURE 28.5.

An example of a disk-intensive application displayed with Performance Monitor on logical drives.

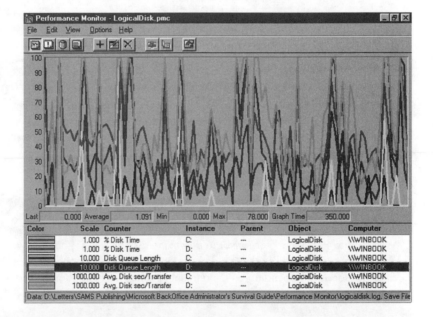

> **NOTE**
>
> Remember that DiskHog.EXE is a simulation designed to overload your disk I/O subsystem. It cannot be used to demonstrate a normal usage pattern for a file server. It is designed to illustrate detection of performance bottlenecks with the Performance Monitor.

28

TUNING THE SERVER

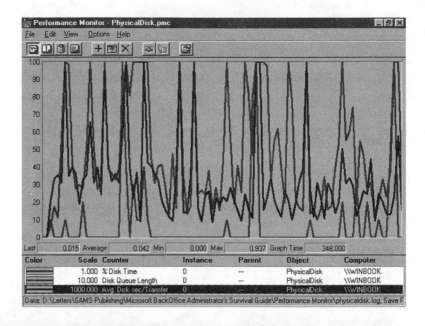

CAUTION

If you run this program and place the data file on a compressed drive, it will most likely run to completion and write almost a gigabyte of data, even if you have fewer than a couple of hundred megabytes free on the drive. This is because the data block it writes is composed of 1MB blocks of asterisks (*) and is easily compressible.

TIP

When using Performance Monitor to determine disk activities, you may want to change the default capture rate. I break mine down into intervals of 5 seconds, 1 second, $\frac{1}{10}$ second, and $\frac{1}{100}$ second, depending on the amount of data I want to capture and the server activity.

If you find a bottleneck, there are several options for you to implement aside from those mentioned in the beginning of this section:

■ Create a mirror set. This can double your read performance if your disk driver can support multiple asynchronous I/O requests. This rules out most IDE and EIDE controllers, which use the default ATDISK driver.

■ Create a striped set with or without parity. This can increase both read and write performance if your disk driver can support multiple asynchronous I/O requests. Your best bet is to use a 32-bit SCSI bus master controller.

■ If your budget is limited, spend your money on a fast SCSI controller and average disk drives (in terms of seek time) because the SCSI controller has more of an impact on a two-drive system.

■ If you have sufficient funds, purchase drives with the lowest possible seek time to optimize your disk subsystem. This is because the time spent seeking tracks (to find the data) versus the time spent transferring the data is on the order of 10 to 1 or higher. That simply means your disk drives spend more time searching for data than they do transferring the data. Faster seek times mean there will be less time wasted looking for the data and more time spent transferring the data.

■ Distribute the work load (one reason to use the LogicalDisk.PMW example) to place highly accessed data files on different drives. For example, you can place the application files for Microsoft Office on your first physical drive and your SQL Server databases on your second physical drive. Do not place them on different logical drives on the same physical drive because this will defeat the purpose of distributing the load.

■ If you use a FAT file system, defragment it occasionally. This will prevent the multiple seeks required to read or write data to the disk.

■ If you have volumes larger than 400MB, you should choose the NTFS file system. NTFS partitions make more efficient use of the disk to provide better performance. For example, a FAT partition can support a maximum of 65,536 clusters. On a large partition, the cluster size may be as large as 64KB. A cluster is the minimum allocation unit, so if you store a 512-byte file, you have wasted 63.5KB. NTFS partitions can have up to 2^{64} clusters to access the partition, so the cluster size can be much smaller and therefore waste less space.

NOTE

Executive Software has a disk defragmenter called DiskKeeper that runs as a Windows NT service. It can defragment both your NTFS and FAT partitions.

Finding Network Bottlenecks

Chapter 4, "Choosing a Platform for Windows NT Server," discusses most of the network performance-tuning options provided by the graphical interface tools such as the Control Panel applets and the hardware alternatives. However, you may want to look in Appendix C, "The Registry Editor and Registry Keys," which includes some other mechanisms for configuring the Windows NT services. Keep in mind that altering any of the registry keys may prevent a Windows NT service from automatically tuning itself for maximum performance. I have included another sample Performance Monitor workspace file, displayed in Figure 28.7, called `Network.PMW`. This includes a chart, alert, and report view to aid you in your network diagnostics.

FIGURE 28.7.

Using Performance Monitor to isolate network bottlenecks.

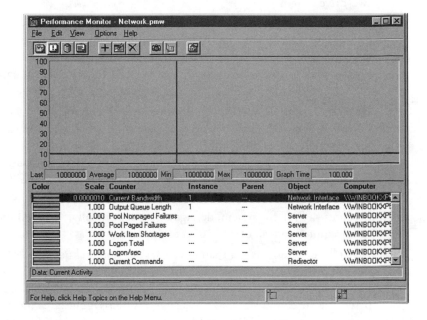

The performance object counters included in the chart and alert views are provided to give you a means to monitor how busy your server is and to determine basic network utilization. The object counters I consider important for these determinations are summarized in Table 28.4.

Table 28.4. Summary of network performance counters.

Counter	Instance	Description
Network Interface Object		
Current Bandwidth	Per interface	An estimated value of the current network utilization in bits per second.
Network Segment Object		
Network Utilization	Per adapter	An estimated value of the percentage of the network bandwidth currently in use on the network segment.

Counter	Instance	Description
Server Object		
Pool Nonpaged Failures	N/A	The number of times allocations from the nonpaged memory pool have failed.
Pool Paged Failures	N/A	The number of times allocations from the paged memory pool have failed.
Work Item Shortages	N/A	The number of times a work item could not be allocated. This counter can indicate that the `InitWorkItems` and `MaxWorkItems` parameters for the LanMan Server service need to be increased.
Logons Total	N/A	A total count since the computer was last rebooted of all interactive logons, remote logons, service logons, and failed logons.
Logons/sec	N/A	The rate at which all interactive logons, remote logons, service logons, and failed logons are occurring.
Server Work Queues Object		
Work Item Shortages	Per processor	The number of failed work-item allocations. A number greater than 1 indicates that the `MaxWorkItem` parameter should be increased.
Queue Length	Per processor	This counter indicates the current number of requests currently waiting in the server queue. A number consistently higher than 4 indicates that a faster processor could improve performance.

28

TUNING THE SERVER

continues

Table 28.4. continued

Counter	Instance	Description
	Redirector Object	
Current Commands	N/A	The number of outstanding network requests waiting to be serviced. If this number is greater than the number of network adapters installed in the computer, a network bottleneck is present. Adding a network adapter may increase performance.
Network Errors/sec	N/A	Indicates that serious network errors have occurred. These errors are generally logged in the system event log, so you should look there for further information. If an error occurs, you should take immediate notice and attempt to resolve the situation.

> **NOTE**
>
> The Network Interface Current Bandwidth counter is available only if you install the Network Monitor Agent. It can be used to determine whether your network is overloaded. A value of 50000000.0000 is the 50 percent mark, which indicates that you should consider segmenting your network. Some network administrators prefer to plan for additional growth and will split the network segment at the 30 to 40 percent mark. The Network Segment Network Utilization counter applies only if you have the TCP/IP protocol installed. This counter is in fractional percentages, and at an indication of 50 percent or higher, the network segment should be split as well.

Finding IIS Bottlenecks

Depending on the size and activity of your Internet Information Server installation, you may run into a few performance-related problems. But before you try to configure the IIS services for better performance, you should try using the Performance Monitor to look at processor, memory, disk, or network bottlenecks, as described in the previous sections. Only after you have done your best to solve those problems should you move on to optimizing your IIS services. The good news is that you can use several IIS counters to determine just how heavy a load your IIS server is carrying, as well as counters to scrutinize each service.

You should start your performance tuning with the general IIS counters, described in Table 28.5, to get a basic look at how well your IIS server is performing. To determine how well a specific service is performing, you can use the counters in Table 28.6 for your WWW Publishing service, Table 28.7 for your FTP Publishing service, and Table 28.8 for your Gopher Publishing service. You should pay particular attention to the global cache counters mentioned in Table 28.5 because you may modify the size of this cache by modifying the registry key `HKEY_LOCAL_MACHINE\System\CurrentControlSet\Services\InetInfo\Parameters\MemoryCacheSize`. The default is to allocate 3MB (3072000 bytes), and the legal values range from 0 (which disables caching entirely) to FFFFFFF (or 4GB). If you are encountering large numbers of cache flushes or misses or if you have a poor hit ratio, increasing this value may improve performance. You should be careful, however, to make sure that you only use physical memory that is not required by the base operating system or SQL Server; otherwise, you may affect these systems and cause poor IIS performance.

Table 28.5. Summary of global IIS performance counters.

Counter	Description
Cache Flushes	Specifies how often a cached memory region expired due to changes in IIS files or the directory tree.
Cache Hits	Specifies how often a reference to a file, a directory tree, or an IIS-specific object was found in the cache.
Cache Hits %	Specifies the hit ratio of all cache requests.
Cache Misses	Specifies how often a reference to a file, a directory tree, or an IIS-specific object was not found in the cache.
Cache Size	Specifies the size of the shared memory cache.
Cache Used	Specifies the total number of bytes in use (file handles, IIS-specific objects, and so on) in the cache.
Cached File Handles	The total number of file handles contained in the cache.
Current Blocked Async I/O Requests	The total number of current asynchronous I/O requests blocked by the bandwidth throttle.
Directory Listings	Specifies the total number of directory listings contained in the cache.

continues

28

TUNING THE
SERVER

Table 28.5. continued

Counter	Description
Measured Async I/O Bandwidth Usage	Specifies the total amount of asynchronous I/O bandwidth average over a minute.
Objects	Specifies the total number of objects (file handle objects, directory listing objects, and so on) contained in the cache.
Total Allowed Async I/O Requests	The total number of asynchronous I/O requests permitted by the bandwidth throttle.
Total Blocked Async I/O Requests	The total number of asynchronous I/O requests blocked by the bandwidth throttle.
Total Rejected Async I/O Requests	The total number of asynchronous I/O requests rejected by the bandwidth throttle.

Table 28.6. Summary of HTTP service performance counters.

Counter	Description
Bytes Received/sec	Specifies the rate (in bytes per second) at which the HTTP server is receiving data.
Bytes Sent/sec	Specifies the rate (in bytes per second) at which the HTTP server is transmitting data.
Bytes Total/sec	Specifies the total amount of data that is being transmitted, or received, by the HTTP server in bytes/second.
CGI Requests	Specifies the number of Common Gateway Interface (CGI) requests received by the HTTP server.
Connection Attempts	Specifies the total number of attempts made to connect to the HTTP server.
Connections/sec	Specifies the number of connections to the HTTP server per second.
Current Anonymous Users	Specifies how many anonymous users are currently connected to the HTTP server.

Counter	Description
Connection Attempts	Specifies the number of times a connection to the server was attempted.
Current CGI Requests	Specifies how many CGI requests are currently being processed by the HTTP server.
Current Connections	Specifies the current number of connections to the HTTP server.
Current ISAPI Extension Requests	Specifies the current number of ISAPI requests being processed by the server.
Current NonAnonymous Users	Specifies the total number of users currently connected to the HTTP server using a domain user account.
File Received	Specifies the total number of files received by the HTTP server.
File Sent	Specifies the total number of files transmitted by the HTTP server.
File Total	Specifies the sum of the total number of files transmitted and received.
Get Requests	Specifies the total number of HTTP requests using the GET method.
Head Requests	Specifies the total number of HTTP requests using the HEAD method.
ISAPI Extension Requests	Specifies the total number of ISAPI requests being processed by the server.
Logon Requests	Specifies the total number of logon attempts that have been made by the HTTP server.
Maximum Number of Anonymous Users	Specifies the maximum number of simultaneously connected anonymous users.
Maximum CGI Requests	Specifies the maximum number of simultaneous CGI requests processed by the HTTP server.
Maximum Connection	Specifies the maximum number of simultaneous connections to the HTTP server.

continues

28

TUNING THE SERVER

Table 28.6. continued

Counter	Description
Maximum ISAPI Extension Requests	Specifies the maximum number of simultaneous ISAPI requests processed by the HTTP server.
Maximum NonAnonymous Users	Specifies the maximum number of simultaneously connected users using a domain user account.
Not Found Errors	Specifies the total number of requests that failed because of a missing document.
Other Requested Methods	Specifies the total number of HTTP requests that do not use the GET, HEAD, or POST methods. This can include PUT, DELETE, LINK, or other methods.
Post Requests	Specifies the total number of HTTP requests using the POST method.
Total Anonymous Users	Specifies the total number of anonymous users that have ever connected to the HTTP server.
Total NonAnonymous Users	Specifies the total number of users that have ever connected to the HTTP server using a domain user account.

Table 28.7. Summary of the FTP server performance counters.

Counter	Description
Bytes Received/sec	Specifies the rate (in bytes per second) at which the FTP server is receiving data.
Bytes Sent/sec	Specifies the rate (in bytes per second) at which the FTP server is transmitting data.
Bytes Total/sec	Specifies the total amount of data that is being transmitted, or received, by the FTP server in bytes per second.
Current Anonymous Users	Specifies how many anonymous users are currently connected to the FTP server.

Counter	Description
Current Connections	Specifies the current number of connections to the FTP server.
Current NonAnonymous Users	Specifies the total number of users currently connected to the FTP server using a domain user account.
File Received	Specifies the total number of files received by the FTP server.
File Sent	Specifies the total number of files transmitted by the FTP server.
Logon Attempts	Specifies the total number of logon attempts that have been made by the FTP server.
Maximum Anonymous Users	Specifies the maximum number of simultaneously connected anonymous users.
Maximum Connections	Specifies the maximum number of simultaneous connections to the FTP server.
Maximum NonAnonymous Users	Specifies the maximum number of simultaneous connected users using a domain user account.
Total Anonymous Users	Specifies the total number of anonymous users that have ever connected to the FTP server.
Total NonAnonymous Users	Specifies the total number of users that have ever connected to the FTP server using a domain user account.

28

TUNING THE SERVER

Table 28.8. Summary of Gopher service performance counters.

Counter	Description
Aborted Connections	Specifies the total number of connections that failed due to errors or over-limit requests made to the Gopher server.
Bytes Received/sec	Specifies the rate (in bytes per second) at which the Gopher server is receiving data.

continues

Table 28.8. continued

Counter	Description
Bytes Sent/sec	Specifies the rate (in bytes per second) at which the Gopher server is transmitting data.
Bytes Total/sec	Specifies the total amount of data that is being transmitted, or received, by the Gopher server in bytes per second.
Connection Attempts	Specifies the total number of attempts made to connect to the Gopher server.
Connections in Error	Specifies the number of errors that occurred while being processed by the Gopher server.
Current Anonymous Users	Specifies how many anonymous users are currently connected to the Gopher server.
Current Connections	Specifies the current number of connections to the Gopher server.
Current NonAnonymous Users	Specifies the total number of users currently connected to the Gopher server using a domain user account.
Directory Listing Sent	Specifies the total number of directory listings transmitted by the Gopher server.
File Sent	Specifies the total number of files transmitted by the Gopher server.
File Total	Specifies the sum of the total number of files transmitted and received.
Gopher Plus Requests	Specifies the total number of Gopher Plus requests received by the Gopher server.
Logon Requests	Specifies the total number of logon attempts that have been made by the Gopher server.
Maximum Anonymous Users	Specifies the maximum number of simultaneously connected anonymous users.
Maximum NonAnonymous Users	Specifies the maximum number of simultaneously connected users using a domain user account.
Maximum Connections	Specifies the maximum number of simultaneously connected users to the Gopher server.

Counter	Description
Searches Sent	Specifies the total number of searches performed by the Gopher server.
Total Anonymous Users	Specifies the total number of anonymous users which have ever connected to the Gopher server.
Total NonAnonymous Users	Specifies the total number of users that have ever connected to the Gopher server using a domain user account.

Configuring SQL Server

After you optimize Windows NT Server to provide the best possible performance, you can turn your attention to configuring SQL Server. After you change your SQL Server configuration, you might need to change your Windows NT Server configuration to fine-tune its performance. The easiest way to modify SQL Server's configuration is with the SQL Enterprise Manager; however, you can use an ISQL command-line prompt if you prefer. This section looks at the various options and describes both the good and bad sides of these options. The next section explains how the Performance Monitor can help you determine whether your configuration choices are working as well as expected.

The first step is to load the SQL Enterprise Manager. Next click a registered server to connect to the SQL Server installation you want to configure. Then right-click the server name and choose Configure from the pop-up menu. The Server/Configuration dialog box will appear. Choose the Configuration tab to display the available options on the properties sheet. To change the current value, enter a new value in the Current column for the specific option. Repeat this step for each option you want to change. After you make all your modifications, click the OK button to return to the SQL Enterprise Manager main window. Table 28.9 lists the options you can change.

> **TIP**
>
> To set any of these options from an ISQL command prompt, you can use the stored procedure sp_configure. The basic syntax follows:
>
> ```
> sp_configure 'option', 'value'
> ```
>
> where option and value are specified in Table 28.9.

Table 28.9. The SQL Server configuration options.

Option	Minimum Value	Maximum Value	Default Value	Requires Restart to be Placed in Effect	Description
allow updates	0	1	0	No	Specifies that users with appropriate permissions will be able to modify system tables directly. Use this option with care because it is possible to damage system tables and corrupt a database quite easily.
backup buffer size	1	10	1	No	Specifies the size (in 32-page increments) of the dump and load buffers used to increase the backup performance.
backup threads	0	32	5	Yes	Specifies the number of threads to be reserved for striped operations (such as a dump or load).
database size	2	10,000	2	Yes	Specifies the default size, in megabytes, for newly created databases. This minimum size is based on the model database. If you make a change to the model database, it determines the minimum size of all databases created after the change.
default language	0	9,999	0	Yes	Specifies the default language to use with SQL Server. It is best (and easiest) to set this value using the SQL Server Setup utility.

Option	Minimum Value	Maximum Value	Default Value	Requires Restart to be Placed in Effect	Description
fill factor	0	100	0	Yes	Specifies how full (a percentage from 0 to 100, where 0 specifies the SQL Server default) the data page will be whenever SQL Server creates a new index. You can override this value by using the CREATE INDEX command.
language in cache	3	100	3	No	Specifies the maximum number of languages that can be held simultaneously in the system cache.
LE threshold maximum	2	500,000	200	N/A	Specifies the maximum number of page locks that can be held before escalating to a table lock.
LE threshold percent	0	100	0	N/A	Specifies the percentage of page locks that can be held on a table before escalating to a table lock.
locks	5000	2,147,483,647	5000	Yes	Specifies how many locks are available for use by SQL Server. Each lock requires about 32 bytes of memory. If you run out of locks, a process fails or it is suspended until a lock is available. I recommend that you specify a minimum of 50,000 locks.

28

TUNING THE SERVER

continues

Table 28.9. continued

Option	Minimum Value	Maximum Value	Default Value	Requires Restart to be Placed in Effect	Description
					You may need more if you have complex stored procedures or queries, or a large number of users accessing SQL Server.
logwrite sleep	1	500	0	N/A	Specifies the time, in milliseconds, before a write to the log that a delay will occur if the buffer is not full.
max async IO	1	50	8	Yes	Specifies the maximum number of asynchronous I/O requests that can be issued by SQL Server. Increase this value if you have a stripe set, a stripe set with parity, or a RAID 5 hardware array. I recommend that you increase this value by half the number of spindles in the system. If you have five disk drives, for example, the entry should be 20 [(5 × 8) /2 = 20)]. You can increase this value if you have an exceptionally fast I/O subsystem.
max text repl size	0	2,147,483,647	65,536	N/A	Specifies the maximum size, in bytes, of text or image data that can be added to a replicated column in a single insert, update, writetext, or updatetext statement.

Option	Minimum Value	Maximum Value	Default Value	Requires Restart to be Placed in Effect	Description
max worker threads	10	1,024	255	Yes	Specifies the maximum number of threads SQL Server can use to support client connections and perform internal maintenance. Increasing this value if you have more than one processor installed on the system can improve performance.
media retention	0	365	0	Yes	Specifies the time you plan to keep each disk used for a database or transaction log.
memory	1000	1,048,576	Based on amount of memory installed	Yes	Specifies the number of 2KB units to be used by SQL Server. This is the number one item to change for maximum performance. I recommend that you allocate as much memory as possible for SQL Server's usage. You should leave a minimum of 16MB for Windows NT Server, however. If you have additional services, such as Services for Macintosh, Gateway Services for NetWare, DHCP, WINS, and so on, plan on allocating an additional 2MB per service. You can allocate any leftover memory to

28

TUNING THE SERVER

continues

Table 28.9. continued

Option	Minimum Value	Maximum Value	Default Value	Requires Restart to be Placed in Effect	Description
					SQL Server. In a 64MB system, for example, I generally allocate between 32MB and 48MB to SQL Server.
nested triggers	0	1	1	Yes	Specifies whether nested triggers are enabled (1) or disabled (0).
network packet size	512	32,767	4096	No	Specifies the size, in bytes, of the network packet size to use. This value can be overridden by the client application.
open databases	5	32,767	20	Yes	Specifies the maximum number of databases that can be opened simultaneously. Each database allocation consumes about 1KB of system memory.
open objects	100	2,147,483,647	500	Yes	Specifies the maximum number of database objects that can be opened simultaneously. Each object allocation consumes about 70 bytes.
procedure cache	1	99	30	Yes	Specifies the amount of memory (a percentage from 0 to 100 percent) to allocate to the procedure cache after the SQL Server allocation demands have been

Option	Minimum Value	Maximum Value	Default Value	Requires Restart to be Placed in Effect	Description
					satisfied. If you modify the default settings for memory allocations as recommended, you also may want to change this value. In a high-memory system (64MB or more), I recommend a value between 30 and 40 percent, depending on the number of users and active stored procedures.
RA worker threads	0	255	3	N/A	Specifies the number of read-ahead worker threads to allocate.
recovery flags	0	1	0	Yes	Specifies what information SQL Server displays during the recovery process. If you are having problems, setting this value to 1 enables additional diagnostic messages that may help to isolate the problem.
recovery interval	1	32,767	5	No	Specifies the maximum number of minutes SQL Server can use to recover a database. Increase this value if you have very complex or large databases.
remote access	0	1	0	Yes	Specifies that remote SQL Servers can access this server (1) or cannot access this server (0).

28

TUNING THE SERVER

continues

Table 28.9. continued

Option	Minimum Value	Maximum Value	Default Value	Requires Restart to be Placed in Effect	Description
remote conn timeout	-1	32,767	10	N/A	Specifies the maximum number of minutes to wait before closing inactive server-to-server connections.
tempdb	0	2044	0	Yes	Specifies the size (in MB) of RAM to allocate for temporary databases. This is the second most important performance option that you can use because the temporary database is constantly in use for temporary objects (tables, procedures, sorts, and so on). Use this option with care, however, because it directly affects the amount of available RAM that can be used by other system processes. If you have more than 64MB of RAM, it certainly will benefit you to use an additional 16MB to 64MB of RAM for the temporary database, depending on the type of queries you will be executing.
user connections	5	32,767	10	Yes	Specifies the maximum number of simultaneous user connections that can be established with

Option	Minimum Value	Maximum Value	Default Value	Requires Restart to be Placed in Effect	Description
					this server. Each connection consumes about 37KB of system memory. This value should be based on the number of legal license agreements you have purchased, and, for what it's worth, it is better to have a few too many connections than to run out of available connections. At the very least, you should use the SQL Administrator to check for connections that have been terminated but not removed from SQL Server's connection list and manually terminate them to free up available connections.
user options	0	4,096	0	N/A	Specifies a bit mask to be used to set various user options which may be overridden on a per-user basis using the SET command.

NOTE

Many of the changes you make will be put into effect only after you shut down and restart SQL Server.

28

TUNING THE
SERVER

SQL Server for Windows NT includes performance counters you can use to monitor the activity of your server for informational purposes and to fine-tune the performance of your SQL Server installation. If you look in the SQL Server for Windows NT Program Manager group, you will find a predefined set of performance counters you can use to check the basic activity of your server. It's not always enough to use these settings, however, which is why I have included Table 28.10. You can use this table to determine which counters may be of interest to you.

> **NOTE**
>
> Depending on which version of SQL Server you are using, the counters may be different.

Table 28.10. The SQL Server Performance Monitor counters.

Object	Counter	Description
SQLServer	I/O Log Writes/sec	Specifies the number of log pages written to disk per second. Because almost all database activity is transaction based, which means that changes must be written to the log before they can be applied to the database, this is a good counter to watch to determine whether your disk is a bottleneck for SQL Server performance.
SQLServer	I/O Batch Writes/sec	Specifies the number of asynchronous writes in a single batch (generally as part of the checkpoint process). The higher the value, the better the SQL Server performance. Monitor this value as you make changes to segment and device allocations to see whether your changes are increasing or decreasing performance.
SQLServer	I/O Batch Average Size	Specifies the average number of pages (2KB) written to disk during a batch operation. The higher the value, the better. You can use this counter to determine whether your changes to the max async i/o parameter are effective. If you increase the max async i/o value too much, this counter decreases.

Object	Counter	Description
SQLServer	I/O Batch Max Size	Specifies the maximum number of pages (2KB) that have been written to disk. The higher the value, the better the overall performance. This counter also can be used to determine whether the `max asycn i/o` parameter setting is effective. If this counter lowers after your changes, decrease the value for the `max async i/o` parameter.
SQLServer	I/O Page Reads/sec	Specifies the number of physical disk reads per second. The lower the number, the better. If this value is too high, you can change the procedure cache percentage to increase the amount of memory allocated to the data cache. A larger data cache lowers the number of physical disk reads.
SQLServer	I/O Single page Writes/sec	Specifies the number of physical disk writes per second. Like the I/O Page Reads/sec counter, a lower number is better. If a high value is encountered, it might be beneficial to increase the size of the data cache.
SQLServer	I/O Outstanding Reads	Specifies the number of pending physical disk reads. You can use this value to determine how well your I/O subsystem is performing. A high value over an extended period of time is an indication that the I/O subsystem is a bottle-neck in SQL Server performance.
SQLServer	I/O Outstanding Writes	Specifies the number of pending physical disk writes. Like the I/O Outstanding Reads counter, a high value over an extended period of time is an indication that the I/O subsystem is a bottleneck.
SQLServer	I/O Transactions/sec	Specifies the number of Transact-SQL batches per second. A higher value is better.
SQLServer	I/O - Trans. Per Log Record	Specifies the number of transactions that were packed into a single log record before being written to disk. A higher value is better.

28

TUNING THE SERVER

continues

Table 28.10. continued

Object	Counter	Description
SQLServer	Cache Hit Ratio	Specifies the percentage of time in which requested data was found in the data cache. The higher the value, the better. If your hit rate routinely drops below 60 to 70 percent, increasing the size of the data cache might improve SQL Server performance.
SQLServer	Cache Flushes	Specifies the number of cache buffers that need to be flushed to disk in order to free a buffer for use by the next read. When cache flushes occur, you should increase the size of your data cache or increase the checkpoint frequency to provide additional buffers and increase performance.
SQLServer	Cache - Avg. Free Page Scan	Specifies the average number of buffers that needed to be scanned in order to find a free buffer. When this value increases above 10, increase the size of the data cache or the frequency of the checkpoint process to free additional buffers and increase performance.
SQLServer	Cache - Max Free Page Scan	Specifies the maximum number of buffers that had to be scanned in order to find a free buffer. When this value increases above 10, increase the size of the data cache or the frequency of the checkpoint process to free additional buffers and increase performance.
SQLServer	Cache - Scan Limit Reached	Specifies the number of times the scan limit was reached while searching for free buffers. If this value is consistently high, increase the size of the data cache or the checkpoint frequency to free up additional buffers.
SQLServer	Network Reads/sec	Specifies the number of tabular data stream packets read from the network. A higher value indicates higher network activity.
SQLServer	Network Writes/sec	Specifies the number of tabular data streams written to the network. A higher value is an indication of higher network activity.

Object	Counter	Description
SQLServer	Network Command Queue Length	Specifies the number of outstanding client requests waiting to be serviced by the SQL Server worker threads. A higher value is an indication that increasing the number of worker threads may improve performance. If performance does not increase, it may be an indication that the processor is a bottleneck, and adding an additional processor may increase overall throughput.
SQLServer	User Connections	Specifies the number of current users connected to SQL Server.
SQLServer-Locks	Total Locks	Specifies the total number of locks currently in use by SQL Server.
SQLServer-Locks	Total Exclusive Locks	Specifies the total number of exclusive (meaning no other process can access the locked area) locks in use by SQL Server.
SQLServer-Locks	Total Shared Locks	Specifies the total number of shared (meaning the lock will not prevent other users from reading the locked data) locks in use by SQL Server.
SQLServer-Locks	Total Blocking Locks	Specifies the number of locks blocking other processes from continuing. (A blocked process is one that requires a lock on the same area.)
SQLServer-Locks	Total Demand Locks	Specifies the number of locks blocking other processes that need to obtain a shared lock on the same data area.
SQLServer-Locks	Table Locks - Exclusive	Specifies the number of exclusive locks on tables in use by SQL Server.
SQLServer-Locks	Table Locks - Shared	Specifies the number of shared locks on tables currently in use by SQL Server.
SQLServer-Locks	Table Locks - Total	Specifies the total number of table locks in use by SQL Server.
SQLServer-Locks	Extent Locks - Exclusive	Specifies the number of exclusive extent locks in use on databases (eight pages at a time) that are being allocated or freed.

28

TUNING THE SERVER

continues

Table 28.10. continued

Object	Counter	Description
SQLServer-Locks	Extent Locks - Shared	Specifies the number of shared extent locks in use on databases (eight pages at a time) that are being allocated or freed.
SQLServer-Locks	Extent Locks - Total	Specifies the total number of extent locks in use. An extent lock prevents an exclusive lock from being set.
SQLServer-Locks	Intent Locks - Exclusive	Specifies the total number of exclusive intent locks in use. An intent lock indicates the intention of obtaining the requested type of lock; it does not indicate that the lock has currently been granted. An intent lock prevents an exclusive lock from being granted to another process that needs to lock the same data area.
SQLServer-Locks	Intent Locks - Shared	Specifies the total number of shared intent locks in use.
SQLServer-Locks	Intent Locks - Total	Specifies the total number of intent locks in use by SQL Server.
SQLServer-Locks	Page Locks - Exclusive	Specifies the number of exclusive locks on pages.
SQLServer-Locks	Page Locks - Shared	Specifies the number of shared locks on pages.
SQLServer-Locks	Page Locks - Update	Specifies the number of update locks on pages.
SQLServer-Locks	Page Locks - Total	Specifies the total number of locks on pages.
SQLServer-User	Memory	Specifies the amount of memory (in 2KB units) allocated to a user connection.
SQLServer-User	CPU Time	Specifies the cumulative amount of time allocated to a user connection.
SQLServer-User	Physical I/O	Specifies the number of disk reads/writes for the currently executing Transact-SQL statement.
SQLServer-User	Locks Held	Specifies the number of locks currently held by the user connection.

Object	Counter	Description
SQLServer-Log	%Full	Specifies the amount (in a percentage) of the transaction log that is currently in use. Setting an alert for each transaction log on each database of importance can be a great help because it can provide you with an early warning.
SQLServer-Log	Size	Specifies the current allocation (in MB) of the transaction log.

Summary

In this chapter you learn how to optimize your server using sample Performance Monitor charts, alerts, reports, and workspace files. These files, used with the sample programs, illustrate how to find processor, memory, disk, and network bottlenecks. You also examine the performance counters you can use to determine how well your IIS server and SQL Server installations are performing.

28

TUNING THE
SERVER

VIII

PART

IN THIS PART

■ Glossary *811*

■ HTML Reference *839*

■ The Registry Editor and Registry
Keys *889*

Appendixes

Glossary

access control entry (ACE)   An entry in an access control list. Each access control entry defines the protection or auditing to be applied to a file or other object for a specific user or group of users.

access control list (ACL)   The part of a security descriptor that enumerates both the protections for accessing and the auditing of that accessing applied to an object. The owner of an object has discretionary access control of the object and can change the object's ACL to allow or disallow others to access the object. Access control lists are ordered lists of access control entries.

access right   A permission granted to a process to manipulate a particular object in a particular way (by calling a service, for example). Different object types support different access rights. These access rights are stored in an object's access control list.

access token or **security token**   An object that uniquely identifies a user who has logged on. An access token is attached to all the user's processes and contains the user's security identifier (SID), the SIDs of any groups to which the user belongs, any privileges that the user owns, the default owner of any objects that the user's processes create, and the default access control list to be applied to any objects that the user's processes create. See also *privilege*.

access violation   An attempt to carry out a memory operation that is not allowed by Windows NT memory management. An access violation has nothing to do with the Security Manager's checking of user-mode access rights to objects.

Four basic kinds of actions can cause access violations:

- Attempting an invalid operation, such as writing to a read-only buffer.
- Attempting to access memory beyond the limit of the current program's address space (also known as a *length violation*).
- Attempting to access a page to which the system forbids access. (For example, code is not allowed to run in the low-order 64KB of the Windows NT user-mode address).
- Attempting to access a page that is currently resident but is dedicated to the use of an executive component. (For example, user-mode code is not allowed access to a page that the kernel is using.)

address class   In a TCP/IP world, the address class describes the type of network subnet. The three classes are class A address (such as 206.0.0.0), class B address (such as 206.170.0.0), and class C address (such as 206.170.127.0). A class C address can contain only 256 IP addresses (from .0 to .255), a class B address can contain 65,536 IP addresses (from 0.0 to 255.255), and a class A address can contain 16,777,216 IP addresses (from 0.0.0 to 255.255.255).

address space or **virtual address space**   The set of addresses available for a process's threads to use. In Windows NT, every process has a unique address space of 4GB; 2GB of this address space is reserved for the operating system, and 2GB of the address space is available for the process.

administrative alert   A message sent to a computer or user by the Alerter Service to announce a critical problem or low resource supply on a computer, such as a low-disk-space warning.

Alerter Service   A Windows NT service designed to send alert messages. This service requires that the Windows NT Messenger Service also be running in order to actually send an alert to a computer or user.

algorithm   In its most general sense, an algorithm is any set of instructions that can be followed to carry out a particular task. In computer usage, an algorithm is a set of instructions within a program. If you choose the Network option in the Control Panel, for example, you see the message `A binding algorithm failed`. This message means that the program was unable to execute a set of instructions designed to bind together elements necessary for a functional network configuration.

allocation units   See *clusters* or *allocation units*.

anonymous-level security token   The type of security token used when a server impersonates a client. When the client calls the server, if the client specifies an anonymous impersonation mode, the server cannot access any of the client's identification information, such as its security identifier or privileges. The server will have to use an anonymous-level security token when representing the client in successive operations. See also *access token* or *security token*.

application programming interface (API)   A set of routines an application program uses to request and carry out lower-level services performed by the operating system.

Programming code is built using a series of function calls, or *routines*, that perform certain actions. For example, suppose that every workday you get up at 7 a.m., shower, dress, fix and eat breakfast, brush your teeth, and then drive to work. If you were a computer and never deviated from this pattern, a programmer could write a program for you called `DAILY_ROUTINE` that would perform these actions automatically. Instead of having to specify each action, the programmer could just write `DAILY_ROUTINE` in the code and the actions would be carried out. In this example `DAILY_ROUTINE` is an API.

archive bit   An attribute stored on the disk to indicate that a directory or file has changed. Backup programs use this bit to determine whether to copy a file to a backup medium (such as a tape). After a file is copied, this bit is reset. See also *hidden bit, read-only bit,* and *system bit.*

asymmetric multiprocessing (AMP)   A multiprocessing methodology that uses one processor to execute the operating system and another processor to execute applications. See also *symmetric multiprocessing.*

audit   The ability to record information about object access. An object could be a file, a directory, a process, or another auditable object. This auditing information is stored in the Security event log and may be viewed by an administrator using the Event Viewer.

audit policy   A set of rules that specifies the type of information to be audited. Many audit policies include user authentication (to know who has logged on to your system) and object access (to determine who is using your computer).

A

GLOSSARY

To enable systemwide auditing, use the Audit option from the Policy menu on User Manager for Domains. To enable directory or file auditing, use File Manager or the Windows Explorer. To enable printer auditing, use Print Manager.

authentication package   A subsystem that verifies that the logon information a user supplies matches the information stored in a security database.

AUTOEXEC.NT files and **CONFIG.NT files**   Windows NT configures the MS-DOS environment by reading the AUTOEXEC.BAT file when you log on and by reading the AUTOEXEC.NT and CONFIG.NT files when you start an application in a new command window. The AUTOEXEC.NT and CONFIG.NT files are the Windows NT versions of AUTOEXEC.BAT and CONFIG.SYS.

When you log on to Windows NT, the path and environment variables stored in the AUTOEXEC.BAT file are appended to the Windows NT path and environment settings. Because this portion of the operating environment is established at logon, the values set for the path and environment variables are available to each application you use. If you change these values, you must log off from Windows NT and then log on again for the changes to take effect.

When you start an MS-DOS–based or a 16-bit Windows-based application in a new command window, Windows NT reads the CONFIG.NT and AUTOEXEC.NT files to configure the environment for the application. If you change an application's driver in the CONFIG.NT file, for example, restarting the application puts the change into effect. You can edit these files just as you would CONFIG.SYS and AUTOEXEC.BAT. The files are located in the *SystemRoot*\SYSTEM32 directory, where *SystemRoot* is the root directory of your Windows NT installation (generally, C:\WINNT35).

backup domain controller (BDC)   For a Windows NT Server domain, the BDC is a server that contains a copy of the security policy and the master database for a domain and, along with the primary domain controller, authenticates domain logons. See also *primary domain controller.*

bad-sector mapping   A technique used by the Windows NT file system to handle write errors. When an error is detected, the file system takes a free block, writes the data to that block instead of to the bad block, and updates a bad-block map. A copy of this map is written to disk.

basic input/output system (BIOS)   A system component, generally a ROM or flash memory chip, that contains processor instructions to operate a system peripheral, such as a disk controller, keyboard, or video controller. The BIOS is an intermediary device that provides device independence. An operating system can call a BIOS function instead of controlling the device directly. Windows NT, however, generally uses the BIOS only to boot the computer and instead requires a specific device driver to control the peripheral. See also *flash memory* and *read-only memory.*

batch file   A text file containing commands to be noninteractively processed in a logical order. AUTOEXEC.NT is an example of a batch file.

batch process   A process (application) that executes in the background without user intervention. The Windows NT Scheduler service can be used to initiate a batch process, such as a backup program, at a specific time.

bayonet nut connector   A T-shaped connector in a thin Ethernet–based network that connects the network adapter to the network segment. The base of the connector attaches to the network adapter, and the input/output network cable attaches to the top of the connector.

binding   A series of bound paths from the upper-layer network services and protocols to the lowest layer of adapter card device drivers. Each network component can be bound to one or more network components above it or below it to make the component's services available to any component that can benefit from them.

boot partition   The boot partition for Windows NT is a volume, formatted for a Windows NT file system (NTFS) or a file allocation table (FAT) file system, that has the Windows NT operating system and its support files. The boot partition can be (but does not have to be) the same as the system partition. It cannot be part of a stripe set or volume set, but it can be part of a mirror set. See also *system partition*.

browse   A process of enumerating network resources—for example, a list of shared directories or printers. See also *enumeration operation*.

browser   See *Web browser*.

C2-level security   A standard implemented by the U.S. government's National Computer Security Council that requires discretionary access to computer resources and auditing.

chat   An application with multiple windows that displays text communications among users. A chat can be one to many or many to many. See also *Internet Relay Chat*.

Common Gateway Interface (CGI)   An application interface used to customize the behavior of a Web page. A CGI application executes as a separate process. It is commonly used with Web-based forms to capture client information.

circular dependency   A dependency in which an action that appears later in a chain is contingent on an earlier action. Suppose that three services (A, B, and C) are linked. A is dependent on B to start. B is dependent on C to start. A circular dependency results when C is dependent on A to start. See also *dependency*.

client/server application   An application divided into two or more components at the API level—usually a client application that executes on a network client computer and a server application that executes on a different computer. Distributing the load can improve performance by using a fast computer to run the server, which processes the data, and a client computer to display the data.

A

GLOSSARY

clusters or **allocation units**   In data storage, a *cluster* is a disk-storage unit consisting of a fixed number of sectors (storage segments on the disk) that the operating system uses to read or write information. Typically, a cluster consists of between two and eight sectors, each of which holds a certain number of bytes (characters).

A formatted disk is divided into sectors, and a cluster is a set of contiguous sectors allocated to files as a single unit. Clustering of sectors reduces disk fragmentation but may result in wasted space within the cluster.

Under both the NTFS and the FAT system, the size of a cluster is based on the size of the partition. With NTFS, however, you can override this default with a switch, which forces a smaller (or larger) cluster size. For example, the command FORMAT D: /fs:NTFS /v:D_Drive / a:512 formats the D: drive as NTFS with a sector size of 512 bytes and labels the drive as D_Drive. With a FAT partition, the size of a cluster cannot be changed; the larger the partition, the more sectors you have per cluster. Therefore, with a FAT partition you can have 1, 2, 4, 8, 16, 32, and 64 sectors per cluster.

CONFIG.NT files   See *AUTOEXEC.NT files* and *CONFIG.NT files*.

control set   All Windows NT startup-related data not computed during startup is saved in one of the registry hives. This startup data is organized into control sets, each of which contains a complete set of parameters for starting up devices and services. The registry always contains at least two control sets, each of which contains information about all the configurable options for the computer: the current control set and the LastKnownGood control set. See also *LastKnownGood control set*.

cooperative multitasking   A multitasking methodology that can halt the execution of one process and start the execution of another process only at the discretion of the currently executing application. See also *preemptive multitasking*.

corrupted data   Data in memory or on disk that has been unintentionally changed, thereby altering or obliterating its meaning.

current control set   The control set used most recently to start the computer, which contains any changes made to the startup information during the current session. See also *LastKnownGood control set*.

cyclic redundancy check (CRC)   A procedure used on disk drives to ensure that the data written to a sector is read correctly later.

This procedure also is used when checking for errors in data transmission. The procedure is known as a *redundancy check* because each data transmission includes not only data but also extra (redundant) error-checking values. The sending device generates a number based on the data to be transmitted and sends its result along with the data to the receiving device. The receiving device repeats the same calculation after transmission. If both devices obtain the same result, the transmission is assumed to be error free.

Data Source Name   Specifies a name to an ODBC data source. The data source defines the connection characteristics between the application using the data source and the ODBC database. These characteristics might include the filename of an Access database, a username to log on to the database, time-out values, buffer sizes, or other information relevant to accessing the database.

deadlock condition   A runtime-error condition that occurs when two threads of execution are blocked. Each is waiting to acquire a resource that the other holds, and neither is able to continue running.

debugger breakpoints   Set by the user of the Kernel Debugger (KD) before running the Windows NT Executive, a breakpoint is put into the Executive code at an instruction. Then, when the Executive is run, if and when that instruction is executed, execution stops and the current values of registers and flags are displayed. KD breakpoints are sticky in the sense that they remain in the program until explicitly removed. Consequently, code can have breakpoints in it that were never explicitly removed. See also *Kernel Debugger.*

default gateway   Specifies a host (a router, or another computer) to forward TCP/IP packets outside of the local subnet. A gateway is generally a point where two networks interface. You may, for example, have two subnets (called A and B). For these subnets to be accessible from each other, they would be joined using a router. Network clients in subnets A and B would use the IP address of this router as the default gateway.

dependency   A situation in which one action must take place before another can happen. If action A does not occur, for example, action D cannot occur. Some Windows NT drivers have dependencies on other drivers or groups of drivers. For example, driver A will not load unless some driver from the G group loads first. See also *circular dependency.*

device driver   A low-level (usually kernel mode) operating system component that provides the software interface to a hardware device. A device driver is an individual file that facilitates replacing a hardware device. Some device drivers (such as the 4mm DAT driver) are loaded dynamically any time by the operating system, whereas other device drivers (such as a disk controller driver) are loaded only at boot time. The AHA174x.SYS device driver, for example, provides the software (operating system) interface to the hardware (I/O ports, registers, and so on) for my Adaptec 1742/a SCSI controller.

dial-up networking   The client side of a client/server service to provide network access to physically remote network clients using modems, ISDN, and X.25 adapters. Generally the dial-up networking client uses a modem and standard phone line to connect to the network. The modem acts as a network adapter to transmit and receive network packets from the attached network (or Internet). The dial-up networking client supports the PPP and SLIP interfaces and the TCP/IP, IPX/SPX, and NetBEUI network transport protocols.

A

GLOSSARY

Directory Replicator Service   A Windows NT service used to export or import a directory tree. Only a Windows NT Server computer can act as a directory export server, although any Windows NT computer can act as a directory import partner. The most common use of this service is to replicate the logon scripts from one domain controller (not necessarily the primary domain controller) to all the other domain controllers in the domain. See also *export path* and *import path*.

disk duplexing   A fault-tolerant capability provided with Windows NT Server that uses a second disk or partition on a physically separate disk controller to create a redundant copy of a disk or partition. If the primary disk controller or disk drive fails, the second copy can keep the system up and running.

disk mirroring   A fault-tolerant capability provided with Windows NT Server that uses a second disk or partition to make a redundant copy of a disk or partition in case the primary disk or partition fails.

disk striping   See *striped set* and *striped set with parity*.

dongle   An adapter that connects to the parallel port and contains a software key. Protected software often uses this type of mechanism to prevent software piracy.

domain   For Windows NT Server, a collection of computers that share a common-accounts database and security policy. Each domain has a unique name. A domain is a set of servers and workstations grouped together for efficiency and security and is the basic administrative unit in Windows NT Server. For example, a network can be divided into domains by department, workgroup, or building floor.

Domains keep large networks manageable. Users displaying a list of servers see only the servers for their domain. But they still can access resources on servers in any domain if they have been granted the necessary rights.

domain controller   See *primary domain controller*.

domain name   A UNIX-based operating system defines a common name for a group of computers, very similar in concept to a Windows NT domain. A domain name is a mechanism used for address resolution. You Web server may be known as www.*yourdomainname*.com, or your e-mail address may be *YourName@YourDomain*.com. In both cases, the hostname will be converted to a specific IP address to establish a connection.

domain name service (DNS)   An RFC-defined service under TCP/IP-based service for resolving NetBIOS computer names to TCP/IP IP addresses. A DNS server uses several host files, such as LMHOST, which is an ASCII file that contains computer names and IP addresses. See also *Dynamic Host Configuration Protocol, Windows Internet Naming Service,* and *WINS proxy agent*.

domain synchronization   A process for keeping a consistent copy of the account database on all domain controllers. The primary domain controller contains the original copy of the account database and is responsible for copying these changes to the backup domain controllers. After a change is made, the domain controller informs the backup domain controllers that an update has been made. Then the backup domain controllers request the updates to maintain a consistent copy of the account database. This process prevents a user from gaining access to the network on the basis of stale data.

down level   An earlier operating system, such as Windows for Workgroups or LAN Manager, that still can interoperate with Windows NT Workstation or Windows NT Server.

Dynamic Host Configuration Protocol (DHCP)   A client/server mechanism for automatically configuring TCP/IP IP addresses on networked client computers using the TCP/IP protocol. Windows NT Server includes the DHCP service, which supplies a TCP/IP address to a network client that includes a DHCP client, such as Windows NT Workstation, Windows NT Server, Windows 95, Windows for Workgroups, and MS-DOS clients using the MS-DOS connection. See also *Windows Internet Naming Service.*

dynamic link library (DLL)   A library of routines that user-mode applications access through ordinary procedure calls. The operating system automatically modifies the user's executable image to point to DLL procedures at runtime. That way, the code for the procedures does not have to be included in the user's executable image and may be shared with other executable images.

enumeration operation   The counting, accessing, or listing of an entire set of similar objects. When the last object in the set is counted, accessed, or listed, the enumeration operation is complete.

error logging   The process by which errors that cannot readily be corrected by the majority of end users are written to a file instead of being displayed onscreen. System administrators, support technicians, and users can use this log file to monitor the condition of the hardware in a Windows NT computer, to tune the configuration of the computer for better performance, and to debug problems as they occur.

exception   A synchronous error condition resulting from the execution of a particular computer instruction. Exceptions can be hardware-detected errors, such as division by zero, or software-detected errors, such as a guard-page violation. See also *guard-page protection.*

Executive   The part of the Windows NT operating system that runs in kernel mode. Kernel mode is a privileged processor mode in which a thread has access to system memory and to hardware. (In contrast, user mode is a nonprivileged processor mode in which a thread can access system resources only by calling system services.) The Windows NT Executive provides process structure, thread scheduling, interprocess communication, memory management, object management, object security, interrupt processing, I/O capabilities, and networking.

The Windows NT kernel is the part of the Windows NT Executive that manages the processor. It performs thread scheduling and dispatching, interrupt and exception handling, and

A

GLOSSARY

multiprocessor synchronization. It also provides primitive objects to the Windows NT Executive, which uses them to create user-mode objects.

executive messages   Two types of character-mode messages occur when the Windows NT kernel detects an inconsistent condition from which it cannot recover: stop messages and hardware-malfunction messages.

Character-mode stop messages always are displayed on a full character-mode screen rather than in a Windows-mode message box. They also are uniquely identified by a hexadecimal number and a symbolic string, as in the following example:

```
*** STOP: 0x00000001
APC_INDEX_MISMATCH
```

The content of the symbolic string may suggest, to a trained technician, the part of the kernel that detected the condition from which there was no recourse but to stop. However, keep in mind that the cause actually may be in another part of the system.

Character-mode hardware-malfunction messages are caused by a hardware condition detected by the processor. The first one or two lines of a hardware-malfunction message may differ, depending on which company manufactured the computer. These lines always convey the same idea, however, as shown in the following example for an *x*86-based computer:

```
Hardware malfunction Call your hardware vendor for support.
```

The additional lines in each manufacturer's message screen also differ in format and content.

The Executive displays a Windows-mode status message box when it detects conditions within a process (generally, an application) that you should know about. Status messages can be divided into three types:

- System-information messages. All you need to do is read the information in the message box and click the OK button. The kernel continues running the process or thread.

- Warning messages. Some advise you to take an action that will enable the kernel to keep running the process or thread. Others warn you that although the process or thread will continue running, the results may not be correct.

- Application-termination messages. These warn you that the kernel is about to terminate a process or a thread.

export path   The local path on a Windows NT Server computer that contains the directories and files to copy to import partners. An *import partner* is a Windows NT computer that has an executing Directory Replicator Service and specifically has been configured to copy the directories and files in the export path. See also *Directory Replicator Service* and *import path*.

extended attribute   Windows NT file allocation table files have four basic parts: the data, the file system attributes (such as creation time and date, and file allocation table attributes), the security descriptors, and the extended attributes (EAs). EAs make up the set of extended information about a file and are structured as name/value pairs. Typical Windows NT system uses of EAs are actions, such as storing the icon of an executable image or indicating that the file is a symbolic link.

extended partition This partition is created from free space on a hard disk and can be subpartitioned into zero or more logical drives. The free space in an extended partition also can be used to create volume sets or other kinds of volumes for fault-tolerance purposes. Only one of the four partitions allowed per physical disk can be an extended partition, and no primary partition can be present.

family set A group of tapes containing the same tape name and one or more backup sets created by NTBACKUP. A family set can be thought of as a single logical tape, even though it consists of more than one physical tape.

file control block (FCB) In MS-DOS, a 36-byte block of memory that contains all the information MS-DOS needs to know about an open file, such as the filename, what drive it is on, current file size, and date and time of creation.

File Transfer Protocol (FTP) A language used to send or receive files over the Internet using a client/server architecture.

flash memory A set of memory chips installed on the computer that stores instructions for a computer to execute or data to be read by the processor. Flash memory is similar to ROM in that its purpose is to support read-only operations. It can be written to, however, by using a special program to change its contents. Flash memory generally is used to contain your system BIOS and is a better choice than ROM because it enables the user to upgrade the system BIOS. See also *basic input/output system, random access memory,* and *read-only memory.*

Fully Qualified Domain Name (FQDN) A hostname with the domain name appended. If your computer name is roadtrip and your domain name is nt-guru.com, for example, then your FQDN would be roadtrip.nt-guru.com.

gateway See *default gateway.*

global group A series of one or more user accounts logically grouped into a single unit and available to the whole domain. Global groups are available only on a Windows NT domain. See also *local group.*

globally unique identifier (GUID) See *universally unique identifier.*

guard-page protection The Windows NT Virtual Memory Manager can put a guard page at the end of a data structure, such as a dynamic array, and generate a warning message when a user-mode thread accesses the guard-page memory. The user-mode process can respond appropriately, for example, by extending the array.

handle In general, a unique identifier (often an integer) by which a client refers to an object in the Windows NT operating system. Clients call servers to get the handle of the object on

which the client wants to operate. Then the client sends requests for operations to the object, referring to the object by its handle. The server actually performs the operation. This sequence ensures that the client does not operate on the object directly.

In the registry, each of the first-level key names begins with HKEY to indicate to software developers that it is a handle that can be read by a program. A *handle* is a value that provides a unique identifier for a resource so that a program can access it.

hardware abstraction layer (HAL)   The lowest layer of the Windows NT operating system and part of the Executive. The HAL is used to provide platform independence. It communicates directly with the expansion bus, motherboard cache, programmable interrupt controller, and other system-specific components. All that is needed to convert Windows NT from a uniprocessor (single CPU) to a multiprocessor version of Windows NT is to use a supported motherboard with two or more CPUs and a multiprocessor HAL. The rest of the operating system components remain the same.

hexadecimal   A base-16 number system that consists of the digits 0 through 9 and the uppercase and lowercase letters A (equivalent to decimal 10) through F (equivalent to decimal 15).

hidden bit   An attribute stored on the disk to indicate that a directory or file should not be displayed. File Manager, for example, does not display hidden files unless the View Hidden | System Files option is enabled. System files required for the operation of your computer often are hidden. The BOOT.INI file, for example, which Windows NT requires to determine the location of the operating system to boot, is normally hidden. See also *archive bit, read-only bit,* and *system bit.*

high memory area (HMA)   A 64KB memory block located just above the 1MB address in a virtual DOS machine (VDM). This memory becomes visible when the A20 address line is turned on, enabling 21-bit addressing in the VDM.

hive   The registry is divided into parts called hives, which are analogous to the cellular structure of a beehive. A hive is a part of the registry that maps to a file on your hard disk. Each user profile is a separate hive, which means that it is also a separate file. Therefore, an administrator can copy a user profile as a file and then view, repair, or copy entries using the Registry Editor on another computer.

home directory   A local or shared directory specified as the user's default directory with User Manager.

hotkey   In a user interface, hotkeys provide an alternative to the mouse for manipulating interface objects. Instead of using the mouse, for example, you can press the key combination Alt+F to open the File menu on the menu bar. Alt+F is a hotkey.

Hypertext Markup Language (HTML)   A set of rules that utilize ASCII-based tags to format text, display objects, and create links within a document or Web page.

Hypertext Transfer Protocol (HTTP)   The common protocol, or language, used by World Wide Web (WWW) servers and Web browsers as the communication link between client and server.

Hypertext Transfer Protocol Secure (HTTPS)   The protocol, or language, used by World Wide Web (WWW) servers and Web browsers as a secure communication link between client and server. This secure link is obtained through the use of data encryption.

impersonation   The capability of a thread in one process to take on the security identity of a thread in another process and to perform operations on the other thread's behalf. The Windows NT environment subsystems and network services use impersonation to access remote resources on behalf of client applications.

import path   The local path on a Windows NT Server computer that has an executing Directory Replicator Service. The directories and files of the export partner are copied to this relative path. See also *Directory Replicator Service* and *export path*.

INF file   One of a set of files that the setup program uses during Windows NT installation, maintenance setup, or both. An INF file generally contains a script for the setup program to follow, along with configuration data that ends up in the registry.

input/output address   All peripherals connected to your expansion bus use one or more I/O ports to communicate with a device driver to control the physical device, to transfer data to/from the system and the device, or both. A communication port (COM1), for example, has a base I/O address of 03F8h and eight I/O ports for communicating with the device and to transfer data.

input/output bus   A hardware path inside a computer for transferring information to and from the processor and various input and output devices.

input/output control (IOCTL)   An IOCTL command enables a program to communicate directly with a device driver, for example, by sending a string of control information recognized by the driver. None of the information passed from the program to the device driver is sent to the device itself (in other words, the printer does not display the control string sent to a printer driver).

installable file system (IFS)   A file system that can be loaded into the operating system dynamically. Windows NT can support multiple installable file systems at one time, including the file allocation table file system, the high-performance file system, the Windows NT file system, and the CD-ROM file system. Windows NT automatically determines the format of a storage medium and reads and writes files in the correct format.

Internet access provider (IAP)   A company that provides you with a raw Internet connection. In contrast to an Internet service provider, an IAP does not provide any associated services. See also *Internet service provider*.

A

GLOSSARY

Internet Database Connector   An Internet Information Service extension. The extension is an ISA application that provides a customizable interface to an ODBC database from an HTML document.

Internet Locator Service   A Microsoft service used by Microsoft NetMeeting to maintain a database of NetMeeting users currently logged on to the server. This service enables NetMeeting users to find and connect to each other, even though their IP address changes dynamically. See also *NetMeeting*.

Internet Protocol (IP)   A low-level network protocol that provides a means of identifying a particular host. Every host on the Internet requires a unique IP address.

Internet Relay Chat (IRC)   An Internet protocol that supports multiple-participant text communications. As with most Internet applications, an IRC server and an IRC client are required to provide this service.

Internet Server Application Programming Interface (ISAPI)   A set of APIs used by developers to customize the behavior of the IIS Web server. Its purpose is similar to the Common Gateway Interface (CGI) except that ISAPI applications execute within the same process as the Web server, rather than as a separate process. This behavior can provide a substantial performance increase over CGI applications.

Internet service provider (ISP)   A company that provides you with your Internet connection and services. These services can include domain name registration, IP address allocation, and Web-site hosting.

interrupt   An asynchronous operating system condition that disrupts normal execution and transfers control to an interrupt handler. Both software and hardware devices requiring service from the processor can issue an interrupt. When software issues an interrupt, it calls an interrupt service routine. When hardware issues an interrupt, it signals an interrupt request line.

interrupt request level (IRQL)   A ranking of interrupts by priority. A processor has an interrupt request level setting that threads can raise or lower. Interrupts that occur at or below the processor's IRQL setting are masked, whereas interrupts that occur above the processor's IRQL setting are not. The priority of software interrupts is almost always lower than the priority of hardware interrupts.

IP address   A 32-bit number represented as a series of numbers between 0 and 255 separated by periods. For example, the IP address for my server is `206.170.127.65`.

ISA   Usually means an Industry Standard Architecture I/O bus. However, ISA also stands for Internet Server Application. An Internet Server Application is an ISAPI application that extends the functionality of the HTTP server.

JavaScript   A programming language designed as part of the Microsoft ActiveX development efforts. JavaScript applications are executable code embedded as an object within HTML documents, which can provide interactive Web pages. JavaScript is based on the Java language by Sun Microsystems, which in turn is based on the C++ object model.

kernel   The Windows NT kernel is the part of the Windows NT Executive that manages the processor. It performs thread scheduling and dispatching, interrupt and exception handling, and multiprocessor synchronization. It also provides primitive objects to the Windows NT Executive, which uses them to create user-mode objects.

Kernel Debugger (KD)   The Windows NT Kernel Debugger is a 32-bit application used to debug the kernel and device drivers and to log the events leading up to a Windows NT Executive stop, status, or hardware-malfunction message.

The Kernel Debugger runs on another Windows NT host computer connected to your Windows NT target computer. The two computers send debugging (troubleshooting) information back and forth through a communications port that must be running at the same baud rate on each computer. See also *debugger breakpoints, system debugger,* and *WINDBG.EXE.*

kernel mode   See *Executive.*

keyword   A special type of command parameter that includes a value. For example, the syntax of the width keyword is width = 40.

LastKnownGood (LKG) control set   The most recent control set that correctly started the system and resulted in a successful startup. The control set is saved as the LKG control set when you have a successful logon.

A copy of the control set used to start the system also is stored as the Clone subkey in the registry. At startup time, the Service Control Manager copies the Clone subkey to the LastKnownGood control set before any new changes are made to the control set. This procedure helps to ensure that the computer always contains a working control set. See also *current control set.*

local area network (LAN)   A group of computers physically located in a single area and connected to each other over a high-speed medium to shared resources. See also *wide area network.*

local group   A series of one or more user accounts logically grouped into a single unit and available either throughout a domain or only on the local Windows NT Workstation. See also *global group.*

local procedure call (LPC)   A local procedure call performs exactly like a remote procedure call except that it is used only on a single computer. It provides a means of building distributed applications by testing them on a single computer. To initiate an LPC call for a distributed application, change the computer name to a single period for the connection string. For example, use

```
\\.\pipe\sql\query
```

instead of

```
\\computername\pipe\sql\query
```

to connect a SQL client application to the SQL Server that is on the same computer as the SQL Server application.

local security authority (LSA)   A component of the Windows NT security system that maintains all aspects of local security on a system. This collection of information is known as the *local security policy.* The local security policy identifies, among other things, domains trusted to authenticate logon attempts, who may access the system, how they may access it (locally, from the network, or as a service), who is assigned privileges, and what security auditing is to be performed.

mandatory user profile   A user profile that cannot be changed by the user and, therefore, may be shared by multiple users. See also *user profile.*

mapped I/O or **mapped file I/O**   File I/O performed by reading and writing to virtual memory backed by a file.

memory control block (MCB)   MS-DOS organizes available memory as a pool of blocks maintained as a chain (or linked list). The MCB occupies the bottom 16 bytes of each memory block and, among other things, points to the next memory block in the chain. If an MCB is corrupted, MS-DOS cannot find the next block in the chain and does not know which memory blocks have been allocated and which have not.

mounting a volume   Finding a file system that recognizes the format of a volume and associating the file system with the volume. Windows NT performs this task automatically the first time a program accesses a volume (or, for other forms of removable media such as floppy disks or CD-ROMs, each time the user reinserts the floppy disk or CD into a drive and performs I/O on it). A volume must be mounted before I/O operations can be performed on it.

multihomed   A computer with more than one TCP/IP IP address assigned to it. A multihomed computer has more than one network adapter, with each network adapter assigned a unique IP address. A multihomed computer is often used to combine separate physical network segments into a single logical network by forwarding IP packets between the two segments.

multiprocessing   The capability to execute more than one program at a time by dividing the processor cycles among several applications.

multithreading   The capability to subdivide a process into one or more executable components. See also *thread.*

named pipe   An interprocess communication mechanism that enables one process to send data to another local or remote process. See also *pipe.*

NetBIOS Extended User Interface (NetBEUI)   A network transport protocol supported by all Microsoft network operating systems and some IBM network operating systems. It has a maximum number of 255 simultaneous computer connections and has been superseded by the NetBEUI Frame (NBF) Protocol, which does not have the 255-computer connection limit.

NetMeeting   A Microsoft application that can provide real-time voice communications, text communications, and a shared whiteboard over the Internet or intranet.

Network Basic Input/Output System (NetBIOS)   A network API set, rather than a network transport protocol, defined for use by applications for utilization of network resources.

network control block (NCB)   A block of fixed-length sequential data. This data includes an operation code that indicates the operation to be performed and elements that indicate the status of the operation. See also *opcode.*

network news transfer protocol (NNTP)   Specifies a network protocol used to support the online bulletin board system (BBS) functionality of Internet newsgroups.

network transport   Can be a particular layer of the Open System Interconnect (OSI) reference model between the network layer and the session layer or a communications protocol between two different computers on a network.

object   A single runtime instance of a Windows NT–defined object type. It contains data that can be manipulated only by using a set of services provided for objects of its type.

In Windows NT Performance Monitor, an object is a standard mechanism for identifying and using a system resource. Objects are created to represent individual processes, sections of shared memory, and physical devices. Performance Monitor groups counters by object type. Each object type also can have several instances. The Processor object type, for example, has multiple instances if a system has multiple processors. The Physical Disk object type has two instances if a system has two disks. Some object types (such as Memory and Server) do not have instances.

opcode   An operation code is usually a number that specifies an operation to be performed. An opcode is often the first component in a contiguous block of data; it indicates how other data in the block should be interpreted. See also *network control block.*

Open Database Connectivity (ODBC)   ODBC provides a logical mechanism to access an ODBC-aware database. An ODBC-aware database is any database (such as Microsoft SQL Server or Microsoft Access) that you create that has an ODBC driver. The ODBC driver functions as a layer between your application and the database and provides a uniform mechanism to access any ODBC database. Therefore, you can build a database using Microsoft Access and switch it to a Microsoft SQL Server database just by building the SQL Server database and supplying a new definition for the Data Source Name (DSN). Your application will remain the same.

paging file or **swap file**   A system file containing the contents of virtual pages that have been temporarily removed from physical memory by the Virtual Memory Manager.

With virtual memory under Windows NT, some of the program code and other information is kept in RAM, whereas other information is temporarily swapped to a virtual-memory paging file. When that information is required again, Windows NT pulls it back into RAM and, if necessary, swaps other information to virtual memory. This activity is invisible, although you might notice that your hard disk is working. The benefit is that you can run more programs at one time than your system's RAM usually would allow. See also *virtual memory.*

A

GLOSSARY

parameter   Parameters customize commands entered at the Windows NT command prompt. For example, the MS-DOS `COPY` command has two parameters: the path to the file to copy and the path to where the copy will be placed. These two parameter values can be any valid path; by changing these parameters each time you use the `COPY` command, you are customizing the command.

parity   A mechanism that ensures data integrity. The basic methodology combines (using an `XOR` algorithm) the binary values in an element and then sets a parity bit based on the result. This result bit is a `1` if the `XOR` result was `1`, or a `0` if the `XOR` result was `0`. The parity bit can be used to determine the data changes.

partition   A portion of a physical disk that functions as though it were a physically separate unit. You can use a partitioning program, such as `FDISK` for the MS-DOS and OS/2 operating systems and Disk Administrator for Windows NT, to create these unformatted units. You then must use the `FORMAT` command (from the command prompt or from within Disk Administrator) to format the disk for use with a specific file system. A partition usually is referred to as a *primary* or an *extended partition*. See also *volume*.

partition table   A structure on a disk that the operating system uses to divide a disk into logical divisions called *partitions*, which then can be formatted to a specific file system. Primary partitions are defined by a data entry in the main partition table of a hard disk. Extended partitions are defined by a nondata entry in the main partition table.

permission   A rule associated with an object (usually a directory, file, or printer) in the form of a discretionary access control list (DACL) that regulates which users or groups can have access to the object and in what manner. You can set file and directory permissions only on drives formatted to use the Windows NT File System. See also *right*.

pipe   An interprocess communication (IPC) mechanism. Writing to and reading from a pipe is much like writing to and reading from a file except that the two processes actually are using a shared memory segment to communicate data. An unnamed pipe is a local IPC methodology and can be used only among processes running on the same computer. See also *named pipe*.

Point-to-Point Protocol (PPP)   A protocol definition used to link two networks (or individual computers). The Microsoft implementation supports PPP connections using TCP/IP, IPX/SPX, or NetBEUI network transport protocols.

preemptive multitasking   A multitasking methodology that can halt the execution of a process and start the execution of another process at the discretion of the operating system. Generally, a preemptive multitasking operating system, such as Windows NT, is based on a timeslice in which each process executes for a specific number of CPU cycles. See also *cooperative multitasking* and *timeslice*.

primary domain controller (PDC)   For a Windows NT Server domain, the server that maintains the original copy of the security policy and master database for a domain and, along with backup domain controllers, authenticates domain logons. Any changes made to the account policies and account database have to occur on the primary domain controller. These changes then are replicated to the backup domain controllers. See also *backup domain controller* and *replication.*

primary partition   A portion of a physical disk that can be marked as active for use by an operating system. *Active* means that the power-on self-test routine can locate a boot sector on the partition. A physical disk can contain up to four primary partitions (or up to three if there is already an extended partition). A primary partition cannot be subpartitioned.

privilege   The representation of most user rights in access tokens. For example, holders of the backup privilege are allowed to bypass file system security to backup and restore data on a disk. In a secure system, not all users have that privilege. See also *access token* or *security token.*

privileged instruction   Instructions that have access to system memory and the hardware.

process   A logical division of labor in an operating system. A Windows NT process is created when a program runs. A process can be an application (such as Microsoft Word or CorelDRAW!), a service (such as Event Log or Computer Browser), or a subsystem (such as POSIX). In Windows NT a process comprises a virtual address space, an executable program, one or more threads of execution, some portion of the user's resource quotas, and the system resources that the operating system has allocated to the process's threads. A process is implemented as an object. See also *object.*

random access memory (RAM)   A set of memory chips installed in the computer that store either computer instructions to be loaded and executed by the processor or data. RAM can be read from or written to an unlimited number of times. See also *flash memory* and *read-only memory.*

read-only bit   An attribute stored on the disk to indicate that a directory or file cannot be modified (written to). System files required for the operation of your computer often are marked as read-only. The NTLDR file required by Windows NT to load the operating system to boot, for example, normally is marked as read-only. See also *archive bit, hidden bit,* and *system bit.*

read-only memory (ROM)   A set of memory chips installed on the computer that stores either instructions for a computer to execute or data to be read by the processor. ROM cannot be written to—hence the name *read-only*—and generally stores boot instructions that the processor uses to initialize and access a physical device. Your system ROM boots the computer, for example, but your video ROM draws data on the computer screen. See also *flash memory* and *random access memory.*

registry   A secure, unified database that stores application-configuration data, hardware-configuration data (such as device-driver configuration data, network protocol, and adapter card settings), and user data in a hierarchical form for a Windows NT Workstation or Windows NT Server computer.

registry key   The configuration data in the registry is stored in a hierarchical form, and keys are the building blocks of this hierarchy. The registry has four top-level keys that contain per computer and per user databases. Each key can contain data items, called *value entries*, and additional subkeys. In the registry structure, keys are analogous to directories, and the value entries are analogous to files. See also *value entries*.

Remote Access Software (RAS)   The server side of a client/server service to provide network access to physically remote network clients using modems, ISDN, and X.25 adapters. The client side of the service is referred to as *dial-up networking*.

remote procedure call (RPC)   A message-passing facility that enables a distributed application to call services available on various computers in a network without regard to their locations. Remote network operations are handled automatically. RPC provides a procedural, rather than a transport-centered, view of networked operations. See also *local procedure call*.

remote procedure call (RPC) binding   A logical connection between the client and server, or the process by which the client establishes a logical connection to the server.

remote procedure call (RPC) connection   A transport-level virtual circuit between the client and server. The RPC runtime establishes the circuit when the client binds to the server interface instance. Connections are not visible to the client. A client may have more than one connection to the server.

remote procedure call (RPC) endpoint   An endpoint identifies a specific server instance (or address space) on a host. The format of the endpoint depends on the transport protocol used. *Well-known endpoints* are registered in the name service database. *Dynamic endpoints* are assigned to server instances at runtime.

remote procedure call (RPC) protocol sequence   A character string that identifies the network protocols used to establish a relationship between a client and a server. The protocol sequence contains a set of options that the RPC runtime must know about to establish a binding. These options include the RPC protocol, the format of the network address, and the transport protocol. For example, a sample protocol sequence string might be as follows:

```
ncacn_ip_tcp
```

remote procedure call (RPC) server   The program or computer that processes remote procedure calls from a client.

replication   The process of copying the original account policies, account database, and logon scripts from the primary domain controller to the backup domain controllers in a Windows NT domain. See also *backup domain controller, Directory Replicator Service,* and *primary domain controller*.

request for comment (RFC)   A document that defines a specification for interaction, or functionality, of a TCP/IP component.

revision level   A revision level is built into many Windows NT data structures, such as security descriptors and access control lists. This feature enables the structure to be passed between systems or stored on disk, even though it is expected to change in the future.

right   Authorizes a user to perform certain actions on the system. In most situations, rights should be provided to a user by adding that user's account to one of the built-in groups that already possesses the needed rights, instead of by administering the user-rights policy. Rights apply to the system as a whole and are different from permissions, which apply to specific objects. See also *permission*.

root directory   In a file system structured as a hierarchy of directories on a partition or volume, the root directory is the parent of all the other directories. The root directory name in the File Allocation Table (FAT), High Performance File System (HPFS), and New Technology File System (NTFS) is a backslash (\).

route   When discussed in the presence of a network protocol, a route is the path that the source computer uses to transmit information to the destination computer.

router   A hardware device that combines two network segments. The router passes data addressed to a host outside the local segment to the intended recipient. You can also use software in combination with your server's hardware to emulate a router. However, a dedicated router can support more users than a software emulation can.

Routing for the Internet Protocol (RIP)   A Windows NT service that provides dynamic update capabilities to the TCP/IP routing table. See also *route*.

secrets   Encrypted pieces of information.

Secure Socket Layer (SSL)   A network protocol enhancement used to provide a secure method to transfer data between a Web browser and Web server. A Web server that accepts credit card numbers, for example, would do so using SSL.

security accounts manager (SAM)   A Windows NT–protected subsystem that maintains the security accounts database.

security descriptor   A data structure that houses all the security information related to an object. It contains a discretionary access control list, a system access control list that controls auditing on the object, an owner, and a primary group of the object.

security identifier (SID)   A number that identifies a user, a global group of users, a local group of users, or a domain within Windows NT.

security token   See *access token* or *security token*.

semaphore   Generally, semaphores are signaling devices or mechanisms. However, in Windows NT, system semaphores are objects that synchronize activities on an interprocess level. When two or more processes share a common resource such as a printer, video screen, or memory segment, for example, semaphores control access to those resources so that only one process can alter them at any particular time.

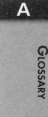

serial line Internet protocol (SLIP)   An older protocol definition that uses the TCP/IP network transport protocol to link two networks (or individual computers).

server message block (SMB)   A block of data containing a work request from a workstation to a server or containing the response from the server to the workstation. SMBs are used for all communications that go through the server or workstation service, such as file I/O, creating and removing remote connections, or performing any other network function that the redirector needs to carry out.

Microsoft network redirectors use this structure to send remote requests or information over the network to a remote computer, which can be a Windows NT Workstation, Windows NT Server, or other Microsoft Network–compatible computer.

sharepoint   A shared directory or printer on a Windows NT computer that network clients can connect to in order to access the resource.

Simple Mail Transfer Protocol (SMTP)   Defines a protocol for sending or receiving e-mail messages to or from other SMTP mail servers. The SMTP protocol is used almost exclusively for providing Internet mail capabilities.

Simple Network Management Protocol (SNMP)   Defines a protocol for reporting statistical information, configuring software components, or configuring hardware components from an SNMP management console (like HP OpenView).

single system image (SSI)   A domain that has the logon service running and that propagates its user accounts database throughout the domain.

standalone   A workstation or server that is not currently a member of a domain. Or a workstation or server at which a logon server does not validate logon requests.

striped set   A unit created by combining multiple physical disk drives into a single logical unit. This logical unit is divided into blocks that are split among the disk drives to increase disk throughput by reading or writing multiple blocks in a single operation.

striped set with parity   A fault-tolerant implementation of a striped set that uses a single-parity block for each stripe to increase disk throughput and provide protection from a single disk failure. If a single disk drive fails, the parity block can be exclusively combined (XOR) with the remaining data blocks to re-create the missing data block and provide access to the data with only a slight performance penalty.

Structured Query Language (SQL)   A standardized programming language that accesses data stored in an application database. Generally, SQL accesses SQL Server databases, but it can also be used by an application to access data stored in a proprietary database, such as a Microsoft Access database.

subnet   A subcomponent of a larger network component. In a TCP/IP–based network, a subnet is part of a larger subnet based on its class definition. For example, my class C address 206.170.127.64 is a subnet of another class C address 206.170.127.25. See also *address class*.

swap file   See *paging file* or *swap file.*

switch   A special type of command parameter denoted by a leading slash (/) or leading dash (-). Switches normally are used for parameters that are simple toggles (on/off switches). In the CHKDSK command, for example, an optional parameter is the /f switch. If it is used, CHKDSK attempts to fix any problems it finds on a disk. If it is not used, CHKDSK only reports the problems and does not attempt to fix them.

symmetric multiprocessing (SMP)   A multiprocessing methodology that uses all processors installed on the computer to execute the operating system and all applications. See also *asymmetric multiprocessing.*

syntax   The rules governing the structure and content of commands entered into the computer. When you enter commands at the Windows NT command prompt, for example, if the structure and content of a command violate the syntax rules, the Windows NT command processor cannot interpret the command and generates a syntax error message.

system bit   An attribute stored on the disk to indicate that a directory or file is reserved for use by the operating system. The NTDETECT.COM file, for example, which is required by Windows NT to detect the hardware on your system as part of the operating system boot procedure, normally is marked as a system file. See also *archive bit, hidden bit,* and *read-only bit.*

system debugger   The Windows NT system debugger (NTSD) is a 32-bit application that supports the debugging of user mode applications and dynamic link libraries. NTSD can read and write paged and nonpaged memory and also supports multiple-thread debugging and multiprocess debugging.

NTSD enables you to display and execute program code, set breakpoints that stop the execution of your program, examine and change values in memory, and refer to data and instructions by name rather than by address. It can access program locations through addresses, global symbols, or line-number references, making it easy to locate and debug specific sections of code. You can debug C programs at the source-file level as well as at the machine-code level. You also can display the source statements of a program, the disassembled machine code of the program, or a combination of source statements and disassembled machine code.

In contrast to NTSD, the Windows NT Kernel Debugger (KD) supports the debugging of kernel-mode code. It cannot be used to set breakpoints in user mode or to read or write paged-out memory. KD also does not provide support for threads. However, it does support multiprocess debugging.

You therefore would use NTSD for debugging user-mode programs and KD for debugging the kernel and device drivers. See also *Kernel Debugger* and *WINDBG.EXE.*

system files   Files used by the operating system or the file system to store special system data. NTFS uses them to store special data on the file system.

A

GLOSSARY

Operating systems use these files to store information and programs that start the computer and load the operating system. MS-DOS system files include IO.SYS, MSDOS.SYS, and COMMAND.COM. Windows NT system files include NTLDR, NTDETECT.COM, BOOT.INI, and several of the files in the *SystemRoot*\SYSTEM32 directory.

system partition   The system partition for Windows NT is the volume that has the hardware-specific files needed to load Windows NT. On *x*86-based computers, it must be a primary partition that has been marked as active for startup purposes and must be located on the disk that the computer accesses when starting up the system. Only one active system partition can exist at a time, and it is denoted onscreen by an asterisk. If you want to use another operating system, you first must mark its system partition as active before restarting the computer.

Partitions on a RISC-based computer are not marked active. Instead, they are configured by a hardware-configuration program supplied by the manufacturer. On RISC-based computers, the system partition must be formatted for the file allocation table file system. On either type of computer, the system partition can never be part of a stripe set or volume set, but it can be part of a mirrored set. See also *boot partition*.

T connector   In network terminology this type of connector reflects a physical attribute. The top of the T is considered the network segment, and the base of the T is the connection between the network segment and the network adapter. This connection looks like the letter *T*.

TCP/IP   The combination of the Transmission Control Protocol with the Internet Protocol. In essence, TCP is concerned with the data, whereas IP is concerned with the delivery of the data from the source to destination computers. TCP/IP is the most widely used combination of network protocols for connecting large networks or for connecting any network to the Internet.

terminated process   In Windows NT a *process object* is a program invocation, including the address space and resources required to run the program. When the Windows NT Executive terminates a process, it quits running the program and returns the address space and resources to the system. From the user's point of view, the application is no longer running.

thread   An executable entity that belongs to one (and only one) process. It comprises a program counter, a user-mode stack, a kernel-mode stack, and a set of register values. All threads in a process have equal access to the process's address space, object handles, and other resources.

In Windows NT Performance Monitor, threads are objects within processes that execute program instructions. They allow concurrent operations within a process and enable one process to execute different parts of its program on different processors simultaneously. Each thread running on a system shows up as an instance for the Thread object type and is identified by association with its parent process. If Print Manager has two active threads, for example, Performance Monitor identifies them as Thread object instances Printman ==> 0 and Printman ==> 1.

timeslice   An operating system algorithm used in process management. The basic mechanism assigns each process a time limit (usually in nanoseconds). When the time limit is reached, the active process is suspended, and an inactive process is resumed. When the time limit is up for this resumed process, it too will be suspended to allow the next inactive process to execute. When the last process executes and uses its timeslice, the first process will be executed and the loop restarted.

Transmission Control Protocol (TCP)   A high-level network protocol that provides a reliable transmission pathway between hosts.

transport driver interface (TDI)   A Windows NT interface for network redirectors and servers for sending network-bound requests to network transport drivers. This interface provides transport independence by abstracting transport-specific information.

trap   A processor's mechanism for capturing an executing thread when an unusual event (such as an exception or interrupt) occurs and then transferring control to a fixed location in memory where the handler code resides. The trap handler determines the type of condition and transfers control to an appropriate handling routine.

trust relationship   A link between domains that enables passthrough authentication, in which a user has only one user account in one domain, yet can access the entire network. User accounts and global groups defined in a trusted domain can be given rights and resource permissions in a trusting domain, even though those accounts don't exist in the trusting domain's database. A trusting domain honors the logon authentications of a trusted domain.

universal naming convention (UNC) name   A name given to a device, computer, or resource to enable other users and applications to establish an explicit connection and access the resources over the network. Also known as the *uniform naming convention*. The syntax of a UNC name is

```
\\<computername>\<sharename>\<filename>
```

universal resource identifier (URI)   A unique identifier to indicate the type of resource to be acquired and the protocol to be used to acquire the resource. A Web page URL (such as `http://www.nt-guru.com`) uses the `http` URI, which specifies that the Hypertext Transfer Protocol be used to retrieve the resource (the default HTML document for the `www.nt-guru.com` site). URIs come in many flavors, such as `https` (for Hypertext Transfer Protocol Secure resources), `file` (for locally defined resources), and `mailto` (for electronic mail).

universal resource locator (URL)   A unique identifier to locate a resource on the Internet. The following example shows the syntax for the Web server, FTP server, and Gopher server that are maintained on my server:

```
http://www.nt-guru.com
```

```
ftp://ftp.nt-guru.com
```

```
gopher://gopher-nt-guru.com
```

universally unique identifier (UUID)   A unique identification string associated with the remote procedure call interface. Also known as a *globally unique identifier.*

These identifiers consist of 8 hexadecimal digits followed first by a hyphen, then by three groups of 4 hexadecimal digits with each group followed by a hyphen, and finally by 12 hexadecimal digits. The following identifier is syntactically correct:

```
12345678-1234-1234-1234-123456789ABC
```

The identifiers on the client and server must match in order for the client and server to bind.

User Datagram Protocol (UDP)   A high-level network protocol that provides an unreliable transmission pathway between hosts. This method is fast, but should be used only in low-error networks or when data coherency is not required.

user mode   See *Executive.*

user profile   A profile is a copy of the user environment (Program Manager groups, desktop settings, and application-configuration information) and is stored both locally on the user's computer and on a server in the domain if so configured in User Manager. A profile initially is created with the User Profile Editor and saved as a file on a server. See also *mandatory user profile.*

value entries   The value for a specific entry under a key or subkey in the registry. Value entries appear as a string with three components: a name, a type, and the value. See also *registry key.*

VBScript   A programming language designed as part of the Microsoft ActiveX development efforts. VBScript applications are executable code embedded as an object within an HTML document. These applications can provide interactive Web pages. VBScript is based on the Microsoft Visual Basic language.

virtual address space   See *address space* or *virtual address space.*

virtual device driver   An emulation of a physical device. Whereas a device driver provides an interface to control a real physical device, a virtual device driver provides an interface to a logical (not physically present) device. For example, you use a virtual device driver every time you run a console application. While each application thinks it has an 80×24 character physical display screen assigned for its exclusive use, in reality the application is writing to a virtual screen. This screen is wrapped up in a window frame provided by the operating system. See also *device driver.*

virtual DOS machine (VDM)   Provides a complete MS-DOS environment and a character-based window in which to run an MS-DOS–based application. Any number of VDMs can run simultaneously.

virtual memory   A logical view of memory that does not necessarily correspond to the memory's physical structure.

Normally, virtual memory is the space on your hard disk that Windows NT uses as if it were actually memory. Windows NT does so through the use of the paging file. Virtual memory also can be unused address space that is allocated to a process but not yet in use. In this case, the memory will not physically exist anywhere until it is actually used (that is, until data or code is loaded into it).

The benefit of using virtual memory is that you can run more applications at one time than your system's physical memory would otherwise allow. The drawbacks are the disk space required for the virtual-memory paging file and the decreased execution speed when swapping is required. See also *paging file* or *swap file*.

volume   A file-based medium that has been initialized with a file system structure (for example, a floppy disk, a hard disk, a tape reel, or a particular partition on a hard disk). A disk partition or collection of partitions that have been formatted for use by a file system and that also can be used as volume sets, stripe sets, and mirrored sets. See also *partition*.

Web browser   The client component of a client/server application that utilizes the HTTP protocol to communicate with the Web server. A Web browser is often a GUI application that provides an interface to Internet services, which can include the WWW, FTP, and Gopher services.

Web server   The server component of a client/server application used to display content on a Web browser using HTTP as the linkage between client and server. A Web server's capabilities may be customized using application programming interfaces such as ISAPI, CGI, ActiveX, and languages such as C/C++, Visual Basic, and Perl.

wide area network (WAN)   A group of computers or a group of LANs physically located in a separate area and connected to each other over a low-speed medium to share resources. WANs generally use low-speed phone lines or leased lines to connect, although higher-speed lines are available. See also *local area network*.

WINDBG.EXE   The Windows NT debugger is a 32-bit application that you can use, along with a collection of DLLs, for debugging the kernel, device drivers, and applications. This application also can be used on all hardware platforms, although each platform has its own build. WINDBG.EXE can be used for remote or local debugging and also with the System Recovery option in the Control Panel.

Windows Internet Naming Service (WINS)   A client/server mechanism for resolving NetBIOS computer names for network clients using the TCP/IP protocol. WINS performs a similar service as domain name service for UNIX-based systems except that you do not have to manually modify a host file because WINS automatically updates its internal database of computer names to IP addresses. Windows NT Server includes the WINS service, which is the server side of the application. WINS supplies a TCP/IP IP address to a network client that includes a WINS client when a request is made to access to a computer by name rather than by IP address. Current WINS clients include Windows NT Workstation, Windows NT Server, Windows 95, Windows for Workgroups, and MS-DOS clients using the MS-DOS connection. See also *domain name service, Dynamic Host Configuration Protocol,* and *WINS proxy agent*.

WINS proxy agent   Acts as an interpreter for computers that use the TCP/IP protocol but do not support the WINS protocol. When a computer makes a request by computer name, the proxy agent queries the WINS server to obtain the TCP/IP IP address. This IP address then is forwarded to the requesting computer. A WINS proxy agent can be a Windows NT Server, Windows NT Workstation, or Windows for Workgroups 3.11 computer.

working set   The set of virtual pages in physical memory at any moment for a particular process. In a virtual memory system such as Windows NT, a memory management system provides a large address space to each process by mapping the process's virtual addresses into physical addresses as the process's threads use them. When physical memory becomes full, the memory management system swaps selected memory contents to disk, reloading them from disk on demand.

World Wide Web (WWW)   An Internet-derived service. The service consists of two components: a WWW server and a WWW client (or Web browser). A Web server transmits the requested document, or Web page, when requested by a Web browser. The document may contain text, graphics, audio-video clips, or links to additional documents. See also *File Transfer Protocol, Hypertext Markup Language,* and *Hypertext Transfer Protocol.*

HTML Reference

IN THIS APPENDIX

■ How This Reference Is Structured *840*

■ HTML Element List *841*

■ Defining Special Characters on Your Web Page *875*

■ HTML Summary for the Internet Information Server and the Internet Assistant for Word for Windows *880*

APPENDIX B

The Hypertext Markup Language (HTML) is in constant flux. This appendix focuses on the HTML elements that are currently in use, including

- HTML 2.0 tags, which are specified in RFC 1866
- Some of the proposed tags for HTML 3.2
- Some HTML tag extensions supported by the Microsoft Internet Explorer version 3.01

This appendix is meant to be an easy-to-use reference for the major HTML tags. It is by no means a definitive HTML reference; an entire book would be needed for that. Of course, any book devoted to HTML will probably be out of date by the time you read it.

> **TIP**
>
> For the latest information on the HTML specification, check out http://www.w3.org. For the latest HTML extensions supported by the Microsoft Internet Explorer, use http://www.microsoft.com/workshop/author/newhtml/default.htm. For the latest on Netscape Navigator HTML extensions, take a look at http://home.netscape.com.

This reference is divided into two major sections. The first section is an HTML reference that includes HTML tags and extensions currently supported by the Microsoft Internet Explorer and Netscape Navigator. The second section contains two tables that list the HTML tags supported by the Internet Information Server and Internet Assistant for Microsoft Word, respectively. This format should make life a little easier when you are creating WWW pages that may be used by multiple Web browsers.

How This Reference Is Structured

The elements (or *tags*, if you prefer) are listed in alphabetical order to make searching for the tag a little easier. Within each element definition, the minimum attributes for the element are described, as are all possible attributes. If an element allows other elements to be embedded within it, or if an element is restricted to the context of a set of elements, this, too, is mentioned. To make this list a little shorter and more descriptive (it is possible for groups to contain other groups that more fully display the nesting and recursion that can occur within a group), this reference uses the group definitions defined in RFC 1866. These groups include the following:

- BLOCK—Includes the groups BLOCK.FORMS, LIST, PREFORMATTED, and TABLE, and the entities DL and P.
- BLOCK.FORMS—Contains the BLOCKQUOTE, FORM, and ISINDEX entities.

■ BODY.CONTEXT—Can contain the groups BLOCK, HEADING, and TEXT, and the HR and ADDRESS entities. According to the HTML specification, this group should contain only the BLOCK, HEADING, TEXT, HR, ADDRESS, and IMG entities. Therefore, all text within a body should be enclosed in a block.

Instead of this format:

```
<H1>HEADING</H1>
Textual Information
```

the HTML specification suggests using the following format:

```
<H1>Heading</H1>
<P>Textual information</P>
```

■ FONT—Contains the TT, B, and I entities.

■ HEADING—Contains the H1, H2, H3, H4, H5, and H6 entities.

■ LIST—Contains the DIR, MENU, OL, and UL entities.

■ PHRASE—Contains the EM, CITE, CODE, KBD, SAMP, STRONG, and VAR entities.

■ PREFORMATTED—Contains the LISTING, PRE, and XMP entities.

■ TEXT—Contains the PHRASE and FONT groups, the A, IMG, and BR entities, and parsed character data. Parsed character data is any valid character data after the data has been parsed and all special character entities have been replaced.

NOTE

The internationalization proposal also suggests the BDO, Q, SPAN, SUB, and SUP entities be included in the TEXT group.

HTML Element List

<A>

Description: Anchors a piece of text and/or image that is identified as a hypertext link. This element must have either an HREF or a NAME attribute. The HREF attribute defines a URL as the destination target. A NAME attribute defines a destination target within the current document. To associate a target in an external document, an HREF attribute may be used with the #name suffix on the URL. This syntax will load the associated document and position the display at the selected location of the NAME tag. You can also use an HREF attribute with a URL consisting solely of #name to jump to a location within the current document. If the REL attribute is present in a document/object (A) that has an HREF to a document/object (B), the REL attribute identifies a relationship that B has to A, which A recognizes/verifies/authorizes. If the REV attribute is present in document/object B with an HREF to document/object A, the REV attribute identifies a relationship that B has to A, but which must be verified by checking with A.

Minimum Attributes: `<A HREF="...">`*CharacterData...*`</A>`

All Attributes: `<A NAME="...">`*CharacterData...*`</A>`

Elements Allowed Within: `<A HREF="..." NAME="..." REL="..." REV="..." URN="..." TITLE="..." METHODS="..." LANG="..." DIR=LTR¦RTL CHARSET="..." ID="..." CLASS="..." MD="..." TARGET=... SHAPE="...">`*CharacterData...*`</A>`

Allowed in Context of: Members of groups HEADING and TEXT, but not element `<A>`.

Notes: Any element that permits group TEXT.

The internationalization proposal introduced the LANG, DIR, and CHARSET attributes. The CHARSET attribute is a hint as to which character set should be used by the hyperlink. Prior proposals suggested changing the NAME attribute to the ID attribute, thus declaring the NAME attribute as obsolete. The ID attribute would then be added to various elements that previously used the NAME attribute. However, with the current style sheet proposal (which includes the ID, MD, and CLASS attributes), this syntax is very likely to change. The REL and REV attributes are rarely used or supported. These relationships are more commonly identified in the document HEAD using the LINK element. The URN attribute is for a Universal Resource Number and is currently not used or supported. TITLE and METHODS are also rarely used or supported. TARGET is a Netscape 2.0 extension. The SHAPE attribute is proposed to provide a mechanism to define multiple `<A>` elements, with corresponding hotzones in the proposed FIG element. This syntax would perform the same basic function as the ISMAP element without developing a cgi-bin application. An alternative proposal is defined by the MAP element.

<ABBREV>

Description: Changes the character rendering of the contents to logically represent abbreviations.

Minimum Attributes: `<ABBREV>`*CharacterData...*`</ABBREV>`

All Attributes: `<ABBREV LANG="..." DIR=LTR¦RTR ID="..." CLASS="...">`*CharacterData...* `</ABBREV>`

Elements Allowed Within: TBD.

Allowed in Context of: TBD.

<ACRONYM>

Description: Changes the character rendering of the contents to logically represent acronyms.

Minimum Attributes: `<ACRONYM>`*CharacterData...*`</ACRONYM>`

All Attributes: `<ACRONYM LANG="..." DIR=LTR¦RTR ID="..." CLASS="...">`*CharacterData...* `</ACRONYM>`

Elements Allowed Within: TBD.

Allowed in Context of: TBD.

<ADDRESS>

Description: Defines a separated multiline set of text to be rendered for address/contact information.

Minimum Attributes: `<ADDRESS>`*`CharacterData...`*`</ADDRESS>`

All Attributes: `<ADDRESS LANG="..." DIR=LTR¦RTR ALIGN=LEFT¦RIGHT¦CENTER¦JUSTIFY ID="..."` `CLASS="..." CLEAR=LEFT¦RIGHT¦ALL¦"..." NOWRAP>`*`CharacterData...`*`</ADDRESS>`

Elements Allowed Within: Members of group `TEXT` or element `<P>`.

Allowed in Context of: Any element that permits members of the group `BODY.CONTENT`.

Notes: Text within an address is generally rendered in italics. The internationalization proposal introduced the `LANG`, `DIR`, and `ALIGN` attributes.

<APP>

See `<APPLET>`.

<APPLET>

Description: This element replaces the `APP` element, which is used to invoke a Java application. Web browsers that support the `APP` element will ignore all `APPLET` attributes except for the `PARAM` attribute. Web browsers that do not support the `APPLET` element should ignore both it and the `PARAM` element and should instead process the element content. So in essence, the alternative HTML is the content of the `APPLET` element. The file that contains the compiled applet subclass is named `CODE`. This name is relative to the base URL of the applet and cannot be an absolute URL. The `WIDTH` and `HEIGHT` elements provide the initial width and height, in pixels, of the applet's display area. `CODEBASE` specifies the base URL for the applet; `ALT` specifies the parsed character data to be displayed if the Web browser supports the `APPLET` element but cannot or will not run the applet; `NAME` specifies an applet instance; `ALIGN` specifies the display alignment; and `VSPACE` and `HSPACE` specify the reserved space around the applet in pixels.

Minimum Attributes: `<APPLET CODE="..." WIDTH="..." HEIGHT="...">`*`CharacterData...`* `</APPLET>`

All Attributes: `<APPLET CODE="..." WIDTH="..." HEIGHT="..." CODEBASE="..." ALT="..."` `NAME="..." ALIGN=LEFT¦RIGHT¦TOP¦TEXTTOP¦MIDDLE¦ABSMIDDLE¦BASELINE¦BOTTOM¦ABSBOTTOM` `VSPACE="..." HSPACE="...">`*`CharacterData...`*`</APPLET>`

Elements Allowed Within: <PARAM> element and any other elements that would have been allowed in the document at this point.

Allowed in Context of: TBD.

Notes: The APPLET element is a Netscape Navigator 2.0 extension.

<AREA>

Description: Specifies a single area of an image that, if selected, will jump to the hypertext link identified by the HREF attribute. COORDS specifies the position of an area, in pixels, of the image in comma-separated x,y coordinates (the upper-left corner is defined as 0,0). For the SHAPE attribute, RECT (the default) is left, top, right, bottom; a CIRCLE is center x, center y, radius; a POLYGON is successive x and y vertices. The NOHREF attribute specifies that the region should not generate a link. The ALT attribute defines optional parsed character data to describe the area that can be displayed by Web browsers that do support images.

Minimum Attributes: <AREA COORDS="...">

All Attributes: <AREA COORDS="..." SHAPE=RECT¦CIRCLE¦POLYGON HREF="..." NOHREF ALT="...">

Elements Allowed Within: None.

Allowed in Context of: <MAP>.

Notes: There is no corresponding end tag. The AREA element is a proposed enhancement to support client-side image maps. This element is a Netscape 2.0 extension that currently supports only the SHAPE=RECT attribute, and ALT is not defined.

<AU>

Description: Changes the character rendering of the contents to logically represent an author's name.

Minimum Attributes: <AU>*CharacterData*...</AU>

All Attributes: <AU LANG="..." DIR=LTR¦RTR ID="..." CLASS="...">*CharacterData*...</AU>

Elements Allowed Within: TBD.

Allowed in Context of: TBD.

<B>

Description: Displays rendered text in a bold font.

Minimum Attributes: <B>*CharacterData*...</B>

All Attributes: <B LANG="..." DIR=LTR¦RTL ID="..." CLASS="">*CharacterData*...</B>

Elements Allowed Within: Members of group TEXT.

Allowed in Context of: Any element that permits group FONT.

Notes: A Web browser that does not support the BOLD element may render the text in another fashion. This rendering, however, must be distinct from the rendering produced by the <I> element.

<BANNER>

Description: A proposal for corporate logos, navigational aids, disclaimers, or other informational material that should not be scrolled with the rest of the document.

Minimum Attributes: `<BANNER>`*CharacterData*`...</BANNER>`

All Attributes: `<BANNER LANG="..." DIR=LTR¦RTR ID="..." CLASS="...">`*CharacterData*`...</BANNER>`

Elements Allowed Within: TBD.

Allowed in Context of: `<BODY>`.

<BASE>

Description: Specifies an absolute URL to be used by relative URLs within the document. It must be a complete file name, and it is normally the original URL of the document.

Minimum Attributes: `<BASE HREF="...">`

All Attributes: `<BASE HREF="..." TARGET="...">`

Elements Allowed Within: N/A.

Allowed in Context of: `<HEAD>`.

<BASEFONT>

Description: Specifies a base font size to be used within the document instead of the default of 3.

Minimum Attributes: `<BASEFONT SIZE=1¦2¦3¦4¦5¦6¦7>`

All Attributes: `<BASEFONT SIZE=1¦2¦3¦4¦5¦6¦7>`

Elements Allowed Within: TBD.

Allowed in Context of: TBD.

Notes: The BASEFONT element is a Netscape Navigator extension.

B

HTML REFERENCE

`<BDO>`

Description: Used as a directional override to deal with unusual pieces of text where the directionality cannot be specifically determined. The DIR attribute is required but is different in context than when used for inline text markup. For BDO, the DIR attribute specifies the directionality of all characters, including those with strong directional context.

Minimum Attributes: `<BDO DIR=LTR¦RTR>CharacterData...</BDO>`

All Attributes: `<BDO LANG="..." DIR=LTR¦RTR>CharacterData...</BDO>`

Elements Allowed Within: Members of group TEXT.

Allowed in Context of: Any element that permits members of group TEXT.

Notes: A proposed element of the internationalization of HTML.

`<BGSOUND>`

Description: Plays an audio file as a background sound. SRC specifies the location of the file to be played, and LOOP specifies the number of iterations.

Minimum Attributes: `<BACKGROUND SRC="...">`

All Attributes: `<BACKGROUND SRC="..." LOOP="...">`

Elements Allowed Within: None.

Allowed in Context of: TBD.

Notes: Microsoft Internet Explorer 2.0 extension.

`<BIG>`

Description: Specifies that the physical rendering of the font be increased if practical.

Minimum Attributes: `<BIG>CharacterData...</BIG>`

All Attributes: `<BIG LANG="..." DIR=LTR¦RTR ID="..." CLASS="...">CharacterData...</BIG>`

Elements Allowed Within: TBD.

Allowed in Context of: TBD.

Notes: A Netscape Navigator 2.0 extension.

`<BLINK>`

Description: Specifies that the physical rendering of the enclosed text be a blinking font.

Minimum Attributes: `<BLINK>CharacterData...</BLINK>`

All Attributes: `<BLINK>CharacterData...</BLINK>`

Elements Allowed Within: TBD.

Allowed in Context of: TBD.

Notes: A Netscape 1.1 extension. Most Web browsers ignore this element.

`<BLOCKQUOTE>`

Description: Specifies that a multiline set of text be rendered as quoted text.

Minimum Attributes: `<BLOCKQUOTE>CharacterData...</BLOCKQUOTE>`

All Attributes: `<BLOCKQUOTE LANG="..." DIR=LTR¦RTR ALIGN=LEFT¦RIGHT¦CENTER¦ JUSTIFY>CharacterData...</BLOCKQUOTE>`

Elements Allowed Within: Members of `BODY.CONTENT`.

Allowed in Context of: Any element that permits members of group `BODY.FORMS`.

Notes: Typically rendered in enclosed quotes or as an indented paragraph in an italic font.

`<BODY>`

Description: Specifies the actual content of the document, as opposed to `HEAD`, which contains information about the document itself. All displayable elements should be within the body of the document. `BACKGROUND` specifies a path/filename to an image to be used as a tiled background bitmap. `BGCOLOR` specifies a background color.

Minimum Attributes: `<BODY>CharacterData...</BODY>`

All Attributes: `<BODY LANG="..." DIR=LTR¦RTR ID="..." CLASS="..." BACKGROUND="..." BGCOLOR="..." BGPROPERTIES=FIXED TEXT="RRGGBB" LINK="RRGGBB" VLINK="RRGGBB" ALINK="RRGGBB">CharacterData...</BODY>`

Elements Allowed Within: Members of `BODY.CONTENT`.

Allowed in Context of: HTML.

Notes: Netscape Navigator requires a `RRGGBB` (red green blue) format for the color elements. Microsoft Internet Explorer 2.0 can accept `BLACK`, `MAROON`, `GREEN`, `OLIVE`, `NAVY`, `PURPLE`, `TEAL`, `GRAY`, `SILVER`, `RED`, `LIME`, `YELLOW`, `BLUE`, `FUCHSIA`, `AQUA`, and `WHITE` instead of an RGB value. The `TEXT`, `LINK`, `ALINK`, and `VLINK` attributes are Netscape Navigator extensions that also work with Internet Explorer 2.0. In addition, Internet Explorer 2.0 supports the `BGPROPERTIES` (only with the `FIXED` attribute) to specify a nonscrolling background image.

`<BQ>`

Description: Specifies a multiline set of text to be rendered as quoted text.

Minimum Attributes: `<BQ>`*CharacterData...*`</BQ>`

All Attributes: `<BQ LANG="..." DIR=LTR¦RTR ID="..." CLASS="..." CLEAR=LEFT¦RIGHT¦ALL¦"..." NOWRAP>`*CharacterData...*`</BQ>`

Elements Allowed Within: `<CREDIT>`. Others TBD.

Allowed in Context of: `<BQ>`. Others TBD.

`<BR>`

Description: Specifies a new line without separating the text with additional vertical space.

Minimum Attributes: `<BR>`

All Attributes: `<BR CLEAR=LEFT¦RIGHT¦ALL¦"..." ID="..." CLASS="...">`

Elements Allowed Within: None.

Allowed in Context of: Any element that permits group TEXT.

Notes: A Netscape Navigator 1.1 extension.

`<CAPTION>`

Description: Specifies a label for a table or figure. The ALIGN attribute specifies where the caption should be placed.

Minimum Attributes: `<CAPTION>`*CharacterData...*`</CAPTION>`

All Attributes: `<CAPTION ALIGN=TOP¦BOTTOM¦LEFT¦RIGHT LANG="..." DIR=LTR¦RTR ID="..." CLASS="...">`*CharacterData...*`</CAPTION>`

Elements Allowed Within: TBD.

Allowed in Context of: `<FIG>` `<TABLE>`.

Notes: Netscape Navigator 1.1 extension.

`<CENTER>`

Description: CENTER encloses text between the left and right margins.

Minimum Attributes: `<CENTER>`*CharacterData...*`</CENTER>`

All Attributes: `<CENTER>`*CharacterData...*`</CENTER>`

Elements Allowed Within: TBD.

Allowed in Context of: `<A>`. Others TBD.

Notes: A Netscape Navigator 1.1 extension. This element has been replaced by the `ALIGN=CENTER` attribute in Netscape Navigator 2.0.

`<CITE>`

Description: Changes the character rendering of the text to logically display a citation.

Minimum Attributes: `<CITE>CharacterData...</CITE>`

All Attributes: `<CITE DIR=LTR¦RTR ID="..." CLASS="...">CharacterData...</CITE>`

Elements Allowed Within: Members of group `TEXT`.

Allowed in Context of: Any element that permits elements of group `PHRASE`.

Notes: Typically rendered in an italic font.

`<CODE>`

Description: Changes the character rendering of the text to logically display computer code. It is intended for short words or phrases. The `PRE` element is recommended for multiline listings.

Minimum Attributes: `<CODE>CharacterData...</CODE>`

All Attributes: `<CODE DIR=LTR¦RTR ID="..." CLASS="...">CharacterData...</CODE>`

Elements Allowed Within: Members of group `TEXT`.

Allowed in Context of: Any element that permits elements of group `PHRASE`.

Notes: Typically displayed in a fixed-width font.

`<COL>`

Description: Specifies column-based defaults for a table. `SPAN` specifies how many columns are contained within the table with a default of 1. `WIDTH` specifies the width of the column in pixels (although you can override this setting by appending a two-character code to the unit; `pt` = points, `pi` = picas, `in` = inches, `cm` = centimeters, `mm` = millimeters, `em` = em units, and `px` = pixels) in the span. `ALIGN` and `VALIGN` specify the horizontal and vertical alignment of text within a cell. If `ALIGN=CHAR`, the `CHAR` specifies a character to be used for alignment. The default is a decimal point. `CHAROFF` specifies an offset from the alignment character.

Minimum Attributes: `<COL>`

All Attributes: `<COL LANG="..." DIR=LTR¦RTR ID="..." CLASS="..." SPAN=nn WIDTH="..." ALIGN=LEFT¦RIGHT¦CENTER¦JUSTIFY¦CHAR CHAR="." CHAROFF+"..." VALIGN=TOP¦BOTTOM¦ MIDDLE¦BASELINE>`

Elements Allowed Within: None.

Allowed in Context of: `<COLGROUP>` and `<TABLE>`.

Notes: Part of the new specification and not currently widely implemented.

`<COLGROUP>`

Description: Specifies a group of one or more columns and assigns defaults for all the columns in the group. `CHAROFF` specifies an offset from the alignment character, in pixels (although this may be overridden by appending a two-character code to the unit; `pt` = points, `pi` = picas, `in` = inches, `cm` = centimeters, `mm` = millimeters, `em` = em units, and `px` = pixels) in the span. `ALIGN` and `VALIGN` specify the horizontal and vertical alignment of text within a cell. If `ALIGN=CHAR`, then `CHAR` specifies a character to be used for alignment. The default is a decimal point.

Minimum Attributes: `<COLGROUP>`*CharacterData*`...</COLGROUP>`

All Attributes: `<COLGROUP LANG="..." DIR=LTR¦RTR ID="..." CLASS="..." ALIGN=LEFT¦RIGHT¦CENTER¦JUSTIFY¦CHAR CHAR="." CHAROFF+"..." VALIGN=TOP¦BOTTOM¦MIDDLE¦BASELINE>`*CharacterData*`...</COLGROUP>`

Elements Allowed Within: `<COL>`.

Allowed in Context of: `<TABLE>`.

Notes: Part of the new specification and not currently widely implemented.

`<CREDIT>`

Description: Specifies the name of a source of a block quotation or figure.

Minimum Attributes: `<CREDIT>`*CharacterData*`...</CREDIT>`

All Attributes: `<CREDIT LANG="..." DIR=LTR¦RTR ID="..." CLASS="...">`*CharacterData*`...</CREDIT>`

Elements Allowed Within: TBD.

Allowed in Context of: `<BQ>` `<FIG>`.

`<DD>`

Description: Specifies the separate multiline definition of a definition list (`<DL>`).

Minimum Attributes: `<DD>`*CharacterData*`...</DD>`

All Attributes: `<DD LANG="..." DIR=LTR¦RTR ID="..." CLASS="...">`*CharacterData*`...</DD>`

Elements Allowed Within: Members of groups BLOCK and TEXT.

Allowed in Context of: <DL>.

Notes: Generally rendered as indented text in a normal font.

<DEL>

Description: Specifies that text be physically rendered to logically represent deleted text.

Minimum Attributes: <DEL>*CharacterData*...</DEL>

All Attributes: <DEL LANG="..." DIR=LTR¦RTR ID="..." CLASS="...">*CharacterData*...</DEL>

Elements Allowed Within: TBD.

Allowed in Context of: TBD.

Notes: Proposed as a replacement to the <S> and <STRIKE> elements.

<DFN>

Description: Specifies a logical rendering of the text to represent a definition in a term/definition pair.

Minimum Attributes: <DFN>*CharacterData*...</DFN>

All Attributes: <DFN LANG="..." DIR=LTR¦RTR ID="..." CLASS="...">*CharacterData*...</DFN>

Elements Allowed Within: TBD.

Allowed in Context of: TBD.

Notes: Usually rendered in bold text.

<DIR>

Description: Specifies an unordered list of single-line <LI> items.

Minimum Attributes: <DIR></DIR>

All Attributes: <DIR COMPACT LANG="..." DIR=LTR¦RTR ALIGN=LEFT¦RIGHT¦CENTER¦JUSTIFY></DIR>

Elements Allowed Within: <LI>, but not any elements of group BLOCK.

Allowed in Context of: Any element of group LIST.

<DIV>

Description: A proposed element, to be used with the CLASS attribute, for specifying different types of containers (chapters, sections, abstracts, or appendixes).

Minimum Attributes: `<DIV>CharacterData...</DIV>`

All Attributes: `<DIV LANG="..." DIR=LTR¦RTR ALIGN=LEFT¦RIGHT¦CENTER¦JUSTIFY  ID="..." CLASS="..." NOWRAP CLEAR=LEFT¦RIGHT¦ALL¦"...">CharacterData...</DIV>`

Elements Allowed Within: TBD.

Allowed in Context of: `<BODY>`.

<DL>

Description: Specifies a definition list. Each item in the list is expected to have two components, which are identified by the `<DT>` and `<DD>` elements.

Minimum Attributes: `<DL></DL>`

All Attributes: `<DL COMPACT LANG="..." DIR=LTR¦RTR ALIGN=LEFT¦RIGHT¦CENTER¦JUSTIFY></DL>`

Elements Allowed Within: `<LH>`, `<DT>`, and `<DD>`.

Allowed in Context of: Any element that permits group BLOCK.

<DT>

Description: Specifies the term in a definition list.

Minimum Attributes: `<DT>CharacterData...</DT>`

All Attributes: `<DT LANG="..." DIR=LTR¦RTR>CharacterData...</DT>`

Elements Allowed Within: Members of group TEXT.

Allowed in Context of: `<DL>`.

Notes: Typically rendered in a bold font.

<EM>

Description: Changes the character rendering to assume an emphasized attribute.

Minimum Attributes: `<EM>CharacterData...</EM>`

All Attributes: `<EM LANG="..." DIR=LTR¦RTR ID="..." CLASS="...">CharacterData...</EM>`

Elements Allowed Within: Members of group TEXT.

Allowed in Context of: Any element that permits group PHRASE.

Notes: Typically rendered in an italic font.

<EMBED>

Description: Specifies a container for inserting objects directly into an HTML page. Embedded objects are supported by application-specific plug-ins.

Minimum Attributes: `<EMBED SRC="...">`

All Attributes: `<EMBED SRC="..." HEIGHT="..." WIDTH="..." attribute_1="..." attribute_2= "..." >CharacterData...</EMBED>`

Elements Allowed Within: `<NOEMBED>`.

Allowed in Context of: TBD.

Notes: A Netscape Navigator 2.0 extension.

<FIG>

Description: An advanced form of the IMG element that specifies an image with optional overlays, text, and hotzones.

Minimum Attributes: `<FIG SRC="...">`

All Attributes: `<FIG SRC="..." LANG="..." DIR=LTR¦RTR ID="..." CLASS="..." CLEAR=LEFT¦ RIGHT¦ALL¦"..." NOFLOW MD="..." ALIGN=LEFT¦RIGHT¦CENTER¦JUSTIFY¦BLEEDLEFT WIDTH=Value HEIGHT=Value UNITS="..." IMAGEMAP="..."></FIG>`

Elements Allowed Within: `<OVERLAY>`, `<CAPTION>`, and `<CREDIT>`. All others TBD.

Allowed in Context of: TBD.

<FN>

Description: Specifies the rendering of text as a logical footnote. The reference location for a footnote is expected to be an A element with an HREF attribute that references the ID of the FN element.

Minimum Attributes: `<FN ID="...">CharacterData...</FN>`

All Attributes: `<FN LANG="..." DIR=LTR¦RTR ID="..." CLASS=...">CharacterData...</FN>`

Elements Allowed Within: TBD.

Allowed in Context of: TBD.

<FONT>

Description: Specifies the size of the font used for the following text in one of the seven defined sizes or as a plus/minus of the BASEFONT.

Minimum Attributes: <FONT SIZE=1¦2¦3¦4¦5¦6¦7>

All Attributes: <FONT SIZE=1¦2¦3¦4¦5¦6¦7 COLOR="..." FACE="...">

Elements Allowed Within: TBD.

Allowed in Context of: TBD.

Notes: Netscape Navigator requires an RRGGBB (red green blue) format for the color elements. Microsoft Internet Explorer 2.0 can accept BLACK, MAROON, GREEN, OLIVE, NAVY, PURPLE, TEAL, GRAY, SILVER, RED, LIME, YELLOW, BLUE, FUCHSIA, AQUA, and WHITE instead of an RGB value. FACE is an Internet Explorer 2.0 extension that is currently not defined.

<FORM>

Description: Creates a fill-in form that is displayed on the Web browser. The browser then sends the information to an application on the server, which is identified as a URL by the AC-TION attribute. If the METHOD=GET (the default), the information is appended to the ACTION URL, which on most systems becomes the environment value QUERY_STRING. If METHOD=POST (the preferred method), the input is sent in a data body, available as stdin, with the data length set in the environment variable CONTENT_LENGTH. Form data is a stream of name/value pairs separated by the & character. Each name/value pair is a URL encoded in hexadecimal form. At least one of the following is expected in the FORM contents: INPUT, SELECT, or TEXTAREA.

Minimum Attributes: <FORM></FORM>

All Attributes: <FORM ACTION="..." METHOD=GET¦POST ENCTYPE="..." LANG="..." DIR=LTR¦RTR ACCEPT-CHARSET="..." SCRIPT="..."></FORM>

Elements Allowed Within: Members of group BODY.CONTENT and any of the elements <INPUT>, <SELECT>, and <TEXTAREA>, but not element <FORM>.

Allowed in Context of: Any element that permits members of group BLOCK.FORM.

<FRAME>

Description: Specifies a single frame in a frameset. The SRC value is a URL of the document to be displayed within the frame. The NAME element assigns a name to the frame that will be used as the target of a hypertext link. The SCROLLING attribute defines whether the frame should have a scrollbar and defaults to the value AUTO. If the NORESIZE attribute is present, the user cannot resize the frame.

Minimum Attributes: <FRAME>

All Attributes: `<FRAME SRC="..." NAME="..." MARGINWIDTH="..." MARGINHEIGHT="..." SCROLLING=YES¦NO¦AUTO NORESIZE>`

Elements Allowed Within: None.

Allowed in Context of: `<FRAMESET>`.

Notes: A Netscape Navigator 2.0 extension that defines multiple windows for viewing a document. The following entries are reserved for the NAME attribute: _BLANK, _SELF, _PARENT, and _TOP. These entries have the following definitions: new unnamed window, load in the same window, load in the parent window, and load in the top window, respectively. The units defined for MARGINWIDTH and MARGINHEIGHT are in pixels.

<FRAMESET>

Description: Used instead of the BODY element in an HTML document to define the layout of sub-HTML documents, or frames, that make up the page. The ROWS and COLS values are comma-separated lists defining the row height and column width of the frames.

Minimum Attributes: `<FRAMESET>`*CharacterData...*`</FRAMESET>`

All Attributes: `<FRAMESET ROWS="..." COLS="...">`*CharacterData*`</FRAMESET>`

Elements Allowed Within: `<FRAME>`, `<FRAMESET>`, and `<NOFRAMES>`.

Allowed in Context of: `<HTML>`.

Notes: A Netscape Navigator 2.0 extension. The ROWS and COLS values are restricted to integer values with an optional suffix to define the unit of measure.

<H1>

Description: A level-1 heading.

Minimum Attributes: `<H1>`*CharacterData...*`</H1>`

All Attributes: `<H1 LANG="..." DIR=LTR¦RTR ALIGN=LEFT¦RIGHT¦CENTER¦JUSTIFY ID="..." CLASS="..." CLEAR=LEFT¦RIGHT¦ALL¦"..." SEQNUM=`*nnn* `SKIP=`*nnn* `DINGBAT=`*entity-name* `SRC="..." MD="..." NOWRAP>`*CharacterData...*`</H1>`

Elements Allowed Within: Members of group TEXT.

Allowed in Context of: Any element that permits members of group HEADING.

<H2>

Description: A level-2 heading.

Minimum Attributes: `<H2>`*CharacterData...*`</H2>`

All Attributes: `<H2 LANG="..." DIR=LTR¦RTR ALIGN=LEFT¦RIGHT¦CENTER¦JUSTIFY ID="..." CLASS="..." CLEAR=LEFT¦RIGHT¦ALL¦"..." SEQNUM=`*nnn* `SKIP=`*nnn* `DINGBAT=`*entity-name* `SRC="..." MD="..." NOWRAP>`*CharacterData...*`</H2>`

Elements Allowed Within: Members of group TEXT.

Allowed in Context of: Any element that permits members of group HEADING.

<H3>

Description: A level-3 heading.

Minimum Attributes: `<H3>`*CharacterData...*`</H3>`

All Attributes: `<H3 LANG="..." DIR=LTR¦RTR ALIGN=LEFT¦RIGHT¦CENTER¦JUSTIFY ID="..." CLASS="..." CLEAR=LEFT¦RIGHT¦ALL¦"..." SEQNUM=`*nnn* `SKIP=`*nnn* `DINGBAT=`*entity-name* `SRC="..." MD="..." NOWRAP>`*CharacterData...*`</H3>`

Elements Allowed Within: Members of group TEXT.

Allowed in Context of: Any element that permits members of group HEADING.

<H4>

Description: A level-4 heading.

Minimum Attributes: `<H4>`*CharacterData...*`</H4>`

All Attributes: `<H4 LANG="..." DIR=LTR¦RTR ALIGN=LEFT¦RIGHT¦CENTER¦JUSTIFY ID="..." CLASS="..." CLEAR=LEFT¦RIGHT¦ALL¦"..." SEQNUM=`*nnn* `SKIP=`*nnn* `DINGBAT=`*entity-name* `SRC="..." MD="..." NOWRAP>`*CharacterData...*`</H4>`

Elements Allowed Within: Members of group TEXT.

Allowed in Context of: Any element that permits members of group HEADING.

<H5>

Description: A level-5 heading.

Minimum Attributes: `<H5>`*CharacterData...*`</H5>`

All Attributes: `<H5 LANG="..." DIR=LTR¦RTR ALIGN=LEFT¦RIGHT¦CENTER¦JUSTIFY ID="..." CLASS="..." CLEAR=LEFT¦RIGHT¦ALL¦"..." SEQNUM=`*nnn* `SKIP=`*nnn* `DINGBAT=`*entity-name* `SRC="..." MD="..." NOWRAP>`*CharacterData...*`</H5>`

Elements Allowed Within: Members of group TEXT.

Allowed in Context of: Any element that permits members of group HEADING.

\<H6>

Description: A level-6 heading.

Minimum Attributes: `<H6>`*CharacterData*`...</H6>`

All Attributes: `<H6 LANG="..." DIR=LTR¦RTR ALIGN=LEFT¦RIGHT¦CENTER¦JUSTIFY ID="..." CLASS="..." CLEAR=LEFT¦RIGHT¦ALL¦"..." SEQNUM=`*nnn* `SKIP=`*nnn* `DINGBAT=`*entity-name* `SRC="..." MD="..." NOWRAP>`*CharacterData*`...</H6>`

Elements Allowed Within: Members of group TEXT.

Allowed in Context of: Any element that permits members of group HEADING.

\<HEAD>

Description: Defines general information about the document. None of the elements are displayed.

Minimum Attributes: N/A

All Attributes: `<HEAD LANG="..." DIR=LTR¦RTR></HEAD>`

Elements Allowed Within: `<TITLE>`, `<ISINDEX>`, `<BASE>`, `<META>`, `<LINK>`, and `<NEXTID>`.

Allowed in Context of: `<HTML>`.

\<HP*n*>

Description: Specifies a set of HP*n* elements, where *n* = 1, 2, 3, 4, 5, or 6 and corresponds to the heading levels H1 to H6. This tag specifies the font size of the text and highlights the text as well.

Minimum Attributes: `<HPn>`*CharacterData*`...</HPn>`

All Attributes: `<HPn>`*CharacterData*`...</HPn>`

Elements Allowed Within: N/A.

Allowed in Context of: N/A.

Notes: This element is rarely used and should be considered obsolete.

\<HR>

Description: Defines a horizontal divider (or rule), which is a line between sections of text. You can use the SRC attribute to specify a custom image for the rule.

Minimum Attributes: `<HR>`

All Attributes: `<HR DIR=LTR¦RTR ALIGN=LEFT¦RIGHT¦CENTER¦JUSTIFY ID="..." CLASS="..."` `CLEAR=LEFT¦RIGHT¦ALL¦"..." SRC="..." MD="..." SIZE=Number WIDTH=Number¦Percent NOSHADE>`

Elements Allowed Within: None.

Allowed in Context of: Any element that permits members of group `BODY.CONTENT`.

Notes: Netscape Navigator 2.0 extensions include the `SIZE`, `WIDTH`, `ALIGN`, and `NOSHADE` attributes, although only the `ALIGN=LEFT¦RIGHT¦CENTER` options are implemented.

`<HTML>`

Description: Defines the HTML document. All elements must be bracketed within the `<HTML>` `</HTML>` tags.

Minimum Attributes: `<HTML></HTML>`

All Attributes: `<HTML VERSION="..." LANG="..." DIR=LTR¦RTR></HTML>`

Elements Allowed Within: `<HEAD>`, `<BODY>`, and `<PLAINTEXT>`.

`<I>`

Description: Specifies that rendered text be displayed in an italic font.

Minimum Attributes: `<I>`*CharacterData*`...</I>`

All Attributes: `<I LANG="..." DIR=LTR¦RTR ID="..." CLASS="...">`*CharacterData*`...</I>`

Elements Allowed Within: Members of group `TEXT`.

Allowed in Context of: Any element that permits members of group `FONT`.

`<IMG>`

Description: Defines an image file to be inserted into the current document with associated text. The `ALT` attribute defines the parsed character data to be displayed in place of the image for Web browsers that do not support image insertion. The `ISMAP` attribute is meaningful only if the `IMG` element is within the contents of an `A` element. A corresponding `cgi-bin` application will receive the `HREF` input values when the client clicks a selectable portion of the image.

Minimum Attributes: `<IMG SRC="...">`

All Attributes: `<IMG SRC="..." ALT="..." ISMAP LANG="..." DIR=LTR¦RTR ID="..." CLASS="..."` `MD="..." ALIGN=LEFT¦RIGHT¦TOP¦MIDDLE¦BOTTOM¦TEXTTOP¦ABSMIDDLE¦BASELINE¦ABSBOTTOM` `HEIGHT=`*Value*` WIDTH=`*Value*` UNITS="..." BORDER=`*Value*` LOWSRC="..." HSPACE=`*Value*` Vspace=`*Value*` USEMAP="..." DYNSRC="..." START=FILEOPEN¦MOUSEOVER CONTROLS LOOP=`*Number*`¦INFINITE¦-1` `LOOPDELAY=`*Number*`>`

Elements Allowed Within: None.

Allowed in Context of: Any element that permits group TEXT.

Notes: The BORDER, HEIGHT, WIDTH, HSPACE, VSPACE, and LOWSRC attributes are Netscape Navigator 1.1 extensions. The DYNSRC, START, CONTROLS, LOOP, and LOOPDELAY attributes are Internet Explorer 2.0 extensions. DYNSRC identifies a video clip or VRML world to be displayed. If START=MOUSEOVER, the image is displayed until the mouse is over the image. CONTROLS will display a set of controls under the animation image. LOOP is defined as the number of times the image will be replayed when activated. If LOOP is set to INFINITE or -1, the video clip will play indefinitely. LOOPDELAY determines the time, in milliseconds, between replays of the video clip.

<INPUT>

Description: Specifies an input field as part of the contents in a form. TYPE=TEXT is the default. NAME defines the symbolic name of the returned field to the server upon submission. This attribute must be present except when TYPE=SUBMIT¦RESET. For TYPE=CHECKBOX¦RADIO, the name may be the same for multiple INPUT elements. TYPE=RADIO ensures that only one name is selected. For TYPE=PASSWORD, the value should be obscured, generally by an asterisk (*), so that the actual password is not readable onscreen when entered. VALUE defines the label for a push button. CHECKED specifies that the push button, or radio INPUT, be preconfigured to a selected state. TYPE=IMAGE defines an image specified in the URL and defined in the SRC attribute, which, when clicked, submits the form and sends the x,y coordinates to the receiving URL. The SIZE and MAXLENGTH attributes are used only with a TYPE=TEXT or TYPE=PASSWORD attribute, where SIZE is the physical size of the displayed input field expressed in characters and rows and MAXLENGTH is the maximum number of characters that will be accepted as input.

Minimum Attributes: <INPUT>

All Attributes: <INPUT TYPE="TEXT¦PASSWORD¦CHECKBOX¦RADIO¦SUBMIT¦RESET¦HIDDEN¦ IMAGE¦FILE¦RANGE¦SCRIBBLE¦JOT" LANG="..." DIR=LTR¦RTR ID="..." CLASS="..." NAME="..." VALUE="..." SRC="..." CHECKED SIZE="..." MAXLENGTH=*Number* ALIGN=LEFT¦RIGHT¦TOP¦MIDDLE¦ BOTTOM ACCEPT="..." DISABLED ERROR="..." MIN=*Number* MAX=*Number* MD="...">

Elements Allowed Within: None.

Allowed in Context of: <FORM>.

<INS>

Description: Specifies that rendered text be displayed as logically inserted text.

Minimum Attributes: <INS>*CharacterData*...</INS>

All Attributes: `<INS LANG="..." DIR=LTR¦RTR ID="..." CLASS="...">`*CharacterData...*`</INS>`

Elements Allowed Within: TBD.

Allowed in Context of: TBD.

<ISINDEX>

Description: A precursor to the `<FORM>` element and usually created by a server-side script. When placed in the BODY of a document, the ISINDEX requires the ACTION attribute to point to a cgi-bin application to handle a query. A simple INPUT field with the prompt `This is a searchable index. Enter search keywords:` is produced. When placed in the HEAD of a document, the ISINDEX informs the Web browser that the document is an index document that can be examined using a keyword search.

Minimum Attributes: `<ISINDEX>`

All Attributes: `<ISINDEX LANG="..." DIR=LTR¦RTR ACTION="..." PROMPT="...">`

Elements Allowed Within: None.

Allowed in Context of: The element `<HEAD>` and any element that permits members of group BLOCK.FORMS.

<KBD>

Description: Specifies that rendered text be displayed as keyboard input.

Minimum Attributes: `<KBD>`*CharacterData...*`</KBD>`

All Attributes: `<KBD LANG="..." DIR=LTR¦RTR ID="..." CLASS="...">`*CharacterData...*`</KBD>`

Elements Allowed Within: Members of group TEXT.

Allowed in Context of: Any element that permits members of group PHRASE.

Notes: Typically displayed with a fixed-width font.

<LANG>

Description: Changes the default language context for subsequent elements. A LANG attribute on an element will override the default language context for the particular element.

Minimum Attributes: `<LANG>`*CharacterData...*`</LANG>`

All Attributes: `<LANG ID="..." CLASS="...">`*CharacterData...*`</LANG>`

Elements Allowed Within: TBD.

Allowed in Context of: TBD.

\<LH>

Description: Defines a list header to be used as a title for a list.

Minimum Attributes: `<LH>`*`CharacterData`*`...</LH>`

All Attributes: `<LH LANG="..." DIR=LTR¦RTR ID="..." CLASS="...">Character Data...</LH>`

Elements Allowed Within: TBD.

Allowed in Context of: `<DL>`, `<OL>`, and `<UL>`.

\<LI>

Description: Defines a list item.

Minimum Attributes: `<LI>`*`CharacterData`*`...`

All Attributes: `<LI LANG="..." DIR=LTR¦RTR ALIGN=LEFT¦RIGHT¦CENTER¦JUSTIFY` within OL `TYPE=DISK¦CIRCLE¦SQUARE` within OL `TYPE=A¦I` within OL `VALUE=`*`n`*`>`*`CharacterData`*`...</LI>`

Elements Allowed Within: Members of group TEXT and BLOCK.

Allowed in Context of: `<DIR>`, `<MENU>`, `<OL>`, and `<UL>`.

Notes: The TYPE and VALUE attributes are Netscape Navigator extensions.

\<LINK>

Description: Specifies that a relationship between this document and another document exists. Multiple LINK elements may exist within a document. If the REL attribute is present in document/object (A) with an HREF to a document/object (B), LINK identifies a relationship that B has to A, which A recognizes/verifies/authorizes. If the REV attribute is present in document/object (B) with an HREF to a document/object (A), LINK identifies a relationship that B has to A, which must be verified by checking with A.

Minimum Attributes: `<LINK HREF="...">`

All Attributes: `<LINK HREF="..." REL="..." REV="..." LANG="..." DIR=LTR¦RTR CHARSET="..." URN="..." TITLE="..." METHODS-"...">`

Elements Allowed Within: None.

Allowed in Context of: `<HEAD>`.

\<LISTING>

Description: Specifies that separated multiline text be rendered as it exists, with all line breaks intact.

Minimum Attributes: `<LISTING>`*CharacterData*`...</LISTING>`

All Attributes: `<LISTING WIDTH="...">`*CharacterData*`...</LISTING>`

Elements Allowed Within: None.

Allowed in Context of: Any element that permits members of group `BLOCK`.

Notes: Assumed width is 132 characters. Some Web browsers no longer support this attribute.

`<MAP>`

Description: Specifies a name and description for a client-side image map. An *image map* is a set of areas on the image that may be used to select specific hypertext links. `NAME` defines the map name to be used with the `USEMAP` attribute on an `IMG` element.

Minimum Attributes: `<MAP NAME="..."></MAP>`

All Attributes: `<MAP NAME="..."></MAP>`

Elements Allowed Within: `<AREA>`.

Allowed in Context of: TBD.

`<MARQUEE>`

Description: Defines an area in which visual scrolling will be used to display the content of the element.

Minimum Attributes: `<MARQUEE>`*CharacterData*`...</MARQUEE>`

All Attributes: `<MARQUEE ALIGN=LEFT¦RIGHT¦TOP¦MIDDLE¦BOTTOM BEHAVIOR=SCROLL¦SLIDE¦ ALTERNATE BGCOLOR="RRBBGG"¦COLORNAME DIRECTION=LEFT¦RIGHT HEIGHT=`*Number*`¦`*NumberPercent* `HSPACE=`*Number* `LOOP=`*Number*`¦INFINITE¦-1 SCROLLAMOUNT=`*Number* `SCROLLDELAY=`*Number* `VSPACE=`*Number*`>`*CharacterData*`...</MARQUEE>`

Elements Allowed Within: TBD.

Allowed in Context of: TBD.

Notes: A Microsoft Internet Explorer 2.0 extension. The `BGCOLOR` attribute can accept `BLACK`, `MAROON`, `GREEN`, `OLIVE`, `NAVY`, `PURPLE`, `TEAL`, `GRAY`, `SILVER`, `RED`, `LIME`, `YELLOW`, `BLUE`, `FUCHSIA`, `AQUA`, and `WHITE`. The `BEHAVIOR` attribute specifies how the text will scroll (`SCROLL`), completely in and out; slide (`SLIDE`), in and stay; or bounce (`ALTERNATE`) between the sides of the marquee. The `DIRECTION` attribute specifies in which direction the text will flow; the `HEIGHT` attribute specifies how high the marquee should be; the `HSPACE` and `VSPACE` determine, in pixels, the amount of surrounding whitespace; and the `LOOP` attribute specifies how many iterations of the marquee to play. `SCROLLAMOUNT` specifies the number of pixels in the marquee text, and `SCROLLDELAY` specifies the number of milliseconds between repeated redraws of the marquee text.

\<MENU>

Description: Defines an unordered list consisting of separate multiline \<LI> (list item) elements.

Minimum Attributes: `<MENU></MENU>`

All Attributes: `<MENU COMPACT LANG="..." DIR=LTR¦RTR ALIGN=LEFT¦RIGHT¦CENTER¦JUSTIFY>` `</MENU>`

Elements Allowed Within: Element \<LI>, but not members of group BLOCK.

Allowed in Context of: Any element that permits members of group LIST.

\<META>

Description: Used within the HEAD element to embed meta information into the document that is not defined by any HTML element. The HTTP-EQUIV element binds the element to an HTTP response header. If present, the NAME attribute identifies this meta information. It should not be used within the HTTP response header. If the NAME attribute is not present, you can assume that the name is the same as the value of HTTP-EQUIV. The CONTENT attribute defines the meta-information content to be associated with the given name of the HTTP response header.

Minimum Attributes: `<META CONTENT="...">`

All Attributes: `<META HTTP-EQUIV="..." NAME="..." CONTENT="..." URL="...">`

Elements Allowed Within: None.

Allowed in Context of: \<HEAD>.

Notes: The URL attribute is a Netscape Navigator extension. Netscape Navigator 1.1 has added an automatic refresh capability by assigning the HTTP-EQUIV attribute to REFRESH, the CONTENT attribute to a number of seconds, and the URL attribute to a file to load.

\<NEXTID>

Description: Specifies the only attribute (N) as the number to be used by automatic-hypertext editors.

Minimum Attributes: `<NEXTID N="...">`

All Attributes: `<NEXTID N="...">`

Elements Allowed Within: None.

Allowed in Context of: \<HEAD>.

Notes: RFC 1866 recommends not using this element.

<NOBR>

Description: Specifies that line breaks cannot be inserted within the enclosed tags.

Minimum Attributes: `<NOBR>`*CharacterData*`...</NOBR>`

All Attributes: `<NOBR>`*CharacterData*`...</NOBR>`

Elements Allowed Within: TBD.

Allowed in Context of: TBD.

Notes: This element is a Netscape Navigator 1.1 extension.

<NOEMBED>

Description: Specifies alternative content to be displayed by Web browsers that do not support embedded content.

Minimum Attributes: `<NOEMBED>`*CharacterData*`...</NOEMBED>`

All Attributes: `<NOEMBED>`*CharacterData*`...</NOEMBED>`

Elements Allowed Within: TBD.

Allowed in Context of: `<EMBED>`.

Notes: A Netscape Navigator 2.0 extension to supported specific application plug-ins.

<NOFRAMES>

Description: Specifies content to be displayed by Web browsers that do not support frames.

Minimum Attributes: `<NOFRAMES>`*CharacterData*`...</NOFRAMES>`

All Attributes: `<NOFRAMES>`*CharacterData*`...</NOFRAMES>`

Elements Allowed Within: TBD.

Allowed in Context of: `<FRAMESET>`.

Notes: A Netscape Navigator 2.0 extension.

<NOTE>

Description: Specifies that rendered text be displayed as a logical note. The SRC attribute specifies an image to be displayed before the note.

Minimum Attributes: `<NOTE>`*CharacterData*`...</NOTE>`

All Attributes: `<NOTE LANG="..." DIR=LTR¦RTR ID="..." CLASS="..." CLEAR=LEFT¦RIGHT¦CENTER¦ALL¦"..." SRC="..." MD="..."></NOTE>`

Elements Allowed Within: TBD.

Allowed in Context of: TBD.

<OL>

Description: Defines an ordered (such as a numbered) list.

Minimum Attributes: <OL></OL>

All Attributes: <OL COMPACT LANG="..." DIR=LTR¦RTR ALIGN=LEFT¦RIGHT¦CENTER¦JUSTIFY ID="..." CLASS="..." CLEAR=LEFT¦RIGHT¦CENTER¦ALL¦"..." CONTINUE SEQNUM=*Value* START=*Value* TYPE=A¦I¦1></OL>

Elements Allowed Within: <LH> and <LI>.

Allowed in Context of: Any element of group LIST.

Notes: Both TYPE and START are Netscape Navigator extensions.

<OPTION>

Description: Specifies a choice in a SELECT element. SELECTED specifies that the option is selected by default.

Minimum Attributes: <OPTION>*CharacterData*...

All Attributes: <OPTION SELECTED VALUE="..." LANG="..." DIR=LTR¦RTR ID="..." CLASS=..." DISABLED ERROR="..." SHAPE="...">*CharacterData*...</OPTION>

Elements Allowed Within: May contain only parsed character data.

Allowed in Context of: <SELECT>.

<OVERLAY>

Description: Specifies one or more images to be overlayed on a FIG element.

Minimum Attributes: <OVERLAY SRC="...">

All Attributes: <OVERLAY SRC="..." MD="..." UNITS=PIXELS¦EN X=*Value* Y=*Value* WIDTH=*Value* HEIGHT=*Value* IMAGEMAP="...">

Elements Allowed Within: None.

Allowed in Context of: <FIG>.

`<P>`

Description: Specifies a paragraph break and separates two blocks of text with vertical whitespace.

Minimum Attributes: `<P>`

All Attributes: `<P ALIGN=LEFT¦RIGHT¦CENTER¦JUSTIFY¦INDENT WRAP=ON¦OFF NOWRAP CLEAR=LEFT¦RIGHT¦ALL¦"..." LANG="..." DIR=LTR¦RTR ID="..." CLASS="...">` *CharacterData...*`</P>`

Elements Allowed Within: Members of group `TEXT`.

Allowed in Context of: Any element that permits members of group `BLOCK`.

`<PARAM>`

Description: Defines a general-purpose mechanism to pass parameters to an `APPLET` application, where `NAME` is the name of the parameter and `VALUE` is the data to be obtained by the `APPLET` application using the `getParameter()` method.

Minimum Attributes: `<PARAM NAME="..." VALUE="...">`

All Attributes: `<PARAM NAME="..." VALUE="...">`

Elements Allowed Within: None.

Allowed in Context of: `<APPLET>`.

`<PERSON>`

Description: Specifies the rendering of text on the display to logically represent the names of personnel, thus allowing automatic extraction by indexing programs.

Minimum Attributes: `<PERSON>`*CharacterData...*`</PERSON>`

All Attributes: `<PERSON LANG="..." DIR=LTR¦RTR ID="..." CLASS="...">`*CharacterData...*`</PERSON>`

Elements Allowed Within: TBD.

Allowed in Context of: TBD.

`<PLAINTEXT>`

Description: Specifies that separated multiline text be rendered as it exists, with all line breaks intact, and that all HTML tags within the enclosed elements be ignored.

Minimum Attributes: `<PLAINTEXT>`*CharacterData...*`</PLAINTEXT>`

All Attributes: `<PLAINTEXT WIDTH="..." LANG="..." DIR=LTR¦RTR>`*CharacterData...*`</PLAINTEXT>`

Elements Allowed Within: None.

Allowed in Context of: `<HTML>`.

Notes: Typically displayed in a fixed-width font. Some Web browsers no longer support this attribute.

`<PRE>`

Description: Specifies that separated multiline text be rendered as it exists, with all line breaks intact.

Minimum Attributes: `<PRE>`*CharacterData...*`</PRE>`

All Attributes: `<PRE WIDTH=`*Number* `LANG="..." DIR=LTR¦RTR ID="..." CLASS="..."` `CLEAR=LEFT¦RIGHT¦ALL¦"...">`*CharacterData...*`</PRE>`

Elements Allowed Within: Elements `<A>`, `<HR>`, `<BR>`, and parsed character data.

Allowed in Context of: Any element that permits members of group BLOCK.

Notes: Typically displayed in a fixed-width font.

`<Q>`

Description: Specifies that rendered text be displayed as a logical short quotation.

Minimum Attributes: `<Q>`*CharacterData...*`</Q>`

All Attributes: `<Q LANG="..." DIR=LTR¦RTR ID="..." CLASS="...">`*CharacterData...*`</Q>`

Elements Allowed Within: Members of group TEXT.

Allowed in Context of: Any element that permits members of group TEXT.

Notes: A proposed element that is to be displayed in those quotation marks appropriate to the specified language.

`<S>`

Description: Specifies that rendered text be displayed with a strikeout character.

Minimum Attributes: `<S>`*CharacterData...*`</S>`

All Attributes: `<S LANG="..." DIR=LTR¦RTR ID="..." CLASS="...">`*CharacterData...*`</S>`

Elements Allowed Within: TBD.

Allowed in Context of: TBD.

Notes: A proposed element to replace the STRIKE element.

B

HTML REFERENCE

<SAMP>

Description: Specifies that rendered text be displayed as a logical sequence of literal characters.

Minimum Attributes: `<SAMP>CharacterData...</SAMP>`

All Attributes: `<SAMP LANG="..." DIR=LTR¦RTR ID="..." CLASS="...">CharacterData...</SAMP>`

Elements Allowed Within: Members of group TEXT.

Allowed in Context of: Any element that permits members of group PHRASE.

Notes: Typically rendered with a fixed-width font.

<SELECT>

Description: Defines a menu of a series of input in a FORM, each identified with the OPTION element. At least one OPTION element is expected within the SELECT contents. The NAME is a symbolic name returned to the server. The SIZE determines the number of OPTION statements physically visible when the form is displayed by the Web browser.

Minimum Attributes: `<SELECT NAME="...">CharacterData...</SELECT>`

All Attributes: `<SELECT NAME="..." SIZE=Value MULTIPLE LANG="..." DIR=LTR¦RTR ID="..." CLASS="..." ALIGN=TOP¦MIDDLE¦BOTTOM¦LEFT¦RIGHT DISABLED ERROR="..." SRC="..." MD="..." WIDTH=Value HEIGHT=Value UNITS=PIXELS¦EM>CharacterData...</SELECT>`

Elements Allowed Within: `<OPTION>`.

Allowed in Context of: `<FORM>`.

<SMALL>

Description: Specifies that rendered text be displayed with a smaller font, if practical.

Minimum Attributes: `<SMALL>CharacterData...</SMALL>`

All Attributes: `<S LANG="..." DIR=LTR¦RTR ID="..." CLASS="...">CharacterData...</S>`

Elements Allowed Within: TBD.

Allowed in Context of: TBD.

Notes: A Netscape Navigator 2.0 extension.

<SPAN>

Description: Specifies a generic container to set language characteristics for container content.

Minimum Attributes: `<SPAN>CharacterData...</SPAN>`

All Attributes: `<SPAN LANG="..." DIR=LTR¦RTR>CharacterData...</SPAN>`

Elements Allowed Within: Members of group TEXT.

Allowed in Context of: Any element that permits members of group TEXT.

Notes: Another internationalization proposal.

<STRIKE>

Description: Specifies that rendered text be displayed with a strikeout character.

Minimum Attributes: `<STRIKE>CharacterData...</STRIKE>`

All Attributes: `<STRIKE>CharacterData...</STRIKE>`

Elements Allowed Within: TBD.

Allowed in Context of: TBD.

<STRONG>

Description: Specifies that rendered text be displayed with stronger emphasis.

Minimum Attributes: `<STRONG>CharacterData...</STRONG>`

All Attributes: `<STRONG LANG="..." DIR=LTR¦RTR ID="..." CLASS="...">CharacterData...`
`</STRONG>`

Elements Allowed Within: Members of group TEXT.

Allowed in Context of: Any element that permits members of group PHRASE.

Notes: Typically rendered as bold text.

<STYLE>

Description: Specifies the rendering of information contained within a document.

Minimum Attributes: `<STYLE>`

Maximum Attributes: `<STYLE> TITLE=CharacterData TYPE=MimeType></STYLE>`

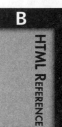

B

HTML REFERENCE

All Attributes: `<STYLE> TITLE=`*`CharacterData`* `TYPE=`*`MimeType`*`...></STYLE>`

Elements Allowed Within: Parsed character data.

Allowed in Context of: Any element that permits members of group TEXT.

<SUB>

Description: Specifies that rendered text be displayed as a subscript.

Minimum Attributes: `<SUB>`*`CharacterData`*`...</SUB>`

All Attributes: `<SUB LANG="..." DIR=LTR¦RTR ID="..." CLASS="...">`*`CharacterData`*`...</SUB>`

Elements Allowed Within: Parsed character data.

Allowed in Context of: Any element that permits members of group TEXT.

<SUP>

Description: Specifies that rendered text be displayed as a superscript.

Minimum Attributes: `<SUP>`*`CharacterData`*`...</SUP>`

All Attributes: `<SUP LANG="..." DIR=LTR¦RTR ID="..." CLASS="...">`*`CharacterData`*`...</SUP>`

Elements Allowed Within: Parsed character data.

Allowed in Context of: Any element that permits members of group TEXT.

<TAB>

Description: Aligns text according to a defined horizontal position. Text is positioned by using the TO and/or ALIGN attributes or by using the INDENT attribute.

Minimum Attributes: `<TAB>`*`CharacterData`*`...`

All Attributes: `<TAB ID="..." INDENT=`*`ens`* `TO="..." ALIGN=LEFT¦RIGHT¦CENTER¦DECIMAL DP="...">`*`CharacterData`*`...`

Elements Allowed Within: TBD.

Allowed in Context of: TBD.

<TABLE>

Description: Defines a series of rows of table cells. The order in the sequence is important and consists of at least one TR element, possibly some COL or COLGROUP elements, at most one THEAD, at most one TFOOT, at most one TBODY, and at most one CAPTION element.

Minimum Attributes: `<TABLE></TABLE>`

All Attributes: `<TABLE LANG="..." DIR=LTR¦RTR ID="..." CLASS="..." ALIGN=LEFT¦RIGHT¦`
`CENTER¦JUSTIFY¦BLEEDLEFT¦BLEEDRIGHT WIDTH="..." COLS=Number BORDER="..."`
`FRAME=VOID¦ABOVE¦BELOW¦HSIDES¦LHS¦RHS¦VSIDES¦BOX¦BORDER RULES=NONE¦BASIC¦ROWS¦COLS¦ALL`
`CELLSPACING="..." CELLPADDING="..." CLEAR=LEFT¦RIGHT¦ALL¦"..." NOFLOW UNITS=EN¦RELATIVE¦`
`PIXELS COLSPEC="..." DP="..." NOWRAP></TABLE>`

Elements Allowed Within: `<CAPTION>`, `<COL>`, `<COLGROUP>`, `<THEAD>`, `<TFOOT>`, `<TBODY>`, and `<TR>`.

Allowed in Context of: Any element that permits members of group `BLOCK`.

`<TBODY>`

Description: Defines a series of table-row definitions and specifies the defaults for all rows in the group. Table rows within a `TABLE` content are grouped into at most one `THEAD`, at most one `TFOOT`, and at least one `TBODY` (in that order).

Minimum Attributes: `<TBODY>`

All Attributes: `<TBODY LANG="..." DIR=LTR¦RTR ID="..." CLASS="..." ALIGN=LEFT¦RIGHT¦`
`CENTER¦JUSTIFY¦CHAR CHAR="..." CHAROFF="..." VALIGN=TOP¦BOTTOM¦MIDDLE¦BASELINE>`
`CharacterData...</TBODY>`

Elements Allowed Within: `<TR>`.

Allowed in Context of: `<TABLE>`.

`<TD>`

Description: Defines a data cell as part of a `TABLE`. The AXIS and AXES attributes define concise labels for cells. The ROWSPAN and COLSPAN attributes define the number of rows and columns spanned by a cell.

Minimum Attributes: `<TD>`

All Attributes: `<TD LANG="..." DIR=LTR¦RTR ID="..." CLASS="..." AXIS="..." AXES="..."`
`NOWRAP ROWSPAN=Value COLSPAN=Value ALIGN=LEFT¦RIGHT¦CENTER¦JUSTIFY¦CHAR¦DECIMAL`
`CHAR="... CHAROFF="..." DP="..." VALIGN=TOP¦MIDDLE¦BOTTOM¦BASELINE WIDTH=Value`
`BGCOLOR="...">CharacterData...</TD>`

Elements Allowed Within: Members of group `BODY.CONTENT`.

Allowed in Context of: `<TR>`.

Notes: An extension in both Netscape Navigator and the Microsoft Internet Explorer 2.0. The values JUSTIFY¦CHAR are new and not widely implemented. The BGCOLOR attribute can accept BLACK, MAROON, GREEN, OLIVE, NAVY, PURPLE, TEAL, GRAY, SILVER, RED, LIME, YELLOW, BLUE, FUCHSIA, AQUA, and WHITE.

<TEXTAREA>

Description: Specifies a multiline input field as part of a FORM element, where NAME defines a symbolic name to be returned to the server upon submission of the form.

Minimum Attributes: <TEXTAREA NAME="..." ROWS="..." COLS="..."></TEXTAREA>

All Attributes: <TEXTAREA NAME="..." ROWS="..." COLS="..." LANG="..." ID="..." CLASS="..." WRAP=OFF¦VIRTUAL¦PHYSICAL ALIGN=LEFT¦RIGHT¦TOP¦MIDDLE¦BOTTOM DISABLED ERROR="...">*CharacterData*...</TEXTAREA>

Elements Allowed Within: Only parsed data.

Allowed in Context of: <FORM>.

<TFOOT>

Description: Encloses a series of table-row definitions and specifies defaults for all rows in the group. Table rows grouped within this TABLE element have at most one THEAD, at most one TFOOT, and at least one TBODY.

Minimum Attributes: <TFOOT>

All Attributes: <TFOOT LANG="..." DIR=LTR¦RTR ID="..." CLASS="..." ALIGN=LEFT¦RIGHT¦ CENTER¦JUSTIFY¦CHAR CHAR="..." CHAROFF="..." VALIGN=TOP¦MIDDLE¦BOTTOM¦BASELINE> *CharacterData*...</TFOOT>

Elements Allowed Within: <TR>.

Allowed in Context of: <TABLE>.

<TH>

Description: Defines a header cell as part of the TABLE construct.

Minimum Attributes: <TH>

All Attributes: <TH LANG="..." DIR=LTR¦RTR ID="..." CLASS="..." AXIS="..." AXES="..." NOWRAP ROWSPAN=*Value* COLSPAN=*Value* ALIGN=LEFT¦RIGHT¦CENTER¦JUSTIFY¦CHAR¦DECIMAL CHAR="..." CHAROFF="..." DP="..." VALIGN=TOP¦MIDDLE¦BOTTOM¦BASELINE WIDTH=*Value* BGCOLOR="...">*CharacterData*...</TH>

Elements Allowed Within: Members of group BODY.CONTENT.

Allowed in Context of: <TR>.

Notes: An extension both in Netscape Navigator and the Microsoft Internet Explorer 2.0. The values JUSTIFY¦CHAR are new and not widely implemented. The BGCOLOR attribute can accept BLACK, MAROON, GREEN, OLIVE, NAVY, PURPLE, TEAL, GRAY, SILVER, RED, LIME, YELLOW, BLUE, FUCHSIA, AQUA, and WHITE.

<THEAD>

Description: Encloses a series of table-row definitions, and specifies defaults for all rows in the group. Table rows grouped within this TABLE element have at most one THEAD, at most one TFOOT, and at least one TBODY.

Minimum Attributes: <THEAD>

All Attributes: <THEAD LANG="..." DIR=LTR¦RTR ID="..." CLASS="..." ALIGN=LEFT¦RIGHT¦CENTER¦JUSTIFY¦CHAR CHAR="..." CHAROFF="..." VALIGN=TOP¦MIDDLE¦BOTTOM¦BASELINE>*CharacterData*...</THEAD>

Elements Allowed Within: <TR>.

Allowed in Context of: <TABLE>.

<TITLE>

Description: Defines a label commonly used by Web browsers to display a document tile on the caption.

Minimum Attributes: <TITLE>*CharacterData*...</TITLE>

All Attributes: <TITLE LANG="..." DIR=LTR¦RTR>*CharacterData*...</TITLE>

Elements Allowed Within: Only parsed data.

Allowed in Context of: <HEAD>.

<TR>

Description: Defines a table row.

Minimum Attributes: <TR>

All Attributes: <TR LANG="..." DIR=LTR¦RTR ID="..." CLASS="..." ALIGN=LEFT¦RIGHT¦CENTER¦JUSTIFY¦CHAR¦DECIMAL CHAR="..." CHAROFF="..." VALIGN=TOP¦MIDDLE¦BOTTOM¦BASELINE DP="...">*CharacterData*...</TR>

Elements Allowed Within: <TD> and <TH>.

Allowed in Context of: <TBODY>, <TFOOT>, and <THEAD>.

<TT>

Description: Specifies that rendered text be displayed as a fixed-width teletype font.

Minimum Attributes: `<TT>`*CharacterData*`...</TT>`

All Attributes: `<TT LANG="..." DIR=LTR¦RTR ID="..." CLASS="...">`*CharacterData*`...</TT>`

Elements Allowed Within: Members of group TEXT.

Allowed in Context of: Any element that permits members of group FONT.

<U>

Description: Specifies that rendered text be displayed in an underlined font.

Minimum Attributes: `<U>`*CharacterData*`...</U>`

All Attributes: `<U LANG="..." DIR=LTR¦RTR ID="..." CLASS="...">`*CharacterData*`...</U>`

Elements Allowed Within: TBD.

Allowed in Context of: TBD.

Notes: Generally rendered as an underlined font; however, some Web browsers will display this as an italic font.

<UL>

Description: Defines an unordered (such as a bulleted) list.

Minimum Attributes: `<UL></UL>`

All Attributes: `<UL COMPACT LANG="..." DIR=LTR¦RTR ALIGN=LEFT¦RIGHT¦CENTER¦JUSTIFY ID="..." CLASS="..." CLEAR=LEFT¦RIGHT¦CENTER¦ALL¦"..." PLAIN SRC="..." MD="..." DINGBAT="..." WRAP=VERT¦HORIZ TYPE=DISK¦CIRCLE¦SQUARE></UL>`

Elements Allowed Within: `<LH>` and `<LI>`.

Allowed in Context of: Any element of group LIST.

<VAR>

Description: Specifies that rendered text be displayed as a logical variable name.

Minimum Attributes: `<VAR>`*CharacterData*`...</VAR>`

All Attributes: `<VAR LANG="..." DIR=LTR¦RTR ID="..." CLASS="...">`*CharacterData*`...</VAR>`

Elements Allowed Within: Members of group TEXT.

Allowed in Context of: Any element that permits members of group PHRASE.

Notes: Typically rendered in an italic font.

<WBR>

Description: Specifies a line break in a no-break zone.

Minimum Attributes: <WBR>

All Attributes: <WBR>

Elements Allowed Within: None.

Allowed in Context of: <NOBR>.

Notes: A Netscape Navigator 2.0 extension.

<XMP>

Description: Specifies that a separated multiline text be rendered as it exists, with the same line breaks as in the source document.

Minimum Attributes: <XMP>*CharacterData*...</XMP>

All Attributes: <XMP WIDTH="..." LANG="..." DIR=LTR¦RTR ID="..." >*CharacterData*... </XMP>

Elements Allowed Within: None.

Allowed in Context of: Any element that permits members of group BLOCK.

Notes: Typically rendered in a fixed-width font with an assumed width of 80 characters. Some Web browsers no longer support this element.

Defining Special Characters on Your Web Page

When you develop your Web page, you may run into an occasional problem in which you need to define a special character. The format to do so is to concatenate an &, a #, a two-digit number, and a ;, as specified in Table B.1. You may also use a few additional special character sequences, including &copy for the copyright symbol, &reg for the trademark symbol, &shy for a soft hyphen,   for a nonbreaking space, &quot for a quotation mark, &lt for a less-than symbol, &gt for the greater-than symbol, and &amp for the ampersand symbol.

Table B.1. The HTML coded character set.

Key Value	Description
&#00;-&#08;	Unused
&#09;	Horizontal tab
&#10;	Line feed
&#11;-	Unused
&#13;	Carriage return
&#14;-&#31;	Unused
&#32;	Space
&#33;	Exclamation point
&#34;	Quotation mark
&#35;	Number sign
&#36;	Dollar sign
&#37;	Percent sign
&#38;	Ampersand
&#39;	Apostrophe
&#40;	Left parenthesis
&#41;	Right parenthesis
&#42;	Asterisk
&#43;	Plus sign
&#44;	Comma
&#45;	Hyphen
&#46;	Period (full stop)
&#47;	Solidus (slash)
0-9	Digits 0–9
&#58;	Colon
&#59;	Semicolon
&#60;	Less than
&#61;	Equal sign
&#62;	Greater than
&#63;	Question mark
&#64;	Commercial at
A-Z	Letters A–Z

Key Value	Description
`&#91;`	Left square bracket
`&#92;`	Reverse solidus (backslash)
`&#93;`	Right square bracket
`&#94;`	Caret
`&#95;`	Horizontal bar (underscore)
`&#96;`	Acute accent
`&#97;`-`&#122;`	Letters a–z
`&#123;`	Left curly brace
`&#124;`	Vertical bar
`&#125;`	Right curly brace
`&#126;`	Tilde
`&#127;`-`&#159;`	Unused
` `	Nonbreaking space
`&#161;`	Inverted exclamation
`&#162;`	Cent sign
`&#163;`	Pound sterling
`&#164;`	General currency sign
`&#165;`	Yen sign
`&#166;`	Broken vertical bar
`&#167;`	Section sign
`&#168;`	Umlaut (dieresis)
`&#169;`	Copyright
`&#170;`	Feminine ordinal
`&#171;`	Left-angle quote, guillemotleft
`&#172;`	Not sign
`&#173;`	Soft hyphen
`&#174;`	Registered trademark
`&#175;`	Macron accent
`&#176;`	Degree sign
`&#177;`	Plus or minus
`&#178;`	Superscript two

continues

B

HTML REFERENCE

Table B.1. continued

Key Value	Description
&#179;	Superscript three
&#180;	Acute accent
&#181;	Micro sign
&#182;	Paragraph sign
&#183;	Middle dot
&#184;	Cedilla
&#185;	Superscript one
&#186;	Masculine ordinal
&#187;	Right-angle quote, guillemotright
&#188;	Fraction one-fourth
&#189;	Fraction one-half
&#190;	Fraction three-fourths
&#191;	Inverted question mark
&#192;	Capital A, grave accent
&#193;	Capital A, acute accent
&#194;	Capital A, circumflex accent
&#195;	Capital A, tilde
&#196;	Capital A, dieresis or umlaut mark
&#197;	Capital A, ring
&#198;	Capital AE diphthong (ligature)
&#199;	Capital C, cedilla
&#200;	Capital E, grave accent
&#201;	Capital E, acute accent
&#202;	Capital E, circumflex accent
&#203;	Capital E, dieresis or umlaut mark
&#204;	Capital I, grave accent
&#205;	Capital I, acute accent
&#206;	Capital I, circumflex accent
&#207;	Capital I, dieresis or umlaut mark
&#208;	Capital Eth, Icelandic
&#209;	Capital N, tilde

Key Value	*Description*
&#210;	Capital O, grave accent
&#211;	Capital O, acute accent
&#212;	Capital O, circumflex accent
&#213;	Capital O, tilde
&#214;	Capital O, dieresis or umlaut mark
&#215;	Multiplication sign
&#216;	Capital O, slash
&#217;	Capital U, grave accent
&#218;	Capital U, acute accent
&#219;	Capital U, circumflex accent
&#220;	Capital U, dieresis or umlaut mark
&#221;	Capital Y, acute accent
&#222;	Capital THORN, Icelandic
&#223;	Small sharp s, German (sz ligature)
&#224;	Small a, grave accent
&#225;	Small a, acute accent
&#226;	Small a, circumflex accent
&#227;	Small a, tilde
&#228;	Small a, dieresis or umlaut mark
&#229;	Small a, ring
&#230;	Small ae dipthong (ligature)
&#231;	Small c, cedilla
&#232;	Small e, grave accent
&#233;	Small e, acute accent
&#234;	Small e, circumflex accent
&#235;	Small e, dieresis or umlaut mark
&#236;	Small i, grave accent
&#237;	Small i, acute accent
&#238;	Small i, circumflex accent
&#239;	Small i, dieresis or umlaut mark
&#240;	Small eth, Icelandic
&#241;	Small n, tilde

B

HTML REFERENCE

continues

Table B.1. continued

Key Value	Description
&#242;	Small o, grave accent
&#243;	Small o, acute accent
&#244;	Small o, circumflex accent
&#245;	Small o, tilde
&#246;	Small o, dieresis or umlaut mark
&#247;	Division sign
&#248;	Small o, slash
&#249;	Small u, grave accent
&#250;	Small u, acute accent
&#251;	Small u, circumflex accent
&#252;	Small u, dieresis or umlaut mark
&#253;	Small y, acute accent
&#254;	Small thorn, Icelandic
&#255;	Small y, dieresis or umlaut mark

HTML Summary for the Internet Information Server and the Internet Assistant for Word for Windows

Neither the Internet Information Server nor the Internet Assistant for Word for Windows support all the tags described in the preceding section. So to make life just that much easier for you, I have listed the supported tags for these applications in Tables B.2 and B.3, respectively.

Table B.2. HTML tags supported by the Internet Information Server.

Begin Tag	End Tag	Description
<!>	N/A	Defines an author comment.
<!DOCTYPE>	N/A	Specifies the HTML version used within the document.
<A HREF=#X>	</A>	Creates a hypertext link where *X* is a reference to a bookmark.

Begin Tag	End Tag	Description
`<A HREF=X>`	`</A>`	Creates a hypertext link where *X* is a URL pointing to another document, file, or bookmark.
`<A NAME>`	`</A>`	Creates a bookmark anchor, a reference for other hypertext links to jump to.
`<ADDRESS>`	`</ADDRESS>`	Creates an address that usually contains the author's name, street address, and e-mail address.
`<APPLET>`	`</APPLET>`	Embeds a Java applet in an HTML document.
`<AREA>`	`</AREA>`	Defines an area on the screen to be used as a hotspot.
`<B>`	`</B>`	Displays the enclosed text in bold.
`<BASE>`	`</BASE>`	Defines the document's URL.
`<BASEFONT>`	N/A	Sets the default font.
`<BGSOUND>`	N/A	Specifies a default sound track for the document.
`<BIG>`	`</BIG>`	Increases the size of the displayed font by an order of magnitude.
`<BLOCKQUOTE>`	`</BLOCKQUOTE>`	Delineates a block of text quoted from another source.
`<BODY>`	`</BODY>`	Marks the beginning and ending of the document content and specifies document attributes.
` `	N/A	Creates a line break. Note that there is no corresponding end tag.
`<CAPTION>`	N/A	Specifies a table caption or header. Must be used within a table tag.
`<CENTER>`	`</CENTER>`	Centers enclosed text.
`<CITE>`	`</CITE>`	Defines a citation, which is generally displayed as italic text.
`<CODE>`	`</CODE>`	Defines a line of source code. Note that this text is usually displayed as monospaced text.
`<COL>`	N/A	Specifies the properties of one or more columns in a table.
`<COLGROUP>`	N/A	Specifies the properties of one or more columns within a column in a table.
`<COMMENT>`	N/A	Specifies a comment within the document that is not displayed on the client's screen.

continues

Table B.2. continued

Begin Tag	End Tag	Description
`<DD>`	N/A	Specifies the following text as a term definition in a term (`<DT>`) definition (`<DD>`) tag pair.
`<DFN>`	`</DFN>`	Creates a definition for an item that you are describing for the first time, which is usually displayed as bold text.
`<DIR>`	`</DIR>`	Creates a directory list.
`<DIV>`	`</DIV>`	Specifies a container (such as a chapter, section, abstract, or appendix) within an HTML document.
`<DL>`	`</DL>`	Creates a definition list consisting of two columns. The term is on the left, and the term description is on the right.
`<DL COMPACT>`	N/A	Creates a compact definition list, which means no vertical space appears between the term and the term description. Note that the `<DL>`...`</DL>` tags are automatically applied.
`<DT>`	N/A	Specifies the following text is a term in a term (`<DT>`) definition (`<DD>`) tag pair.
`<EM>`	`</EM>`	Displays text with extra emphasis. Usually displayed in italic or bold type.
`<EMBED>`	`</EMBED>`	Inserts an embedded object within a document. This tag is maintained for backward compatibility. If possible, use the `<OBJECT>` tag instead.
`<FONT>`	`</FONT>`	Changes the displayed font.
`<FORM>`	`</FORM>`	Creates a form field used to capture information entered by the client.
`<FRAME>`	N/A	Defines a single frame within a frameset.
`<FRAMESET>`	`</FRAMESET>`	Defines the host (or container if you prefer) for frames. For Web browsers that do not support frames, you can use the optional `<NOFRAMES>` tag to specify a document to be displayed.
`<H1>`	`</H1>`	Creates a document header level 1.
`<H2>`	`</H2>`	Creates a document header level 2.
`<H3>`	`</H3>`	Creates a document header level 3.
`<H4>`	`</H4>`	Creates a document header level 4.

Begin Tag	End Tag	Description
<H5>	</H5>	Creates a document header level 5.
<H6>	</H6>	Creates a document header level 6.
<HEAD>	</HEAD>	Marks the beginning and ending of the document header.
<HR>	N/A	Inserts a line on the page. Usually used to provide a visual break between information on the screen. No corresponding end tag.
<HTML>	</HTML>	Marks the beginning and ending of an HTML document.
<I>	</I>	Displays the enclosed text in italics.
<IFRAME>	</IFRAME>	Defines a floating frame.
<IMG>	N/A	Inserts an inline graphic image in either a GIF or JPG format. No corresponding end tag.
<INPUT>	N/A	Specifies a form control. No corresponding end tag.
<ISINDEX>	N/A	Indicates that a searchable index is present. No corresponding end tag.
<KBD>	</KBD>	Displays text you want the user to type on the screen. Usually displayed as a monospaced font.
<LI>	</LI>	Indicates a single item in a list. Used within a <OL></OL> or <UL></UL> tag pair.
<LINK>	N/A	Specifies a hierarchical organization between a set of HTML documents.
<LISTING>	</LISTING>	Displays text in a fixed-width typeface.
<MAP>	</MAP>	Specifies a series of hotspots.
<MARQUEE>	</MARQUEE>	Creates a scrolling or sliding text marquee within a document.
<MENU>	</MENU>	Creates a list of items to display.
<META>	N/A	Specifies non-HTML information to be used by browsers, search engines, or other applications. Note: This text is not displayed within the client browser.
<NOBR>	</NOBR>	Disables automatic line breaks.

continues

Table B.2. continued

Begin Tag	End Tag	Description
`<NOFRAMES>`	N/A	Specifies the content to be displayed by Web browsers that do not support frames.
`<OBJECT>`	`</OBJECT>`	Inserts an object (such as another document or an image) into the current document.
`<OL>`	`</OL>`	Creates an ordered (such as a numbered) list.
`<OPTION>`	`</OPTION>`	Defines a choice in a list box.
`<P>`	N/A	Marks the end of a paragraph. There is no corresponding end tag.
`<PARAM>`	`</PARAM>`	Sets the properties of an object to a given value.
`<PLAINTEXT>`	`</PLAINTEXT>`	Displays text onscreen in a fixed-width font without processing the text for embedded HTML tags.
`<PRE>`	`</PRE>`	Displays preformatted text.
`<PRE WIDTH=X>`	`</PRE>`	Displays preformatted text but overrides the default width (80 characters).
`<S>`	`</S>`	Identifies deleted text. This text usually appears with a line through the middle.
`<SAMP>`	`</SAMP>`	Displays a sample item. This text appears in a monospaced font and is enclosed with single quote marks.
`<SCRIPT>`	`</SCRIPT>`	Specifies the contained text is a VBScript, or JavaScript, script.
`<SELECT>`	`</SELECT>`	Specifies a list box or a drop-down list.
`<SMALL>`	`</SMALL>`	Decreases the size of the displayed font by an order of magnitude.
`<SPAN>`	`</SPAN>`	Specifies style information to be applied to text or other HTML elements within a document.
`<STRIKE>`	`</STRIKE>`	Identifies deleted text. This text usually appears with a line through the middle.
`<STRONG>`	`</STRONG>`	Displays text with extra emphasis (more emphasis than the `<EM>` tag displays). This text usually appears in bold type.

Begin Tag	End Tag	Description
`<STYLE>`	`</STYLE>`	Specifies the way a document will be rendered (displayed) on a client's Web browser. A style is much more powerful than a frame in that a style overrides the user's preferences to display the document as the author intended.
`<SUB>`	`</SUB>`	Displays the enclosed text as a subscript.
`<SUP>`	`</SUP>`	Displays the enclosed text as a superscript.
`<TABLE>`	`</TABLE>`	Specifies the beginning and ending of a table. Note that the supported tags and structure are based on the HTML 3.2 draft standard and may change in the future.
`<TBODY>`	`</TBODY>`	Defines multiple sections for use when rules are needed between multiple tables within a document.
`<TD>`	`</TD>`	Defines a cell within a table row.
`<TEXTAREA>`	`</TEXTAREA>`	Defines a multiline editable text field.
`<TFOOT>`	`</TFOOT>`	Specifies a table footer.
`<TH>`	N/A	Defines a table row or column heading within a table.
`<THEAD>`	N/A	Defines the table heading.
`<TITLE>`	`</TITLE>`	Marks the beginning and ending of the document title. The title appears on the Web browser's caption bar.
`<TR>`	`</TR>`	Defines a table row.
`<TT>`	`</TT>`	Displays text in a fixed-width typeface.
`<U>`	`</U>`	Displays the enclosed text with an underline.
`<UL>`	`</UL>`	Creates a bulleted list.
`<VAR>`	`</VAR>`	Displays a variable name, usually entered by the user. Generally displayed in italics.
`<WBR>`	N/A	Enables automatic line breaks within a nobreak `<NOBR></NOBR>` section. No corresponding end tag.
`<XMP>`	`</XMP>`	Displays text in a fixed-width font.

B

HTML REFERENCE

Table B.3. HTML tags supported by the Internet Assistant for Word.

Begin Tag	End Tag	Description
`<A HREF=#X>`	`</A>`	Creates a hypertext link where *X* is reference to a bookmark.
`<A HREF=X>`	`</A>`	Creates a hypertext link where *X* is a URL pointing to another document, file, or bookmark.
`<A NAME>`	`</A>`	Creates a bookmark anchor, a reference for other hypertext links to jump to.
`<ADDRESS>`	`</ADDRESS>`	Creates an address. This usually contains the authors name, address, and e-mail address.
`<B>`	`</B>`	Displays the enclosed text in bold.
`<BLOCKQUOTE>`	`</BLOCKQUOTE>`	Delineates a block of text quoted from another source.
`<BODY>`	`</BODY>`	Marks the beginning and ending of the document content and specifies document attributes.
` `	N/A	Creates a line break. No corresponding end tag.
`<CENTER>`	`</CENTER>`	Centers enclosed text.
`<CITE>`	`</CITE>`	Defines a citation, which is generally displayed as italic text.
`<CODE>`	`</CODE>`	Defines a line of source code. Usually displayed as monospaced text.
`<DFN>`	`</DFN>`	Creates a definition for an item that you are describing for the first time. Usually displayed as bold text.
`<DIR>`	`</DIR>`	Creates a directory list.
`<DL>`	`</DL>`	Creates a definition list consisting of two columns. The term is on the left, the term description on the right.
`<DL COMPACT>`	N/A	Creates a compact definition list, which means there will be no vertical space between the term and term description. The `<DL>`...`</DL>` tags are automatically applied.
`<EM>`	`</EM>`	Displays text with extra emphasis. Usually displayed in italic or bold type.
`<FORM>`	`</FORM>`	Creates a form field used to capture information entered by the client.

Begin Tag	End Tag	Description
`<H1>`	`</H1>`	Creates a document header level 1.
`<H2>`	`</H2>`	Creates a document header level 2.
`<H3>`	`</H3>`	Creates a document header level 3.
`<H4>`	`</H4>`	Creates a document header level 4.
`<H5>`	`</H5>`	Creates a document header level 5.
`<H6>`	`</H6>`	Creates a document header level 6.
`<HEAD>`	`</HEAD>`	Marks the beginning and ending of the document header.
`<HR>`	N/A	Inserts a line on the page. Usually used to provide a visual break between information on the screen. No corresponding end tag.
`<HTML>`	`</HTML>`	Marks the beginning and ending of an HTML document.
`<I>`	`</I>`	Displays the enclosed text in italics.
`<IMG>`	N/A	Inserts an in-line graphic image. The image must be in either a GIF or JPG format. No corresponding end tag.
`<KBD>`	`</KBD>`	Displays text you want the user to type on the screen. Usually displayed as a monospaced font.
`<MENU>`	`</MENU>`	Creates a list of items to display.
`<META>`	N/A	Defines non-HTML-related information. Usually inserted automatically by the Word Internet Assistant.
`<OL>`	`</OL>`	Creates an ordered (such as a numbered) list.
`<P>`	N/A	Marks the end of a paragraph. No corresponding end tag.
`<PRE>`	`</PRE>`	Displays preformatted text.
`<PRE WIDTH=X>`	`</PRE>`	Displays preformatted text, but overrides the default width (80 characters).
`<SAMP>`	`</SAMP>`	Displays a sample item. Usually displayed in a monospaced font enclosed with single quote marks.
`<STRIKE>`	`</STRIKE>`	Identifies text that has been struck out. Usually appears with a line through the middle of the text.
`<STRONG>`	`</STRONG>`	Displays text with extra emphasis (more emphasis than the `<EM>` tag). Usually displayed in bold type.

continues

Table B.3. continued

Begin Tag	End Tag	Description
`<TITLE>`	`</TITLE>`	Marks the beginning and ending of the document title. Note that the title is displayed on the Web browser's caption bar.
`<TT>`	`</TT>`	Displays text in a fixed-width typeface.
`<U>`	`</U>`	Displays the enclosed text with an underline.
`<UL>`	`</UL>`	Creates a bulleted list.
`<VAR>`	`</VAR>`	Displays a variable name, usually entered by the user. Generally displayed in italics.

The Registry Editor
and Registry Keys

IN THIS APPENDIX

- The Registry   890
- The Registry Editor   892
- Useful Registry Keys   895

APPENDIX C

Although Microsoft has made the Registry Editor available as a tool to help you when you call for technical support, it is not an officially supported application. Therefore, you will not see the Registry Editor in any of your program groups. However, I find this tool so useful that the first thing I do after I have installed Windows NT Server is add this tool to my Administrative Tools group. You, too, can add the Registry Editor by creating a new program item for the Administrative Tools group and specifying Registry Editor for the Description and REGEDT32.EXE for the command line. Windows NT 4.0 installs the Windows 95 version of the Registry Editor (regedit.exe) if it does not detect a shared Windows 3.*x* and Windows NT installation. I prefer to use regedt32.exe because it provides more control, but it lacks the capability to search the registry by value. So when I'm looking for a specific key, I use regedit.exe. The rest of this discussion focuses on using regedt32.exe.

WARNING

The Registry Editor is a powerful tool that you should use with extreme care. All the configuration information for Windows NT is stored in the registry (in binary format). If you inadvertently delete a registry key or value that is required, Windows NT may refuse to load. Your only recourse at that point is to restore the original registry from a recent tape backup or to use the repair process.

Before you start hacking away with the Registry Editor, an explanation of the registry is in order. Once that is out of the way, you take a look at how to use the Registry Editor. Then this appendix describes the registry keys that you can use to modify the configuration of the various services. Finally, you learn other little tidbits that can be handy from time to time.

The Registry

The registry is the central storehouse for all configuration information for Windows NT Server. The registry replaces the Windows 3.*x* INI files, although applications can still use INI files if desired. The registry contains information about the hardware platform, performance data, the installed software, all configuration settings for the services and device drivers, and all OLE, DDE, and file associations. Some of this information is backed up by files stored on your hard disk in your *SystemRoot*\System32\Config subdirectory, whereas the rest of the keys are created and stored only in memory. Table C.1 summarizes the relationship between the primary registry keys and the files that are used to store these keys. The registry, like the NTFS file system or a SQL Server database, uses a transaction log (the version of the file with the .LOG extension) to make sure any change to the registry either succeeds or fails entirely. This method ensures the integrity of the registry. Another interesting registry file is the SYSTEM.ALT file, which contains a copy of the previous system registry hive since the last time a user logged on to the system. The Last Known Good operation uses this file to replace a failed or corrupted system registry hive.

Table C.1. The registry keys and associated files.

Registry Key	Filename
SOFTWARE	SOFTWARE, SOFTWARE.LOG
SYSTEM	SYSTEM, SYSTEM.LOG, SYSTEM.ALT
SAM	SAM, SAM.LOG
SECURITY	SECURITY, SECURITY.LOG
USER	AAAAA###, AAAAA###.LOG *
DEFAULT	DEFAULT, DEFAULT.LOG

*User profiles are stored in the following form: the first five characters of the user name, plus three digits (starting with 000) to create a unique filename. For example, my user name is Arthur; my local user profile is stored in the files ARTHU000 and ARTHU000.LOG, and my domain user profile is stored in the files ARTHU001 and ARTHU001.LOG. I use the same user name for both my local and domain user accounts. Only users who have logged on to the computer locally or who are configured to use a roaming profile will have these registry files. The registry is basically composed of seven hives. A registry hive is a collection of registry keys, subkeys, values, and data. HKEY_LOCAL_MACHINE, the root key for the configuration information of a computer, has several important subkeys:

- ■ HARDWARE—This key contains information about the detected hardware on your system, including your processor, disk controller, video adapter, and serial and parallel ports.

- ■ SAM—This key, an acronym for Security Account Manager, contains all the user and group data.

- ■ SECURITY—This key contains system-security-related data.

CAUTION

The SAM and SECURITY keys are protected keys, which is why they are displayed as a gray, rather than yellow, folder in the Registry Editor. As such, they are inaccessible. The only way to see the data in these keys is to take ownership of them. However, if you do that, the operating system will be unable to access those keys, essentially making your computer unusable. You can restore the protected keys from a repair disk or a previous tape backup (on which you also backed up the registry).

- ■ SOFTWARE—This key contains all systemwide configuration data for the software installed on a computer.

- ■ SYSTEM—This key contains all system-specific configuration data for system services and device drivers installed on a computer.

- ■ HKEY_CLASSES_ROOT—This subkey of HKEY_LOCAL_MACHINE\SOFTWARE contains all the OLE, DDE, and file-association information.

- HKEY_CURRENT_CONFIG—This key is a copy of the HKEY_LOCAL_MACHINE\ CurrentControlSet\Hardware Profiles\Current registry key. It includes information (such as your video driver state) about the currently loaded profile.

- HKEY_USERS—This key is the root key for all user-specific configuration data for a computer. It contains the user profiles of all users who have logged on locally to the computer. HKEY_CURRENT_USER is a subkey of HKEY_USERS and contains a profile of any currently logged on user.

The Registry Editor

Administrators use the Registry Editor to tune the performance of your server, to configure your installation, and to solve client-related problems. As mentioned in the previous section, the registry is composed of keys, subkeys, values, and data. Each data element is one of the following types:

- REG_SZ—A regular string.

- REG_MULTI_SZ—A multiple string value where each string is separated by a carriage return.

- REG_EXPAND_SZ—An expanded string. This type of string will expand an embedded environment string into its actual value. For example, if you include the value %SystemRoot% in your string, the value of %SystemRoot% (normally C:\WINNT35) is inserted into the string at the specified location.

- REG_BINARY—A binary data element.

- REG_DWORD—A 32-bit data value.

The first time you use the Registry Editor, the screen contains four tiled windows. Each window is a shortcut to a specific registry key. For convenience, I have tiled my view in Figure C.1. Notice that this view appears quite similar to the view in the File Manager. You have expandable folders, which are like directories, in the left window; a split bar in the middle; and a right window that displays the subkeys, which are like subdirectories. Values are displayed in the right window with their associated data, which are like files. If you want to expand or compress a folder, simply double-click it. Similarly, just double-click a value (in the right window only) to edit its data.

TIP

The first time you use the Registry Editor, you should set it on read-only mode via the Options | Read Only Mode menu option. This setting prevents you from accidentally deleting any keys or other elements while you browse through the registry.

FIGURE C.1.

The Registry Editor in tiled-display mode.

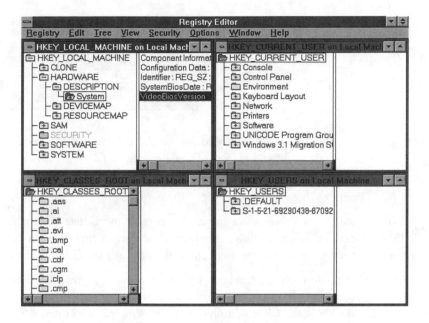

The primary purpose of the Registry Editor is to manipulate registry keys and values. If you want to create a new key or add a new subkey to a existing key, follow these steps:

1. Select and highlight the key in the left window under which you want to create the subkey.
2. Select Edit | Add Key, and the dialog shown in Figure C.2 will appear.

FIGURE C.2.

The Add Key dialog.

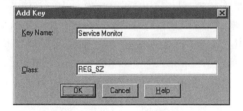

3. Enter the name of the new key in the Key Name: field. Then enter a class type (REG_SZ, REG_MULTI_SZ, REG_EXPAND_SZ, REG_BINARY, or REG_DWORD) in the Class: field. Click the OK button.

If you want to add a new value to a key, follow these steps:

1. Select and highlight the desired key in the left window.
2. Select Edit | Add Value, and the dialog shown in Figure C.3 will appear.

FIGURE C.3.
The Add Value dialog.

3. Enter the name of the new value in the Value Name: field. Then select the data type from the drop-down list in the Data Type: field. Click the OK button.

4. The Edit dialog will appear. Enter the value for the item and press the OK button. The new value and data appear in the right window.

To delete a key or value, select the item and press the Delete key, or use the menu option Edit | Delete. To delete a value's data item, double-click the value (in the right window) and press the backspace key for the highlighted entry in the Edit dialog. Then click the OK button.

Before you go overboard deleting registry keys and values, you should save them. You can do so by selecting the key in the left window and then using the menu option Registry | Save Key. If you make a mistake while editing the key or value, you can use the Registry | Restore menu option to restore the key you just saved. You can use the Registry | Load Hive menu option to load a complete registry hive file under a new key. You will specify the name of the registry key in the Key Name: field of the Load Hive dialog. Here are a few other menu options that can come in handy:

■ Registry | Select Computer—Use this option to open and manipulate a remote computer's registry, just as you would your own local registry.

■ Registry | Close—Use this option to close a remote or local registry.

■ Registry | Open Local—Use this option to reopen your registry if you had previously closed it.

■ Registry | Print Subtree—Use this option to print a copy of the selected registry key.

■ Registry | Save Subtree As—Use this option to save a copy of the selected subtree in text format.

■ View | Display Binary Data—When this option is checked, you will be able to view selected binary data in a split-hex dump format rather than in the raw format.

■ View | Find Key—Use this menu option to search through the registry for a specific key.

■ Security | Permissions—Use this option to view or specify security settings for a selected key.

■ Security | Auditing—When selected, this option displays the dialog shown in Figure C.4. You can use this dialog to enable auditing of the selected registry key. If you want to enable auditing of all keys, select HKEY_LOCAL_MACHINE and the Security | Auditing option.

FIGURE C.4.

The Registry Key Auditing dialog.

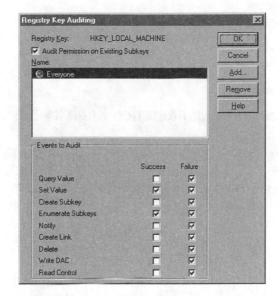

■ Security | Owner—Use this option to take ownership of a registry key.

Useful Registry Keys

This section is divided into four parts. Each part contains tables of registry keys that you can use to manually configure various aspects of a service, including the Internet Information Server services. The first part discusses basic network services, the second discusses NBF transport protocol settings, the third discusses some of the memory-related registry keys, and the fourth includes miscellaneous registry keys that may be useful.

> **TIP**
>
> You can use the Repair Disk utility (RDISK.EXE) to create a backup of your existing registry before you make any system modifications. This way, you can restore your entire configuration and reenable the self-tuning capabilities.

> **NOTE**
>
> I have not included all the keys that are available. If you want more information, I suggest purchasing the *Windows NT Resource Kit* (Microsoft Press) because it includes a help file that provides additional information about some of the keys in the following tables as well as about some other keys. However, I have included some extra information, based on my experience working with Windows NT Server, that may not be documented in the Resource Kit.

System Service Configuration Registry Keys

This section covers registry keys for system services that are not configurable from a Control Panel applet. There registry settings are configurable from Control Panel applets, and whenever possible you should use that interface to modify a setting. However, before you modify any system-service settings in the following tables, you should be aware that modifying a system-service entry may make you responsible for the tuning of your server. Normally Windows NT Server is self-tuning, but adding a key may disable the self-tuning capability. Modifying an existing key, however, generally will not disable Windows NT Server's self-tuning capability.

The Internet Information Server registry entries are divided into four types. The general keys are summarized in Table C.2. The server-specific keys are summarized in Tables C.3 through C.5. The keys listed in Tables C.2 through C.5 are not all the registry keys; rather, these are the keys that I think are important and that cannot be set through any other interface (such as the Internet Service Manager). For more information on the IIS service registry keys, take a look at 10_IIS.HTM, which is located in your *IISRoot*\Admin\htmladoc directory.

The keys listed in Tables C.6 through C.7 are also not all the registry keys for the various add-on services, but, once again, they cannot be set through any other interface. The Server service is responsible for sharing resources on the network; Table C.8 includes a listing of registry keys that you can use to change the default behavior of the Server service. The Workstation service accesses shared resources on the network; Table C.9 includes a listing of registry keys you can use to modify the default behavior of the Workstation service. The NetLogon service replicates the user/group account information from the primary domain controller (PDC) to the backup domain controllers (BDCs) on the network; Table C.10 includes a listing of the registry keys and descriptions that you can modify to change the behavior of the NetLogon service. Table C.11 includes miscellaneous registry keys and descriptions that you can modify to change other system service configurations.

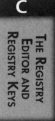

Table C.2. Internet Information Server service registry keys.

Default	Minimum	Maximum	Description
HKEY_LOCAL_MACHINE\SYSTEM\CurrentControlSet\Services\InetInfo\Parameters\ListenBackLog			
15	1	Unlimited	Specifies the number of active connections to remain in a queue waiting to be serviced. A very active site might improve its site performance by changing this value to 50.
HKEY_LOCAL_MACHINE\SYSTEM\CurrentControlSet\Services\InetInfo\Parameters\LogFileBatchSize			
65536	0	0xFFFFFFFF	Specifies the size of the log file cache. Log file writes are cached at the server until the number of log records to be written exceeds this size. A very active site may obtain a performance benefit by increasing this value.
HKEY_LOCAL_MACHINE\SYSTEM\CurrentControlSet\Services\InetInfo\Parameters\MemoryCacheSize			
3145728	0	0xFFFFFFFF	Specifies the size of the Internet Information Server cache. The Internet Information Server caches file handles, directory listings, and other objects. A very active site with sufficient physical RAM may obtain a performance benefit by increasing this value.
HKEY_LOCAL_MACHINE\SYSTEM\CurrentControlSet\Services\InetInfo\Parameters\ObjectCacheTTL			
30	0	0xFFFFFFFF	Specifies the time, in seconds, that objects in the Internet Information Server cache will be retained. A very active site may obtain a performance benefit by increasing this value. To obtain the maximum performance benefit, you should increase the size of your cache by changing the MemoryCacheSize key as well.

Table C.3. World Wide Web Publishing service registry keys.

Default	Minimum	Maximum	Description
			`HKEY_LOCAL_MACHINE\SYSTEM\CurrentControlSet\Services\W3CSVC\Parameters\AllowGuestAccess`
1	0	1	Specifies that guest logons are accepted (the default), or rejected (0) for the HTTP server. Whenever a user logs on to the system, the HTTP server either accepts or rejects a user authentication for non-domain members based on the setting of this flag. Under Windows NT, the Guest account's default configuration may have too many permissions available to the account. This condition could cause site administration problems and possible security breaches. For added security, you should set the `AllowGuestAccess` key to 0 to prevent possible abuse.
			`HKEY_LOCAL_MACHINE\SYSTEM\CurrentControlSet\Services\W3CSVC\Parameters\AllowSpecialCharInShell`
0	0	1	Specifies that clients may use special characters (such as the & character, which is used to separate multiple batch commands) in batch files. You can use these types of special characters to execute random commands on the server. Because this setting can cause a security breach, I recommend leaving this option disabled (the default) unless you really must provide this type of access to your server.
			`HKEY_LOCAL_MACHINE\SYSTEM\CurrentControlSet\Services\W3CSVC\Parameters\CacheExtensions`
1	0	1	Specifies that IIS extensions (dynamic link libraries such as the `dbWeb` extension `dbwebc.dll`) be cached (1) or not cached (0) by the HTTP server. Because it offers a performance improvement at the cost of physical memory, one of the few reasons to disable caching is to free up some memory for other applications.

Default	*Minimum*	*Maximum*	*Description*

HKEY_LOCAL_MACHINE\SYSTEM\CurrentControlSet\Services\W3CSVC\Parameters\CheckForWAISDB

| 0 | 1 | 1 | Specifies that the HTTP server will support the Wide Area Information Server (WAIS) Toolkit searches. The WAIS Toolkit is included with the Windows NT Resource Kit and is not normally supported by IIS. The HTTP server decides to support WAIS Toolkit searches by setting this flag to 1 and then checking for `waislook.exe` on the system path. The default is 0, no WAIS Toolkit searches supported. |

HKEY_LOCAL_MACHINE\SYSTEM\CurrentControlSet\Services\W3CSVC\Parameters\CreateProcessAsUser

| 0 | 1 | 1 | Specifies that the HTTP server will execute CGI processes using the system context rather than the user context when enabled (1). You should not change the default (0) arbitrarily. Allowing CGI applications to execute using the more powerful privileges assigned to the system increases the potential for a serious security breach. |

HKEY_LOCAL_MACHINE\SYSTEM\CurrentControlSet\Services\W3CSVC\Parameters\CreateProcessWithNewConsole

| 0 | 1 | 1 | Specifies that the HTTP server will execute CGI in process with a new console. This key is particularly useful when your CGI scripts include I/O redirection (such as that used with the \| symbol). However, the default is 0 because this option also degrades overall system performance. |

HKEY_LOCAL_MACHINE\SYSTEM\CurrentControlSet\Services\W3CSVC\Parameters\ReturnURLUsingHostName

| 0 | 1 | 1 | When enabled (1), this option specifies that the HTTP server will supply a hostname, rather than an IP address, whenever the server is requested to supply a hostname. This setting is valid only if a hostname has been entered in the DNS property sheet of the Microsoft TCP/IP Properties dialog. |

Table C.4. FTP Publishing service registry keys.

Default	Minimum	Maximum	Description

Default	Minimum	Maximum	Description
`HKEY_LOCAL_MACHINE\SYSTEM\CurrentControlSet\Services\MSFTPSVC\Parameters\EnablePortAttack`			
0	1	1	When enabled (1), this option specifies that the FTP server support access to FTP ports (as defined in the FTP RFC) other than the default of 20 (the FTP data port). The reason this option is disabled (0) by default is that allowing clients to connect to other FTP ports (less than 20, or between 21 and 1024) creates higher security risks.
`HKEY_LOCAL_MACHINE\SYSTEM\CurrentControlSet\Services\MSFTPSVC\Parameters\AnnotateDirectories`			
0	1	1	When enabled (1), this option specifies that the FTP server supply additional information to describe the current directories. This information is contained in a hidden file in each root directory called ~ftpsvc~.ckm.

Table C.5. Gopher Publishing service registry keys.

Default	Minimum	Maximum	Description
`HKEY_LOCAL_MACHINE\SYSTEM\CurrentControlSet\Services\GopherSVC\Parameters\CheckForWAISDB`			
0	1	1	Specifies that the Gopher Server will support Gopher-based searches. The WAIS Toolkit, included with the Windows NT Resource Kit, can supply the search capabilities. The Gopher Server decides to support WAIS Toolkit searches by setting this flag to 1 and then looking for the waislook.exe on the system path. The default is 0, no WAIS Toolkit searches supported.

Table C.6. News Server service registry keys.

Default	Minimum	Maximum	Description
HKEY_LOCAL_MACHINE\SYSTEM\CurrentControlSet\Services\NntpSvc\DisableNewnews			
0	0	1	When set to 1, this flag prevents an unauthorized user from sending multiple simultaneous feeds.
HKEY_LOCAL_MACHINE\SYSTEM\CurrentControlSet\Services\NntpSvc\Parameters\AdminEmail			
None	N/A	N/A	Specifies the administrator's e-mail alias (default is Admin@Corp.com).
HKEY_LOCAL_MACHINE\SYSTEM\CurrentControlSet\Services\NntpSvc\Parameters\AdminName			
None	N/A	N/A	Specifies a text string to be associated with the administrator's e-mail alias (see above).
HKEY_LOCAL_MACHINE\SYSTEM\CurrentControlSet\Services\NntpSvc\Parameters\DisableNewnews			
1	0	1	Denies any client the ability to issue newnews commands.

Table C.7. Internet Location Server service registry keys.

Default	Minimum	Maximum	Description
HKEY_LOCAL_MACHINE\SYSTEM\CurrentControlSet\Services\LdapSvc\Parameters\AdminEmail			
None	N/A	N/A	Specifies the administrator's e-mail alias (default is Admin@Corp.com).
HKEY_LOCAL_MACHINE\SYSTEM\CurrentControlSet\Services\LdapSvc\Parameters\AdminName			
None	N/A	N/A	Specifies a text string to be associated with the administrator's e-mail alias (see above).

Table C.8. Server service registry keys.

Default	Minimum	Maximum	Description
HKEY_LOCAL_MACHINE\SYSTEM\CurrentControlSet\Services\LanmanServer\Parameters\InitConnTable			
8	1	128	This value's data establishes the initial number of tree connections to be allocated in the connection table. The Server service automatically increases this value as needed. However, you should increase this value for better

continues

Table C.8. continued

Default	*Minimum*	*Maximum*	*Description*
			initial performance. The overhead involved in increasing this value as part of the self-tuning characteristics is higher in terms of resource usage.

`HKEY_LOCAL_MACHINE\SYSTEM\CurrentControlSet\Services\LanmanServer\Parameters\InitFileTable`

Default	*Minimum*	*Maximum*	*Description*
16	1	256	This value's data entry specifies the initial number of file entries to be pre-allocated in the file table of each server connection. Set this value higher if your users use more files on a frequent basis. The Server service automatically adjusts the number of file-table entries upward if needed; however, preallocating them can improve performance.

`HKEY_LOCAL_MACHINE\SYSTEM\CurrentControlSet\Services\LanmanServer\Parameters\InitSessTable`

Default	*Minimum*	*Maximum*	*Description*
4	1	64	This value specifies the initial allocation of session entries in the session table for each server connection.

`HKEY_LOCAL_MACHINE\SYSTEM\CurrentControlSet\Services\LanmanServer\Parameters\InitWorkItems`

Default	*Minimum*	*Maximum*	*Description*
Depends on system configuration	1	512	This value specifies an initial allocation of work items for the Server service to use. This value will increase as needed, but preallocating a higher value can increase performance. A work item is a receive buffer used to contain a user data request.

`HKEY_LOCAL_MACHINE\SYSTEM\CurrentControlSet\Services\LanmanServer\Parameters\MaxMpxCbt`

Default	*Minimum*	*Maximum*	*Description*
50	1	100	This value specifies a suggested maximum number of outstanding simultaneous requests to the server. Increasing this value can improve performance, but at the expense of work item usage.

Default	*Minimum*	*Maximum*	*Description*

HKEY_LOCAL_MACHINE\SYSTEM\CurrentControlSet\Services\LanmanServer\Parameters\MaxWorkItems

Depends on system config- uration	1	512	This value specifies the maximum number of work items to be used by the Server service. If this number is reached, the server will initiate a flow-control algorithm and you will notice a performance decrease.

HKEY_LOCAL_MACHINE\SYSTEM\CurrentControlSet\Services\LanmanServer\Parameters\MaxWorkItemIdleTime

300	10	1800	This value specifies the maximum time, in seconds, that a work item has to be idle before it is freed for reuse. Decreasing this value can improve performance on systems that have reached their maximum allocation of work items and that have a significant amount of idle network requests.

HKEY_LOCAL_MACHINE\SYSTEM\CurrentControlSet\Services\LanmanServer\Parameters\RawWorkItems

Depends on system config- uration	1	512	This value specifies the number of work items to be allocated by the Server service. A higher value can improve performance but at the expense of system memory.

HKEY_LOCAL_MACHINE\SYSTEM\CurrentControlSet\Services\LanmanServer\Parameters\MaxRawWorkItems

Depends on system config- uration	1	512	This value specifies the maximum number of work items to be used by the Server service to service raw I/O requests. Raw I/O has less over head than standard I/O and offers the potential for increased performance. If the maximum number of raw work items is reached, then raw I/O requests will be rejected.

HKEY_LOCAL_MACHINE\SYSTEM\CurrentControlSet\Services\LanmanServer\Parameters\MinFreeWorkItems

2	0	10	This value specifies the minimum number of available work items that must be available before a potentially blocking server message block (SMB) is

continues

C

THE REGISTRY
EDITOR AND
REGISTRY KEYS

Table C.8. continued

Default	Minimum	Maximum	Description
			processed. You can use a higher value to ensure that more work items are available for nonblocking requests, but this setting may cause a blocking request to fail.

`HKEY_LOCAL_MACHINE\SYSTEM\CurrentControlSet\Services\LanmanServer\Parameters\MinRcvQueue`

Default	Minimum	Maximum	Description
2	0	10	This value specifies the minimum number of available work items necessary before the server will begin allocating additional work items. A higher value can ensure the availability of work items for processing client requests, but a value too high will not use the system resources efficiently.

`HKEY_LOCAL_MACHINE\SYSTEM\CurrentControlSet\Services\LanmanServer\Parameters\ScavTimeOut`

Default	Minimum	Maximum	Description
30	1	300	This value specifies the time, in seconds, that it takes for the scavenger to wake up for service requests. A smaller value can increase performance but at the expense of processor usage.

`HKEY_LOCAL_MACHINE\SYSTEM\CurrentControlSet\Services\LanmanServer\Parameters\ThreadCountAdd`

Default	Minimum	Maximum	Description
Depends on the system configuration (generally 1)	0	10	This value's data specifies how many threads per processor the Server service should use. Increasing this value can increase performance but will require additional memory.

`HKEY_LOCAL_MACHINE\SYSTEM\CurrentControlSet\Services\LanmanServer\Parameters\ThreadPriority`

Default	Minimum	Maximum	Description
1	0	15	Specifies the server thread priorities in relation to the base priority of the server process. Increasing this value can improve server performance at the cost of interactive responsiveness. Values can be 0 (normal), 2 (background), 1

The Registry Editor and Registry Keys

APPENDIX C

905

C

THE REGISTRY
EDITOR AND
REGISTRY KEYS

Default	Minimum	Maximum	Description
			(foreground), and 15 (real-time). Setting your server thread priority to the real-time setting is not really a good idea because it will consume the majority of the CPU cycles and may prevent other threads from executing in an acceptable fashion.

HKEY_LOCAL_MACHINE\SYSTEM\CurrentControlSet\Services\LanmanServer\Parameters\BlockingThreads

Default	Minimum	Maximum	Description
Depends on system configuration	1	9999	This value specifies the number of threads that are reserved to service a potentially blocking request. A higher value can increase performance but at the expense of system memory. Too many allocated threads can impede performance because of excessive task switching.

HKEY_LOCAL_MACHINE\SYSTEM\CurrentControlSet\Services\LanmanServer\Parameters\NonBlockingThreads

Default	Minimum	Maximum	Description
Depends on system configuration	1	9999	This value specifies the number of threads that are reserved for service requests that will not block the service thread for a significant period of time. A higher value can increase performance but at the expense of system memory. Too many allocated threads can impede performance because of excessive task switching.

HKEY_LOCAL_MACHINE\SYSTEM\CurrentControlSet\Services\LanmanServer\Parameters\Hidden

Default	Minimum	Maximum	Description
0	0	1	Set this value's data entry to 1 to hide a server from client browse requests on the network. Users will not see this as an available resource, but they can still connect to it if they know the server name and resource name. Set it to 0 (default) to allow the server to be visible in browse requests.

continues

Table C.8. continued

Default	Minimum	Maximum	Description
HKEY_LOCAL_MACHINE\SYSTEM\CurrentControlSet\Services\LanmanServer\Parameters\SizReqBuf			
4356	512	65536	This value specifies the size of the Server service request buffers. A higher value may increase performance but at the cost of system memory.

Table C.9. Workstation service registry keys.

Default	Minimum	Maximum	Description
HKEY_LOCAL_MACHINE\SYSTEM\CurrentControlSet\Services\LanmanWorkstation\Parameters\MaxCmds			
15	0	255	This value's data specifies the number of work buffers that the redirector will reserve to service network requests. Increasing this value may increase performance, but at the expense of nonpaged memory pool usage. Each additional command allocates about 1KB, but this memory will not be consumed unless the client actually uses the additional buffers.
HKEY_LOCAL_MACHINE\SYSTEM\CurrentControlSet\Services\LanmanWorkstation\Parameters\MaxCollectionCount			
16	0	65535	Writes to character-mode named pipes less than this value will be buffered. Increasing this value above the default of 16 may improve performance for network applications that utilize character-mode named pipes. Changing this value will not affect SQL Server performance.
HKEY_LOCAL_MACHINE\SYSTEM\CurrentControlSet\Services\LanmanWorkstation\Parameters\CharWait			
3600	0	65535	This value specifies the time, in milliseconds, for an instance of a named pipe to become available when a client open request is issued. If your named pipe application server is very busy, increasing this value can improve the likelihood that your client application will connect. However, increasing this value also may increase the time a client spends waiting for the application to error out if no named pipes are available.

The Registry Editor and Registry Keys

APPENDIX C

907

C

THE REGISTRY
EDITOR AND
REGISTRY KEYS

Default	Minimum	Maximum	Description
HKEY_LOCAL_MACHINE\SYSTEM\CurrentControlSet\Services\LanmanWorkstation\Parameters\CollectionTime			
250	0	65535000	This value specifies the time, in milliseconds, that character-mode named pipes with write-behind caching will allow the data to remain in the pipe. Increasing this value above the default may increase performance of the application. Changing this value does not affect SQL Server performance.
HKEY_LOCAL_MACHINE\SYSTEM\CurrentControlSet\Services\LanmanWorkstation\Parameters\SizCharBuf			
512	64	4096	This value's data entry specifies the maximum number of bytes that will be written into a character-mode named-pipe buffer. Increasing this value may improve performance of named pipe applications and does not affect SQL Server performance.
HKEY_LOCAL_MACHINE\SYSTEM\CurrentControlSet\Services\LanmanWorkstation\Parameters\CacheFileTimeout			
10	0	N/A	This value specifies the maximum time, in seconds, for data to remain in the file cache. If your clients repeatedly reuse (close, then reopen) data files beyond the 10 second default, then increasing this value may improve client performance.
HKEY_LOCAL_MACHINE\SYSTEM\CurrentControlSet\Services\LanmanWorkstation\Parameters\ServerAnnounceBuffers			
20	0	N/A	This value specifies the number of buffers to be used for server announcements. If you have many servers and are losing announcement messages (check your event log), increasing this value can improve the ability to receive and process server announcements.
HKEY_LOCAL_MACHINE\SYSTEM\CurrentControlSet\Services\LanmanWorkstation\Parameters\MailslotBuffer			
5	0	Limited by available memory	If your application is losing mail slot messages, increase this value above the default of 5 buffers.

Table C.10. NetLogon service registry keys.

Default	Minimum	Maximum	Description
HKEY_LOCAL_MACHINE\SYSTEM\CurrentControlSet\Services\NetLogon\Parameters\MaximumMailslotMessages			
500	0	4294967295	This value specifies the maximum number of mail slot messages that the NetLogon service can queue for processing. If you have a heavily congested network, increasing this value can improve your network's capability to receive and process mail slot messages sent to the NetLogon service. Each mail slot message consumes about 1,500 bytes of nonpaged memory until it is processed by the NetLogon service.
HKEY_LOCAL_MACHINE\SYSTEM\CurrentControlSet\Services\NetLogon\Parameters\MaximumMailslotTimeout			
10	5	4294967295	This value specifies the maximum time, in seconds, a mail slot message is held. Messages older than this time will be ignored. This parameter should be changed only on a heavily congested network because each mail slot is generally processed in a fraction of a second. However, if the server is severely overloaded, it may discard mail slot messages that are older than 10 seconds (default) because it cannot process them quickly enough.
HKEY_LOCAL_MACHINE\SYSTEM\CurrentControlSet\Services\NetLogon\Parameters\MailslotDuplicateTimeout			
2	0	5	This value specifies the time, in seconds, that the NetLogon service will use to compare received mail slot messages and discard duplicates. If your server can receive but not respond to mail slot messages, set this value to 0 to disable the discard function. Such a situation could occur if a bridge or router is filtering outgoing network packets. In such a situation, the server can receive the messages, but cannot respond to them.

Default	Minimum	Maximum	Description

HKEY_LOCAL_MACHINE\SYSTEM\CurrentControlSet\Services\NetLogon\Parameters\Pulse

| 300 | 60 | 3600 | This value specifies the time, in seconds, the NetLogon service has to group changes to the domain controller's account database. Only after this time has expired will the changes be sent to the backup domain controllers. |

HKEY_LOCAL_MACHINE\SYSTEM\CurrentControlSet\Services\NetLogon\Parameters\PulseConcurrency

| 20 | 1 | 500 | This value specifies the maximum number of pulses the domain controller will send to backup domain controllers. Increasing this value can decrease the time required to replicate the domain controller's account changes to the BDCs, but it can place a significant load on the server. Decreasing this value lowers the load on the server, but increases the time required to replicate the account modifications. |

HKEY_LOCAL_MACHINE\SYSTEM\CurrentControlSet\Services\NetLogon\Parameters\PulseMaximum

| 7200 | 60 | 86400 | This value specifies the time, in seconds, to wait before sending a pulse to a BDC. Each BDC will be sent a pulse at this frequency, whether its account database is up-to-date or not. Increasing this value can be useful for networks that have little or no user account modifications, or for heavily congested networks, to delay the user account replication process. |

HKEY_LOCAL_MACHINE\SYSTEM\CurrentControlSet\Services\NetLogon\Parameters\PulseTimeout1

| 5 | 1 | 120 | This value specifies the maximum time, in seconds, a BDC should take to respond to a pulse from the PDC. If a BDC fails to respond in this time frame, it is considered unresponsive. An unresponsive BDC is not considered (doesn't increment the pulse counter) in the maximum number of pulses limited by the PulseConcurrency settings. If the BDC is unresponsive, another pulse will be sent to a different BDC. If and when the first BDC |

continues

Table C.10. continued

Default	Minimum	Maximum	Description
			responds, it will partially replicate the account changes and add to the load on the PDC. So if you have several slow BDCs or a congested network, increasing this time setting can improve overall PDC response by limiting the number of simultaneous pulses the PDC must respond to.

HKEY_LOCAL_MACHINE\SYSTEM\CurrentControlSet\Services\NetLogon\Parameters\PulseTimeout2

Default	Minimum	Maximum	Description
300	60	3600	This value specifies the maximum time, in seconds, in which a BDC should complete a partial replication of the account database. Even though a BDC has responded in the time frame specified by the PulseTimeout2 setting, it must continue to respond at the interval specified in this setting or be considered unresponsive. This setting is valid only when many changes have occurred on the PDC and more than one RPC call is required from the BDC to obtain all the changes.

HKEY_LOCAL_MACHINE\SYSTEM\CurrentControlSet\Services\NetLogon\Parameters\Randomize

Default	Minimum	Maximum	Description
2	1	120	This value specifies the maximum time, in seconds, that a BDC will delay before requesting the account changes from the PDC. As a pulse is received, the BDC will wait between 0 and the Randomized value before responding to the PDC. This value must be less than PulseTimeout1.

HKEY_LOCAL_MACHINE\SYSTEM\CurrentControlSet\Services\NetLogon\Parameters\ReplicationGoverner

Default	Minimum	Maximum	Description
100	0	100	This value (a percentage) specifies the size of the data and the frequency of the calls to the BDC for replication to occur. For example, a value of 25 uses a 32KB buffer instead of the default of 128KB and therefore has an outstanding replication call only 25 percent of the time. Setting this value too low may prevent

The Registry Editor and Registry Keys

APPENDIX C

911

C

THE REGISTRY
EDITOR AND
REGISTRY KEYS

Default	Minimum	Maximum	Description
			replication from completing. Setting this value to 0 prevents replication from occurring at all.
			HKEY_LOCAL_MACHINE\SYSTEM\CurrentControlSet\Services\NetLogon\Parameters\Update
Yes	Yes	No	This value specifies that the NetLogon service should replicate the entire database each time it is started.

Table C.11. Miscellaneous service registry keys.

Default	Minimum	Maximum	Description
			HKEY_LOCAL_MACHINE\SYSTEM\CurrentControlSet\Services\Browser\Parameters\MaintainServerList
Auto	Yes	No	This value determines the possibility of a server or workstation becoming a browse master. A browse master is a computer that caches computer and shared resource names that other computers can access to view resources (that is, browse) on the network. If this value is set to Auto, then the Master Browse Server determines whether a requesting computer will become a backup browse master. If set to Yes, the computer is always a backup browse master. If set to No, the computer is never a backup browse master.
			HKEY_LOCAL_MACHINE\SYSTEM\CurrentControlSet\Services\Rdr\Parameters\Connect
300	0	N/A	This value specifies the maximum number of seconds to wait for a network connect or disconnect operation to complete.
			HKEY_LOCAL_MACHINE\SYSTEM\Print\Printers*Printer Name*\SpoolDirectory
N/A	N/A	N/A	Set this value to the directory you wish to use for all of your printer spooling for a specific printer. The *Printer Name* entry above is a placeholder for the name of the printer you installed (for example, HP DeskJet 310).

NetBEUI Frame Protocol Configuration Registry Keys

For the most part, Windows NT is completely self-tuning in its management of network transport protocols, and for the average network, you should never have to change any of the following settings. However, if you are experiencing problems or have WAN connections, I have included some of the configurable registry settings for NetBEUI Frame (NBF) in Table C.12.

Table C.12. NBF protocol configuration registry keys.

Default	Minimum	Maximum	Description
			HKEY_LOCAL_MACHINE\SYSTEM\Services\NBF\Parameters\DefaultT1Timeout
6000000	0	N/A	This value specifies the initial time, in 100 nanosecond units, to use for T1 time-outs. The T1 time specifies the time that NBF waits for a response after sending a logical link control (LLC) poll packet before resending it. Although NBF will adapt over time, it may be useful to increase this value if NBF will be connecting over a congested network or low network bandwidth (such as a WAN link) or connecting to slow computers.
			HKEY_LOCAL_MACHINE\SYSTEM\Services\NBF\Parameters\DefaultT2Timeout
1500000	0	N/A	This value specifies the initial time, in 100 nanosecond units, to use for T2 time-outs. A T2 time-out is the maximum amount of time to wait after receiving an LLC poll packet before responding. It must be significantly less than DefaultT1Timeout; one-half or less is a good rule of thumb. Increasing this value may improve performance if NBF will be connecting over a congested network or low network bandwidth (such as a WAN link) or connecting to slow computers.
			HKEY_LOCAL_MACHINE\SYSTEM\Services\NBF\Parameters\DefaultTiTimeout
300000000	0	N/A	This value specifies the initial time, in 100 nanosecond units, to use for Ti time-outs. A Ti time-out is the maximum time for NBF

Default	Minimum	Maximum	Description
			to wait before sending an LLC poll packet to ensure that the link is still active. Increasing this value may prove useful if NBF will be connecting over a congested network or low network bandwidth (such as a WAN link) or to slow computers.

`HKEY_LOCAL_MACHINE\SYSTEM\Services\NBF\Parameters\LLCMaxWindowSize`

Default	Minimum	Maximum	Description
10	0	Number of frames	This value specifies the number of LLC I frames that NBF can send before polling and waiting for a response. Adjusting this value can be useful for network connections that have variable reliability problems.

`HKEY_LOCAL_MACHINE\SYSTEM\Services\NBF\Parameters\LLCRetries`

Default	Minimum	Maximum	Description
8	1	N/A	This value specifies the number or retry attempts that NBF will make after a T1 time-out before closing the connection. Setting this value to 0 forces a continuous retry operation. Adjusting this value can be useful for network connections that have high reliability problems.

`HKEY_LOCAL_MACHINE\SYSTEM\Services\NBF\Parameters\AddNameQueryRetries`

Default	Minimum	Maximum	Description
3	0	Number	This value is used to specify the number of retry attempts for NBF when sending ADD_NAME_QUERY and ADD_GROUP_NAME_QUERY frames. If your network drops many packets, increasing this value can improve address registration.

`HKEY_LOCAL_MACHINE\SYSTEM\Services\NBF\Parameters\AddNameQueryTimeout`

Default	Minimum	Maximum	Description
5000000	0	Number	This value specifies the time-out, in 100 nanosecond units, that NBF will wait before sending successive ADD_NAME_QUERY and ADD_GROUP_NAME_QUERY frames. If your network drops many packets, increasing this value can improve address registration.

continues

Table C.12. continued

Default	Minimum	Maximum	Description
			HKEY_LOCAL_MACHINE\SYSTEM\Services\NBF\Parameters\GeneralRetries
3	0	Number	This value specifies the number of retry operations that NBF will use when sending STATUS_QUERY and FIND_NAME frames. If your network drops many packets, increasing this value can improve network operations.
			HKEY_LOCAL_MACHINE\SYSTEM\Services\NBF\Parameters\GeneralTimeout
5000000	0	Number	This value specifies the time-out, in 100 nanosecond units, that NBF will use in retry operations when sending successive STATUS_QUERY and FIND_NAME frames. If your network drops many packets, increasing this value can improve network operations.
			HKEY_LOCAL_MACHINE\SYSTEM\Services\NBF\Parameters\NameQueryRetries
3	0	Number	This value specifies the number of retry operations that NBF will use when sending NAME_QUERY frames. If your network drops many packets, increasing this value can improve network operations.
			HKEY_LOCAL_MACHINE\SYSTEM\Services\NBF\Parameters\NameQueryTimeout
5000000	Number	Number	This value specifies the time-out, in 100 nanosecond units, that NBF will use in retry operations when sending successive NAME_QUERY frames. If your network drops many packets, increasing this value can improve network operations.
			HKEY_LOCAL_MACHINE\SYSTEM\Services\NBF\Parameters\QueryWithoutSourceRouting
0	0	1	Setting this value to 1 will specify that half of the packets sent over the network will not include source-routing information. This is useful for bridges that cannot forward frames containing source-routing information.

Default	Minimum	Maximum	Description
HKEY_LOCAL_MACHINE\SYSTEM\Services\NBF\Parameters\WanNameQueryRetries			
5	0	Number	This value specifies the number of retry operations that NBF will use when sending NAME_QUERY frames when connected to a server using a Remote Access Service (RAS) link. If your connection drops many packets, increasing this value can improve network operations.

Memory-Related Registry Keys

You can gain one of the biggest performance benefits for your server by manually tuning the various memory settings to increase the performance of a particular service. The settings listed in Table C.13 can aid you in tuning your server. However, these settings will generally override the self-tuning characteristics of Windows NT Server, so you should use them with care. You should also be prepared for failure messages from other services that use the paged and nonpaged memory pools. These error messages generally show up in the system log, but third-party applications may also use these memory pools. If a third-party application generates an error, it will most likely be in the application log.

TIP

If you start your memory-tuning efforts with a single service and test this setting for at least a week before modifying any other service, you can achieve better results than if you try to manipulate more than one service at a time. Start with your most essential service and then move to your least essential service. With this approach, when an error message does occur, you can just reset the service to its previous configuration.

Pay particular attention to your logs, and use the Performance Monitor (I suggest setting alerts) to track the various services. These services include paged-pool and nonpaged-pool memory-related failures settings, such as the Server object Pool Paged Failures and Pool Nonpaged Failures counters. These features can tell you when you have gone too far with a particular service. If these errors start to occur, you should lower the memory settings you have changed or increase the overall system-pool settings. Keep in mind that your system has can allocate only so much physical RAM to the system-nonpaged-memory pool; therefore, you cannot increase the nonpaged-memory-pool settings indefinitely.

Table C.13. Memory-related registry keys.

Default	Minimum	Maximum	Description
			HKEY_LOCAL_MACHINE\SYSTEM\CurrentControlSet\Control\Session Manager\Memory Management\IoPageLockLimit
512KB	0	Physical Memory —Padding	This value specifies the amount of memory, in bytes, that can be locked for I/O operations. Increasing this value can increase I/O performance on an I/O-bound server. The maximum value is determined by the physical memory minus a padding factor. This padding is about 7MB for small systems and increases as the physical memory increases. For a 64MB system, the padding is about 16MB; for a 512MB system, the padding is about 64MB.
			HKEY_LOCAL_MACHINE\SYSTEM\CurrentControlSet\Control\Session Manager\Memory Management\NonPagedPoolSize
0	0	80 percent of physical memory	This value determines the amount of physical memory that is allocated to the nonpaged memory pool. System services and various API calls use this memory pool to allocate memory that is not paged to disk. The default setting of 0 specifies that the system uses a pool size based on the amount of physical memory installed on the computer.
			HKEY_LOCAL_MACHINE\SYSTEM\CurrentControlSet\Control\Session Manager\Memory Management\PagedPoolSize
0	0	128MB	This value specifies the size of the paged memory pool. System services and various API calls use the paged memory pool to allocate memory that can be paged to disk. A default setting of 0 will allocate 32MB for the paged memory pool.

The Registry Editor and Registry Keys

APPENDIX C

917

C

THE REGISTRY
EDITOR AND
REGISTRY KEYS

Default	Minimum	Maximum	Description
HKEY_LOCAL_MACHINE\SYSTEM\CurrentControlSet\Services\LanmanServer\Parameters\MaxNonpagedMemoryUsage			
Depends on system and server configuration	1MB	Variable depending on size of system physical memory	This value specifies the the Server service's usage of the nonpaged memory pool. Increasing this can increase performance at the expense of physical memory used and may cause another system to fail for lack of nonpageable memory.
HKEY_LOCAL_MACHINE\SYSTEM\CurrentControlSet\Services\LanmanServer\Parameters\MaxPagedMemoryUsage			
Depends on system and server configuration	1MB	Variable depending on size of system page files	This value specifies the Server service's usage of the paged memory pool. Increasing this value can increase performance at the expense of pageable memory used and may cause another system to fail for lack of pageable memory. If you specify a value for *MaxNonPagedUsage*, you should specify a value here as well.
HKEY_LOCAL_MACHINE\SYSTEM\CurrentControlSet\Services\MacFile\Parameters\PagedMemLimit			
0x4e20 (20000KB)	0x3e8 (1000KB)	0x3e800 (256000KB)	This value specifies the amount of paged pool memory that the Services for Macintosh will use. Performance will increase as this value increases, but the paged pool memory is a limited resource. Therefore, increasing this value may cause a failure in another service. This value should not be set lower than 1000KB.
HKEY_LOCAL_MACHINE\SYSTEM\CurrentControlSet\Services\MacFile\Parameters\NonPagedMemLimit			
0xfa0 (4000KB)	0xff (256KB)	0x3e80 (16000KB)	This value specifies the amount of nonpaged pool memory (physical RAM) that the Services for Macintosh will use. Performance will increase as

continues

Table C.13. continued

Default	Minimum	Maximum	Description
			this value increases, but the nonpaged memory pool is a limited resource. Therefore, increasing this value may cause a failure in another service.

Miscellaneous Registry Keys

Table C.14 describes registry keys you can modify to configure items such as the Windows NT source installation path, the ability to log on automatically, the ability to display a user splash screen at logon, and other miscellaneous settings.

Table C.14. Miscellaneous registry keys.

Default	Minimum	Maximum	Description
\multicolumn{4}{l}{HKEY_LOCAL_MACHINE\SOFTWARE\Windows NT\Current Version\Winlogon\ShutdownWithoutLogon}			
0	0	1	Set this value to 1 to add the Shutdown button to the Logon dialog so that anyone can shut down the server without logging on to the system. Set this value to 0 (default) to require a logon to the system in order to shut down the system.
\multicolumn{4}{l}{HKEY_LOCAL_MACHINE\SOFTWARE\Windows NT\Current Version\Winlogon LegalNoticeCaption}			
N/A	N/A	N/A	Set this value's data string to the text you want displayed in a message box whenever a user logs on to the system. Use this message as a disclaimer to protect yourself from unauthorized users. In order to make this message box visible, you must also set `LegalNoticeText` to a nonnull value.
\multicolumn{4}{l}{HKEY_LOCAL_MACHINE\SOFTWARE\Windows NT\Current Version\Winlogon LegalNoticeText}			
N/A	N/A	N/A	Set this value's data string to the text you want displayed in the caption bar of the message box whenever a user logs on to the system. In order to make this message box visible, you must also set *LegalNoticeCaption* to a nonnull value.

Default	Minimum	Maximum	Description
			HKEY_LOCAL_MACHINE\SOFTWARE\Windows NT\Current Version\Winlogon\AutoAdminLogon
0	0	1	Set this value's data to 1 to automatically log on to the system and bypass the logon dialog. Set it to 0 to restore the original settings and require a user logon via the logon dialog box. In order to perform this action, you will need to create the AutoAdminLogon key with the Registry Editor with a data type of REG_SZ. This value must be used in conjunction with the DefaultUserName and DefaultPassword values.
			HKEY_LOCAL_MACHINE\SOFTWARE\Windows NT\Current Version\Winlogon\DefaultPassword
N/A	N/A	N/A	Set this value's data to the password for the user name you want to use to automatically log on to the system. This setting will bypass the logon dialog. In order to perform this action, you will need to create the DefaultPassword key with the Registry Editor. Set the type to REG_SZ. This data value is unprotected and is thereby visible to all users who log on to the system. Therefore, any user can thereby obtain the username and password. This value must be used with the DefaultUserName and AutoAdminLogon values.
			HKEY_LOCAL_MACHINE\SOFTWARE\Windows NT\Current Version\Winlogon\DefaultUserName
N/A	N/A	N/A	Set this value's data to the default user name you want to use in the automatic log on process. This value must be used with the AutoAdminLogon and DefaultPassword values.
			HKEY_LOCAL_MACHINE\SOFTWARE\Windows NT\Current Version\IniFileMapping
N/A	N/A	N/A	This key contains information related to the mapping of configuration data entries. You will find references to USR:, which specifies that the configuration information is contained in HKEY_CURRENT_USER, or SYS:, which is a reference to the HKEY_LOCAL_MACHINE\SOFTWARE key. For example, the MSMAIL32.INI entry is USR:Software\Microsoft\Mail, which means

continues

Table C.14. continued

Default	Minimum	Maximum	Description
			that when Microsoft Mail starts, it will look in HKEY_CURRENT_USER\Software\Mail for configuration data.
HKEY_LOCAL_MACHINE\SOFTWARE\Windows NT\Current Version\SourcePath			
N/A	N/A	N/A	Change this value's data if you want to change the source media path, which is used to copy the device drivers whenever you add new hardware or software to your system. The preferred method is to use a UNC filename (such as \\SRV\CD-ROM\I386) instead of a mapped drive letter (such as E:\I386).
HKEY_LOCAL_MACHINE\SYSTEM\CurrentControlSet\Control\SessionManager\RegisterProcessors			
4	1	Number of CPUs supported by OEM kernel	If you have a multiprocessor kernel installed on your system, you can change this value's data to support more than the maximum (default) of 4 processors for Windows NT Server.
HKEY_LOCAL_MACHINE\SYSTEM\CurrentControlSet\Control\WOW\LPT_timeout			
15	0	None	Change this value's data from 15 (default) to increase the number of seconds that a 16-bit Windows application will wait before timing out. If your 16-bit Windows application experiences printer time-out problems, increasing this value in 5-second increments might solve the problem.
HKEY_LOCAL_MACHINE\SYSTEM\CurrentControlSet\Control\WOW\DefaultSeparateVDM			
0	0	1	Set this value to 1 to have 16-bit Windows applications run in separate address spaces by default. Set it to 0 (default) to use a shared address space.

INDEX

Symbols

* (asterisk) wildcard notation, 613
+ addition operator (VBScript), 533
- subtraction operator (VBScript), 533
{ } (ending braces), 623
3D objects
    CorelWeb.Gallery, 474-476
    CorelWeb.Transit, 476-477
    home pages, creating with Web 3D, 469-472
    rendering, 466
    Web 3D, 466-469
    Web.Designer, 473-474
56KB leased line, 11

A

<A HREF> HTML tag, Internet Explorer, 880
<A NAME> HTML tag
    Internet Explorer, 881
    Internet Assistant for Word, 886
<A> (anchor) HTML tag, 399, 841-842
<ABBREV> HTML tag, 842
Aborted Connections counter, 791
About dialog box subroutine (VBScript), 556
About filename property (dbWeb), 658
Abs function (VBScript), 545
Abstract Windowing ToolKit (AWT), 613
access
    rights, 812, 831
        Internet, restricting, 211-212
        privileges, 829
        user accounts, security, 285
    tokens, 812
    violations, 812
Access 95, Web publishing, 446-451

Access 97, Web publishing, 444-445
Access Control Entries (ACEs), 53, 812
Access Control Lists (ACLs), 53, 812
Access Web site, 445
accessing
    Internet sites, limiting, 336-338
    networks, firewalls, 280-282
    objects, enumeration operations, 819
    systems, 306
Accessories command (Start menu), 298
Accessories dialog box, 171
Accessories menu commands, Dial-Up Networking, 176
Account command (Policies menu), 286
Account Policy dialog box, 286
    Account Lockout option, 287
accounts
    domains, 61
        Guest, 286
    users
        configuring policies, 286-288
        displaying, 294
        protecting, 285
        security, 285-286
ACEs (Access Control Entries), 53, 812
ACLs (Access Control Lists), 53, 812
<ACRONYM> HTML tag, 842
Activate command (Scope menu), 234
active content home pages, security, 277-278
Active Leases command (Scope menu), 239-241
active links, HTML documents, 498
Active Server Pages, see ASPs
ActiveX, 31, 278
    digital certificates, 189
ActiveX Streaming Format (ASF), 638

adapters
    buses, 74
    dongles, 818
    networks
        adding, 85-90
        bayonet nut connectors, 815
        security, 90
        segments, 90
Add and Read option (permissions), 291
Add command (Server menu), 231
Add Data Source dialog box, 661
Add DHCP Server on the Server List dialog box, 231
Add Key dialog box, 893
Add option (permissions), 290
Add Reservations command (Scope menu), 240
Add Reserved Clients dialog box, 240
Add Static Mappings dialog box, 257
Add to Alert dialog box, 762
Add to Chart command (Edit menu), 753, 758, 771
Add to Log command (Edit menu), 756
Add to Report command (Edit menu), 758, 761
Add To Item dialog box, 752
Add Users and Groups dialog box, 293, 309
Add Value dialog box, 894
Add WINS Server command (Server menu), 250
Add/Remove Programs applet, 171
AddDigit subroutine (VBScript), 560
adding
    buttons, 486
    CD-ROMs, 78
    counters, 752
    DHCP servers, 231
    networks, adapters, 85-90
    processors, 91, 774

registry keys, 893
scopes
configurations, 237
DHCP client reservations,
240
servers, WINS, 250, 255
addition operator (VBScript),
533
address class, 812
address toolbar (Internet
Explorer), 175
<ADDRESS> HTML tag, 843
Internet Assistant for Word,
886
Internet Explorer, 881
addresses
e-mail, troubleshooting, 206
input/output, 823
IP, 7, 10, 217, 824
DHCP, 221-223
Exchange Server, 209
firewalls, 281
networks, 265
routable, 35
scopes, 217
static, 222
subnets, 233
SMTP, 207
space, 812
TCP/IP, 217
URLs, 495
WINS, mapping, 244
administrative alerts, 813
Administrative Tools group,
890
Administrator, dbWeb, 655
properties, 655-657
Administrator Preferences
dialog box, 655, 658
Administrator Properties
dialog box, 660
administrators, 57
Advanced IP Addressing
dialog box, 302
TCP/IP utilities, installing,
103
Advanced Research Projects
Agency (ARPA), 4, 6
advertising Web sites, 15, 37
newsgroups, 38
agents, proxy, 838
WINS, 245-248

Alert command (Options
menu), 763
Alert Options dialog box, 763
Alert view, 761
Performance Monitor, 751
Alerter Service, 813
alerts
administrative, 813
creating, 760-766
NTFS (NT File System), 288
object counters, 764-766
selecting, 762
viewing, 751
Alerts command (View menu),
761
algorithms, 813
timeslices, 835
alignment (HTML documents),
382-383
ALIGN keyword, 396
headers, 387
All Events command (View
menu), 316
ALL HTTP (CGI variable), 737
ALL HTTP extension, 704
allocation units, 813, 816
Allow Anonymous Connec-
tions option (FTP Publishing
service), 152
Allow Only Anonymous
Connections option (FTP
Publishing service), 153
AMP (Asymmetric Multipro-
cessing), 813
anchors (links), 399
AND operator (VBScript), 534
anonymous-level security
tokens, 813
antiquated systems, 76
APIs (Application Program-
ming Interfaces), 813
ISAPI, 824
<APPLET> HTML tag, 607,
626, 843-844
applets
Add/Remove Programs, 171
Java, 605-606
alpha versions, 607
compiling, 624-625
creating, 608-624

embedding in HTML,
625-626
initializing, 615-618
painting, 619-621
threads, 622-624
Marquee
code for, 610-613
color values, 617-618
embedding, 625
parameters, 609-610
run method, 623
start method, 622
stop method, 622
Application Programming
Interfaces, see APIs
<APPLICATION> HTML tag,
843
application-termination
messages, 820
ApplicationName switch, 44
applications
CGI, 511
creating, 587
programming languages,
572
client/servers, 815
clients, 216
disk-intensive applications
logical drives, 781
physical drives, 782
e-mail, changing, 182
HotDog Pro, customizing,
487-495
infected systems, recovering,
278-279
Internet, security, 274-277
ISAPI, 30-31, 511-512
defined, 510
testing, 512
third-party, 512
ISAs, 513, 521-524
logs, 312
multiprocessing, 826
processor intensive, 772-774
starting, 774
Remote Access Admin, 120
shortcut keys, customizing,
846-847
TAPI, 46

trojan horses, 277
VBScript
    *function and control
        structure examples,
        555-570*
    Hello World, 529-570
viruses, removing, 279
Windows NT Server, 44
archive bits, 813
archiving, events, 316
<AREA> HTML tag, 844
    Internet Explorer, 881
**arguments, command-line,
    displaying options, 641**
**ARPA (Advanced Research
    Projects Agency), 4, 6**
**ARPA-###.REV configuration
    file, 265, 270**
ARPAnet, 6
Array function (VBScript), 545
arrays
    declaring with Dim statement
        dynamic, 538
        multidimentional, 538
        static, 538
    encapsulated, 237
Asc function (VBScript), 545
ASCII text, 377
**ASF (ActiveX Streaming
    Format), 638**
ASF Editor (NetShow Live)
    displaying, 643-646
    multimedia files, creating,
        642
**ASPs (Active Server Pages),
    628-629**
    browsers, compatibility, 645
    creating, 629-633
    documentation Web site, 628
    files, inserting, 633-635
    include directive, 634
    installing, 126-128
    objects, embedded, 645
    permissions, 635
    scripting, language support,
        628
**ASPs: including files (listing),
    633**
ASPSample.ASP (listing), 631
**assigning permissions,
    WinSock Proxy Service,
    340-342**

associating files, 181-186
    editing associations, 183
    installation, 182
    viewing associations, 183
**Asymetrix Web 3D, see Web
    3D**
**Asymmetric Multiprocessing
    (AMP), 813**
**ATM (Asynchronous Transfer
    Mode), 12**
Atn function (VBScript), 546
attributes
    extended, 820
    fonts, changing in Word 97,
        437
    HTML tags
        <A>, 842
        <ABBREV>, 842
        <ACRONYM>, 842
        <ADDRESS>, 843
        <APPLET>, 843
        <AREA>, 844
        <AU>, 844
        <B>, 844
        <BACKGROUND>, 846
        <BANNER>, 845
        <BASE>, 845
        <BASEFONT>, 845
        <BDO>, 846
        <BIG>, 846
        <BLINK>, 846
        <BLOCKQUOTE>, 847
        <BODY>, 847
        *
, 848*
        <CAPTION>, 848
        <CENTER>, 848
        <CITE>, 849
        <CODE>, 849
        <COL>, 849
        <COLGROUP>, 850
        <CREDIT>, 850
        <DD>, 850
        <DEL>, 851
        <DFN>, 851
        <DIR>, 851
        <DIV>, 852
        <DL>, 852
        <DT>, 852
        <EM>, 852
        <EMBED>, 853
        <FIG>, 853

        <FN>, 853
        <FONT>, 854
        <FORM>, 854
        <FRAME>, 854
        <FRAMESET>, 855
        <H1>, 855
        <H2>, 855
        <H3>, 856
        <H4>, 856
        <H5>, 856
        <H6>, 857
        <HEAD>, 857
        <HPn>, 857
        <HR>, 857
        <HTML>, 858
        <I>, 858
        <IMG>, 858
        <INPUT>, 859
        <INS>, 859
        <ISINDEX>, 860
        <KBD>, 860
        <LANG>, 860
        <LH>, 861
        <LI>, 861
        <LINK>, 861
        <LISTING>, 862
        <MAP>, 862
        <MARQUEE>, 862
        <MENU>, 863
        <META>, 863
        <NEXTID>, 863
        <NOBR>, 864
        <NOEMBED>, 864
        <NOFRAMES>, 864
        <NOTE>, 864
        <OL>, 865
        <OPTION>, 865
        <OVERLAY>, 865
        <P>, 866
        <PARAM>, 866
        <PERSON>, 866
        <PLAINTEXT>, 866
        <PRE>, 867
        <Q>, 867
        <S>, 867
        <SAMP>, 868
        <SELECT>, 868
        <SMALL>, 868
        <SPAN>, 869
        <STRIKE>, 869
        <STRONG>, 869
        <SUB>, 870

<SUP>, 870
<TAB>, 870
<TABLE>, 870
<TBODY>, 871
<TD>, 871
<TEXTAREA>, 872
<TFOOT>, 872
<TH>, 872
<THEAD>, 873
<TITLE>, 873
<TR>, 873
<TT>, 874
<U>, 874
<UL>, 874
<VAR>, 874
<WBR>, 875
<XMP>, 875
permissions
directories, 292-293
files, 292-293
Web pages, FrontPage Editor, 421
<AU> HTML tag, 844
audio only stream file formats, 640
Audio Video Interleave (AVI) files, 174, 466
Audit command (Policies menu), 307, 814
auditing, 813
directories, 308-311
enabling, configuring systems, 307-308
events, 307
files, 308-311
groups, 308
logoffs, 308
logons, 308
objects, 308
permissions, 309
policies, 813
printers, 814
processes, tracking, 308
restarting, 308
security, policies, 308
shutdowns, 308
systems, 308
user rights, 308
users, 308
Auditing command (Policies menu), 309
Auditing command (Security menu), 307, 895

AUTH TYPE (CGI variable), 737, 851
AUTH TYPE extension, 704
authenticating domains, 91
authentication
encrypting, 298-299
packages, 814
RAS, troubleshooting, 118
Author (meta tag), 729
auto-dial
configuring, 176, 342-343
Internet connections, 176
auto-replies on the Internet, preventing, 212
AUTOEXEC.NT files, 814
autorun scripts, 482
available bytes counter, 775-777
Avg. Disk Transfer/sec counter, 780
AVI files (Audio-Video Interleave), 174, 466
AWT (Abstract Window ToolKit), 613

B

B-nodes, DHCP, 220-221
<B> (bold) HTML tag, 384, 844
Internet Assistant for Word, 886
Internet Explorer, 881
Backbone Network Service (vBNS), 6
backgrounds, 467
graphics, 497
HTML documents, 388-390, 497
Internet Assistant for Word, modifying, 448
Word 97, changing color, 436-437
Backup Domain Controller (BDC), 62, 92, 814
BackupDirPath (Registry key), 262
backups
archive bits, 813
DHCP servers, 222

bad-sector mapping, 814
Balance option (Server dialog box), 94
bandwidth, 12
graphics, 467
multimedia, 639
<BANNER> HTML tag, 845
banners, HTML documents, 496
<BASE> HTML tag, 845
Internet Explorer, 881
<BASEFONT> HTML tag, 845
Internet Explorer, 881
Basic command, Internet Services Manager, 142
Basic Input/Output System, see BIOS
Basic Rate Interfaces (BRIs), 12
batch files, 815
batch processes, 815
bayonet nut connectors, 815
BBSs (Bulletin Board Systems), 29
newsgroups, 38
BDC (Backup Domain Controller), 62, 92, 814
<BDO> HTML tag, 846
<BDSOUND> HTML tag, 846
Beep on error property (dbWeb), 658
BeginDetail extension, 704
<%BeginDetail%> (HTX file variable), 741
bgcolor option, 609
<BGSOUND> HTML tag, Internet Explorer, 881
<BIG> HTML tag, 846
binary data type, defined, 237
binary subtraction operator (VBScript), 533
bindings, 86, 815
RPCs, 830
Bindings property sheets, 87-89
BIOS (Basic Input/Output System), 814
Intel, 73, 83
Windows NT, 45
see also flash memory; ROM

bits
archive, 813
hidden, 822
read-only, 829
system, 833
Blat (e-mail utility), 599
<BLINK> HTML tag, 846
<BLOCKQUOTE> HTML tag, 393, 847
Internet Assistant for Word, 886
Internet Explorer, 881
blocks
ECBs, formats, 515-516
NCB, 827
SMBs, 832
body (HTML documents), 378
<BODY> HTML tag, 379, 847-848
Internet Assistant for Word, 886
Internet Explorer, 881
bold text, 377
HTML documents, 384
books (guest books), 687-691
Boolean operators (VBScript), 534
BOOT configuration file, 265-267
boot partitions, 815
boot sectors, viruses, 275
borders (HTML documents), 398
frames, 401
bottlenecks
disks
budgets, 783
finding, 780-783
mirror sets, 782
striped sets, 783
troubleshooting, 782
IIS, finding, 786-793
memory, finding, 774-780
networks
finding, 783-786
Performance Monitor, 784
processors
finding, 769-774
Performance Monitor, 771
**
 HTML tag, 848**
Internet Assistant for Word, 886
Internet Explorer, 881

breakpoints, debugger, 817
BRIs (Basic Rate Interfaces), 12
broadcasts, 220
WINS, 245
browse, 815
browsers, 837
ActiveX, 278
ASPs (Active Server Pages), compatibility, 645
AVI (audio-video) files, 174
backgrounds, 467
CGI scripts, creating custom, 594-599
color
default, 174
links, 174
displaying graphics, 173
Hot Java, 606
OLE, 278
scripting, 278
security, 277-278
views, text-only, 173
WWW, 28
see also Internet Explorer
browsing domains, 245
BtnDelete_OnClick subroutine (VBScript), 559
BtnEvaluate_OnClick subroutine, 559
BtnHello subroutine, 530
BtnHello_OnClick subroutine, 530
BtnTime_OnClick subroutine, 531
buffering, double (animation), 73
Build External Hypertext Link dialog box, 500
building queries, 714
bulleted lists (HTML documents), 390-391
Bulletin Board Systems (BBSs), 29
buses
adapters, 74
DMA, 74
double buffering, 73
EISA, 74, 84
I/O, 72-76, 823
ISA, 73
MCA, 74

PCI, 75
PCMCIA, 75
speed, 73
troubleshooting, 73, 76
VLBs, 74
Windows NT Server, 76
businesses
ISPs, 15-16
references, 16
ordering, 33
publishing, 33
button bars (HotDog Pro), customizing, 484-486
buttons
adding, 486
Calculator program
Delete, 559
Evaluate, 556, 559
deleting, 486
moving, 486
bytes, data types, 237
Bytes Received/sec counter, 788-791
Bytes Sent/sec counter, 788-792
Bytes Total/sec counter, 788-792

C

C programming language
CGI, accessing variables, 592-593
Hello World script, 590-591
C2-level security, 815
Cache-Avg. Free Page Scan counter, 804
Cache-Max Free Page Scan counter, 804
Cache-Scan Limit Reached counter, 804
CACHE configuration file, 265-268
Cache Faults/sec counter, 775-777
Cache Flushes counter, 787, 804
Cache Hit Ratio counter, 804
Cache Hits % counter, 787
Cache Hits counter, 787
Cache Manager, 84

Cache Misses counter, 787
Cache Size counter, 787
Cache Used counter, 787
Cached File Handles counter, 787
caches
    upgrading, 774
    validating, 254
    Web Proxy Service, options, 332-335
caching (Internet Explorer), configuration, 193-194
Call statement (VBScript), 537
calls
    functions, routines, 813
    LPCs, 825
    RPCs, 49, 830
        bindings, 830
        connections, 830
        endpoints, 830
        Exchange Server, 210
        protocol sequences, 830
        servers, 830
<CAPTION> HTML tag, 848
    Internet Explorer, 881
cascading style sheets (CSS), 403
catalogs, 712
    publishing, 19-20
CBool function (VBScript), 546
CByte function (VBScript), 546
CD-ROM
    adding, 78
    HotDog Pro, 482
CDate function (VBScript), 546
CDbl function (VBScript), 546
<CENTER> HTML tag, 848
    Internet Assistant for Word, 886
    Internet Explorer, 881
centralized administration, 56
CGI (Common Gateway Interface), 31-32, 815
    applications
        compared to ISAPI applications, 510-511
        creating, 587
    benefits, 573-574
    browsers, creating custom scripts, 594-599
    capabilities, 572-574
    content type, 586

directories, controlling access, 579
    feedback forms, creating, 599-601
    file locking, 579-580
    Hello World script, 588-592
    overview, 572-577
    passwords, OTP, 580
    Perl, 584-585
    programming languages, 572
    scripts
        interactive, 577
        noninteractive, 575
        server response, 575
    security, 578-579
    security considerations, 580
    system performance, 579
    users, validating, 580
    variables, 580, 737-739
        accessing, 592-594
        AUTH TYPE, 581
        CONTENT LENGTH, 581
        CONTENT TYPE, 581
        GATEWAY INTERFACE, 581
        HTTP ACCEPT, 581
        HTTP USER AGENT, 582
        PATH INFO, 582
        PATH TRANSLATED, 582
        QUERY STRING, 582
        REMOTE ADDR, 582
        REMOTE HOST, 583
        REMOTE IDENT, 583
        REMOTE USER, 583
        REQUEST METHOD, 583
        SCRIPT NAME, 583
        SERVER NAME, 584
        SERVER PORT, 584
        SERVER PROTOCOL, 584
        SERVER SOFTWARE, 584
CGI Requests counter, 788
challenge-response authentication mechanisms, 285
Change Folder dialog box, 654

Change option (permissions), 291
Change Option Type dialog box, 237
Channel Service Unit/Data Service Unit (CSU/DSU), 11
character sets, Internet Explorer, 175
character-modes, executive messages, 820
Chart command (Options menu), 757
Chart command (View menu), 752
Chart Option dialog box, 754
Chart view, Performance Monitor, 750-752
charts
    creating, 752-755
    viewing, 751
Chat command (Options menu), 754
chat rooms, creating persistent, 353-359
Choose a Table dialog box, 664
Choose Destination Location dialog box, 651
Choose Permissions commands (Security menu), 292
Choose Program Group dialog box, 654
Chr function (VBScript), 546
CiBookMark (HTX file read-only variable), 743
CiBookMarkSkipCount (HTX file variable), 742
CiCatalog (user configurable variable), 735
CiColumns (user configurable variable), 735
CiContainsFirstRecord (HTX file read-only variable), 743
CiContainsLastRecord (HTX file read-only variable), 743
CiCurrentPageNumber (HTX file read-only variable), 743
CiCurrentRecord (HTX file variable), 742
CiCurrentRecordNumber (HTX file read-only variable), 743

CiDeferNonIndexedTrimming (user configurable variable), 735
CiErrorMessage (HTX file read-only variable), 743
CiErrorNumber (HTX file read-only variable), 743
CiFirstRecordNumber (HTX file read-only variable), 743
CiFlags (user configurable variable), 735
CiForceUseCi (user configurable variable), 735
CiLastRecordNumber (HTX file read-only variable), 743
CiLocale (user configurable variable), 735
    codes, 736-737
CiMachedRecordCount (HTX file read-only variable), 744
CiMatchedRecordCount (HTX file variable), 742
CiMaxRecordsInResultSet (user configurable variable), 736
CiMaxRecordsPerPage (user configurable variable), 736
CiMaxRecordsPerPage variable, 733
CInt function (VBScript), 546
CiOutOfDate (HTX file read-only variable), 744
CiQueryComplete (HTX file read-only variable), 744
CiQueryDate (HTX file read-only variable), 744
CiQueryTime (HTX file read-only variable), 744
CiQueryTimeOut (HTX file read-only variable), 744
CiQueryTimeZone (HTX file read-only variable), 744
circuit-switched networks, 5
circular dependency, 815
CiRecordsNextPage (HTX file read-only variable), 744
CiRestriction (user configurable variable), 736
CiScope (user configurable variable), 736
CiScope variable, 733

CiSort (user configurable variable), 736
CiSort variable, 733
<CITE> (citation) HTML tag, 384, 849
    Internet Assistant for Word, 886
    Internet Explorer, 881
CiTemplate (user configurable variable), 736
CiTotalNumberOfPages (HTX file read-only variable), 744
classes (Java)
    address class, 812
    defining, 614
    importing, 613-614
Client Properties dialog box, 239
Client stub name property (dbWeb), 658
clients, 27
    applications, 216, 815
    ASFs (Active Server Pages), displaying, 643-646
    database models, 27
    DHCP, 223, 238
        configurations, 223-225
        configuring, 238
        IDs, 225
        leases, 239
        overlays, 225
        reservations, 240
    dial-up networking, 817
    non-WINS clients, subnet networks, 247
    RAS, allowing connections, 120-121
    software, configuring, 344-345
    supporting with Internet service, 9
    viruses, 213
    WINS, 248, 257-258
        registrations, 244
CLng function (VBScript), 546
Clone subkey, 825
Close command (Registry menu), 894
clusters, 816
code
    Java, comments, 613
    Marquee applet, 610-613
    VBScript, hiding, 529

<CODE> HTML tag, 384, 849
    Internet Assistant for Word, 886
    Internet Explorer, 881
codecs (multimedia), 639
codes
    HTML, input forms, 696-697
    opcodes, 827
<COL> HTML tag, 849
<COLGROUP> HTML tag, 850
collecting data, 21-22
Color dialog box, 498
colors
    HTML documents, 497
        backgrounds, 389
        fonts, 384
    links, 498
        browser defaults, 174
    object counters, 754
    Word 97, changing background, 436-437
columns
    dbWeb, queries, 665
    QBE, 673
    tabular forms, 677
command-line
    arguments, displaying options, 641
    programs (IPCONFIG), syntax, 238
commands
    Accessories menu, Dial-Up Networking, 176
    DHCP Options menu
        Defaults, 236
        Scope, 235
    Edit menu
        Add Key, 893
        Add to Chart, 753, 771
        Add to Log, 756
        Add to Report, 758, 761
        Add Value, 893
        Delete, 894
        Preferences, 655, 658
        Tag Information, 500
    File menu
        New, 469
        New Chart, 758
        New Other, 210
        Open, 469, 755
        Open Project, 506

Project Manager, 506
Properties, 204
Publish Document, 505
Save, 687
Save Chart Settings, 755
Save Log Setting As, 758
Save Report Settings As,
760
Save Workspace, 755
Format menu, Document,
495
Help menu, Contents, 483
Insert menu
Hypertext Target, 500
Image, 501
Image Advanced, 502
Jump to Document, 500
Jump Within this
Document, 500
Launch an Internet Service,
504
Table, 502
Internet Services Manager
Basic, 142
Connect to Server, 139
Connection Timeout, 141
Find All Servers, 139
Maximum Connections,
142
Sort by Comment, 140
Sort by Server, 140
Sort by Service, 140
Sort by State, 140
JScript, 632
keywords, 825
Log menu
Log Settings, 316
Log Type, 316
Save As, 316
Mappings menu
Initiate Scavenging, 259
Static Mappings, 257
Models menu
Create Simple Model, 471
Create Text Models, 471
Options menu
Alert, 763
Chart, 754, 757
Data From, 758
Global, 235
Preferences, 253

Read Only Mode, 892
Update Now, 755-757,
760
parameters, 828
switches, 833
Permissions menu, Security,
293
Policies menu
Account, 286
Audit, 307, 814
Auditing, 309
User Rights, 286
Registry menu
Close, 894
Load Hive, 894
Open Local, 894
Print Subtree, 894
Restore, 894
Save Key, 894
Save Subtree, 894
Select Computer, 894
Scene menu, Generate
Snapshot, 471
Scope menu
Activate, 234
Active Leases, 239-241
Add Reservations, 240
Create, 232
Deactivate, 234
Delete, 234
Scope Properties menu,
DHCP Options, 223
Security menu
Auditing, 307, 895
Choose Permissions, 292
Owner, 296, 895
Permissions, 894
Server menu
Add, 231
Add WINS Server, 250
Configuration, 250, 262
Delete WINS Server, 250
Replication Partners, 255
Start menu, Accessories, 298
syntax, 833
Tools menu
Customize Button Bar,
484
Options, 213, 487
Shortcut Keys, 486
Template from Document,
505

View menu
Alerts, 761
All Events, 316
Chart, 752
Database, 253
Display Binary Data, 894
Filter Events, 314
Find Key, 894
Log, 756
Report, 758
Special Characters, 499
Tags, 499
Comment option
FTP Publishing service, 153
NetShow On-Demand
service, 161
<COMMENT> HTML tag,
Internet Explorer, 881
comments
Java code, 613
RFCs, 830
Commercial Internet Server
Web site, 320
Committed Bytes counter,
775-777
Common Gateway Interface,
see CGI
compacting
DHCP databases, 241
WINS databases, 258
companies
ISPs, 15-16
references, 16
ordering, 33
publishing, 33
comparison operators
(VBScript), 536
compatibility
ASPs (Active Server Pages),
browsers, 645
FrontPage, servers, 408
HotDog Pro, 480
Internet Assistants, Office 97,
434
protocols, RAS, 114
Windows NT Server, 46
compilers, 605
compiling Java applets,
624-625
components, events, 313
compressing folders, 892
compression support, 53

Computed Column Expression Builder dialog box, 673-680
computer management, Windows NT, 56-58
concatenating strings (VBScript), 531
conditions, deadlock, 817
config directive, 634
CONFIG.NT files, 814
configuration
  auto-dial (Internet connection), 176, 342-343
  connections (Internet), 176-179
  data locations, installing IIS, 99
  DHCP, clients, 223-225, 238
  client software, 344-345
  frame protocols, 912
  FTP Publishing service, 151-156
    directories, 154-156
    messages, 153-154
    properties, 152
  Gopher service, 156-159
    directories, 158-159
    properties, 157-158
  IMC, 202-211
    startup values, 209
  Internet Explorer, 172-195
    advanced settings, 191-195
    caching options, 193-194
    interface, 173-176
    miscellaneous settings, 194-195
    search pages, 179-181
    security rating, 187-189
    Start page, 179-181
  Internet Services Manager
    Allow Anonymous, 142-143
    Anonymous Logon, 142
    Password Authentication, 142
    Password field, 142
    Username, 142
    Windows NT Challenge/ Response, 143
  Microsoft Internet Chat Server, 348-352

Microsoft Proxy Server, 326-328
NBF protocol configurations, 912-915
NetShow On-Demand service, 160-163
  directories, 161-162
  log files, 162-163
ports, FrontPage Server, 411
RAS, 119-120
Registry keys, WINS servers, 262-263
scopes, 235-236
  adding, 237
  creating new options, 236-237
security rating system, 187
servers, PPTP packets, 301
software, 92-95
SQL Server, 793-802
system services, registry keys, 896
systems, enabling audits, 307-308
TCP/IP, 217
user accounts
  policies, 286-288
  security, 285-286
Web Proxy Service, 328-345
Windows NT Server, firewalls, 300-306
WINS, 220
  WINS Manager, 250-257
WinSock Proxy Service, 338-342
WWW Publishing service, 141-151
  directories, 143-148
Configuration command (Server menu), 250, 262
configuration files
  BOOT, 265-267
  CACHE, 265-268
  DNS, 265
    ARPA-###.REV, 265, 270
  PLACE.DOM, 265, 268-269
Configuration Manager, 49
confirming download, 185
Connect to Server command (Internet Services Manager), 139

connecting
  Exchange Server sites, 209-210
  IIS, Windows NT Server, 8-9
  Internet, 6, 10
    56KB leased lines, 11
    auto-dial, 176
    bandwidths, 12
    configuration, 176-179
    dial-up, 11
    Dial-Up Networking, 176
    frame relay, 12
    FTP Server, 9
    Gopher Server, 9
    hardware, 10
    IAPs, 14-15
    ISDN, 12-13
    ISPs, 14-17
    setting up networks, 7-8
    WWW Server, 8
  RPCs, 830
Connection Attempts counter, 788-792
Connection Timeout command (Internet Services Manager), 141
Connection Timeout option (FTP Publishing service), 152
Connections in Error counter, 792
Connections/sec counter, 788
connectors
  bayonet nut, 815
  IMC, 200
  Internet Database Connector, 824
  T, 834
  see also IDC
constraints, 669-672
Constraints dialog box, 671
CONTAINS (HTX file variable), 742
CONTAINS extension, 704
CONTENT LENGTH (CGI variable), 581, 737
CONTENT LENGTH extension, 704
CONTENT TYPE (CGI variable), 581, 738
CONTENT TYPE extension, 704
Content-Type (meta tag), 730

Content-Type parameter (IDC), 703

Contents command (Help menu), 483

Context switches/sec counter, 770

Control Panel, Add/Remove Programs, 171

Control Panel dialog box, 653

Control Panel System Properties dialog box, 93

control sets, 816
current, 816
LastKnownGood, 825

control structures
VBScript, 537
For Each/Next, 540
For/Next, 540
While/Wend, 545

controllers, 62-63
disk subsystems, single, 79-81
DMA, 74
domains, 818
backup, 62
creating, 63
primary, 62
synchronizing, 818
PDCs, 828
replications, 830

conversion tools, NetShow Live, 638

converting
e-mail messages, trouble-shooting, 206
RPCs, 49
strings to numbers (Java applets), 617

cookies, 193

cooperative multitasking, 816
see also preemptive multitasking

Copying Files dialog box, 172

Corel, 473

CorelWeb.Gallery, 474-476

CorelWeb.Transit, 476-477
HTML Transit, 477

corporate directories, 33

corporations
ISPs, 15-16
references, 16
ordering, 33
publishing, 33

corrupted data, 816

Cos function (VBScript), 546

counters
adding, 752
alerts, 764-766
colors, 754
deleting, 752
FTP, 790-791
Gopher, 791-793
HTTP, 788-790
IIS, 787-788
instances, 759
memory, 775
Network Interface Current Bandwidth, 786
networks, 784
objects, Performance Monitor, 260
Performance Monitor, 750
processors, 770
ranges, 754
scales, 754
SQL Server, Performance Monitor, 802-807
systems, 779
updating, 752

counting objects, enumeration operations, 819

CPU Time counter, 806

CRC (Cyclic Redundancy Check), 816

Create command (Scope menu), 232

Create HotDog Program Group dialog box, 483

Create Hypertext Link dialog box, 504

Create Scope dialog box, 232

Create Simple Model command (Models menu), 471

Create Table dialog box, 502-504

Create Template dialog box, 505

Create Text Models command (Models menu), 471

credit card numbers, 186

<CREDIT> HTML tag, 850

Crystal Reports, 720
installing, 131-132
log files, 721-722

ODBC databases, 722
servers, 723-726
type-related messages, 723

CSnet, 6

CSng function (VBScript), 547

CSS (cascading style sheets), 403

CStr function (VBScript), 547

CSU/DSU (Channel Service Unit/Data Service Unit), 11

Current Anonymous Users counter, 788-792

Current Bandwidth counter, 784

Current Blocked Async I/O Requests counter, 787

Current Commands counter, 786

Current Connections counter, 789-792

current control sets, 816

Current ISAPI Extension Requests counter, 789

Current NonAnonymous Users counter, 789-792

Current Sessions option (FTP Publishing service), 153

CurrentRecord extension, 704

Custom access header property (dbWeb), 660

Custom secure header property (dbWeb), 660

Customize Button Bar command (Tools menu), 484

Customize Button Bar dialog box, 484

Customize Shortcut Keys dialog box, 486

customizing
HotDog Pro, 481, 484
application shortcut keys, 486-487
applications, 487-495
button bars, 484-486
message boxes, 551

CVErr function (VBScript), 547

Cyclic Redundancy Check (CRC), 816

D

DARPA (Defense Advanced Research Projects Agency), 6
data, 17-21
   corrupted, 816
   snooping, 186
   sources
      dbWeb system, creating, 663
      ODBC, 660-664
Data From command (Options menu), 758
Data Source dialog box, 661
Data Source Name, 817
data source name (ODBC), dbWeb, 659
data types, 237, 892
Database command (View menu), 253
databases
   backups, DHCP servers, 222
   DHCP, compacting, 241
   IIS site activity
      adding permissions, 165
      logging, 163-164
   Internet Database Connector, 824
   models
      client/servers, 27
      monolithic, 27
      dbWeb, creating, 664-667
   ODBC, 827
      Crystal Reports, 722
      dbWeb, 650-653
   ordering, 713
   registry, 829
   replications, DHCP servers, 222
   schema
      constraints, 669-672
      joins, 669-672
   schema properties, 667-668
   troubleshooting, 668
   WINS, compacting, 258
Datasource parameter (IDC), 702
Date dialog box (VBScript), 531
Date function (VBScript), 547
DateSerial function (VBScript), 547

DateValue function (VBScript), 547
Day function (VBScript), 547
DbFileNm (Registry keys), 261
dbWeb, 650
   Administrator, 655
      properties, 655-657
   columns, queries, 665
   data sources (system), creating, 663
   database schema
      creating, 664-667
      tables, 664
   directories, 653
   drilldown links, 666
   guest books, creating, 687-691
   help files, 657, 690
   installing, 650-655
   IP logging, 659
   ODBC
      data source name, 659
      data source profiles, 663-664
      data sources, creating, 660-662
      installing, 654
   passwords, 659
   QBE, properties, 672-674
   schema
      constraints, 669-672
      database properties, 667-668
      delete forms, 682-684
      freeform form properties, 679-682
      HTML form properties, 686-687
      insert forms, 682-684
      joins, 669-672
      properties, 656
      tables, 669
      tabular form properties, 676-679
      update forms, 682-684
   servers
      internal properties, 659
      properties, 657-660
   setup wizard, 651
   TCP/IP printing services, 653
   users, IDs, 659
   Web site, 650

dbWeb License Agreement dialog box, 651
DBX Editor dialog box, 687
<DD> HTML tag, 850
DDLs (Dynamic Link Libraries), 30
Deactivate command (Scope menu), 234
deadlock conditions, 817
debugger
   breakpoints, 817
   NTSD, 833
debugging, 817, 825
declaring
   dynamic arrays, 538
   multidimensional arrays, 538
   multiple variables, 538
   static arrays, 538
   variant variables, 538
default colors, browsers, 174
default gateways, 817
Default Parameters parameter (IDC), 702
Default Values DHCP Options dialog box, 236
Defaults command (DHCP Options menu), 236
Defense Advanced Research Projects Agency (DARPA), 6
defining
   joins, 670
   ODBC data sources, 661-662
   properties, HTML documents, 495-498
   special characters, 875, 880
definition files, IDC, 702
<DEL> HTML tag, 851
Delete button, Calculator program, 559
Delete command (Edit menu), 894
Delete command (Scope menu), 234
delete forms
   properties, 682-684
   property sheets, 685-686
Delete WINS Server command (Server menu), 250
deleting
   buttons, 486
   counters, 752
   joins, 671

objects, 471
permissions, 295
scopes, 232-234
WINS, servers, 248
see also removing
**delivering e-mail messages,
208**
**denial of service, Exchange
Server, 211**
dependency, 817
circular, 815
Description (meta tag), 729
descriptors, security, 831
**design models, Windows NT
Server, 47-50**
designing
DHCP protocols, 217-222
DNS, 263-264
Web pages, FrontPage Editor,
421-428
Web sites, 466
CorelWeb.Gallery,
474-476
Web 3D, 466-467
Web.Designer, 473-474
WINS, 244-245
destination
hosts, e-mail, 206
IP address, firewalls, 281
IP ports, firewalls, 281
device drivers, 817
virtual, 836
<DFN> HTML tag, 851
Internet Assistant for Word,
886
Internet Explorer, 882
**DHCP (Dynamic Host
Configuration Protocol),
100, 216, 819**
B-nodes, 220-221
client reservations, adding,
240
clients, 223, 238
configuration, 223-225,
238
IDs, 225
leases, 239
overlays, 225
reservations, 240
databases, compacting, 241
DNS, 263-264
servers, 223

H-nodes, 221
installing, 106-108, 219-230
IP addresses, 221-223
lease expirations, 222-223
M-nodes, 221
NetBIOS, 224
overlays, 225
P-nodes, 221
protocols, designing, 217-222
rebinding, 218, 225
renewals, 224
RFCs, routers, 220-223
scopes, 217, 230-231
configuring, 235-236
creating, 232-234
deleting, 232-234
options, creating, 236-237
properties, 235-236
servers, 222-225
adding, 231
backups, 222
database replication, 222
DHCP Manager, 230-231
Registry keys, 242-243
static IP addresses, 222
subnets, 233
masks, 223
WINS, 223, 263-264
configuring, 220
see also subnets
DHCP Manager, 58
servers, 230-231
**DHCP Manager Active Leases
dialog box, 239**
**DHCP Options command
(Scope Properties menu),
223**
**DHCP Options dialog box,
235**
**DHCP Options menu com-
mands**
Defaults, 236
Scope, 235
dial-up connections, 11
Dial-Up Networking, 817
command (Accessories
menu), 176
dialog box, 176, 298-299
Internet connection, 176
RAS servers, contacting, 119
security, 296-300

dialog boxes
Accessories, 171
Account Policy, 286
Active Leases, 239-241
Add Data Source, 661
Add DHCP Server on the
Server List, 231
Add Key, 893
Add Reserved Clients, 240
Add Static Mappings, 257
Add to Alert, 762
Add to Chart, 753, 758
Add To Item, 752
Add to Log, 756
Add to Report, 758
Add Users and Groups, 293,
309
Add Value, 894
Add WINS Server, 250
Administrator Preferences,
655, 658
Administrator Properties, 660
Advanced IP Addressing, 302
installing TCP/IP utilities,
103
Alert Options, 763
Audit Policy, 307
Build External Hypertext
Links, 500
Change Folder, 654
Change Option Type, 237
Chart Option, 754
Choose a Table, 664
Choose Destination Location,
651
Choose Program Group, 654
Client Properties, 239
Color, 498
Computed Column
Expression Builder, 673,
677-680
Constraints, 671
Control Panel, 653
Control Panel System
Properties, 93
Copying Files, 172
CorelWeb.Transit, 477
Create HotDog Program
Group, 483
Create Hypertext Link, 504
Create Scope, 232
Create Table, 502-504

Create Template, 505

Customize Button Bar, 484

Customize Shortcut Keys, 486

Data From, 758

Data Source, 661

Date (VBScript), 531

DBX Editor, 687

Default Values DHCP Options, 236

DHCP Manager Active Leases, 239

DHCP Options, 235

Dial-Up Networking, 176, 298-299

Directory Auditing, 309

Directory Permissions, 292-294

Drilldown Automatic Link, 665

Edit, 894

Edit Item Entry, 752

Edit Tag Information, 500

Enter schema name, 666

Enter Target ID, 500

Event Detail, 314

Event Viewer Filter, 315

Exchange Server Setup, 201

File Option, 716

File Permissions, 295-296

File Save As, 755

Filter, 314

Format Document, 495

Formatting, 717

Generate Snapshot, 471-472

Global Group Membership, 294

Hello World! (VBScript), 530

HotDog Pro Welcome, 484

HotDog Select Picture, 485

Insert Image, 501

Installation Complete, 483

Installation Status, 172

Internet Connector Properties, 211

Internet Mail Connector Properties, 204, 208

Joins, 670

Local Group Membership, 294

Log Options, 757

Log Settings, 316

Microsoft TCP/IP Properties, 301

Modify Surface and Color, 470

Network, 87, 297, 301

Network Configuration, 297-298

Network Settings Change, 297

New Phonebook Entry, 298

New Schema, 664

Notifications, 206

ODBC Data Sources, 663

ODBC Driver Pack 3.0 Custom, 654

ODBC Driver Pack 3.0 Setup, 654

ODBC SQL Server Setup, 661

Operability, 206

Options, 487

Internet Explorer, 173

Policy, 286

Preferences, 251

Project Manager, 506

Project Manager Links, 506

Properties, 673

Pull Properties, 256

Push Properties, 256

RAS Server Protocol Configuration, 297

Registration Details, 482

Registry Key Auditing, 895

Remote Access Setup, 297

Replication Partners, 255

Save As, 316

Scheduling, 715

Schema Name, 667

Security Add, 302

Select Components to Install, 482

Select Destination Directory, 482

Select Folder, 483

Select Hypertext Target, 500

Server, 94

Server/Configuration, 793

Service, 209

Set Up Files, 476

Site Services Account, 202

SMTP Properties, 207

Snapshot and Animation Settings, 472

Special Access, 296

Special Directory Access, 295

Special File Access, 295

Static Mappings, 257

System Data Sources, 661

Tags, 499-500

TCP/IP Security, 302

Time (VBScript), 531

Virtual Memory, 93-94

Welcome to HotDog!, 483

WINS Server Configuration, 251, 262

WWW Service Properties, 141

Digital AltaVista Web site, 37

digital certificates, ActiveX, 189

Dim statement (VBScript), 537

declaring multidimensional arrays, 538

declaring multiple variables, 538

declaring static arrays, 538

dynamic arrays, 538

<DIR> HTML tag, 391, 851

Internet Assistant for Word, 886

Internet Explorer, 882

Directory Auditing dialog box, 309

Direct Memory Access (DMA), 74

direction option, 609

directives (HTML), inserting files, 634

directories, 33, 37-38

auditing, 308-311

backups, archive bits, 813

CGI, controlling access, 579

dbWeb, 653

export paths, 820

FTP Publishing service, configuring, 154-156

Gopher service, configuring, 158-159

home, 822

NetShow On-Demand service, configuring, 161-162

permissions, 292
  attributes, 292-293
  setting, 290-296
root, 831
sharepoints, 832
virtual, creating, 143
WWW Publishing service
  configuring, 143-148
  properties, 144-145
Directory Browsing Allowed option (WWW Publishing service), 144
Directory Listing Sent counter, 792
Directory Listings counter, 787
Directory Permissions dialog box, 292-294
Directory Replicator Service, 818
  cxport paths, 820
  import paths, 823
directory trees, 818
disabling
  graphics display, browsers, 173
  WINS protocols, 90
disk duplexing, 54-55
disk mirroring, 54-55
Disk Queue Length counter, 780
disk striping with parity, 54-55
  drives, 81
  troubleshooting, 81
disk subsystems, 76-78
  antiquated systems, 76
  Disk Time counter, 780
  EIDE, 77
  hardware, RAID, 84-85
  IDE, 77
  multiple, 81-82
  network adapters, adding, 85-90
  SCSI, 82
  single, 79-81
DiskKeeper, 783
disks
  bottlenecks
    budgets, 783
    finding, 780-783
    mirror sets, 782

  striped sets, 783
  troubleshooting, 782
duplexing, 818
mirroring, 818
partitioning, 55, 828
striped sets, 832
striping, 818
Display Binary Data command (View menu), 894
displaying
  ASFs (Active Server Pages), clients, 643-646
  graphics, browsers, 173
  links, colors, 498
  message boxes, 551
    source code, HTML documents, 384
  user accounts, 294
<DIV> HTML tag, 852
division operator (VBScript), 533
<DL COMPACT> HTML tag
  Internet Assistant for Word, 886
  Internet Explorer, 882
<DL> HTML tag, 852
  Internet Assistant for Word, 886
  Internet Explorer, 882
DLLs (Dynamic Link Libraries), 30, 819
  ActiveX, 278
  ISAPI applications, 510
  loading/unloading, 511
DMA (Direct Memory Access), 74, 769
DNS (Domain Name Service), 77, 100, 216, 263, 304, 818
  configuration files, 265
    ARPA-###.REV, 270
    BOOT, 265-267
    CACHE, 265-268
    PLACE.DOM, 265-269
  designing, 263-264
  DHCP, 263-264
  domains, lookup file, 268
  FQDN, 269
  installing, 109-110, 264
  records, SOA, 269
  servers, 223
  subnets, lookup files, 269

Do/Loop control structure, 539
DoBackupOnTerm (Registry keys), 262
Document command (Format menu), 495
document type declaration (DTD), 377
documentation
  Active Server Pages Web site, 628
  Response objects, locating, 632
documents
  ASPs (Active Server Pages), creating, 629-633
  entering text, 498-499
  external, inserting links, 501
  HotDog Pro, 495
  HTML, 376-379
    ASPs (Active Server Pages), 628
    colors, 497-498
    creating templates, 505
    creating with HotDog Pro, 495-496
    creating with IIS SDK, 510
    defining properties, 495-498
    HotDog Pro, 480
    links, 498
    searchable indexes, 497
    text, 498
  HTML tags, inserting, 499-501
  infected systems, recovering, 278-279
  inserting
    hypertext links, 500-501
    graphics, 501-502
  Internet
    security, 274-277
    types, 628
  Internet command, inserting, 504
  projects, 506
  publishing, 505
  tables, inserting, 502-504
  titles, 495
Domain Guests user group, 142

Domain Name Service, see DNS

domain names, registering (virtual servers), 148

domains, 61, 818
  accounts, 61
    Guest, 286
  authenticating, 91
  BOOT configuration file, 266
  controllers, 818
    backup, 62
    primary, 62
  creating, 63
  DNS, records, 269
  FQDN, 821
  lookup file, 268
  master model, 64-67
  models, 63
  names, 10, 35, 223, 818
    ISPs, 15
    registering, 14
  PDCs, 828
  records, SOA, 269
  Server Manager, 58
  servers, single models, 63-64
  synchronizing, 818
  trust relationships, 61, 67, 835
  User Manager, 59
  Windows NT, 60
  WINS, 245

dongles, 818

DoStaticDataInit (Registry keys), 261

double buffering, 73

down levels, 819

downloading
  files
    confirmation, 185
    security, 275
  HotDog Pro, 480
  Internet Explorer, installation, 171-172

DRAM (Dynamic Random Access Memory), 83

drawing rectangles, 620
  see also rendering

drawRect method, 620

drawString method, 621

Drilldown Automatic Link dialog box, 665

drilldown links, 666

drivers
  devices, 817
  fault-tolerant, 55
  virtual device drivers, 836

drives
  disk subsystems, single, 79-81
  RAID, selecting, 85
  striping with parity, 81

drop boxes, FTP, 14

DSN, interactive web pages, 695

<DT> HTML tag, 852

DTD (document type declaration), 377

duplexing, 54, 818

dynamic arrays
  declaring with Dim statement, 538
  ReDim statement, 539

dynamic endpoints, 830

Dynamic Host Configuraion Protocol, see DHCP

Dynamic Link Libraries, see DLLs

Dynamic Random Access Memory, see DRAM

dynamic Web pages, 20, 694

E

e-mail, 10
  addresses
    HTML documents, 393
    troubleshooting, 206
  changing applications, 182
  destination hosts, 206
  IMC, 200
  ISPs, 15
  messages
    conversions, 206
    delivering, 208
    flames, 211
    protecting, 212-213
  protocols, errors, 206
  relay hosts, 203, 208
  sending, 200
  timeout errors, 207

EAs (Extended Attributes), 820

ECBs (Extension Control Blocks), 513
  formats, 515-516

echo directive, 634

Edit dialog box, 894

Edit Item Entry dialog box, 752

Edit menu commands
  Add Key, 893
  Add to Chart, 753, 771
  Add to Log, 756
  Add to Report, 758, 761
  Add Value, 893
  Delete, 894
  Preferences, 655, 658
  Tag Information, 500

Edit Tag Information dialog box, 500

editing
  file associations, 183
  Web pages, 417

editors
  Registry, 242
    troubleshooting, 261
  WYSIWYG, 695

EIDE (Enhanced Integrated Drive Electronics), 77

EISA (Enhanced Industry Standard Architecture), 71, 74, 84

electronic mail, see e-mail

else extension, 704

<%Else%> (HTX file variable), 741

<EM> (emphasis) HTML tag, 384, 852
  Internet Assistant for Word, 886
  Internet Explorer, 882

<EMBED> HTML tag, 853

embedded objects, ASPs (Active Server Pages), 645

embedding
  Java applets in HTML, 625-626
    <APPLET> HTML tag, 626
    <PARAM> HTML tag, 626
  Marquee applet, 625

Enable File Level Access option (NetShow On-Demand service), 161
enabling
    audits, configuring systems, 307-308
    printers, audits, 814
encapsulated arrays, 237
encrypting, 285
    authentications, 298-299
    ISPs, 298-299
    plain text, 298
    secrets, 831
encryption, setting (RAS), 118
<%EndDetail%> (HTX file variable), 705, 741
endif extension, 704
<%EndIf%> (HTX file variable), 741
ending braces ({ }), 623
endpoints, RPCs, 830
Enhanced Industry Standard Architecture (EISA), 71, 74, 84
Enhanced Integrated Drive Electronics (EIDE), 77
Enhanced Run Length Limited (ERLL), 76
Enhanced Small Device Interface (ESDI), 76
Enter schema name dialog box, 666
Enter Target ID dialog box, 500
    entering text, documents, 498-499
enumeration operations, 819
environmental subsystems, Windows NT, 50-52
EQ (HTX file variable), 705, 742
equivalence operator (VBScript), 536
Erase statement (VBScript), 539
ERLL (Enhanced Run Length Limited), 76
error checking (VBScript), 558
error messages (NetShow On-Demand Server), installing, 130

errors
    bad-sector mapping, 814
    CRC, 816
    Crystal Reports, type-related messages, 723
    cxccptions, 819
    logging, 819
    protocols, 206
    timeout, 207
<%EscapeHTML VariableText%> (HTX file variable), 741
<%EscapeRaw VariableText%> (HTX file variable), 741
<%EscapeURL VariableText%> (HTX file variable), 741
ESDI (Enhanced Small Device Interface), 76
Ethernet, 11
Evaluate button, Calculator program, 556, 559
Event Detail dialog box, 314
Event Viewer, 56
    Windows NT, 312-313
Event Viewer Filter dialog box, 315
events
    archiving, 316
    auditing, 307
    components, 313
    filtering, 314-316
    OnChange, 558
    Performance Monitor, 750, 757
    viewing, 313-314
Excel 97, Web publishing, 438-441
Excel Web site, 441, 453
exception handling, Java applets, 623-624
exceptions, 819
Exchange Server, 200
    e-mail messages, protecting, 212-213
    IMC, 200
        configuring, 202-209
        installing, 201-202
    Internet, 200-206
        connecting sites, 209-210
    IP addresses, 209
    MIME, 203

    protocols, troubleshooting, 206
    RPCs, 210
    security, 210-213
        denial of service, 211
        viruses, 213
    servers, 200
    SMTP, 200
    timeout errors, 207
Exchange Server Setup dialog box, 201
Excite web site, 37
exec directive, 634
Executive, 819
    HAL, 822
    kernel modes, 825
executive messages, 820
Executive Software, DiskKeeper, 783
Exit For statement (VBScript), 540
Exit Function statement (VBScript), 541
Exit statement (VBScript), 540
Exp function (VBScript), 548
expanding folders, 892
expansions
    I/O buses, 72
    ISA, 73
expirations (leases), DHCP, 222-223
Expires parameter (IDC), 703
exponential operator (VBScript), 533
export paths, 820
exporting
    directory trees, 818
    extensions, 513
    snapshots, 467
extended attributes (EAs), 820
extended partitions, 821
extensible platforms, 30-31
Extension Control Blocks, see ECBs
extensions
    exporting, 513
    HTML, Web site, 840
    HTX, 704
    servers, FrontPage Server Administrator, 412-416
Extent Locks - Exclusive counter, 805

Extent Locks - Shared counter, 806

Extent Locks - Total counter, 806

external documents, inserting links, 501

external tools, HotDog Pro, 481

F

Failed Queries/sec object counter, 260

Failed Releases/sec object counter, 260

family sets, 821

FAT

clusters, 816
files, disk bottlenecks, 783

fault-tolerant

capabilities, 54-56
drivers
disk duplexing, 55
disk mirroring, 55
disk striping with parity,
55
network adapters, 56
Windows NT, 45

FCBs (File Control Blocks), 821

feedback forms, creating (CGI scripts), 599-601

fgcolor option, 609

<FIG> HTML tag, 853

file locking, CGI, 579-580

File Manager, 57

File menu commands

New, 469
New Chart, 758
New Other, 210
Open, 469, 755
Open Project, 506
Project Manager, 506
Properties, 204
Publish Document, 505
Save, 687
Save Chart Settings, 755
Save Log Setting As, 758
Save Report Settings As, 760
Save Workspace, 755

File Option dialog box, 716

File Permissions dialog box, 295-296

File Received counter, 789-791

File Save As dialog box, 755

File Sent counter, 789-792

File Total counter, 789-792

File Transfer Protocol, see FTP

filenames

HotDog Pro, 482
NTFS, 53

files

ASP (Active Server Pages),
628-629
inserting, 633-635
associating, 181-186
editing associations, 183
installation, 182
viewing associations, 183
associations, descriptions, 184
auditing, 308-311
AUTOEXEC.NT, 814
AVI, 466
backups, archive bits, 813
batch, 815
bits, read-only, 829
CONFIG.NT, 814
configuration, DNS, 265-270
definitions, IDC, 702
downloading
confirmation, 185
security, 275
export paths, 820
help, dbWeb, 657, 690
HTX (HTML Extension),
728
creating, 739-741
read-only variables,
743-744
variables, 741-742
I/O mappings, 826
IDC, Sign-In-IDC.HTX,
706, 708
IDQ (Internet Data Query),
728
creating, 734
IFS, 823
INF, 823
.ini, 890
inserting, directives, 634
interfaces, creating, 700-703

log, Crystal Reports,
721-722
multimedia
creating streams, 641-642
formats, 640
paging, 827
parsing, 378
partitioning, boot, 815
paths, relative compared to
virtual, 633
permissions, 292
attributes, 292-293
setting, 290-296
registry keys, 891
SearchGuestBook.HTX, 709
Sign-In-IDC.IDC, 700-701
snapshots, exporting, 467
swap, 827
SYSTEM.MDB, 241-242
systems, 833
WINDBG.EXE, 837

fillRect method, 620

Filter dialog box, 314

Filter Events command (View menu), 314

filtering, events, 314-316

filters, ISAPI, 31

Find All Servers command (Internet Services Manager),
139

Find Key command (View menu), 894

finding bottlenecks

disks, 780-783
IIS, 786-793
memory, 774-780
networks, 783-786
processors, 769-774

fingering, 305

firewalls, 280-282

configuring, Windows NT
Server, 300-306
destination IP address, 281
destination IP ports, 281
protocols, 281
source IP addresses, 281
source IP ports, 281

Fix function (VBScript), 549

fixed-width fonts (HTML documents), 380, 386-387

fixed-width fonts (Internet Explorer), 175

flames, 211
flash memory, 821
#flastmod directive, 634
floating-point division
 operator, 533
<FN> HTML tag, 853
folders, Registry Editor, 892
<FONT> HTML tag, 384, 854
 Internet Explorer, 882
fonts
 fixed-width, HTML
  documents, 380, 386-387
 HTML documents, 497
  color, 384
  size, 384
 Internet Assistant for Word,
  449
 Internet Explorer, 175
  fixed-width, 175
  proportional, 175
 proportional, HTML
  documents, 380
 reading, Java applets, 621
 selecting for Java applets, 615
 setting current, Java applets,
  619-620
 Word 97, changing
  attributes, 437
For Each/Next control
 structure (VBScript), 540
For/Next control structure
 (VBScript), 540
Forcibly Disconnect Remote
 Users from Server, 288
<FORM> HTML tag, 854
 Internet Assistant for Word,
  886
 Internet Explorer, 882
Format Document dialog box,
 495
Format menu commands,
 Document, 495
formats, ECBs, 515-516
formatting
 dialog box, 717
 documents, text, 498
 tables, Internet Assistant for
  Word, 450
forms
 CGI scripts, creating,
  599-601
 creating for Web pages,
  695-696

delete, properties, 682-684
freeforms
 properties, 679-682
 property sheets, 681-682
 HTML, properties, 686-687
 inputs, creating, 696-700
 insert, properties, 682-684
 orders, 712
 search, Index Information
  Server, 730-733
 tabular, properties, 676-679
 update, properties, 682-684
FQDN (Fully Qualified
 Domain Name), 269, 821
frame relay, 12
 bandwidths, 12
<FRAME> HTML tag, 854
frames
 FrontPage Editor, 422-424
 HTML documents, 394,
  401-403
frames protocol configuration
 registry keys, 912
<FRAMESET> HTML tag, 855
framesets, 401
freeform forms
 properties, 679-682
 property sheets, 681-682
 queries, 715
FrontPage, 695
 Editor, 421
  attributes, 421
  designing, 421-428
  frames, 422-424
  scripts, 427-429
  tables, 425-427
  templates, 430
 Explorer, 416
  Summary View, 418
  Web pages, editing, 417
 installing, 408-409
 links, verifying, 420
 Personal Web Server,
  installing, 408
 Server, 410
  *ports, changing default,
  411*
  server extensions, 412-416
 Server Administrator,
  412-416
 Server Extensions, installing,
  132-133

servers, compatibility, 408
To Do List, 419
fsize directive, 634
FTP (File Transfer Protocol),
 821, 304
 drop box, 14
 performance counters,
  790-791
 registry keys, 900
 sites, security, 274
FTP Publishing service
 Allow Anonymous Connec-
  tions option, 152
 Allow Only Anonymous
  Connections option, 153
 Comment option, 153
 configuring, 151-156
 Connection Timeout option,
  152
 Current Sessions option, 153
 directories, configuring,
  154-156
 Maximum Connections
  option, 152
 messages, configuring,
  153-154
 Password option, 153
 properties, configuring, 152
 Username option, 152
FTP Server, 27
 Internet, connecting to, 9
 publishing services, 29
Full Control option (Permis-
 sions), 291
%Full counter, 807
Fully Qualified Domain Name
 (FQDN), 269, 821
Function statement (VBScript),
 541
functions
 GetExtensionVersion,
  513-515
 GetServerVariable, 514,
  517-519
 HttpExtensionProc, 513-517
 ReadClient, 514, 519
 routines, 813
 ServerSupportFunction, 514,
  520-521
 VBScript, 545-570
  Abs, 545
  Array, 545

Asc, 545
Atn, 546
CBool, 546
CByte, 546
CDate, 546
CDbl, 546
Chr, 546
CInt, 546
CLng, 546
Cos, 546
CSng, 547
CStr, 547
CVErr, 547
Date, 547
DateSerial, 547
Day, 547
Exp, 548
Fix, 549
Hex, 548
Hour, 548
InputBox, 548
Instr, 548
Int, 549
IsArray, 549
IsDate, 546, 549
IsEmpty, 549
IsError, 549
IsNull, 549
IsNumeric, 549
IsObject, 549
LBound, 550
LCase, 550
Left, 550
Len, 550
Log, 550
LTrim, 550
Mid, 550
Minute, 550
Month, 550
MsgBox, 551
Now, 552
Oct, 552
Right, 552
Rnd, 552
RTrim, 550
Second, 552
Sgn, 552
Sin, 552
Sqr, 553
Str, 553
StrComp, 553
String, 553
Tan, 553

Time, 553
TimeValue, 553
Trim, 550
UBound, 554
UCase, 554
Val, 554
VarType, 554
Weekday, 555
Year, 555
VBScript, DateValue, 547
WriteClient, 514, 519-520

G

Gallery option (Chart Options dialog box), 755
GATEWAY INTERFACE (CGI variable), 581, 705, 738
gateways, defaults, 817
General property sheet, 174
Generate Snapshot command (Scene menu), 471-472
Get Requests counter, 789
GetExtensionVersion function (ISAs), 513-515
GetServerVariable function (ISAs), 514, 517-519
GIF (Graphical Interchange Format) files
    background images, 388
    snapshots, exporting, 467
Global command (Options menu), 235
Global Group Membership dialog box, 294
global groups, 821
    see also local groups
Gopher, 304
    performance counters, 791-793
    publishing text, 21
    registry keys, 900
Gopher Plus Requests counter, 792
Gopher Server, 9, 27
    publishing services, 29
Gopher service
    configuring, 156-159
    directories, configuring, 158-159
    properties, configuring, 157-158

granting permissions, access rights, 812
graphics
    3D, designing, 470
    backgrounds, 497
    bandwidths, 467
    browsers, displaying, 173
    CorelWeb.Gallery, 474-476
    CorelWeb.Transit, 476-477
    HTML documents, 394-396
    inserting into documents, 501-502
    labeling in VBScript, 566
    objects, inserting into home pages, 471
    ray traced, 471
    realistic with shadows, 471
    rendering, 471
    solid models, 471
    Web 3D, 467-469
    Web.Designer, 473-474
    wireframes, 471
greater than operator (VBScript), 537
greater than or equal to operator (VBScript), 537
Group Conflicts/sec object counter, 260
Group Registrations/sec object counter, 260
Group Renewals/sec object counter, 260
groups
    auditing, 308
    local, 825
        Guests, 286
GT (HTX file variable), 705, 742
guard-page protection, 821
Guest domains, accounts, 286
guest books, creating with dbWeb, 687-691
Guests local group, 286

H

H-nodes, 221
<H1> HTML tag, 855
    Internet Assistant for Word, 887
    Internet Explorer, 882

\<H2\> HTML tag, 855
  Internet Assistant for Word, 887
  Internet Explorer, 882
\<H3\> HTML tag, 856
  Internet Assistant for Word, 887
  Internet Explorer, 882
\<H4\> HTML tag, 856
  Internet Assistant for Word, 887
  Internet Explorer, 882
\<H5\> HTML tag, 856
  Internet Assistant for Word, 887
  Internet Explorer, 883
\<H6\> HTML tag, 857
  Internet Assistant for Word, 887
hackers, 186
HAL (Hardware Abstraction Layer), 50, 91, 822
handles, 821
hard drives, disk subsystems, 79-81
hardware, 10, 15
  RAID, 84-85
  upgrades, 83
  Windows NT Server, 71
Hardware Abstraction Layer (HAL), 50, 91, 822
HARDWARE registry key, 891
Haynes & Company Web site, 36
head (HTML documents), 378
Head Requests counter, 789
\<HEAD\> HTML tag, 857
  Internet Assistant for Word, 887
  Internet Explorer, 883
headers (HTML documents), 387-388
  centered, 398
  tables, 397
Hello World application, 588-592
  listing, 532
  with VBScript, 529-570
Hello World! dialog box (VBScript), 530
help desks, 33
help files, dbWeb, 657, 690

Help menu commands, Contents, 483
Hex function (VBScript), 548-549
hexadecimals, 822
hidden bits, 822
Hide, 696, 702
hiding VBScript code, 529
High Memory Area (HMA), 822
history file (Internet Explorer), 181
hives, 822
HKEY CLASSES ROOT registry key, 891
HKEY CURRENT CONFIG registry key, 892
HKEY USERS registry key, 892
HMA (High Memory Area), 822
home directories, 822
home pages
  creating with Web 3D, 469-472
  Microsoft VBScript, 528
  objects, inserting, 471
Horizontal Grid option (Chart Options dialog box), 755
horizontal lines (HTML documents), 393
hosting, servers, 14
hostnames, networks, 265
hosts, IP addresses, 10
Hot Java, 606
hot keys, 822
hot swapping, 85
HotDog Pro, 480-481
  compatibility, 480
  customizing, 481, 484
    application shortcut keys, 486-487
    applications, 487-495
    button bars, 484-486
  documents, 495
    defining properties, 495-498
    entering text, 498-499
    HTML, creating, 495-496
    inserting HTML tags, 499-501
    inserting hypertext links, 500-501
    inserting tables, 502-504

external tools, 481
filenames, 482
graphics, inserting into documents, 501-502
HTML, 481
  syntax checker, 481
HTML documents, 480
  creating templates, 505
  publishing, 505
installing, 481-483
projects, 481, 506
spell checker, 481
templates, 495
tutorial, 483
HotDog Pro Select Picture dialog box, 485
HotDog Pro Welcome dialog box, 484
HotSpot subroutine (VBScript), 567
Hour function (VBScript), 548
\<HPn\> HTML tag, 857
\<HR\> (horizontal rule) HTML tag, 393, 857
  Internet Assistant for Word, 887
  Internet Explorer, 883
HSE STATUS ERROR status code, 517
HSE STATUS PENDING status code, 517
HSE STATUS SUCCESS AND KEEP CONN status code, 517
HSE STATUS SUCCESS status code, 517
HSE VERSION INFO structure, 514
HTML (HyperText Markup Language), 376, 822, 840
  bold text, 377
  codes, input forms, 696-697
  compared to SGML, 378
  documents
    ASPs (Active Server Pages), 628
    colors, 497
    colors of links, 498
    creating templates, 505
    creating with HotDog Pro, 495-496
    creating with IIS SDK, 510

defining properties,
  495-498
HotDog Pro, 480
inserting hypertext links,
  500-501
links, 498
projects, 506
publishing, 505
searchable indexes, 497
text, 498
embedding Java applets in,
  625-626
  <APPLET> HTML tag,
    626
  <PARAM> HTML tag,
    626
extensions Web site, 840
forms, properties, 686-687
HotDog Pro, 481
  syntax checker, 481
insert statement, 633
parsing files, 378
skeleton, 378
special characters, defining,
  875, 880
syntax, 376
tags, 840
  <A>, 841-842
  <ABBREV>, 842
  <ACRONYM>, 842
  <ADDRESS>, 843
  <APPLET>, 607, 626,
    843-844
  <AREA>, 844
  <AU>, 844
  <B>, 844
  <BANNER>, 845
  <BASE>, 845
  <BASEFONT>, 845
  <BDO>, 846
  <BGSOUND>, 846
  <BIG>, 846
  <BLINK>, 846
  <BLOCKQUOTE>, 847
  <BODY>, 847-848

, 848
  <CAPTION>, 848
  <CENTER>, 848
  <CITE>, 849
  <CODE>, 849
  <COL>, 849
  <COLGROUP>, 850
  <CREDIT>, 850

<DD>, 850
<DEL>, 851
<DFN>, 851
<DIR>, 851
<DIV>, 852
<DL>, 852
<DT>, 852
<EM>, 852
<EMBED>, 853
<FIG>, 853
<FN>, 853
<FONT>, 854
<FORM>, 854
<FRAME>, 854
<FRAMESET>, 855
<H1>, 855
<H2>, 855
<H3>, 856
<H4>, 856
<H5>, 856
<H6>, 857
<HEAD>, 857
<HPn>, 857
<HR>, 857
<HTML>, 858
<I>, 858
<IMG>, 858-859
<INPUT>, 859
<INS>, 859
inserting into documents,
  499-501
Internet Assistant for Word,
  886-888
Internet Explorer, 880-885
<ISINDEX>, 860
<KBD>, 860
<LANG>, 860
<LH>, 861
<LI>, 861
<LINK>, 861
<LISTING>, 861
<MAP>, 862
<MARQUEE>, 862
<MENU>, 863
<META>, 729-730, 863
<NEXTID>, 863
<NOBR>, 864
<NOEMBED>, 864
<NOFRAMES>, 864
<NOTE>, 864
<OBJECT>, 645
<OL>, 865

<OPTION>, 865
<OVERLAY>, 865
<P>, 866
<PARAM>, 626, 866
<PERSON>, 866
<PLAINTEXT>, 866
<PRE>, 867
<Q>, 867
<S>, 867
<SAMP>, 868
<SCRIPT>, 632
<SELECT>, 868
<SMALL>, 868
<SPAN>, 869
<STRIKE>, 869
<STRONG>, 869
<SUB>, 870
<SUP>, 870
<TAB>, 870
<TABLE>, 870
Tags dialog box, 499-500
<TBODY>, 871
<TD>, 871
<TEXTAREA>, 872
<TFOOT>, 872
<TH>, 872
<THEAD>, 873
<TITLE>, 873
<TR>, 873
<TT>, 874
<U>, 874
<UL>, 874
<VAR>, 874
<WBR>, 875
<XMP>, 875
templates, creating, 703-712
tutorial, 483
Word 97, creating Web
  pages, 434
**HTML code for displaying ASP
  documents (listing), 630**
**HTML code for IDQ file
  (listing), 734**
**HTML code from an HTX file
  (listing), 739-740**
HTML documents, 376-379
  advanced techniques,
    394-405
  alignment, 382-383
    headers, 387
  background, 388-390
    color, 389

body, 378
borders, 398
    frames, 401
cascading style sheets, 403
display, maximum character
    amount, 387
e-mail addresses, 393
fonts
    color, 384
    fixed-width, 380-387
    proportional, 380
    size, 384
frames, 394, 401-403
graphics, 394-396
head, 378
headers, 387-388
    alignment, 387
    centered, 398
    tables, 397
horizontal lines, 393
indentation, 383
justification, 383
line breaks, 393
links, 399-400
    anchors, 399
lists, 391-392
    bulleted lists, 390-391
    numbered lists, 390-391
live video, 395
meta tags, 404-405
page attributes, 388-390
paragraph attributes, 382-383
paragraph breaks, 381
quotes, 393
source code, displaying, 384
style sheets, 403
styles, 404
tables, 381, 397-399
    headers, 397
    rows, 397
testing, 376
text
    attributes, 383, 386
    bold, 384
    italic, 384
titles, 379
**HTML Extension files, see HTX
files**
**HTML Header Type property
(dbWeb), 659**
HTML Transit, 477

<HTML> HTML tag, 379, 858
    Internet Assistant for Word,
    887
    Internet Explorer, 883
**HTMLQueryForm variable,
733**
**HTTP (HyperText Transfer
Protocol), 28, 400, 823**
    performance counters,
    788-790
    servers, ISAs, 513
**HTTP ACCEPT (CGI variable),
581, 738**
HTTP ACCEPT extension, 705
**HTTP USER AGENT CGI
variable, 582**
**HttpExtensionProc function
(ISAs), 513-517**
**HTTPS (HyperText Transfer
Protocol Secure), 400, 823**
**HTX (HTML Extension) files,
728**
    creating, 739-741
    variables, 741-742
        read-only, 743-744
HTX extensions, 704
**HTX file (HTML code), listing,
740**
hypertext links, see links
**HyperText Markup Language,
see HTML**
**Hypertext Target command
(Insert menu), 500**
**HyperText Transfer Protocol
Secure (HTTPS), 400, 823**
**HyperText Transfer Protocol,
see HTTP**

I

I/O
    buses, 72-76, 823
        adapters, 74
        DMA, 74
        double buffering, 73
        EISA, 74
        expansions, 72
        ISA, 73
        MCA, 74
        PCI, 75
        PCMCIA, 75

    servers, 75
    troubleshooting, 73, 76
    VLBs, 74
    Windows NT Server, 76
    mappings, 826
**I/O - Trans. Per Log Record
counter, 803**
**I/O Batch Average Size
counter, 802**
**I/O Batch Max Size counter,
803**
**I/O Batch Writes/sec counter,
802**
**I/O Log Writes/sec counter,
802**
I/O Manager, 50
**I/O Outstanding Reads
counter, 803**
**I/O Outstanding Writes
counter, 803**
**I/O Page Reads/sec counters,
803**
**I/O Single page Writes/sec
counter, 803**
**I/O Transactions/sec counter,
803**
<I> (italic) HTML tag, 384, 858
    Internet Assistant for Word,
    887
    Internet Explorer, 883
**IAPs (Internet Access Provid-
ers), 14-15, 823**
ICMP, 303
**IDC (Internet Database
Connector), 686, 694**
    files
        definitions, 702
        *SearchGuestBook.HTX,
        709*
        *Sign-In-IDC.HTX,
        706-708*
    HTML templates, creating,
    703-712
    interface files, creating,
    700-703
    layout, 694
    parameters, 701-702
    SQL Server, Web Assistant,
    712-718
    Web pages, creating forms,
    695-696

IDE (Integrated Drive Electronics), 77
identifiers
  handles, 821
  SIDs, 831
  URIs, 835
  UUID, 836
IDQ (Internet Data Query) files, 728
  creating, 734
IDs
  DHCP, clients, 225
  users, dbWeb, 659
IE (Internet Explorer), 20
if extension, 705
<%If%> (HTX file variable), 741
If/Then/Else statement (VBScript), 542
IFS (Installable File System), 823
IIS (Internet Information Server), 26, 32
  bottlenecks, finding, 786-793
  defined, 26
  extensible platforms, 30-31
  FTP Server, 9
  Gopher Server, 9
  hosts, IP addresses, 10
  installing, 123-133, 652
    connection considerations, 98-99
    cost considerations, 98-99
    data location configurations, 99
    performance considerations, 124
    planning, 98-100
    software requirements, 100-102
  logs, 317
  performance counters, 787-788
  performance levels, 35-36
  registry keys, 897
  security, user accounts, 285-286
  servers
    FTP, 27
    Gopher, 27
    WWW, 26

site activity
  logging, 163-167
  ODBC data sources, 165-167
TCP/IP, 26
version 2, installing, 124
version 3, installing, 126-133
Web site, 123
Windows NT Server, 8-9, 70
  robust, 44
  security, 284
WWW Server, 8
IIS SDK, 510
  ISAPI, applications, 510
illustrated audio stream file formats, 640
Image Advanced command (Insert menu), 502
Image command (Insert menu), 501
ImageMapGraphic_MouseMove subroutine, 567
images
  backgrounds, Internet Assistant for Word, 448
  CorelWeb.Gallery, 474-476
  CorelWeb.Transit, 476-477
  HTML documents
    alignment, 396
    <IMG> tag, 399
  inserting, Internet Assistant for Word, 450
  inserting into documents, 501-502
  labeling in VBScript, 566
  objects, inserting into home pages, 471
  ray traced, 471
  realistic with shadows, 471
  rendering, 471
  solid models, 471
  SSIs, 832
  tables, Internet Assistant for Word, 450
  three-dimensional, designing, 470
  Web 3D, 467-469
  Web.Designer, 473-474
  wireframes, 467-471
IMC (Internet Mail Connector), 200
  configuring, 202-211
    startup values, 209

Exchange Server, 200
installing, 201-202
messages, notifications, 207
MIME, 203
protocols, troubleshooting, 206
SMTP, 210
timeout errors, 207
<IMG> (image) HTML tag, 399, 858-859
  Internet Assistant for Word, 887
  Internet Explorer, 883
impersonations, 823
import partners, export paths, 820
import paths, 823
  export paths, 823
import statement, importing Java classes, 613-614
importing
  directory trees, 818
  Java classes, 613-614
    defining, 614
include directive, 634
<%Include VariableText%> (HTX file variable), 742
indentation (HTML documents), 383
Index Information Server, 728
  IDQ file, creating, 734-735
  installing, 130-131
  meta tags, 729-730
  sample search page (listing), 731-733
  search forms, 730-733
Index Internet Server (HTX files)
  creating, 739-741
  read-only variables, 743-744
  variables, 741-742
indexes, HTML documents, 497
Industry Standard Architecture (ISA), 73
INF files, 823
infected systems, recovering, 278-279
infinite loops, 623
.ini files, 890

init method
  font selection, 615
  initializing Java applets, 615-618
  parameters, 615-616
  testing strings, 616-617
initializing
  Java applets, 615-618
    converting strings to numbers, 617
    length of strings, 617-618
    parameters, 615-616
    selecting fonts, 615
    substrings, 617-618
    testing strings, 616-617
Initiate Scavenging command (Mappings menu), 259
InitTimePause (Registry keys), 261
input
  addresses, 823
  BIOS, 814
  I/O, buses, 823
input forms, creating, 696-700
Input/Output Control (IOCTL), 823
<INPUT> HTML tag, 859
  Internet Explorer, 883
InputBox function (VBScript), 548
<INS> HTML tag, 859
insert forms
  properties, 682-684
  property sheets, 685-686
Insert Image dialog box, 501
Insert menu commands
  Hypertext Target, 500
  Image, 501
  Image Advanced, 502
  Jump to Document, 500
  Jump Within this Document, 500
  Launch an Internet Service, 504
  Table, 502
insert statement (HTML), 633
inserting
  files
    ASPs (Active Server Pages), 633-635
    directives, 634
  graphics into documents, 501-502

  HTML tags
    into documents, 499-501
    Tags dialog box, 499-500
  Internet command into documents, 504
  links into external documents, 501
  objects
    into home pages, 471
    Word 97, 437-438
  special characters, 499
  tables
    Internet Assistant for Word, 450
    into documents, 502-504
  video, Internet Assistant for Word, 450
Installable File System (IFS), 823
Installation Complete dialog box, 483
Installation Status dialog box (Internet Explorer), 172
installing
  ASPs, 126-128
  Crystal Reports, 131-132
  dbWeb, 650-655
  DHCP, 106-108, 219-230
  DNS, 109-110
  FrontPage, 408-409
  FrontPage 97 Server Extensions, 132-133
  HotDog Pro, 481-483
  IIS, 123-133, 652
    connection considerations, 98-99
    cost considerations, 98-99
    data location configurations, 99
    performance considerations, 124
    planning, 98-100
    software requirements, 100-102
    version 2, 124
    version 3, 126-133
  IMC, 201-202
  Index Information Server, 130-131
  Internet Assistant for Excel, 453-454

  Internet Assistant for PowerPoint, 457
  Internet Assistant for Word, 446-447
  Internet Explorer, 171-172
  Microsoft Internet Chat Server, 347-348
  Microsoft News Server, 364-366
  Microsoft Office 97, 433-434
  Microsoft Proxy Server, 321-326
  Microsoft TCP/IP Printing, 112-113
  modems, RAS, 116
  NetShow On-Demand Server, 128-130
    error messages, 130
  ODBC, 654
  Perl, 585
  RAS, 114-119
  RIP for Internet Protocol, 108-109
  server extensions, FrontPage Server, 412-413
  Service Pack 1, Windows NT, 128
  Simple TCP/IP Service, 112
  SNMP, 110-112
  TCP/IP, 102-106
  WINS, 108, 245-250
instances
  object counters, 759
  Performance Monitor, 750
Instr function (VBScript), 548
instructions, privileged, 829
integer-division operator (VBScript), 534
integratability, Windows NT Server, 46
Integrated Drive Electronics (IDE), 77
Integrated Services Digital Networks (ISDNs), 12-13
Intel
  BIOS, 83
  I/O buses, 73
Intent Locks - Exclusive counter, 806
Intent Locks - Shared counter, 806

Intent Locks - Total counter, 806

interactive sites, 604

interactive web pages
DSN, 695
ODBC, 695

interfaces
APIs, 813
BRIs, 12
CGIs, 31-32
default gateways, 817
ESDI, 76
files, creating, 700-703
Internet Explorer, configuration, 173-176
ISAPI, 30-31, 512-513, 824
NetBEUI, 826
ODBC databases, 650
PRIs, 12
SCSI, 77
TAPI, 46
TDI, 835
see also CGI

interleaved audio video stream file formats, 640

internal properties (dbWeb servers), 659

Internet, 17
access rights, restricting, 211-212
applications, security, 274-275
ARPA, 4
ARPAnet, 6
auto-replies, preventing, 212
circuit-switched networks, 5
collecting data, 21-22
commands, inserting into documents, 504
connecting to, 6, 10
56KB leased lines, 11
bandwidths, 12
dial-up, 11
frame relay, 12
FTP Server, 9
Gopher Server, 9
IAPs, 14-15
ISDNs, 12-13
ISPs, 14-17
setting up networks, 7-8
WWW Server, 8

connections
configuration, 176-179
Dial-Up Networking, 176
modifying Registry keys, 122
RAS, 99
routing tables, 123
CSnet, 6
documents
security, 274-275
types, 628
domains, names, 10
e-mail, 10
events
archiving, 316
components, 313
Exchange Server, 200-201, 206
connecting sites, 209-210
hardware, 10
history of, 4-6
hosts, IP addresses, 10
IIS, defined, 26
messages, troubleshooting, 211
networks
protocols, 284
switches, 5
wrappers, 5
newsgroups, 14
NSFnet, 6
packet-switched network protocol, 5
packets, routing, 5
protocols
compatibility with RAS, 114
SNMP, 101
publishing, 17-21, 32-35
catalogs, 19-20
text, 20-21
RAS, connections, 121-123
routers, 9
security, 35, 274
browsers, 277-278
challenge-response, 285
configuring user accounts, 285-286
dial-up networking, 296-300
enabling audits, 307-308
encrypting, 285

firewalls, 280-282
NTFS, 288-290
passwords, 285
proxy agents, 280, 283-284
recovering infected systems, 278-279
trojan horses, 275-277
user accounts, 285
viruses, 213, 275-277
security issues, 98
selling products, 22-23
service providers, 4
requirements, 9-10
see also ISPs
TCP/IP, 6
technical support, 17-19
vBNS, 6
Web Proxy Service, limiting site access, 336-338
Windows NT Server, security, 284
WINS server, 258
see also WWW

Internet Access Providers (IAPs), 14-15, 823

Internet Assistant for Access, publishing Web pages, 459-463

Internet Assistant for Excel
installing, 453-454
spreadsheets, publishing, 452-455
Web pages, publishing, 453
Web site, 453

Internet Assistant for PowerPoint
installing, 457
Web pages, publishing, 456-459
Web site, 457

Internet Assistant for Word
backgrounds, modifying, 448
fonts, 449
images, inserting, 450
installing, 446-447
tables
formatting, 450
inserting, 450
video, inserting, 450
Web pages, creating, 447-451
Web site, 446

Internet Assistants
  compatibility, Office 97, 434
  HotDog Pro, 480-481
Internet Chat Server, 345-346
  chat rooms
    creating, 351
    creating persistent,
      353-359
  configuring, 348-352
  installing, 347-348
  properties, 349-352
  security, 359-363
Internet Connector Properties dialog box, 211
Internet Data Query files (IDQ files), 728
Internet Database Connector, 31, 824
  IDC, 686
Internet Explorer (IE), 20, 170
  address toolbar, 175
  character sets, 175
  configuration, 172-195
    advanced settings, 191-195
    caching options, 193-194
    interface, 173-176
    miscellaneous settings,
      194-195
    search pages, 181
    security rating, 187-189
    Start page, 181
  downloading, installation, 171-172
  fonts, 175
    fixed-width, 175
    proportional, 175
  history file, 181
  HTML tags, 880-885
  installation, 171-172
  languages, 176
  links toolbar, 175
  MIME, 175-176
  search pages, 179-181
  security, 186-191
    destructive code, 190-191
    warnings, 191-192
  setup, 172
  sounds, 174
  standard toolbar, 174
  Start page, 179-181
  toolbars, 195-197
  see also browsers

Internet Explorer Administration Kit, 172
Internet Information Server (IIS), 26
Internet Mail Connector Properties dialog box, 204-208
Internet Mail Connector (IMC), 200
Internet Protocol, see IP
Internet Server Application Programming, 30-31, 824
Internet Server Applications (ISAs), 513
Internet Server Manager, 57
Internet Service Providers (ISPs), 264, 824
Internet services, 400
Internet Services Manager, 138
  Allow Anonymous, configuring, 142-143
  Anonymous Logon, configuring, 142
  commands
    Basic, 142
    Connect to Server, 139
    Connection Timeout, 141
    Find All Servers, 139
    Maximum connections, 142
    Sort by Comment, 140
    Sort by Server, 140
    Sort by Service, 140
    Sort by State, 140
  FTP Publishing service, configuring, 151-156
  Gopher service, configuring, 156-159
  NetShow On-Demand service, configuring, 160-163
  Password Authentication, configuring, 142
  Password field, configuring, 142
  security, limiting access, 150-151
  services, adding, 139
  site management, View menu, 140
  Username, configuring, 142

  Web Proxy Server, configuring, 328
  Windows NT Challenge/Response, configuring, 143
InterNIC, IP addresses, 7
interoperating with non-WINS clients, 245
Interrupt ReQuest Level (IRQL), 824
interrupts, 824
Interrupts/sec counter, 770
intranets
  publishing, 32-35
  security, 35
invalid operations, access violations, 812
inventory, 33
IOCTL (Input/Output Control), 823
IP (Internet Protocol), 6, 100, 824
  addresses, 7, 10, 217, 824
    configuring in Web Proxy Server, 330
    DHCP, 100, 221-223
    Exchange Server, 209
    firewalls, 281
    networks, 265
    routable, 35
    scopes, 217
    static, 222
    subnets, 233
  logging, dbWeb, 659
  ports, 303
    firewalls, 281
IP Address Only option (Preferences dialog box), 253
IP log property (dbWeb), 659
IPCONFIG command-line program syntax, 238
IRC, 306
  servers, 345
IRQL (Interrupt ReQuest Level), 824
ISA (Industry Standard Architecture), 73, 824
  double buffering, 73
  expansions, 73

ISAPI (Internet Server Application Server Interface), 30-31, 824
applications, 511-512
CGIs, 511
defined, 510
testing, 512
CGIs, 31-32
creating with IIS SDK, 510
DLLs, 30
filters, 31
interfaces, 512-513
Internet Database Connector, 31
third-party applications, 512
ISAPI Extension Requests counter, 789
IsArray function (VBScript), 549
ISAs (Internet Server Applications), 513, 521-524
ECBs, formats, 515-516
functions
GetExtensionVersion, 514-515
GetServerVariable, 514, 517-519
HttpExtensionProc, 514-517
ReadClient, 514-519
ServerSupportFunction, 514, 520-521
WriteClient, 514-520
HTTP servers, 513
IsDate function (VBScript), 546, 549
ISDNs (Integrated Services Digital Networks), 12-13
ISEMPTY (HTX file variable), 742
IsEmpty function (VBScript), 549
IsError function (VBScript), 549
<ISINDEX> HTML tag, 860
Internet Explorer, 883
IsNull function (VBScript), 549
IsNumeric function (VBScript), 549
IsObject function (VBScript), 549

ISPs (Internet Service Providers), 14-15, 264, 824
businesses, 15-16
domain names, 15
registration, 14
e-mail, 15
encrypting, 298-299
FTP drop box, 14
hardware, 15
Internet, connecting to, 17
newsgroups, 14
references, 16
security, encrypting, 285
servers
hosting, 14
virtual, 14
technical support, 16
ISTYPEEQ (HTX file variable), 742
italic text, HTML documents, 384

J

Java, 604-608
applets, 605-606
alpha versions, 607
code for marquee applet, 610-613
color values of Marquee, 617-618
compiling, 624-625
creating, 608-624
embedding in HTML, 625-626
initializing, 615-618
painting, 619-621
parameters for marquee applet, 609-610
threads, 622-624
capabilities, 607-608
classes, importing, 613-614
code, comments, 613
compilers, 605
defining classes, 614
Hot Java, 606
initializing
converting strings to numbers, 617
length of strings, 617-618
parameters, 615-616

substrings, 617-618
testing strings, 616-617
object-oriented programming, 606
robustness, 607
security, 607
JavaScript, 824
joins, 669-672
creating, 670
defining, 670
deleting, 671
Joins dialog box, 670
JPEG (Joint Picture Experts Group) files
background images, 388
snapshots, exporting, 467
JPG files, 174
JScript, 628
commands, 632
Jump to Document on Another System command (Insert menu), 500
Jump Within this Document command (Insert menu), 500
justification (HTML documents), 383

K

<KBD> HTML tag, 860
Internet Assistant for Word, 887
Internet Explorer, 883
KD (Kernel Debugger), 817, 825
kernel modes, 825
Executive, 819
executive messages, 820
kernels, 50
Key Manager, 213
keys, creating, 893
keywords, 825
HTML documents, ALIGN, 396
users, 497
VBScript
Nothing, 544
Private, 543
Public, 543
Static, 544
Keywords (meta tag), 729

L

Label Image program (listing), 568-570
labeling images in VBScript, 566
<LANG> HTML tag, 860
Language option (security rating), 188
languages
  Internet Explorer, 176
  Java, 604-608
    applets, 605-606
    capabilities, 607-608
    defining classes, 614
    importing classes, 613-614
    initializing, 615-618
    object-oriented programming, 606
    robustness, 607
    security, 607
  JavaScript, 824
  markup languages, 377
  VBScript, 836
LANS (Local Area Networks), 825
LastKnownGood control set, 816, 825
Launch an Internet Service command (Insert menu), 504
launching Web Assistant, 714
layout, IDC, 694
LBound function (VBScript), 550
LCase function (VBScript), 550
lease expirations, DHCP, 222-223
leased lines, 56KB, 11
leases (DHCP), clients, 239
Left function (VBScript), 550
Legend option (Chart Options dialog box), 755
Len function (VBScript), 550
length violations, 812
less than operator (VBScript), 536
less than or equal to operator (VBScript), 537
Let statement (VBScript), 542
<LH> HTML tag, 861
<LI> HTML tag, 861
  Internet Explorer, 883

libraries, DLLs, 30, 819
line breaks (HTML documents), 393
linear chains, replication (WINS servers), 248
<LINK> HTML tag, 861
linking, DLLs, 819
links, 399
  browsers, 174
  colors, 498
  documents, inserting into, 500-501
  drilldown, 666
  HTML documents, 399-400, 498
    anchors, 399
  hypertext, inserting into documents, 500-501
  inserting into external documents, 501
  verifying, FrontPage, 420
links toolbar (Internet Explorer), 175
listing objects, enumeration operations, 819
<LISTING> HTML tag, 861
  Internet Explorer, 883
listings
  ASPs: including files, 633
  ASPSample.ASP, 631
  Calculator Web page, 561-570
  code for Marquee.java, 610-613
  directories, 37-38
  DOS batch file for compiling Java applets, 625
  embedding the Marquee applet, 625
  Hello World! Web page (VBScript example), 532
  HTML code for displaying ASP documents, 630
  HTML code for IDQ file, 734
  HTML code from an HTX file, 739-740
  HTX file (HTML code), 740
  Index Information Server sample search page, 731-733
  Label Image program, 568-570

run method (threads in a Java applet), 623
  Skeleton.C source code, 522
  Skeleton.DEF source code, 524
  Skeleton.H source code, 522
lists
  ACEs, 812
  ACLs, 812
  HTML documents, 390-392
live video, HTML documents, 395
LKG control set, 825
Load Hive command (Registry menu), 894
loading DLLs, 511
Local Area Networks (LANs), 825
Local Group Membership dialog box, 294
local groups, 825
  Guests, 286
Local IPC Manager, 49
Local Procedure Calls (LPCs), 825
Local Security Authority (LSA), 826
Locks Held counter, 806
Log command (View menu), 756
Log Event in Application option (Alert Options dialog box), 763
log files
  creating, WWW Publishing service, 149-150
  Crystal Reports, 721-722
  IIS, site activity, 163-167
  NetShow On-Demand service, configuring, 162-163
  Web Proxy Service, 335-336
Log function (VBScript), 550
Log menu commands
  Log Settings, 316
  Log Type, 316
  Save As, 316
Log Options dialog box, 757
Log Settings command (Log menu), 316
Log Type command (Log menu), 316

Log view, Performance
Monitor, 751, 756
LogDetailedEvents (Registry
key), 262
LogFilePath (Registry key),
261
logging
errors, 819
IP, dbWeb, 659
logging on, auditing, 308
LoggingOn (Registry key),
262
logical drives, disk-intensive
applications (Performance
Monitor), 781
logoffs, auditing, 308
Logon Attempts counter, 791
Logon Requests counter,
789-792
Logon Script, 60
Logons Total counter, 785
Logons/sec counter, 785
logs
administrators, 57
applications, 312
creating, 756
IIS, 317
saving, 758
security, 312
systems, 312
updating, 757, 760
long filenames
HotDog Pro, 482
NTFS, 53
long integer data type, 237
lookup files, subnets (DNS),
268
loop statement (VBScript), 539
loops, infinite, 623
LPCs (Local Procedure Calls),
49, 825
LSA (Local Security Authority),
826
LSet statement (VBScript), 542
LT (HTX file variable), 742
LT extension, 705
LTrim function (VBScript), 550

M

M-nodes, DHCP, 221
MAC (Media Access Control),
239
macros, viruses, 276
mail, see e-mail; SMTP
management sites
Internet Services Manager,
140
View menu, 140
mandatory user profiles, 826
<MAP> HTML tag, 862
Internet Explorer, 883
mapping
bad-sectors, 814
I/O, 826
WINS, addresses, 244
Mappings menu commands
Initiate Scavenging, 259
Static Mappings, 257
markup languages, 377
tag pairs, 377
Marquee applet
color values, 617-618
embedding, 625
run method, 623
start method, 622
stop method, 622
<MARQUEE> HTML tag, 862
masks, subnets, 223
Master Boot Record (MBR),
275
master domains, 64-67
MaxFieldSize parameter
(IDC), 703
Maximize Throughput for File
Sharing option, 94
Maximize Throughput for
Network Applications, 94
Maximum Anonymous Users
counter, 791-792
Maximum CGI Requests
counter, 789
Maximum Clients option
(NetShow On-Demand
service), 160
Maximum concurrent users
property (dbWeb), 658

Maximum Connections
command
FTP Publishing service, 152
Internet Services Manager,
142
Maximum Connections
counter, 789-791
Maximum File Bitrate option
(NetShow On-Demand
service), 161
Maximum ISAPI Extension
Requests counter, 790
Maximum NonAnonymous
Users counter, 790-792
Maximum Number of
Anonymous Users counter,
789
Maximum Password Age
option (Account Policies
menu), 286
MaxRecords extension, 705
MaxRecords HTTP (CGI
variable), 703, 738
MBONE, 303
MBR (Master Boot Record),
275
MCA (Microchannel Architec-
ture), 74
McastIntvl (Registry key), 261
McastTtl (Registry key), 261
MCB (Memory Control Block),
826
MDI (multiple document
interface), 401
Media Access Control (MAC),
239
MemHog.EXE program, 778
memory
access violations, 812
bottlenecks, finding, 774-780
Cache Manager, 84
DMA, 769
DRAM, 83
FCB, 821
flash, 821
HMA, 822
object counters, 775
paging files, 827
RAM, 829
registry keys, 915-917
ROM, 829

SRAM, 83
swap files, 827
troubleshooting, 778
upgrades, 83-84
virtual, 836
Virtual Memory Manager, 49
Memory Control Block (MCB),
826
Memory counter, 806
Memory Pages/sec counter,
780
<MENU> HTML tag, 391, 863
Internet Assistant for Word,
887
Internet Explorer, 883
message boxes
customizing, 551
displaying, 551
messages
administrative alerts, 813
application-termination, 820
e-mail
conversions, 206
delivering, 208
protecting, 212-213
executive, 820
flames, 211
IMC, notifications, 207
Internet, troubleshooting,
211
SMBs, 832
system-information, 820
warning, 820
meta tags, Index Information
Server, 729-730
meta tags (HTML documents),
404-405
<META> HTML tag, 863
Index Information Server,
729-730
Internet Assistant for Word,
887
methods
drawRect, 620
drawString, 621
fillRect, 620
init
font selection, 615
initializing Java applets,
615-618
parameters, 615-616
testing strings, 616-617

paint, 619
repaint, 623
Response object, locating
documentation, 632
run, Java applet threads, 623
setFont, 619-620
start, Java applet threads, 622
stop, Java applet threads, 622
substring, 618
MFM (Modified Frequency
Modulation), 76
Microchannel Architecture
(MCA), 74
Microsoft dbWeb, see dbWeb
Microsoft dbWeb License
Agreement dialog box, 651
Microsoft Exchange Server,
see Exchange Server
Microsoft Exchange Server
Setup dialog box, 201
Microsoft FrontPage, see
FrontPage
Microsoft Internet Chat Server,
see Internet Chat Server
Microsoft News Server, see
News Server
Microsoft Office 95, see Office
95
Microsoft Office 97, see Office
97
Microsoft Proxy Server, see
Proxy Server
Microsoft TCP/IP Printing, 101
installing, 112-113
Microsoft TCP/IP Properties
dialog box, 301
Microsoft VBScript, 528
Microsoft VBScript home
page, 528
Microsoft VBScript information
Web site, 528
Microsoft VM for Java, Web
sites, 628
Microsoft Word 95, see Word
95
Microsoft Word 97, see Word
97
Mid function (VBScript), 550
Mid statement (VBScript), 542
MigrateOn (Registry key),
263
MIME, 203
Internet Explorer, 175-176

Minimize Memory User option
(Server dialog box), 94
Minimum Password Age
option (Account Policies
menu), 286
Minimum Password Length
option (Account policies
menu), 287
Minute function (VBScript),
550
mirror sets, disk bottlenecks,
782
mirroring disks, 54, 818
MOD operator (VBScript), 534
models, domains, 63
Models menu commands
Create Simple Model, 471
Create Text Models, 471
modems, installing (RAS), 116
Modified Frequency Modula-
tion (MFM), 76
Modify Surface and Color
dialog box, 470
monitoring, protocols
(WinSock Proxy Service),
338-340
monitors, see Performance
Monitor
monolithic database model,
27
Month function (VBScript),
550
mounting volumes, 826
moving, buttons, 486
MS.Category (meta tag), 729
MS.Locale (meta tag), 729
MsgBox function (VBScript),
551
multidimensional arrays,
declaring with Dim state-
ment, 538
multihomed servers, 300, 826
WINS Server, 258
multimedia
bandwidth, 639
codecs, 639
file formats, 640
NetShow Live
features, 638-639
stream types, 640
streaming, 638-639
creating files, 641-642

Multimedia Marketing Group Web site, 38
multiple variables, declaring with Dim statement, 538
multiplication operator (VBScript), 533
multiprocessing, 826
  AMP, 813
  symmetric, 833
multitasking
  cooperative, 816
  preemptive, 828
multithreading, 826
  Windows NT Server, 46
  see also threads

N

named pipes, 826
names
  domains, 10, 35, 223, 818
    ISPs, 15
    registering, 14
    WINS, resolving, 243
  NBF protocol configuration, registry keys, 912-915
  NCB (Network Control Block), 827
NCBs (Network Control Blocks), 827
  see also opcodes
NetBEUI (NetBIOS Extended User Interface), 826
  frame protocol configuration, 912
NetBIOS (Network Basic Input/Output System), 224-243, 827
  name resolutions, 100
Netlogon, registry keys, 908-911
NetShow Live
  conversion tools, 638
  features, 638-639
  multimedia files
    creating, 642
    streaming, 639
  stream types, 640
NetShow On-Demand Player, 638

NetShow On-Demand Server, 638
  Administration Utilities, 638
  error messages, 130
  installing, 128-130
NetShow On-Demand Service
  Comment option, 161
  configuring, 160-163
  directories, configuring, 161-162
  Enable File Level Access option, 161
  log files, configuring, 162-163
  Maximum Clients option, 160
  Maximum file Bitrate option, 161
network adapters, 56
Network Alert option (Alert Options dialog box), 763
Network Basic Input/Output System, see NetBIOS
Network Command Queue Length counter, 805
Network Configuration dialog box, 297-298
Network Control Blocks, see NCBs
Network dialog box, 87, 297, 301
Network Errors/sec counter, 786
Network File System (NFS), 306
Network Interface Current Bandwidth counter, 786
Network News Transfer Protocol (NNTP), 827
Network Reads/sec counter, 804
Network Settings Change dialog box, 297
Network Time Protocol (NTP), 306
Network Utilization counter, 784
Network Writes/sec counter, 804
networking, dial-up, 817
  security, 296-300

networks
  adapters
    adding, 85-90
    security, 90
  bindings, 815
  bottlenecks
    finding, 783-786
    Performance Monitor, 784
  CACHE configuration file, 265-267
  circuit-switched, 5
  connectors, bayonet nut, 815
  CSnet, 6
  DARPA, 6
  default gateways, 817
  DNS, 264
  domains, 818
    names, 10
    single models, 63-64
  Ethernet, 11
  firewalls, 280-282
  FTP Server, 9
  hostnames, 265
  hosts, IP addresses, 10
  Internet, history of, 6
  IP addresses, 265
  ISPs, support services, 16
  LANs, 825
  NetBIOS, 827
  NNTP, 827
  NSFnet, 6
  packet-switched, 5
  packets, routing, 5
  performance counters, 784
  processors, adding, 91
  protocols, 284
    TCP, 835
    TCP/IP, 834
  routers, 831
  routes, 831
  security, proxy agents, 283-284
  segments, 90
  servers, selecting, 91-92
  setting up connections, 7-8
  subnets, 832
    address class, 812
  switches, 5
  transporting, 827
  vBNS, 6
  WANs, 28, 837

wrappers, 5
WWW Server, 8
New Chart command (File menu), 758
New command (File menu), 469
New Other command (File menu), 210
New Phonebook Entry dialog box, 298
New Push Parameter Default Configuration option, 255
New Schema dialog box, 664
New Technology File System, see NTFS
News Server, 363-364
  installing, 364-366
  newsgroups
    creating, 366-368
    creating feeds, 368-370
    setting message expiration, 368
newsgroups, 14
  creating, Microsoft News Server, 366-368
  feeds, creating, 368-370
  message expiration, setting, 368
  publicizing Web sites, 38
Next statement (VBScript), 540
<NEXTID> HTML tag, 863
NFS (Network File System), 306
NFSnet, 6
NNTP (Network News Transfer Protocol), 305, 827
No Access option (permissions), troubleshooting, 290
<NOBR> HTML tag, 864
  Internet Explorer, 883
nodes
  B-nodes, 220
  H-nodes, 221
  M-nodes, 221
  P-nodes, 221
<NOEMBED> HTML tag, 864
<NOFRAMES> HTML tag, 864
NoOfWrkThds (Registry key), 262
NOT operator (VBScript), 535
<NOTE> HTML tag, 864

Nothing keyword (VBScript), 544
notifications, IMC, 207
Notifications dialog box, 206
Now function (VBScript), 552
NTFS (New Technology File System), 52
  compression support, 53
  filenames, 53
  security, 53, 288-290
NTP (Network Time Protocol), 305
NTSD (Windows NT System Debugger), 833
nudity option (security rating), 188
numbered lists (HTML documents), 390-391
numbers, converting strings to, 617

O

Object Manager, 48
object-oriented programming, 606
object-reference operator (VBScript), 536
<OBJECT> HTML tag, 645
objects, 827
  3D
    creating home pages with Web 3D, 469-472
    Web 3D, 466-469
  auditing, 308, 813
  CorelWeb.Gallery, 474-476
  CorelWeb.Transit, 476-477
  counters
    adding, 752
    alerts, 764-766
    colors, 754
    deleting, 752
    instances, 759
    memory, 775
    processors, 770
    ranges, 754
    scales, 754
    systems, 779
    updating, 752
    WINS, Performance Monitor, 260

  deleting, 471
  embedded, ASPs (Active Server Pages), 645
  enumeration operations, 819
  graphical, Web sites, 467
  inserting, 471
    Word 97, 437-438
  Performance Monitor, 750
  processes, 829, 834
  ray traced, 471
  realistic with shadows, 471
  Response, locating method documentation, 632
  semaphores, 831
  solid models, 471
  Web.Designer, 473-474
  wireframes, 471
Oct function (VBScript), 552
ODBC (Open DataBase Connectivity), 827
  Data Source Name, 817
  data sources
    creating, 660-662
    defining, 661-662
    profile properties, 663-664
  databases, 650
    Crystal Reports, 722
  dbWeb, 653
    data source name, 659
    installing, 650-655
    passwords, 659
  IIS site activity, adding permissions, 165-167
  installing, 654
  interactive web pages, 695
ODBC Data Sources dialog box, 663
ODBC Driver Pack 3.0 Custom dialog box, 654
ODBC Driver Pack 3.0 Setup dialog box, 654
ODBC SQL Server Setup dialog box, 661
Office 95, Web publishing, 446
Office 97
  compatibility (Internet Assistants), 434
  installing, 433-434
  Web publishing, 432-445
Office Web site, 432, 446
OK dialog boxes, 551

**<OL> (ordered list) HTML tag,
390, 865**
  Internet Assistant for Word,
   887
  Internet Explorer, 884
OLE
  applications, file associations,
   182
  browsers, 278
**On Error Resume Next
statement (VBScript), 543**
OnChange event, 558
**one-time passwords (OTP),
580**
online catalogs, 712
opcodes, 827
  see also NCBs
**Open command (File menu),
469, 755**
**Open DataBase Connectivity,
see ODBC**
**Open Local command
(Registry menu), 894**
**Open Market Commercial
Sites Index Web site, 37**
**Open Project command (File
menu), 506**
Operability dialog box, 206
operating systems
  device drivers, 817
  domains, names, 818
  down levels, 819
  HAL, 822
  processors, adding, 91
  servers, selecting, 91-92
**OperatorBox_OnChange
subroutine (VBScript), 558**
operators, VBScript, 533-570
  addition, 533
  AND, 534
  Boolean, 534
  comparison, 536
  division, 533
  equivalence, 536
  exponential, 533
  greater than, 537
  greater than or equal to, 537
  integer-division, 534
  less than, 536
  less than or equal to, 537
  MOD, 534

  multiplication, 533
  NOT, 535
  object-reference, 536
  OR, 534
  string-concatenation, 534
  subtraction, 533
  unequal, 536
  XOR, 535
option overlays, 225
<OPTION> HTML tag, 865
  Internet Explorer, 884
**Options command (Tools
menu), 213, 487**
Options dialog box, 487
  Internet Explorer, 173
Options menu commands
  Alert, 763
  Chart, 754, 757
  Data From, 758
  Global, 235
  Preferences, 253
  Read Only Mode, 892
  Update Now, 755-757, 760
OR operator (VBScript), 534
order forms, 712
ordering, 33
  databases, 713
organizations
  ISPs, 15-16
    references, 16
  ordering, 33
  publishing, 33
**Other Requested Methods
counter, 790**
**OTP (one-time passwords),
580**
  Web site, 580
output
  addresses, 823
  BIOS, 814
  I/O, 74
    buses, 823
<OVERLAY> HTML tag, 865
overlays, DHCP, 225
**Owner command (Security
menu), 296, 895**

P

P-nodes, 221
**<P> (paragraph) HTML tag,
380, 866**
  Internet Explorer, 884
  Internet Assistant for Word,
   887
packages, authentication, 814
**packet-switched network
protocols, 5**
packets
  routing, 5
  wrappers, 5
**page attributes (HTML
documents), 388-390**
**Page Faults/sec counter,
775-777**
**Page Locks - Exclusive
counter, 806**
**Page Locks - Shared counter,
806**
**Page Locks - Total counter,
806**
**Page Locks - Update counter,
806**
Pages/sec counter, 775-777
paging, files, 827
paint method, 619
**painting, Java applets,
619-621**
  reading fonts, 621
  setting current font,
   619-620
  writing text, 620-621
**paragraph attributes (HTML
documents), 382-383**
<PARAM> HTML tag, 626, 866
parameters, 828
  IDC, 701-702
  Java applets, 615-616
  keywords, 825
  pull partners, 251
  push partners, 252
  SQL Server, Web Assistant,
   714
  switches, 833
parity, 828
  striped sets, 832
  see also disk striping with
   parity

parsing files, 378
partitioning, 828
    boot, 815
    disks, 55
    extended, 821
    primary, 829
    systems, 834
    tables, 828
    see also volumes
partners, import (export
    paths), 820
Password option (FTP
    Publishing service), 153
Password parameter (IDC),
    703
Password Uniqueness option
    (Account Policies menu), 287
passwords, 285
    CGI, OTP, 580
    dbWeb, 659
    domains, 61
    RAS, 122
    Web Assistant, 714
    WWW Publishing service,
        security considerations, 143
PATH INFO CGI variable, 582
PATH INFO extension, 705
Path to client stub property
    (dbWeb), 658
Path to HTML dir property
    (dbWeb), 658
PATH TRANSLATED CGI
    variable, 582, 738
PATH TRANSLATED extension,
    705
paths
    export, 820
    import, 823
    relative compared to virtual,
        633
pausing, services, 139
PCI (Peripheral Component
    Interconnect), 71, 75
    servers, 75
    VLBs, 74
PCMCIA (Personal Computer
    Memory Card Interface
    Adapter), 75
PDCs (Primary Domain
    Controllers), 92, 828

performance counters
    FTP, 790-791
    Gopher, 791-793
    HTTP, 788-790
    IIS, 787-788
Performance Monitor, 750
    alerts
        creating, 760-766
        object counters, 764-766
    bottlenecks
        networks, 784
        processors, 771
    charts, creating, 752-755
    counters, 750
        instances, 759
    disk-intensive applications
        logical drives, 781
        physical drives, 782
    events, 750, 757
    instances, 750
    logs
        creating, 756
        updating, 757, 760
    objects, 827
    performance tuning, 768-769
    processor intensive applica-
        tions, 772-774
    reports
        creating, 758-760
        saving, 760
    SQL Server, counters,
        802-807
    toolbar, 751
    views, 750
        Alert, 761
        Chart, 752
        Log, 756
        Report, 759
        saving, 755
    WINS, object counters, 260
performance tuning, 768-769
Peripheral Component
    Interconnect, see PCI
Perl (Practical Extraction and
    Report Language), 584-585
    CGI, accessing variables,
        593-594
    Hello World script, 588-590
    installing, 585
    Web sites, 585-586
permissions, 828
    access rights, 812
    ASPs, 635

    assigning, WinSock Proxy
        Service, 340-342
    auditing, 309
    deleting, 295
    directories, 292
        attributes, 292-293
        setting, 290-296
    files, 292
        attributes, 292-293
        setting, 290-296
    granting, RAS servers, 120
    IIS site activity, adding to
        database, 165
    Microsoft Proxy Server,
        326-328
    Web Proxy Service, assigning,
        330-332
Permissions command
    (Security menu), 894
Permissions menu commands,
    Security, 293
<PERSON> HTML tag, 866
Personal Computer Memory
    Card Interface Adapter
    (PCMCIA), 75
Personal Web Server,
    installing, 408
PersonaNonGrata (Registry
    key), 263
phonebook (RAS), creating
    entries, 120
physical drives (disk-intensive
    applications), Performance
    Monitor, 782
Physical I/O counter, 806
PICS (Platform and Internet
    Content Selection), 187
pictures
    3D (Web 3D), 466-467
    snapshots, 466
pipes, 828
    named, 826
PLACE.DOM configuration file,
    265, 268-269
Plain Old Telephone System
    (POTS), 11
plain text, encrypting, 298
<PLAINTEXT> HTML tag, 866
    Internet Explorer, 884
platforms, extensible, 30-31
Point-to-Point Protocol, see PPP

policies
  audits, 813
  security, auditing, 308
  user accounts, configuring,
    286-288
Policies menu commands
  Account, 286
  Audit, 307
  Auditing, 309
  User Rights, 286
Policy dialog box, 286
**Policy menu commands,
  Audit, 814**
**Pool Nonpaged Bytes
  counter, 779**
**Pool Nonpaged Failures
  counter, 785**
**Pool Paged Bytes counter,
  779**
**Pool Paged Failures counter,
  785**
ports, 179
  FrontPage, changing default,
    411
  IP, 303
    firewalls, 281
  mappers, 305
Post Requests counter, 790
PostMaster Web site, 37
**POTS (Plain Old Telephone
  System), 11**
PowerPoint
  slide shows, converting to
    HTML, 458-459
  Web site, 444, 457
**PowerPoint 97, Web publish-
  ing, 441-443**
**PPP (Point-to-Point Protocol),
  119, 828**
  multiple connections, RAS,
    119
**PPTP packets, configuring
  (servers), 301**
**Practical Extraction and
  Report Language, see Perl**
<PRE> HTML tag, 386, 867
  Internet Assistant for Word,
    887
  Internet Explorer, 884

<PRE WIDTH> HTML tag
  Internet Assistant for Word,
    887
  Internet Explorer, 884
preemptive multitasking, 828
  see also cooperative
    multitasking
**Preferences command (Edit
  menu), 655, 658**
**Preferences command
  (Options menu), 253**
Preferences dialog box, 251
**preventing Internet auto-
  replies, 212**
**Primary Domain Controllers
  (PDCs), 62, 828**
  synchronizing, 818
primary partitions, 829
**Primary Rate Interfaces (PRIs),
  12**
Print Manager, 57
**Print Subtree command
  (Registry menu), 894**
printers, auditing, 814
printing services, dbWeb, 653
**PriorityClassHigh (Registry
  keys), 262**
**PRIs (Primary Rate Interfaces),
  12**
**Private keyword (VBScript),
  543**
privileged instructions, 829
privileges, 829
  rights, 831
  SIDs, 812
**procedures, stored (queries),
  715**
Process Manager, 49
processes, 46, 829
  batch, 815
  impersonations, 823
  objects, 834
  terminated, 834
  threads, 834
  tracking, 308
processing queries, URLs, 497
**processor intensive applica-
  tions, 772-774**
  starting, 774
**Processor queue length
  counter, 770**
processor time counter, 770

processors
  adding, 91, 774
  bottlenecks
    finding, 769-774
    Performance Monitor, 771
  I/O, selecting buses, 72-76
  object counters, 770
  RISC, 71
  upgrading, 774
  Windows NT Server, 71-72
products, selling, 22-23
**profile properties, ODBC data
  sources, 663-664**
profiles, 59
  users, 836
    mandatory, 826
programming
  ISAPI, 30-31
  languages
    CGI applications, 572
    VBScript, 836
    JavaScript, 824
    see also Java
  object-oriented, 606
  TAPI, 46
**programs, command-line
  (IPCONFIG), 238**
**Project Manager command
  (File menu), 506**
**Project Manager dialog box,
  506**
**Project Manager Links dialog
  box, 506**
projects, 506
  HotDog Pro, 481
properties
  databases, schema, 667-668
  dbWeb
    Administrator, 655-657
    schema, 656
    servers, 657-660
  defining, HTML documents,
    495-498
  forms
    delete, 682-684
    freeforms, 679-682
    HTML, 686-687
    insert, 682-684
    tabular, 676-679
    update, 682-684
  General property sheet, 174
  Gopher service, configuring,
    157-158

Microsoft Internet Chat Server, 349-352
ODBC data sources, profiles, 663-664
QBE, 672-674
scopes, 235-236
security, 187
snapshots, 471
Web Proxy Server, 329
Windows NT Setup, 171
WWW Publishing service, directories, 144-145
Properties command (File menu), 204
Properties dialog box, 673
property sheets
    Bindings, 87-89
    forms
        delete, 685-686
        freeforms, 681-682
        insert, 685-686
        tabular, 679
        update, 685-686
    QBE, 676
proportional fonts (HTML documents), 380
proportional fonts (Internet Explorer), 175
protected registry keys, 891
protecting
    clients, viruses, 213
    e-mail, messages, 212-213
    networks
        firewalls, 280-281
        NTFS, 288-290
    servers, Exchange Server, 210
    user accounts, 285
protocols
    compatibility, RAS, 114
    DCHP, 58, 216, 224
        B-nodes, 220
        client configurations, 223-230
        client reservations, 240-241
        clients, 238
        compacting databases, 241
        creating new scope options, 236-237
        database backups, 222
        databases, 241
        deleting scopes, 234
        H-nodes, 221

        installing, 219
        lease expirations, 222
        M-nodes, 221
        P-nodes, 221
        properties of scopes, 235-236
        rebinding, 225
        renewals, 224
        routers, 223
        scopes, 224
        servers, 222
        static IP addresses, 222
        subnets, 233
        WINS configurations, 220
    DNS, 304
    errors, 206
    fingering, 305
    firewalls, 281
    frame protocols, configuring, 912
    FTP, 304, 821
    Gopher, 304
    HTTP, 28, 400, 823
    HTTPS, 400, 823
    ICMP, 303
    IP, 6, 824
        DHCP, 100
    MBONE, 303
    monitoring, WinSock Proxy Service, 338-340
    NBF protocol configurations, 912-915
    networks, security, 284
    NFS, 306
    NNTP, 305, 827
    NTP, 305
    packet-switched network, 5
    PPP, 828
    rebinding, 225
    RIPs, 831
    routes, 831
    sequences, RPCs, 830
    SLIP, 832
    SMTP, 832
    SNMP, 101, 304-305, 832
    TCP, 6, 304, 835
    TCP/IP, 26, 219, 303, 834
    Telnet, 304
    UDP, 836
    WAIS, 305
    WINS, 243
        disabling, 90
    WWW, 305

providers, see ISPs
proxy agents, 280, 838
    networks, security, 283-284
    WINS, 245-248
Proxy Server
    configuring, 326-328
    Enable Access Control, 326
    enhancements, Web site, 321
    installing, 321-326
    permissions, 326-328
    user groups, 321
    Web site, 320
proxy servers, 177-179
Public keyword (VBScript), 543
publicizing Web sites, 37
    newsgroups, 38
Publish Document command (File menu), 505
publishing
    catalogs, 19-20
    data, 17-21
    documents, 505
    Internet, 32-35
        connections, 99
    intranets, 32-35
    newsgroups, 38
    text, 20-21
publishing services
    FTP Server, 29
    Gopher Server, 29
    WWW Server, 28
pull partners, 248
    parameters, 251
    WINS servers, 248
Pull Properties dialog box, 256
pullIPAddress (Registry key), 263
push partners, 248
    parameters, 252
    WINS, servers, 248
Push Properties dialog box, 256

Q

<Q> HTML tag, 867
QBE (Query By Example)
    columns, 673
    properties, 672-674
    property sheet, 676

queries, 694
building, 714
dbWeb, columns, 665
freeform text, 715
processing, URLs, 497
SQL, 832
stored procedures, 715
Queries/sec object counter, 260
QUERY STRING CGI variable, 582, 738
QUERY STRING extension, 705
Queue Length counter, 785
quotes (HTML documents), 393

R

RAID (Redundant Array of Inexpensive Disks), 70
drives, selecting, 85
hardware, 84-85
hot swapping, 85
RAM (Random Access Memory), 829
see also flash memory; ROM
Randomize statement (VBScript), 543
ranges (object counters), selecting, 754
RAS (Remote Access Server), 99-101, 113
Administrator, 57
authentication, troubleshooting, 118
clients, allowing connections, 120-121
configuring, 119-120
connections, monitoring, 121
encryption settings, 118
installing, 114-119
Internet connections, 99, 121-123
modifying Registry keys, 122
modems, installing, 116
passwords, 122
phonebook, creating entries, 120

protocols, compatibility, 114
servers
Dial-UP-Networking, 119
granting connections, 120
UARTS, requirements, 114
RAS Server Protocol Configuration dialog box, 297
rating options, security, 186-187
ray traced images, 471
Read Only Mode command (Options menu), 892
Read option (permissions), 291
read-only bits, 829
Read-Only Memory (ROM), 829
read-only variables, HTX files, 743-744
ReadClient function (ISAs), 514, 519
reading fonts, Java applets, 621
rebinding, 218
DHCP, 225
records
auditing, 813
databases, troubleshooting, 668
DNS, 269
SOA, 269
recovering, infected systems, 278-279
rectangles, drawing, 620
ReDim statement, dynamic arrays, 539
Reduced Instruction Set Computer (RISC), 71
redundancy check, CRC, 816
Redundant Array of Inexpensive Disks, see RAID
reflections, realistic with shadows, 471
RefreshInterval (Registry key), 263
REG BINARY data type, 892
REG DWORD data type, 892
REG EXPAND SZ data type, 892
REG MULTI SZ data type, 892
REG SZ data type, 892
registering domain names, 14

Registration Details dialog box, 482
registrations, WINS clients, 244
Registry, 829
hives, 822
keys, 830, 895, 911, 918-920
creating, 893
DHCP, servers, 242-243
files, 891
FTP, 900
Gopher, 900
IIS, 897
memory, 915-917
Netlogon, 908-911
protected, 891
servers, 261-263, 901-906
system service configuration, 896
workstations, 906-907
WINS, configuring, 262-263
WWW, 898-899
modifying, Internet connections, 122
Registry Editor, 242
Administrative Tools group, 890
data types, 892
.ini files, 890
keys, creating, 893
troubleshooting, 261, 890
windows, 892
Registry Key Auditing dialog box, 895
Registry menu commands
Close, 894
Load Hive, 894
Open Local, 894
Print Subtree, 894
Restore, 894
Save Key, 894
Save Subtree, 894
Select Computer, 894
relationships, trust, 61, 835
domains, 67
relative paths, compared to virtual, 633
relay hosts, 203, 208
releases (WINS), users, 244
Releases/sec object counter, 260

Rem statement (VBScript), 543
Remote Access Admin application, 120
Remote Access Server Administrator (RAS), 57
Remote Access Service, see RAS
Remote Access Setup dialog box, 297
REMOTE ADDR CGI variable, 582, 738
REMOTE ADDR extension, 705
REMOTE HOST CGI variable, 583, 738
REMOTE HOST extension, 705
REMOTE IDENT CGI variable, 583
Remote Procedure Calls, see RPCs
REMOTE USER CGI variable, 583, 738
REMOTE USER extension, 706
removing
    viruses, 278-279
    WINS, servers, 255
    see also deleting
rendering
    images, 471
    three-dimensional objects, 466
    see also drawing
renewals, 245
    DHCP, 224
repaint method, 623
Repair Disk utility, 895
replicating databases, DHCP servers, 222
Replication Interval option, 255
Replication Partners command (Server menu), 255
Replication Partners dialog box, 255
replications, 830
Report command (View menu), 758
Report view, Performance Monitor, 751, 759
reports
    creating, 758-760
    saving, 760
    viewing, 751

Request for Comments, see RFCs
REQUEST METHOD CGI variable, 583, 738
REQUEST METHOD extension, 706
RequiredParameters parameter (IDC), 703
requirements, service providers, 9-10
reservations, DHCP clients, 240
resolving WINS names, 243
Response object methods, locating documentation, 632
restarting, audits, 308
Restore command (Registry menu), 894
restricting access rights, 211-212
    networks, firewalls, 280-282
revision levels, 831
RFCs (Request for Comments), 216, 830
    DHCP, routers, 220
Right function (VBScript), 552
rights, 831
    access rights, 812
    users, auditing, 308
RIP (Routing Protocol for the Internet Protocol), 101, 831
    installing, 108-109
RISC (Reduced Instruction Set Computer), 71
RLL (Run Length Limited), 76
Rnd function (VBScript), 552
robust, 44
robustness, Java, 607
ROM (Read-Only Memory), 829
    see also flash memory; RAM
root directories, 831
routable IP addresses, 35
routers, 9-11, 831
    DHCP, 220, 223
    RFCs, 220
routes, 831
routines, APIs, 813
routing packets, 5
Routing Protocol for the Internet Protocol (RIP), 831
routing tables, Internet connections, 123

rows (tables), HTML documents, 397
RPCs (Remote Procedure Calls), 49, 830
    bindings, 830
    connections, 830
    endpoints, 830
    Exchange Server, 210
    protocol sequences, 830
    servers, 830
    see also LPCs
RplOnlyWCnfPnrs (Registry key), 263
RSAC (Recreational Software Advisory Council), 187
RSet statement (VBScript), 544
RTrim function (VBScript), 550
Run Length Limited (RLL), 76
run method, Java applet threads, 623

S

<S> HTML tag, 867
    Internet Explorer, 884
safe in communications (security), 189-190
SAM (Security Accounts Manager), 831
    registry key, 891
<SAMP> HTML tag, 868
    Internet Assistant for Word, 887
    Internet Explorer, 884
Sausage Software Web site, 480
Save As command (Log menu), 316
Save As dialog box, 316
Save Chart Settings command (File menu), 755
Save command (File menu), 687
Save Key command (Registry menu), 894
Save Log Setting As command (File menu), 758
Save Report Settings As command (File menu), 760
Save Subtree command (Registry menu), 894

Save Workspace command (File menu), 755
saving
  logs, 758
  Performance Monitor, views, 755
  reports, 760
scalability, 45
scales, object counters, 754
Scene menu commands, Generate Snapshot, 471
Scheduling dialog box, 715
schema
  constraints, 669-672
  databases, properties, 667-668
  dbWeb, databases, 664
  forms
    delete, 682-684
    insert, 682-684
    update, 682-684
  freeform forms, properties, 679-682
  HTML forms, properties, 686-687
  joins, 669-672
  properties, dbWeb, 656
  QBE, properties, 672-674
  tables, 669
  tabular forms, properties, 676-679
Schema Name dialog box, 667
Scope command (DHCP Options menu), 235
Scope menu commands
  Activate, 234
  Active Leases, 239-241
  Add Reservations, 240
  Create, 232
  Deactivate, 234
  Delete, 234
Scope Properties menu commands, DHCP Options, 223
scopes
  configurations, adding, 237
  configuring, 235-236
    creating new options, 236-237
  creating, 232-234
  deleting, 232-234

DHCP, 230-231
  client reservations, adding, 240
  IP addresses, 217
  properties, 235-236
<SCRIPT LANGUAGE=VBS> tag, 528
SCRIPT NAME CGI variable, 583, 738
SCRIPT NAME extension, 706
<SCRIPT> HTML tag, 632
scripting
  browsers, 278
  languages
    ASPs (Active Server Pages), support, 628
    JScript, 628
scripts
  autorun, 482
  CGI
    controlling directory access, 579
    creating applications, 587
    creating feedback forms, 599-601
    file locking, 579-580
    Hello World, 588-592
    interactive, 577
    noninteractive, 575
    passwords, 580
    Perl, 584-585
    security considerations, 580
    server response, 575
    system performance, 579
    validating users, 580
    variables, 580-584
  CGI content type, 586
  Web pages, FrontPage Editor, 427-429
SCSI (Small Computer Systems Interface), 54, 77-78, 82
search engines, meta tags, 404
search forms, Index Information Server, 730-733
search pages (Internet Explorer), 179-181
searchable indexes, HTML documents, 497
Searches Sent counter, 793
SearchGuestBook.HTX file, 709

Second function (VBScript), 552
secrets, 831
sectors
  bad-sector mapping, 813
  boot, viruses, 275
  clusters, 816
Secure Socket Layer (SSL), 22-23, 285, 831
security, 98
  ACLs, 812
  administrative alerts, 813
  Alerter Service, 813
  anonymous-level security tokens, 813
  ASPs, permissions, 635
  auditing
    directories, 308-311
    files, 308-311
  browsers, 277-278
  C2-level, 815
  CGI, 578-580
  checking site credentials, 186
  cookies, 193
  credit card numbers, 186
  data snooping, 186
  descriptors, 831
  dial-up networking, 296-300
  domains, 818
  e-mail messages, protecting, 212-213
  encrypting, plain text, 298
  events
    archiving, 316
    components, 313
    filtering, 314-316
    viewing, 313-314
  Exchange Server, 210-213
    denial of service, 211
  guard-page protection, 821
  hackers, 186
  Internet, 35, 274
    applications, 274-275
    challenge-response authentication, 285
    configuring user accounts, 285-286
    destructive code, 190-191
    dial-up networking, 296-300
    documents, 274-275
    enabling audits, 307-308

encrypting, *285*
firewalls, *280-282*
NTFS, *288-290*
preventing auto-replies,
212
proxy agents, *280*
recovering infected systems,
278-279
restricting access rights,
211-212
trojan horses, *275-277*
viruses, *275-277*
Internet Chat Server,
359-363
chat rooms, 355
Internet Explorer, 186-191
warnings, 191-192
Internet Services Manager,
limiting access, 150-151
intranets, 35
Java, 607
limiting access, rating system,
187
logs, 312
LSA, 826
network adapters, 90
networks
protocols, 284
proxy agents, 283-284
NTFS, 53, 288-290
permissions, 828
policies, auditing, 308
privileges, 829
properties, 187
Proxy Server, permissions,
326-328
proxy servers, 178-179
rating options, 186-187
revision levels, 831
safe communications,
189-190
SAM, 831
server extensions, FrontPage
Server, 415
SIDs, 812
SSLs, 831
tokens, 831
user accounts, 285-286
passwords, 285
viruses
protecting, 213
removing, 279

Windows NT, 45
Windows NT Server, 284
workgroups, 61
**Security Accounts Manager,
see SAM**
Security Add dialog box, 302
**Security command (Permis-
sions menu), 293**
**Security Identifiers (SIDs) 812,
831**
Security menu commands
Auditing, 307, 895
Choose Permissions, 292
Owner, 296, 895
Permissions, 894
**Security Reference Manager,
48**
SECURITY registry key, 891
security tokens, 812
segments, 90
**Select Components to Install
dialog box, 482**
**Select Computer command
(Registry menu), 894**
**Select Destination Directory
dialog box, 482**
Select Folder dialog box, 483
**Select Hypertext Target dialog
box, 500**
Select Picture dialog box, 485
<SELECT> HTML tag, 868
Internet Explorer, 884
selecting
alerts, 762
drives, RAID, 85
fonts for Java applets, 615
I/O, buses, 72-76
object counters, ranges, 754
servers, 91-92
selling products, 22-23
semaphores, 831
sending e-mail, 200
**Serial Line Internet Protocol
(SLIP), 832**
Server dialog box, 94
**server extensions (FrontPage
Server)**
installing, 412-413
security, 415
uninstalling, 414
upgrading, 414-416
Server Manger, domains, 58

Server menu commands
Add, 231
Add WINS Server, 250
Configuration, 250, 262
Delete WINS Server, 250
Replication Partners, 255
**Server Message Blocks
(SMBs), 832**
**SERVER NAME CGI variable,
584, 738**
SERVER NAME extension, 706
**SERVER PORT CGI variable,
584, 739**
SERVER PORT extension, 706
**SERVER PORT SECURE
extension, 706**
**SERVER PROTOCOL CGI
variable, 379, 584**
**SERVER PROTOCOL exten-
sion, 706**
Server service, 86
**SERVER SOFTWARE CGI
variable, 584, 739**
**SERVER SOFTWARE exten-
sion, 706**
server-side includes, see SSIs
**Server/Configuration dialog
box, 793**
servers, 27, 62-63
applications, 216, 815
compatibility, FrontPage, 408
configuring, PPTP packets,
301
Crystal Reports, 723-726
database models, 27
dbWeb
internal properties, 659
properties, 657-660
DHCP, 222, 225
adding, 231
backups, 222
Registry keys, 242-243
replications, 222
subnets, 233
DHCP Manager, 230-231
dial-up networking, 817
DNS, 77, 223, 263
designing, 263
records, 268-269
domains
authenticating, 91
single models, 63

Exchange Server, 200
RPCs, 210
security, 210-213
extensions, FrontPage Server
Administrator, 412-416
FTP, 27
publishing services, 29
FTP Server, connecting to
the Internet, 9
Gopher, 9, 27
publishing services, 29
hosting, ISPs, 14
HTTP, ISAs, 513
IIS, 26
IRC, 345
ISAPI, 30-31
ISAs, 513, 521-524
multihomed, 300
PCI, 75
proxy servers, 177-179
Registry Editor, 892
registry keys, 901-906
RPCs, 830
tuning, 768
virtual, 14, 143
Windows NT
buses, 76
design models, 47-50
disk subsystems, 76-78
hardware, 71
performance, 79
selecting, 91-92
Windows NT Server, 44
compatibility, 46
configuring firewalls,
300-306
IIS, 8-9, 70
integratability, 46
multithreading, 46
processors, 71-72
robust, 44
security, 284
WINS, 258
adding, 250, 255
databases, 258-259
deleting, 248
Internet, 258
multihomed, 258
pull partners, 248
push partners, 248
Registry keys, 261-263

WWW, 26, 837
HTTP, 28
publishing services, 28
WWW Server, connecting to
the Internet, 8
see also Exchange Server
ServerSupportFunction
function (ISAs), 514,
520-521
Service dialog box, 209
Service Pack 1 (Windows NT),
installing, 128
service providers, 4
56KB leased lines, 11
bandwidths, 12
dial-up connections, 11
frame relay, 12
ISDNs, 12-13
requirements, 9-10
see also ISPs
services
adding, Internet Service
Manager, 139
pausing, 139
Server, 86
Workstation, 86
WWW Publishing, configur-
ing, 141-151
Set statement (VBScript), 544
Set Up Files dialog box, 476
setFont method, 619-620
sets, working, 838
settings
advanced, Internet Explorer,
191-195
permissions
directories, 290-296
files, 290-296
setup, Internet Explorer, 172
setup wizards, dbWeb, 651
sex option (security rating),
188
SGML
compared to HTML, 378
tag pairs, 377
SGML (Standard Generalized
Markup Language), 377
Sgn function (VBScript), 552
shadows, realistic with
shadows, 471
sharepoints, 832
shareware, HotDog Pro, 480

Shiloh Consulting Web site, 36
shortcut keys
applications, 486-487
creating, 486
HotDog Pro, customizing,
484
Shortcut Keys command
(Tools menu), 486
shortcuts, see hot keys
shutdowns, auditing, 308
SIDs (Security Identifiers),
812, 831
see also privileges
Sign-In-IDC.HTX file, 706-708
Sign-In-IDC.IDC file, source
code, 700-701
Simple Calculator Web page,
556
Simple Mail Transfer Protocol,
see SMTP
Simple Network Management
Protocol, see SNMP
Simple TCP/IP Service, 101
installing, 112
Sin function (VBScript), 552
single disk subsystems, 79-81
single domains, 63-64
Single System Images, see
SSIs
site credentials (security), 186
Site Services Account dialog
box, 202
sites
Exchange Server, connecting,
209-210
FTP sites, security, 274
interactive, 604
management
Internet Service Manager,
140
View menu, 140
Web sites, 716
backgrounds, 467
bandwidths, 467
CorelWeb.Gallery,
474-476
CorelWeb.Transit,
476-477
dbWeb, 650
designing, 466
Digital AltaVista, 37
directories, 37-38

Excite, 37
Haynes & Company, 36
HTML tags, 840
Multimedia Marketing
Group, 38
Open Market Commercial
Sites Index, 37
PostMaster, 37
publicizing, 37
ray traced, 471
realistic with shadows, 471
rendering images, 471
Sausage Software, 480
security, 277-278
Shiloh Consulting, 36
snapshot properties, 471
solid models, 471
Submit It, 37
Web 3D, 466-469
Web.Designer, 473-474
Webaholics Top 50 Links,
37
whitepapers, 36
wireframes, 471
Yellow Page of the Entire
United States, 38
Size counter, 807
skeleton code, HTML, 378
Skeleton.C source code listing,
522
Skeleton.DEF source code
listing, 524
Skeleton.H source code listing,
522
slide shows (PowerPoint),
converting to HTML,
458-459
SLIP (Serial Line Internet
Protocol), 832
Small Computer Systems
Interface (SCSI), 77
<SMALL> HTML tag, 868
SMBs (Server Message
Blocks), 832
SMDS (Switched Multimegabit
Data Service), 12
SMP (Symmetric
MultiProcessing), 833
SMTP (Simple Mail Transfer
Protocol), 832
addresses, 207
Exchange Server, 200
IMC, 210

SMTP Properties dialog box,
207
Snapshot Animation Settings
dialog box, 472
snapshots, 466
exporting, 467
properties, 471
SNMP (Simple Network
Management Protocol), 101,
304-305, 834
installing, 110-112
SOA record (Start of Authoritative), 269
software
clients, configuring, 344-345
configurations, 92-95
HotDog Pro, 480
RAS, 830
installing, 116
requirements, installing IIS,
100-102
SOFTWARE registry key, 891
solid models, 471
Sort by Comment command
(Internet Services Manager),
140
Sort by Server command
(Internet Services Manager),
140
Sort by Service command
(Internet Services Manager),
140
Sort by State command
(Internet Services Manager),
140
sounds, Internet Explorer, 174
source code
HTML documents,
displaying, 384
Sign-In-IDC.IDC file,
700-701
Skeleton.C listing, 522
Skeleton.DEF listing, 524
Skeleton.H listing, 522
source IP address, firewalls,
281
source IP ports, firewalls, 281
<SPAN> HTML tag, 869
SPAP (Standard Internet
Encryption Method), 298
Special Access dialog box,
296

special characters
defining, 875, 880
inserting, 499
Special Characters command
(View menu), 499
Special Directory Access
dialog box, 295
Special Directory Access
option (Permissions), 291
Special File Access dialog
box, 295
Special File Access option
(Permissions), 291
speed of buses, 73
troubleshooting, 73
speed option, 609
spell checker, HotDog Pro,
481
spreadsheets, publishing,
452-455
SQL (Structured Query
Language), 832
SQL Server
configuring, 793-802
dbWeb, creating guest books,
689
Performance Monitor,
counters, 802-807
Web Assistant, 712-718
parameters, 714
SQL Server Web Assistant File
Option dialog box, 716
SQL Server Web Assistant
Formatting dialog box, 717
SQL Server Web Assistant
Scheduling dialog box, 715
SQLStatement parameter
(IDC), 703
Sqr function (VBScript), 553
SRAM (Static Random Access
Memory), 83
SSIs (server-side includes),
632
ASPs (Active Server Pages),
inserting into HTTP
stream, 632
Web site, 635
SSIs (Single System Images),
832
SSL (Secure Socket Layer),
22-23, 285, 831
standalones, 832

Standard Internet Encryption
  Method (SPAP), 298
standard links, HTML
  documents, 498
standard toolbar (Internet
  Explorer), 174
Start menu commands,
  Accessories, 298
start method, Java applet
  threads, 622
Start of Authoritative (SOA),
  269
Start page (Internet Explorer),
  179-181
start time option (Preferences
  dialog box), 255
starting
  HotDog Pro, 481-483
  processor intensive applica-
    tions, 774
startup data, control sets, 816
  current, 816
startup values (IMC),
  configuring, 209
statements
  import, importing Java
    classes, 613-614
  insert, HTML, 633
  ReDim, dynamic arrays, 539
  VBScript
    Call, 537
    Dim, 537
    Do/Loop, 539
    Erase, 539
    Exit, 540
    Exit For, 540
    Exit Function, 541
    Function, 541
    If/Then/Else, 542
    Let, 542
    loop, 539
    LSet, 542
    Mid, 542
    Next, 540
    *On Error Resume Next,
      543*
    Randomize, 543
    Rem, 543
    RSet, 544
    Set, 544
    Step, 540
    Sub, 541, 544

static arrays, declaring with
  Dim statement, 538
static IP addresses, 222
Static keyword (VBScript),
  544
static mappings, WINS, 257
Static Mappings command
  (Mappings menu), 257
Static Mappings dialog box,
  257
Static Random Access
  Memory (SRAM), 83
static Web pages, 20
status codes
  HSE STATUS ERROR, 517
  HSE STATUS PENDING,
    517
  HSE STATUS SUCCESS,
    517
  HSE STATUS SUCCESS
    AND KEEP CONN, 517
Step statement (VBScript), 540
stop method, Java applet
  threads, 622
stored procedures, queries,
  715
storing, clusters, 816
Str function (VBScript), 553
StrComp function (VBScript),
  553
streaming
  multimedia, 638-639
    creating files, 641-642
  NetShow Live, stream types,
    640
<STRIKE> (strikethrough)
  HTML tag, 384, 869
  Internet Explorer, 884
  Internet Assistant for Word,
    887
String function (VBScript), 553
string-concatenation operator
  (VBScript), 534
strings
  concatenating (VBScript),
    531
  converting to numbers, Java
    applets, 617
  length, 617-618
  substrings, 617-618
  testing, Java applets, 616-617

striped sets, 832
  disk bottlenecks, 783
  parity, 832
striping, 818
  with parity, drives, 81
<STRONG> HTML tag, 384,
  869
  Internet Explorer, 884
  Internet Assistant for Word,
    887
Structured Query Language
  (SQL), 832
structures, HSE VERSION
  INFO, 514
style sheets (HTML docu-
  ments), 403
styles (HTML documents), 404
Sub statement (VBScript),
  541, 544
<SUB> HTML tag, 870
Subject (meta tag), 729
subkeys
  Clone, 825
  creating, 893
Submit It Web site, 37
subnets, 832
  default gateways, 817
  DHCP, servers, 233
  DNS, lookup files, 268
  IP addresses, 233
  masks, 223
  networks, address class, 812
  WINS, proxy agents,
    247-248
subroutines, VBScript
  About dialog box, 556
  AddDigit, 560
  BtnDelete_OnClick, 559
  BtnEvaluate_OnClick, 559
  BtnHello, 530
  BtnHello_OnClick, 530
  BtnTime_OnClick, 531
  HotSpot, 567
  ImageMapGraphic_
    MouseMove, 567
  OperatorBox_OnChange,
    558
substring method, 618
substrings, Java applets,
  617-618

subsystems, 79-81
subtraction operator
(VBScript), 533
Successful Queries/sec object
counter, 260
Successful Releases/sec object
counter, 260
Summary View, FrontPage
Explorer, 418
<SUP> HTML tag, 870
support services
Internet, 17-19
Internet services, 9
ISPs, 16
professionals, 16
swap files, 827
Switch to Alert View option
(Alert Options dialog box),
763
Switched Multimegabit Data
Service (SMDS), 12
switches, 5, 833
ApplicationName, 44
wrappers, 5
symmetric multiprocessing
(SMP), 45-56, 833
see also AMP
synchronizing domains, 818
syntax, 833
command-line programs
(IPCONFIG), 238
syntax checker (HTML),
HotDog Pro, 481
system bits, 833
System calls/sec counter, 770
system data sources, creating,
663
System Data Sources dialog
box, 661
system files, 833
SYSTEM registry key, 891
system service configuration,
registry keys, 896
system-information messages,
820
SYSTEM.MDB files, 241-242
systems
accessing, 306
auditing, 308
configuring, enabling audits,
307-308
infected systems, recovering,
278-279

logs, 312
memory, upgrades, 83-84
object counters, 779
partitioning, 834

T

T connectors, 834
<TAB> HTML tag, 870
Table command (Insert menu),
502
Table Locks - Exclusive
counter, 805
Table Locks - Total counter,
805
<TABLE> HTML tag, 397, 870
Internet Explorer, 885
tables
constraints, 671
dbWeb, database schema,
664
formatting, Internet Assistant
for Word, 450
HTML documents, 381,
397-399
rows, 397
inserting
Internet Assistant for Word,
450
into documents, 502-504
Internet Assistant for Word
formatting, 450
inserting, 450
joins, 670
partitions, 828
schema, 669
Web pages, FrontPage Editor,
425-427
tabular forms, properties,
676-679
Tag Information command
(Edit menu), 500
tags
HTML, 377, 840
<A>, 841, 842
<ABBREV>, 842
<ACRONYM>, 842
<ADDRESS>, 843
<APPLET>, 607, 626,
843-844
<AREA>, 844

<AU>, 844
<B>, 844
<BANNER>, 845
<BASE>, 845
<BASEFONT>, 845
<BDO>, 846
<BGSOUND>, 846
<BIG>, 846
<BLINK>, 846
<BLOCKQUOTE>, 847
<BODY>, 847-848
*
, 848*
<CAPTION>, 848
<CENTER>, 848
<CITE>, 849
<CODE>, 849
<COL>, 849
<COLGROUP>, 850
<CREDIT>, 850
<DD>, 850
<DEL>, 851
<DFN>, 851
<DIR>, 851
<DIV>, 852
<DL>, 852
<DT>, 852
<EM>, 852
<EMBED>, 853
<FIG>, 853
<FN>, 853
<FONT>, 854
<FORM>, 854
<FRAME>, 854
<FRAMESET>, 855
<H1>, 855
<H2>, 855
<H3>, 856
<H4>, 856
<H5>, 856
<H6>, 857
<HEAD>, 857
<HPn>, 857
<HR>, 857
<HTML>, 858
<I>, 858
<IMG>, 858-859
<INPUT>, 859
<INS>, 859
inserting into documents,
499-501
inserting with Tags dialog
box, 499-500

<ISINDEX>, 860
<KBD>, 860
<LANG>, 860
<LH>, 861
<LI>, 861
<LINK>, 861
<LISTING>, 861
<MAP>, 862
<MARQUEE>, 862
<MENU>, 863
<META>, 729-730, 863
Index Information Server,
729-730
<NEXTID>, 863
<NOBR>, 864
<NOEMBED>, 864
<NOFRAMES>, 864
<NOTE>, 864
<OBJECT>, 645
<PARAM>, 626
<SCRIPT>, 632
<SCRIPT
LANGUAGE=VBS>,
528
<OL>, 865
<OPTION>, 865
<OVERLAY>, 865
<P>, 866
<PARAM>, 866
<PERSON>, 866
<PLAINTEXT>, 866
<PRE>, 867
<Q>, 867
<S>, 867
<SAMP>, 868
<SELECT>, 868
<SMALL>, 868
<SPAN>, 869
<STRIKE>, 869
<STRONG>, 869
<SUB>, 870
<SUP>, 870
<TAB>, 870
<TABLE>, 870
<TBODY>, 871
<TD>, 871
<TEXTAREA>, 872
<TFOOT>, 872
<TH>, 872
<THEAD>, 873
<TITLE>, 873
<TR>, 873

<TT>, 874
<U>, 874
<UL>, 874
<VAR>, 874
<WBR>, 875
<XMP>, 875
meta, Index Information
Server, 729-730
pairs, 377
VBScript program defini-
tions, 528
Web site, 840
Internet Assistant for Word,
886-888
**Tags command (View menu),
499**
Tags dialog box, 499-500
Tan function (VBScript), 553
tapes, family sets, 821
TAPI, 46
Task Manager, 776
<TBODY> HTML tag, 871
**TCP (Transmission Control
Protocol), 6, 304, 835**
**TCP/IP (Transmission Control
Protocol/Internet Protocol),
6, 26, 834**
address class, 812
addresses, 217
auto-dial, 176
configuring, 217
dbWeb, 653
multihomed, 826
protocols, 303
utilities, installing, 102-106
**TCP/IP Properties dialog box,
301**
**TCP/IP Security dialog box,
302**
<TD> HTML tag, 871
**TDI (Transport Driver
Interface), 835**
technical support
Internet, 17-19
ISPs, 16
**Telephone Application
Programming, 46**
Telnet, 304
**Template from Document
command (Tools menu), 505**
**Template parameter (IDC),
703**

TemplateName variable, 733
templates
creating, from HTML
documents, 505
home pages, creating with
Web 3D, 469-472
HotDog Pro, 495
HTML, creating, 703-712
Web pages, FrontPage Editor,
430
terminated processes, 834
testing
ISAPI, 512
strings, Java applets, 616-617
text
attributes (HTML docu-
ments), 383, 386
bold, 377
encrypting, 298
entering, documents,
498-499
HTML documents, 498
alignment, 382-383
bold, 384
italic, 384
strikethrough, 384
publishing, 20-21
writing Java applets, 620-621
text option, 609
**text-only view (browsers),
173**
<TEXTAREA> HTML tag, 872
<TFOOT> HTML tag, 872
<TH> HTML tag, 872
<THEAD> HTML tag, 873
**theft, e-mail messages,
212-213**
themes, 505
**third-party ISAPI applications,
512**
threads, 46, 834
defined, 614
Executive, 819
impersonations, 823
Java applets, 622-624
exception handling,
623-624
run method, 623
start method, 622
stop method, 622
multithreading, 826

three-dimensional objects
CorelWeb.Gallery, 474-476
CorelWeb.Transit, 476-477
home pages, creating,
469-472
Web 3D, 466-469
Web.Designer, 473-474
Time dialog box (VBScript),
531
Time function (VBScript), 553
timeout errors, 207
timeslices, 835
TimeValue function (VBScript),
553
<TITLE> HTML tag, 379, 873
Internet Assistant for Word,
888
Internet Explorer, 885
titles
documents, 495
HTML documents, 379
tokens
access, 812
anonymous-level security,
813
security, 812, 831
TombstoneInterval (Registry
key), 263
TombstoneTimeout (Registry
key), 263
toolbars
Internet Explorer, 195-197
Performance Monitor, 751
Tools menu commands
Customize Button Bar, 484
Options, 213, 487
Shortcut Keys, 486
Template from Document,
505
Total Allowed Async I/O
Requests counter, 788
Total Anonymous Users
counter, 790-793
Total Blocked Async I/O
Requests counter, 788
Total Blocking Locks counter,
805
Total Demand Locks counter,
805
Total Exclusive Locks counter,
805
Total NonAnonymous Users
counter, 790-793

Total Number of Conflicts/sec
object counter, 260
Total Number of Registra-
tions/sec object counter, 260
Total Number of Renewals/
sec object counter, 260
total processor time counter,
770
Total Rejected Async I/O
Requests counter, 788
Total Shared Locks counter,
805
<TR> HTML tag, 873
tracking
IP addresses, 7
processes, 308
Transmission Control Protocol
(TCP), 6, 835
Transmission Control Proto-
col/Internet Protocol, see
TCP/IP
Transport Driver Interface,
835
transporting, networks, 827
traps, 835
trees, see directory trees
Trim function (VBScript), 550
trojan horses, 275-277
troubleshooting, protocols,
206
troubleshooting
authentication, RAS, 118
backgrounds, 467
buses, 73
databases, 668
disk bottlenecks, 782
disk striping with parity, 81
e-mail
addresses, 206
message conversions, 206
flames, 211
I/O buses, 76
Internet, messages, 211
memory, 778
permissions, No Access
option, 290
Registry Editor, 261, 890
registry keys, 891
timeout errors, 207
viruses, 213
Web Proxy Service, assigning
permissions, 331

trust relationships, 61, 835
domains, 67
truth table for VBScript
equivalence operator, 536
<TT> HTML tag, 384, 874
Internet Explorer, 885
Internet Assistant for Word,
888
tuning
performance, 768-769
servers, 768
tutorial, HotDog Pro, 483
types of variables, determining with VarType function,
554

U

<U> HTML tag, 874
Internet Assistant for Word,
888
Internet Explorer, 885
UARTS (Universal Asynchronous Receiver/Transmitters),
114
RAS, installing, 114
UBound function (VBScript),
554
UCase function (VBScript),
554
UDP (User Datagram
Protocol), 836
<UL> (unnumbered list) HTML
tag, 390, 874
Internet Assistant for Word,
888
Internet Explorer, 885
unary minus operator
(VBScript), 533
UNC (Universal Naming
Convention), 835
unequal operator (VBScript),
536
uninterruptable power supply,
56
Unique Conflicts/sec object
counter, 260
unique identifiers, handles,
821
Unique Registrations/sec
object counter, 260

Unique Renewals/sec object
  counter, 260
units, allocation, 816
Universal Asynchronous
  Receiver/Transmitters, see
  UARTS
Universal Naming Convention
  (UNC), 835
Universal Resource Identifiers
  (URIs), 835
Universal Resource Locators,
  see URLs
Universally Unique Identifiers,
  see UUID
unloading, DLLs, 511
UNMAPPED REMOTE
  extension, 706
Update Count option
  (Preferences dialog box),
  255
update forms
  properties, 682-684
  property sheets, 685-686
Update Now command
  (Options menu), 755-760
Update Time option
  Alert Options dialog box, 763
  Chart Options dialog box,
  755
updating
  counters, 752
  logs, 757, 760
upgrading
  caches, 774
  hardware, 83
  memory, 83-84
  processors, 774
  server extensions, FrontPage
  Server, 414-416
URIs (Universal Resource
  Identifiers), 835
URL extension, 706
URLs (Universal Resource
  Locators), 835
  addresses, 495
  processing queries, 497
Usage counter, 775-777
Usage Peak counter, 775-778
user configurable variables,
  735-736
User Connections counter, 805
USER extension, 706

user groups
  Domain Guests, 142
  Microsoft Proxy Server, 321
user management, Windows
  NT, 59-60
User Manger for Domains, 59
User Profile Editor, 59
Username option, FTP
  Publishing service, 152
UserName parameter (IDC),
  703
users
  accessing, systems, 306
  accounts
    configuring policies,
    286-288
    displaying, 294
    protecting, 285
    security, 285-286
  auditing, 308
  IDs, dbWeb, 659
  keywords, 497
  profiles, 59, 836
    mandatory, 826
  rights, auditing, 308
  WINS, releases, 244
Users Must Log On in Order
  to Change Password option,
  288
UseSelfFndPnrs (Registry key),
  262
utilities
  e-mail, Blat, 599
  Repair Disk, 895
  TCP/IP, installing, 102-106
UUID (Universally Unique
  Identifiers), 836

V

Val function (VBScript), 554
validating caches, 254
validation, CGI, 580
Value Bar option (Chart
  Options dialog box), 755
value entries, 836
  see also registry keys
<VAR> HTML tag, 874
  Internet Assistant for Word,
  888
  Internet Explorer, 885

variables
  CGI, 580, 737-739
    accessing, 592-594
    AUTH TYPE, 581
    CONTENT LENGTH,
    581
    CONTENT TYPE, 581
    GATEWAY INTERFACE,
    581
    HTTP ACCEPT, 581
    HTTP USER AGENT,
    582
    PATH INFO, 582
    PATH TRANSLATED,
    582
    QUERY STRING, 582
    REMOTE ADDR, 582
    REMOTE HOST, 583
    REMOTE IDENT, 583
    REMOTE USER, 583
    REQUEST METHOD,
    583
    SCRIPT NAME, 583
    SERVER NAME, 584
    SERVER PORT, 584
    SERVER PROTOCOL,
    584
    SERVER SOFTWARE,
    584
  CiMaxRecordsPerPage, 733
  CiScope, 733
  CiSort, 733
  HTMLQueryForm, 733
  HTX files, 741-742
    read-only, 743-744
  multiple, declaring with Dim
    statement, 538
  TemplateName, 733
  types, determining with
    VarType function, 554
  user configurable, 735-736
  variant, with Dim statement,
    538
variant variables, 538
VarType function (VBScript),
  554
vBNS (Backbone Network
  System), 6
VBScript, 528, 836
  applications
    function and control
    structure examples,
    555-570
    Hello World, 529-570

code, hiding, 529
control structures, 537
   For Each/Next, 540
   For/Next, 540
   While/Wend, 545
Date dialog box, 531
error checking, 558
functions, 545-570
Hello World! Web page
  example, 532
keywords
   Nothing, 544
   Private, 543
   Public, 543
   Static, 544
labeling images, 566
operators, 533-570
statements
   Call, 537
   Dim, 537
   Do/Loop, 539
   Erase, 539
   Exit, 540
   Exit For, 540
   Exit Function, 541
   Function, 541
   If/Then/Else, 542
   Let, 542
   loop, 539
   LSet, 542
   Mid, 542
   Next, 540
   On Error Resume Next, 543
   Randomize, 543
   Rem, 543
   RSet, 544
   Set, 544
   Step, 540
   Sub, 541, 544
strings, concatenating, 531
subroutines
   About dialog box, 556
   AddDigit, 560
   BtnDelete_OnClick, 559
   BtnEvaluate_OnClick, 559
   HotSpot, 567

   ImageMapGraphic_ MouseMove, 567
   OperatorBox_OnChange, 558
   Time dialog box, 531
VBScript information Web site, 528
VDM (Virtual DOS Machine), 836
VerifyInterval (Registry keys), 263
Vertical Grid option (Chart Options dialog box), 755
Vertical Labels option (Chart Options dialog box), 755
Vertical Maximum option (Chart Options dialog box), 755
video files, inserting (Internet Assistant for Word), 450
Video Local Buses (VLBs), 74
vidtoasf.exe (NetShow Live), 638
  command-line arguments, 641
View menu
  commands
   Alerts, 761
   All Events, 316
   Chart, 752
   Database, 253
   Display Binary Data, 894
   Filter Events, 314
   Find Key, 894
   Log, 756
   Report, 758
   Special Characters, 499
   Tags, 499
  sites, management, 140
viewers, see Event Viewer
viewing
  alerts, 751
  charts, 751
  events, 313-314
  file associations, 183
  reports, 751
views
  Alert, 761
  browsers, text-only, 173
  Chart, 752
  Log, 756

  Performance Monitor, 750
   Report, 759
   saving, 755
violations, access rights, 812
violence option (security rating), 188
virtual address space, 812
Virtual Bytes Peak counter, 779
virtual directories, creating, 143
  WWW Publishing service, 145-146
Virtual DOS Machine (VDM)
virtual memory
  paging files, 827
  swap files, 827
Virtual Memory dialog box, 93-94
Virtual Memory Manager, 49
  guard-page protection, 821
virtual paths, compared to relative, 633
Virtual Private Networks (VPNs), see VPNs
virtual servers, 143
  creating, WWW Publishing service, 146-148
  domain names, WWW Publishing service, 148
viruses, 275-277
  boot sectors, 275
  clients, 213
  infected systems, recovering, 278-279
  macros, 276
  removing, 278-279
  Windows NT, 276
virutal device drivers, 836
virutal memory, 836
virutal servers, 14
visited links, HTML documents, 498
Visual C++, Windows NT Server, 47
VLBs (Video Local Buses), 74
volumes, 837
  mounting, 826
VPNs (Virtual Private Networks), 300

W

WAIS, 305
WANs (Wide Area Net-
works), 28, 113, 837
  creating, 113
warning messages, 820
warnings (security), 191-192
wavtoasf.exe (NetShow Live),
638
  command-line arguments,
  642
<WBR> HTML tag, 875
  Internet Explorer, 885
Web 3D, 466-469
  home pages, creating,
  469-472
Web Assistant
  launching, 714
  passwords, 714
  SQL Server, 712-718
    parameters, 714
Web browsers, Hot Java, 606
Web pages
  attributes, FrontPage Editor,
  421
  creating, Internet Assistant
  for Word, 447-451
  designing, FrontPage Editor,
  421-428
  editing, 417
  frames, FrontPage Editor,
  422-424
  Hello World! VBScript
  example, 532
  Java applets
    code for marquee applet,
    610-613
    compiling, 624-625
    creating, 608-624
    embedding in HTML,
    625-626
    importing classes, 613-614
    initializing, 615-618
    painting, 619-621
    parameters for Marquee
    applet, 609-610
    threads, 622-624
  Microsoft VBScript, 528
  publishing
    Access 95, 446-451
    Access 97, 444-445

Excel 97, 438-441
Internet Assistant for
  Access, 459-463
Internet Assistant for Excel,
  453
Internet Assistant for
  PowerPoint, 456-459
Office 95, 446
Office 97, 432-445
PowerPoint 97, 441-443
Word 95, 451
Word 97, 434-438
  scripts, FrontPage Editor,
  427-429
  Simple Calculator, 556
  tables, FrontPage Editor,
  425-427
  templates, FrontPage Editor,
  430
Web Proxy Server, properties,
329
Web Proxy Service
  caching options, 332-335
  configuring, 328-345
  Internet sites, limiting access,
  336-338
  log files, 335-336
  permissions, assigning,
  330-332
  Web sites, caching, 334
Web sites
  Access, 445
  ASPs (Active Server Pages),
  documentation, 628
  Blat e-mail utility, 600
  caching, Web Proxy Service,
  334
  Commercial Internet Server,
  320
  Excel, 441, 453
  IIS, 123
  Internet Assistant for Excel,
  453
  Internet Assistant for
  PowerPoint, 457
  Internet Assistant for Word,
  446
  management, FrontPage
  Explorer, 416
  Microsoft Office, 432
  Microsoft Proxy Server, 320
    third-party enhancements,
    321

Microsoft VBScript
  information, 528
Microsoft VM for Java, 628
Office, 446
one-time passwords, 580
Perl, 585-586
PowerPoint, 444, 457
SSIs, 635
WinZip, 585
Word, 436
Web.Designer, 473-474
Webaholics Top 50 Links Web
site, 37
Weekday function (VBScript),
555
Welcome dialog box, 484
Welcome to HotDog! dialog
box, 483
well-known endpoints, 830
While/Wend control structure
(VBScript), 545
whitepapers, Web site, 36
Wide Area Networks
(WANs), 28, 113, 837
wildcard (*) notation, 613
WINDBG.EXE file, 837
windows, Registry Editor, 892
Windows Internet Naming
Service, see WINS
Windows NT, 50-52
  BIOS, 45
  compression support, 53
  computer management,
  56-58
  Configuration Manager, 49
  controllers, 62-63
    backup domain, 62
    domains, 62
  DHCP Manager, 58
  disk duplexing, 54-55
  disk mirroring, 54-55
  disk striping with parity,
  54-55
  domains, 60-61
    master model, 64-66
    multiple master model,
    66-67
    single models, 63-64
    trust relationships, 67
  environmental subsystems,
  50-52
  Event Viewer, 56, 312-313

fault-tolerant capabilities, 45, 54-56
File Manager, 57
FTP Server, publishing services, 29
Gopher Server, publishing services, 29
I/O Manager, 50
IIS, 70
Internet Server Manager, 57
Local IPC Manager, 49
Logon Script, 60
network adapters, 56
NTFS, 52
    filenames, 53
    security, 53
Object Manager, 48
Print Manager, 57
Process Manager, 49
RAS Administrator, 57
scalability, 45
security, 45
Security Reference Manager, 48
Server Manager, domains, 58
servers, 62-63
    FTP, 27
    Gopher, 27
    WWW, 26
Service Pack 1
    installing, 128
Setup properties, 171
software, configurations, 92-95
symmetric multiprocessing, 45, 56
TCP/IP, 26
uninterruptable power supply, 56
user management, 59-60
User Manager for Domains, 59
User Profile Editor, 59
users, profiles, 59
Virtual Memory Manager, 49
viruses, 276
WINS Manager, 58
workgroups, 60-61
    security, 61
WWW Server, publishing services, 28

Windows NT Server, 44, 60
buses, 76
CD-ROMs, adding, 78
compatibility, 46
configuring, firewalls, 300-306
design models, 47-50
disk striping with parity, 81
disk subsystems, 76-78
    multiple, 81-82
    SCSI, 82
    single, 79-81
EIDE, 77
hardware, 71
    upgrades, 83
IDE, 77
IIS, 8-9
integratability, 46
memory, upgrades, 83-84
multithreading, 46
network adapters, adding, 85-90
performance, 79
processors, 71-72
    adding, 91
robust, 44
security, 284
selecting, 91-92
Web publishing, 99
Windows NT System Debugger (NTSD)
Windows NT Task Manager, 776
Windows on Win32 (WOW), 51
WINS (Windows Internet Naming Service), 58, 100, 216, 837
addresses, mapping, 244
clients, 248, 257-258
    registrations, 244
configurations, 220
configuring, with WINS Manager, 250-257
databases, compacting, 258
designing, 244-245
DHCP, 223, 263-264
domains, 245
installing, 108, 245-250
Internet, 258
names, resolving, 243
NetBIOS, 243

non-WINS clients, subnet networks, 247
protocols, disabling, 90
proxy agents, 245-248, 838
pull partners, 248
push partners, 248
renewals, 224
servers
    adding, 250, 255
    deleting, 248
    multihomed, 258
    Registry keys, 262-263
static mappings, 257
users, releases, 244
WINS Manager, 58
configuring, 250-257
WINS Server Configuration dialog box, 251-262
WinSock Proxy Service
configuring, 338-342
permissions, assigning, 340-342
protocols, monitoring, 338-340
WinZip Web site, 585
wireframes, 471
images, 467
wizards, dbWeb setup, 651
Word Web site, 436
Word 95, Web pages, publishing, 451
Word 97
backgrounds, changing color, 436-437
fonts, changing attributes, 437
objects, inserting, 437-438
Web publishing, 434-438
Internet Assistant for Word, HTML tags, 886-888
Work Item Shortages counter, 785
workgroups, 60-61
security, 61
Windows NT, 60
Working Set counter, 779
Working Set Peak counter, 779
working sets, 838
Workstation service, 86
workstations
registry keys, 906-907
standalones, 832

World Wide Web, see WWW
WOW (Windows on Win32),
  51
wrappers, 5
WriteClient function (ISAs),
  514, 519-520
writing
  Java applets, 608-624
    code for marquee applet,
      610-613
    parameters for marquee
      applet, 609-610
  text, Java applets, 620-621
WWW (World Wide Web), 4,
305, 838
  advertising, 15
  browsers, 28, 837
    Hot Java, 606
    security, 277-278
  Crystal Reports, 723-726
  directories, 37-38
  pages
    creating forms, 695-696
    creating input forms,
      696-700
    defining special characters,
      875, 880
    DSN, 695
    dynamic, 20, 694
    ODBC, 695
    static, 20
    WYSIWYG editor, 695
  registry keys, 898-899
  security, recovering infected
    systems, 278-279
  servers, 837
  sites, 716
    backgrounds, 467
    bandwidths, 467
    CorelWeb.Gallery,
      474-476
    CorelWeb.Transit,
      476-477
    dbWeb, 650
    designing, 466
    Digital AltaVista, 37
    Excite, 37
    Haynes & Company, 36
    HTML tags, 840
    Multimedia Marketing
      Group, 38
    Open Market Commercial
      Sites Index, 37

  PostMaster, 37
  publicizing, 37
  ray traced, 471
  realistic with shadows, 471
  rendering images, 471
  Sausage Software, 480
  security, 277-278
  Shiloh Conulting, 36
  snapshot properties, 471
  solid models, 471
  Submit It, 37
  Web 3D, 466-469
  Web.Designer, 473-474
  Webaholics Top 50 Links,
    37
  whitepapers, 36
  wireframes, 471
  Yellow Page of the Entire
    United States, 38
WWW Publishing service
  configuring, 141-151
  directories
    configuring, 143-148
    properties, 144-145
  Directory Browsing Allowed
    option, 144
  log files, creating, 149-150
  security considerations, 143
  virtual directories, creating,
    145-146
  virtual servers, creating,
    146-148
WWW Server, 26
  HTTP, 28
  Internet, connecting to, 8
  publishing services, 28
WWW Service Properties
  dialog box, 141
WWW sites, interactive, 604
WYSIWYG (What-You-See-Is-
  What-You-Get), 695

X-Y-Z

<XMP> HTML tag, 875
  Internet Explorer, 885
XOR operator (VBScript), 535

Yahoo!, 37
Year function (VBScript), 555
Yellow Page of the Entire
  United States Web site, 38

MACMILLAN COMPUTER PUBLISHING USA

A VIACOM COMPANY

Technical ---- Support:

If you need assistance with the information in this book or with a CD/Disk accompanying the book, please access the Knowledge Base on our Web site at **http://www.superlibrary.com/general/support**. Our most Frequently Asked Questions are answered there. If you do not find the answer to your questions on our Web site, you may contact Macmillan Technical Support **(317) 581-3833** or e-mail us at **support@mcp.com**.

Microsoft SMS Administrator's Survival Guide

James Farhatt, et al.

This book covers everything system administrators need to know to implement, plan, and manage the Systems Management Server. Reduce the loss of revenue associated with network downtime by quickly integrating SMS with other BackOffice products. Coverage focuses on management, troubleshooting, and expansion planning.

CD-ROM includes scripting and programs that add efficiency to SMS management.

$59.99 USA/$84.95 CDN	*0-672-30984-X*	*700 pp.*
Client/Server	*Accomplished—Expert*	*03/01/97*

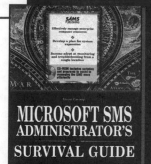

Designing and Implementing Microsoft Proxy Server

David Wolfe

Microsoft Proxy Server works in client/server environments and also can be adapted to place data on an Internet or intranet site. As the newest member of Microsoft's BackOffice suite, Microsoft Proxy Server had more than 10,000 users register to download the beta version in the first week of its release. *Designing and Implementing Microsoft Proxy Server* shows users how to maximize the full power of this server, both in client/server and Internet environments.

Teaches how to implement both internal client/server security and external Internet security using firewalls. Shows how to use protocols and products from HTTP to RealAudio and VDOLive.

$39.99 USA/$56.95 CDN	*1-57521-213-7*	*288 pp.*
Internet/Networking/Servers	*Accomplished*	*02/01/97*

Designing and Implementing Microsoft Index Server

Mark Swank & Drew Kittel

Microsoft Index Server allows companies to automate their indexing of crucial data, organizing and maintaining large amounts of information. Its integration with Windows NT and Internet Information Server opens the doors to a large market of corporate NT and IIS users that will want to automate their indexing. Everything from installation to implementation is discussed in detail, including ways of integrating Microsoft Index Server into existing systems. Coverage includes maintenance, administration, and security issues.

$39.99 USA/$56.95 CDN	*1-57521-212-9*	*350 pp.*
Internet/Networking/Servers	*Accomplished*	*12/01/96*

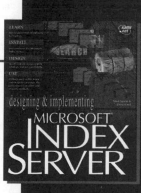

Microsoft BackOffice 2 Unleashed

Joe Greene, et al.

An instrumental tool for anyone in charge of developing or managing BackOffice. It covers the individual pieces of BackOffice as well as key phases in the development, integration, and administration of the BackOffice environment.

Contains coverage on using BackOffice as the infrastructure of an intranet or for the Internet. Instructs readers on integrating individual BackOffice products. CD-ROM includes source code, third-party products, and utilities. Covers BackOffice.

$59.99 USA/$84.95 CDN	*0-672-30816-9*	*1,264 pp.*
Client/Server	*Accomplished—Expert*	*11/01/96*

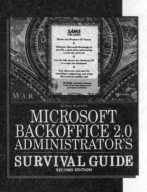

Microsoft BackOffice 2 Administrator's Survival Guide, Second Edition

Arthur Knowles

This all-in-one reference describes how to make the components of BackOffice version 2 work best together and with other networks. BackOffice is Microsoft's complete reference for networking, database, and system management products. Contains the fundamental concepts required for daily maintenance, troubleshooting, and problem solving. CD-ROM includes product demos, commercial and shareware utilities, and technical notes from Microsoft vendor technical support personnel. Covers version 2.

$59.99 USA/$84.95 CDN	*0-672-30977-7*	*1,200 pp.*
Client/Server	*Accomplished*	*11/01/96*

Microsoft SQL Server 6.5 Unleashed, Second Edition

David Solomon, et al.

This comprehensive reference details the steps needed to plan, design, install, administer, and tune large and small databases. In many cases, the readers will use the techniques in this tome to create and manage their own complex environment. CD-ROM includes source code, libraries, and administration tools. Covers programming topics, including SQL, data structures, programming constructs, stored procedures, referential integrity, large table strategies, and more. Includes updates to cover all new features of SQL Server 6.5 including the new transaction processing monitor and Internet/database connectivity through SQL Server's new Web Wizard.

$59.99 USA/$84.95 CDN	*0-672-30956-4*	*1,272 pp.*
Databases	*Accomplished—Expert*	*10/01/96*

Windows NT 4 Server Unleashed

Jason Garms, et al.

The Windows NT Server has been gaining tremendous market share over Novell NetWare, and the new upgrade—which includes a Windows 95 interface—is sure to add momentum to its market drive. To that end, *Windows NT 4 Server Unleashed* is written to meet that growing market. It provides information on disk and file management, integrated networking, BackOffice integration, and TCP/IP protocols. CD-ROM includes source code from the book and valuable utilities. Focuses on using Windows NT as an Internet server. Covers security issues and Macintosh support.

$59.99 USA/$84.95 CDN	*0-672-30933-5*	*1,100 pp.*
Networking	*Accomplished—Expert*	*08/01/96*

Windows NT 4 Workstation Unleashed

Sean Mathias, et al.

NT Workstation is expected to become the platform of choice for corporate America! This new edition focuses on NT Workstation's new-and-improved features as a high-end graphics workstation and scalable development platform. Provides in-depth advice on installing, configuring, and managing Windows NT Workstation. Features comprehensive, detailed advice for NT. CD-ROM includes Windows NT utilities, demos, and more. Covers Windows NT 4 Workstation.

$39.99 USA/$56.95 CDN	*0-672-30972-6*	*696 pp.*
Operating Systems	*Accomplished—Expert*	*11/01/96*

Add to Your Sams.net Library Today
with the Best Books for Internet Technologies

ISBN	Quantity	Description of Item	Unit Cost	Total Cost
0-672-30984-X		Microsoft SMS Administrator's Survival Guide (Book/CD-ROM)	$59.99	
1-57521-213-7		Designing and Implementing Microsoft Proxy Server	$39.99	
1-57521-212-9		Designing and Implementing Microsoft Index Server	$39.99	
0-672-30816-9		Microsoft BackOffice 2 Unleashed (Book/CD-ROM)	$59.99	
0-672-30977-7		Microsoft BackOffice 2 Administrator's Survival Guide, Second Edition (Book/CD-ROM)	$59.99	
0-672-30956-4		Microsoft SQL Server 6.5 Unleashed, Second Edition (Book/CD-ROM)	$59.99	
0-672-30933-5		Windows NT 4 Server Unleashed (Book/CD-ROM)	$59.99	
0-672-30972-6		Windows NT 4 Workstation Unleashed (Book/CD-ROM)	$39.99	
		Shipping and Handling: See information below.		
		TOTAL		

Shipping and Handling: $4.00 for the first book, and $1.75 for each additional book. If you need to have it NOW, we can ship the product to you in 24 hours for an additional charge of approximately $18.00, and you will receive your item overnight or in two days. Overseas shipping and handling adds $2.00. Prices subject to change. Call between 9:00 a.m. and 5:00 p.m. EST for availability and pricing information on latest editions.

201 W. 103rd Street, Indianapolis, Indiana 46290

1-800-428-5331 — Orders   1-800-835-3202 — Fax   1-800-858-7674 — Customer Service

Book ISBN 1-57521-271-4

What's on the CD-ROM

This book's companion CD-ROM contains an assortment of third-party tools and product demos. The CD-ROM creates a new program group for this book and uses Windows Explorer. Using the icons in the program group and Windows Explorer, you can view information concerning products and companies, and you can install programs with just a few clicks of the mouse.

Some of the utilities and programs mentioned in this book are included on this CD-ROM. If they are not, a reference to a Web site or FTP location may be provided in the text. If a reference is missing, up-to-date information can almost always be obtained from comprehensive shareware sites such as Microsoft's main site (http://www.microsoft.com) for late-breaking Microsoft Internet Information Server news or, similarly, Beverly Hills Software (http://www.bhs.com) for third-party Windows NT products.

Windows 95/NT Installation Instructions

To create the program group for this book, follow these steps:

1. Insert the CD-ROM into your CD-ROM drive.

2. With Windows NT installed on your computer and the AutoPlay feature enabled, a program group for this book is automatically created whenever you insert the CD-ROM into the CD-ROM drive. Follow the directions provided in the installation program.

   If AutoPlay is not enabled, using Windows Explorer, choose Setup.exe from the root level of the CD-ROM to create the program group for this book.

3. Double-click the Browse the CD-ROM icon in the newly created program group to access the installation programs of the software or the reference material included on the CD-ROM.

   To review the latest information about this CD-ROM, double-click the About this CD-ROM icon.

> **NOTE**
>
> For best results, set your monitor to display between 256 and 64,000 colors. A screen resolution of 640×480 pixels is also recommended. If necessary, adjust your monitor settings before using the CD-ROM.

Technical Support

If you need assistance with the information in this book or with the CD-ROM accompanying this book, access the Knowledge Base on our Web site:

http://www.superlibrary.com/general/support

Our most Frequently Asked Questions are answered there. If you do not find the answer to your questions on our Web site, you may contact Macmillan Technical Support at (317) 581-3833 or e-mail us at support@mcp.com.